Toward Nuclear Disarmament and Global Security:
A Search for Alternatives

STUDIES ON A JUST WORLD ORDER

Other Titles in This Series

Also of Interest

†Available in hardcover and paperback.

Toward Nuclear Disarmament and Global Security: A Search for Alternatives

edited by Burns H. Weston

with the assistance of
Thomas A. Hawbaker and Christopher R. Rossi

This text is designed to provide students and others with a theoretical and factual base for understanding the complex questions posed by continued reliance on nuclear weapons to protect geopolitical interests.

In Part One, the authors examine the destructiveness and cost of modern nuclear arsenals and offer both normative and systemic explanations for the proliferation of nuclear armaments. They investigate the causes of past public unwillingness to come to grips with the nuclear weapons crisis and go on to consider some of the main arguments behind the accelerating transnational antinuclear movement. Part Two develops a critical analysis of the doctrines and perceptions that fuel the expansion of the world's nuclear forces.

The two parts that follow constitute a search for alternative security arrangements. In Part Three, the authors look at multiple approaches to the process of nuclear arms reduction and disarmament. In Part Four, they identify a variety of national defense strategies, supranational institutions, and structural political transformations that offer the potential for genuine global security. The book concludes with an assessment of opportunities to develop an international grassroots commitment to a denuclearized world.

Intended for use as a basic text in world order studies, peace studies, national security studies, and global issues courses, and as a supplementary text in international law and relations, international organization, and modern diplomatic and military history, this collection encourages its readers to assess their own perceptions and values and the objectives of their own governments. The seminal articles and original essays make it a valuable resource for scholars, researchers, libraries, and citizen groups, as well as students. In addition to the readings, each chapter contains an introduction, discussion questions, and a selected bibliography.

Burns H. Weston is Bessie Dutton Murray Distinguished Professor of Law at The University of Iowa. A specialist in international law and international affairs, he is a Senior Fellow of the World Policy Institute and a Fellow of the World Academy of Art and Science. Weston is editor of *Toward World Order and Human Dignity: Essays in Honor of Myres S. McDougal* (1976) and author of *International Law and World Order: A Problem-Oriented Coursebook* (1980).

Thomas A. Hawbaker and Christopher R. Rossi are recent graduates of The University of Iowa College of Law.

To
Timothy,
Holly,
Rebecca,
Heather,
Natasha,
and
Eric

STUDIES ON A JUST WORLD ORDER, NO. 4

Toward Nuclear Disarmament and Global Security: A Search for Alternatives

edited by Burns H. Weston

with the assistance of
Thomas A. Hawbaker and Christopher R. Rossi

WESTVIEW PRESS / BOULDER, COLORADO

Studies on a Just World Order

Copyright © 1984 by Westview Press, Inc.

Published in 1984 in the United States of America by
Westview Press, Inc.
5500 Central Avenue
Boulder, Colorado 80301
Frederick A. Praeger, President and Publisher

Library of Congress Cataloging in Publication Data
Main entry under title:
Toward nuclear disarmament and global security.
(Studies on a just world order; v. 4)
Includes bibliographies and index.
1. Atomic weapons and disarmament—Addresses, essays, lectures. 2. Security, International—Addresses, essays, lectures. I. Weston, Burns H., 1933– . II. Hawbaker, Thomas A. III. Rossi, Christopher R. IV. Series.
JX1974.7.T68 1984   327.1'74   83-16653
ISBN 0-86531-642-2
ISBN 0-86531-643-0 (pbk.)

Printed and bound in the United States of America

Contents

PART TWO
RETHINKING SOME BASIC ASSUMPTIONS

Chapter 6
Rethinking "The Enemy"

PART THREE
OPTING FOR NUCLEAR DISARMAMENT

Chapter 7
Overcoming Distrust and Competition

Chapter 8
Breaking the Momentum Toward Nuclear War

Chapter 9
Curbing the Nuclear Danger

PART FOUR
PURSUING ALTERNATIVE GLOBAL SECURITY

Chapter 10
Relying on Alternative Defense Strategies

Chapter 11
Enhancing World Security Arrangements

Chapter 12
Promoting Systemic Transformation

Acknowledgments

There can be no full accounting of my debt to all the people who have contributed to this volume since it first came to mind around the time of the United Nations General Assembly's First Special Session on Disarmament in 1978, but they know who they are and will recognize their input here and there. To them, my thanks.

For dialogue, feedback, and encouragement, I especially want to thank Louis René Beres, Jeff Dumas, and Bruce Russett. I also am grateful to the following colleagues and students (past and present) who helped in the discovery, review, and processing of the materials contained herein: Chin Choon Fong, Linda Friedman, Candace Goldman, David Huscher, John Redick, Lawrence Ross, Sherle Schwenninger, Laura Schisgall, Eric Sloter, Marek Thee, and Mark Wilson. For sustained intellectual creativity and commitment to this project, I particularly want to acknowledge Sherle Schwenninger of the World Policy Institute; at his request, he is not recorded as a coeditor, but he should be.

Joan McMains, my secretary, showed truly extraordinary dedication and brought much-needed skill to the preparation of the manuscript. She gave of herself, always with kindness, far beyond what I had a right to expect.

I am much indebted also to The University of Iowa College of Law and to the World Policy Institute for funding that helped underwrite such expenses as the hiring of student assistants and the acquisition and reproduction of needed materials. Their generosity is greatly appreciated.

Finally, I want to underscore what I already have acknowledged on the title page, namely, the incalculable contributions of my former research assistants Thomas A. Hawbaker and Christopher R. Rossi, each living proof that the opportunity to engage in painstaking research and exhaustive analysis constitutes the best graduate curriculum available. Without their prodigious efforts during the past two years, my work would have been rendered far more arduous, if not impossible. Except for my wife, Kay, whose unflagging friendship and support is always an inspiration, I extend to them my deepest appreciation of all.

Burns H. Weston

Credits

I would like to thank all of the authors and publishers who granted permission to include their material in this book. A complete list of credits follows, numbered by reading:

1. "Imagine One Nuclear Bomb" is excerpted from *This is the Way the World Will End, This is the Way You Will End, Unless . . .* by Harold Freeman. Copyright © 1982 by Schenkman Publishing Company. Reprinted by permission of the publisher.
2. "Effects of the Use of Nuclear Weapons" is excerpted with minor revision from *General and Complete Disarmament—Comprehensive Study on Nuclear Weapons,* Report of the Secretary-General, UN Doc. A/35/392, September 12, 1980.
3. "A Republic of Insects and Grass" is excerpted from *The Fate of the Earth* by Jonathan Schell. Copyright © 1982 by Jonathan Schell. Originally appeared in *The New Yorker.* Reprinted by permission of Alfred A. Knopf, Inc.
4. "Why Do Arms Races Occur?" is excerpted with minor revision from *The Prisoners of Insecurity* by Bruce Russett. Copyright © 1983 by W. H. Freeman and Company. Reprinted by permission of the publisher.
5. "Political Distrust as Generator of the Arms Race: Prisoners' and Security Dilemmas" is excerpted from *Arms Control and Peacekeeping* by Ralph M. Goldman. Copyright © 1982 by Random House, Inc. Reprinted by permission of the publisher.
6. "SALT II: A Symptom of the Arms Race," by Robert C. Johansen, is based on research reported in Chapter 2 of his book *The National Interest and the Human Interest: An Analysis of U.S. Foreign Policy* (Princeton: Princeton University Press, 1980).
7. "Beyond Psychic Numbing: A Call to Awareness," by Robert Jay Lifton, appeared originally in the *American Journal of Orthopsychiatry,* Vol. 52, No. 4 (October 1982). Copyright © 1982 by the American Orthopsychiatric Association, Inc. Reprinted by permission of the publisher.

8. "Pastoral Letter on War and Peace—The Challenge of Peace: God's Promise and Our Response," by the National Council of Catholic Bishops, is an abridgment of an article bearing the same title that appeared originally in *Origins,* Vol. 13, No. 1 (May 19, 1983). Copyright © 1983 by the National Catholic News Service. Reprinted by permission of the publisher.

9. "Statement on the Illegality of Nuclear Weapons" was drafted by Elliott L. Meyrowitz and John H. E. Fried and approved by the Lawyers Committee on Nuclear Policy on November 24, 1981.

10. "Myths and Realities of Security" is excerpted from Robin Luckham, "Regional Security and Disarmament in Africa," *Alternatives,* vol. 9, no. 2 (Fall 1983). Copyright © 1983 by Robin Luckham. Reprinted by permission of the author.

11. "The Illusion of Security," by Richard J. Barnet, is reprinted with minor revision and permission from *Foreign Policy,* No. 3 (Summer 1971). Copyright © 1971 by the Carnegie Endowment for International Peace.

12. "Military Spending and Economic Decay," by Lloyd J. Dumas, appeared originally in Lloyd J. Dumas, ed., *The Political Economy of Arms Reduction* (Boulder, CO: Westview Press, Inc., 1982). Copyright © 1982 by the American Association for the Advancement for Science. Reprinted by permission of Westview Press, Inc.

13. "Nuclear Weapons and the End of Democracy," by Richard A. Falk, abridged and reprinted by permission of *Praxis International,* Vol. 2, No. 1 (April 1982).

14. "Deterrence and Its Contradictions," by Allan Krass, is an abridgment of "The Evolution of Military Technology and Deterrence Strategy," in *World Armaments and Disarmament, SIPRI Yearbook 1981* (Cambridge, MA: Oelgeschlager, Gunn & Hain, 1981). Copyright © 1981 by the Stockholm International Peace Research Institute (SIPRI). Reprinted with permission from SIPRI.

15. "Nuclear Strategy and World Order: The United States Imperative," by Louis René Beres, is reprinted with minor revision and permission from *Alternatives—A Journal of World Policy,* Vol. 8, No. 2 (Fall 1982). Copyright © 1982 by the Institute for World Order (renamed the World Policy Institute) and the Center for the Study of Developing Societies.

16. "The Prospects for Deterrence" is reprinted with minor revision and permission from Hedley Bull, "Future Conditions of Strategic Deterrence," *The Future of Strategic Deterrence, Part I,* Adelphi Paper 160 (London: International Institute for Strategic Studies, Autumn 1980).

17. "Soviet Perceptions of the U.S.—Results of a Surrogate Interview Project" is abridged from a Research Memorandum prepared by Gregory Guroff for the Office of Research, U.S. International Communications Agency, Washington, DC (June 27, 1980).

18. "Relations Between the United States and the Soviet Union—Accuracy of U.S. Perceptions," by Georgi A. Arbatov, appeared

Kriesberg, appeared originally in Carolyn M. Stephenson, ed., *Alternative Methods for Security* (Washington, DC: University Press of America, Inc., 1982). Copyright © 1982 by the University Press of America, Inc. Reprinted by permission of the publisher.

39. "Toward an Alternative Security System," by Robert C. Johansen, is abridged from "Toward an Alternative Security System: Moving Beyond the Balance of Power in the Search for World Security," *World Policy Paper No. 24* (New York: World Policy Institute, 1983). Copyright © 1983 by the Institute for World Order (renamed the World Policy Institute). Reprinted by permission of the publisher.

40. "Elements of a Programme for Arms Control and Disarmament: Strengthening the United Nations Security System, Regional Approaches to Security, and Economic Security" is excerpted from *Report on the Independent Commission on Disarmament and Security Issues: Common Security—A Programme for Disarmament.* Copyright © 1982 by the Independent Commission on Disarmament and Security Issues. Reprinted by permission of Simon & Schuster, a division of Gulf & Western Corporation.

41. "The Establishment of a World Authority: Working Hypothesis," by Silviu Brucan, is reprinted with permission from *Alternatives—A Journal of World Policy,* Vol. 8, No. 2 (Fall 1982). Copyright © 1982 by the Institute for World Order (renamed the World Policy Institute) and the Center for the Study of Developing Societies.

42. "Survival in an Age of Transformation," by Rajni Kothari, is reprinted with minor revision and permission from *Gandhi Marg,* Vol. 4, Nos. 2–3 (May–June 1982). Copyright © 1982 by the Gandhi Peace Foundation. This article also appears in Agrawal and Radhakrishna, eds., *Arms and Survival* (Bombay: Gandhi Peace Foundation, 1982).

43. "Disarmament: The Armament Process in Reverse," by Mary Kaldor, appeared originally in E. P. Thompson and Dan Smith, eds., *Protest and Survive* (New York: Monthly Review Press, 1981). Copyright © 1981 by E. P. Thompson and Dan Smith. Reprinted by permission of Mary Kaldor.

44. "Reconstructing Human Polities: Collective Security in the Nuclear Age" is an original essay by Chadwick F. Alger.

45. "Obtain the Possible: Demand the Impossible" is excerpted with minor revision from *Indefensible Weapons: The Political and Psychological Case Against Nuclearism,* by Robert Jay Lifton and Richard A. Falk. Copyright © 1982 by Basic Books, Inc. Reprinted by permission of the publisher.

Toward Nuclear Disarmament and Global Security:
A Search for Alternatives

General Introduction:
The Machines of Armageddon

On September 25, 1961, John J. McCloy, on behalf of the United States, and Valerian A. Zorin, on behalf of the Soviet Union, submitted to the United Nations (UN) General Assembly a "Joint Statement of Agreed Principles for Disarmament Negotiations."[1] Popularly known as the McCloy-Zorin Agreement, this joint statement, which was adopted unanimously by the General Assembly, called for multilateral negotiations to design and implement an internationally acceptable program of general and complete disarmament that would lead to the eventual dissolution of national armed forces, the creation of a standing UN peacekeeping force, and the establishment of effective and reliable mechanisms for the peaceful settlement of international disputes in accordance with the Charter of the United Nations.[2]

Now, some twenty years later, fulfillment of the broad principles set forth in the McCloy-Zorin Agreement seems a distant goal. To be sure, some important (although deficient) arms control measures have been undertaken by the two superpowers and other states[3]—for example, the 1963 Partial Test Ban Treaty (PTB) imposing restrictions on nuclear weapon testing;[4] the 1968 Nuclear Non-proliferation Treaty (NPT) prohibiting, inter alia, the transfer of nuclear weapons from states with such weapons to non–nuclear weapon states;[5] and the 1971-1972 SALT I accords.[6] Additionally, a series of treaties now prohibit nuclear weapons in Antarctica, Latin America, outer space, and on the seabed beyond the limit of national territorial seas.[7] Nevertheless, unable or unwilling to reconcile their geopolitical differences, the Soviet Union and the United States find themselves locked in a deadly competition to achieve the means necessary to fight *and prevail* in a protracted nuclear war; and to fight and "win" such a war, each state has developed and deployed a complex array of "strategic" and "theater" nuclear weapons capable not only of massive "countervalue" attacks that would crush the socioeconomic and political vitality of their potential adversaries but also of increasingly effective "counterforce" strikes that would eliminate an adversary's military (especially nuclear) installations. In short, far from observing the principles set forth in the McCloy-Zorin Agreement, the two superpowers and their allies have worked steadily to make resort to nuclear weapons an increasingly admissible policy option in a variety of confrontational contexts.

The remainder of this general introduction—and its primary purpose—is to depict as accurately as public information allows the nuclear capabilities of the United States and the Soviet Union, as well as the capabilities of other at least self-confirmed nuclear-weapon states. Before proceeding, however, we need to define the terms "strategic," "theater," "countervalue," and "counterforce." All figure prominently in any discussion about nuclear warfare, inasmuch as all help to make up the tangled doctrinal web that we popularly call "nuclear deterrence." (For further details concerning these and other nuclear warfare terms and abbreviations, see Appendix A: Glossary of Terms.)

Strategic nuclear weapons are designed to disrupt an adversary's overall capacity to wage war through the destruction of its economic, political, and military infrastructure (or to defend against weapons with such capability); theater nuclear weapons are intended to suppress an adversary's ability to wage war (conventional or nuclear) in a particular region, such as Europe or the Middle East. Thus, strategic nuclear weapons and delivery systems may be seen to include intercontinental ballistic missiles (ICBMs), submarine-launched ballistic missiles (SLBMs), and intercontinental heavy bombers (with and without cruise missiles), whereas theater nuclear weapons and delivery systems generally are understood to include intermediate-range ballistic missiles (IRBMs), medium-range ballistic missiles (MRBMs), and medium-range bombers and other strike aircraft, plus "battlefield" nuclear weapons such as short-range ballistic missiles (SRBMs), rockets, howitzers, mortars, and demolition mines. It is important to understand, however, that these distinctions are not without ambiguity. For example, although theater nuclear weapons may not possess the range of their strategic counterparts, some of them possess accuracies, yields, side effects, and potential targets that render them in many ways indistinguishable from strategic nuclear weapons. What ultimately matters for definitional purposes is more the reasons for which nuclear weapons are used than their performance capabilities and characteristics per se.

Similar ambiguities attend the distinction between the countervalue and counterforce doctrines of nuclear warfare. Generally speaking, countervalue targeting, as embodied in the doctrine of Mutual Assured Destruction (MAD), refers to nuclear attacks upon an adversary's cities and industries; counterforce targeting refers to attacks upon an enemy's military (primarily nuclear) forces. In point of fact, however, there is no neat dividing line between countervalue and counterforce targeting. The central concern, once again, is the ultimate purpose for which the particular weapon or weapon system is to be used. The essential purpose of counterforce targeting is to threaten military *defeat* (or "denial") as a deterrent to potential aggression or escalation of hostilities; the primary aim of countervalue targeting is to threaten massive *punishment* by way of societal destruction.

Now, with these initial clarifications in mind, let us review briefly the instruments of war that publicly are known to exist in the United States, in the USSR, and in other confirmed nuclear arsenals. (For quick reference, see the chart on nuclear weapons set forth in Appendix B.) It should go without saying that these weapons are awesome indeed and are capable of destroying almost everything in target countries many times over. A typical nuclear weapon by today's standards is a device in the one-megaton (1-Mt) range, with a blast effect equivalent to one million tons of TNT—70 to 80 times the intensity and scale of the kiloton (kt) bombs dropped on Hiroshima and Nagasaki, about 13 kt (or 13,000 tons of TNT) and 22 kt (or 22,000 tons of TNT) respectively.

U.S. NUCLEAR FORCES

U.S. Strategic Offensive Forces

The United States maintains three separate but complementary strategic offensive nuclear-strike forces: land-based ICBMs; sea-based SLBMs and sea-launched cruise missiles (SLCMs); and heavy bombers armed with short-range attack missiles (SRAMs), gravity bombs, and air-launched cruise missiles (ALCMs).[8]

Land-Based Systems. There are presently 1,052 missiles in the U.S. ICBM force: 550 Minuteman IIIs, 450 Minuteman IIs, and 52 Titan IIs. The Minuteman III carries three multiple independently targetable reentry vehicles (MIRVs), which means that each Minuteman III is armed with three nuclear warheads capable of destroying three separate targets. The Minuteman II and the Titan II each carry a single warhead. During the 1980s, the United States plans to increase substantially the counterforce capabilities of its ICBM arsenal.

The first element of this modernization program consists of "militarily significant" modifications of existing Minuteman IIIs. When first deployed, all 550 Minuteman IIIs carried 170-kt warheads, but starting in 1981 the United States began to "retrofit" 300 of these missiles with Mark 12A reentry vehicles (RVs) armed with 350-kt warheads. Nine hundred 170-kt warheads are thus being replaced by 900 350-kt warheads, a fact of major military significance because the heavier warheads possess a superior hard-target kill capability. This upward revision in the destructive power of 900 Minuteman III warheads has been accompanied, moreover, by improvements that sharpen the missile's expected accuracy—or "circular error probable" (CEP)—from 300 to 190 meters. This advancement in accuracy means that a single 170-kt warhead has a better than 50 percent chance of destroying a Soviet missile silo and that two such warheads fired in succession have about an 80 percent chance (barring "fratricide" effects). The hard-target kill probability of a single Mark 12A warhead is around 57 percent, and close to 95 percent when two of these warheads are used in tandem.

There are two other major elements in the U.S. ICBM modernization program. First, the United States plans to replace 50 single-warhead Minuteman IIs with 50 MIRVed Minuteman IIIs, which translates to a net increase of 100 warheads suitable for counterforce missions. Second, and more widely publicized, is the plan to deploy 100 "Peacekeeper" (MX) ICBMs. The so-called Peacekeeper is a high-yield, highly accurate MIRVed weapon system; its 10 to 12 335-kt/500-kt warheads possess a single-shot hard-target kill probability of 97 percent. Thus, theoretically, the 1,000 to 1,200 warheads aboard the MX missile force could destroy the bulk of the Soviet Union's 1,398 ICBM silos in a preemptive first strike, and thus also, when combined with the counterforce potential of the Minuteman IIIs, the United States theoretically could destroy all 1,398 of the Soviet ICBMs, eliminating 72 percent of the USSR's strategic warheads. This scenario causes many to challenge the deployment of the MX because its first-strike potential is likely to compel the Soviets to upgrade their strategic forces to a launch-on-warning alert status, hence increasing the possibility of accidental nuclear war.

These elements of the ongoing U.S. ICBM modernization program— advancements in the yield and accuracy of Minuteman III warheads, replacement of 50 Minuteman IIs with 50 Minuteman IIIs, and deployment of 100 MX missiles—are accompanied by a steady deactivation of the Titan II ICBMs. Retirement of these obsolete, liquid-fueled missiles is expected to be completed by 1986, leaving the U.S. ICBM force based entirely on solid-fuel propulsion systems.[9]

Sea-Based Systems. The United States land-based ICBM force is complemented by some 550 SLBMs aboard the U.S. Navy's nuclear ballistic missile submarine (SSBN) fleet. At present, there are 33 SSBNs in the U.S. nuclear arsenal: 31 Poseidon SSBNs and 2 Trident SSBNs. Eight additional Tridents are scheduled for deployment during the 1980s and 1990s, and the Reagan administration plans to build one more.

Each Poseidon submarine carries 16 SLBM launching tubes, and each Trident carries 24. At present, 19 Poseidon SSBNs are armed with the Poseidon C-3 missile, a MIRVed weapon system carrying 10 40-kt warheads. The other 12 Poseidons as well as the 2 operational Tridents are armed with the Trident C-4 SLBM carrying 8 100-kt MIRVed warheads. Until recently, the relative inaccuracy of SLBMs rendered them unreliable for preemptive strikes against an adversary's strategic nuclear forces and command structures, although adequate for strikes against countervalue targets, airfields, and conventional force bases and training centers. Upon deployment of the forthcoming Trident D-5 SLBM aboard all the Trident SSBNs, however, the United States will possess approximately 3,000 sea-launched warheads with accuracies comparable to those possessed by warheads aboard its land-based missiles, clearly a significant advancement in the capacity of the United States to destroy an adversary's means of nuclear attack.

The nuclear strike capability of the U.S. Navy will be upgraded even further with the scheduled deployment of some 1,720 sea-launched cruise missiles (SLCMs) aboard major surface warships and attack submarines. The cruise missile, which may be equipped with conventional or nuclear warheads and which may be targeted for land attack as well as antiship missions, is a small, subsonic, long-range weapon system possessing exceptional accuracy, and because it flies at surface-hugging altitudes it is extremely difficult to detect. The navy plans to procure 1,720 Tomahawk SLCMs during fiscal years 1983 and 1984.

Airbreathing Systems. Long-range manned bombers compose the third strategic assault force available to U.S. policymakers. Some 330 B-52s and 65 FB-111s are currently available for deep penetration air strikes against the Soviet Union, and some 30 percent of these aircraft are prepared for immediate launch at all times. Nuclear armaments aboard these strategic bombers consist of gravity bombs and short-range attack missiles (SRAMs). Private sources estimate the number of gravity bombs at 1,400 and the number of SRAMs at 1,020. Current plans call for 316 B-52s to remain operational into the next century, together with 65 U.S.-based FB-111s.

The capacity of the B-52s to avoid exposure to increasingly effective Soviet air defense systems will be significantly enhanced by the deployment of an estimated 3,300 air-launched cruise missiles (ALCMs) aboard some 120 to 150 of these aircraft during the 1980s. Armed with 200-kt warheads, these ALCMs have a range exceeding 2,500 kilometers (km), thus enabling their parent aircraft to launch nuclear strikes against hardened targets from positions along the periphery of Soviet air defenses. However, according to government sources, deployment of these ALCMs will not obviate the need for a manned bomber capable of penetrating deeply into Soviet airspace. Citing a need to prevent the USSR from focusing its air defense efforts solely on the ALCM-armed bombers, as well as a need to attack mobile military assets critical to Soviet wartime objectives, United States policymakers plan to deploy 100 B-1B supersonic bombers during the 1980s and an unspecified number of radar-elusive "stealth" aircraft—known officially as the Advanced Technology Bomber (ATB)—during the 1990s.

U.S. Strategic Defense Systems

Strategic defense systems are defined here as those forces that do not rely on land-attack missions to diminish an enemy's capacity to attack U.S. civilian and military assets of strategic value. Specifically, this definition encompasses antisubmarine warfare (ASW) forces, ballistic missile defenses (BMD), antisatellite (ASAT) systems, and antiaircraft defenses.

Air Defense Forces. Strategic antiaircraft defenses include 120 F-106 long-range interceptors and some 100 Nike-Hercules surface-to-air missiles (SAMs). Each F-106 is armed with 2 1-kt Genie air-to-air missiles; each Nike-Hercules SAM is armed with a single 1-kt warhead. The F-106s are assigned to the North American Aerospace Command (NORAD) and are supported by Tactical Air Command (TAC) interceptors that presently maintain ground alert at sites around the periphery of the forty-eight contiguous states, in Alaska, and in Canada. About half of the F-106s are slated for replacement by the more advanced F-15 Fighting Falcons.

Antisatellite Capabilities. Disruption of an enemy's capacity to fight a protracted nuclear war requires diminution of its ability to target strategic assets through satellite surveillance. To gain an effective ASAT capability, the U.S. Air Force plans to deploy the Air-Launched Miniature Vehicle (ALMV), which is launched by F-15s against enemy satellites. To support an ASAT capability beyond the 1980s, the United States is currently assessing the feasibility of space-based laser weapons.

Antisubmarine Warfare Forces. The United States currently maintains the world's most advanced antisubmarine capability. The ASW network consists of long-range aircraft, nuclear attack submarines, and surface vessels. These systems, supported by underwater surveillance mechanisms, rely on nuclear torpedoes, nuclear depth charges, and nuclear-tipped missiles to destroy an adversary's ballistic missile and hunter-killer submarine forces. The bulk of the ASW force is composed of 24 active and 13 reserve squadrons of P-3 land-based aircraft (9 planes per squadron) and some 69 nuclear attack submarines (SSNs). Eventually there will be some 40 additional attack submarines in the U.S. fleet, i.e., 40 SSN-668 LOS ANGELES–class vessels armed with SLCMs as well as ASW weapons (nuclear or conventional).

Ballistic Missile Defenses. Ballistic missile defense (BMD) technology has been publicly acknowledged to have been developed to the point where, should the need arise, the United States could field an advanced and highly effective BMD system quickly. Private sources are of the opinion that this BMD system would involve the use of one tier of missiles armed with nuclear or conventional warheads to attack enemy reentry vehicles (RVs) at altitudes above 300,000 feet, and a second tier of nuclear-armed missiles to attack surviving RVs at altitudes below 50,000 feet. Research and development of ground-based and orbital BMD systems exploiting charged-particle-beam and laser technologies also is under way.

U.S. Theater Nuclear Forces

As noted earlier, theater nuclear forces (TNF) include weapon systems intended to suppress an adversary's ability to wage war (conventional or nuclear) in a particular area. Theater nuclear forces generally include intermediate-range ballistic missiles (IRBMs) possessing ranges between

1,000 and 5,500 km, medium-range ballistic missiles (MRBMs) capable of striking targets 200 to 1,000 km away, and "dual-capable" aircraft with combat ranges under 3,000 km. Theater nuclear forces also include nuclear weapons with ranges below 200 km. These systems, known as tactical systems, are designed for "battlefield" operations. Currently, there are 6,000 U.S. nuclear warheads aboard land-based and airbreathing systems slated for combat in the European theater. When sea-based nuclear systems are taken into account, the total number of warheads maintained by the United States for a nuclear war in Europe is estimated at 15,000.

Long-Range Theater Nuclear Forces. Long-range theater nuclear forces (LRTNF) capabilities include weapon systems with ranges above 1,000 km. At present, the LRTNF arsenal of the United States is composed solely of aircraft with combat radii near or above the 1,000-km range. These LRTNF aircraft are divided into two categories: (a) "primary" LRTNF aircraft, with combat radii well over 1,000 km and with low-level, all-weather capabilities to ensure penetration of enemy air defenses; and (b) "marginal" LRTNF aircraft, with combat radii of about 800 to 1,200 km and a limited low-level, all-weather capability. In Europe, U.S. long-range theater forces include 164 F-111 bombers (characterized as primary LRTNF systems) and 254 F-4 Phantom fighter-bombers plus 68 A6/7 attack aircraft (considered marginal LRTNF systems). In addition, there are 264 aircraft stationed aboard U.S. carriers operating in the Atlantic and the Mediterranean that are capable of attacking the Soviet homeland.

The United States does not presently maintain an intermediate-range ballistic missile (IRBM) system capable of striking Soviet territory from bases in Europe. However, unless diplomatic or political developments dictate otherwise, this situation will change significantly in late 1983 when Pershing II IRBMs begin to replace, on a one-for-one basis, at least 108 of the 216 shorter-range Pershing IA missiles currently stationed in West Germany. The Pershing II is a highly accurate, single-warhead missile that will be mounted aboard the 108 Pershing IA mobile launchers based in the Federal Republic. Its deployment is to be accompanied by the simultaneous deployment of 464 Tomahawk ground-launched cruise missiles (GLCMs).

Medium- and Short-Range Theater Nuclear Forces. These TNF categories include Pershing IA missiles and marginal LRTNF combat aircraft. As noted, starting in 1983, the United States plans to retire the Pershing IA force, replacing these weapons with new, longer-range Pershing IIs. In addition, the F-15 Fighting Falcon is scheduled to replace the less capable, aging fleet of F-4 fighter-bombers.

Tactical (Battlefield) Nuclear Forces. U.S. battlefield nuclear weapons include some 950 Lance short-range ballistic missiles (SRBMs), 36 of them in Europe. At present, the United States is stockpiling enhanced-radiation (ER) warheads (i.e., so-called neutron bombs) compatible with the Lance delivery system. Other nuclear systems intended for use in ground operations include 2,000 8-inch and 155-mm howitzers capable of firing nuclear-tipped, rocket-assisted artillery shells, and some 300 atomic demolition munitions (ADMs), commonly known as nuclear land mines.

The United States also possesses a wide variety of sea-based tactical weapons with which to engage hostile naval forces, including shorter-range antiair, antisubmarine, and antiship weapons (such as the Terrier surface-to-air missiles), plus antisubmarine rockets, air-delivered nuclear depth bombs, and gravity bombs delivered by carrier-based aircraft.

SOVIET NUCLEAR FORCES

Soviet Strategic Offensive Forces

The Soviet Union, like the United States, maintains three strategic nuclear attack capabilities: land-based, sea-based, and airbreathing systems. However, considerable differences exist between the two superpowers in the overall composition of these strategic forces.[10]

Land-Based Systems. Soviet land-based strategic forces consist of 1,398 ICBMs under the control of the Strategic Rocket Force (SRF): 580 SS-11s, 60 SS-13s, 150 SS-17s, 308 SS-18s, and about 300 SS-19s. The great majority of the SS-17s, SS-18s, and SS-19s are armed with multiple independently targetable reentry vehicles (MIRVs), which means that the Soviet Union's 1,398 ICBMs carry more than 5,100 warheads, or approximately 72 percent of the Soviet strategic warhead inventory of 7,800.

The SS-17 is armed with four MIRVed warheads estimated at over 200 kt each. The SS-17 employs a "cold-launch" technique that delays main engine ignition until the missile has exited its hardened silo. This technique minimizes launch damage to the silo and is consistent with developing a reload/refire capability during a protracted nuclear conflict.

The SS-18, which is the backbone of the Soviet Union's much publicized first-strike capacity to destroy a high percentage (80 to 95 percent) of the U.S. ICBM force, is the largest of the current Soviet ICMBs. It is deployed in single- and multiple-warhead versions, and also uses a cold-launch technique. The yield of the weapon aboard the single-warhead SS-18 is believed to be in the 25 to 50 Mt range, and it possesses the accuracy necessary to destroy any known fixed target with high probability. The MIRVed versions of the SS-18 carry 8 to 10 warheads with yields estimated at 1 or 2 Mt apiece, and with expected accuracies (CEPs) of approximately 180 meters. The explosive power and accuracy of these warheads appear to render futile any realistic effort to protect a target through "hardening."

The SS-19 uses a hot-launch technique with engine ignition occurring while the missile is in its silo. Like the SS-18, there are both single-

and multiple-warhead versions of this ICBM. The yield of the single-warhead version is unspecified in publicly available defense literature, but is likely to be between 10 to 25 Mt. The MIRVed version is believed to be capable of delivering 6 warheads, with yields estimated to vary between 200 kt and 1 Mt per warhead.

At present, the USSR is testing a new generation of ICBMs and preparing to modify existing systems. The anticipated changes will include a switch from liquid- to solid-fuel propulsion systems and a reduction in the size of individual reentry vehicles (RVs) so as to allow each missile to carry a greater number of warheads. The first modification should provide the Soviet Union with additional flexibility in handling and in basing its ICBM force; the second will heighten its hard-target kill capabilities and possibly reduce the prospects for collateral damage. Enhanced warhead accuracy should also be expected.

Sea-Based Systems. The Soviet fleet of nuclear-powered ballistic missile submarines (SSBNs) includes 24 YANKEE-class SSBNs, 38 DELTA-class SSBNs, 8 HOTEL-class SSBNs, and 1 TYPHOON-class SSBN. Thirty of these SSBNs have been built since 1975. In general, the Soviets have increased the range of their submarine-launched ballistic missiles (SLBMs) and the number of SLBMs per submarine.

The HOTEL-class SSBN was first deployed in the early 1960s. Three versions are operational at present: 6 HOTEL-IIs, 1 HOTEL-III, and 1 HOTEL-IV. The HOTEL-II SSBN is armed with 3 single-warhead, liquid-fueled SS-N-5s with a range of 700 nautical miles (nm); the HOTEL-III is armed with 6 single-warhead, liquid-fueled SS-N-6s with a range of 1,300 nm; and the HOTEL-IV is armed with 6 single-warhead, liquid-fueled SS-N-8s with a range of 4,300 nm. All of the warheads aboard the HOTEL-class SSBNs have a 1-Mt yield.

The YANKEE-class SSBN was deployed in two versions in the late 1960s and early 1970s. There are 23 YANKEE-I SSBNs armed with 16 SS-N-6s each and carrying either a single 1-Mt warhead or two 200-kt multiple reentry vehicles (MRVs) or warheads. The range of the SS-N-6 varies between 1,300 and 1,600 nm depending on the payload aboard. Also operational is one YANKEE-II SSBN armed with 12 1-Mt, single-warhead SS-NX-17 SLBMs.

The DELTA-class SSBN first appeared in 1973. The USSR's 12 DELTA-I and 11 DELTA-II SSBNs are armed with 12 and 16 SS-N-8 SLBMs respectively. The SS-N-8 has a range of 4,300 nm and carries a single warhead in the 1-Mt range. In addition, there are 9 DELTA-III SSBNs, each armed with 16 SS-N-18s, the first Soviet SLBM to demonstrate a MIRV capability. This SLBM's range varies between 6,500 and 8,000 km depending on the payload aboard, and thus is capable of attacking North American strategic targets from Soviet home waters, substantially reducing the risk of SSBN losses at the hands of highly advanced enemy antisubmarine forces. The SS-N-18 is believed typically to carry 3 200-kt MIRVed warheads.

In 1980, the USSR launched a new and very large strategic submarine, the Typhoon, which is believed to carry 20 to 24 SLBMs known as the SS-NX-20. This missile carries 7 to 12 MIRVed warheads at the 200-kt level and, like the SS-N-18, has the range necessary to attack counterforce targets deep in the United States from the relative safety of Soviet coastal waters.

Soviet Airbreathing Systems. Unlike the United States, the Soviet Union does not maintain a large contingent of manned strategic bombers, although there are reports that the USSR is developing a new intercontinental attack aircraft. At present, the USSR possesses some 140 M-4 Bison and Tu-9 Bears of considerable age and vulnerability. However, the deployment of 150 Backfire bombers, which are being produced at a rate of 30 per year and which are capable of one-way nuclear attacks on North American targets, has clouded the picture somewhat. Moreover, as Soviet in-flight refueling capabilities grow, the capacity of Soviet Backfires to attack intercontinentally will be enhanced significantly. Nuclear armaments aboard these aircraft are armed with gravity bombs and air-launched cruise missiles (ALCMs) and, overall, comprise approximately 3 to 4 percent of the Soviet Union's inventory of strategic warheads.

Soviet Strategic Defense Systems

Soviet Air Defense Forces (PVO-Strany) possess some 7,000 radar stations, 2,600 interceptor aircraft, an estimated 10,000 SAM launchers, and 64 Galosh ABMs centered around Moscow. An additional 36 Galosh launchers and associated radar systems are under construction, and there are official Western reports of a hypersonic SAM intended to intercept enemy short-range attack missiles (SRAMs). Soviet antiaircraft weapons carry either nuclear or conventional warheads; all Soviet antiballistic missiles are nuclear tipped.

A reliable antisatellite (ASAT) capability is also a high Soviet priority. Research in hunter-killer satellite systems is being accompanied by intense efforts to develop an operational particle-beam or laser-based ballistic missile defense (BMD) system.

To challenge the survivability of the sea-based leg of the U.S. strategic deterrent, the Soviet Union maintains a large fleet of some 220 hunter-killer submarines. About 60 of them are nuclear-powered and armed with nuclear-tipped antiship and antisubmarine torpedoes; newer versions also will carry rocket-delivered antisubmarine weapons. The antiship and antisubmarine capabilities of the nuclear-powered attack submarine fleet are augmented by similar weapons carried aboard 50 nuclear-powered cruise missile submarines (SSGNs) and 20 diesel-powered cruise missile submarines (SSGs).

Soviet Theater Nuclear Forces

The Soviet Union, like the United States, is anticipated to continue to modernize and expand its theater nuclear forces during the 1980s.

Western public awareness of this expansion is relatively recent and has tended to focus largely on the longer-range elements of the force, especially the SS-20 and the Tu-26 Backfire bomber. In fact, improvements in the Soviet Union's ability to carry out nuclear strikes against theater and peripheral targets have been steady over the years and have applied to short- and medium-range as well as long-range systems.

Long-Range Theater Nuclear Forces. The long-range Soviet theater nuclear forces (LRTNF) consist of intermediate-range ballistic missiles (IRBMs) and medium-range ballistic missiles (MRBMs) under the control of the Strategic Rocket Force (SRF), plus bombers assigned to Long-Range Aviation and Naval Aviation.

The land-based missile component of the Soviet LRTNF consists of SS-4 MRBMs and SS-5 and SS-20 IRBMs. First deployed in 1959, the SS-4 is a liquid-fuel missile that carries a single 1-Mt warhead to a maximum range of 1,900 km. Some 340 SS-4s are believed still to be operational. The SS-5 is also a liquid-fuel system, carrying a single 1-Mt warhead to a maximum range of 4,100 km. Initially deployed in 1961, approximately 40 SS-5s still are in service. Due to the relative inaccuracy and vulnerability of the SS-4s and SS-5s, the Soviet Union has been compelled to assign a significant portion of its land-based intercontinental missiles to theater warfare missions.

The SS-20 weapon system includes a mobile launcher with a rapid reload/relaunch capability that fires a MIRVed IRBM armed with 3 200-kt warheads. At present, 324 of a projected 350 to 500 SS-20 weapon systems are operational. The accuracy of the SS-20 warheads, which have a circular error probable (CEP) of 300 m, is an immense improvement over the CEPs of the SS-4 and SS-5 warheads, which in some cases exceed 1.5 km. This heightened accuracy gives the SS-20 a highly effective first-strike capability against NATO's nuclear and conventional forces, thus freeing theater hard-target missiles for intercontinental missions. Also, the SS-20 poses a special problem for arms control verification. By the simple addition of a third stage, the SS-20 can be transformed into an SS-16 ICBM, capable of striking targets deep in North America. The SS-20 launching system is fully compatible with the SS-16 missile, and the canisters in which the SS-20 and the SS-16 repose can be made to look identical. At present, however, it is unclear whether the USSR has developed the launch technologies and guidance systems to overcome the targeting problems associated with ICBM mobility.

The principal Soviet long-range, nuclear-capable theater bombers are the Tu-16 Badger, the Tu-22 Blinder, and the Tu-26 Backfire. Deployment of these aircraft is divided between Long-Range Aviation (LRA) and Soviet Naval Aviation (SNA).

The Badger (with its 2,800 km range) and the Blinder (with its 3,100 km range) are old systems (first deployed in 1955 and 1962 respectively), but they are being equipped with improved air-to-surface missiles and, very probably, improved low-level guidance and control systems to penetrate an adversary's air defenses. Roughly 715 of these bombers remain in service at this time.

The Tu-26 Backfire, which as previously noted might be used for intercontinental warfare, has an unrefueled combat radius of at least 4,200 km, allowing it to cover, from bases in the USSR, all of NATO Europe as well as large areas of adjacent oceans. Perhaps equally important, it gives the aircraft increased "loiter time" at shorter ranges, and thus a heightened capacity for seeking out mobile targets. The Backfire can carry either bombs or air-to-surface missiles, and enjoys a low-level supersonic dash capability.

Short-Range Systems. Principal missile systems in this category are the SS-12 Scaleboard, the Scud B, and the FROG (free rocket over ground). First deployed in 1969, the land-mobile SS-12 short-range ballistic missile (SRBM) has an estimated range of 900 km, but it is being replaced by the newer SS-22 which has an equivalent range. Some 120 SS-12s and SS-22s are in service at the present time, and, so far as is known, all are deployed on Soviet territory in peacetime. In contrast, the Scud and FROG systems are integrated into Soviet forces in Eastern Europe. The SS-1c Scud B, first deployed in 1965, has a 300-m range and is a land-mobile system. About 410 are deployed with Soviet forces, although they are expected to be replaced by the SS-X-23 SRBM, which has greater accuracy and range and shorter reaction and reload times. The 680 FROG systems, which have an estimated maximum range of 60 to 75 km, also are due to be retired in favor of a more accurate system—the SS-21. The SS-21 first entered service in 1978, but only a few have been deployed so far.

Perhaps more noteworthy than the modifications in Soviet SRBMs are the improvements over the past decade in the nuclear ground-attack capabilities of Soviet tactical aircraft. The most significant new system is the Su-24 Fencer, which entered into service in 1974 as the first modern Soviet system designed specifically for ground attack. Though estimates vary, the Fencer's combat radius is well in excess of 1,000 km and may be as high as 1,800 km. Combined with its high payload, this range capability (and commensurate loiter time) makes the Fencer especially appropriate for strikes against mobile systems (including mobile weapon launchers) from bases in the western USSR—characteristics that have caused the aircraft to be procured in large numbers (approximately 600 to date, produced at a pace of some 60 aircraft per year). The Soviet Union has even larger numbers of the nuclear-capable MiG-23/-27 Flogger and Su-7/-17 Fitter, each fighter-bombers capable of ground attack.

Finally, the Soviet Union is believed to have given some of its 203 mm and 240 mm artillery pieces a nuclear capability. All such dual-capable artillery is believed to be deployed exclusively on Soviet territory; but, since the older towed artillery is being replaced by self-propelled models, these systems presumably could be brought to bear against NATO Europe without much difficulty.

OTHER NUCLEAR-WEAPON STATES

In addition to the United States and the Soviet Union, there are three other self-confirmed nuclear-weapon states: France, the People's Republic of China, and the United Kingdom. These three countries all maintain independent nuclear forces.

France currently deploys 5 SSBNs, each armed with 16 MSBS M-20 SLBMs. This system has a 1-Mt warhead and a range of some 3,000 km. A sixth nuclear submarine is due to enter service in 1985 with the MRVed M-4 missile (4,000 km range, 6 to 7 150-kt warheads). The entire French SSBN fleet will convert to the M-4 by 1989. France also maintains 18 land-based MRBMs, and 24 medium-range bombers. A mobile IRBM is expected to replace the increasingly vulnerable French bomber force.

The present Chinese nuclear force consists of 2 to 4 ICBMs and approximately 100 IRBMs and MRBMs. The People's Republic has no SLBMs and is widely considered to be twenty to forty years behind the United States and the Soviet Union both quantitatively and qualitatively in developing and deploying large numbers of ICBMs and SLBMs. However, the Chinese medium-range and intermediate-range missiles probably could destroy the top forty Soviet cities in a first strike.

The United Kingdom's nuclear forces include 4 RESOLUTION-class SSBNs, each armed with 16 Polaris A-3 SLBMs carrying 3 200-kt MRV warheads apiece, and 40 aging Vulcan medium-range bombers. Both components will be upgraded significantly in the next two decades. The UK's air-attack capacity will be improved through a continuing deployment of Tornado fighter-bombers possessing low-altitude and all-weather, deep-strike capabilities. The British SLBM force will be expanded quantitatively and qualitatively with the forthcoming deployment of 4 or 5 new SSBNs carrying 16 or 24 Trident D-5 SLBMs.

Although West Germany is not a confirmed nuclear-weapon power, its military establishment possesses nuclear-capable aircraft, Pershing IA missiles, and Lance and Honest John SRBMs. Nuclear warheads for these forces are kept in U.S. custody.

Other states believed to possess nuclear weapons or to be capable of producing them within a few months are India, Israel, South Africa, and Pakistan. India has conducted a peaceful nuclear explosion (PNE), and possesses nuclear-capable aircraft. Argentina, Brazil, and Libya are widely cited as future nuclear-weapon states, as are Iraq, Taiwan, and South Korea.

SUMMARY AND CONCLUSION

The nuclear arsenals of the superpowers possess the capacity to devastate whole societies in a matter of hours, if not minutes. Even if the use of nuclear weapons were restricted to limited counterforce strikes, the collateral damage would cause casualties and physical damage of unprecedented magnitude. Still, the Soviet Union and the United States have worked persistently to further their nuclear war-fighting capabilities. Their competitive quest for nuclear military supremacy seems unending as both strive not only to improve their offensive nuclear forces but also to deploy laser and particle-beam weaponry to defend against such forces. And as the primary nuclear-weapon states race to improve their nuclear force postures, regional powers also are developing the means to launch nuclear attacks, and thus the possibility of nuclear war proliferates.

There are some who believe that these trends make nuclear war inevitable. But there are some, too, who may have recalled the wisdom of the late Arnold Toynbee:

The dead civilizations are not dead by fate; and therefore a living civilization is not doomed inexorably in advance *migrare ad plures:* to join the majority of its kind that have suffered shipwreck. Though sixteen civilizations may have perished already to our knowledge, and nine others may be now at the point of death, and though Nature, in her wanton prodigality, may be wont to slay the representatives of a species, not by tens or scores, but by thousands and tens of thousands, before she rouses herself to create a new specific mutation, we need fear no evil from the encompassing shadow of Death; for we are not compelled to submit our fate to the blind arbitrament of statistics. The divine spark of creative power is instinct in ourselves; and if we have the grace to kindle it into flame, then the stars in their courses cannot defeat our efforts to attain the goal of human endeavors.[11]

Increasingly, people the world over are refusing to accept the possibility of what would be the most severe social and biological catastrophe of all time. Increasingly, they are refusing to abdicate their compassion, their reason, and their will.

In the last few years, the complex questions surrounding nuclear weapons and warfare have emerged from the inner chambers of the physicists, the engineers, and the strategists to become psychologically and politically visible to the common man and woman. In the West, an increasingly powerful antinuclear movement has arisen and become a central feature of domestic politics among the NATO countries. To some albeit minor extent, it also has begun to take root among the peoples of the Soviet bloc. And the near uniform reaction is a demand for significant change.

This book is about such change. Its purpose is to examine critically the basic assumptions and perceptions that underlie the worldwide profusion of nuclear armaments and to help initiate the search for new arrangements and structures that bear the promise of reversing the nuclear arms race while simultaneously ensuring the community of nations against the threat of military coercion. It raises many difficult questions for which, in all probability, no single persuasive answer will be found. But escape from the nuclear dilemma surely requires that each of us give serious attention to the quest for alternative security systems and to the evolution of transformative policies and programs that can ensure long-term human survival. Clearly the time has come for all men and women, especially those with the freedom to call into question the policies of their governments, to give responsible consideration to the preciousness of life and to the possibilities for safeguarding human existence.

NOTES

1. "Joint Statement of Agreed Principles for Disarmament Negotiations," *U.S.-USSR Report to the General Assembly,* UN Doc. A/4879, reprinted in the *Department of State Bulletin,* Vol. 45, No. 1163 (Oct. 9, 1961), pp. 589–590.

2. The full text of the "Joint Statement," note 1, *supra,* reads as follows:

Having conducted an extensive exchange of views on disarmament pursuant to their agreement announced in the General Assembly on 30 March 1961,

Noting with concern that the continuing arms race is a heavy burden for humanity and is fraught with dangers for the cause of world peace,

Reaffirming their adherence to all the provisions of the General Assembly resolution 1378 (XIV) of 20 November 1959,

Affirming that to facilitate the attainment of general and complete disarmament in a peaceful world it is important that all States abide by existing international agreements, refrain from any actions which might aggravate international tensions, and that they seek settlement of all disputes by peaceful means,

The United States and the USSR have agreed to recommend the following principles as the basis for future multilateral negotiations on disarmament and to call upon other States to co-operate in reaching early agreement on general and complete disarmament in a peaceful world in accordance with these principles.

1. The goal of negotiations is to achieve agreement on a programme which will ensure that (a) disarmament is general and complete and war is no longer an instrument for settling international problems, and (b) such disarmament is accompanied by the establishment of reliable procedures for the peaceful settlement of disputes and effective arrangements for the maintenance of peace in accordance with the principles of the United Nations Charter.

2. The programme for general and complete disarmament shall ensure that States will have at their disposal only those non-nuclear armaments, forces, facilities, and establishments as are agreed to be necessary to maintain internal order and protect the personal security of citizens and that States shall support and provide agreed manpower for a United Nations peace force.

3. To this end, the programme for general and complete disarmament shall contain the necessary provisions, with respect to the military establishment of every nation, for:

(a) Disbanding of armed forces, dismantling of military establishments, including bases, cessation of the production of armaments as well as their liquidation or conversion to peaceful uses;

(b) Elimination of all stockpiles of nuclear, chemical, bacteriological, and other weapons of mass destruction and cessation of the production of such weapons;

(c) Elimination of all means of delivery of weapons of mass destruction;

(d) Abolishment of the organizations and institutions designed to organize the military effort of States, cessation of military training, and closing of all military training institutions;

(e) Discontinuance of military expenditures.

4. The disarmament programme should be implemented in an agreed sequence, by stages until it is completed, with each measure and stage carried out within specified time-limits. Transition to a subsequent stage in the process of disarmament should take place upon a review of the implementation of measures included in the preceding stage and upon a decision that all such measures have been implemented and verified and that any additional verification arrangements required for measures in the next stage are, when appropriate, ready to operate.

5. All measures of general and complete disarmament should be balanced so that at no stage of the implementation of the treaty could any State or group of States gain military advantage and that security is ensured equally for all.

6. All disarmament measures should be implemented from beginning to end under such strict and effective international control as would provide firm assurance that all parties are honouring their obligations. During and after the implementation of general and complete disarmament, the most thorough control should be exercised, the nature and extent of such control depending on the requirements for verification of the disarmament measures being carried out in each stage. To implement control over and inspection of disarmament, an International Disarmament Organization including all parties to the agreement should be created within the framework of the United Nations. This International Disarmament Organization and its inspectors should be assured unrestricted access without veto to all places as necessary for the purpose of effective verification.

7. Progress in disarmament should be accompanied by measures to strengthen institutions for maintaining peace and the settlement of international disputes by peaceful means. During and after the implementation of the programme of general and complete disarmament, there should be taken, in accordance with the principles of the United Nations Charter, the necessary measures to maintain international peace and security, including the obligation of States to place at the disposal of the United Nations agreed manpower necessary for an international peace force to be equipped with agreed types of armaments. Arrangements for the use of this force should ensure that the United Nations can effectively deter or suppress any threat or use of arms in violation of the purposes and principles of the United Nations.

8. States participating in the negotiations should seek to achieve and implement the widest possible agreement at the earliest possible date. Efforts should continue without interruption until agreement upon the total programme has been achieved, and efforts to ensure early agreement on and implementation of measures of disarmament should be undertaken without prejudicing progress on agreement on the total programme and in such a way that these measures would facilitate and form part of that programme.

3. For quick summary reference, see Jozef Goldblat, "Multilateral and Bilateral Arms Control Agreements," in *The Arms Race and Arms Control,* ed. Stockholm International Peace Research Institute (London: Taylor & Francis, 1982). For the full text of arms control agreements and the status of their implementation, see Jozef Goldblat, *Agreements for Arms Control: A Critical Survey* (London: Taylor & Francis, 1982).

4. Treaty Banning Nuclear Weapon Tests in the Atmosphere, in Outer Space and Under Water, *done* Aug. 5, 1963, *entered into force* Oct. 10, 1963, 14 UST 1313, TIAS No. 5433, 480 UNTS 43 (ratified by 110 states as of Dec. 31, 1982).

5. Treaty on the Non-proliferation of Nuclear Weapons, *done* July 1, 1968, *entered into force* Oct. 5, 1970, 21 UST 483, TIAS No. 6839, 729 UNTS 161 (ratified by 119 states as of Jan. 31, 1983).

6. The SALT I accords include the following four instruments: Agreement Between the United States of America and the Union of Soviet Socialist Republics on Measures to Improve the USA-USSR Direct Communications Link, *done*

Sept. 30, 1971, *entered into force* Sept. 30, 1971, 22 UST 1598, TIAS No. 7187, 806 UNTS 402; Agreement on Measures to Reduce the Risk of Outbreak of Nuclear War Between the United States of America and the Union of Soviet Socialist Republics, *done* Sept. 30, 1971, *entered into force* Sept. 30, 1971, 22 UST 1590, TIAS No. 7186, 807 UNTS 57; Treaty Between the United States of America and the Union of Soviet Socialist Republics on the Limitation of Anti-Ballistic Missile Systems, *done* May 26, 1972, *entered into force* Oct. 3, 1972, 23 UST 3435, TIAS No. 7503; and Interim Agreement Between the United States of America and the Union of Soviet Socialist Republics on Certain Measures With Respect to the Limitation of Strategic Offensive Arms, *done* May 26, 1972. *Entered into force,* Oct. 3, 1972, *expired,* Oct. 3, 1977, 23 UST 3462, TIAS No. 7504.

7. *See* the Antarctic Treaty, Arts. I & V, *done* Dec. 1, 1959, *entered into force* June 23, 1961, 12 UST 794, TIAS 4780, 402 UNTS 71 (ratified by 26 states as of Dec. 31, 1982); Treaty for the Prohibition of Nuclear Weapons in Latin America, *done* Feb. 14, 1967, *entered into force* for 24 states as of Dec. 31, 1982, 634 UNTS 281; Treaty on Principles Governing the Activities of States in the Exploration and Use of Outer Space, Including the Moon and Other Celestial Bodies, Art. IV, *done* Jan. 27, 1967, *entered into force* Oct. 10, 1967, 18 USTY 2410, TIAS 6347, 610 UNTS 205 (ratified by 81 states as of Dec. 31, 1982); Treaty on the Prohibition of the Emplacement of Nuclear Weapons and Other Weapons of Mass Destruction on the Seabed and the Ocean Floor and in the Subsoil Thereof, *done* Feb. 11, 1971, *entered into force* for 70 states as of Dec. 31, 1982, 23 UST 701, TIAS No. 7337.

8. Sources of information on U.S. nuclear forces include the following: Center for Defense Information, "U.S.-Soviet Military Facts," *Defense Monitor,* Vol. 11, No. 6 (1982); Anthony H. Cordesman, *Deterrence in the 1980s: Part I— American Strategic Forces and Extended Deterrence,* Adelphi Paper No. 175 (London: International Institute for Strategic Studies, 1982); Randall Forsberg, "A Bilateral Nuclear Weapon Freeze," *Scientific American,* Vol. 247, No. 5 (Nov. 1982), pp. 52–61; Harold Freeman, *This Is the Way the World Will End, This Is the Way You Will End, Unless . . .* (Edmonton, Canada: Hurtig Publishers, 1983); Ground Zero, *Nuclear War; What's in It for You?* (New York: Pocket Books, 1982); Jan Lodal, "U.S. Strategic Nuclear Forces," in *America's Security in the 1980s: Part I,* Adelphi Paper No. 173 (London: International Institute for Strategic Studies, 1982); Thomas Millar, *The East-West Strategic Balance* (London: George Allen & Unwin, 1981); North Atlantic Assembly's Special Committee on Nuclear Weapons in Europe, *Second Interim Report on Nuclear Weapons in Europe,* Report to the Committee on Foreign Relations, United States Senate (Washington, DC: Government Printing Office, 1983); North Atlantic Treaty Organization, *NATO and Warsaw Pact Force Comparisons* (Brussels: NATO, 1982); Stockholm International Peace Research Institute (SIPRI), *The Arms Race and Arms Control* (London: Taylor & Francis, 1982); Kosta Tsipis, and John David Isaacs, "Instruments of War," in *The Final Epidemic: Physicians and Scientists on Nuclear War,* ed. Ruth Adams and Susan Cullen (Chicago: University of Chicago Press, 1981); United Nations, *General and Complete Disarmament—Comprehensive Study on Nuclear Weapons: Report of the Secretary-General,* 35 UN, GAOR Annex [Provisional Agenda Item 48(b)], UN Doc. A/35/392 (1980); and U.S. Department of Defense, *Report of Secretary of Defense Caspar W. Weinberger to the Congress on the FY 1984 Budget, FY 1985 Authorization Request and FY 1984–88 Defense Programs* (Washington, DC: Government Printing Office, 1983).

8. Solid-fuel propulsion systems are considered superior to liquid-fuel systems because the former are simpler and safer to maintain, and do not require extended preparation for launch.

9. Sources of information on Soviet nuclear forces include the following: International Institute for Strategic Studies (IISS); *Strategic Balance Survey 1971–1982* (Colchester, UK: Spottiswoode & Ballantyne, 1982); Fred M. Kaplan, *Dubious Specter—A Skeptical Look at the Soviet Nuclear Threat* (Washington, DC: Institute for Policy Studies, 1980); Jeff McCauseland, "The SS-20: Military and Political Threat?" *Fletcher Forum,* Vol. 6, No. 1 (Winter 1982), pp. 1–32; Stewart Menaul, *Russian Military Power* (New York: Bonanza Books, 1982); and U.S. Department of Defense, *Soviet Military Power* (Washington, DC: Government Printing Office, 1981). In addition, see the sources cited in note 8 above for further information pertaining to Soviet nuclear forces.

10. Arnold Toynbee, *A Study of History,* Vol. 4 (New York and London: Oxford University Press, 1939), p. 39.

PART ONE

CONFRONTING THE NUCLEAR CRISIS

CHAPTER 1

Facing up to
Nuclear Extinction

On August 6, 1945, a 12.5-kt atomic weapon was detonated at low altitude over Hiroshima, Japan. The explosion killed 70,000 to 100,000 inhabitants and completely destroyed 13 square kilometers of the city. Three days later, at Nagasaki, a second nuclear attack caused some 40,000 civilian deaths and destroyed approximately 7 square kilometers completely. Thereafter, in the vicinity of both cities, for literally months after the bombings, tens of thousands succumbed to radiation poisoning.

The bombs dropped on Hiroshima and Nagasaki thus wrought a profound and terrible transformation in the conduct and meaning of war. The unending search for decisive military advantage had yielded a weapon of unprecedented destructiveness, enabling a single aircraft in but a few brief moments to inflict damage on a scale previously achieved only by massive air strikes involving hundreds of conventionally armed heavy bombers.

Yet compared to modern military nuclear capabilities, the bombs that devastated Hiroshima and Nagasaki were primitive. In terms of destructive power, accuracy, and means of delivery, nuclear weapons have undergone radical "improvement." The Soviet Union and the United States have deployed thousands of nuclear warheads many hundreds—even thousands and millions—of times more powerful than the weapons used against Japan. Warheads with yields comparable to the Hiroshima and Nagasaki bombs are no longer directed at strategically significant metropolitan areas; such weapons are now earmarked for tactical use against "mere" battlefield targets. And what was once a maximum capability of attacking a limited number of urban-industrial centers with propeller-driven aircraft has today become a hair-triggered network of weapon systems possessing the speed, precision, and power to shred within minutes the entire socioeconomic fabric of a target state. Should a general nuclear war break out, total casualties are expected to number in the hundreds of millions, accompanied by species-threatening ecological and genetic damage, pestilence, and famine.

Despite these ominous developments and projections, military leaders and civilian elites appear to think and act as if the nuclear weapon is "just one more weapon," only somewhat more destructive. Worse, there are many others who share this belief, or act as if they do. The notion of overkill has become commonplace; instead of confronting squarely the realities of nuclear war, we have grown accustomed to ignoring the danger.

This chapter is intended to remove nuclear weapons and warfare from the realm of the abstract and unimaginable. The essay by Harold Freeman bids us to comprehend the capabilities of a thermonuclear warhead as an engine of destruction, explaining, on the basis of actual case studies, the characteristics of a nuclear explosion and the various lethal forces it unleashes. The extract from the United Nations Secretary-General's report on nuclear weapons draws upon leading scientific and military studies to portray the consequences of nuclear conflict at the "theater" and "intercontinental" levels of confrontation. The final selection, from Jonathan Schell's major work *The Fate of the Earth,* represents one person's search for the human meaning of nuclear war, to discover in the words of Hiroshima's survivors what it means to enter, and emerge from, a fission-made holocaust.

1. Imagine One Nuclear Bomb . . .

Harold Freeman

A twenty-year-old man received extensive third-degree burns when the gasoline tank of his car exploded. He was taken to Massachusetts General, the only hospital in Boston with a burn care unit. Over the period of his hospitalization he received 281 units of fresh-frozen plasma, 147 units of fresh-frozen red blood cells, 37 units of platelets, and 36 units of albumin. He underwent six operations, during which 85% of his body surface was covered with skin grafts. He was kept on artificial respiration because his lungs had been scorched out. Treating him stretched to the limit the resources of the burn care unit.

On the thirty-third day he died.

BOSTON: ONE TWENTY-MEGATON BOMB

Now imagine that one twenty-megaton[1] nuclear bomb is dropped on Boston. Of those who survive, one million will receive second- or third-degree flash burns from ignited clothing. As at Hiroshima, much of their skin will hang in shreds. For them there will be no plasma, no skin grafts. There will be no hospitals. Most of them will die painfully; morphine will not reach them.

In the United States there are three burn care units with a total of ninety beds. They were meant for children.[2] Construction and operation were financed by the Shriners. Costs were so high that no more units could be built. Between $200,000 and $400,000 is needed to treat one severe burn case. Treatment includes thirty to fifty operative procedures, anesthesia every other day, infection-proof enclosures, constant attention. At most a burn care unit can handle three fresh severe cases at once.

Dr. John Constable of Massachusetts General Hospital writes that thermal injuries from a *one*-megaton nuclear bomb "will completely overwhelm what we consider to be the most lavish and well-developed medical facilities in the world." (If in fact any such facilities would be left standing, which is unlikely.) "The medical facilities of the nation would choke totally on even a fraction of the burn casualties alone."

From experience in wartime London, the International Physicians for the Prevention of War estimate that acute treatment of 34,000 serious burn cases would require 170,000 health professionals and 8,000 tons of medical supplies. When the bomb falls there will be neither.

Burned survivors will be only a part of the picture. Within a radius of four miles of a twenty-megaton bomb burst, Greater Boston will literally disappear. It will be replaced by rubble. More than 750,000 will die outright, from concussion, heat, or fire. Many of them will be vaporized. Fire-wind storms resembling winter blizzards will originate in a fireball hotter than the sun, and will sweep a radius of twenty miles. Within that radius 2,200,000 will die outright. Another 500,000 will be disabled and in shock. Their injuries will include deep chest wounds, ruptured internal organs, compound fractures, radiation sickness, and blindness. On the last, anyone who looks at the explosion from a distance of forty miles or less will likely be blinded.

Epidemic disease, carried by radiation-resistant flies and mosquitoes and by hunger-crazed animals, will end the suffering of more than 25% of the weakened survivors. In the judgment of several authorities, such diseases from the past as polio, dysentery, typhoid fever, and cholera will reappear.

Of the dead, 300,000 will neither be vaporized nor incinerated. The Pentagon has asked the National Funeral Directors Association of the United States to prepare to handle mass burials; the president of the association has asked for a training course in embalming radioactive corpses. One thing is certain. Unburied, buried, incinerated, or vaporized, the dead will continue to be radioactive—forever.

Occupants of shelters will die in assorted ways. By crushing if the shelter is vulnerable to bomb blast. By incineration if the shelter is reached by the firestorm, or by asphyxiation if the firestorm absorbs all available oxygen. By starvation or dehydration in the likely absence of radiation-free food or water. By radiation if the air within the shelter cannot be continuously filtered. MIT physicists estimate that appearance outside a shelter for more than three minutes will produce fatal third-degree burns from intense ultraviolet light.

Of Greater Boston's 6,000 doctors, 5,100 will be incapacitated or dead. That leaves 900 to treat the injured. The Dean of the Harvard School of Public Health writes:

The ratio of injured persons to physicians is thus in excess of 1,700 to 1. If a physician spends an average of only fifteen minutes with each injured person and works sixteen hours each day . . . it will take from sixteen to twenty-six days for each casualty to be seen once.

Doctors will have to treat the maimed where they lie, in the radioactive rubble. And with little more than bare hands. There will be no anesthesia, no bandages, few drugs.[3] Consider blood alone. Close to ten million units would be needed. On one recent day the total blood inventory of the Northeast Region of the American Red Cross was 11,000 units.

Even if every injured person in the city could miraculously be lifted out of the rubble by helicopter, all the hospitals in the United States would be insufficient in resources to handle them. In fact, the majority of the injured—those suffering from severe radiation—might not be admitted to a hospital. At an early stage, it is not possible to separate mild and severe cases of radiation sickness. Reliable tests are not available. The victims look and behave alike. Here are instructions from the British Civil Defense Manual:

Hospitals should accept only those casualties who would be likely to be alive after seven days with a fair chance of eventual recovery. . . . People suffering from radiation sickness only should not be admitted. There is no specific treatment for radiation injury. . . . Treatment of a person exposed to heavy radiation would probably include bone-marrow transplants, blood transfusions, and continuous use of antibiotics. None would likely be available.

Death by radiation could require a month. Here is one description of the process:

The first symptoms of radiation poisoning are headache, nausea, dizziness and frequent vomiting, then acute diarrhea and fatigue. This lasts several days and is followed by apparent recovery, but two or three weeks later the symptoms return together with internal hemorrhaging. Breathing becomes difficult, hair falls out, sores appear under and on the skin; there is fever, total fatigue, and finally death.

THE NEUTRON BOMB

But death by radiation may not always be that easy. Consider the neutron bomb, now close to operational in the United States, now in early construction stage in (socialist) France. It is easily built. It causes death by radiation (neutron and gamma particles), not by heat or blast. Representative Barbara Mikulski of Maryland has reported her conversation with Dr. Edward Buddemeyer, a nuclear physicist at the University of Maryland:

He [Buddemeyer] said that the neutron bomb explodes and blows so many holes in your nerve cells that your brain ceases to function. If it does not, you will collapse and you will lose control of your body functions. You will die within minutes or perhaps hours, and while you are lying there waiting for death to call, you will lie in your own wastes, in your own feces, with rapid convulsions and shaking.

The second cause of death, if you are a little further away, will come from something called the GI syndrome. At first you will retch and vomit. Then the nausea will pass, but you will not feel like eating because the cells in your digestive tract, extending from your mouth down through your throat and down into your stomach, will continue to divide and die, and by that time your digestive tract will become an open sore.

Your heart will weaken, your kidneys will fail, your fever will climb and you are going to hallucinate. As you lie there dying, the very insides of your body will be rotting.

The third way to die will be from the blood syndrome. If you are lucky, you will die of anemia. This will be the more peaceful option, because the neutron will attack the blood cells so they will no longer be able to reproduce. If anemia does not claim a victim on the periphery of a neutron bomb blast, death will be prolonged and agonizing. A mere hangnail will become a green ulcer, since disease defense mechanisms will be destroyed by the neutron radiation. Your gums will bleed and your mouth will hemorrhage. Microbes will grow in your lungs and they will lose their elasticity. Fluid will begin to gather and, in effect, your own lungs will become a swamp within your body.

As you gasp and struggle for breath, your liver will fail and your skin will turn yellow. You will then perhaps die or drown from your own contaminated body fluids contained in your lungs and your liver. This will take four to five weeks, while you are lying there.

We append two notes on the neutron bomb:

1. *The* (Manchester) *Guardian* reports that the United States Navy has already experimented with high doses (2,500 to 20,000 rems[4]) of neutron-gamma radiation. Within 132 hours monkeys in the experiments died very painful deaths. Much of the experimentation took place at the Armed Forces Radiobiology Research Institute at Bethesda, Maryland.
2. Former Secretary of State Alexander Haig remarks that the "great emotional complaints" that have arisen over this weapon are "ludicrous." Secretary of Defense Caspar Weinberger says, "The opportunity that this weapon gives to strengthening theater nuclear forces is one that we very probably want to make use of."

A ONE-MEGATON BOMB

Now consider a one-megaton nuclear bomb. It is the equal of seventy Hiroshima bombs. "It would take a train 300 miles long to transport the equivalent dynamite," writes Dr. Kosta Tsipis of MIT. One such bomb could vaporize ten million tons of ice. One such bomb equals half of the total destructive power of all bombs used by the Western Allies in Europe during all of World War II. Bombs of this size are currently stockpiled by the thousands in the United States and the Soviet Union.

Consider the radioactive fallout of one bomb. Following explosion at ground level, all unprotected people within an area of 1,000 square miles will die. Within 2,000 square miles there will be substantial risk of death or severe injury. Further out, with specific areas depending on prevailing winds, death from radiation will take longer. A breeze as light as twenty miles an hour can carry lethal fallout hundreds of miles from the burst. Death will arrive via such diseases as leukemia (particularly for children), ulceration of the intestines, cancer of the lungs, thyroid, breast, and intestine, and bone cancer. For longer-term survivors there will be other consequences—genetic damage, abnormalities in new births, psychological trauma of every description, mental retardation, and concentration of plutonium in testicles and ovaries (for 50,000 years); the living may very well envy the dead.

Physicists differ in their appraisals of nuclear bomb damage. At a recent conference of physicists and doctors, an independent judgment was reached of the impact on New York City of the detonation of a one-megaton bomb. It is estimated that 2,250,000 will die, 1,000,000 of them within eleven seconds. Most will be vaporized. About 3,600,000 will suffer crushing injuries and ruptured internal organs.

The fallout will be one thousand times greater than the fallout of the worst conceivable nuclear power reactor accident. It will likely blanket 1,000 square miles, causing additional casualties in the hundreds of thousands over a longer period of time. Food, water, and air will be lethally radioactive. Few will be able to enter the area to help survivors.

The fireball, hotter than the sun, will be about one-and-one-half miles in diameter. The resulting firestorm will cover about 100 square miles. Third-degree burns are likely for those within a radius of 8 miles of the burst; second-degree burns will be common over an additional 250 square miles. Shelters in the larger area will become ovens, incinerating their occupants.

Skyscrapers will topple. It is unlikely that a single metropolitan hospital will remain standing. New York City will be replaced by acres of highly radioactive rubble. There will be no communication, no transport, no medicines, no edible food, no drinkable water.

Some species will survive, notably cockroaches. They will be blind but they will continue to reproduce.

A more recent estimate, for a one-megaton airburst 8,500 feet over the Empire State Building, follows. All buildings within a radius of 4.6 miles (66 square miles) will be flattened, with death to almost all occupants. All buildings within a radius of 8 miles (201 square miles) will be heavily damaged. At 2 miles from the point of explosion, winds will be 400 miles per hour, at 4 miles, 180 miles per hour. *Initial* nuclear radiation will kill all unprotected persons within 6 square miles. Second-degree burns, likely fatal, will afflict almost all within a radius of 9.5 miles (284 square miles).

If the bomb is a twenty-megaton, the blast wave created by the fireball will destroy almost all buildings (and almost all of their occupants) within a radius of 12 miles (452 square miles), and second-degree burns will afflict almost all within a radius of 28 miles (2,463 square miles).

Is there any defence? No. Rear Admiral Gene LaRocque, United States Navy (Ret.), director of the Center for Defense Information, writes that annihilation could come in

fifteen minutes from the submarines sitting off the coast right now with nuclear weapons aimed at Boston and New York. There is no defense against Soviet missiles, absolutely none.

OMAHA: ONE FIFTEEN-MEGATON BOMB

A probable target is the Strategic Air Command, fifteen miles from Omaha. The Command is the control centre for all American strategic nuclear weapons; the long list of targets in the Soviet Union is housed there. Here is the likely effect on the Command of the explosion of a fifteen-megaton bomb.

In the seconds following detonation, the bomb would create a huge fireball with temperatures of twenty to thirty million degrees Fahrenheit. Anyone even glancing at the fireball—from as far away as thirty-five miles—would be blinded by retinal burning. Tens of thousands of people on the side of Omaha closest to the SAC base would suffer third-degree burns.

The shock wave created by the explosion would cause skull fractures, ruptured lungs, and crushing injuries to the chest. There would be broken backs, deep lacerations from flying debris, and massive hemorrhaging. Even at eleven or twelve miles from ground zero, the overpressure would be great enough to turn an ordinary window into a lethal weapon as thousands of pieces of glass exploded at one hundred miles per hour.

These injuries do not include the many who would be killed by random spontaneous fires fueled by gasoline stations, natural gas lines. . . .

CHICAGO: ONE TWENTY-MEGATON BOMB

Another scenario and another likely target—Chicago. One twenty-megaton nuclear bomb explodes just above ground level, at the corner of LaSalle and Adams. In less than one millionth of a second the temperature rises to 150,000,000 degrees Fahrenheit, four times the temperature of the centre of the sun. A roar follows but no one is alive to hear it.

Chicago has disappeared. The crater is 600 feet deep, one-and-one-half miles in diameter. Within a five-mile radius, skyscrapers, apartment buildings, roads, bridges, trains, subways, planes, hospitals, ambulances, automobiles, gas mains, trees, earth, animals, people—all have vanished. For inner city people it was instant, painless death, occurring before the firestorm or the shockwave began to move out.

The fireball is brighter than five thousand suns. The firestorm roars out in all directions, absorbing all available oxygen, thereby suffocating or incinerating all the living in its path. Before it burns out it will devastate 1.4 million acres and most of the people on them.

The firestorm is followed by the shockwave, the latter at close to the speed of sound. Then the mushroom cloud, reaching twenty miles in height, and the beginning of lethal radioactive fallout. If the prevailing wind is from the west, and it usually is, 50% of the residents of Kalamazoo, one hundred miles away, will be dead in fifteen hours, 100% will be dead in twenty-four hours. Detroit is 230 miles east of Chicago and will survive longer; within three weeks 50% will die, within one year 100% will be dead. But, as the authors of this official scenario note, this last calculation is probably irrelevant; Detroit has already been hit.[5]

For a twenty-megaton nuclear bomb, an independent estimate has been made for Chicago. Briefly, (1) all property within 4 miles of burst reduced to rubble, (2) immediate death to all persons within 10 miles of burst, (3) life expectancy for those 10 to 20 miles away will be less than four minutes, (4) a 10% survival rate for those 20 to 30 miles away, (5) within 150 miles of Chicago, all will eventually die of radiation, within 300 miles, 90% will die.

Add in the emotional trauma which accompanies these massive numbers. Along with knowing that nameless millions are suffering horrors, survivors will have to live with doubts about family members and close friends, nearby and further away. What about the daughter visiting friends? The husband driving home from work? If Chicago is bombed, what is happening to grandparents in Kalamazoo during the twenty-four hours before 100% of the people in Kalamazoo are themselves dead?

MONTREAL: ONE TWENTY-MEGATON BOMB

We apply to Montreal estimates of loss of life and property recently published by Physicians for Social Responsibility.

A twenty-megaton nuclear bomb is exploded at ground level on Dominion Square. At point of burst, temperatures will reach 20 million to 30 million degrees Fahrenheit. In downtown Montreal all things and all living beings will be vaporized.

The fireball will be nearly 3 miles in radius. Within 6 miles of the epicentre, roughly out to St.-Léonard-de-Port-Maurice to the north,

Bronx Park to the south, and St.-Laurent to the west, all persons will be killed by a silent heat flash; the flash will travel at the speed of light. Winds of 225 miles per hour and a supersonic shock wave will collapse buildings, including all hospitals.

Within a 10-mile radius, out to Ville de Laval to the northwest, a combination of blast wave, 100-mile-per-hour wind, and fire will leave 50% of the population dead and 40% injured; many of the injured will be burned. At 20 miles from the epicentre, that is, as far out as St.-Jean to the southeast, 50% of the population will be killed or injured, by blast pressure or by direct thermal radiation.

A 20-mile-per-hour wind will carry radioactive fallout 150 miles from the burst. All exposed persons will probably acquire lethal doses of radiation in twenty-four hours, with death likely in one to two weeks.

NOTES

1. One megaton is equivalent to one million tons of TNT, one kiloton to one thousand tons of TNT.

2. In addition, there are one thousand less specialized "burn beds" in the United States.

3. When asked how he would allocate federal money in the period immediately following the bomb, one doctor replied, "Use it all on morphine." The U.S. federal authorities may not be in total disagreement with this view. They have stockpiled 71,000 pounds of opium (morphine is a derivative of opium) for critical civilian use, and have recently requested 59,000 additional pounds. The Reagan administration has delayed adding to this stockpile to avoid a war-ready image.

4. A rem is a unit of radiation dosage used in connection with human exposure.

5. For a detailed account of devastation if Detroit (or Leningrad) is hit by a one-megaton or a twenty-five-megaton bomb, see *The Effects of Nuclear War* by the Office of Technology Assessment of the United States Congress. (*One* twenty-five-megaton nuclear bomb has considerably greater destructive power than the 1906 earthquake which destroyed San Francisco.)

2. Effects of the Use of Nuclear Weapons

Group of Experts,
Report of the UN Secretary-General

Nuclear weapons are weapons of mass destruction. Their various effects may cover vast areas and the destruction of the intended target within this area, whether military or civilian, can be made as complete as desired through the choice of weapon yield and the point of explosion. There is therefore no target strong enough to resist the intense effects of nuclear weapons, no effective defense against a determined attack. Protection in a nuclear war, when it exists, does so because of limits imposed on the strength of the attack. In this sense, mankind is faced with the absolute weapon.

At the same time, it is the very strength of the effects of nuclear explosives that make them difficult to use as war-fighting weapons in the traditional sense. It is a fact that there are today megaton weapons in existence each of which releases an energy greater than that of all conventional explosives ever used since gunpowder was invented. If this enormous power were ever to be used, the consequences in terms of human casualties and physical destruction would be virtually incomprehensible. Figures and rough estimates may be given, as indeed they will in the following, but there exists an uncertain limit beyond which such data have little meaning except as a categorical imperative that nuclear war must never happen.

The existing knowledge of the effects of the use of nuclear weapons is far from complete. Although numerous tests have been carried out, forming a basis for the understanding of the physical explosion phenomena, there are only two instances when these weapons have been used in war, on 6 August 1945 against Hiroshima and on 9 August 1945 against Nagasaki. The outcome of these explosions has been painstakingly investigated, in particular with regard to the number of people killed or injured, and yet considerably different data are given by different sources, as will be illustrated below.

Furthermore, any assessment of a hypothetical future situation based on the Japanese data would have to rest on interpretation and sometimes extrapolation, as today's arsenals contain weapons that are a thousand times more powerful than the two used in Japan, but also smaller and, in some cases, specialized weapons. . . . Thus there are uncertainties as to the effects of one single explosion.

It is a well-established fact that the explosion of a nuclear weapon causes damage through several effects: a powerful blast wave, intense heat radiation and nuclear radiation from the fireball, and from radioactive fallout. There is also a pulse of electromagnetic radiation not directly harmful to living creatures. However, the size of the area affected by these various phenomena, their strength—in absolute terms and relative to each other—and the extent of the damage they cause will depend strongly on the explosive yield but also on a number of other factors specific to each situation. Among these are the height above ground of the explosion, weather conditions, and (particularly for explosions close to the ground) wind velocity, and, of course, the nature of target. The design of the weapon will also influence the outcome.

Should large numbers of nuclear weapons ever come to be used, the total effect would be much more complex than the sum of individual cases. This is in some part due to interactions of a direct and physical nature, for instance on electrical or other networks, but the most important additional uncertainties pertain to the overall social, economic, and political consequences of the sudden and widespread devastation that a nuclear war would entail. The accounts given below should therefore be considered only as probable indications of the magnitude of the effects of nuclear war.

*   *   *

EFFECTS OF A LIMITED NUCLEAR ATTACK

The term "limited nuclear attack" can be interpreted only in a specific context. In general, however, the term implies a certain degree of restraint in the execution of an attack, thus limiting the damage. It is open to debate whether a nuclear war between the major nuclear powers could be conducted with such restraint, and there will always be a very large risk of escalation. However, some studies refer to "limited attacks" in a central strategic context, and this subject will be reviewed in a later section.[1]

In addition, one could conceive of other "limited" scenarios, which might have less likelihood but which are technically feasible and occasionally mentioned in the literature. These will be the topic of this section. Some of them are clearly related to a superpower conflict, but the majority pertain to nuclear aggression against non-nuclear-weapon States. If nuclear weapons are further proliferated, and if no interventions or other sanctions have to be feared, that sort of aggression might become a realistic alternative in future conflicts. In those hypothetical cases, nuclear weapons use may be limited because the aggressor has limited nuclear means.

At present, however, the basic situation would be one where a State with an abundance of nuclear weapons decided to use some of these weapons to enforce its will upon a non-nuclear-weapon State. (To decide to do so, one would require a virtual certainty that the action did not trigger a large nuclear conflict.) In this case, other limitations could apply.

Such limitations should not be thought of as simply a matter of the number of weapons employed, as the launching of even one nuclear weapon represents a most serious decision. Political and military constraints would most probably apply to the decision and determine what restrictions might exist concerning the nature and location of the targets. This could, for instance, imply that certain areas or certain types of facilities would be excluded from targeting. There could thus be large differences in the consequences of various hypothetical nuclear attacks, but there is no distinct gap between the different categories. The consequences for the victim may vary from the slightest to the most severe.

The lowest level of nuclear violence could be an implicit or outspoken threat to use nuclear weapons. Such a threat could next be emphasized by means of a "demonstration explosion" giving only some slight effects on the ground and delayed radiation effects from global fallout. Or a target could be chosen, so located that a nuclear weapon could destroy it without causing any appreciable immediate damage to other areas. Such "solitary" targets could be satellites in space, ships at sea, remote air or naval bases, and isolated military or commercial installations.

Satellite nuclear warfare, which would be mainly an affair between the superpowers, would involve high-altitude bursts, creating electromagnetic pulse damage over large parts of the earth's surface (and hence possibly for many uninvolved nations), and late effects from global fallout. Long-range radio communications might be disturbed for an extended period of time, and power or telephone shutdowns could occur locally or regionally. Many of the other types of target indicated above would be destroyed by fairly low-yield weapons. In particular, surface vessels at sea are relatively "easy" targets for modern guided missiles and could be sunk immediately with a small nuclear warhead.

There is in modern military literature some discussion regarding procedures and planning for the use of nuclear weapons against military targets in a zone of combat and possibly military and military support targets over a larger area (a "theatre of war"). The planning is done within a framework of tactical and military policy considerations regarding guidelines for the use of nuclear and conventional resources in a theatre of war. But this would in turn be subject to decisions at a political level as to whether nuclear weapons should be used at all and if so, in what manner.

In general, the employment of nuclear weapons against military targets would produce considerable "collateral" (i.e., unintended and undesired) damage to large areas of civilian society, particularly if surface bursts were used. This would occur even if political directives emphasized the importance of avoiding collateral damage as far as possible.

As an example of "limited-theatre use" of nuclear weapons, one might assume that military operations were launched in the face of defending ground forces with a strength of four army divisions (around 80,000 men). The ground defence might be supported by approximately 100 aircraft operating from 10 or more bases. This is a significant defence, yet one possessed by many non-nuclear-weapon States. To break through by conventional force only, a traditional estimate is that an attacker must assign at least 12 army divisions[2] and several hundred aircraft to the operation. The same result could be achieved by using some tens of weapons of 1 to 10 kt yield against important elements of the ground forces and up to 10 weapons of 20 to 100 kt yield to reduce the opponent's air force.

For each of the low-yield shots against army units in the field, immediate civilian casualties would vary within wide limits, with a possible average of about 1,000 (in a fairly densely populated rural district). A total of 50,000 to 100,000 dead or severely injured civilians due to the direct effects could be the outcome of this part of the campaign. The attacks on air force bases would perhaps add another 100,000 people to these figures, especially if some of these bases were also ordinary airports, relatively close to population centres.

In addition, it is likely some of the strikes would be (intentionally or otherwise) surface bursts causing severe radioactive contamination in some areas. Under assumptions believed to be realistic, regarding the radiation-shielding properties of ordinary buildings and time spent outdoors, this could mean anything between 10,000 and 50,000 additional radiation casualties.[3]

Assuming some intermediate values in the ranges indicated, the total sum of fatalities and severe injuries in this campaign could come out as follows:

Cause	*Civilian*	*Military*
Immediate nuclear-weapon effects	150,000	30,000
Fallout radiation	30,000	5,000
Total	180,000	35,000

If some protective measures were considered, in terms of possible evacuation, warning, and access to shelters, the casualties could be reduced by a factor of 3–5. There is a very wide margin of error to these figures. However, this does not invalidate the most conspicuous conclusion that can be drawn from the table: even when only military targets are selected, and even if protection is provided, the civilian casualties may far outnumber the military ones.

Other immediate effects, which could add to the number of casualties and create additional difficulties during a rescue period, would include disruption of medical care, of power and telecommunication networks, and of ground and air transport; tree felling and possibly forest fires; and, to a lesser extent, induced radioactivity in the ground near the explosion points. In addition to the immediate consequences, there would be several thousands of late radiation deaths over several decades, and a similar number of genetic effects. (Some of these would occur outside the attacked country.) Agricultural and industrial activity could certainly be seriously disrupted, but to what extent and with what consequences would depend on the specific attack conditions.

In spite of the large numbers of civilians killed and injured, and in spite of other late effects (not only on health, nutrition, and medical care but also on the economy and the morale of the victimized population), military planners might consider this to be a limited attack, which could be followed by another and yet another if military resistance were to continue.

If a military campaign with nuclear weapons were ever to take place in a developing country, there would be important differences with regard to the general conditions of living and their influence on collateral damage and on the potential for survival. The means available to the civilian population for their physical protection against weapons effects would be much less adequate than in a developed country. Primitive and perhaps fragile houses would afford little protection against even weak blast waves and moderate fallout. In a warm climate, scant clothing could give rise to a higher incidence of both thermal burns and skin injuries from radioactive particles in the fallout. Tree felling and large forest fires could occur in any country but would be more difficult to deal with where there was a scarcity of various kinds of equipment.

In the military discussion of nuclear war it is common practice to distinguish "strategic" nuclear weapons from "tactical" or "theatre" ones. Whereas it is true that weapons denoted "strategic" have, on the average, higher explosive yields and longer ranges than the others, it is also important to realize that the distinction does not primarily rest with the weapons themselves but with the objectives for their use.

Strategic attack is often defined as aiming at the elimination of the attacked nation as a war-fighting unit, either as a consequence of the devastation wrought upon it or because it surrenders in order to avoid further destruction. Nuclear weapons have added new dimensions to this concept. In the Second World War strategic bombing was an instrument for the attrition of the enemy's industrial potential, particularly the arms industry, and for the demoralization of the enemy population. This was a lengthy process and seen as a supplement rather than an alternative to ordinary military operations. With long-range nuclear weapons it has become possible to wreak near-complete eradication of a nation's population and devastation of its economy in less than a day's time and on less than an hour's notice. It is worth noting that even what is termed a limited nuclear attack would have the most deleterious consequences.

Another new factor is that some of the nuclear means for strategic use are themselves regarded as strategic targets. Accordingly, two different strategic modes for nuclear-weapon employment have emerged: "counterforce" against these weapons, and "counter-value" corresponding to the classical strategic attack. Possibilities and probabilities concerning the nuclear exchange between the superpowers in either or both of these modes are extensively studied and publicly discussed. This discussion, however, should not be allowed to obscure the fact that States other than the superpowers, including non-nuclear countries, could be targets for a nuclear strategic attack against value targets and, in effect, one using weapons other than those commonly called strategic. In the context of the power-bloc balance this is reflected by the distinction that is sometimes made between "central strategic" and "Eurostrategic" systems. . . . But the core of the matter is that a wide spectrum of nuclear weapons can now be put to strategic use.

The effects of one nuclear explosion against a city have been described above. A limited strategic attack could, however, involve the targeting of several cities. The most important fact is then that a simple addition of casualties or destroyed facilities would not give a true picture of the extent of the devastation. After a single city attack, a national effort could conceivably be organized to rescue and aid survivors and to compensate for the loss of industrial capacity. With five major cities obliterated simultaneously and casualties in one day running to perhaps 10 percent of the nation's population, both the physical capacity and the psychological strength to launch such an effort might be in doubt. The number of people in need of medical care would be much larger than could be coped with, not only in the targeted cities but in the entire country. Some key industrial branches might have been destroyed and this could become an immediate difficulty if, for instance, some basic foods or medical supplies were among the items that could not be produced. Administrative problems of an unprecedented nature and magnitude would arise and cause extreme difficulties for the national, regional, and local governments.

Effects of Extensive Use
of Tactical Nuclear Weapons

At present, the most obvious danger of an extensive use of tactical or theatre nuclear weapons would exist if there were a superpower conflict in Europe. Here there are large, diversified, and militarily integrated nuclear arsenals that could be used for extensive theatre employment. In Europe, there is also the strong political commitment, the geographic proximity between bloc territories and the concentration of forces—conventional as well as nuclear—that could constitute the possible setting for a large-scale confrontation. In the future, however, similar dangers may present themselves also in other areas of the world, since the number of available weapons in the superpower arsenal continues to increase.

If such a war should occur, the probability is that it could not be kept at theatre level. On the contrary, a crisis which had escalated beyond the use of a few theatre nuclear weapons could be in imminent danger of reaching the level of "strategic exchange," owing to the magnitude of political objectives which by necessity would underlie a conflict of such tension. In particular, this could be the case if an extensive theatre nuclear war should turn out to be of considerable disadvantage to one of the two sides. A technical factor indicating the ease with which escalation could occur from the theatre to the strategic level is that the same weapon systems could be used for either purpose.

No analysis of a large-scale theatre nuclear war has so far been made public. A comprehensive study of the consequences of a nuclear war in the Federal Republic of Germany was published in 1971.[4] But it is not possible to describe the effects of a nuclear war in a detailed and accurate manner. The consequences are too vast and complex.

The situation being considered is one in which both sides had mobilized and deployed forces in the range of 50 to 100 divisions each, and where these and their supporting tactical air forces had been issued their nuclear munitions.

The assumption is further that the priority targets would be the adversary's nuclear delivery means in the theatre, i.e., field artillery, rocket and guided missile units, and air bases. Thus, the exchange would basically be a duel between the opposing nuclear systems. In addition, armoured units and command posts would be targeted and rear-area targets other than army forces and air bases would not be excluded per se. They would be less important to the outcome of a nuclear campaign of short duration, but might still add appreciably to the number of casualties. Attacks on targets at sea might take place but would cause little collateral damage except for global fallout.

The weaponry available to the two sides is today somewhat asymmetrical. To reflect this, the average yield of weapons for battlefield targets might be 1 kt on one side and 5 kt on the other. It is further assumed that command and communication centres, air bases and other rear-area targets would be attacked only with missiles equipped with 100 kt warheads. The situation described might lead to a nuclear-weapon employment as follows:

Side	Ground forces targets	Air bases, etc.
A	1,000 weapons, average yield 1 kt	100 weapons, average yield 100 kt
B	500 weapons, average yield 5 kt	100 weapons, average yield 100 kt

The ensuing civilian casualties would vary with the distribution of people in the targeted areas and the locations of ground zeros with respect to this distribution. A lower estimate could be based on the same assumption as in the preceding section, that there were no military targets except air bases in the vicinity of major cities. For the battle area, the average population density could be 100 persons/km^2.

The worst case would occur when the shots from both sides were distributed without any regard to the civilian settlements in the battle area, i.e., non-restrictive employment. The consequences would be less severe if one or both of the belligerents were restrictive, i.e., deliberately tried to avoid hitting these settlements.

The resulting casualty figures (dead and severely injured civilians) for the employment of the low-yield weapons against ground forces can be calculated as follows:

Employment characteristics	Civilian casualties
A and B restrictive	0.1 million

A non-restrictive, B restrictive   0.5 million
A restrictive, B non-restrictive   0.6 million
A and B non-restrictive   1.0 million

The casualties would be caused by blast effects, thermal radiation and fire, initial radiation, and combinations of these. One could expect that virtually all of those with severe injuries would die, as adequate medical treatment would not be available.

The major part of the collateral damage against the civilian society would not be caused by the 100-kt weapons. Even though the targets for these weapons would not as a rule be located within urban areas and, in addition, would presumably be surrounded by an uninhabited safety zone, a population density of 300 persons/km² is assumed, bearing in mind that the population density in large European cities is about 10 times that figure. With this assumption, each of the 100-kt weapons might kill or injure about 25,000 civilians, which would lead to a total of up to 5 million casualties. Thus the conclusion would be that the immediate effects of this nuclear war would be between 5 and 6 million civilian lives. This would hold only as long as the weapons were properly aimed, however. Each missile going astray and hitting an urban area instead of the intended target would add another quarter of a million to the total.

It is assumed that some of the 1,700 explosions would be surface bursts, producing local radioactive fallout, acutely hazardous to the population in areas downwind from the burst. The size of such areas, and, consequently, the number of people exposed to the hazard, would increase with the explosive yield (see Fig. 1). For this reason, fallout from one of the 1-kt or 5-kt weapons on the battlefield would add very little to the overall casualty figures. If no more than 10 percent of these explosions were surface bursts, an estimate would be that 20,000 to 50,000 additional deaths would be caused by fallout therefrom. The number is highly dependent on population density and availability of shelters.

Fallout from the 200 weapons of 100 kt would constitute a more serious problem, as each weapon would release a much larger amount of radioactivity. A larger proportion of the explosions might also be surface bursts, and the population density in the fallout areas would be higher. If half of these explosions were surface bursts, a total of about 0.7 million people could be expected to receive radiation doses causing death within about a month, even if it were assumed that they made reasonable efforts to stay in shelter.

In addition to high dose effects, there would be a number of late somatic and genetic injuries caused primarily by the fallout from surface bursts. These would occur over a period of some decades after the war. The number of late cancers, including leukemia, could be about 400,000 in the countries where the explosions took place. These would mainly

38

FIGURE 1. Fallout Areas From Tactical Nuclear Weapons

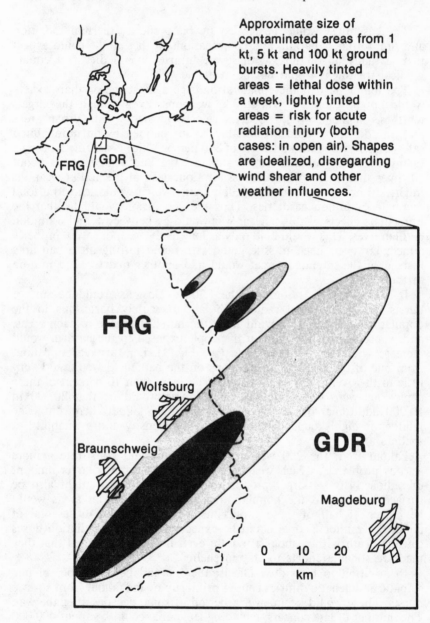

Approximate size of contaminated areas from 1 kt, 5 kt and 100 kt ground bursts. Heavily tinted areas = lethal dose within a week, lightly tinted areas = risk for acute radiation injury (both cases: in open air). Shapes are idealized, disregarding wind shear and other weather influences.

TABLE 1. Total Casualties (Dead and Severely Injured) in the Theatre Nuclear War Described

Weapons (all fission):	200 x 100 kt	1,500 x low yield	
Population density, km^{-2}:	300	100	
Percentage of surface bursts:	50	10	
Civilian			*Approx. total*
Immediate effects	5 mill.	0.1-1 mill.	5-6 million
Early fallout	0.7 mill.	0.02-0.05 mill.	0.7 million
Late radiation	0.4 mill.	0.01 mill.	0.4 million
Total civilian	6.1 mill.	0.1-1.1 mill	6-7 million
Military			
All causes			0.4 million

be caused by the 100-kt explosions, with perhaps some 10,000 cases originating from the fallout from the lower-yield weapons or from initial radiation among those who survived the direct effects of an explosion. The total casualties are summarized in Table 1.

In the above scenario the total yield delivered (23.5 Mt) is a small fraction of the destructive power available to the superpowers, the individual weapon yields are all far below those which are common in the weapons denoted strategic, and targeting restrictions have been observed. Although the plausibility of the scenario may be doubted, it offers a very conservative setting for a description of possible effects of nuclear war-fighting. Nevertheless, the important point emerges that civilian casualties could hardly be reduced below a certain very high level, given the collateral effects of the nuclear attacks against the enemy's air force and other long-range systems. In addition to the civilian casualties, large military forces would have been virtually obliterated and thousands of nuclear weapons spent (but the overall nuclear strength of the superpowers would still remain essentially intact). The civilian casualties would, however, outnumber the military ones by more than 12 to 1.

EFFECTS OF A TOTAL NUCLEAR WAR, A NUCLEAR EXCHANGE

A total nuclear war is the highest level of human madness. Perhaps it is, therefore, not surprising that many studies of this have been carried out, analysing the consequences in some detail. The results of course vary with the assumptions made regarding targets, the numbers and yields of weapons, their mode of employment, the meteorological conditions and the existence (or nonexistence) of protective measures. The conclusion which may be drawn from the outcome of these studies is, however, that nuclear weapons must never be used.

In these studies various scenarios have been described. They are generally of two kinds: either a counterforce or counter-value strike is assumed. A counterforce strike is aimed at destroying the opponent's missile silos, strategic bomber and submarine bases, aircraft carriers, and, to the extent that their positions are known, the strategic submarines at sea. Important military command, communication, and surveillance centres might also be included on the target list. In counter-value scenarios, industrial and population centres are assumed to be directly attacked in an attempt to cause unacceptable destruction to the opponent's industrial and human resources. Military facilities might then be targeted or not, depending on the situation.

These studies often neglect consequences other than direct physical damage to human and material resources, such as the effect of the elimination of key industrial sectors in a counter-value attack on the capacity of other industrial production, consequences of loss of transportation facilities and food shortage due to reduction in livestock and crop caused by early fallout radiation and to processing and distribution failures. Food shortage in turn would have consequences on the efficiency of reconstruction labour, the general health of the survivors, the ability to recover for those injured, etc.

Even more difficult to predict, and hence largely omitted in these studies, are the psychological, social, and political consequences of the enormous strains imposed on a society which has been subjected to a large-scale nuclear attack. Demoralization of the surviving population may well occur, and could result in erratic, non-social behaviour, aggressiveness, or apathy. Disorientation, fear, doubt and antipathy against authorities could occur when strains on a population were severe. Conflicting loyalties with respect to family and to society would add to the staggering organizational problems in an attacked region. Conflicts that exist even in peacetime between ethnic, racial, and religious groups, and possibly even political factions within certain countries, could come out in the open following the deprivations, stresses and disorganization of the post-attack period. Political, legal, and monetary institutions would, if they survive, most likely be severely weakened and it is in doubt whether an organized central control could be maintained.

The Counterforce Attack

In a counterforce attack, surface bursts would probably be used in large numbers, as they maximize the probability of destroying hard military targets, e.g., ICBM silos. The major collateral damage would then be caused by early fallout (cf. Fig. 2). Attacks against strategic bomber bases and strategic submarine bases might use air bursts, and, to the extent that these facilities were located close to population centres, blast

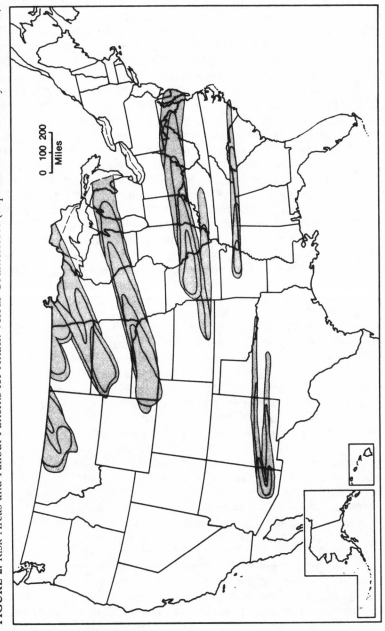

FIGURE 2. Risk Areas and Fallout Patterns for Attack Versus Counterforce (Representative Westerly March Winds)

0 100 200
Miles

and thermal effects would cause considerable collateral damage in such areas.

The Office of Technology Assessment study published in 1979 quotes United States Government studies indicating that between 2 million and 20 million Americans would be killed within 30 days after a counter-silo attack on the United States ICBM sites. Another recent study[5] states that in a counterforce attack on the United States, 8 to 12 million fatalities would result if the attack occurred without warning and 5 to 8 million fatalities if there were warning. The OTA study concludes that a comprehensive counterforce attack on the United States would produce about 14 million dead even if the present fallout shelter capability were utilized. According to the same source, a United States counterforce strike against the USSR would result in somewhat similar numbers of casualties, i.e., from 2 million to 10 million people killed in a counter-silo strike and 2 million to 13 million in a full counterforce strike. The majority of fatalities within 30 days in a counterforce attack would be caused by radiation due to early fallout from surface bursts.

In the studies referred to above, extensive sheltering of the civilian population is assumed. An uninterrupted stay in shelter during several weeks would be required to avoid still larger casualties. This would cause serious problems of sanitation, food and water supply, air filtration, health, communication to the outer world, psychological tensions, etc. Longer periods of outdoor stay could be considered "safe under the circumstances" after these first weeks, but even after 2 to 3 months the radiation levels would still be far higher than "safe" peacetimes levels.

Assuming a "pure" counterforce strike, most productive resources would survive with little material damage. Yet, for some time the economic life would be expected to have collapsed due to the heavy casualties from fallout and other weapon effects and due to fear that still another attack might be imminent. The fact that there might be little material damage to the civilian society would not mean that there would be little economic disturbance. Economic activities, especially in contaminated areas, would be disrupted for months and perhaps years. Long-term damage to the economy would be caused by deaths and long-lasting injuries to the working force, key persons in various or-ganizations, etc. It would take decades before the people killed could be replaced in either the demographic or economic sense.

Radioactive fallout would cause serious problems to agriculture. Livestock would have little protection against fallout. A severe decline in meat supply would therefore result after a certain period of time, and many years would be required to build up new livestock. A considerable decline in the supply of milk, cheese, and butter would result. Radiation effects on crops would depend on the season, an attack in spring causing more damage than one in the summer or early autumn. Radioactive elements filtering down into the ground water would be taken up by plants and, through grazing, by cattle and other animals.

Quantities of radioactivity could then enter the human system through consumption of crop, meat, and milk products from contaminated areas, and this would take its toll through late cancers in the surviving population and genetic defects in future generations.

Public health would be lowered for a long time after the attack, causing extra demands on a nation's medical care facilities. Individuals would be exposed to unknown radiation risks, since enough instruments to measure total radiation received by a person might not be available. Fallout could cause irreversible adverse effects on ecological systems, and genetic mutations changing the ecosystem in unpredictable ways could not be ruled out. Wild animal populations might likewise be considerably affected. But most important, it should be remembered that the attacked country, devastated as it may be, would still have a more than sufficient nuclear capability remaining to deliver a devastating blow to the attacker. This would be, according to the logic of deterrence, a counter-value attack.

The Counter-Value Attack

A massive counter-value attack would aim at destroying the very basis of a nation's entire existence by striking at its industrial assets and major urban centres and killing a large fraction of its population. Though military installations might be targeted as well, the destruction of these would not be the primary purpose of this type of attack. The point is rather that a counter-value attack is easier to carry out than a counterforce attack, since less precision is required to strike urban and industrial areas than to destroy missile silos and since the number and size of weapons needed to cause "unacceptable destruction" is less demanding in a counter-value strike. According to former United States Secretary of Defense Robert McNamara, "unacceptable destruction" would require one-fourth to one-third fatalities to a population of a large industrialized nation and the destruction of one-half to two-thirds of its industrial capacity. According to one report,[6] this was at the time believed to require 400 Mt equivalent[7] megatonnage in a counter-value attack on the USSR and roughly the same yield in a similar attack on the United States.

In the light of more recent studies, less than 400 equivalent megatons would suffice to cause "unacceptable destruction" of either the USSR or the United States. Thus a number of reports[8] indicate that very heavy damage could be inflicted on either superpower by relatively few weapons aimed at crucial targets. This is illustrated by Table 2. The report[9] from which these tables have been taken also indicates that the nuclear arsenals needed to launch even the heaviest attacks given in the table would be available even after a surprise counterforce attack. In particular, each of the three major types of delivery system (long-range bombers, ICBMs or SLBMs) would retain the number of nuclear weapons necessary to inflict very heavy damage.

TABLE 2. Vulnerability to Counter-value Attack

Tables have been adapted from A. Katz (*op. cit.*). The asymmetry in the data given reflects the different assumptions made: the United States is considered subject to a given (simultaneous) attack. For comparison, the requirement for attacks with similar consequences on the USSR are examined.

Assumed attacks against the United States

Attack number[a]	Total warheads and bombs required	Total megaton equivalents	Total[b] casualties (mill)	Percentage of total industry destroyed
1	300−400	144−166	40−60	25−35
2	400−500	244−266	50−70	35−45
3	500−600	344−366	60−80	45−60
4	700−800	544−566	70−90	60−65

Assumed attacks against the USSR

Attack number	Total population at risk (mill)	Percentage of total industry at risk	Total warheads[c] and bombs required	Total megaton[c] equivalents
1	15[d]	15	26 (181)	26 (25)
2	20	25	90 (300)	90 (40)
3	45	50	144 (631)	144 (86)
4	75	62	303 (1 014)	303 (138)

a. The attacks 1−4 assume 100, 200, 300 and 500 1 Mt weapons respectively aimed at the 70 largest metropolitan and industrial centres in the United States. To each case another 200−300 weapons of 100 kt yield have been added.

b. Casualties were estimated from the 1 Mt weapons only.

c. Numbers outside the parentheses refer to a hypothetical attack with 1 Mt weapons only, whereas those within parentheses assume an attack with 50 kt weapons only. Attack No. 4 assumes the 200 largest metropolitan and industrial areas of the USSR to be targeted, and attack No. 1 the 10 largest areas excluding Moscow.

d. Numbers have been rounded to the nearest five.

With regard to the longer-range consequences of a counter-value attack, the larger part of the key industries would have been eliminated. There would therefore be a crucial race between the depletion of remaining supplies of virtually everything and economic recovery under the most adverse conditions. Considering the complexity and interdependence of industrialized society, the shortage of food, energy, transportation, human resources, various machines and vehicles, and complex electronic and electrical systems, and considering as well the disorganization, the human despair and social disruption from starvation, illness, and other traumatic experiences, it is obvious that the enormous task of rebuilding society will not be attained within many years—if it ever will.

The national capacity for food production, processing and distribution would be much more severely affected than by a counterforce strike. Destruction of storage facilities, processing plants, and transport facilities would result in a general food shortage within a short period of time. This would be likely to continue even after a year or more, as a result of lack of fuel and other energy sources, lack of fertilizers and pesticides, and the general destruction or disruption of the infrastructure. Common crop yields in advanced agricultural areas could be reduced by about 50 percent if no fertilizers and pesticides were available. Radiation hazards and loss of livestock would further aggravate the situation. Malnutrition would in turn affect the general health of the population and impede the reconstruction work. Competition for food would result in starvation and antisocial behaviour.

The destruction of virtually all petroleum capacity, pipeline systems, etc., would have immediate consequences for transportation, heating, and electrical power production. Sufficient substitution by coal or natural gas or reconstruction of refineries would take many years. The race between the recovery of industrial output and the depletion of surviving resources would therefore crucially depend on the limited surviving energy supply.

The most demanding immediate medical tasks would be treatment of shock, burn injuries, mechanical injuries, and radiation injuries. Many people would suffer from combined injuries. A disproportionately large number of people with medical education would have been killed, since most hospitals are located in urban areas. Lack of sanitation, drugs, antibiotics, and modern medical facilities would add to the difficulties, and the food shortage would further degrade the general health conditions.

For the nation as a whole, a most serious problem would be the destruction of many social and political institutions at a time when demands would far exceed the normal capacity of such institutions, had they remained viable. A counter-value attack could well entail the successive decay, if not the sudden collapse, of societal structure.

GLOBAL ASPECTS

Environmental Effects

The consequences of a major nuclear war would not be restricted to the nuclear-weapon States. Even if there were no direct nuclear attack against any non-nuclear-weapon State, there are probable collateral effects from a nuclear war between the superpowers. In a longer perspective, fallout radiation after a large nuclear war would affect the whole world (although predominantly the hemisphere in which the war was fought). The same could hold true from some other physical effects influencing the environment, such as the dispersal of nitrous oxides and dust in the atmosphere.

Of the worldwide effects associated with nuclear warfare, that of global fallout is the most thoroughly studied and known. The different ways in which airborne radioactivity (including tritium and carbon-14, which are not deposited on the ground) can reach and irradiate humans have largely been derived from empirically established fallout intensities produced by atmospheric tests. The transport of waterborne activity with ocean currents has also been investigated. These surveys have been supplemented by laboratory research regarding the effects of ionizing radiations on living organisms.

The result of this knowledge has been applied to an "unrestricted" nuclear war in a number of studies,[10] and the corresponding toll of the world's population over the years (including future generations) has been estimated. As an example, global fallout from a total explosive yield of 10,000 Mt, i.e., well over half of what presently exists in the world's nuclear stockpiles, would cause of the order of 5 to 10 million additional deaths from cancer within the next 40 years. In addition, a similar amount of (non-lethal) thyroid cancers would result. Genetic damage would appear in about as many instances as lethal cancers, half of which would be manifest in the following two generations and the rest in generations thereafter.

Extensive early fallout (i.e., from surface bursts) over nations not directly involved in a nuclear war may also occur. To quantify estimates of short- and long-term radiation injuries from this fallout is much more difficult than for global fallout, as they depend on meteorological conditions and protective measures taken. Under adverse conditions, cases of late cancers and hereditary defects would run into some millions.

Ionizing radiation could possibly also cause many mutations in plants and animals. There has been speculation that some of these mutations might change the ecosystem in unpredictable ways, but too little is known about the physical and biological processes involved to make predictions in this field.

A large nuclear war would cause the injection of substantial quantities of nitrogen oxides into the upper atmosphere, especially if a multitude of explosions in the megaton range were to occur. These oxides would then reach the ozone layer in the stratosphere and might, through chemical reactions, partially destroy it in a few months. A period of about 5 years is believed to be required to restore the layer again. Since ozone is an effective barrier to solar ultraviolet radiation, a depletion of the ozone column would result in an increase of this radiation at the surface of the earth. Unfortunately, the full biological implications of an increased ultraviolet radiation to ecosystems at various latitudes are not known. However, the incidence of skin cancer is thought to be related to the amount of ultraviolet radiation received. Mutations in plants and animals might also increase.

The extent to which the release of a given quantity of nitrogen oxides would deplete the ozone layer is at present not entirely clear. A 1975 study by the United States National Academy of Sciences reported a 30 to 70 percent reduction of the ozone layer if a total yield of 10,000 Mt were to be exploded. Later investigations have led to a better understanding of the chemistry involved. It is now believed that such a heavy depletion could occur only if most of the total yield derived from multi-megaton weapons.

A sizable change of ozone concentration in the stratosphere would seriously affect stratospheric heating. This in turn would change temperature conditions in the troposphere and hence cause possible climatic changes at the earth's surface. Large amounts of dust injected in the atmosphere might further add to these changes. It has been estimated that 10,000 Mt would pollute the stratosphere with 10^7-10^8 tons of material, i.e., of the same order as that injected by the eruption of Krakatoa.[11] Climatic changes would be expected to be smaller in tropical and subtropical zones and larger at higher latitudes. In the latter regions, however, even small changes, such as a cooling of 1° C, would have serious consequences. (It is estimated that the Krakatoa event at most caused a temperature reduction of 0.5° C over a few years.) The 1° C cooling could severely hamper wheat growing in Canada and parts of the USSR, for instance, due to a reduction of the number of frost-free days. Although the recovery time associated with possible global climatic changes due to a large nuclear war would probably be only a few years, present knowledge is insufficient to definitely rule out more persistent effects.

Social, Economic, and Political Effects

Whereas many physical and biological effects of nuclear war can be identified and to some extent investigated, the worldwide economic and social disruption that would be an unavoidable consequence of a large nuclear war is more difficult to examine. Today's world is characterized by a large and increasing international interdependency. A substantial number of important products are made up of parts and components from all over the world. Financially, the business activities in various countries are highly interrelated through agreements as well as flows of currencies and credits. And the nuclear powers are also the major nodes in this international network of trade.

To describe coherently even the main effects of a large nuclear war on the economic and social world situation is not possible. In this context it seems particularly prudent to quote the Office of Technology Assessment report mentioned previously: "The effects of a nuclear war that cannot be calculated are at least as important as those for which calculations are attempted." Some general ideas could be inferred from the study of past wars as well as of peacetime crises; examples in the latter category would include the collapse of the United States stock market in 1929, but also recent distress situations such as those following the widespread crop failures in 1972 and 1974. However, historical evidence dwindles beside the possible aftermath of a large nuclear war.

An analysis of the consequences for world trade in general and supply of essential commodities in particular would have to take into account both decreasing production volumes and the possible breakdown of the organization of world commerce and communications. When there are serious problems in both these respects, they would soon have an impact on everyday conditions for most people on the globe.

Most critical would be the world food supply: in many developing countries, famine is an ever-present threat even under stable and peaceful conditions, and a large and continuous international grains trade is needed to prevent starvation.[12] In addition, modern agriculture increasingly uses inputs from many different branches of industry. Among these are various kinds of tools and machinery as well as pesticides and herbicides, but above all fertilizers from the chemical industry which—together with energy—are required continuously and are absolutely necessary if land resources are limited.

The world food situation some time after the war could be crudely assessed by recalling that wheat is the most important grain—and consequently foodstuff—in international trade. The importance of the North American exports is well known. During 1979, for instance, the United States alone exported about 37 million tons of wheat, which is almost half the world trade in wheat. In addition the United States and Canada have about 40 million tons of the wheat stocks, and if they were unavailable after a nuclear war the world food situation would become disastrous in a very short time. This could mean that famine would spread to hundreds of millions of people.

The major cause of hunger today is poverty—the lack of resources with which to buy enough food or enough fertilizers, fuels, machinery, etc., for an adequate indigenous production. This would be even more pronounced after a large nuclear war. As exports are necessary to pay for imports, the loss of substantial export markets—detrimental to most nations—would be disastrous for the poor, food-importing countries, and there would be severe disruptions of this kind if the United States and the USSR were devastated to an extent that eliminated them as partners in trade for even a couple of years.

The United States is one of the largest trading countries in the world. Very few countries have less than 10 percent of their export market in the United States, and some have between 50 percent and 70 percent of their export destined to the United States. Likewise, the United States is the largest single contributor both to development aid and to international organizations like the United Nations. The foreign trade of the Soviet Union is about one third of that of the United States, and about half of all Soviet trade is within the Council for Mutual Economic Assistance (CMEA). For the East European countries, a loss of the USSR as a trading partner would be a disaster, as the USSR takes 33 percent of their total export. The CMEA economies are also highly coordinated with the Soviet economy. Some non-CMEA nations have from 20 to 40 percent of their export market in the USSR, and there are also a number of countries very heavily dependent on Soviet development assistance.

All countries in the world would suffer a drastic reduction of foreign trade, entailing difficulties and economic losses. There are interactive effects of different kinds:

(a) Eliminated countries may be major suppliers or exclusive manufacturers of many technology-intensive products and services;
(b) Export items are inputs in other countries' export products;
(c) Downgraded foreign trade might cause shortages of essential equipment, semi-manufactures, spare parts, etc., which no longer could be paid for, thereby reducing the domestic output;
(d) Decreased income per capita and increased unemployment would result in redistribution of consumption patterns and hence of demand, supply, and production in many countries.

The annihilation of the major financial and trading centres of the world, such as New York, London, Moscow, and other such cities, would inevitably lead to the destruction of the elaborate system of international finance and trade as it is now constituted, thus eliminating the orderly transfer of goods and services that characterize international economic relations.

Globally, the physical means of transport and communication would probably not be too severely affected. When properly organized after the initial confusion, remaining resources for shipping, land and air transport, and telecommunications would prove adequate for the reduced post-war world trade, possibly even if some kind of international relief programmes were instituted. By securing spare parts through "cannibalism," it should be possible to keep even advanced aircraft functioning for several years. All this is under the assumption that oil (and other energy resources) were available. However, the physical consequences of the war do not include an additional deficit of oil in the world as a whole, as the United States imports oil while the USSR is currently slightly more than self-sustaining.

In the general hardship and unrest that would follow a nuclear war, countries with a grain surplus might not act for the benefit of starving people in distant countries. Their surplus might instead be used, for example, for bilateral bartering for raw materials. In a somewhat longer perspective, the fertilizer situation would be a serious problem, as the United States and the USSR are major producers of fertilizers. Even though most of their production is for domestic consumption, the unavailability of large quantities of essential agricultural inputs would be a more severe problem than the loss of grain surplus nations, because it would threaten the capability of all fertilizer importers to produce food.

If almost all major nations in Europe were impaired or eliminated in addition to the United States and the USSR, an analysis of the consequences on world affairs sounds euphemistic, as there would probably be very little business to transact, at least between these regions and the rest of the world. The economic importance of these countries to the world community stands out by noting that together they could account for between one-half and two-thirds of the world's gross national product and trade.

A major difference in comparison with the previous scenario is the impossibility of heavy relief programmes for the devastated countries, as the surviving industrialized countries would not possess the capability for such a task. This would be an aggravating circumstance which could rule out any chance of international economic recovery for a long time. Furthermore, many of the non-belligerents would be developing countries which were suppliers of raw materials and agricultural products of less immediate importance after a large nuclear war. These might expect an almost total cessation of foreign trade.

In addition to this, there would probably be a total breakdown in the multilateral system of payments and in the United Nations and World Bank organizations. Important sections and main stations of the international telecommunications system via cable and satellite would also be out of order along with major urban areas in Europe.

Food would be in very short supply, especially after some time when the shortages of fertilizers had reduced the yield in most parts of the world. These fertilizer shortages would be much more severe in this scenario. The result might well be that hundreds of millions would starve to death. The global disaster would be further aggravated by the scarcity of transport equipment, pharmaceuticals, and pesticides, which would increase the horror and the plagues.

All surviving countries trying to switch over their domestic production to an increased level of self-sufficiency would have to accomplish this change in a race with time before stocks ran out completely. A failure to achieve viability (i.e., production at least equalling consumption plus depreciation) would result in many additional deaths and much additional economic, political, and social deterioration. Thus a downward self-feeding spiral might start. Which way the economy in a particular region or country would go is unpredictable, however.

The discussion above has focused on a few quantifiable items. It must be borne in mind, however, that there are innumerable other aspects to be investigated, some of an intangible nature and all interactive. A local war or threat of war in any region might divert industry and materials into producing for the war effort and away from the economy and standard of living. A breakdown of law and order in some regions of the world might severely hamper the recuperation of international trade. Tremendous importance must also be attached to the political and social institutions affecting both the motivation of individuals and the overall efficiency with which a nation's human, financial, and natural resources would be used in agricultural production and the way the food would be distributed.

The motivation of people to come to grips with the huge and seemingly hopeless task of rebuilding a world destroyed would perhaps be the decisive factor in some cases. One should have no high expectations in this regard, if the cultural, social, and political values which are today the driving forces behind a great deal of evolution suddenly lost their meaning.

In fact, there is very little reason to believe that the political and social situation in any country would be unchanged after a large nuclear war. Many nations among those we know would probably disappear. Others might be virtually depopulated by famine and mass migration. The system of international security would have been destroyed, and so would to a large extent the traditional pattern of those States, nations, and societies which might survive.

*   *   *

CIVIL DEFENCE

A number of nations have organized a civil defence to meet the demands of a conventional war, with or without additional features specifically designed for nuclear war situations. Traditionally, civil defence comprises measures to avoid civilian casualties, like sheltering, warning, and evacuation to limit immediate damage, and firefighting and rescue efforts to give immediate relief to the injured and homeless.

Some of these measures could help to limit the number of fatalities caused by a nuclear attack. In view of the large devastation caused, especially if nuclear weapons are used directly against the population, available resources for post-attack relief could prove totally inadequate, however. What matters most then is the potential for long-term survival, recovery, and reconstruction. These long-term aspects would become particularly important after large attacks, when the survival of the entire population would be in jeopardy. For this reason, traditional civil defence should be discussed in conjunction with other measures designed to allow or facilitate national recovery after a nuclear war.

Civil defence is sometimes regarded between the superpowers as a component of the strategic balance and it is then even maintained that a strong civil defence effort could upset that balance. This seems to be an exaggeration of current civil defence capabilities, as in our time no civil defence system could provide reliable protection for most of the citizenry under all circumstances. The possible value depends largely on the attack scenario. Civil defence could, for instance, be very effective in saving lives which would otherwise be lost to fallout in a limited attack against hard targets. On the other hand, it would be far less effective in a war involving strikes against industry in cities, or against the civilian population as such. This holds true for non-nuclear-weapon States as well as nuclear-weapon States in a nuclear war. Even in countries which do not themselves come under nuclear attack, civil defence would be needed to deal with fallout from large numbers of nuclear explosions in neighbouring countries.

Civil Defence Methods

The two means most commonly considered for protecting the population from nuclear-weapon effects are evacuation and sheltering. Evacuation of population from areas expected to come under attack has to be planned very carefully in advance. Apart from transportation and housing of evacuees, this planning must include at least short-term provisions for the relocated population. Information and instructions to the general public would have to be issued in advance. Even if instructions were available, however, the execution of an evacuation would probably be accompanied by confusion and panic. Large-scale evacuation is therefore, in most cases, no attractive option.

To start an evacuation too early would mean an unnecessary disruption of everyday activities; to start too late would worsen the prospects for those evacuated, as their vulnerability would be highest during the transfer phase. The very fact that an evacuation had started might even precipitate the attack, and there is also the possibility of targeting the relocated population. These constraints are valid in any type of war, but in a nuclear war they would be more severe. In addition, there is the particular problem of radioactive fallout, as available radiation shielding can generally be expected to be inferior in rural areas. Furthermore, the location of serious fallout areas cannot be predicted in advance.

Sheltering, which is a very expensive protective measure, implies hardening against nuclear-weapon effects rather than avoiding them. In nuclear war, shelters would have to protect against ionizing radiation as well as blast, collapsing buildings and flying debris, thermal radiation, and fire. Shelters that offer reasonable protection against mechanical loads would, generally speaking, give adequate radiation shielding. Special shelter design features would be necessary, however, to deal with the extended air blast of nuclear weapons. Difficult problems would also be the long-lasting thermal load on a shelter buried under a large heap of smouldering rubble and the ventilation of the shelter under these conditions. Filtration of the incoming air would be desirable to keep out radioactive dust and toxic gases. Ordinary filters do not, however, remove the carbon monoxide generated by smouldering fires.

Food, water, and sanitation would have to be available as people might have to stay in shelter for a long time after a nuclear attack to avoid the effects of fallout radiation or because rescue work was seriously impeded. Under heavy fallout conditions, as would prevail for instance about 30 km downwind of a 1-Mt fission surface burst, people could leave their shelters after two days, provided that they could leave the contaminated area immediately and be outside it in an hour or two. If such evacuation were not possible and they had to remain on the spot for a couple of days, they would have to stay in shelters for a month if acute radiation injuries were to be avoided. One hundred km downwind, the corresponding times would be a few hours and a week respectively. In both these instances, there would be a high incidence of late radiation cancers among the survivors, even if the proper sheltering periods could be observed.

Rescue efforts in a nuclear war would pose special problems because of the enormity of the operation involved and because of the possible existence of residual radiation. There would be many fires to extinguish and large masses of debris from collapsed buildings to remove. It would not be possible to assign such resources that all survivors trapped in shelters or basements could be saved, even if sophisticated disaster plans had been prepared in advance.

The presence of fallout would necessitate equipment and routines for surveying the contaminated area and monitoring the radiation. There would be a large need of fallout shelters which, however, could be produced more easily and more cheaply than blast shelters. Even in non-belligerent countries, problems might be posed by fallout from explosions elsewhere in the world. After megaton surface bursts and in unfavourable weather conditions, outdoor doses large enough to cause acute radiation injuries could occur up to about 1,000 km from the targeted areas.

Long-Term Survival and Recovery

After a nuclear attack (and to some extent after fallout contamination originating from an attack elsewhere), domestic production and distribution of various commodities would be disturbed and international trade disrupted. Among the most important factors would be those related to food, energy, medical supplies, clothing, and provisional housing. Crisis stockpiling of basic supplies would be an important precaution for dealing with these difficulties during the first days or weeks. However, distribution problems could quickly become critical.

The most urgent problem would be to ensure the continuous production of food. This production may have to be independent of imported goods, which could cause particular difficulties in countries where agriculture was highly mechanized. Fallout would have taken a toll of the livestock, partly because of difficulties to tend the animals properly and partly as a consequence of radiation injuries to them. An additional difficulty would be that some farmland and pastures might have been rendered useless for years due to radioactive contamination.

The superpowers have reportedly held discussions at the national level regarding systematic protection of the industrial base through hardening and dispersion. Hardening would mean protection of the buildings and machines up to a certain level of overpressure. Significant increase in hardness is particularly difficult for some industries, such as oil refineries. Dispersion is more expensive and could evidently come about only as a result of long-range planning. It is doubtful whether any such effort is worthwhile. The hardening of a targeted industry could be countered by detonating weapons at lower altitudes or by increasing weapon accuracy. Similarly, dispersion could be rendered insufficient by new developments in numbers of warheads and weapons accuracy. No country is known to have attempted significant hardening or dispersion of industry.

In endeavouring to reconstruct both agriculture and other basic industry, the overriding problem would be to reach a production rate at least equal to a minimum consumption rate before stockpiles were entirely depleted. However, the organized effort necessary to master this awesome task would require an unequalled level of determination and insight among both the population and the leadership.

Existing and Potential
Civil Defence Programmes

A complete civil defence programme consists of a number of components which have to operate together. There are doubts, however, concerning the effectiveness of even a well-balanced and largely implemented complete system in a nuclear war. This is due partly to the basic uncertainties concerning characteristics of the attack, behaviour of the population, object response to weapons effects, influence of weather, climatic conditions, etc., and partly to the enormous force of nuclear weapons, which allows the attacker to neutralize the effect of any civil defence effort simply by employing a few more, and somewhat larger, nuclear weapons. Unless it was presumed that the attacker's objective was to kill as many civilians as possible, however, civil defence could help substantially to lessen the consequences of an attack and to ameliorate conditions after it. Thus, civil defence is warranted by humanitarian concern, notwithstanding the doubts of its capacity to deal with all situations.

To estimate the actual cost of various national civil defence efforts is very difficult. Costs are calculated and accounted for differently in different countries. Furthermore, comparisons between differently com- posed programmes may be misleading, particularly as all programmes are not solely or primarily nuclear-oriented. The examples given in Table 3 should be examined with these qualifications in mind.

There are, however, two additional and more important caveats to be remembered. One is that very little is or even could be known about the actual value of existing civil defence programmes in a large nuclear war, as fortunately they have not yet been tested. The other is that there are a large number of nations in the world which cannot afford to spend anything at all on civil defence, even if they were convinced

TABLE 3. Some Examples of Annual Civil Defense Costs

Nation	Approximate costs per capita (US dollars)
Switzerland ⎫ Norway ⎬ Israel ⎭	more than 10
Sweden	9[a]
USSR	8[b]
Finland ⎫ Denmark ⎭	4
Federal Republic of Germany	3.5
Netherlands	2.5
United States	0.5[c]

Source: DCPA *Information Bulletin*, 5 April 1979, No. 303.

a. Amount quoted covers traditional civil defense, including radiological defense, but no crisis stockpiling.

b. Amount quoted covers personnel costs, shelter construction and operation of some military installations of civil defence importance. See also Soviet Civil Defense, the Department of State, United States of America, Special Report No. 47, September 1978.

c. Mainly administration and planning for protection against nuclear effects.

of the favourable cost-effectiveness ratio of the various measures necessary.

NOTES

1. Numerical estimates of casualties, etc., in this and the following section were made at the Swedish National Defense Research Institute.

2. This 3:1 relationship can be found in many military works published during the last 50 years. A recent reference is *United States Army Field Manual FM 100-5: Operations.*

3. With a given population density and average shielding factor, the number of casualties is almost directly proportional to the fission yield in surface bursts. For instance, with 100 persons/km^2 and an average shielding factor of 0.3, there would be about 70 early radiation deaths per kiloton fission yield exploded close to the ground.

4. C. F. von Weizsäcker, ed., *Kriegsfolgen und Kriegsverhütung,* Munich, 1971.

5. R. Sullivan et al., *Civil Defense Needs of High-Risk Areas of the United States,* System Planning Corporation, Arlington, Va., SP 409, 1979.

6. A. Katz, "Economic and Social Consequences of Nuclear Attacks on the United States," United States Senate, Committee on Banking, Housing and Urban Affairs, 96th Congress, First Session (March 1979).

7. The concept of "equivalent megatonnage" has been introduced to take account of the fact that the area covered by blast does not increase linearly with weapon yield. It is defined as the 2/3 power of the actual yield expressed in Mt. For instance, if the yield is 100 kt = 0.1 Mt, then the equivalent megatonnage is $0.1^{2/3} = 0.22$.

8. (a) "Data Base and Damage Criteria for Measurements of Arms Limitation Effects on War Supporting Industry," ACDA/WEC-242, 1974. (b) Office of Technology Assessment, *The Effects of Nuclear War* (Washington, D.C.: Government Printing Office, 1979). (c) G. Kemp, "Nuclear Force for Medium Powers, Part I. Targets and Weapon Systems, Part II and III. Strategic Requirements and Options"; Adelphi Papers 106 and 107, International Institute for Strategic Studies, London, 1974.

9. United States Senate, Committee on Banking, Housing and Urban Affairs, op. cit.

10. See, for instance, "Long-Term Worldwide Effects of Multiple Nuclear-Weapons Detonations," National Academy of Sciences, Washington, D.C., 1975.

11. Krakatoa is a small volcanic island in the Sunda Straits which was almost completely blown to pieces by underwater explosions when the volcano erupted in August 1883. This is the largest recorded volcanic event.

12. The total production of grains in the world is equivalent to about 365 kg per person and year while the minimum subsistence level is somewhere between 200 and 250 kg, unless complementary diet is available. However, the annual production per capita is very different in different regions, running from a high of more than 1,200 kg in North America to a low of less than 150 kg in Africa. The figures are for 1976 according to the FAO *Production Yearbook, 1977.*

3. A Republic of Insects and Grass

Jonathan Schell

[The following is excerpted from an extensive discussion of the ecological, societal, and personal consequences of a general nuclear war.   —*Ed.*]

The yardsticks by which one can measure the destruction that will be caused by weapons of different sizes are provided by the bombings of Hiroshima and Nagasaki and American nuclear tests in which the effects of hydrogen bombs with up to sixteen hundred times the explosive yield of the Hiroshima bomb were determined. The data gathered from these experiences make it a straightforward matter to work out the distances from the explosion at which different intensities of the various effects of a bomb are likely to occur. . . . [Of course, projected facts] and figures, can . . . tell us nothing of the human reality of nuclear destruction. Part of the horror of thinking about a holocaust lies in the fact that it leads us to supplant the human world with a statistical world; we seek a human truth and come up with a handful of figures.

The only source that gives us a glimpse of that human truth is the testimony of the survivors of the Hiroshima and Nagasaki bombings. Because the bombing of Hiroshima has been more thoroughly investigated than the bombing of Nagasaki, and therefore more information about it is available, I shall restrict myself to a brief description of that catastrophe.

On August 6, 1945, at 8:16 A.M., a fission bomb with a yield of twelve and a half kilotons was detonated about nineteen hundred feet above the central section of Hiroshima. By present-day standards, the bomb was a small one, and in today's arsenals it would be classed among the merely tactical weapons. Nevertheless, it was large enough to transform a city of some three hundred and forty thousand people into hell in the space of a few seconds. "It is no exaggeration," the authors of "Hiroshima and Nagasaki" tell us, "to say that the whole city was ruined instantaneously." In that instant, tens of thousands of people were burned, blasted, and crushed to death. Other tens of thousands suffered injuries of every description or were doomed to die of radiation sickness. The center of the city was flattened, and every part of the city was damaged. The trunks of bamboo trees as far away as five miles from ground zero—the point on the ground directly under the center of the explosion—were charred. Almost half the trees within a mile and a quarter were knocked down. Windows nearly seventeen miles away were broken. Half an hour after the blast, fires set by the thermal pulse and by the collapse of the buildings began to coalesce into a firestorm, which lasted for six hours. Starting about 9 A.M. and lasting until late afternoon, a "black rain" generated by the bomb (otherwise, the day was fair) fell on the western portions of the city, carrying radioactive fallout from the blast to the ground. For four hours at midday, a violent whirlwind, born of the strange meteorological conditions produced by the explosion, further devastated the city. The number of people who were killed outright or who died of their injuries over the next three months is estimated to be a hundred and thirty thousand. Sixty-eight percent of the buildings in the city were either completely destroyed or damaged beyond repair, and the center of the city was turned into a flat, rubble-strewn plain dotted with the ruins of a few of the sturdier buildings.

In the minutes after the detonation, the day grew dark, as heavy clouds of dust and smoke filled the air. A whole city had fallen in a moment, and in and under its ruins were its people. Among those still living most were injured, and of these most were burned or had in some way been battered or had suffered both kinds of injury. Those within a mile and a quarter of ground zero had also been subjected to intense nuclear radiation, often in lethal doses. When people revived enough from their unconsciousness or shock to see what was happening around them, they found that where a second before there had been a city getting ready to go about its daily business on a peaceful, warm

August morning, now there was a heap of debris and corpses and a stunned mass of injured humanity. But at first, as they awakened and tried to find their bearings in the gathering darkness, many felt cut off and alone. In a recent volume of recollections by survivors called "Unforgettable Fire," in which the effects of the bombing are rendered in drawings as well as in words, Mrs. Haruko Ogasawara, a young girl on that August morning, recalls that she was at first knocked unconscious. She goes on to write:

How many seconds or minutes had passed I could not tell, but, regaining consciousness, I found myself lying on the ground covered with pieces of wood. When I stood up in a frantic effort to look around, there was darkness. Terribly frightened, I thought I was alone in a world of death, and groped for any light. My fear was so great I did not think anyone would truly understand. When I came to my senses, I found my clothes in shreds, and I was without my wooden sandals.

Soon cries of pain and cries for help from the wounded filled the air. Survivors heard the voices of their families and their friends calling out in the gloom. Mrs. Ogasawara writes:

Suddenly, I wondered what had happened to my mother and sister. My mother was then forty-five, and my sister five years old. When the darkness began to fade, I found that there was nothing around me. My house, the next door neighbor's house, and the next had all vanished. I was standing amid the ruins of my house. No one was around. It was quiet, very quiet—an eerie moment. I discovered my mother in a water tank. She had fainted. Crying out, "Mama, Mama," I shook her to bring her back to her senses. After coming to, my mother began to shout madly for my sister: 'Eiko! Eiko!"
I wondered how much time had passed when there were cries of searchers. Children were calling their parents' names, and parents were calling the names of their children. We were calling desperately for my sister and listening for her voice and looking to see her. Suddenly, Mother cried "Oh Eiko!" Four or five meters away, my sister's head was sticking out and was calling my mother. . . . Mother and I worked desperately to remove the plaster and pillars and pulled her out with great effort. Her body had turned purple from the bruises, and her arm was so badly wounded that we could have placed two fingers in the wound.

Others were less fortunate in their searches and rescue attempts. In "Unforgettable Fire," a housewife describes a scene she saw:

A mother, driven half-mad while looking for her child, was calling his name. At last she found him. His head looked like a boiled octopus. His eyes were half-closed, and his mouth was white, pursed, and swollen.

Throughout the city, parents were discovering their wounded or dead children, and children were discovering their wounded or dead parents. Kikuno Segawa recalls seeing a little girl with her dead mother:

A woman who looked like an expectant mother was dead. At her side, a girl of about three years of age brought some water in an empty can she had found. She was trying to let her mother drink from it.

The sight of people in extremities of suffering was ubiquitous. Kinzo Nishida recalls:

While taking my severely wounded wife out to the riverbank by the side of the hill of Nakahiro-machi, I was horrified, indeed, at the sight of a stark naked man standing in the rain with his eyeball in his palm. He looked to be in great pain, but there was nothing that I could do for him.

Many people were astonished by the sheer sudden absence of the known world. The writer Yoko Ota later wrote:

I just could not understand why our surroundings had changed so greatly in one instant. . . . I thought it might have been something which had nothing to do with the war—the collapse of the earth, which it was said would take place at the end of the world, and which I had read about as a child.

And a history professor who looked back at the city after the explosion remarked later, "I saw that Hiroshima had disappeared."

As the fires sprang up in the ruins, many people, having found injured family members and friends, were now forced to abandon them to the flames or to lose their own lives in the firestorm. Those who left children, husbands, wives, friends, and strangers to burn often found these experiences the most awful of the entire ordeal. Mikio Inoue describes how one man, a professor, came to abandon his wife:

It was when I crossed Miyuki bridge that I saw Professor Takenaka, standing at the foot of the bridge. He was almost naked, wearing nothing but shorts, and he had a ball of rice in his right hand. Beyond the streetcar line, the northern area was covered by red fire burning against the sky. Far away from the line, Ote-machi was also a sea of fire.

That day, Professor Takenaka had not gone to Hiroshima University, and the A-bomb exploded when he was at home. He tried to rescue his wife, who was trapped under a roofbeam, but all his efforts were in vain. The fire was threatening him also. His wife pleaded, "Run away, dear!" He was forced to desert his wife and escape from the fire. He was now at the foot of Miyuki Bridge.

But I wonder how he came to hold that ball of rice in his hand. His naked figure, standing there before the flames with that ball of rice, looked to me as a symbol of the modest hopes of human beings.

In "Hiroshima," John Hersey describes the flight of a group of German priests and their Japanese colleagues through a burning section of the city:

The street was cluttered with parts of houses that had slid into it, and with fallen telephone poles and wires. From every second or third house came the voices of people buried and abandoned, who invariably screamed, with formal politeness, *"Tasukete kure!* Help, if you please!" The priests recognized several ruins from which these cries came as the homes of friends, but because of the fire it was too late to help.

And thus it happened that throughout Hiroshima all the ties of affection and respect that join human beings to one another were being pulled and rent by the spreading firestorm. Soon processions of the injured—processions of a kind that had never been seen before in history—began to file away from the center of the city toward its outskirts. Most of the people suffered from burns, which had often blackened their skin or caused it to sag off them. A grocer who joined one of these processions has described them in an interview with Robert Jay Lifton which appears in his book "Death in Life":

> They held their arms bent [forward] . . . and their skin—not only on their hands but on their faces and bodies, too—hung down. . . . If there had been only one or two such people . . . perhaps I would not have had such a strong impression. But wherever I walked, I met these people. . . . Many of them died along the road. I can still picture them in my mind—like walking ghosts. They didn't look like people of this world.

The grocer also recalls that because of people's injuries "you couldn't tell whether you were looking at them from in front or in back." People found it impossible to recognize one another. A woman who at the time was a girl of thirteen, and suffered disfiguring burns on her face, has recalled, "My face was so distorted and changed that people couldn't tell who I was. After a while I could call others' names but they couldn't recognize me." In addition to being injured, many people were vomiting—an early symptom of radiation sickness. For many, horrifying and unreal events occurred in a chaotic jumble. In "Unforgettable Fire," Torako Hironaka enumerates some of the things that she remembers:

1. Some burned work-clothes.
2. People crying for help with their heads, shoulders, or the soles of their feet injured by fragments of broken window glass. Glass fragments were scattered everywhere.
3. [A woman] crying, saying "Aigo! Aigo!" (a Korean expression of sorrow).
4. A burning pine tree.
5. A naked woman.
6. Naked girls crying, "Stupid America!"
7. I was crouching in a puddle, for fear of being shot by a machine gun. My breasts were torn.
8. Burned down electric power lines.

9. A telephone pole had burned and fallen down.
10. A field of watermelons.
11. A dead horse.
12. What with dead cats, pigs, and people, it was just a hell on earth.

Physical collapse brought emotional and spiritual collapse with it. The survivors were, on the whole, listless and stupefied. After the escapes, and the failures to escape, from the firestorm, a silence fell over the city and its remaining population. People suffered and died without speaking or otherwise making a sound. The processions of the injured, too, were soundless. Dr. Michihiko Hachiya has written in his book "Hiroshima Diary":

> Those who were able walked silently toward the suburbs in the distant hills, their spirits broken, their initiative gone. When asked whence they had come, they pointed to the city and said, "That way," and when asked where they were going, pointed away from the city and said, "This way." They were so broken and confused that they moved and behaved like automatons.
>
> Their reactions had astonished outsiders, who reported with amazement the spectacle of long files of people holding stolidly to a narrow, rough path when close by was a smooth, easy road going in the same direction. The outsiders could not grasp the fact that they were witnessing the exodus of a people who walked in the realm of dreams.

Those who were still capable of action often acted in an absurd or an insane way. Some of them energetically pursued tasks that had made sense in the intact Hiroshima of a few minutes before but were now utterly inappropriate. Hersey relates that the German priests were bent on bringing to safety a suitcase, containing diocesan accounts and a sum of money, that they had rescued from the fire and were carrying around with them through the burning city. And Dr. Lifton describes a young soldier's punctilious efforts to find and preserve the ashes of a burned military code book while people around him were screaming for help. Other people simply lost their minds. For example, when the German priests were escaping from the firestorm, one of them, Father Wilhelm Kleinsorge, carried on his back a Mr. Fukai, who kept saying that he wanted to remain where he was. When Father Kleinsorge finally put Mr. Fukai down, he started running. Hersey writes:

> Father Kleinsorge shouted to a dozen soldiers, who were standing by the bridge, to stop him. As Father Kleinsorge started back to get Mr. Fukai, Father LaSalle called out, "Hurry! Don't waste time!" So Father Kleinsorge just requested the soldiers to take care of Mr. Fukai. They said they would, but the little, broken man got away from them, and the last the priests could see of him, he was running back toward the fire.

In the weeks after the bombing, many survivors began to notice the appearance of petechiae—small spots caused by hemorrhages—on their skin. These usually signalled the onset of the critical stage of radiation sickness. In the first stage, the victims characteristically vomited repeatedly, ran a fever, and developed an abnormal thirst. (The cry "Water! Water!" was one of the few sounds often heard in Hiroshima on the day of the bombing.) Then, after a few hours or days, there was a deceptively hopeful period of remission of symptoms, called the latency period, which lasted from about a week to about four weeks. Radiation attacks the reproductive function of cells, and those that reproduce most frequently are therefore the most vulnerable. Among these are the bone-marrow cells, which are responsible for the production of blood cells. During the latency period, the count of white blood cells, which are instrumental in fighting infections, and the count of platelets, which are instrumental in clotting, drop precipitously, so the body is poorly defended against infection and is liable to hemorrhaging. In the third, and final, stage, which may last for several weeks, the victim's hair may fall out and he may suffer from diarrhea and may bleed from the intestines, the mouth, or other parts of the body, and in the end he will either recover or die. Because the fireball of the Hiroshima bomb did not touch the ground, very little ground material was mixed with the fission products of the bomb, and therefore very little local fallout was generated. (What fallout there was descended in the black rain.) Therefore, the fatalities from radiation sickness were probably all caused by the initial nuclear radiation, and since this affected only people within a radius of a mile and a quarter of ground zero, most of the people who received lethal doses were killed more quickly by the thermal pulse and the blast wave. Thus, Hiroshima did not experience the mass radiation sickness that can be expected if a weapon is ground-burst. Since the Nagasaki bomb was also burst in the air, the effect of widespread lethal fallout on large areas, causing the death by radiation sickness of whole populations in the hours, days, and weeks after the blast, is a form of nuclear horror that the world has not experienced.

In the months and years following the bombing of Hiroshima, after radiation sickness had run its course and most of the injured had either died of their wounds or recovered from them, the inhabitants of the city began to learn that the exposure to radiation they had experienced would bring about a wide variety of illnesses, many of them lethal, throughout the lifetimes of those who had been exposed. An early sign that the harm from radiation was not restricted to radiation sickness came in the months immediately following the bombing, when people found that their reproductive organs had been temporarily harmed, with men experiencing sterility and women experiencing abnormalities in their menstrual cycles. Then, over the years, other illnesses, including cataracts of the eye and leukemia and other forms of cancer, began to appear in larger than normally expected numbers among the exposed population. In all these illnesses, correlations have been found between nearness to the explosion and incidence of the disease. Also, fetuses exposed to the bomb's radiation in utero exhibited abnormalities and developmental retardation. Those exposed within the mile-and-a-quarter radius were seven times as likely as unexposed fetuses to die in utero, and were also seven times as likely to die at birth or in infancy. Surviving children who were exposed in utero tended to be shorter and lighter than other children, and were more often mentally retarded. One of the most serious abnormalities caused by exposure to the bomb's radiation was microcephaly—abnormal smallness of the head, which is often accompanied by mental retardation. In one study, thirty-three cases of microcephaly were found among a hundred and sixty-nine children exposed in utero.

What happened at Hiroshima was less than a millionth part of a holocaust at present levels of world nuclear armament. The more than millionfold difference amounts to more than a difference in magnitude; it is also a difference in kind. The authors of "Hiroshima and Nagasaki" observe that "an atomic bomb's massive destruction and indiscriminate slaughter involves the sweeping breakdown of all order and existence—in a word, the collapse of society itself," and that therefore "the essence of atomic destruction lies in the totality of its impact on man and society." This is true also of a holocaust, of course, except that the totalities in question are now not single cities but nations, ecosystems, and the earth's ecosphere. Yet with the exception of fallout, which was relatively light at Hiroshima and Nagasaki (because both the bombs were air-burst), the immediate devastation caused by today's bombs would be of a sort similar to the devastation in those cities. The immediate effects of a twenty-megaton bomb are not different in kind from those of a twelve-and-a-half-kiloton bomb; they are only more extensive. (The proportions of the effects do change greatly with yield, however. In small bombs, the effects of the initial nuclear radiation are important, because it strikes areas in which people might otherwise have remained alive, but in larger bombs—ones in the megaton range—the consequences of the initial nuclear radiation, whose range does not increase very much with yield, are negligible, because it strikes areas in which everyone will have already been burned or blasted to death.) In bursts of both weapons, for instance, there is a radius within which the thermal pulse can ignite newpapers: for the twelve-and-a-half-kiloton weapon, it is a little over two miles; for the twenty-megaton weapon, it is twenty-five miles. (Since there is no inherent limit on the size of a nuclear weapon, these figures can be increased indefinitely, subject only to the limitations imposed by the technical capacities of the bomb builder—and of the earth's capacity to absorb the blast. The Soviet Union, which has shown a liking for sheer size in so many of its undertakings, once detonated a sixty-megaton bomb.) Therefore, while the total effect of a holocaust is qualitatively different from the total effect of a single bomb, the experience of individual people in a holocaust would be, in the short term (and again excepting the presence of lethal fallout wherever the bombs were ground-burst), very much like the experience of individual people in Hiroshima. The Hiroshima people's experience, accordingly, is of much more than historical interest. It is a picture of what our whole world is always poised to become—a backdrop of scarcely imaginable horror lying just behind the surface of our normal life, and capable of breaking through into that normal life at any second. Whether we choose to think about it or not, it is an omnipresent, inescapable truth about our lives today that at every single moment each one of us may suddenly become the deranged mother looking for her burned child; the professor with the ball of rice in his hand whose wife has just told him "Run away, dear!" and died in the fires; Mr. Fukai running back into the firestorm; the naked man standing on the blasted plain that was his city, holding his eyeball in his hand; or, more likely, one of millions of corpses. For whatever our "modest hopes" as human beings may be, every one of them can be nullified by a nuclear holocaust.

Questions for Reflection and Discussion

1. What would be the most likely consequences of a nuclear war? At the intercontinental level? The regional level? Is it reasonable to think that nuclear war can be localized? On the basis of existing technology, is there any circumstance in which nuclear weapons would be no more destructive than conventional arms? Would nuclear war be a "war" or a "holocaust"? What about Hiroshima and Nagasaki?

2. Do you believe it is possible to survive a nuclear war? You personally? Your family? Your community? Your country? What would it mean to "survive" a nuclear war?

3. Do you support a substantial commitment to civil defense? Why? Why not? Should your local, state, and national governments make preparations to function after a nuclear attack? If so, what steps should they take and what functions should they seek to safeguard?

4. Is it possible to reduce the destructiveness of nuclear war in a meaningful way? If so, would we thereby increase or decrease the likelihood that nuclear weapons would be purposefully used?

5. Under what circumstances, if any, should national leaders *threaten* resort to nuclear weapons? Is there any occasion in which the *use* of nuclear weapons would be justified? What standards would you employ to make these determinations? Would you distinguish between civilian and military targets? Should collateral damage to noncombatant states be taken into account? The natural environment? Would such differentiations be possible?

6. What role do your images of the Hiroshima-Nagasaki bombings play in your answers to the foregoing questions? What role should they play?

Selected Bibliography

Abrams, Herbert L., and William von Kaenel. "Medical Problems of Survivors of Nuclear War." *New England Journal of Medicine* (Nov. 12, 1981), pp. 1226–1232.

Ball, Desmond. *Can Nuclear War Be Controlled?* Adelphi Paper No. 169. London: International Institute for Strategic Studies, 1981.

Bates, Don G. "The Medical and Ecological Effects of Nuclear War." *McGill Law Journal,* Vol. 28, No. 3 (July 1983), pp. 716–731.

Beres, Louis René. *Apocalypse: Nuclear Catastrophe in World Politics.* Chicago: University of Chicago Press, 1980.

Briggs, Raymond. *When the Wind Blows.* New York: Schocken Books, 1982.

Calder, Nigel. *Nuclear Nightmares.* New York: Viking Press, 1979.

Clayton, Bruce D. *Life After Doomsday: A Survivalist Guide to Nuclear War and Other Major Disasters.* New York: Dial Press, 1980.

Committee for the Compilation of Materials on Damage Caused by the Atomic Bombs in Hiroshima and Nagasaki. *Hiroshima and Nagasaki: The Physical, Medical, and Social Effects of the Atomic Bombings.* New York: Basic Books, 1981.

Drell, Sidney D., and Frank von Hippel. "Limited Nuclear War." *Scientific American,* Vol. 235, No. 5 (Nov. 1976), pp. 27–37.

Freeman, Harold. *This Is the Way the World Will End, This Is the Way You Will End, Unless . . .* Edmonton, Canada: Hurtig Publishers, 1983.

Geiger, H. Jack. "Addressing Apocalypse NOW: The Effects of Nuclear Warfare as a Public Health Concern." *American Journal of Public Health,* Vol. 70, No. 9 (Sept. 1980), pp. 958–961.

Glasstone, Samuel, and Phillip J. Dolan, eds. *The Effects of Nuclear Weapons.* 3rd ed. Washington, DC: Government Printing Office, 1977.

Griffiths, Franklyn, and John C. Polanyi, eds. *The Dangers of Nuclear War: A Pugwash Symposium.* Toronto and Buffalo: University of Toronto Press, 1979.

Ground Zero. *Nuclear War: What's In It For You?* New York: Pocket Books, 1982.

Hersey, John. *Hiroshima.* New York: Alfred A. Knopf, 1946.

International Physicians for the Prevention of Nuclear War. *Last Aid: The Medical Dimensions of Nuclear War.* San Francisco: W. H. Freeman and Co., 1982.

Joyce, James Avery. *The War Machine: The Case Against the Arms Race.* New York: Avon Books, 1980.

Katz, Arthur M. *Life After Nuclear War: The Economic and Social Impacts of Nuclear Attacks on the United States.* Cambridge, MA: Ballinger Publishing Co. 1982.

Kraybill, Don. *Facing Nuclear War.* Paradise, CA: Herald Press, 1982.

Lewis, K. N. "The Prompt and Delayed Effects of Nuclear War." *Scientific American,* Vol. 241 (1979), pp. 27–39.

Lifton, Robert Jay. *Death in Life: Survivors of Hiroshima.* New York: Random House, Vintage edition, 1968.

McNamara, Robert S. *The Essence of Security: Reflections in Office.* New York: Harper & Row, 1968.

Medvedev, Zhores A. *Nuclear Disaster in the Urals.* New York: Vintage Books, 1979.

Office of Technology Assessment, U.S. Congress. *The Effects of Nuclear War.* Washington, DC: Government Printing Office, 1979.

Osada, Arata, ed. *Children of Hiroshima.* New York: Harper & Row, 1982.

Schell, Jonathan. *The Fate of the Earth.* New York: Alfred A. Knopf, 1982.

Silberner, Joanne. "Psychological A-Bomb Wounds." *Science News,* Vol. 120, No. 19 (Nov. 7, 1981), pp. 296–298.

Stockholm International Peace Research Institute. *Nuclear Radiation in Warfare.* London: Taylor & Francis, 1981.

Stonier, Tom. *Nuclear Disaster.* Cleveland and New York: Meridian Books, 1964.

United States Arms Control and Disarmament Agency. *The Effects of Nuclear War.* Washington, D.C.: Government Printing Office, 1979.

Zuckerman, Solly. *Nuclear Illusion and Reality.* New York: Viking Press, 1982.

CHAPTER 2

Understanding
the Arms Race

Since World War II, governments have spent approximately 9 trillion dollars on defense, with the Soviet Union and the United States spearheading the drift toward militarism. Together, these two nations, representing only 11 percent of the world's population, spend approximately one-half the world's military budget (which in 1982 alone exceeded $600 billion). Also, they export 58 percent of the arms moving in international trade and control 96 percent of the world's nuclear weapons. And, rather than showing signs of abatement, the armaments competition between them accelerates.

The Soviet Union remains committed to the complete overhaul of its land-based intercontinental missile force, replacing single-warhead missiles with SS-17s, SS-18s, and SS-19s. The majority of these newer missiles will carry multiple and independently targeted reentry vehicles or warheads (MIRVs), and thus improve significantly the offensive capabilities of the Soviet land-based strategic weapons force. Soviet intermediate-range capabilities also have been upgraded substantially by the deployment of the SS-20 (a three-warhead, solid-fuel missile mounted aboard a mobile launcher believed to possess a reload capability) and by the marked expansion of armored forces equipped for the irradiated battlefield. Additionally, a new generation of Soviet nuclear submarines, each armed with approximately 20 missiles carrying 12 warheads apiece, are on the production line.

On the U.S. side, in addition to the creation of a Rapid Deployment Force (RDF), a massive shipbuilding effort aimed at putting a 600-ship navy to sea by the late 1980s, and the deployment of a new generation of land and naval attack aircraft, enormous resources have been committed to a new round of quantitative and qualitative "improvements" in U.S. nuclear capabilities. One hundred eight Pershing II intermediate-range missiles and 574 Tomahawk ground-launched cruise missiles (GLCMs) are scheduled for deployment in Western Europe. Eight new Trident missile submarines, about twice the size of the currently deployed

Poseidon-Polaris missile submarines, are being built; each is to carry 24 ballistic missiles (SLBMs) with a range of 7,500 km, and 8 100-kt MIRVed warheads, some with first-strike capability. And as soon as a politically acceptable basing mode is selected, it is likely that the United States will also deploy a new land-based intercontinental ballistic missile, the MX.

Quantitative and qualitative improvements in strategic and theater-level offensive capabilities have not been the only subject of superpower competition, however. The pursuit of superior nuclear war-fighting capabilities has come to include, as well, a race to prevent retaliatory strikes through destruction of the adversary's command structure and the development of sophisticated defense systems and weaponry such as antiballistic missile systems and space-age laser and particle-beam weapons. A secure retaliatory-strike capability was once considered essential to mutual deterrence because independent possession of such a capability was believed to eliminate the incentive to launch a strategic first strike in a crisis. Now, both the United States and the Soviet Union strive to reduce one another's retaliatory power.

Why? Why are the superpowers seemingly locked into an ever-escalating process of armaments acquisition and refinement? A leading explanation was advanced by Robert S. McNamara, Secretary of Defense during the Kennedy and Johnson administrations:

What is essential to understand [about the arms race] is that the Soviet Union and the United States mutually influence one another's strategic plans. Whatever be their intentions, actions—or even realistically potential actions—on either side relating to the buildup of nuclear forces, be they either offensive or defensive weapons, necessarily trigger reactions on the other side. It is precisely this action-reaction phenomenon that fuels an arms race.[1]

This "action-reaction" theory, although often cited as the basic explanation of the arms race, has proven more heuristic than definitive, however. If McNamara had been correct, the arms race would have slowed when nuclear equilibrium between the superpowers was essentially established in the 1970s. Thus, to grasp more clearly the factors responsible for the quantitative and qualitative armaments competition, it is necessary to look further, beyond the weapons themselves.

The readings selected for this chapter form a composite of alternative perspectives concerning the dynamics that fuel the arms race. Bruce Russett argues that the U.S.-USSR military rivalry has been caused and maintained both by geopolitical considerations and by a domestic military-bureaucratic-economic-scientific alliance in both countries whose political strength rests on continuous armaments competition. Ralph M. Goldman highlights the "prisoners' dilemma" model to demonstrate that political distrust also lies behind the deadly armaments spiral. In the last selection, Robert C. Johansen advances the postscript that even the arms control process (at least as so far revealed) institutionalizes the arms race by shifting the locus of weapons competition to systems not covered by the negotiated agreements.

NOTES

1. "The Dynamics of Nuclear Strategy," *Department of State Bulletin,* Vol. 57, No. 1476 (Oct. 9, 1967), p. 446.

4. Why Do Arms Races Occur?

Bruce Russett

Why do countries arm themselves, and how might an arms race possibly be controlled? The idea of a spiraling arms race represents an advance over the ideas prevalent in the early cold war years, when it seemed to many Americans that the phenomenon of action and reaction was all one way—that is, that America was reacting to Soviet aggressive actions and militarism. But when the period of isolation under Stalin drew to a close and Soviet and American scientists began to make contact with each other, it became apparent that Soviet citizens typically held a mirror image of that view; that is, they saw the Soviet Union simply as reacting to American threats. From this exchange, people developed a more general understanding that, in some real sense, each side was reacting to the other. It is very hard to sort out particular causes, especially once the action-reaction process is well under way.

After the first shocks of the cold war in the early post–World War II years, the Soviet and American military spending levels were more or less constant for a long time, not showing a clear upward move again until the 1960s. An arms race, of course, need not imply an upward spiral, but it does imply competition. If two long-distance runners maintain a steady pace, we consider them to be in a race just as much as if their speed were continually increasing; it is the element of competition, or interaction, that makes the race.

In some degree, at least, that interaction is present in Soviet and American behavior—not a steady interaction, perhaps, but more likely one that moves in fits and starts in response to particular acts that seem especially provocative. The notion of a race surely does not explain every element of this behavior. It may tell us about the fact of interaction in arms spending but not about the level at which the interaction takes place; that is, the Soviet-American arms race might conceivably occur at spending levels of less than $50 billion a year instead of more than $200 billion. Something other than mere interaction must be affecting that level. Moreover, the idea of interaction does not explain what happened in the 1970s. The idea of interaction would lead us to expect

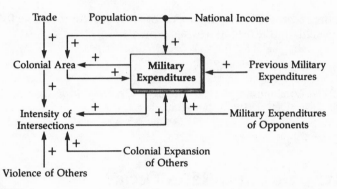

FIGURE 1.
A model of the causes of military expenditures. [Adapted from Nazli Choucri and Robert C. North, *Nations in Conflict: National Growth and International Violence* (San Francisco: W. H. Freeman and Company. Copyright © 1975), p. 168.]

the Soviet Union to moderate its military spending once the Americans slowed down after Vietnam. No such moderation occurred; rather, quite the contrary. Again, something else was going on. A variety of domestic and international pressures played a role.

International hostility may help get an arms race started and maintain it once it has begun, but varoius kinds of domestic influences also help maintain high levels of military spending. To understand further what drives this infernal machine, we must consider several kinds of explanations.

INTERNATIONAL INFLUENCES

Figure 1 is a schematic representation of the causes of military expenditures. It has been adapted from a diagram that Nazli Choucri and Robert C. North devised to provide a comprehensive framework for the causes of World War I.[1] Choucri and North were not so much concerned with explanations why particular decision makers behaved as they did in the course of the August 1914 crisis. Rather, they were trying to identify the larger conditions within governments, societies, and the whole international system that brought about the crisis.

This is a complex diagram, as international politics really is very complex. Each of the arrows with a plus sign (+) indicates a causal relationship, where an increase in a factor or variable helps produce an increase in the factor or variable to which the arrow points. In some cases, changes in a variable are caused by changes in two or more other variables. For example, the box labeled *Military Expenditures* has five arrows pointing to it. One arrow leads from *Military Expenditures of Opponents*. Considering the Soviet-American antagonism, we have a reference to one of the kinds of arms race phenomena that we have been discussing.

Obviously, the largest, most important, and potentially most threatening opponents are most relevant to military spending decisions. The plural *opponents* reminds us that we should not see all arms races purely as bilateral or two-country phenomena. In the contemporary world, the Soviet Union has to be concerned also with the power and behavior of its close neighbor China and devotes a significant part of its military effort to coping with that problem. And it was not many years ago that United States strategic delivery vehicles were pointed at China so that the United States could strike at China as well as at Russia in the event of a Soviet attack on America.

Conflicts over Spheres of Influence

Two other arrows come from *Colonial Area* and *Intensity of Intersections*. For Choucri and North, the latter term refers to the "intensity of violence in specifically colonial conflicts between the actor state and other major powers."[2] In the late twentieth century, there are few colonial territories as such; most areas of the world are composed of formally sovereign states. Yet most major powers clearly do have "spheres of influence" consisting of states over which, to one degree or another, they exert substantial control. The Western Hemisphere (except for Cuba and maybe Nicaragua, which are very sore points) is such a sphere for the United States. Eastern Europe, with many Communist states that are often referred to as satellites of the Soviet Union, is of course the major Soviet sphere of influence. But the two powers compete sharply with each other in these and other areas of the world. They are deeply involved in this competition, using economic, political, and military means in Africa, the Middle East, and Asia. In these contemporary intersections states frequently move from one power's sphere of influence to the other's in a process that often involves a great deal of military violence. Or, one power may repulse an effort to shift a state out of its sphere of influence, again often using substantial military force.

The Vietnam War is perhaps the most vivid example, but there are many others. Within the past few years, Ethiopia shifted from an American to a Soviet client, and its enemy and neighbor, Somalia, made the opposite shift in the course of a long and devastating war between them. After a long national liberation struggle, Angola ceased to be a colony of America's NATO ally, Portugal. Its struggle was heavily assisted by the Russians and the Chinese, who each supported different, bitterly opposed local leaders. The United States and France later intervened to preserve their influence on Angola's African neighbor, Zaire, when there seemed to be some threat to it from Angola. Zimbabwe (Rhodesia) was long wracked by civil war. The government was dominated in various degrees by the white minority, who looked—not always successfully—to the West for help, and by the black guerrillas, who were helped, though not dominated, by the USSR. Western-backed Yemen fought Soviet-supported South Yemen on the Arabian peninsula. Of course, the United States and the Soviet Union have been deeply enmeshed in the Arab-Israeli conflict, sending arms to various and sometimes shifting allies. The Soviet Union helped engineer a coup against a fairly neutralist regime in Afghanistan to bring that country securely into its sphere of influence. The new regime proved highly unpopular, and the Russians found themselves increasingly drawn into that civil war. In Indochina, the Soviet Union helped the Vietnamese overthrow a government in Cambodia that had been allied with China.

Colonial or sphere-of-influence expansion and intense intersections feed into a demand for more military expenditures: If a big power has colonies or spheres of influence, it will need troops to police them. They may be troops of the big power itself or local client forces armed and supplied by the big power. If wars are going on or are threatened in various parts of the globe, the big states need arms and troops. If they don't fight directly, they still need arms to supply their small-power clients and money to support their clients' armed forces in war.

In each of these two relationships (military expenditures and colonial area; military expenditures and intersections) there are two arrows running between the pairs, one arrow in either direction. This indicates that two variables interact with each other in a positive way, creating feedback whereby not only does high intensity of intersection create a need or demand for more arms but the military expenditures also create the possibility of further intense intersections. With a large, well-trained, well-equipped, and mobile military establishment, there comes a potential—and perhaps a temptation—to use it. Many critics of American foreign and security policy have maintained that the Vietnam War was made possible by, and in some sense perhaps caused by, the fact that the United States had developed a great capacity for fighting counter-insurgent or antiguerrilla wars in faraway places. These critics therefore tried to reduce the size of the American military establishment, and especially its capacity for fighting conventional wars, as a means of making it less likely that the United States would get involved in such wars. Whatever the merits of their evaluation of the Vietnam situation, it does seem reasonable that there would be a positive interaction between these two variables—local conflicts being made possible by, as well as stimulating, military expenditures.

Intersections may also escalate into serious military conflicts between major powers. This has rarely happened in the post–World War II international system. The United States and the Soviet Union so far have avoided head-on military violence, but the Soviet Union and China did fight a limited direct conflict on their common border, the Ussuri River, in 1969. Such violent superpower confrontations, if they do not lead immediately to all-out war, provide a further impetus to arms acquisitions for both contending powers.

Action-Reaction Processes

The idea of an arms race captures the sense that opposing states may be driven, from fear of permitting the other to gain an advantage, into an even sharper and perhaps ultimately self-defeating competition. This perspective on competition emerges also in the action-reaction perspective on arms races associated with the work of Lewis Frye Richardson.[3] Richardson was an English mathematician, physicist, and meteorologist (as well as a member of the Society of Friends) who in the 1930s turned his skills to understanding the causes of international conflict. His work provided innovations in both theory building and statistical hypothesis testing, but he is probably most famous for the set of equations for arms races that now are typically referred to as "Richardson processes." In their simplest form, the equations read:

$$\Delta X = kY - aX + g \tag{1}$$
$$\Delta Y = lX - bY + h \tag{2}$$

In this two-nation arms race, the changes (Δ) in the military allocations of the nations (X and Y) are influenced by three major factors: (1) the military expenditures of the other state (k and l represent reaction coefficients); (2) the economic burden of paying for previous decisions to purchase military goods (a and b represent "fatigue" coefficients to indicate the weight of this burden); and (3) the underlying "grievance" held by each state against the other (g and h).

By this formulation, changes in state X's spending result, in the first term, from the degree of threat produced by the level of military expenditures of Y. This raises the level of X's expenditures, which thereby leads to an increase in Y's military spending. So too do the grievances—basic sources of political, economic, and ideological hostility. The result from these two terms alone would be a never-ending spiral, which of course does not happen in reality. Rather, the arms race may end in violent conflict—war—or it may for some reason be brought under control and stabilized or may even be reversed.

The last term in each of the equations is meant to indicate influences that affect the possibility of nonviolent damping of the race. The fatigue coefficients for the burden of expenditures represent the fact that arms spending diverts resources from civilian needs (consumption and investment) and cannot proceed to the point where it consumes the entire economy. Instead, the economic drain will stimulate political responses that, in the absence of war, can slow and ultimately stop the military expansion. The operation of such possible constraints can be seen faintly in the political efforts during 1982 to hold down military spending, efforts which were begun soon after congressional approval of administration tax cuts and budgetary requests, as the economic burden of the military budget increases became more apparent. Similarly, there is repeated speculation about the ability of the Soviet government to extract further resources for the military out of its civilian economy, especially in the face of stagnating growth and the possibility of civilian unrest, as demonstrated in its neighbor Poland.

These fatigue constraints, however, may not be very powerful, especially at the relatively low levels of military spending experienced in the superpowers at present. Currently, the United States is spending about 7 percent of its GNP for military purposes; it spent about 13 percent during the height of the Korean War and over 40 percent at the peak of World War II. States under the direst threat may persuade their citizens to spend even more. Britain and the Soviet Union spent as much as 60 percent of their total product on defense during the worst of World War II; by that standard the current figure of about 14 percent for the USSR may not seem high. Israel has maintained a defense burden above 25 percent of its GNP for quite a few years (though with a good deal of foreign assistance contributing to its defense budget). Thus it is not clear how effective these constraints may currently be, particularly if the national sense of threat, or grievance, is high or can be made high.

This last reminds us of the importance of domestic *and* international politics in affecting arms races. Domestic elites may try to rally their people to meet a foreign threat. The Soviet government, with its relatively comprehensive control over the mass media of its people, can effectively propagandize about threats to socialism or Soviet national interests. American elites may, even without such tight control of the media, try the same, as in Senator Arthur Vandenberg's advising President Truman, at the beginning of the cold war, to "go and scare hell out of the country." Once these popular passions are unleashed, policymakers may even become more constrained by it than they wish to be: Recall the witch hunting and fears of the Joseph McCarthy era. Some Americans are afraid that the current revival of cold war sentiments may escalate into a new wave of virulent domestic anticommunism. The greater the sense of economic burden (fatigue), the greater the temptation to elites to justify that burden by fanning popular fears and grievances. Fatigue, therefore, cannot be depended upon to slow modern arms races.

DOMESTIC INFLUENCES

Shift now in Figure 1 to the influence, at the upper right corner, labeled *Previous Military Expenditures.* Pressures to maintain and to increase military expenditures arise within a country in at least three different ways.

Bureaucratic Politics

The leader of any large organization must be deeply concerned with the interests of his or her organization. A leader will be most reluctant to see the size of the organization shrink or its budget cut. Furthermore, the leader is likely to feel that the organization is doing important jobs for society—if he didn't think so, he probably would do something else for a living. If it is doing an important job and fulfilling an important function, then it would do even better with more people and resources at its disposal.

Moreover, the leader's own power in the government and in society at large depends heavily on the size of the organization. Leaders of big and growing organizations receive more respect than do leaders of small or shrinking ones. A leader will, therefore, vigorously resist any effort to cut the budget or personnel level of the organization and do his best to expand them. Research on budget making has long established that just about the best predictor of the size of an organization's budget in any year is the size of its last budget (with, especially in an expanding economy, an incremental increase).

Military organizations are by no means unique in this characteristic, but neither are they immune from it. Personal self-interest, interests of the organization one leads, and images of societal self-interest all influence the leader to ask for a higher budget. After all, if the Air Force Chief of Staff doesn't speak up to be sure that the Air Force gets a fair share of society's resources, who will? This also means that when one major weapons system becomes outmoded or obsolete, there will be a built-in interest group pressing either to modernize it and somehow keep it going or to replace it with something else that will do a similar job and keep the same people and resources employed.

When the B-52 bomber becomes obsolete, Air Force generals will look around for a new bomber, such as the B-1, to replace it. They think the bombing mission is important and vital to American security: How can there be a good Air Force if there are no big, glamorous planes to fly? Who would enlist in the Air Force only to be a missile command officer in a silo hundreds of feet underground? Air Force evaluations of the merits of a proposed new strategic bomber are unlikely, therefore, to be entirely objective and disinterested.

The Air Force's major mission has evolved to one of strategic nuclear deterrence, which depends on land-based missiles. Air Force generals will be loath to see that element of the strategic triad abandoned as obsolete. They will look hard for something like the MX and a means to deploy it. Once a weapon has gone far through the process of research and development, it becomes politically and bureaucratically very difficult not to produce and deploy it in large numbers. For example, the MIRV was developed largely to ensure that some American retaliatory vehicles would be able to penetrate Soviet defenses even if the USSR should deploy an effective ABM system. The 1972 ABM Treaty between the United States and the USSR, however, very sharply limited ABM construction and made MIRVs unnecessary for the main purpose for which they were designed. Nevertheless, production and deployment of MIRV went ahead.

The Navy, too, has its own interests. Admirals like to maintain big surface ships like aircraft carriers as well as the limited-mission and not-so-glamorous nuclear submarines. It's hard to "join the Navy and see the world" from under the sea.

This is not to imply that such leaders are corrupt or that their advice to maintain or acquire a weapons system is necessarily mistaken: Their evaluation of the national interest and that of most objective observers might well coincide. But it does imply that the allocation of resources within a government—or the total allocation of society's resources to all government activities—is strongly resistant to change, especially in any downward direction. This year's military budget is a good predictor (along with such external factors as intersections and opponents' spending) of next year's military budget.

Technological Momentum

Bureaucratic inertia is buttressed by technological momentum. Military research and development employs a half million of the best-qualified scientists and engineers worldwide and absorbs one-third to one-half of the world's human and material resources devoted generally to research and development. The research is intellectually challenging—and highly competitive. Individuals compete with one another, corporations and military services compete with their counterparts, and, of course, their countries compete. The incentives, privileges, and rewards are high. The work, however, takes a long time. Lead times of 10 years or more are typical from conceptualization through design, model production, improvement, repeated testing, evaluation, prototype production, training, and final deployment. This scientific inertia intertwines with bureaucratic inertia to make it very difficult to halt a promising project once it gets under way, even if its initial purpose (as with MIRV) has been lost.

The MIRV system had its origins in satellite-launching systems of the early 1960s. It began principally in government organizations: the Advanced Research Projects Agency of DOD, the Space Technology Laboratory, and the Air Force Space and Missile System Office. Once many of the pieces were available, it then became almost inevitable that they would be put together as a multiple-warhead delivery system, and private aerospace companies combined with the government laboratories and military chiefs to promote the project. As Herbert York, who observed the process from inside, remarked, "Once the technology was developed MIRV assumed a momentum of its own; the chances of halting it were by then slim."[4]

MIRV perhaps had its origin in technological momentum and was preserved, first, by action-reaction forces and, finally, by bureaucratic inertia. Sometimes a project may be stopped even though it is far down the technological ways, but that happens only rarely. Even ABM deployment, which was halted by the 1972 treaty, is not a clear case. In the forms under development up to that time, it clearly was a loser—technically incapable of effectively doing the job for which it was being developed. Recently, however, a new generation of technological possibilities, such as laser beams, are being touted for ABM application, and pressures to perfect and deploy them are apparent.

The Military-Industrial Complex

The third kind of domestic pressure, one that arises from the society and economy at large, is what is often referred to as the "military-industrial complex." In his last public address as President, Dwight Eisenhower warned about the political influence of a newly powerful military-industrial complex:

We have been compelled to create a permanent armaments industry of vast proportions. Added to this, three-and-a-half million men and women were directly engaged in the defense establishment. We annually spend on military security alone more than the net income of all United States corporations.

Now this conjunction of an immense military establishment and a large arms industry is new in the American experience. The total influence—economic, political, even spiritual—is felt in every city, every state house, every office of the federal government. . . . In the councils of government, we must guard against the acquisition of unwarranted influence, whether sought or unsought, by the military/industrial complex. The potential for the disastrous rise of misplaced power exists and will persist.

The phrase *military-industrial complex,* especially if interpreted broadly to include the labor unions and political leaders (such as members of Congress with defense industries or military bases in their districts, who would benefit directly from military spending) is now a commonly used expression. It represents the understanding that whether or not the American economic system benefits from assertive foreign or military policies, particular interest groups certainly do benefit. Even if the American economy as a whole could prosper without military spending, some industries and some geographical areas would suffer severe short- or medium-term damage from any reduction of military expenditures.

Controversy surrounds the question of whether profits in the defense industries are higher than in comparable nondefense industries; overall there seems to be no conclusive evidence that they are.[5] Nevertheless, a cutback, disrupting production and marketing in these industries and forcing their firms to make and find buyers for alternative products, would cause sharp, temporary losses. Defense-industry corporations, aided by the technical and political knowledge of former military officers who become defense-industry employees (see Table 1), try hard to maintain their business and to add new contracts. They are helped by government policies that seek to maintain a mobilization base in defense industries, especially the aerospace industry. It is important, for instance, to have several firms capable of manufacturing modern military aircraft.

TABLE 1.
Personnel Transfers Between Department of Defense (DOD) and
Major Military Contractors, 1970–1979

Company	Total Flow	Flow to Company DOD Military	DOD Civilian	Flow To DOD
Boeing	398	316	35	37
General Dynamics	239	189	17	32
Grumman	96	67	5	16
Lockheed	321	240	30	34
McDonnell-Douglas	211	159	12	29
Northrop	360	284	50	16
Rockwell	234	150	26	47
United Technologies	83	50	11	12
Total	1942	1455	186	233

Source: Adapted from Gordon Adams, *The Iron Triangle: The Politics of Defense Contracting*
(New York: Council on Economic Priorities, 1981), p. 84.

When one of Lockheed's aviation contracts is finished, a new contract
will be needed if the company's experience, skilled labor, and capital
equipment are not to be scattered and lost.

Increasingly, sales of arms abroad, especially to allies and the Third
World, rival in economic importance the sales of many countries' arms
manufacturers to their domestic governments. Especially during the
post–Vietnam War years, arms exports became a major prop to the
military-industrial complex. United States arms exports of $10 billion
in 1974 and 1975 amounted to over half as much as the total of U.S.
government arms purchases for the American armed forces. Foreign
sales can make the difference between short production lines (building
perhaps a few hundred tanks per year at high cost) or longer production
lines (turning out a thousand or more tanks with the lower unit costs
of mass production). These efficiencies of scale are especially important
to smaller countries like France, who could not buy enough for their
own armed forces to keep costs at a competitive level. Arms sales also
are useful to help the balance of payments. American and European
arms sales to Iran and the Arab states made a significant contribution
to paying the increased costs of oil imports from those same countries.
Both to sustain a healthy domestic arms industry and to help the
balance of payments, governments of exporting countries often want to
encourage arms exports at the same time that, for other reasons (such
as the unsavory nature of some of the the recipients' authoritarian
regimes), they may wish to discourage them. Figure 2 shows the major
arms exporting countries and the destinations of their weapons.

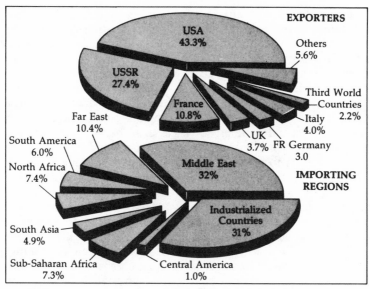

FIGURE 2.
Shares of world exports (by country) and world imports (by region) of major weapons, 1977–1980. [Stockholm International Peace Research Institute (SIPRI), *World Armaments and Disarmament*, SIPRI Yearbook 1981 (London: Taylor and Francis, 1981), p. xxi.]

On the demand side, the governments of exporting countries usually want to use arms sales or military assistance programs to build up their foreign allies. South Korea and Saudi Arabia are very important allies of the United States, and the demands of American national security seem to override doubts about arming governments that will use those arms at least partly to oppress their own populations. Any government policy that tries to limit international arms sales always bumps up against these political and economic realities. And in most cases, if one country (the United States, for instance) refuses to sell arms to a Third World state, some other country (for example, France or the Soviet Union) will gladly oblige.

Thus a variety of pressures help maintain a heavy flow of military sales and assistance to Third World countries. Add the desire of many governments for modern arms and policy primarily as instruments to control their own population (rather than to deter their neighbors) and the desire of industrialized countries to help prop up the governments of their friends (whether by the Russians in Afghanistan, Angola, or Ethiopia, or the Americans in Morocco, the Philippines, or Zaire), and the result is a powerful constellation of interests maintaining the world's biggest industries.

Certainly someone stands to gain from every dollar spent on arms; some industries do benefit from military spending and would suffer from its reduction. The important question for military-industrial complex theories is how broad and deep that suffering would be compared with the benefits that might go to other industries if resources were taken away from military ends. The disarmament damage to military industries (and probably to certain regional labor markets as well) would exceed the gains going to any other single sector of industry; that is, while military spending does not necessarily benefit the economy as a whole, the gains from defense spending are greater to a few industries than are the costs to any one sector when spread among all the sectors of the civilian economy. Toy makers, citrus growers, and home builders all lose a little business when more money is spent for fighter planes. But if less money were spent for fighters, McDonnell-Douglas Corporation would lose heavily—and resist mightily. In democracies, pressure groups concentrate their activities on those issues that promise them the greatest gains and will not deeply resist efforts of other groups pursuing their most important special interests when those efforts involve modest costs (as long as the prospective costs *remain* modest). Each looks out for gaining something for himself and tolerates similar activities by others.

This essentially political explanation would account for continuing excessive levels of military spending (and perhaps even maintenance of an ideological climate of fear and hostility necessary to support such a defense posture), despite the fact that economic gains were limited to but a small segment of the economy. This view fits with the findings of a major study of American businessmen's attitudes toward tariff issues. According to the study's authors: "The men who feared loss from a tariff cut were more in favor of raising tariffs than were those who explicitly asserted that they would gain by the increase. We see that fear of loss is a more powerful stimulus than prospect of gain."[6]

Of course, similar interests are powerful in the Soviet Union. While there are no capitalists in that economy, certainly state industrial managers have interests in promoting the growth, power, prosperity, and technological preeminence of the arms manufacturing plants they control. They too share interests with their clients in the Red Army and Strategic Rocket Forces and with hawkish ideologues in the Communist Party. A cold war—though not necessarily a hot one—helps to maintain their privileges and central roles in Soviet society. In both countries, therefore, entrenched economic and political interests serve to maintain the momentum of established hard-line policies and to resist change. In a perverse way, the military-industrial complex of each country helps the other. Each embodies the foreign threat that its counterpart in the other country needs to justify its own activities.

A more radical argument holds that military spending undergirds modern industrial capitalist economies. By this line of reasoning, if it were not for the prop provided by military spending, industrial capitalism would quickly collapse into underconsumption. To absorb "surplus capital," the government must increase its spending and taxing. "Welfare state" spending is opposed by conservatives because it is thought to damage work incentives in the labor market and to compete unfairly with private enterprise. Expanded public spending for civil purposes therefore is not acceptable, but military spending is, precisely because it does not compete with big private vested interests.

It is difficult to make a satisfactory test of this idea. Nearly everyone agrees that rearmament for World War II provided a stimulus to the American economy that brought it out of the Depression. Since World War II, military spending as a proportion of GNP has been at a level previously unprecedented in peacetime, coinciding with a long period of prosperity. But other kinds of government spending, taxation, and monetary policy (as informed by modern economics) probably deserve more credit as causes of that prosperity. Some other countries, notably Japan and West Germany, have had even more expansive economies with much less military spending. Nevertheless, it is now well known that political leaders like to increase government spending just before elections to create at least short bursts of prosperity that will impress voters favorably. Military spending is one that is relatively easy to increase and at most times is considered a proper function of government. Arthur Burns advised President Eisenhower of this in March 1960: "Burns' conclusion was that unless some decisive governmental action were taken, and taken soon, we were heading for another dip (in the economy), which would hit its low point just before the elections. . . . He urgently recommended that two steps be taken immediately: by loosening up credit and, where justifiable, increasing spending for national security."[7]

In an analysis of year-to-year military spending changes in the postwar United States, Miroslav Nincic and Thomas Cusack found that "military spending cut back at an expected rate of $2 billion per annum after on-year (presidential) elections and expanded at a similar rate in the two years prior to those elections."[8] Thus, although the underconsumption thesis seems not very plausible in general, political leaders will sometimes boost military spending for reasons that have more to do with politics and economics than with strictly military needs.

CONVERGENT PRESSURES

All these influences help explain . . . the lines for military spending . . . [which] generally [maintain] their levels or [rise] fairly steadily. Periods of significant reduction in military spending, while not totally absent, are rare. Usually a "ratchet effect" occurs from a war. After the level of military effort has been geared up to a high wartime level, a "ratchet" of bureaucratic and political-economic pressure keeps it from dropping down all the way to its prewar level. The new expenditure floor is usually well above that previous level. This happened in the United States after all its major wars in the last 90 years except the Vietnam War (that is, after the Spanish-American War, the two world wars, and the Korean War).

Finally, note in Figure 1 the fifth arrow leading to the *Military Expenditures* box. This one comes from *Population* interacting with *National Income.* We have not talked much about this particular influence, though we may take it as a suggestion of various domestic influences. Here, it chiefly implies that economic and population growth provide the means for expanding the military establishment: A big country can support a big army. In a growing economy, more resources can be devoted to military purposes without necessarily reducing anyone's share of the expanding pie; maintaining large armed forces becomes relatively painless.

Population and income growth also remind us of some explanations—indicated at the upper left by the arrows leading to growth of *Colonial Area*—for imperialism. Growth not only provides the possibility of military expansion, it may also provide the need for it—a need for assured food supplies to feed a growing population or a need for assured raw materials to feed a growing economy. Every modern state depends for its popularity on being able to satisfy the rising demands of its citizens for material goods and services. Haunting all democratic governments is the spectre of the Great Depression of the 1930s. Economic failure destroyed democracy and brought Hitler to power in Germany, which raised the threat of dictatorship throughout Europe. The basic ideology of capitalism values economic growth and tolerates inequalities in the interest of providing incentives to ensure growth. The Communist states, as part of an increasingly interlinked world economy, could not escape this same pressure even if they wished. Through media of worldwide communication and the ever-more-porous "Iron Curtain," Soviet and Eastern European citizens are fully aware of the higher living standards of their western counterparts. Communist governments have to make some concessions to their citizens' demands; indeed, their claim to power depends, in large part, on their promise to provide their people with better living conditions than they had under the old capitalist order.

All industrialized countries, capitalist or communist, must have reliable access to supplies of food and raw materials if they are to ensure economic growth and the domestic political peace dependent on that growth. The United States is substantially, and increasingly, dependent on foreign sources of oil and such minerals as chromium, nickel, cobalt, manganese, and platinum (see Figure 3). Western Europe is completely reliant on imports for 10 vital raw materials; Japan, for 11. Many of these are secured from politically unstable areas in the Third World, especially in southern Africa and the Middle East. Decision makers must worry whether Third World governments will band together in

Minerals	Net Import Reliance as a Percent of Apparent Consumption	Major Foreign Sources (1975–1978)
	0% 25% 50% 75% 100%	
Columbium	100	Brazil (67), Canada (9), Thailand (7)
Mica (Sheet)	100	India (80), Brazil (8), Madagascar (7)
Manganese	98	Gabon (23), South Africa (20), Brazil (18), France (11)
Tantalum	96	Thailand (31), Canada (15), Malaysia (11), Brazil (4)
Bauxite and Alumina	93	Jamaica (33), Australia (27), Guinea (15), Suriname (14)
Chromium	90	South Africa (44), USSR (12), Zimbabwe (8), Turkey (8)
Cobalt	90	Zaire (4), Belg.-Lux. (19), Zambia (10), Finland (7)
Platinum-Group Metals	89	South Africa (50), USSR (22), United Kingdom (12)
Tin	81	Malaysia (55), Thailand (16), Indonesia (11), Bolivia (6)

FIGURE 3.
U.S. net import reliance on selected minerals, 1979. [U.S. Bureau of Mines, U.S. Bureau of the Census.]

cartels to raise the price of their raw material exports manyfold or engage in politically motivated boycotts of western consumers. The OPEC cartel for oil, with its higher prices and earlier boycott, is the prime example.

More threatening is the likelihood—or certainty—that many Third World governments will be unstable. If raw materials are to be exported, some government must be able to enforce social order. Mines must be kept open and supplied with electricity. Oil wells must be kept pumping. Railroads or pipelines must reliably carry the material to port, where ship-loading facilities must be maintained. Mass unrest or civil war can endanger the ability to keep these raw materials flowing, as in post-revolutionary Iran, where oil exports fell to hardly more than a tenth of their volume under the Shah. This kind of danger lies behind the demand for military forces able to intervene to prop up weak but "friendly" Third World regimes or possibly to ensure the continued operation of raw material supplies if the Third World government collapses. The American Rapid Deployment Force is designed for precisely this kind of use in the Middle East or elsewhere. It may seem all the more urgent knowing that another great power, such as the Soviet Union, may also intervene either to secure its own materials supplies or to deny vital supplies to the West. Alarmists speak of a "raw materials war," which calls up memories of pre-1914 spheres of influence, colonial expansion, and imperialism. Here, domestic influences—the need to maintain resource supplies for growth and political stability—combine with international pressures leading to similar needs of other states. Together, they produce international pressures of intense intersections such as those noted earlier in the chapter.

All told, domestic influences seem so strong that some analysts say that military establishments are essentially "autistic actors." They take this image from the psychology of autistic children, who shut themselves off almost completely from outside social stimuli and respond overwhelmingly to their own internal psyches. In this view, the arms race is not really a race at all, if by "race" we mean that the relative positions of the participants influence the pace at which they run. The government and industrial leaders in an "autistic" system would maintain a military buildup almost solely as a result of demands and pressures from within their own countries, not as a result of international incidents or military gains by the other racer. By this explanation, we are racing against ourselves; international events are irrelevant, except perhaps as they provide an excuse for societal elites to demand sacrifices for military purposes. What the enemy is doing thus would become useful domestic propaganda to support policies leaders desire on other grounds. Such an explanation would certainly not rule out even some collusion between the elites of the two ostensibly competing countries. For instance, at about the time one country's elites were considering budgetary appropriations or authorizations, the enemy might act aggressively or show off a new weapon to assist the elites in extracting more military funds; the enemy would then look for the same favor in return when its appropriation cycle came around.

Too exclusive a preoccupation with Soviet and American military spending may obscure another fact: Many countries have military establishments that say they are directed toward external enemies but really are chiefly directed toward internal enemies. They are not instruments of foreign war but instruments of internal repression. This is most obviously the case in many Third World countries, but even for the Soviet Union it should not be ignored. Political dissidence still calls forth repression. Half of the citizens of the Soviet Union are not Russians but are members of other European and Asian ethnic groups with a potential for nationalist separatism. The Soviet government would need a substantial army just to ensure internal security.

WHICH INFLUENCES
ARE MOST IMPORTANT?

It is one thing to list these various influences that may promote military spending or militarism and quite another to decide how important each is. Most of the explanations seem plausible in one degree or another, and there is some evidence for each. Choucri and North report that, for the majority of major powers in the years before World War I, most of their arrows to *Military Expenditures* do turn out to identify significant relationships. But they see domestic factors as more powerful than international ones. In their words:

The primary importance of domestic factors . . . does not preclude the reality of arms competition. Two countries whose military establishments are expanding largely for domestic reasons can, and indeed almost certainly will, become acutely aware of each other's spending. Thereafter, although spending may continue to be powerfully influenced by domestic factors, deliberate military competition may increase and even take the form of an arms race (although the race may be over specific military features and may be a very small portion of total military spending).[9]

Richardson applied his model to information on the Anglo-German rivalry immediately preceding World War I, but he had only a handful of data points that could be interpreted to fit a variety of possible equations. Others since then, like Choucri and North, have done better work on the pre-1914 rivalries and on more recent arms races. Most efforts, not surprisingly, have concentrated largely on the post–World War II Soviet-American (or occasionally, NATO–Warsaw Pact) arms race. The basic Richardson equations have been modified to produce political explanations that seem more plausible. For example, instead of saying that the change in military spending depends on the *level* of the rival's spending, one can make it depend on the *change* in the rival's level of spending or on the *ratio* of one's own spending to that of the rival. Or, one can recognize that spending in any one year goes in part to maintain existing forces and in part to add to them. More important than current levels of spending, therefore, may be the existing stock of weapons to which any addition may be made. In periods when the United States maintained a stock of strategic weapons far superior to that of the Soviet Union, American presidents could (perhaps mistakenly) be relaxed about high levels of Soviet spending in any one year—it might take many years of high spending levels to bring the Soviet weapons stock to essential equivalence with that of the United States.

Efforts to take account of the triangular nature of superpower interactions have been especially intriguing. So too have efforts to couple the action-reaction of military spending with the action-reaction of international political and military initiatives. Richard Ashley adapted the Choucri-North model to the U.S.-Soviet-Chinese relationship. He concluded that the United States partly responded to Soviet spending; he also found a large measure of inertia sustained by the domestic military establishment and national security bureaucracy. The Soviet Union's military spending patterns were a little different. They seemed to be dominated by domestic forces and not to respond in any regular way at all to American military spending. Neither country's military budgets seemed to respond much to what Choucri and North called intersections of interest. Ashley, however, measured these as *commercial* intersections, and that may well be too limited a definition, missing the *confrontations* that have occurred between the superpowers in Africa and elsewhere. He did find some Soviet response to *Chinese* military spending after the two great Communist states broke off relations, and he found some Chinese reaction to collisions of interest with the USSR.[10] Other analysts have also found that, in the Soviet-American (or, sometimes, the Soviet-American-Chinese) case, the main effects are exerted by domestic rather than international forces.[11]

These results, derived as they are from somewhat different theories and research procedures, seem to converge on an agreement that international influences on arms races are less powerful than Richardson's early analyses would have us expect. Instead, they drive explanation most importantly to some combination of bureaucratic inertia and the broader *domestic* forces implied by one version or another of military-industrial complex perspectives. Perhaps the superpowers may respond not to "normal" increments in each other's military posture but only to major changes in their bilateral relations.

The United States did react with increased military expenditures to international political reversals on certain occasions: It rearmed after the North Korean attack on South Korea in 1950; it started a crash program in the late 1950s when Soviet space achievements suggested—erroneously—that Russia might be about to get an ICBM first-strike capability; and American foreign policy reversals of the late 1970s, especially in the Middle East, helped stimulate the most recent American arms buildup. The Soviets, for their part, may have boosted their military spending in the 1960s in response to the visible and rather humiliating defeat they suffered in the Cuban missile crisis—"never again" to have to yield. Yet even in those cases, the new arms exertions had already been demanded by many domestic interests. The external political reversals provided a rallying cry, an excuse, as much as a true impetus.

Many problems arise in trying to do a good arms-race analysis. The results can rarely be conclusive. The time period for analysis is relatively short. The data available are highly aggregated; usually one must deal with total military spending rather than, say, spending for strategic arms, which might be the most relevant to an arms race analysis. The quality of the data on Soviet military spending is very poor, subject to wide differences in estimation. Data may be selected to bias the results, and different estimates provide the basis for quite different conclusions. In Western countries, the time lags between request, authorization, and appropriation make it hard to identify a response to any particular external stimulus. Some military programs are undertaken in anticipation of, rather than reaction to, opponents' programs. As a result, any analysis is bound to contain a substantial element of error. Moreover, both the bureaucratic politics and arms race explanations lead us to expect very similar behavior, namely, steady or gradually increasing levels of expenditure for both sides. Given the problems with data quality, few time points, and so forth, it is very hard to pick apart different patterns and to document those differences in a convincing way.

In the present state of the art and science, probably the best we can say is that both domestic and action-reaction international influences do operate and do make a difference. Evidence seems to tip toward giving somewhat greater weight to internal influences. There is also evidence that the Soviet government's arms spending is constrained by inadequate output, particularly at certain phases of the cycle of five-year plans. Civilian needs seem to get greater emphasis at the beginning of each plan and at the end, as producers are trying to meet plan targets; military spending fares best in the middle years. American military spending may be affected by a different kind of internal political cycle—one keyed to election years. Neither of these cyclical patterns, however, is firmly established.

Finally, behavior varies according to who the decision makers are; that is, certain leaders or administrations may be more tolerant of military spending by the other side or less willing to divert funds from domestic civilian needs than are others. Evidence has been found for this during the naval race between the two world wars.[12] Most recently, we see it with the Reagan administration. The current administration has not only decided to initiate a vast increase in military spending, but it has tried to accomplish it by cutting domestic spending while avoiding raising taxes. This was a deliberate political choice; thus it does matter who is in charge.

Since the empirical results are not conclusive, and since each of the "independent" or "causal" influences is itself caused by prior factors in the chain, it becomes very hard to suggest effective ways to reduce arms expenditures and slow what we call the arms race. Some people, accepting one version of the autism argument, insist that only a drastic change in domestic economic, social, and political institutions could make a difference. But since both the United States and the Soviet Union behave similarly despite their very different domestic systems, that prescription becomes questionable. Obviously, some shift in popular and elite preferences and sense of threat would help—but how much?

During the Vietnam War, American popular opinion toward the military shifted enormously. In the earlier cold war years, typically less than 20 percent of the population wanted to see defense expenditures reduced; according to national surveys in 1969 and 1970, that proportion was up to about half the population. Popular opposition to the military played a central role in reducing military expenditures after the Vietnam War; for the first time in over a hundred years, U.S. military spending after a war dropped below the floor typical of the years preceding the war. But by the late 1970s, in response to dramatic American foreign policy reversals in Africa, Iran, and Afghanistan and the absence of any Soviet restraint in military spending, American opinion shifted again. Popular attitudes on this issue shift often and respond strongly to mass media treatment of foreign events. The Iranian hostage affair, for instance, became a television spectacular that importantly fed Americans' determination to recover their military muscle. After it was over and the domestic costs of new arms programs became apparent, enthusiasm for military spending once again waned (see Figure 4).

Further attention to governmental and bureaucratic sources of arms momentum clearly is in order, as is attention to the forces of technological momentum. Would it be easier to restrain scientific research and development than to head off bureaucratic pressures to deploy newly developed systems? Clearly the international side of the explanation deserves attention. New ways to reduce conflict between competing states, to encourage communication, and to verify arms control agreements—so we can see what the Russians are doing and not simply have to trust them (or they us)—are essential. Some possible actions of this sort will be discussed in later chapters.

Negotiations for arms control have proved exceptionally difficult—gestation of the SALT II treaty occupied eight years and produced a stillborn runt. Sometimes there is a role for one-sided acts of self-control—limited acts, to be sure—and for acts that can be reversible if they fail to bring forth corresponding tit-for-tat concessions from the other side. The role of political actions—colonial expansion and intersections as a direct influence on military spending patterns—should not

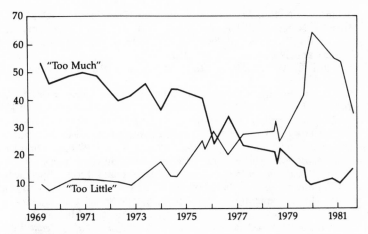

FIGURE 4.
Public preferences for increased or reduced U.S. defense spending, 1969–1981. When two or more surveys were made in the same month, the plotted point represents the average. [Bruce Russett and Donald R. DeLuca, " 'Don't Tread on Me': American Opinion on Foreign Policy in the Eighties," *Political Science Quarterly*, 96, 3 (1981):384; and recent CBS/NYT and NBC/AP surveys.]

be neglected. The increase in American military spending in 1980 seemed to be more in response to Soviet acts in Afghanistan and elsewhere than simply to changes in Soviet spending. In any case, because the arms race is a complex phenomenon, with several causes, we cannot expect to find any single solution.

NOTES

1. Nazli Choucri and Robert C. North, *Nations in Conflict: National Growth and International Violence* (San Francisco: W. H. Freeman and Company, 1975), p. 168.

2. Ibid., p. 169.

3. Lewis F. Richardson, *Arms and Insecurity* (Pittsburgh and Chicago: Boxwood and Quadrangle, 1960).

4. Herbert York, "Multiple Warhead Missiles," *Scientific American* 28, 2 (1973):14–25. See also Ted Greenwood, *Making the MIRV* (Cambridge, Mass.: Ballantine, 1975).

5. Robert J. Art, "Why We Overspend and Underaccomplish: Weapons Procurement and the Military-Industrial Complex," in Steven Rosen, ed., *Testing the Theory of the Military-Industrial Complex* (Lexington, Mass.: D.C. Heath, 1973).

6. Raymond A. Bauer, Ithiel de Sola Pool, and Anthony Dexter, *American Business and Public Policy: The Politics of Foreign Trade* (New York: Atherton, 1963), p. 142.

7. Richard M. Nixon, *Six Crises* (New York: Doubleday, 1962).

8. Miroslav Nincic and Thomas Cusack, "The Political Economy of U.S. Military Spending," *Journal of Peace Research* 16, 2 (1979):101–115.

9. Choucri and North, op. cit., p. 218.

10. Richard K. Ashley, *The Political Economy of War and Peace* (London: Frances Pinter, 1980).

11. See Hans Rattinger, "Armaments, Détente, and Bureaucracy," *Journal of Conflict Resolution* 19, 4 (1975):571–595; A.F.K. Organski and Jacek Kugler, *The War Ledger* (Chicago: University of Chicago Press, 1980); Jean Christian Lambelet and Urs Luterbacher, "Dynamics of Arms Races: Mutual Stimulation vs. Self-Stimulation," *Journal of Peace Science* 4, 1 (1979):49–66; Miroslav Nincic, *The Arms Race* (New York: Praeger, 1982); Steven Majeski and David Jones, "Arms Race Modelling: Causality Analysis and Model Specification," *Journal of Conflict Resolution* 25, 2 (1981):259–288; Thomas Cusack and Michael Don Ward, "Military Spending in the United States, Soviet Union, and China," *Journal of Conflict Resolution* 25, 3 (1981):429–469; and Michael D. Wallace and J. M. Wilson, "Non-Linear Arms Race Models," *Journal of Peace Research* 25 (1978):175–192.

12. Charles Lucier, "Changes in the Value of Arms Race Parameters," *Journal of Conflict Resolution* 23, 1 (1979):17–39.

5. Political Distrust as Generator of the Arms Race: Prisoners' and Security Dilemmas

Ralph M. Goldman

The phenomena of trust and distrust are among the most frequently mentioned and least dealt with elements in the problem of security and arms control. Distrust clearly leads to worst-case analysis, military buildups, and acceleration of the arms race; we have a great deal of evidence of how this process works. We have much less evidence to support a prediction that international political trust would produce arms control, security, and peace. This chapter will describe some of the components of trust and distrust that are identified in behavioral theory. The decision-making predicament of the policymaker responsible for security will be analyzed and illustrated by the case of the Prisoners' Dilemma. Some examples of security policies that generate distrust and others that promote trust and cooperation will be given. The chapter will conclude with an argument favoring greater attention to the trust-distrust aspect of the arms race.

The Prisoners' Dilemma, which is a special case of the theory of games of strategy, affords an excellent model for better understanding some of the difficulties associated with the question of security and

Figure 1. Prisoners' Dilemma Payoff Matrix

		Prisoner II	
		Confess	Not Confess
Prisoner I	Confess	5, 5	½, 10
	Not Confess	10, ½	1, 1

safety in this world. In the usual formulation of the Prisoners' Dilemma, two prisoners have been caught and charged with some crime such as armed robbery. Lacking evidence, the district attorney realizes that he has a weak case against the two, whereupon he has the prisoners placed in separate cells and held incommunicado. He then offers each prisoner the following deal. "The evidence against you is not complete, so each of you has a choice of confessing or not confessing to the crime. If you both confess, your sentences will be five years each. If neither of you confesses, your sentences will be one year each. If one of you confesses, the one who confesses will get a light sentence of only half a year for helping us clear up this case, but the other will dealt with harshly and receive a sentence of ten years." Because the prisoners are kept separated, each must make his own decision about confessing without information about what the other prisoner has decided.

In Figure 1, the first number in each cell represents the possible sentence for Prisoner I and the second the possible sentence for Prisoner II. Obviously each prisoner's greatest preference is likely to be the half-year sentence, followed by the one-year sentence, and the five-year sentence next. The least desirable outcome for each prisoner would be a ten-year sentence. "Rational" behavior, by definition, requires that a person strive exclusively for his first preference on a scale of preferences. In this case, a "rational" prisoner must strive exclusively for the payoff that maximizes his own self-interest without regard for the other party, that is, the half-year sentence. However, neither prisoner can escape the hard fact that the outcome for himself is also contingent upon what his partner in crime decides. In other words, the dilemma each has is how to reconcile the two self-interested "rationalities."

Ordinarily, individuals in such a situation proceed to communicate with each other in order to arrive at some *collective* action. Such is the central role that communication plays in the achievement of coop- eration in human affairs. In our hypothetical Prisoners' Dilemma, however, communication is not possible, and each must consider other factors in arriving at his own decision to confess or not confess.

Each prisoner must consider two antecedent questions. First, what will be the other prisoner's *probable behavior*? Second, will that probable behavior have *positive or negative consequences* for oneself? These two questions are, in fact, the principal elements of *trust*. "Trust" has been defined as consisting of at least two elements: (a) predictability of another's behavior and (b) the positive or negative consequences of that behavior for the trusting individual.[1]

To predict another's probable behavior requires observation of the past behavior of that individual. This is an *empirical* process. One must also make a judgment as to whether or not the predicted behavior will have positive consequences for oneself. This is a *normative* judgment. Taken together, the empirical and the normative conclusions will generate an attitude of trust or distrust toward the other person. Obviously the possibility of error in predicting how another will behave depends a great deal on how well one knows the other, and such empirical knowledge is rarely perfect or without risk. Further, the extent to which one wishes to risk trusting another may depend a great deal upon the weightiness of the positive or negative consequences for oneself that may ensue from such a trusting attitude.

Thus, in the case of the two prisoners, much will depend on how long they have been partners in crime, how well they have "stuck together" under trying circumstances in the past, the extent to which they share common goals, and the degree to which they like each other. If they trust each other not to confess, each would give up his "rational" first preference for the half-year sentence in favor of a second best, but collective, preference: the one-year sentence. However, if they distrust each other, each is likely to try to "get the jump" on the other by confessing, and both are likely thereby to get their third preference, the five year sentence. If one is trusting of the other while the other is distrusting of him, the trusting (not confessing) prisoner will be "exploited" in that he will receive a ten-year sentence while his partner gets off with only a half year.

Distrust continues to be a major hurdle to cooperation most familiarly in international affairs. In fact, distrust is the central feature of the arms race. Consider the following observations by former U.S. Secretary of Defense Harold Brown in his annual report to the Congress:

There remains the question of how large the collective deterrent should be. The answer to that question depends, in turn, on how we interpret the policies and assess the capabilities of the Soviet Union. . . . We face great uncertainty as to the intentions of [the Soviet] leadership. . . . [After reviewing the growth in Soviet military forces since 1964] the Soviets may be less well-intentioned than we would wish them to be. Our planning must take that possibility into account. . . . Exactly what the Soviets are trying to accomplish with their large and growing capabilities is uncertain.[2]

The secretary of defense has said that the Soviet Union is not to be trusted. Its future behavior cannot be reliably predicted on the basis of its past behavior, particularly in the light of its rapidly growing military forces. The consequences of Soviet behavior for the United States are likely to be negative, that is, reduced American security as well as

Figure 2.   Payoff Matrix In The Security Dilemma

		Nation B			
		Cooperate		*Defect*	
			2		1
	Cooperate	CC		CD	
Nation A					
		2		4	
			4		3
	Defect	DC		DD	
		1		3	

reduced American influence in world politics. Of course, Soviet leaders express a similar analysis, with certain variations, arguing that they are surrounded by past and present enemies, namely, Gemany and NATO on the west and China on the east—not to mention the other superpower in North America.

Thus, the parties to an arms race are in a predicament similar to that described in the Prisoners' Dilemma. Thinking strictly on a unilateral, self-interested, "rational" basis, the leader of a nation might say: "We have two choices: to arm or to disarm. If the other nation disarms, we are better off by remaining armed. If the other nation arms, we are even more obviously better off remaining armed." Hence, in an environment of international distrust, the outcome is an arms race, even though both parties may prefer to use their respective resources for other than military purposes. Robert Jervis has formulated this security dilemma as described in Figure 2.[3]

In Jervis' formulation, the numbers represent the ranked order of preferences of Nations A and B. Thinking strictly in terms of its own maximum self-interest, each nation most prefers—as represented by the numeral 1—to defect and thereby exploit the cooperative inclination of the other nation. At the other extreme, however, each nation would least like—numeral 4—to be exploited for being cooperative while the other nation defects. Each nation's second preference would be to cooperate *if and only if* the other nation can be *trusted* to cooperate as well. However, under conditions of distrust, each nation is likely to defect and go its own way, resulting in the third preference in the defect-defect cell, that is, engage in a competitive arms race.

Jervis' excellent analysis of the security dilemma makes it clear that the essential task of Nations A and B is to do all that is necessary and possible to increase their opponent's incentive to cooperate. In recent years, the popular term for this type of effort has been "confidence building." Nations A and B also need to increase the costs that each nation risks by exploiting the other nation.

What happens to nations that allow themselves to be exploited, as indicated in the DC and CD cells in Figure 2? The most obvious results are loss of territory or loss of sovereignty. A more subtle consequence is the loss of international prestige and influence that, in the volatile and fickle world of international politics, may also have serious consequences for the security and prosperity of the victim. It is the profound fear of such exploitation that drives nations to arm, join alliance systems, or seek protection from superpowers.

NOTES

1. Morton Deutsch, "Trust and Suspicion," *Journal of Conflict Resolution* 2 (1958):265–279.
2. Secretary of Defense, *Annual Report to the Congress: Fiscal Year 1979*, pp. 33–34, 62.
3. Robert Jervis, "Cooperation Under the Security Dilemma," *World Politics* (January 1978):167–214. For a survey and evaluation of the debate about deterrence theory and mutual assured destruction (MAD), see Donald M. Snow, "Current Nuclear Deterrence Thinking: An Overview and Review," *International Studies Quarterly* 23, 3 (September 1979):445–486.

6. SALT II: A Symptom of the Arms Race

Robert C. Johansen

THE FAILURE OF ARMS CONTROL

The success of arms control policy may be judged by the extent to which it slows, stops, or reverses the militarization of the planet. By that standard, arms control has failed. Several thousand diplomatic meetings on armaments between the United States and the Soviet Union over the past thirty-five years have failed to eliminate a single weapon or to reduce the willingness of governments to use military power in diplomacy and combat. Why? Are there genuinely insuperable obstacles? The purpose of this essay is to answer these questions and to suggest a more imaginative approach to arms control. Many of the points raised here about U.S. policies will of course apply to the Soviet Union as well. But the emphasis nonetheless will be on the United States because it is the government presumably most subject to influence by those who read this book.

A detailed examination of arms policies since 1945 suggests three central reasons why efforts to reverse the arms buildup have been largely unsuccessful. If we fail to understand these, we may embark on an arms control journey that will turn out, after wearying years of travel, to be a political dead end. First, despite the purpose of arms control negotiations, the politics surrounding them often spark, rather than dampen, arms buildups. Second, all recent U.S. administrations have simultaneously pursued two contradictory ends: to reduce arms and to acquire more of them.[1] This inconsistency of purpose has made it impossible to implement effective means to curtail armaments. Third, the distribution of political resources in the United States weighs heavily against those seeking to reverse the arms buildup. Each of these constraints will be discussed in turn.

In this examination, the Strategic Arms Limitation Talks (SALT) will serve as a useful focus. They illustrate clearly the somewhat surprising content and direction of most arms control negotiations. They represent the most serious recent initiative to control arms. As such, they also provide the background both for the Reagan administration's proposals in START (Strategic Arms Reduction Talks) and for the national campaign to freeze the growth of nuclear arsenals. SALT began in 1969, produced a SALT I treaty in 1972,[2] and continued until 1980, when President Jimmy Carter, in response to the Soviet invasion of Afghanistan, withdrew a second treaty, SALT II, from the Senate ratification process.

The Escalation of Arms
During Negotiations for Reduction

There are four immediate reasons that explain why arms negotiations since 1945 have never led to reductions. First, because arms negotiations are complex and intensely political, they are prolonged; thus they move far less rapidly than the pace of arms expansion and innovation. After working twelve years in SALT, policymakers could claim only one ratified treaty, in itself almost inconsequential compared to the onrushing proliferation of more destructive and dangerous weapons. The SALT II treaty required eight years to complete, only to be aborted despite its lengthy gestation. From 1969 to 1980, the continuing SALT negotiations legitimized a rapid *expansion* of nuclear arsenals. Both U.S. officials and the public believed that any slackening of military growth might weaken the U.S. negotiating posture. Most people assumed that arms programs should proceed until negotiations halted them. Accordingly, total U.S. and Soviet warheads grew from 5,550 in 1969 to 15,200 in 1980.[3]

Second, the SALT negotiations exaggerated the need to tally the number of weapons in each separate category of arms possessed by Washington and Moscow.[4] Because of nationally biased perceptions in such a highly politicized policymaking process, each country perceived the tallies differently. Both claimed that close comparisons of the two arsenals legitimized the expansion of its own. Each felt a need to acquire additional weapons to become "more equal" to the other. The United States sought to expand its land-based missile arsenal, for example, by adding a newly designed MX, despite a deliberate decision years earlier to forego such extremely heavy intercontinental ballistic missiles (ICBMs). In the late 1970s the Soviet Union had developed missile engines with a huge thrust because Soviet scientists had not yet perfected, as the United States had, a high yield-to-weight ratio for its warheads. Nor had the Soviet Union matched U.S. precision in targeting. Once the USSR had manufactured larger missiles and subsequently developed multiple-warhead technology, the United States reversed its decision not to employ a larger ICBM. Thus the arms negotiations underscored a compulsion to produce nearly every weapon system possessed by the Soviet Union, rather than to be satisfied with similar overall capability. This was true even when, as in the case of the smaller throw weight of U.S. ICBMs, the absence of precise nuclear symmetry had no *security* significance.

When one side perceives its strength to be superior in one category of weaponry, it will not eliminate its competitive edge through nego-tiations. Hard-line critics at home are too willing to damage the political careers of those recommending such policies. Instead of cutting back, therefore, the superior side tries to maintain its lead, hoping to negotiate from a position of such strength that the inferior side will concede points or tire of trying to catch up. But this maneuver almost always fails. In SALT, neither party would accept a treaty provision that might lock it into an inferior position. Thus the United States insisted on its right to develop an entirely new, larger ICBM, the MX, even though the missile itself was so impractical that the Department of Defense could not find, [and has yet to develop,] a satisfactory mode for its deployment.[5]

Although it is an understandable assumption, the idea that arms must continue to play an undiminished role in security policy created a hopelessly negative negotiating context. The diplomatic goal was to develop an agreement that minimized, rather than maximized, restraints on new weapons. The purpose of arms policy, in effect, has been to develop as many weapons as possible in areas not prohibited by any agreement. As a result, officials carefully tailored their negotiating proposals to exempt from limitation those new weapons their own government most wanted. These were usually weapons which, if de-veloped, made the other party ever more reluctant to accept any restrictions on its arsenal. Thus even if the two parties could agree to stabilize one category of weapons, they usually escalated the arms buildup in other areas.

After signing the ban on the atmospheric testing of nuclear weapons in 1963, for example, the United States and the Soviet Union conducted more nuclear tests underground than they had conducted above ground before the ban. Early in the SALT negotiations, the two sides had already deployed a roughly equivalent number of strategic missiles. But as soon as they agreed to set limits on these, the United States, followed five years later by the Soviet Union, began to place multiple warheads on each missile. Malcolm Currie, U.S. director of defense research and engineering, explained to the Senate Armed Services Committee that because a SALT II treaty set limits on the *number* of strategic missiles, "the accord . . . re-enforces our need for *technological* progress."[6] Following this line of argument, many officials coupled their support for ratification of the SALT II treaty with insistence on at least a 5 percent real annual increase in military expenditures. Thus, unregulated arms options have been exploited to skirt any legal barrier to new weapons, even though such barriers were the original, professed goal of arms control itself.

The guiding principle of arms control has therefore been the same in purpose, if not in extent, as that of military procurement: to channel and direct the arms buildup, not to end it. In the SALT II treaty, for example, the upper limit on missiles with multiple warheads—1320 for each party—was publicly announced by Presidents Ford and Brezhnev at Vladivostok in 1974. At that time, the United States had already deployed 832 multiple, independently targetable reentry vehicles (MIRVs). The Soviet Union had none. At that time, the United States did not need more weapons: by the end of 1974, it had deployed a total of 7,940 deliverable nuclear warheads (including non-MIRVed warheads) on its strategic vehicles, while the Soviet Union had deployed only 2,600.[7] But because it was ahead in MIRV technology, the United States refused to seize the last easy opportunity to ban MIRVs completely. Secretary of State Henry Kissinger later admitted that the MIRV ceiling could possibly have been lower but that he made no effort to reduce it below the production level that the United States had already planned even if there were no arms agreement.[8] Time afforded a good opportunity for taking a different path. The Soviet Union did not even *test* MIRVs until 3 years after the United States had begun to deploy them. The failure to prohibit MIRVs has since returned to haunt the United States. Soviet MIRVs, U.S. officials now claim, are sufficiently threatening to U.S. ICBMs that the United States should undertake a vast expansion of its own ICBM arsenal.

Kissinger also confirmed that the Vladivostok agreement did not curtail *any* weapons program then in progress or planned before the agreement.[9] Whenever ceilings were set above the level of exisitng deployments, these ceilings then became production targets for new programs.[10] Overall, the 1974 accord legitimized a total U.S. and Soviet increase of 1,808 MIRVed vehicles, or 217 percent. For arms control negotiations to spur an arms buildup obviously can mislead the citizenry. President Ford told the public that the MIRV limit, specified to last only five years, was "a firm ceiling on the strategic arms race, thus preventing an arms race."[11] Kissinger announced that these ceilings were a "major breakthrough" and would "be seen as one of the turning points in the history of the post–World War II arms race."[12]

Fourth, to gain negotiating power, an apparently irresistible urge to bargain from a position of strength exerts a strong upward pressure on arms levels. The more bargaining chips one can produce and then trade away, the argument goes, the more successful the negotiations will be. The development of new weapons was thus justified as an aid to negotiations. But in fact, later negotiations usually facilitated the deployment of all weapons previously begun.

The politics of preparing U.S. negotiating positions provided arms control justifications for weapons that had no military or security justification. In the early 1970s, for example, no security arguments dictated the development of the MIRV. It could be expected to stimulate counter Soviet deployments; it did not seem likely to increase U.S. ability to deter an attack, and the United States already possessed far more warheads than required for simple deterrence of war, even after suffering a first strike. But officials wanted MIRVs anyway, so they invented an arms control "need" for them.[13] They claimed that a MIRV force would help induce the Soviet Union to limit its antimissile missiles because the larger numbers of warheads made possible by MIRVs could overwhelm any antimissile system.

Antiballistic missiles (ABMs) *were* eventually limited in the 1972 SALT treaty, largely because they were ineffective and because they raised serious domestic political problems in communities selected as deployment sites. Once ABMs had been limited to a militarily insignificant number, there was again no rationale for proceeding with MIRVs. So U.S. officials adopted a new bargaining chip argument. They claimed that proceeding with U.S. MIRVs would make the Soviet Union more eager to halt the development and deployment of Soviet MIRVs. Despite some Soviet interest in restricting MIRVs at that time, U.S. officials lost interest as U.S. deployment proceeded. Senator Edmund Muskie, then chairman of the Arms Control Subcommittee, concluded that by developing and deploying MIRVs "we reduce the possibility of a MIRV limitation."[14]

Similarly, the United States at first sought to develop an air-launched cruise missile as a bargaining chip to trade away if the Soviet Union would agree not to produce mobile land-based missiles. U.S. officials calculated that such missiles would be more advantageous to the Soviet Union, given its greater land mass and internal secrecy, than they would be to the United States. After the Soviet Union agreed to discuss mobile missiles, however, the United States reversed its stance. Washington then began to think it could reap a greater advantage from developing the cruise missile than it could from banning mobile missiles.

Many times during the 1970s military officials tried to entice reluctant members of Congress to appropriate more money for new weapons by emphasizing that bargaining chips were essential for success in SALT. In essence, they argued that more weapons were needed for arms control negotiations than were needed for military security itself. By 1982, President Reagan echoed this theme when he stated that the United States must enlarge its nuclear forces in order to negotiate a START agreement that would be better than SALT II. The Reagan administration opposed citizens' efforts for arms restraint by arguing that public support for a mutual U.S.-Soviet nuclear freeze undermined the efforts of U.S. negotiators attempting to reach an arms control treaty with the Soviet Union. According to this view, more arms are required to reduce arms than are required to maintain security; and more public support for an arms buildup is required if negotiations for arms control are in progress than if they are not.

Contradictory Purposes

The failure of arms control policies also springs from an even more fundamental diplomatic contradiction. Two goals of arms policy are incompatible: Diplomacy that plans to rely primarily on military self-help for security contradicts a diplomacy designed to halt the acquisition of more armaments. In the present world system, where no overarching authority exists to prevent one adversary from taking military advantage of another, each side constantly seeks through military procurement to gain a competitive military edge. Their heavy reliance on arms thus negates efforts to stabilize or reverse the arms race.

To be sure, officials might, in theory, arrange to stop the arms buildup at a point of exact equilibrium between states. But in practice this fails. Adversaries perceive equality differently. Because military power cannot be measured precisely, governments locked in military competition usually want more power. They each seek predominance. Equilibrium, with its uncertain guarantees for security, seems too risky. In short, as long as officials and their publics see arms as the almost exclusive key to security and diplomatic influence, they will never feel they have enough.

A dynamic technology makes matters worse. Pressed forward by fear of an adversary's future technological innovation, officials speed the pace of research on future weapons. The technology of new weapons chronically outpaces negotiations to control existing weapons.[15] Arms control negotiators debate ceilings for what exists, not for what is to come. Because the lead time required to develop a new weapon can be from five to ten years, research and development policies, underscored by lengthy arms control negotiations, actually *invite* a rival government to develop new weapons to counter one's own.

When a decision-making conflict arises between halting the arms buildup and pursuing a military edge to gain security or influence, the latter prevails. This is not because it is more rational, pragmatic, or virtuous, but because it satisfies the immediate political need to appear militarily strong. The conflict between reducing arms and increasing arms, each pursued in the quest for greater security, can be resolved in only one way: by the gradual establishment of means for enhancing security that do not rely primarily on military power. The conflict cannot be resolved by a clever arms control formula or even by wise negotiators as long as they operate within the old intellectual framework of the balance of power.

DISTRIBUTION OF POLITICAL RESOURCES

Throughout SALT, the political resources available to support the arms buildup—money, people, bureaucratic strength, and corporate influence—vastly exceeded the quantity available to support arms reductions.[16] The latter also were more difficult to mobilize because citizens hesitated to challenge their government on security issues. They feared that their actions might make Soviet concessions less likely. Yet, the SALT negotiations demonstrate that unless people are willing to accept the international risks that accompany domestic opposition to the expansion of arsenals, and take steps to avert any potentially dangerous side effects, the public will be forced to accept the insecurity and economic hardship inherent in an unending arms race. To shy away from strong efforts to redirect government priorities means accepting the probability of irretrievable disaster for the human race. No third, less painful, alternative exists.

At no time did the balance of political forces become clearer than after the texts of the two SALT treaties were finally written. The drive for more arms continued and even increased. In return for agreeing to support ratification of the SALT I treaty, the Joint Chiefs of Staff extracted "assurances" from the White House that they would get "a very extensive . . . development program and aggressive improvement and modernization programs. . . ."[17] The decision to proceed with the cruise missile, not a part of the treaty restrictions, was another payoff to gain Pentagon support for SALT I.[18] Several years later, development of the cruise missile complicated and delayed the completion of SALT II. Now it threatens to make the verification of any future ban of nuclear weapons virtually impossible without extremely intrusive on-site inspection.

As part of their price for supporting the second stage of SALT negotiations, Pentagon officials obtained approval for developing the MX missile, even though there was no need for a missile as large and accurate as the MX if the United States wanted simply to deter war rather than to create a new ability to threaten the Soviet Union. The professed purpose of the MX was to overcome the vulnerability of the existing U.S. ICBM force, but other, less costly and more effective steps could have been taken toward this end. Of several different missile models that officials considered in the developmental stage, they selected the one most threatening to the Soviet Union, rather than the one least vulnerable to Soviet attack.[19]

In an attempt to build support for ratification of the SALT II treaty, President Carter tried to placate Senate hawks by agreeing to new military commitments: to proceed with development of the large Trident submarine; to speed the deployment of the Mark 12 maneuvering warhead on Minuteman missiles; to press forward with the Trident II long-range missile; to hasten the decision about deploying the MX; to test and further develop cruise missiles capable of being launched from land, sea, and air; to persuade reluctant NATO governments to increase their military spending by 3 percent annually; and to increase U.S. military expenditures by 25 percent beyond inflation over the succeeding five years.[20] Carter also appointed George Siegnius, a career military officer and frequent opponent of arms control, as director of the Arms Control and Disarmament Agency, thus replacing Paul Warnke, who had negotiated the SALT treaty. In addition, Carter resumed registration for the draft, even against the advice of the selective service. Although the United States could have reduced its strategic nuclear arsenal by more than 90 percent and still retained enough warheads to destroy the Soviet Union two times over even after suffering a first strike, Carter continued to add several warheads each week to the U.S. stockpile. Despite SALT's failure to reduce the number of U.S. warheads, Reagan gained in the 1980 election campaign after criticizing Carter for allowing the United States to become too weak.[21]

The perennial subordination of arms restraint to the drive for more weaponry suggests an unsettling conclusion. The leaders of the world's greatest military powers do not *want* to create a world in which *their* military power will play a diminished role. A careful examination of the history of arms control proposals, for example, demonstrates that U.S. officials have not favored limiting or reducing U.S. military strength except under world conditions that are economically, politically, and militarily advantageous to themselves and to their supporters. Although these conditions may appear reasonable to most U.S. citizens, they usually have been biased enough that rival governments cannot reasonably be expected to accept them.[22]

But, one might ask, does not the successful conclusion of some agreements demonstrate that officials indeed are serious about arms control negotiations? Scrutiny of the negotiations and the carefully tailored agreements they produce suggests that officials *do* try to reach agreements, but not for the purpose of reducing arms in general and decreasing the role of military power in world affairs. When agreements have been reached they have not imposed genuine restrictions on new weapons that military officials want. Ironically, arsenals today are probably no less dangerous than they would have been even if no agreements had been reached. Officials seek to manipulate the arms buildup to their advantage, to restrain their rivals when possible, but not to reduce the overall role of the military ingredient of national power. After all, it is that ingredient which has given them superpower status in worldwide diplomacy. Arms control fails because the people best positioned to create a less militarized code of international conduct are the same people who see, or subconsciously fear, that their own status might be diminished if military strength were reduced or its influence circumscribed by more representative and effective international organizations. Yet such organizations to monitor and eventually to enforce restraints on military power are essential if mutually agreeable arms reductions are to be achieved.

The danger of this predicament will increase in the coming decade, as arms competition will center less on quantitative increases in weapons previously developed than on qualitative improvements to make weapons faster, deadlier, more accurate, and more difficult to detect or to defend against. Particularly destabilizing are those weapons designed for a war-fighting capability. To be useful these must be employed in a surprise attack to destroy an opponent's weapons before they have been launched. They encourage both sides to fire their weapons at the first sign of an attack. Thus, a war-fighting capability allows one's opponent almost no time to verify whether an attack is in progress and to decide how to respond. Computers must therefore be relied upon for much of the decision making. Despite these doomsday prospects, the SALT II negotiators did not seek qualitative restrictions; they aimed instead to impose quantitative limits on a single component of the superpowers' arsenals. Even if it had been ratified, the SALT II treaty would not have prevented a single qualitative development on the drawing boards in the Pentagon or the Kremlin.

Although President Reagan rejected SALT II upon assuming the presidency, his proposals for START are in this respect no different. Even if by some unexpected miracle, the Soviet Union were to accept Reagan's START proposals outright and the Senate were to ratify the treaty, the agreement would not prohibit the planned development and deployment of the new B-1 and Stealth strategic bombers; the Trident submarine; the Trident II missile with silo-destroying precision; the MX; the maneuvering reentry warhead; the neutron (enhanced radiation) warhead; the expanded program in antisatellite weapons and space warfare; and the Pershing II and land-based cruise missiles. Most of these weapons are designed to increase a war-fighting capability.

Despite substantial evidence that the familiar approach to arms control is unlikely to produce positive results, the public has shown a surprising willingness during arms control negotiations to believe that the U.S. government has been doing everything possible to resist militarism and achieve a more secure world. As a result, during SALT people's eyes rested on the anemic negotiations, while elsewhere giant new armaments arose. What SALT I declined to control—the MIRV—expanded the arms race much more than the treaty limited it. What the SALT II process legitimized—the MIRV and the cruise and MX missiles—undermined the future of human security far more than the treaty would have enhanced it, even if it had been ratified.

This is not to say that the treaty should have been rejected by the Senate or that its provisions now should be ignored simply because they remain unratified. The point is that the most important dimensions of the arms race and the most realistic ways of reversing it were never on the negotiating agenda.

Even well-informed people acquiesced in this unrealistic approach. After endorsing the missile ceilings for the SALT II treaty, for example, the editors of the *New York Times* commented that as a result of the agreement, the arms buildup would continue "just about as planned, and possibly a little faster in some areas—legitimized, in fact, by international compact."[23] Upon concluding extensive hearings in the weapons evaluation subcommittee of the Senate Committee on Foreign Relations, Senator Edmund Muskie observed, "My suspicion is that the SALT talks actually stimulated the arms race rather than stabilized it."[24] Because the public chose to believe the government's erroneous claim that SALT, and later START, represented the best possible effort at arms control, the negotiations actually deterred more promising steps toward arms reductions.

NOTES

I would like to thank Sherill Leonard for editorial assistance on an earlier draft of this essay.

1. A similar contradiction plagues Soviet policymakers.

2. For an analysis of the political impact of this treaty see Robert C. Johansen, *The National Interest and the Human Interest: An Analysis of U.S. Foreign Policy* (Princeton: Princeton University Press, 1980), pp. 40–112, 416–417; Mason Willrich and John Rhinelander, eds., *SALT: The Moscow Agreements and Beyond* (New York: Free Press, 1974); William Epstein, *The Last Chance: Nuclear Proliferation and Arms Control* (New York: Free Press, 1976); Alva Myrdal, *The Game of Disarmament: How the United States and Russia Run the Arms Race* (New York: Pantheon Books, 1976). For additional historical perspective, see Bernhard G. Bechhoefer, *Postwar Negotiations for Arms Control* (Washington, D.C.: Brookings, 1961); Richard J. Barnet, *Who Wants Disarmament* (Boston: Beacon Press, 1960); and Herbert York, *Race to Oblivion: A Participant's View of the Arms Race* (New York: Simon and Schuster, 1970).

3. See Stockholm International Peace Research Institute, *World Armaments and Disarmament: SIPRI Yearbook 1974* (Stockholm: Almqvist & Wiksell, 1974), pp. 106–107; and *SIPRI Yearbook 1982* (London: Taylor & Francis, 1982), pp. 276–280.

4. As Fred Charles Iklé, the director of the U.S. Arms Control and Disarmament Agency in the mid-1970s and the Undersecretary of Defense in the Reagan administration, warned: "One of the dangers of prolonged bargaining in arms control negotiations is that if you do not watch out it could lead to agreements to *augment* arms, arms augmentation agreements instead of arms reduction agreements. . . . You compare all these numbers and before you know it you have to level *up* to what the other side has instead of leveling down." U.S. Congress, Senate, Committee on Foreign Relations, *ACDA* [Arms Control and Disarmament Agency] *Authorization* (Washington, D.C.: Government Printing Office, 1974), p. 20. Emphasis added.

5. The Department of Defense considered 30 distinct basing modes for a new ICBM. See *The Defense Monitor,* Vol. 10, No. 6 (1981), pp. 5–12.

6. U.S. Congress, Senate, Committee on Armed Services *Fiscal Year 1976 and July–September 1976 Transition Period Authorization for Military Pro-*

curement, Research and Development, and Active Duty, Selected Reserve, and Civilian Personnel Strengths, Hearings (Washington, D.C.: Government Printing Office, 1975), pp. 2640, 2644, 3998. Emphasis added. Hereafter cited as *Fiscal Year 1976 Authorizations.*

7. *SIPRI Yearbook 1974,* pp. 105–107.

8. *Department of State Bulletin,* Vol. 71 (December 30, 1974), p. 912. Air Force Secretary John McLucas also said that "SALT II proposed ceilings generally consistent with our previously planned programs." U.S. Congress, *Fiscal Year 1976 Authorizations,* p. 469.

9. *New York Times,* November 26, 1974, p. 6.

10. Senator Stuart Symington, a former Secretary of the Air Force and member of both the Armed Services Committee and the Foreign Relations Committee, also concluded that the Vladivostok agreement specified ceilings that were targets for increased deployments. See U.S. Congress, *Fiscal Year 1976 Authorizations* (footnote 7), p. 502.

11. The text is in the *New York Times,* December 3, 1974.

12. "Interview for 'Bill Moyers' Journal.'" *Department of State Bulletin,* Vol. 72 (February 10, 1975), p. 176; "Secretary Kissinger's News Conference of December 7," *Department of State Bulletin,* Vol. 71 (December 30, 1974), p. 910.

13. For documentation of this point, see Johansen, *The National Interest,* pp. 40–116; also the statement by David Packard, the deputy secretary of defense, United States Congress, Senate, Committee on Foreign Relations, Subcommittee on Arms Control, International Law and Organization, *Arms Control Implications of Current Defense Budget* (Washington, D.C.: Government Printing Office, 1971), pp. 181–183. Hereafter cited as *Arms Control Implications.*

14. U.S. Congress, *Arms Control Implications,* p. 183.

15. Marek Thee, "Significance of Military R&D: The Impact of the Arms Race on Society," *The Impact of Science on Society,* Vol. 31 (January/March 1981), pp. 49–59.

16. See Jerry Sanders, *Peddlers of Crisis* (Boston: South End Press, 1983); Richard J. Barnet, *Roots of War* (Baltimore: Penguin, 1973); Richard J. Barnet, *The Economy of Death* (New York: Atheneum, 1970); and Ralph E. Lapp, *The Weapons Culture* (New York: Norton, 1968).

17. U.S. Congress, Senate Committee on Appropriations, *Department of Defense Appropriations, Fiscal Year 1975* (Washington, D.C.: Government Printing Office, 1974), p. 293.

18. Secretary of Defense Melvin Laird suggested cruise missiles as a legal way to evade the restrictive impact of the SALT agreement. He advocated making them part of a package of new "strategic initiatives" to win the support of the Joint Chiefs of Staff. *New York Times,* June 16, 1975; Johansen, *The National Interest,* p. 95.

19. Herbert Scoville, "America's Greatest Construction," *New York Review of Books,* March 20, 1980, pp. 12–17.

20. Most of these innovations increased the degree to which the United States acquired a war-fighting capability.

21. Polls showed that a plurality of the public believed Carter would do a better job than Reagan in dealing with the USSR and in keeping the United States out of war, but a large majority thought Reagan would do better in adding to U.S. military strength. *Gallup Opinion Index,* February 1980, pp. 10, 15; April-May 1980, p. 61; July 1980, pp. 19, 24; September 1980, p. 26.

22. The bias often is for maintaining the geopolitical status quo. That may appear reasonable to the United States, but unjust to many other societies. A good example is the resistance of the United States to establishing a new international economic order. The United States grants substantial security assistance and exerts overseas military influence in part to maintain an old order, often through the support of elites that are insensitive to the plight of the poor in their own lands. Competition with the Soviet Union over influence in these countries is one cause of the arms race even in the strategic area. Soviet intervention in Afghanistan and U.S. fears of Soviet influence in the Persian Gulf helped stimulate the enormous military growth begun by Carter and expanded further by Reagan. The rapid deployment force for the Middle East is only a small part of this expansion.

23. *New York Times,* December 1, 1974.

24. U.S. Congress, *Arms Control Implications,* p. 25. The authors of the *SIPRI Yearbook 1973* also concluded that, as a result of SALT I, "the technological arms race is encouraged and even legitimized (p. 17)." George Rathjens said that the agreement was "more likely to facilitate than to inhibit the acquisition of superfluous strategic arms." See Federation of American Scientists, "Scientists Comment on SALT Agreement" (press release of December 12, 1974), p. 6. Commenting upon an earlier series of negotiations, Freeman Dyson, a leading scientist in the development of nuclear weapons, said "The test ban was indeed a disastrous distraction." At the time in the early 1960s when there was opportunity to consider "drastic steps toward nuclear disarmament, people in responsible positions had no time to think about disarmament because they were too busy with the test ban." Dyson, *Disturbing the Universe* (New York: Harper and Row, 1979), p. 146.

Questions for Reflection and Discussion

1. What is an arms race? Why are Soviet-U.S. military relations characterized as an arms race?

2. How would you describe the current nuclear arms race between the Soviet Union and the United States? Who is responsible for it? Are any other nations contributing to its continuation? Is it likely to accelerate? Was it avoidable? Is it reversible?

3. What factors have been cited as the main causes of the current nuclear arms race? Are there causes not identified by the authors? If so what are they?

4. Who gains and who loses most in the arms race? What are the social costs or benefits?

5. Do you agree with Johansen that the arms control process as currently practiced itself contributes to the arms race? Why? Why not? In what directions did the SALT negotiations funnel U.S. and Soviet weapons and weapon systems? Were the gaps in the SALT II agreements intended to leave open opportunities to deploy new generations of weapon systems or was failure to halt competition in these areas due to difficulties of verification?

Selected Bibliography

Adams, Gordon. *The Iron Triangle: The Politics of Defense Contracting.* New Brunswick, NJ: Transaction Books, 1981.

Allison, G. T. *Questions About the Arms Race: Who's Racing Whom? A Bureaucratic Perspective.* Cambridge, MA: Harvard University Public Policy Program, 1974.

Allison, Graham, and Frederic A. Morris. "Armaments and Arms Control: Exploring the Determinants of Military Weapons." In *Arms, Defence Policy, and Arms Control,* ed. Franklin Long and George Rathjens. New York: W. W. Norton, 1976.

Barne, Richard J. *The Economy of Death.* New York: Atheneum, 1969.

Bertram, Christoph. "Arms Control and Technological Change." In *Armaments, Arms Control and Disarmament,* ed. Marek Thee. Paris: UNESCO Press, 1981, pp. 144–156.

Falk, Richard A., and Samuel S. Kim. *The War System: An Interdisciplinary Approach.* Boulder, CO: Westview Press, 1980.

Fallows, James. *National Defense.* New York: Random House, 1981.

Feld, Bernard T. *Impact of New Technologies on the Arms Race: A Pugwash Symposium.* Cambridge, MA: MIT Press, 1971.

Fox, Ronald J. *Arming America: How the U.S. Buys Arms.* Cambridge, MA: Harvard University Press, 1974.

Gansler, Jacques S. *The Defense Industry.* Cambridge, MA: MIT Press, 1980.

Gray, Colin S. "The Urge to Compete: Rationales for Arms Racing." *World Politics,* Vol. 26, No. 2 (Jan. 1974), pp. 207–233.

Green, Christopher. "Economics of the Arms Race." *McGill Law Journal,* Vol. 28, No. 3 (July 1983), pp. 651–683.

Halliday, Fred. *The Origins of the Second Cold War.* London: Verso Editions and NLB, 1982.

Herz, John H. *International Politics in the Atomic Age.* New York and London: Columbia University Press, 1967.

Kaldor, Mary. *The Baroque Arsenal.* New York: Hill and Wang, 1981.

Kohler, Gernot. "Toward a General Theory of Armaments." *Journal of Peace Research,* Vol. 16, No. 2 (1979), pp. 117–135.

Krell, Gert. "On the Theory of Armaments Dynamics." *Bulletin of Peace Proposals,* Vol. 10, No. 1 (1979), pp. 20–28.

Lock, Peter. "Armament Dynamics: An Issue in Development Strategies." *Alternatives: A Journal of World Policy,* Vol. 6, No. 2 (July 1980), pp. 157–178.

Myrdal, Alva. *The Game of Disarmament: How the United States and Russia Run the Arms Race.* Rev. ed. New York: Pantheon Books, 1982.

Nincic, Miroslav. *The Arms Race: The Political Economy of Military Growth.* New York: Praeger, 1982.

Rathjens, George W. "The Dynamics of the Arms Race," *Scientific American,* Vol. 220, No. 4 (April 1969), pp. 15–25.

Sakamoto, Yoshikazu, and Richard Falk. "World Demilitarized: A Basic Human Need." *Alternatives: A Journal of World Policy,* Vol. 6, No. 1 (March 1980), pp. 1–16.

Senghaas, Dieter. "Arms Race Dynamics and Arms Control in Europe." *Bulletin of Peace Proposals,* Vol. 10, No. 1 (1979), pp. 8–19.

Slater, Jerome, and Terry Nardin. "The Military-Industrial Complex Muddle." *Yale Review,* Vol. 65, No. 1 (1975), pp. 1–23.

Sweet, William. "The Pit and the Pendulum: Domestic Politics of United States Military Policy." *Alternatives: A Journal of World Policy,* Vol. 6, No. 1 (March 1980), pp. 17–57.

Thee, Marek. "The Dynamics of the Arms Race, Military R&D, and Disarmament." *International Social Science Journal,* Vol. 30, No. 4 (1978).

York, Herbert. *Race to Oblivion: A Participant's View of the Arms Race.* New York: Simon and Schuster, 1970.

CHAPTER 3

Combating
the Crime of Silence

In 1955, on the tenth anniversary of the dropping of the first nuclear bomb on Hiroshima, the English philosopher Bertrand Russell, with the prior counsel and endorsement of Albert Einstein, issued a declaration that, it was hoped, would stimulate nations and governments to renounce nuclear weapons and the spiraling arms race. This Russell-Einstein Manifesto, as it came to be called, read in part as follows:

> We are speaking on this occasion, not as members of this or that nation, continent or creed, but as human beings, members of the species man, whose continued existence is in doubt. . . . [W]e want you, if you can, to . . . consider yourselves only as members of a biological species which has had a remarkable history, and whose disappearance none of us can desire.

> * * *

> We have to learn to think in a new way. We have to learn to ask ourselves, not what steps can be taken to give military victory to whatever group we prefer, for there no longer are such steps; the question we have to ask ourselves is: What steps can be taken to prevent a military contest of which the issue must be disastrous to all parties?

> * * *

> Many warnings have been uttered by eminent men of science and by authorities in military strategy. None of them will say that the worst results are certain. What they do say is that these results are possible, and no one can be sure that they will not be realized. We have not yet found that the views of experts depend in any degree upon their politics or prejudices. They depend only, so far as our researches have revealed, upon the extent of the particular expert's knowledge. We have found that the men who know most are the most gloomy.
> Here, then, is the problem which we present to you, stark and dreadful and inescapable: Shall we put an end to the human race; or shall mankind renounce war? People will not face this alternative because it is so difficult to abolish war.

The abolition of war will demand distasteful limitations of national sovereignty. But what perhaps impedes understanding of the situation more than anything else is that the term *mankind* feels vague and abstract. People scarcely realize in imagination that the danger is to themselves and their children and their grandchildren, and not only to a dimly apprehended humanity. They can scarcely bring themselves to grasp that they, individually, and those whom they love are in imminent danger of perishing agonizingly.

*   *   *

Most of us are not neutral in feeling, but, as human beings, we have to remember that if the issues between East and West are to be decided in any manner that can give any possible satisfaction to anybody, whether Communist or anti-Communist, whether Asian or European or American, whether white or black, then these issues must not be decided by war. We should wish this to be understood, both in the East and in the West.

There lies before us, if we choose, continual progress in happiness, knowledge and wisdom. Shall we, instead, choose death, because we cannot forget our quarrels? We appeal, as human beings, to human beings: Remember your humanity and forget the rest. If you can do so, the way lies open to a new paradise; if you cannot, there lies before you the risk of universal death.[1]

Nine world-renowned scientists publicly endorsed this declaration in addition to Russell and Einstein. All but two of the total of eleven were Nobel Prize winners.

Tragically, however, the world community—particularly its governing elites—did not take these words seriously to heart. Indeed, despite the aggravated mutilations we call Hiroshima and Nagasaki, it greeted them with a deafening silence, either refusing to face squarely the catastrophic dangers inherent in nuclear weaponry or relegating these dangers to the periphery of responsible attention whenever the possibility of nuclear confrontation seemed real. For four decades now humanity has been living in the shadow of the valley of death and has done little or nothing about it.

Until recently. In the last few years, the complex questions surrounding nuclear weapons and warfare have emerged from the inner chambers of the physicists, engineers, and strategists to become psychologically and politically visible to the common man and woman. In the West,/ an increasingly powerful antinuclear movement has arisen and become a central feature of domestic politics among the NATO countries. To some albeit minor extent, too, it has begun to take root among the peoples of the Soviet bloc. And the near uniform reaction is a demand for significant change.

The purpose of this chapter is to give substance and contour to the new public challenge to nuclear weapons technologies and policies. The opening essay by Robert Jay Lifton explores the psychological dimensions of past acquiescence to increasing reliance on nuclear weapons for political and military purposes, of past failure to confront squarely the meaning and dangers of specific nuclear weapons programs. The remaining selections—from the worlds of religion and the law—suggest the intellectual and moral foundations upon which at least the Western movement against nuclearism rests. They are intended to give particularity to the broad, often ambiguous considerations that help shape the rising tide against continued quantitative and qualitative advances in nuclear weaponry.

NOTES

1. O. Nathan and H. Norden, eds., *Einstein On Peace* (New York: Schocken Books, 1968), pp. 632–635.

7. Beyond Psychic Numbing: A Call to Awareness

Robert Jay Lifton

Human existence itself may be absurd, as many have claimed, but we live now in a special realm of absurdity; we are haunted by something we can neither see nor imagine. We are afraid of something we call "nuclear holocaust" and at the same time are removed from, and have little awareness of, that threat. So our absurdity has several layers; that's where we have to start.

There is a kind of structural layer to our absurdity: the obvious one, the two great superpowers poised to exterminate each other and the rest of the world in the process. Then there is a second layer that is more or less existential; it is the way that we all live—with the sense that we can be annihilated in a moment, along with everything we've known and loved and experienced in our existence, while at the same time we carry on our everyday activities, business as usual. That's our kind of existential absurdity. The third layer involves the mind's relationship to the things that we can't locate in our images, this thing called "nuclear holocaust." In a way, our task is what Martin Buber called "imagining the real."

To characterize our predicament with regard to nuclear weapons, I would identify three present dangers. First, the danger of war is greater than ever; that's the terrible truth, and there is a lot of evidence that is beyond the scope of this paper. Second, there are manifest and important psychological contributions to that danger which have to do with the expansion of nuclear-weapons systems bureaucratically and technologically to the extent that they are no longer controllable by individuals or groups. There's a certain psychological stance that moves toward resignation: "Well, if it happens it happens." Or, in the more elaborate kind of rationalization I've heard recently in the universities: "What's so special about humankind? Many other species have come and gone; maybe this is our turn." That's a very soft, lovely, above-the-battle kind of idea, but it's not one that I recommend. A more hopeful second psychological tendency, which I'll return to, is increasing disquiet with the rationalizations or justifications given by our leaders for the continuing arms race. People don't quite believe them any more, and that's a starting point for us. But the third element here is the call for more numbing. As the numbing or diminished feeling breaks down, our leaders, along with various leaders in different parts of the world, tell us: "Numb yourselves some more, don't feel; above all, don't question." That is the situation we have to confront.

My perception of these dangers has been intensified and perhaps been rendered even more grotesque by recent work I've done on the psychology of Nazi doctors. I've interviewed both ordinary men who were not inherently demonic and could yet engage in demonic pursuits, and professionals who took pride in their professions and could lend themselves to mass murder. Mass murder was not impossible for others and is not impossible in our society.

This paper will examine three questions. First, is Hiroshima our text? Second, what are the fundamental nuclear illusions? (And this I really want to make the centerpiece of what I have to say—how can we confront these nuclear illusions and what are they? I include here what I take to be the ultimate psychological shell game, the idea of security.) Third, what are these weapons doing to us? I'll focus particularly on what I call nuclear fundamentalism: that is, what these weapons are doing to us without their even being used. Finally, I will address a possible direction of hope in which we are beginning to move.

Is Hiroshima our text? Well, my answer is Yes, No, and Yes. I mean that I am constitutionally unable to talk about nuclear weapons without my base being Hiroshima. Of course, I have a special history: I lived and worked there for six months; I became in a sense a survivor by proxy, which is not to compare my experience with that of survivors but to speak in terms of what one commits oneself to. Let me state very briefly what happened in Hiroshima. One could say that from exposure to that bomb in a split second in time, if one survived, one experienced a lifelong encounter with death; that encounter involved several stages, and it's still going on.

The first stage began immediately after the bomb fell as those who had survived were exposed to a grotesque array of dead and near-dead. The fear they felt most strongly at that time went beyond the imagery of their own death, which of course they feared. The feeling, expressed again and again, was that the whole world was dead, that nobody was alive. Hiroshima was gone, the whole world was dying.

During the second stage, soon after the bomb fell, sometimes weeks, sometimes days, sometimes hours, and often in people who seemed physically untouched, there would appear the grotesque symptoms of acute radiation, which included acute bleeding from all the bodily orifices; bleeding into the skin, particularly the eyes; severe diarrhea; extremely high temperatures; weakness, anorexia, and often death. These symptoms gave the people of Hiroshima the sense that this weapon not only destroyed on an incredible scale but also left behind poison in their bones, as indeed it did. The rumor at that time sweeping the city was not only that people would die if they had been exposed to the bomb, but that, in addition—and people later told this to me with deep feeling—from that day on, trees, grass, flowers would never again grow in Hiroshima, the city would never sustain vegetation of any kind. That rumor signified not only total death but nature drying up altogether, which was even beyond human death.

The third array involved effects not months but years after the bomb fell: the discoveries made, beginning three years after the bomb, of an increased incidence of leukemia in people significantly exposed and then subsequently of an increase of various forms of cancer, including some of the more common ones. They are still making these discoveries in Hiroshima, because some of the delays in radiation effects can be 30, 40, or 50 years for some forms of cancer. It is an endless process, and an endless fear. There is real fear about transmitting radiation effects to subsequent generations, because it is known to be possible. Abnormal chromosomal findings in survivors have worried people, even though a systematic increased incidence of birth defects in the next generation has not been demonstrated in control studies. But when I went back to Hiroshima about a year and a half ago and talked to people, they said, "Well, maybe the second generation is okay, but we don't know about the third generation." In other words, the fear is endless and nobody can guarantee that there won't be these effects of irradiation.

That was the Hiroshima bomb—by present standards just a baby bomb. Thus, it's true that, by present standards, Hiroshima is completely inadequate as a model because individual bombs are a hundred to a thousand times the explosive power of the Hiroshima bomb and the radiation effects. Yet it is also true that Hiroshima teaches us, first, the totality of destruction, a single weapon destroying an entire city; second, the unending lethal influence from radiation effects; and, third, an image of nuclear actuality: *it happened there.* We must confront those images; and indeed, we receive those images with awe and dread—an appropriate response if that awe can inspire us to take the necessary intense action— indeed, spiritual action—that we need in our movement. So Hiroshima, in that sense, is very much our text.

But it is also our text in terms of the differences between Hiroshima and our present situation. The crucial difference, the one we must always insist upon, is that although the city of Hiroshima was destroyed, that destruction was temporary because there was an outside world that could intercede. Others did come in. They brought medical help—all too slowly; people suffered—and an infusion of outside energy that helped gradually to reconstitute the city. But who can believe that there will be any outsiders to help us heal and recover from the next nuclear war?

Radiation lends itself to illusion. It has a quality of mystery—its very invisibility, its association with infinity and, in the case of thermonuclear bombs, with the very source of the sun's energy. There have been illusions about radiation all through its history. But there are certain specific illusions about nuclear war that I think are the responsibility especially of those in the psychological and medical professions to confront. These illusions are obvious, but still need to be spelled out. The first is the illusion of limit and control, which allows for the idea of a tactical, limited nucelar war. The scenario goes something like this: I drop my bomb on Moscow, you drop yours on New York, and then, gentlemen, we shake hands, and nobody drops any more bombs. In spite of what we know about human behavior, that scenario is once again being seriously proposed. It was highly prevalent in the 1950s and 1960s, especially in the forms devised by Edward Teller and Herman Kahn. Some of Teller's scenarios are fascinating; a brilliant man really lapses into incongruity and absurdity in putting forward such fantasies. They're usually about a small country undergoing a revolution somewhere in the Third World; the Soviets are helping it to have a communist revolution, and there are two possibilities. One, you use the bomb, you win the war, you restore the democratic process, and everything is fine. The other, you don't use the bomb, the revolutionaries win, it becomes a Soviet puppet, the next state falls—the domino theory—and then what happens to America in the world? It's always a question of either use the bomb or don't—and if you don't use it, you get into trouble.

The concept of limited nuclear war did go out of favor for quite a while, but it has recently made a comeback, notably under the present Administration, but even under the previous one. There's a lot of talk now about nuclear war. At a press conference, when asked about nuclear war, President Reagan fumbled for a while and then said, "Well, it could take place." He said, "Look, you could have a pessimistic outlook or an optimistic one. I always tend to be optimistic." That illusion, though, is the expression of a desire for control. People—and political leaders more than anyone—want so much to maintain control over collective destinies that they will imagine it even where it cannot exist.

Second is the illusion of foreknowledge; the idea that preparing people psychologically for what will happen will help them. It does in most disasters: in a flood or a tornado, it is very useful to know what to expect; then you can know what to do, and that helps you both psychologically and in performing more constructively. But if you know what's going to happen in a nuclear war, if you happen to be one of the few survivors, and you know that survivors are exposed to the most grotesque radiation effects, and that there's very little indeed to look forward to, how much will that help you?

The third illusion is related: it is the illusion of preparation, which involves elaborate evacuation plans and the shelter programs. It's like paranoid delusions; each step has a kind of logic after the previous step, but each step is absolutely wrong. People don't behave that way, you can't evacuate them, people will seek their own family, you can't get them all out anyhow, and the bomb will fall. The whole scenario is absurd, and certainly the shelters are.

The next illusion, also related, is the one of stoic behavior under nuclear attack: Americans don't panic, we're tough. Herman Kahn[1] has said that in order to intensify stoic behavior, don't permit hypochondriacal behavior, which he's afraid of. He recommends radiation meters attached to everybody's clothing. If a man starts to feel nauseated or vomits, you look at his meter—Kahn's theory being that if one man vomits, everybody vomits—and you say: "Look, you've only received ten roentgens. Why are you vomiting? Pull yourself together and get back to work." Those are his words, I'm not making them up.

Kai Erikson, a sociologist at Yale, and I are attempting to make a reasonable projection of how those few survivors in a massive nuclear war would behave.[2] Based on all evidence, of Hiroshima and everything else we know, the numbing and listless behavior—no panic, but a kind of listless, slow motion as in Hiroshima—would likely be so extreme among that tiny contingent of survivors that people would be numb to the point of immobilization. The mind would shut down, and there would be no community. According to Erikson, people would feel themselves to be particles rather than as cohering in a community, which is what we need for any psychological health. That's the kind of stoical behavior you can expect, Herman Kahn notwithstanding.

Another related illusion is that of recovery. You can take all that stoic energy and apply it to recovery. Kahn has said we can dig out of the ruins, we can recover from the catastrophe; and now other people, like Colin Gray, are telling us the same thing. In all this there is the illusion of rationality—another illusion to which we have always to address ourselves. Gray and Keith Payne[3] have said that if American nuclear power is to support U.S. foreign policy objectives, the United States must possess the ability to wage nuclear war *rationally*. We are dealing not with personal madness here, but with social madness; these are clinically sane people who are advocating this, and that makes it hard. It's the normal people who are always the dangerous ones. So we have to cope with the social madness of this collective illusion and this ideological push. More can be said about what those nuclearists assume to be reasonable behavior, but the present examples should suffice.

The idea of security is what I call the "ultimate psychologism." Clearly, the ultimate psychological and existential fact of the nuclear age is vulnerability. Everybody is vulnerable; nobody anywhere is safe from those weapons. That absolute susceptibility to nuclear exposure creates all sorts of reactions. Psychologically, we know that security means feeling safe, experiencing one's environment as reliable and, generally speaking, as life enhancing. The earliest sense of security is made available to us as infants by adults who structure the environment in such a way as to render it safe and reliable; that same structure provides an element of anticipation—anticipation that the environment will remain safe, that we can strive and even experiment, and that it's not dangerous to do so. It's never total, that sense of security; we carry with us a mix of a legacy of insecurity and our effort to cope with each new environmental challenge or threat. In early life, security is provided for us; as we become older and move toward adulthood, we become increasingly responsible for our own sense of security, and make many choices about our environment and, indeed, about our behavior. This course of personal development, of course, all takes place within a nation-state, and we find ourselves building a concept of national security which, as Richard Barnet[4] has said, has to do both with the notion of the national polity, of protecting the national entity, and also with individual feelings of security within that nation. Strictly speaking, in these terms, national security is simply impossible, as is individual security, because everybody is vulnerable. Therefore the insistence upon more and better nuclear devices is partly an effort on the part of our leaders to deny this unacceptable truth, partly a residuum of prenuclear thinking, and partly an effort to reestablish a psychological sense of security in themselves and in all Americans. Each new bomb system that is developed destabilizes our sense of psychological security; with every attempt to regain it, we're exposed to an ever greater danger of massive annihilation. It's like a thermostat in reverse: ordinarily, if the system is getting very hot and dangerous, the thermostat registers it and turns the heat off; here instead the thermostat doesn't rise but actually may go down. The thermostat manipulators keep the temperature reading low and keep on putting up the heat. People tend to get a false assurance, because in part it works, in that you are "more secure" in a psychological sense if you have more and bigger weapons. That's why I call it the "ultimate psychologism," and urge that we keep addressing it as that, in the hope that, one of these days, our political leaders will have the courage to say exactly that.

Secrecy is very much part of this process. There have been some interesting studies, including one by Edward Shils,[5] who described the relationship of the McCarthy period of the 1950s to secrecy about the bomb. It is infuriating, he wrote, to feel that what one holds sacred is rendered insecure by hidden enemies who, through indifference or design, would give away the secrets on which survival rests. So there comes to be an association of survival with secrecy about the weapons. Even though we now know other countries can indeed make the weapons, the myth of the secret helps maintain illusions about security. It also helps a very small group of bomb managers to assume a priest-like stance as exclusive possessor of secrets too arcane and too sacred to be made available to the rest of us. The assumption holds that if they can protect this secret again, if they can maintain vigilance, they can retain security. But in actuality what they do is increase danger and stifle opposition.

One can say similar things about credibility and stability. Credibility becomes, in a way, a contradiction around nuclear weapons. Even Henry Kissinger has conceded that you cannot consider all-out nuclear war as a meaningful instrument of policy. Yet there are constant threats in a system of so-called deterrence and of buildup, with its destabilizing processes, to carry on this meaningless policy of all-out nuclear war. This creates, as Jonathan Schell has written in an earlier work,[6] a sense of confusion and impotence on the part of executives. He noted that, in the last two Administrations, our presidents have been rather rocky on this issue of credibility. Even Watergate, and the actions that President Nixon took at that time, were related to the Administration's credibility and to the increased sensitivity to domestic opposition.

The imagery of the pitiful helpless giant is very much to the point here. We can say that nuclear weapons make of their possessors either mass murderers or else deceivers and self-deceivers, who fluctuate between feelings of omnipotence and impotence, as they gradually lose their hold on ethical tradition and on existence itself. There are dangerous analogies, even in children's psychological behavior. If one who is challenged or in some way insulted threatens to fight back and doesn't, one experiences a sense of loss of credibility and the onset of anxiety. The impulse then may be to fight back all the more strongly or to lash out in order to overcome those uncomfortable feelings. Moreover, if that goes on all through one's childhood, and one happens to be big and strong but reluctant to fight back or to initiate fights when insulted, one may develop a psychological sense of discomfort, of disbelief in oneself, of being an imposter. These are issues that we must explore and expose, as they apply not only to personal psychology but to national political policies as well.

Nuclear weapons, in addition, lead to what could be called a form of technological terrorism. We've heard a lot about terrorists—militant revolutionaries who seize weapons and seek to achieve their aims by threats of violence, often random violence. We hear less about the technological terror of governments that possess massive weapons and threaten their use against other countries. We all live in a realm of technological terrorism that ought to be examined as we address the irrationality of nuclear weapons offering us something called security. There seems, then, to be a vicious psycho-political circle: the sense of loss of security, the onset of fear, the loss of credibility and of stability, and the desperate but impossible quest to regain these by stockpiling nucelar weapons. Then the existence of a nuclear armamentarium provokes a sense of still greater loss and insecurity and the embrace of more and more weapons. It is this vicious circle that we must interrupt.

The image of extinction became the possession of the common man and woman with the Holocaust of World War II. There had, of course, been such images in the past; there had been imagery of the end of the world, and there had been the Biblical imagery of Armageddon, and the plagues of the Middle Ages. In these cases, especially in the first, there is some structure to Armageddon; it is God's will, it is a kind of punishment for humankind, it fits within a structure of meaning. What is new about the present image is the idea of exterminating ourselves, possibly even as a species, by means of our own technology, by our own hand; and that creates a whole array of additional psychological associations, including dimensions of shame, guilt, and hopelessness.

In order to consider this imagery of extinction, we need a way of looking at it that takes into account our larger human connections. In my own work,[7] without going into it in detail, I have used a model or paradigm for symbolization of life and death, or death in the continuity of life, moving toward that from the more classical psychoanalytical model of instinct and defense. By looking at the ways in which we symbolize life and death, we can get closer to these issues. But we also need both a proximate area, a sense of direct nitty-gritty human behavior which we're used to looking at in psychological terms, and an ultimate area, a sense of larger human connectedness which we're less used to looking at. By that ultimate area, I mean the sense we require, in a normative way, of feeling connected to those who have gone before and to those who will presumably go on after our own limited life span. I've called this the symbolization of historical or biological connectedness, or the "symbolization of immortality."

We have a sense of living on in our children and their children, an endless biological chain of being. Or in our work, small or large, in our influence upon others; or in something we call spiritual attainment, some sort of religious idea or belief; or in the idea of eternal nature, which all societies symbolize in some way. Or else through the experience of transcendence, the psychic state that Freud called the "oceanic feeling," one so intense that time and death disappear. Perhaps the most fundmental impact of nuclear weapons on us, without their use (or without their use again), is the break they represent in the great chain of being, the doubt about our still being links in that chain. From the age of five or six on—and maybe even earlier, the images of nuclear weaponry being so pervasive—who among us can be certain that, with these weapons in the world, we can live on in our children and their children, or in our works, or in our nature, which we know to be susceptible to our weaponry and its pollutions? Or, for that matter, in a spiritual idea? In Hiroshima, for instance, people tried to have recourse to their various religious beliefs—mostly Buddhist, but also Shinto and Christian—but found they just weren't adequate to cope with what they had been through. It would seem that we're constantly in quest of more and broader spiritual support which is less and less able to buttress us in the face of this threat of extinction. There is evidence, too detailed to set forth here, of ways in which precisely those biological or creative or natural areas are indeed threatened, and of responses we have had to those threats.

About five years ago, Michael Carey[8] interviewed people of his generation, now in their thirties, focusing on their experience in the shelter drills during the 1950s. We have heard a lot about the absurd seriousness with which young children were told to put papers over their head to protect them from fallout, or to put their head under the desk, or to do other such life-enhancing acts. Of course, Carey found the children were too smart for that; they didn't believe it, but they didn't know what to believe, and certainly a lot of the questioning of authority since then has stemmed from that experience. The children were overwhelmed with fear and all sorts of vivid images and dreams of annihilation which they suppressed because the culture told them to; they numbed themselves. Then, around adolescence, when kids start asking questions, or through ordinary life experiences involving loss or pain, the images would return; they didn't go away. And they're in the rest of us. Those people who went through the drills are not some special group, they are a metaphor for the whole society.

One can make many interpretations of Carey's work, but I shall just suggest two of the central ones here. One is the loss of distinction between ordinary death, what Kurt Vonnegut calls plain old death which we all have to face, and grotesque, absurd death. So just as the child is trying to understand the first, trying to learn something that we never accept fully, it becomes equated with the second; in a sense, all death then becomes absurd and grotesque. That furthers the break in the life-death relationship. I called my most recent study on these issues *The Broken Connection* exactly for that reason. The related pattern in all this is that we live the double life already mentioned—aware that we may be annihilated at any moment and yet going about business as usual.

Fundamentalism has a history in the Protestant faith, but to put it very simply, fundamentalism originally was a struggle to preserve fundamentals. Very easily that struggle to preserve fundamentals can lapse into a narrow demand for a single closed truth. Certainly in the 1970s and 1980s, we see a worldwide epidemic of fundamentalism, in various forms of religious expression and some cult behavior in this country, and in political and religious forms all over the world—on all sides in the Middle East, for example—and in ways that are indeed extremely dangerous, because of their all-or-nothing dogma. There are many ways in which fundamentalist cults tend to contribute to the imagery of extinction, sometimes even embrace that imagery, and often put forward what I call a method of psychism. It's a more extreme version of the search for security, discussed above: One tries to deal with actual physical dangers by certain exercises of the mind, such as the assumption that only a particular group—say, an End of the World cult—will survive, because its members have seen the truth; everybody else will perish. Such thinking can even embrace the idea of a nuclear holocaust. The contribution of this worldwide epidemic of fundamentalism to a climate of acceptance of nuclear weaponry must be studied and understood, just as we must understand the all too visible contribution of nuclear weapons to the phenomenon of fundamentalist cults.

The worst and most dangerous form of fundamentalism centers around the weapons themselves. This I call "nuclearism," the worship of the weapons as something close to deities. Along with other deities, this god not only has the capacity to destroy everything but also the ability to construct and build, and so we have something like worship in regard to these weapons. One could cite glowing accounts of the test explosions and actual bomb explosions, not only by chaplains but by hard-bitten pilots and airmen. There is something about the experience that leads one either to embrace the weapon or else to reject it and warn people of its danger—as, indeed, many of the scientists did. Some scientists and many political and military leaders unfortunately embraced the bomb. Edward Teller is my bad example. I have nothing against him personally, merely against what he says and does. In this kind of nuclearism, the worship is so manifest that logic fails. Teller knows a lot about phsyics, and this is what he wrote:

Radiation from test fallout is very small, its effect to human beings is so little that if it exists at all it cannot be measured. Radiation from test fallout might be slightly harmful to humans, it might be slightly beneficial, it might have no effect at all.[9]

The worship of the weapons virtually as a force to keep the world going is the outcome of this form of nuclearism. It is visible in various diplomatic efforts as well as among scientists, military people, and, indeed, ordinary people such as ourselves. It is the ultimate fundamentalism of our time. At bottom is the idea of conquering death by massive death, or eliminating death by a massive act of suicide or murder.

Numbing is an overall category that includes the standard psychoanalytic defense mechanisms of denial, suppression, and repression. It's an overall tendency to diminish feeling by unconscious impulse or even by conscious will or with the mix of the two that we frequently find. Our problem isn't repression—it's just not feeling enough in many situations. Of course, we domesticate the weapons and we hear these extraordinary terms—"nuclear exchange" (it sounds sort of like gift-giving), "escalation," "nuclear yields," "megatons," "window of vulnerability," "window of opportunity" are among the latest ones. But these terms are an effort to domesticate, to create an illusion of control over that which we cannot control.

Again, my sense about the significance of numbing has been intensified by my work with Nazi doctors, who could numb themselves by acts of extreme technism. One told me: "The word 'ethics' was never used in Auschwitz by Nazi doctors [of course, not surprisingly], we just asked what worked." That sounds somewhat uncomfortably close to a lot of things that we know. The doctors also went about what I call a doubling process; that is, it isn't just that one is partly numbed and experiences a kind of splitting of oneself, but a whole second self forms in those who engage in this demonic activity—say, American physicists, or Americans in any group who embrace and make nuclear weapons and contribute to their being used.

Our situation is desperate and at the same time hopeful. Desperate because of the danger of war, nuclear war; hopeful because something is really happening in this country and elsewhere. There is the beginning of a change, of a shift in awareness. Awareness traditionally means being on guard, being wary, prepared for danger. But in the present context it also means being alert to sensation, to perception, in sensibility, in consciousness, in realization, and even in illumination—carrying one's knowledge or illumination beyond the given. Something like that is beginning to happen, and it will not require total change in order to be meaningful. In working with Vietnam veterans, for instance, I found that many of them changed dramatically and significantly, even while part of them stayed the same; that partial significant change is possible and imaginable and, indeed, beginning to happen. The need now is to move from the fragmentary awareness that is beginning to take shape, toward more formed awareness, toward awareness that informs, that becomes part of our world view, that influences our actions, our behavior, our commitments, our lives.

Part of becoming human is developing the capacity to imagine the future, to symbolize, to create culture; imagining the future includes being able to imagine one's own death and we perceive this capacity to be in danger. If we can imagine our own death, we can not only imagine an act of mass suicide and murder, the nuclear holocaust—which we must imagine in order to prevent—but we can imagine alternatives to that act. That is what is beginning to happen. Presently, there's a conflict in the culture that we all feel and must articulate and enhance. We need conflict. This conflict is between the comfort people seek through the numbing of everyday life—avoiding any thinking about nuclear weapons and especially about what happens at the other end of those weapons—on the one hand, and on the other hand the tension and the beginning anxiety we need to experience, and embrace, and put to good use in the form of action, in order to bring about collective survival. We need that tension, and that tension is beginning to manifest itself. That's why the situation can be called desperate and yet hopeful; we are seeing now, all over the world, a rising of consciousness, a more formed awareness. We see it in the European peace movement, because people in Europe can now imagine in their gut what nuclear weapons would do to them in their so-called theater. We are just as vulnerable; we, too, have to learn to imagine, to see it. We see it not only in the movement of doctors, represented by groups such as Physicians for Social Responsibility, but in similar movements forming among the clergy, lawyers, students, teachers, and others.

Everyone, people from all professions and from all areas, should be urged to take part in these movements. One can imagine a mass movement in this country both within electoral, political channels and outside of them—a movement that doesn't exist yet, but is beginning to take shape. Strangely enough, when one addresses these issues—and of course, they are grim, and one has to immerse one's imagination in this grimness to imagine the real—there is personal value to be realized. One puts oneself more in touch with actuality, with things as they are, with our world, for better or worse, and, indeed with things that matter to us, such as love, sensuality, creative realization, and life goals that have significance. These are concomitants of commitment to this issue; the issue is deadly serious but our call is not a grim one. It is a call to life.

NOTES

1. Kahn, H. 1961. *On Thermonuclear War.* Princeton University Press, Princeton, N.J.

2. Lifton, R,. and Erikson, K. 1982. "Nuclear War's Effect on the Mind." *N.Y. Times* (Op-Ed column), March 15.

3. Gray, C., and Payne, K. 1980. "Victory is Possible." *Foreign Policy* (Summer):14–27.

4. Barnet, R. 1982. "Fantasy, Reality, and the Arms Race: Dilemmas of National Security and Human Survival." *Amer. J. Orthopsychiat.* 52(4):582–589.

5. Shils, E. 1956. *The Torment of Secrecy: The Background and Consequences of American Security Policies.* Free Press, Glencoe, Ill.

6. Schell, J. 1975. *Time of Illusion.* Knopf, New York.

7. Lifton, R. 1979. *The Broken Connection: On Death and the Continuity of Life.* Touchstone, New York.

8. Carey, M. 1982. "Psychological Fallout." *Bull. Atom. Sci.* 38(1):20–24.

9. Teller, E., and Brown, A. 1962. *Legacy of Hiroshima.* Doubleday, Garden City, N.Y.

8. Pastoral Letter on War and Peace— The Challenge of Peace: God's Promise and Our Response

National Conference of Catholic Bishops

INTRODUCTION

"The whole human race faces a moment of supreme crisis in its advance toward maturity." Thus the Second Vatican Council opened its treatment of modern warfare.[1] Since the council, the dynamic of the nuclear arms race has intensified. Apprehension about nuclear war is almost tangible and visible today. As Pope John Paul II said in his message to the United Nations concerning disarmament: "Currently the fear and preoccupation of so many groups in various parts of the world reveal that people are more frightened about what would happen if irresponsible parties unleash some nuclear war."[2]

As bishops and pastors ministering in one of the major nuclear nations, we have encountered this terror in the minds and hearts of our people—indeed, we share it. We write this letter because we agree that the world is at a moment of crisis, the effects of which are evident in people's lives. It is not our intent to play on fears, however, but to speak words of hope and encouragement in time of fear. Faith does not insulate us from the challenges of life; rather, it intensifies our desire to help solve them precisely in light of the good news which has come to us in the person of Jesus, the Lord of history. From the resources of our faith we wish to provide hope and strength to all who seek a world free of the nuclear threat. Hope sustains one's capacity to live with danger without being overwhelmed by it; hope is the will to struggle against obstacles even when they appear insuperable. Ultimately our hope rests in the God who gave us life, sustains the world by his power and has called us to revere the lives of every person and all peoples.

The crisis of which we speak arises from this fact: Nuclear war threatens the existence of our planet; this is a more menacing threat than any the world has known. It is neither tolerable nor necessary that human beings live under this threat. But removing it will require a major effort of intelligence, courage and faith. As Pope John Paul II said at Hiroshima: "From now on it is only through a conscious choice and through a deliberate policy that humanity can survive."[3]

As Americans, citizens of the nation which was first to produce atomic weapons, which has been the only one to use them and which today is one of the handful of nations capable of decisively influencing the course of the nuclear age, we have grave human, moral and political responsibilities to see that a "conscious choice" is made to save humanity. This letter is therefore both an invitation and a challenge to Catholics in the United States to join with others in shaping the conscious choices and deliberate policies required in this "moment of supreme crisis."

*   *   *

WAR AND PEACE IN THE MODERN WORLD:
PROBLEMS AND PRINCIPLES

Both . . . just-war teaching and non-violence are confronted with a unique challenge by nuclear warfare. This must be the starting point of any further moral reflection: Nuclear weapons particularly and nuclear warfare as it is planned today raise new moral questions. No previously conceived moral position escapes the fundamental confrontation posed by contemporary nuclear strategy. Many have noted the similarity of the statements made by eminent scientists and Vatican II's observation that we are forced today "to undertake a completely fresh reappraisal of war." The task before us is not simply to repeat what we have said before; it is first to consider anew whether and how our religious-moral tradition can assess, direct, contain and, we hope, help to eliminate the threat posed to the human family by the nuclear arsenals of the world. Pope John Paul II captured the essence of the problem during his pilgrimage to Hiroshima: "In the past it was possible to destroy a village, a town, a region, even a country. Now it is the whole planet that has come under threat."[4]

The Holy Father's observation illustrates why the moral problem is also a religious question of the most profound significance. In the nuclear arsenals of the United States or the Soviet Union alone there exists a capacity to do something no other age could imagine: We can threaten the entire planet.[5] For people of faith this means we read the Book of Genesis with a new awareness; the moral issue at stake in nuclear war involves the meaning of sin in its most graphic dimensions. Every sinful act is a confrontation of the creature and the Creator. Today the destructive potential of the nuclear powers threatens the human person, the civilization we have slowly constructed, and even the created order itself.

We live today, therefore, in the midst of a cosmic drama; we possess a power which should never be used, but which might be used if we do not reverse our direction. We live with nuclear weapons knowing we cannot afford to make one serious mistake. This fact dramatizes the precariousness of our position, politically, morally, and spiritually.

A prominent "sign of the times" today is a sharply increased awareness of the danger of the nuclear arms race. Such awareness has produced a public discussion about nuclear policy here and in other countries which is unprecedented in its scope and depth. What has been accepted for years with almost no question is now being subjected to the sharpest criticism. What previously had been defined as a safe and stable system of deterrence is today viewed with political and moral skepticism. Many forces are at work in this new evaluation, and we believe one of the crucial elements is the gospel vision of peace which guides our work in this pastoral letter. The nuclear age has been the theater of our existence for almost four decades; today it is being evaluated with a new perspective. For many the leaven of the Gospel and the light of the Holy Spirit create the decisive dimension of this new perspective.

The New Moment

At the center of the new evaluation of the nuclear arms race is a recognition of two elements: the destructive potential of nuclear weapons and the stringent choices which the nuclear age poses for both politics and morals.

The fateful passage into the nuclear age as a military reality began with the bombing of Nagasaki and Hiroshima, events described by Pope Paul VI as a "butchery of untold magnitude."[6] Since then, in spite of efforts at control and plans for disarmament (e.g., the Baruch Plan of 1946), the nuclear arsenals have escalated, particularly in the two superpowers. The qualitative superiority of these two states, however, should not overshadow the fact that four other countries possess nuclear capacity and a score of states are only steps away from becoming "nuclear nations."

This nuclear escalation has been opposed sporadically and selectively, but never effectively. The race has continued in spite of carefully expressed doubts by analysts and other citizens and in the face of forcefully expressed opposition by public rallies. Today the opposition to the arms race is no longer selective or sporadic, it is widespread and sustained. The danger and destructiveness of nuclear weapons are understood and resisted with new urgency and intensity. There is in the public debate today an endorsement of the position submitted by the Holy See at the United Nations in 1976: The arms race is to be condemned as a danger, an act of aggression against the poor, and a folly which does not provide the security it promises.[7]

Papal teaching has consistently addressed the folly and danger of the arms race; but the new perception of it which is now held by the general public is due in large measure to the work of scientists and physicians who have described for citizens the concrete human consequences of a nuclear war.[8]

In a striking demonstration of his personal and pastoral concern for preventing nuclear war, Pope John Paul II commissioned a study by the Pontifical Academy of Sciences which reinforced the findings of other scientific bodies. The Holy Father had the study transmitted by personal representative to the leaders of the United States, the Soviet Union, the United Kingdom and France, and to the president of the General Assembly of the United Nations. One of its conclusions is especially pertinent to the public debate in the United States:

Recent talk about winning or even surviving a nuclear war must reflect a failure to appreciate a medical reality: Any nuclear war would inevitably cause death, disease and suffering of pandemonic proportions and without the possibility of effective medical intervention. That reality leads to the same conclusion physicians have reached for life-threatening epidemics throughout history: Prevention is essential for control.[9]

This medical conclusion has a moral corollary. Traditionally the church's moral teaching sought first to prevent war and then to limit its consequences if it occurred. Today the possibilities for placing political and moral limits on nuclear war are so minimal that the moral task, like the medical, is prevention: As a people, we must refuse to legitimate the idea of nuclear war. Such a refusal will require not only new ideas and new vision, but what the Gospel calls conversion of the heart.

To say no to nuclear war is both a necessary and a complex task. We are moral teachers in a tradition which has always been prepared to relate moral principles to concrete problems. Particularly in this letter we could not be content with simply restating general moral principles or repeating well-known requirements about the ethics of war. We have had to examine, with the assistance of a broad spectrum of advisers of varying persuasions, the nature of existing and proposed weapons systems, the doctrines which govern their use, and the consequences of using them. We have consulted people who engage their lives in protest against the existing nuclear strategy of the United States, and we have consulted others who have held or do hold responsibility for this strategy. It has been a sobering and perplexing experience. In light of the evidence which witnesses presented and in light of our study, reflection, and consultation, we must reject nuclear war. But we feel obliged to relate our judgment to the specific elements which comprise the nuclear problem.

Though certain that the dangerous and delicate nuclear relationship the superpowers now maintain should not exist, we understand how it came to exist. In a world of sovereign states devoid of central authority and possessing the knowledge to produce nuclear weapons many choices were made, some clearly objectionable, others well-intended with mixed results, which brought the world to its present dangerous situation.

We see with increasing clarity the political folly of a system which threatens mutual suicide, the psychological damage this does to ordinary people, especially the young, the economic distortion of priorities— billions readily spent for destructive instruments while pitched battles are waged daily in our legislatures over much smaller amounts for the homeless, the hungry and the helpless here and abroad. But it is much less clear how we translate a no to nuclear war into the personal and public choices which can move us in a new direction, toward a national policy and an international system which more adequately reflect the values and vision of the kingdom of God.

These tensions in our assessment of the politics and strategy of the nuclear age reflect the conflicting elements of the nuclear dilemma and the balance of terror which it has produced. We have said earlier in this letter that the fact of war reflects the existence of sin in the world. The nuclear threat and the danger it poses to human life and civilization exemplify in a qualitatively new way the perennial struggle of the political community to contain the use of force, particularly among states.

Precisely because of the destructive nature of nuclear weapons, strategies have been developed which previous generations would have found unintelligible. Today military preparations are undertaken on a vast and sophisticated scale, but the declared purpose is not to use the weapons produced. Threats are made which would be suicidal to implement. The key to security is no longer only military secrets, for in some instances security may best be served by informing one's adversary publicly what weapons one has and what plans exist for their use. The presumption of the nation-state system that sovereignty implies an ability to protect a nation's territory and population is precisely the presumption denied by the nuclear capacities of both superpowers. In a sense each is at the mercy of the other's perception of what strategy is "rational," what kind of damage is "unacceptable," how "convincing" one side's threat is to the other.

The political paradox of deterrence has also strained our moral conception. May a nation threaten what it may never do? May it possess what it may never use? Who is involved in the threat each superpower makes: government officials? or military personnel? or the citizenry in whose defense the threat is made?

In brief, the danger of the situation is clear; but how to prevent the use of nuclear weapons, how to assess deterrence and how to delineate moral responsibility in the nuclear age are less clearly seen or stated. Reflecting the complexity of the nuclear problem, our arguments in this pastoral must be detailed and nuanced; but our no to nuclear war must in the end be definitive and decisive.

Religious Leadership and the Public Debate

Because prevention of nuclear war appears from several perspectives to be not only the surest but the only way to limit its destructive potential, we see our role as moral teachers precisely in terms of helping to form public opinion with a clear determination to resist resort to nuclear war as an instrument of national policy. If "prevention is the only cure," then there are diverse tasks to be performed in preventing what should never occur. As bishops we see a specific task defined for us in Pope John Paul II's 1982 World Day of Peace Message:

Peace cannot be built by the power of rulers alone. Peace can be firmly constructed only if it corresponds to the resolute determination of all people of good will. Rulers must be supported and enlightened by a public opinion that encourages them or, where necessary, expresses disapproval.[10]

The pope's appeal to form public opinion is not an abstract task. Especially in a democracy, public opinion can passively acquiesce in policies and strategies or it can through a series of measures indicate the limits beyond which a government should not proceed. The "new moment" which exists in the public debate about nuclear weapons provides a creative opportunity and a moral imperative to examine the relationship between public opinion and public policy. We believe it is necessary for the sake of prevention to build a barrier against the concept of nuclear war as a viable strategy for defense. There should be a clear public resistance to the rhetoric of "winnable" nuclear wars, or unrealistic expectations of "surviving" nuclear exchanges and strategies of "protracted nuclear war." We oppose such rhetoric.

We seek to encourage a public attitude which sets stringent limits on the kind of actions our own government and other governments will take on nuclear policy. We believe religious leaders have a task in concert with public officials, analysts, private organizations and the media to set the limits beyond which our military policy should not move in word or action. Charting a moral course in a complex public policy debate involves several steps. We will address four questions, offering our reflections on them as an invitation to a public moral dialogue:

1. The use of nuclear weapons;
2. The policy of deterrence in principle and in practice;
3. Specific steps to reduce the danger of war;
4. Long-term measures of policy and diplomacy.

The Use of Nuclear Weapons

Establishing moral guidelines in the nuclear debate means addressing first the question of the use of nuclear weapons. That question has several dimensions.

It is clear that those in the church who interpret the gospel teaching as forbidding all use of violence would oppose any use of nuclear weapons under any conditions. In a sense the existence of these weapons simply confirms and reinforces one of the initial insights of the non-violent position, namely, that Christians should not use lethal force since the hope of using it selectively and restrictively is so often an illusion. Nuclear weapons seem to prove this point in a way heretofore unknown.

For the tradition which acknowledges some legitimate use of force, some important elements of contemporary nuclear strategies move beyond the limits of moral justification. A justifiable use of force must be both discriminatory and proportionate. Certain aspects of both U.S. and Soviet strategies fail both tests as we shall discuss below. The technical literature and the personal testimony of public officials who have been closely associated with U.S. nuclear strategy have both convinced us of the overwhelming probability that major nuclear exchange would have no limits.[11]

On the more complicated issue of "limited" nuclear war, we are aware of the extensive literature and discussion which this topic has generated.[12] As a general statement, it seems to us that public officials would be unable to refute the following conclusion of the study made by the Pontifical Academy of Sciences:

> Even a nuclear attack directed only at military facilities would be devastating to the country as a whole. This is because military facilities are widespread rather than concentrated at only a few points. Thus, many nuclear weapons would be exploded.
>
> Furthermore, the spread of radiation due to the natural winds and atmospheric mixing would kill vast numbers of people and contaminate large areas. The medical facilities of any nation would be inadequate to care for the survivors. An objective examination of the medical situation that would follow a nuclear war leads to but one conclusion: Prevention is our only recourse.[13]

Moral Principles and Policy Choices

In light of these perspectives we address three questions more explicitly: (1) counterpopulation warfare; (2) initiation of nuclear war; and (3) limited nuclear war.

1. Counterpopulation Warfare. Under no circumstances may nuclear weapons or other instruments of mass slaughter be used for the purpose of destroying population centers or other predominantly civilian targets. Popes have repeatedly condemned "total war," which implies such use. For example, as early as 1954 Pope Pius XII condemned nuclear warfare "when it entirely escapes the control of man" and results in "the pure and simple annihilation of all human life within the radius of action."[14] The condemnation was repeated by the Second Vatican Council:

> Any act of war aimed indiscriminately at the destruction of entire cities or of extensive areas along with their population is a crime against God and man itself. It merits unequivocal and unhesitating condemnation.[15]

Retaliatory action, whether nuclear or conventional, which would indiscriminately take many wholly innocent lives, lives of people who are in no way responsible for reckless actions of their government, must also be condemned. This condemnation, in our judgment, applies even to the retaliatory use of weapons striking enemy cities after our own have already been struck. No Christian can rightfully carry out orders or policies deliberately aimed at killing non-combatants.[16]

We make this judgment at the beginning of our treatment of nuclear strategy precisely because the defense of the principle of non-combatant immunity is so important for an ethic of war and because the nuclear age has posed such extreme problems for the principle. Later in this letter we shall discuss specific aspects of U.S. policy in light of this principle and in light of recent U.S. policy statements stressing the determination not to target directly or strike directly against civilian populations. Our concern about protecting the moral value of non-combatant immunity, however, requires that we make a clear reassertion of the principle our first word on this matter.

2. *The Initiation of Nuclear War.* We do not perceive any situation in which the deliberate initiation of nuclear warfare on however restricted a scale can be morally justified. Non-nuclear attacks by another state must be resisted by other than nuclear means. Therefore, a serious moral obligation exists to develop non-nuclear defensive strategies as rapidly as possible.

A serious debate is under way on this issue.[17] It is cast in political terms, but it has a significant moral dimension. Some have argued that at the very beginning of a war nuclear weapons might be used, only against military targets, perhaps in limited numbers. Indeed it has long been American and NATO policy that nuclear weapons, especially so-called tactical nuclear weapons, would likely be used if NATO forces in Europe seemed in danger of losing a conflict that until then had been restricted to conventional weapons. Large numbers of tactical nuclear weapons are now deployed in Europe by the NATO forces and about as many by the Soviet Union. Some are substantially smaller than the bomb used on Hiroshima, some are larger. Such weapons, if employed in great numbers, would totally devastate the densely populated countries of Western and Central Europe.

Whether under conditions of war in Europe, parts of Asia or the Middle East, or the exchange of strategic weapons directly between the United States and the Soviet Union, the difficulties of limiting the use of nuclear weapons are immense. A number of expert witnesses advise us that commanders operating under conditions of battle probably would not be able to exercise strict control; the number of weapons used would rapidly increase, the targets would be expanded beyond the military and the level of civilian casualties would rise enormously.[18] No one can be certain that this escalation would not occur even in the face of political efforts to keep such an exchange "limited." The chances of keeping use limited seem remote, and the consequences of escalation to mass destruction would be appalling. Former public officials have testified that it is improbable that any nuclear war could actually be kept limited. Their testimony and the consequences involved in this problem lead us to conclude that the danger of escalation is so great that it would be morally unjustifiable to initiate nuclear war in any form. The danger is rooted not only in the technology of our weapons systems, but in the weakness and sinfulness of human communities. We find the moral responsibility of beginning nuclear war not justified by rational political objectives.

This judgment affirms that the willingness to initiate nuclear war entails a distinct, weighty moral responsibility; it involves transgressing a fragile barrier—political, psychological, and moral—which has been constructed since 1945. We express repeatedly in this letter our extreme skepticism about the prospects for controlling a nuclear exchange, however limited the first use might be. Precisely because of this skepticism, we judge resort to nuclear weapons to counter a conventional attack to be morally unjustifiable.[19] Consequently we seek to reinforce the barrier against any use of nuclear weapons. Our support of a "no first use" policy must be seen in this light.

At the same time we recognize the responsibility the United States has had and continues to have in assisting allied nations in their defense against either a conventional or a nuclear attack. Especially in the European theater, the deterrence of a *nuclear* attack may require nuclear weapons for a time, even though their possession and deployment must be subject to rigid restrictions.

The need to defend against a conventional attack in Europe imposes the political and moral burden of developing adequate, alternative modes of defense to present reliance on nuclear weapons. Even with the best coordinated effort—hardly likely in view of contemporary political division on this question—development of an alternative defense position will still take time.

In the interim, deterrence against a conventional attack relies upon two factors: the not inconsiderable conventional forces at the disposal of NATO and the recognition by a potential attacker that the outbreak of large-scale conventional war could escalate to the nuclear level through accident or miscalculation by either side. We are aware that NATO's refusal to adopt a "no first use" pledge is to some extent linked to the deterrent effect of this inherent ambiguity. Nonetheless, in light of the probable effects of initiating nuclear war, we urge NATO to move rapidly toward the adoption of a "no first use" policy, but doing so in tandem with development of an adequate alternative defense posture.

3. Limited Nuclear War. It would be possible to agree with our first two conclusions and still not be sure about retaliatory use of nuclear weapons in what is called a "limited exchange." The issue at stake is the *real* as opposed to the *theoretical* possibility of a "limited nuclear exchange."

We recognize that the policy debate on this question is inconclusive and that all participants are left with hypothetical projections about probable reactions in a nuclear exchange. While not trying to adjudicate the technical debate, we are aware of it and wish to raise a series of questions which challenge the actual meaning of "limited" in this discussion.

- Would leaders have sufficient information to know what is happening in a nuclear exchange?
- Would they be able under the conditions of stress, time pressures and fragmentary information to make the extraordinarily precise decision needed to keep the exchange limited if this were technically possible?

- Would military commanders be able in the midst of the destruction and confusion of a nuclear exchange to maintain a policy of "discriminate targeting"? Can this be done in modern warfare waged across great distances by aircraft and missiles?
- Given the accidents we know about in peacetime conditions, what assurances are there that computer errors could be avoided in the midst of a nuclear exchange?
- Would not the casualties, even in a war defined as limited by strategists, still run in the millions?
- How "limited" would be the long-term effects of radiation, famine, social fragmentation and economic dislocation?

Unless these questions can be answered satisfactorily, we will continue to be highly skeptical about the real meaning of "limited." One of the criteria of the just-war tradition is a reasonable hope of success in bringing about justice and peace. We must ask whether such a reasonable hope can exist once nuclear weapons have been exchanged. The burden of proof remains on those who assert that meaningful limitation is possible.

A nuclear response to either conventional or nuclear attack can cause destruction which goes far beyond "legitimate defense." Such use of nuclear weapons would not be justified.

In the face of this frightening and highly speculative debate on a matter involving millions of human lives, we believe the most effective contribution or moral judgment is to introduce perspectives by which we can assess the empirical debate. Moral perspective should be sensitive not only to the quantitative dimensions of a question, but to its psychological, human, and religious characteristics as well. The issue of limited war is not simply the size of weapons contemplated or the strategies projected. The debate should include the psychological and political significance of crossing the boundary from the conventional to the nuclear arena in any form. To cross this divide is to enter a world where we have no experience of control, much testimony against its possibility and therefore no moral justification for submitting the human community to this risk.[20] We therefore express our view that the first imperative is to prevent any use of nuclear weapons and our hope that leaders will resist the notion that nuclear conflict can be limited, contained or won in any traditional sense.

DETERRENCE IN PRINCIPLE AND PRACTICE

The moral challenge posed by nuclear weapons is not exhausted by an analysis of their possible uses. Much of the political and moral debate of the nuclear age has concerned the strategy of deterrence. Deterrence is at the heart of the U.S.-Soviet relationship, currently the most dangerous dimension of the nuclear arms race.

*The Concept and Development
of Deterrence Policy*

The concept of deterrence existed in military strategy long before the nuclear age, but it has taken on a new meaning and significance since 1945. Essentially deterrence means "dissuasion of a potential adversary from initiating an attack or conflict, often by the threat of unacceptable retaliatory damage."[21] In the nuclear age deterrence has become the centerpiece of both U.S. and Soviet policy. Both superpowers have for many years now been able to promise a retaliatory response which can inflict "unacceptable damage." A situation of stable deterrence depends on the ability of each side to deploy its retaliatory forces in ways that are not vulnerable to an attack (i.e., protected against a "first strike"); preserving stability requires a willingness by both sides to refrain from deploying weapons which appear to have a first-strike capability.

This general definition of deterrence does not explain either the elements of a deterrence strategy or the evolution of deterrence policy since 1945. A detailed description of either of these subjects would require an extensive essay using materials which can be found in abundance in the technical literature on the subject of deterrence.[22] Particularly significant is the relationship between "declaratory policy" (the public explanation of our strategic intentions and capabilities) and "action policy" (the actual planning and targeting policies to be followed in a nuclear attack).

The evolution of deterrence strategy has passed through several stages of declaratory policy. Using the U.S. case as an example, there is a significant difference between "massive retaliation" and "flexible response," and between "mutual assured destruction" and "countervailing strategy." It is also possible to distinguish between "counterforce" and "countervalue" targeting policies; and to contrast a posture of "minimum deterrence" with "extended deterrence." These terms are well known in the technical debate on nuclear policy; they are less well known and sometimes loosely used in the wider public debate. It is important to recognize that there has been substantial continuity in U.S. action policy in spite of real changes in declaratory policy.[23]

The recognition of these different elements in the deterrent and the evolution of policy means that moral assessment of deterrence requires a series of distinct judgments. They include: an analysis of the *factual character* of the deterrent (e.g., what is involved in targeting doctrine); analysis of the *historical development* of the policy (e.g., whether changes have occurred which are significant for moral analysis of the policy); the relationship of deterrence policy and other aspects of *U.S.-Soviet affairs;* and determination of the key *moral questions* involved in deterrence policy.

The Moral Assessment of Deterrence

The distinctively new dimensions of nuclear deterrence were recognized by policymakers and strategists only after much reflection. Similarly, the moral challenge posed by nuclear deterrence was grasped only after careful deliberation. The moral and political paradox posed by deterrence was concisely stated by Vatican II:

Undoubtedly, armaments are not amassed merely for use in wartime. Since the defensive strength of any nation is thought to depend on its capacity for immediate retaliation, the stockpiling of arms which grows from year to year serves, in a way hitherto unthought of, as a deterrent to potential attackers. Many people look upon this as the most effective way known at the present time for maintaining some sort of peace among nations. Whatever one may think of this form of deterrent, people are convinced that the arms race, which quite a few countries have entered, is no infallible way of maintaining real peace and that the resulting so-called balance of power is no sure genuine path to achieving it. Rather than eliminate the causes of war, the arms race serves only to aggravate the position. As long as extravagant sums of money are poured into the development of new weapons, it is impossible to devote adequate aid in tackling the misery which prevails at the present day in the world. Instead of eradicating international conflict once and for all, the contagion is spreading to other parts of the world. New approaches, based on reformed attitudes, will have to be chosen in order to remove this stumbling block, to free the earth from its pressing anxieties, and give back to the world a genuine peace.[24]

Without making a specific moral judgment on deterrence, the council clearly designated the elements of the arms race: the tension between "peace of a sort" preserved by deterrence and "genuine peace" required for a stable international life; the contradiction between what is spent for destructive capacity and what is needed for constructive development.

In the post-conciliar assessment of war and peace and specifically of deterrence, different parties to the political-moral debate within the church and in civil society have focused on one or another aspect of the problem. For some, the fact that nuclear weapons have not been used since 1945 means that deterrence has worked, and this fact satisfied the demands of both the political and the moral order. Others contest this assessment by highlighting the risk of failure involved in continued reliance on deterrence and pointing out how politically and morally catastrophic even a single failure would be. Still others note that the absence of nuclear war is not necessarily proof that the policy of deterrence has prevented it. Indeed, some would find in the policy of deterrence the driving force in the superpower arms race. Still other observers, many of them Catholic moralists, have stressed that deterrence may not morally include the intention of deliberately attacking civilian populations or non-combatants.

The statements of the NCCB-USCC over the past several years have both reflected and contributed to the wider moral debate on deterrence. In the NCCB pastoral letter "To Live in Christ Jesus" (1976), we focused on the moral limits of declaratory policy while calling for stronger measures of arms control.[25] In 1979 Cardinal John Krol, speaking for the USCC in support of SALT II ratification, brought into focus the other element of the deterrence problem: The actual use of nuclear weapons may have been prevented (a moral good), but the risk of failure and the physical harm and moral evil resulting from possible nuclear war remained.

"This explains," Cardinal Krol stated, "the Catholic dissatisfaction with nuclear deterrence and the urgency of the Catholic demand that the nuclear arms race be reversed. It is of the utmost importance that negotiations proceed to meaningful and continuing reductions in nuclear stockpiles and eventually to the phasing out altogether of nuclear deterrence and the threat of mutual-assured destruction."[26]

These two texts, along with the conciliar statement, have influenced much of Catholic opinion expressed recently on the nuclear question.

In June 1982, Pope John Paul II provided new impetus and insight to the moral analysis with his statement to the U.N. Second Special Session on Disarmament. The pope first situated the problem of deterrence within the context of world politics. No power, he observes, will admit to wishing to start a war, but each distrusts others and considers it necessary to mount a strong defense against attack. He then discusses the notion of deterrence:

Many even think that such preparations constitute the way—even the only way—to safeguard peace in some fashion or at least to impede to the utmost in an efficacious way the outbreak of wars, especially major conflicts which might lead to the ultimate holocaust of humanity and the destruction of the civilization that man has constructed so laboriously over the centuries.

In this approach one can see the "philosophy of peace" which was proclaimed in the ancient Roman principle: *Si vis pacem, para bellum.* Put in modern terms, this "philosophy" has the label of "deterrence" and one can find it in various guises of the search for a "balance of forces" which sometimes has been called, and not without reason, the "balance of terror."[27]

Having offered this analysis of the general concept of deterrence, the Holy Father introduces his considerations on disarmament, especially, but not only, nuclear disarmament. Pope John Paul II makes this statement about the morality of deterrence:

In current conditions "deterrence" based on balance, certainly not as an end in itself but as a step on the way toward a progressive disarmament, may still be judged morally acceptable. Nonetheless in order to ensure peace, it is indispensable not to be satisfied with this minimum, which is always susceptible to the real danger of explosion.[28]

In Pope John Paul II's assessment, we perceive two dimensions of the contemporary dilemma of deterrence. One dimension is the danger of nuclear war with its human and moral costs. The possession of nuclear weapons, the continuing quantitative growth of the arms race, and the danger of nuclear proliferation all point to the grave danger of basing "peace of a sort" on deterrence. The other dimension is the independence and freedom of nations and entire peoples, including the need to protect smaller nations from threats to their independence and integrity. Deterrence reflects the radical distrust which marks international politics, a condition identified as a major problem by Pope John XXIII in "Peace on Earth" and reaffirmed by Pope Paul VI and Pope John Paul II. Thus a balance of forces, preventing either side from achieving superiority, can be seen as a means of safeguarding both dimensions.

The moral duty today is to prevent nuclear war from ever occurring *and* to protect and preserve those key values of justice, freedom, and independence which are necessary for personal dignity and national integrity. In reference to these issues, Pope John Paul II judges that deterrence may still be judged morally acceptable, "certainly not as an end in itself but as a step on the way toward a progressive disarmament."

On more than one occasion the Holy Father has demonstrated his awareness of the fragility and complexity of the deterrence relationship among nations. Speaking to UNESCO in June 1980, he said: "Up to the present, we are told that nuclear arms are a force of dissuasion which have prevented the eruption of a major war. And that is probably true. Still, we must ask if it will always be this way."[29]

In a more recent and more specific assessment Pope John Paul II told an international meeting of scientists on Aug. 23, 1982: "You can more easily ascertain that the logic of nuclear deterrence cannot be considered a final goal or an appropriate and secure means for safeguarding international peace."[30]

Relating Pope John Paul's general statements to the specific policies of the U.S. deterrent requires both judgments of fact and an application of moral principles. In preparing this letter we have tried through a number of sources to determine as precisely as possible the factual character of U.S. deterrence strategy. Two questions have particularly concerned us: 1) the targeting doctrine and strategic plans for the use of the deterrent, particularly their impact on civilian casualties; and 2) the relationship of deterrence strategy and nuclear war-fighting capability to the likelihood that war will in fact be prevented.

Moral Principles and Policy Choices

Targeting doctrine raises significant moral questions because it is a significant determinant of what would occur if nuclear weapons were ever to be used. Although we acknowledge the need for deterrent, not all forms of deterrence are morally acceptable. There are moral limits to deterrence policy as well as to policy regarding use. Specifically, it is not morally acceptable to intend to kill the innocent as part of a strategy of deterring nuclear war. The question of whether U.S. policy involves an intention to strike civilian centers (directly targeting civilian populations) has been one of our factual concerns.

This complex question has always produced a variety of responses, official and unofficial in character. The NCCB committee has received a series of statements of clarification of policy from U.S. government officials.[31] Essentially these statements declare that it is not U.S. strategic policy to target the Soviet civilian population as such or to use nuclear weapons deliberately for the purpose of destroying population centers.

These statements respond, in principle at least, to one moral criterion for assessing deterrence policy: the immunity of non-combatants from direct attack either by conventional or nuclear weapons.

These statements do not address or resolve another very troublesome moral problem, namely, that an attack on military targets or militarily significant industrial targets could involve "indirect" (i.e., unintended) but massive civilian casualties. We are advised, for example, that the U.S. strategic nuclear targeting plan (SIOP—Single Integrated Operational Plan) has identified 60 "military" targets within the city of Moscow alone, and that 40,000 "military" targets for nuclear weapons have been identified in the whole of the Soviet Union.[32] It is important to recognize that Soviet policy is subject to the same moral judgment; attacks on several "industrial targets" or politically significant targets in the United States could produce massive civilian casualties. The number of civilians who would necessarily be killed by such strikes is horrendous.[33] This problem is unavoidable because of the way modern military facilities and production centers are so thoroughly interspersed with civilian living and working areas. It is aggravated if one side deliberately positions military targets in the midst of a civilian population.

In our consultations, administration officials readily admitted that while they hoped any nuclear exchange could be kept limited, they were prepared to retaliate in a massive way if necessary. They also agreed that once any substantial numbers of weapons were used, the civilian casualty levels would quickly become truly catastrophic and that even with attacks limited to "military" targets the number of deaths in a substantial exchange would be almost indistinguishable from what might occur if civilian centers had been deliberately and directly struck. These possibilities pose a different moral question and are to be judged by a different moral criterion: the principle of proportionality.

While any judgment of proportionality is always open to differing evaluations, there are actions which can be decisively judged to be disproportionate. A narrow adherence exclusively to the principle of non-combatant immunity as a criterion for policy is an inadequate moral posture for it ignores some evil and unacceptable consequences. Hence, we cannot be satisfied that the assertion of an intention not to strike civilians directly or even the most honest effort to implement that intention by itself constitutes a "moral policy" for the use of nuclear weapons.

The location of industrial or militarily significant economic targets within heavily populated areas or in those areas affected by radioactive fallout could well involve such massive civilian casualties that in our judgment such a strike would be deemed morally disproportionate, even though not intentionally indiscriminate.

The problem is not simply one of producing highly accurate weapons that might minimize civilian casualties in any single explosion, but one of increasing the likelihood of escalation at a level where many, even "discriminating," weapons would cumulatively kill very large numbers of civilians. Those civilian deaths would occur both immediately and from the long-term effects of social and economic devastation.

A second issue of concern to us is the relationship of deterrence doctrine to war-fighting strategies. We are aware of the argument that war-fighting capabilities enhance the credibility of the deterrent, particularly the strategy of extended deterrence. But the development of such capabilities raises other strategic and moral questions. The relationship of war-fighting capabilities and targeting doctrine exemplifies the difficult choices in this area of policy. Targeting civilian populations would violate the principle of discrimination—one of the central moral principles of a Christian ethic of war. But "counterforce targeting," while preferable from the perspective of protecting civilians, is often joined with a declaratory policy which conveys the notion that nuclear war is subject to precise rational and moral limits. We have already expressed our severe doubts about such a concept. Furthermore, a purely counterforce strategy may seem to threaten the viability of other nations' retaliatory forces, making deterrence unstable in a crisis and war more likely.

While we welcome any effort to protect civilian populations, we do not want to legitimize or encourage moves which extend deterrence beyond the specific objective of preventing the use of nuclear weapons or other actions which could lead directly to a nuclear exchange.

These considerations of concrete elements of nuclear deterrence policy, made in light of John Paul II's evaluation, but applying it through our own prudential judgments, lead us to a strictly conditioned moral acceptance of nuclear deterrence. We cannot consider it adequate as a long-term basis for peace.

This strictly conditioned judgment yields *criteria* for morally assessing the elements of deterrence strategy. Clearly, these criteria demonstrate that we cannot approve of every weapons system, strategic doctrine, or policy initiative advanced in the name of strengthening deterrence. On the contrary, these criteria require continual public scrutiny of what our government proposes to do with the deterrent.

On the basis of these criteria we wish now to make some specific evaluations:

1. If nuclear deterrence exists only to prevent the *use* of nuclear weapons by others, then proposals to go beyond this to planning for prolonged periods of repeated nuclear strikes and counterstrikes, or "prevailing" in nuclear war, are not acceptable. They encourage notions that nuclear war can be engaged in with tolerable human and moral consequences. Rather, we must continually say *no* to the idea of nuclear war.

2. If nuclear deterrence is our goal, "sufficiency" to deter is an adequate strategy; the quest for nuclear superiority must be rejected.

3. Nuclear deterrence should be used as a step on the way toward progressive disarmament. Each proposed addition to our strategic system or change in strategic doctrine must be assessed precisely in light of whether it will render steps toward "progressive disarmament" more or less likely.

Moreover, these criteria provide us with the means to make some judgments and recommendations about the present direction of U.S. strategic policy. Progress toward a world freed of dependence on nuclear deterrence must be carefully carried out. But it must not be delayed. There is an urgent moral and political responsibility to use the "peace of a sort" we have as a framework to move toward authentic peace through nuclear arms control, reductions, and disarmament. Of primary importance in this process is the need to prevent the development and deployment of destabilizing weapons systems on either side; a second requirement is to ensure that the more sophisticated command and control systems do not become mere hair triggers for automatic launch on warning; a third is the need to prevent the proliferation of nuclear weapons in the international system.

In light of these general judgments *we oppose* some specific proposals in respect to our present deterrence posture:

1. The addition of weapons which are likely to be vulnerable to attack, yet also possess a "prompt hard-target kill" capability that threatens to make the other side's retaliatory forces vulnerable. Such weapons may seem to be useful primarily in a first strike;[34] we resist such weapons for this reason and we oppose Soviet deployment of such weapons which generate fear of a first strike against U.S. forces.

2. The willingness to foster strategic planning which seeks a nuclear war-fighting capability that goes beyond the limited function of deterrence outlined in this letter.

3. Proposals which have the effect of lowering the nuclear threshold and blurring the difference between nuclear and conventional weapons.

In support of the concept of "sufficiency" as an adequate deterrent and in light of the present size and composition of both the U.S. and Soviet strategic arsenals, *we recommend:*

1. Support for immediate, bilateral, verifiable agreements to halt the testing, production and deployment of new nuclear weapons systems.[35]

2. Support for negotiated bilateral deep cuts in the arsenals of both superpowers, particularly those weapons systems which have destabilizing characteristics; U.S. proposals like those for START (Strategic Arms Reduction Talks) and INF (Intermediate-Range Nuclear Forces) negotiations in Geneva are said to be designed to achieve deep cuts;[36] our

hope is that they will be pursued in a manner which will realize these goals.

3. Support for early and successful conclusion of negotiations of a comprehensive test ban treaty.

4. Removal by all parties of short-range nuclear weapons which multiply dangers disproportionate to their deterrent value.

5. Removal by all parties of nuclear weapons from areas where they are likely to be overrun in the early stages of war, thus forcing rapid and uncontrollable decisions on their use.

6. Strengthening of command and control over nuclear weapons to prevent inadvertent and unauthorized use.

These judgments are meant to exemplify how a lack of unequivocal condemnation of deterrence is meant only to be an attempt to acknowledge the role attributed to deterrence, but not to support its extension beyond the limited purpose discussed above. Some have urged us to condemn all aspects of nuclear deterrence. This urging has been based on a variety of reasons, but has emphasized particularly the high and terrible risks that either deliberate use or accidental detonation of nuclear weapons could quickly escalate to something utterly disproportionate to any acceptable moral purpose. That determination requires highly technical judgments about hypothetical events. Although reasons exist which move some to condemn reliance on nuclear weapons for deterrence, we have not reached this conclusion for the reasons outlined in this letter.

Nevertheless, there must be no misunderstanding of our profound skepticism about the moral acceptability of any use of nuclear weapons. It is obvious that the use of any weapons which violate the principle of discrimination merits unequivocal condemnation. We are told that some weapons are designed for purely "counterforce" use against military forces and targets. The moral issue, however, is not resolved by the design of weapons or the planned intention for use; there are also consequences which must be assessed. It would be a perverted political policy or moral casuistry which tried to justify using a weapon which "indirectly" or "unintentionally" killed a million innocent people because they happened to live near a "militarily significant target."

Even the "indirect effects" of initiating nuclear war are sufficient to make it an unjustifiable moral risk in any form. It is not sufficient, for example, to contend that "our" side has plans for "limited" or "discriminate" use. Modern warfare is not readily contained by good intentions or technological designs. The psychological climate of the world is such that mention of the term "nuclear" generates uneasiness. Many contend that the use of one tactical nuclear weapon could produce panic, with completely unpredictable consequences. It is precisely this mix of political, psychological, and technological uncertainty which has moved us in this letter to reinforce with moral prohibitions and prescriptions the prevailing political barrier against resort to nuclear weapons. Our support for enhanced command and control facilities, for major reductions in strategic and tactical nuclear forces, and for a "no first use" policy (as set forth in this letter) is meant to be seen as a complement to our desire to draw a moral line against nuclear war.

Any claim by any government that it is pursuing a morally acceptable policy of deterrence must be scrutinized with the greatest care. We are prepared and eager to participate in our country in the ongoing public debate on moral grounds.

The need to rethink the deterrence policy of our nation, to make the revisions necessary to reduce the possibility of nuclear war and to move toward a more stable system of national and international security will demand a substantial intellectual, political, and moral effort. It also will require, we believe, the willingness to open ourselves to the providential care, power, and word of God, which call us to recognize our common humanity and the bonds of mutual responsibility which exist in the international community in spite of political differences and nuclear arsenals.

Indeed, we do acknowledge that there are many strong voices within our own episcopal ranks and within the wider Catholic community in the United States which challenge the strategy of deterrence as an adequate response to the arms race today. They highlight the historical evidence that deterrence has not in fact set in motion substantial processes of disarmament.

Moreover, these voices rightly raise the concern that even the conditional acceptance of nuclear deterrence as laid out in a letter such as this might be inappropriately used by some to reinforce the policy of arms buildup. In its stead they call us to raise a prophetic challenge to the community of faith—a challenge which goes beyond nuclear deterrence, toward more resolute steps to actual bilateral disarmament and peacemaking. We recognize the intellectual ground on which the argument is built and the religious sensibility which gives it its strong force.

The dangers of the nuclear age and the enormous difficulties we face in moving toward a more adequate system of global security, stability, and justice require steps beyond our present conceptions of security and defense policy. . . .

*   *   *

CONCLUSION

As we close this lengthy letter, we try to answer two key questions as directly as we can.

Why do we address these matters fraught with such complexity, controversy and passion? We speak as pastors, not politicians. We are teachers, not technicians. We cannot avoid our responsibility to lift up the moral dimensions of the choices before our world and nation. The nuclear age is an era of moral as well as physical danger. We are the first generation since Genesis with the power to virtually destroy God's creation. We cannot remain silent in the face of such danger. Why do we address these issues? We are simply trying to live up to the call of Jesus to be peacemakers in our own time and situation.

What are we saying? Fundamentally, we are saying that the decisions about nuclear weapons are among the most pressing moral questions of our age. While these decisions have obvious military and political aspects, they involve fundamental moral choices. In simple terms, we are saying that good ends (defending one's country, protecting freedom, etc.) cannot justify immoral means (the use of weapons which kill indiscriminately and threatren whole societies). We fear that our world and nation are headed in the wrong direction. More weapons with greater destructive potential are produced every day. More and more nations are seeking to become nuclear powers. In our quest for more and more security we fear we are actually becoming less and less secure.

In the words of our Holy Father, we need a "moral about-face." The whole world must summon the moral courage and technical means to say no to nuclear conflict; no to weapons of mass destruction; no to an arms race which robs the poor and the vulnerable; and no to the moral danger of a nuclear age which places before humankind indefensible choices of constant terror or surrender. Peacemaking is not an optional commitment. It is a requirement of our faith. We are called to be peacemakers, not by some movement of the moment, but by our Lord Jesus. The content and context of our peacemaking is set not by some political agenda or ideological program, but by the teaching of his church.

Thus far in this pastoral letter we have made suggestions we hope will be helpful in the present world crisis. Looking ahead to the long and productive future of humanity for which we all hope, we feel that a more all-inclusive and final solution is needed. We speak here of the truly effective international authority for which Pope John XXIII ardently longed in "Peace on Earth"[37] and of which Pope Paul VI spoke to the United Nations on his visit there in 1965.[38] The hope for such a structure is not unrealistic, because the point has been reached where public opinion sees clearly that, with the massive weaponry of the present, war is no longer viable. There *is* a substitute for war. There is negotiation under the supervision of a global body realistically fashioned to do its job. It must be given the equipment to keep constant surveillance on the entire earth. Present technology makes this possible. It must have the authority, freely conferred upon it by all the nations, to investigate what seems to be preparations for war by any one of them. It must be empowered by all the nations to enforce its commands on every nation. It must be so constituted as to pose no threat to any nation's sovereignty. Obviously the creation of such a sophisticated instrumentality is a gigantic task, but is it hoping for too much to believe that the genius of humanity, aided by the grace and guidance of God, is able to accomplish it? To create it may take decades of unrelenting daily toil by the world's best minds and most devoted hearts, but it shall never come into existence unless we make a beginning now.

As we come to the end of our pastoral letter we boldly propose the beginning of this work. The evil of the proliferation of nuclear arms becomes more evident every day to all people. No one is exempt from their danger. If ridding the world of the weapons of war could be done easily, the whole human race would do it gladly tomorrow. Shall we shrink from the task because it is hard?

We turn to our own government and we beg it to propose to the United Nations that it begin this work immediately; that it create an international task force for peace; that this task force, with membership open to every nation, meet daily through the years ahead with one sole agenda: the creation of a world that will one day be safe from war. Freed from the bondage of war that holds it captive in its threat, the world will at last be able to address its problems and to make genuine human progress so that every day there may be more freedom, more food and more opportunity for every human being who walks the face of the earth.

Let us have the courage to believe in the bright future and in a God who wills it for us—not a perfect world, but a better one. The perfect world, we Christians believe, is beyond the horizon in an endless eternity where God will be all in all. But a better world is here for human hands and hearts and minds to make.

For the community of faith the risen Christ is the beginning and end of all things. For all things were created through him and all things will return to the Father through him.

It is our belief in the risen Christ which sustains us in confronting the awesome challenge of the nuclear arms race. Present in the beginning as the world of the Father, present in history as the word incarnate and with us today in his word, sacraments, and Spirit, he is the reason for our hope and faith. Respecting our freedom, he does not solve our problems, but sustains us as we take responsibility for his work of creation and try to shape it in the ways of the kingdom. We believe his grace will never fail us. We offer this letter to the church and to all who can draw strength and wisdom from it in the conviction that we must not fail him. We must subordinate the power of the nuclear age to human control and direct it to human benefit. As we do this we are conscious of God's continuing work among us, which will one day issue forth in the beautiful final kingdom prophesied by the seer of the book of Revelation:

Then I saw a new heaven and a new earth; for the first heaven and the first earth had passed away and the sea was no more. And I saw the holy city, new Jerusalem, coming down out of heaven from God, prepared as a bride adorned for her husband; and I heard a great voice from the throne saying, "Behold, the dwelling of God is with men. He will dwell with them, and they shall be his people, and God himself will be with them, he will wipe away every tear from their eyes, and death shall be no more, neither shall there be mourning nor crying nor pain any more, for the former things have passed away." And he who sat upon the throne said, "Behold, I make all things new" (Rv. 21:1–5).

NOTES

1. Vatican II, "The Pastoral Constitution on the Church in the Modern World" (hereafter: "Pastoral Constitution"), 77. Papal and conciliar texts will be referred to by title with paragraph number. Several collections of these texts exist although no single collection is comprehensive; see the following: *Peace and Disarmament: Documents of the World Council of Churches and the Roman Catholic Church* (hereafter: *Documents,* with page number) (Geneva and Rome, 1982); J. Gremillion, *The Gospel of Peace and Justice: Catholic Social Teaching Since Pope John* (Maryknoll, N.Y., 1976); D. J. O'Brien and T. A. Shannon, eds., *Renewing the Earth: Catholic Documents on Peace, Justice and Liberation* (New York, 1977); A. Flannery, ed., *Vatican Council II: The Conciliar and Post Conciliar Documents* (Collegeville, Minn., 1975); W. Abbot, ed., *The Documents of Vatican II* (New York, 1966). Both the Flannery and Abbot translations of the pastoral constitution are used in this letter.

2. John Paul II, Message to the Second Special Session of the United Nations General Assembly Devoted to Disarmament (June 1982), 7 (hereafter: Message UN Special Session 1982).

3. John Paul II, Address to Scientists and Scholars, 4; *Origins* 10 (1981):621.

4. Ibid.

5. Declaration on Prevention of Nuclear War (Sept. 24, 1982).

6. Paul VI, World Day of Peace Message, 1967, in *Documents,* p. 198.

7. Statement of the Holy See to the United Nations (1976), in *The Church and the Arms Race,* Pax Christi-USA (New York, 1976), pp. 23–24.

8. R. Adams and S. Cullen, *The Final Epidemic: Physicians and Scientists on Nuclear War* (Chicago, 1981).

9. Pontifical Academy of Sciences, "Statement on the Consequences of the Use of Nuclear Weapons," in *Documents,* p. 241.

10. John Paul II, World Day of Peace Message 1982, *Origins* 12, 11 (1982):476.

11. The following quotations are from public officials who have served at the highest policy levels in recent administrations of our government:

It is time to recognize that no one has ever succeeded in advancing any persuasive reason to believe that any use of nuclear weapons, even on the smallest scale, could reliably be expected to remain limited. [McG. Bundy, G. F. Kennan, R. S. McNamara and G. Smith, "Nuclear Weapons and the Atlantic Alliance," *Foreign Affairs* 60 (1982):757.]

From my experience in combat there is no way that (nuclear escalation) . . . can be controlled because of the lack of information, the pressure of time and the deadly results that are taking place on both sides of the battle line. [Gen. A. S. Collins, Jr. (former deputy commander in chief of U.S. Army in Europe), "Theatre Nuclear Warfare: The Battlefield," in J. F. Reichart and S. R. Sturn, eds., *American Defense Policy,* 5th ed. (Baltimore, 1982), pp. 359–360.]

None of this potential flexibility changes my view that a full-scale thermonuclear exchange would be an unprecedented disaster for the Soviet Union as well as for the United States. Nor is it at all clear that an initial use of nuclear weapons—however selectively they might be targeted—could be kept from escalating to a full-scale thermonuclear exchange, especially if command-and-control centers were brought under attack. The odds are high, whether weapons were used against tactical or strategic targets, that control would be lost on both sides and the exchange would become unconstrained. [Harold Brown, *Department of Defense Annual Report FY 1979* (Washington, 1978). Cf. also "The Effects of Nuclear War" (Washington: U.S. Government Printing Office, 1979)].

12. For example, cf.: H. A. Kissinger, *Nuclear Weapons and Foreign Policy* (New York, 1957), *The Necessity for Choice* (New York, 1960); R. Osgood and R. Tucker, *Force, Order and Justice* (Baltimore, 1967); R. Aron, *The Great Debate: Theories of Nuclear Strategy* (New York, 1965); D. Ball, "Can Nuclear War Be Controlled?" Adelphi Paper No. 161 (London, 1981); M. Howard, "On Fighting a Nuclear War," International Security 5 (1981):3–17.

13. Statement on the Consequences of the Use of Nuclear Weapons, in *Documents,* p. 243.

14. Pius XII, Address to the VIII Congress of the World Medical Association, in *Documents,* p. 131.

15. "Pastoral Constitution," 80.

16. Ibid.

17. M. Bundy et al., "Nuclear Weapons," cited in K. Kaiser, G. Leber, A. Mertes, F. J. Schulze, "Nuclear Weapons and the Preservation of Peace," *Foreign Affairs* 60 (1982):1157–1170. Cf. other responses to Bundy article in the same issue of *Foreign Affairs.*

18. Testimony given to the NCCB Committee during preparation of this pastoral letter. The testimony is reflected in the quotes found in note 11 above.

19. Our conclusions and judgments in this area, although based on careful study of and reflection on the application of moral principles, do not have, of course, the same force as the principles themselves and therefore allow for different opinions.

20. Undoubtedly aware of the long and detailed technical debate on limited war, Pope John Paul II highlighted the unacceptable moral risk of crossing the threshold to nuclear war in his "Angelus Message" of Dec. 13, 1981: "I have in fact the deep conviction that, in the light of a nuclear war's effects, which can be scientifically foreseen as certain, the only choice that is morally and humanly valid is represented by the reduction of nuclear armaments, while waiting for their future complete elimination, carried out simultaneously by all the parties, by means of explicit agreements and with the commitment of accepting effective controls." In *Documents,* p. 240.

21. W. H. Kincade and J. D. Porro, *Negotiating Security: An Arms Control Reader* (Washington, 1979).

22. Several surveys are available. For example, cf.: J. H. Kahin, *Security in the Nuclear Age: Developing U.S. Strategic Policy* (Washington, 1975); M. Mandelbaum, *The Nuclear Question: The United States and Nuclear Weapons 1946–1976* (Cambridge, England, 1979); B. Brodie, "Development of Nuclear Strategy," *International Security* 2 (1978):65–83.

23. The relationship of these two levels of policy is the focus of an article by D. Ball, "U.S. Strategic Forces: How Would They Be Used?" *International Security* 7 (1982-83):31–60.

24. "Pastoral Constitution," 81.

25. USCC, "To Live in Christ Jesus" (Washington, 1976), p. 34.

26. Cardinal John Krol, Testimony on SALT II, *Origins,* 1979, p. 197.

27. John Paul II, Message UN Special Session (1982), p. 3.

28. Ibid., p. 8.

29. John Paul II, Address to UNESCO (1980), 21.

30. John Paul II, Letter to International Seminar on the World Implications of a Nuclear Conflict, Aug. 23, 1982. Text in NC News Documentary, Aug. 24, 1982.

31. Particularly helpful was the letter of Jan. 15, 1983, of National Security Adviser William Clark to Cardinal Bernardin. Clark stated: "For moral, political and military reasons, the United States does not target the Soviet civilian population as such. There is no deliberately opaque meaning conveyed in the last two words. We do not threaten the existence of Soviet civilization by threatening Soviet cities. Rather, we hold at risk the war-making capability of the Soviet Union—its armed forces, and the industrial capacity to sustain war. It would be irresponsible for us to issue policy statements which might suggest to the Soviets that it would be to their advantage to establish privileged sanctuaries within heavily populated areas, thus inducing them to locate much of their war-fighting capability within those urban sanctuaries." A reaffirmation of the administration's policy is also found in Secretary Weinberger's Annual Report to the Congress (Caspar Weinberger, Annual Report to the Congress, Feb. 1, 1983, p. 55): "The Reagan administration's policy is that under no circumstances may such weapons be used deliberately for the purpose of destroying populations." The letter of Weinberger to Bishop O'Connor of Feb. 9, 1983, has a similar statement.

32. S. Zuckerman, *Nuclear Illusion and Reality* (New York, 1982); D. Ball, cited p. 36; T. Powers, "Choosing a Strategy for World War III," *Atlantic Monthly*, November 1982, pp. 82–110.

33. Cf. the comments in the Pontifical Academy of Sciences "Statement on the Consequences of the Use of Nuclear Weapons" cited above.

34. Several experts in strategic theory would place both the MX missile and Pershing II missiles in this category.

35. In each of the successive drafts of this letter we have tried to state a central moral imperative: that the arms race should be stopped and disarmament begun. The implementation of this imperative is open to a wide variety of approaches. Hence we have chosen our own language in this paragraph, not wanting either to be identified with one specific political initiative or to have our words used against specific political measures.

36. Cf. President Reagan's Speech to the National Press Club (Nov. 18, 1981) and Address at Eureka College (May 9, 1982). Department of State, *Current Policy* 346 and 387.

37. John XXIII, "Peace on Earth" (1963), 137.

38. Paul VI, Address to General Assembly of the United Nations (1965), 2.

9. Statement on the Illegality of Nuclear Weapons

Lawyers Committee on Nuclear Policy

Humanity has entered a critical period in its history as a species. Today's nuclear arsenals have the potential for annihilating a large segment of the world's populations, for devastating and contaminating vast areas of the earth's surface, and for producing unpredictable and uncontrollable biological and environmental consequences. In short, nuclear weapons threaten human survival itself.

Yet, the use of nuclear weapons once considered unthinkable is increasingly being contemplated by U.S. policymakers. In fact, with Presidential Directive 59, the United States has officially adopted a counterforce strategy that envisions the use (including the first use) of nuclear weapons in a variety of conventional as well as nuclear settings. This shift in nuclear strategy is all the more troubling given the Reagan administration's position that the United States must be prepared to intervene, using nuclear capabilities if necessary, to protect U.S. interests wherever threatened. Thus there has developed in U.S. official policy a dangerous acceptance of the legitimacy and efficacy of using nuclear weapons to reverse international situations considered adverse to U.S. national interests.

Rather than preserving international peace as claimed, this nuclear strategy is likely to bring us closer to nuclear war. The insistence on a limited nuclear war option increases dramatically the prospect that nuclear weapons will be used in a crisis situation. Furthermore, the notion that the use of nuclear weapons can be kept from escalating into an all-out nuclear exchange is, as many experts have argued, highly questionable. Consequently, we believe there is a growing spectre of nuclear war, which requires us to undertake a fundamental rethinking of the status of nuclear weapons under international law.

The prevalent belief among the general public as well as policymakers is that nuclear weapons are legal. This belief is based on the assumption that a state may do whatever it is not expressly forbidden from doing. The legality of nuclear weapons, however, cannot be judged solely by the existence or non-existence of a treaty rule specifically prohibiting or restricting their use. Any reasonable legal analysis must take into account all the recognized sources of international law—international treaties, international custom, general principles of law, judicial decisions, and the writings of the most qualified publicists. Of particular relevance to the legality of nuclear weapons are the many treaties and conventions which limit the use of any weapons in war, the traditional distinction between combatant and non-combatant, and the principles of humanity including the prohibition of weapons and tactics that are especially cruel and cause unnecessary suffering. A review of these basic principles supports a conclusion that the threat and use of nuclear weapons is illegal under international law.

A basic source of the laws of war are the Hague Conventions of 1907, particularly the Regulations embodied in Hague Convention IV. The United States Air Force, in its most recent official publication (1976) on international law and armed conflict, states that these Regulations "remain the foundation stones of the modern law of armed conflict."

A fundamental tenet of these Regulations is the prohibition of wanton or indiscriminate destruction. The Regulations forbid, for example, "the attack or bombardment, by whatever means, of towns, villages, (and even individual) dwellings or buildings which are undefended."

The universally accepted Geneva Conventions of 1949 updated and greatly strengthened the 1907 Regulations. In particular, the Convention on "the Protection of Civilian Persons in Time of War" imposes additional detailed obligations on all belligerents to ensure the essential requirements for the health, safety, and sustenance of the civilian population. A primary objective of these Conventions is to assure that "disinterested (outside) aid (can be) given without discrimination to all victims of war including members of the armed forces who on account of their wounds, capture or shipwreck cease to be enemies but become suffering and helpless human beings." The use of nuclear weapons of any type would inevitably result in massive violations of both the 1907 and 1949 rules.

Furthermore, restraints on the conduct of hostilities are traditionally not limited to those given explicit voice in specific treaty stipulations. Aware of the continuous evolution of war technology, the 1907 Hague Regulations contain a general yardstick intended exactly for situations where no specific treaty rule exists to prohibit a new type of weapon or tactic. In such cases, "the inhabitants and the belligerents remain under the protection and the rule of the principles of the laws of nations, as they result from the usages established among civilized peoples, from the laws of humanity, and the dictates of public conscience." In short, this general rule, known as the Martens Clause, makes civilized usages, the demands of humanity, and the dictates of public conscience obligatory by themselves—without the formulation of a treaty specifically prohibiting a new weapon. Any specific Convention solemnly prohibiting a specific new weapon or tactic, of course, would serve to reconfirm and strengthen the existing body of law.

Historically, the principles of humanity have been one of the primary sources of law limiting the violence permissible in war. Ever since the Declaration of St. Petersburg of 1868, the principles of humanity have been asserted as a constraint upon military necessity. The Declaration embodies what may be the twin ground rules of the laws of war: that "the right to adopt means of injuring the enemy is not unlimited" and that "the only legitimate object which States should endeavor to accomplish during a war is to weaken the military forces of the enemy."

The protection of civilians and neutral countries flows logically from the elementary distinction between combatant and non-combatant. The commitment to protect civilians and neutral countries also implies that weapons must be used selectively, and only against military targets. As stated by the International Red Cross Committee in its commentary on the 1949 Geneva Conventions, "the civilian population can never be regarded as a military objective. That truth is the very basis of the whole law of war." Without differentiating between military and non-military targets, the fundamental distinction between combatant and non-combatant becomes meaningless.

It is clear that the use of nuclear weapons in populated areas would result in the indiscriminate and massive slaughter of civilians. Moreover, even if nuclear weapons were used only against an enemy's strategic nuclear forces, the annihilation and extermination of the civilian population of the enemy would be an inevitable by-product. As the experiences of Hiroshima and Nagasaki amply demonstrate, the effects of nuclear weapons because of their very awesome nature cannot be limited to military targets.

The 1949 Geneva Conventions were adopted four years after the advent of the "nuclear age." It would therefore be illogical to assume that their provisions are not applicable to nuclear weapons. Nor did any nuclear-weapons State or any of the 130-odd other States that ratified or acceded to the Geneva Conventions make any reservation to such effect. However, it would be impossible under conditions of nuclear warfare to carry out the obligations of the Geneva Conventions, just as it would also be impossible to live up to the universally binding rules of the Hague Conventions of 1907, all of which aim at preserving the minimum requirements for the continued survivability and viability of all societies involved in armed conflict. Hence, the use of nuclear weapons would inevitably result in the commission of war crimes on an enormous scale. This fact alone is sufficient to prohibit the use of nuclear weapons.

The use of nuclear weapons would also result, directly or indirectly, in the indiscriminate destruction of people of a particular nationality. If, for example, the stated objective were the destruction of a nation-state, then the threat or use of nuclear weapons toward this end would violate at least the spirit of the Genocide Convention of 1948—which made the destruction of groups on racial, religious, or nationality grounds an international crime. To assume the legality of a weapon with the distinct capability to terrorize and to destroy an entire civilian population would make meaningless the entire effort to limit combat through the laws of war. As fragile as the laws of war may be, they must be supported, especially in the present setting where the risks to human survival are so great.

One of the most important law-making treaties, the United Nations Charter, establishes a legal duty for all states to refrain from the threat or use of force in their international relations except in self-defense or under the authority of the United Nations. Furthermore, the principle that a war of aggression warrants the highest degree of international opprobrium, namely, to be branded as an international crime, was affirmed by the Nuremberg Tribunals. These two principles have so often been unanimously reaffirmed by the General Assembly as to have become undisputed axioms of international law.

On the basis of these unquestioned principles of international law, the United Nations has repeatedly condemned the use of nuclear weapons as an "international crime." On November 24, 1961, for example, the General Assembly declared in Resolution 1653 (XVI) that "any State using nuclear or thermonuclear weapons is to be considered as violating the Charter of the United Nations, as acting contrary to the law of humanity, and as committing a crime against mankind and civilization." In Resolution 33/71-B of December 14, 1978, and in Resolution 35/152-D of December 12, 1980, the General Assembly again declared that "the use of nuclear weapons would be a violation of the Charter of the United Nations and a crime against humanity." As evidenced by these actions of the General Assembly, a consensus has been clearly emerging that the use of nuclear weapons contradicts the fundamental humanitarian principles upon which the international law of war is founded.

Yet, there is an influential school of thought which would deny the applicability of the existing laws of war to nuclear warfare. This school asserts that in an era of "total war" even the most fundamental rules can be disregarded if this enhances the chances for victory. This argument was urged in another context by some of the Nuremberg defendants, and indignantly rejected by the international Tribunal. The Tribunal's judgment warns that this "Nazi conception" of total war would destroy the validity of international law altogether. Ultimately, the legitimacy of such a view would exculpate Auschwitz.

In sum, if the goal of the laws of war—to set limits on permissible violence—is to be realized to any serious degree, and if the fundamental principles of humanity are to be of continuing relevance to their interpretation, then it must be concluded that any threat of use of nuclear weapons is illegal. Global "survivability" is so elemental that the prohibition can be reasonably inferred from the existing laws of war. To conclude differently would be to ignore the barbaric and nefarious character of the use of nuclear weapons. As the laws of war embody the minimum demands of decency, exempting nuclear weapons from that body of laws would be abandoning even this minimum standard.

The genetic and environmental effects resulting from the use of nuclear weapons, alone, provide a compelling moral and humanitarian argument against their legality. But, as indicated above, this is not the only basis for concluding that the threat or use of nuclear weapons is illegal. The unnecessary and disproportionate suffering resulting from their use; the indiscriminate nature of their effects for civilians and combatants alike; the uncontrollable radioactive fallout they set off; and their similarity in terms of effects to poison, poison gas, or bacteriological weapons (all of which are prohibited by the Hague Convention of 1907 and the Geneva Gas Protocol of 1925)—each is a sufficient basis for concluding that the threat or use of nuclear weapons is prohibited under existing international law. When taken together, these arguments provide overwhelming support for the conclusion that any threat or use of nuclear weapons is contrary to the dictates of international law.

So too, these arguments provide a sound legal basis for delegitimating and criminalizing the manufacture, possession, and ownership of nuclear weapons. If a course of action is illegal, then the planning and preparation for such an action are, by legal and moral logic, also forbidden. Moreover, the attack on the legality of manufacturing and possessing nuclear weapons is all the more necessary given the increasing prospects for the "accidental" use of nuclear weapons arising out of today's dangerous first-strike strategies.

Our intention is not to score points in a battle of legal wits. What we wish to present to fellow lawyers, to governmental decision makers, and to the public is the view that nuclear warfare would lead to results incompatible with fundamental rules of international law, elementary morality, and contrary to any rational conception of national interest and world order. In short, the very nature of nuclear warfare is destructive of all the values which law obligates us to preserve. While it is accurate to say that international law has not been as effective as it should have been in regulating state acts, international law is important to preserve our sense of humanity and to enhance the prospects for peace.

Reducing the likelihood of nuclear war must obviously, then, be the highest priority of our profession. To this end, the legal community needs to give its urgent attention to the study and implementation of the international law relating to nuclear weapons.

——— **Questions for Reflection and Discussion** ———

1. Why, since the issuance of the Russell-Einstein Manifesto in 1955, has there been so little public resistance to the accumulation, spread, and refinement of nuclear weapons? Lifton speaks of "psychic numbing." What does he mean? Are there other explanations? Is the public silence defensible?

2. What are the basic perceptions and principles of those who now protest the nuclear arms race? Are these perceptions and principles shared by national political leaders? If not, why not? Are different world views involved? If so, what are they?

3. How do you perceive the growing peace movement in the West? Does it influence official policymakers? Does it have any impact on the arms control–disarmament process?

4. Whatever influence the Western antinuclear movement may have, it has yet to gain real control of established political institutions. Why? Is this condition likely to change? What are the prospects for a similar movement in Eastern Europe and the Soviet Union? What measures might enhance such prospects? Would increased private initiatives between East and West be helpful? Would they be likely to influence national political leaders either in the East or the West?

5. What leadership roles have been played by the various professions and other organized groups in the current antinuclear movement? Have some groups been more active than others? Are some conspicuously absent? Which? Should some deliberately avoid taking a public stand? Which? Why?

6. What role should you personally play in relation to the nuclear arms race?

Selected Bibliography

Adams, Ruth, and Susan Cullen, eds. *The Final Epidemic: Physicians and Scientists on Nuclear War.* Chicago: Educational Foundation for Nuclear Science, 1981.

Beachey, Duane. *Faith in a Nuclear Age: A Christian Response to War.* Paradise, CA: Herald Press, 1983.

Brownlie, Ian. "Some Legal Aspects of the Use of Nuclear Weapons." *International and Comparative Law Quarterly,* Vol. 14 (1965), pp. 437–451.

Builder, Carl H., and Morlie H. Graubard. *The International Law of Armed Conflict: Implications for the Concept of Assured Destruction.* Santa Monica, CA: Rand Corporation, 1982.

Falk, Richard. "Toward a Legal Regime for Nuclear Weapons." *McGill Law Journal,* Vol. 28, No. 3 (July 1983), pp. 519–541.

Falk, Richard, Lee Meyrowitz, and Jack Sanderson. "Nuclear Weapons and International Law." *Indian Journal of International Law,* Vol. 20, No. 4 (Oct.-Dec. 1980), pp. 541–595.

Frank, Jerome D. *Sanity and Survival.* New York: Random House, 1968.

Fried, John H. E. "First Use of Nuclear Weapons—Existing Prohibitions in International Law." *Bulletin of Peace Proposals* (Jan. 1981), pp. 21–29.

Gardiner, Robert W. *The Cool Arm of Destruction.* Philadelphia: Westminster Press, 1974.

Goodwin, Geoffrey, ed. *Ethics and Nuclear Deterrence.* New York: St. Martin's Press, 1982.

Heyer, Robert J., ed. *Nuclear Disarmament: Key Statements from the Vatican, Catholic Leaders in North America and Ecumenical Bodies.* New York: Paulist Press, 1982.

Paust, Jordan J. "Controlling Prohibited Weapons and the Illegal Use of Permitted Weapons." *McGill Law Journal,* Vol. 28, No. 3 (July 1983), pp. 608–627.

Rotblat, Joseph, ed. *Scientists, the Arms Race and Disarmament: A UNESCO/ Pugwash Symposium.* London: Taylor & Francis, 1982.

Schell, Jonathan. *The Time of Illusion.* New York: Random House, 1976.

Schwarzenberger, Georg. *The Legality of Nuclear Weapons.* London: Stevens and Sons, 1958.

Singh, Nagendra. *Nuclear Weapons and International Law.* New York: Praeger, 1959.

Stockholm International Peace Research Institute. *The Law of War and Inhumane Weapons.* London: Taylor & Francis, 1978.

Thompson, E. P., and Dan Smith, eds. *Protest and Survive*. New York and London: Monthly Review Press, 1981.

Van Voorst, L. Bruce. "The Churches and Nuclear Deterrence." *Foreign Affairs,* Vol. 61, No. 4 (Spring 1983), pp. 827–852.

Wallis, Jim. *Waging Peace: A Handbook for the Struggle to Abolish Nuclear Weapons*. New York: Harper & Row, 1982.

Weston, Burns H. "Nuclear Weapons Versus International Law: A Contextual Reassessment." *McGill Law Journal,* Vol. 28, No. 3 (July 1983), pp. 542–590.

Zacharias, Jerrold R., Myles Gordon, and Saville R. Davis. *Common Sense and Nuclear Peace*. Newton, MA: Education Development Center, 1983. Reprinted as a special supplement in *Bulletin of the Atomic Scientists,* Vol. 39, No. 4 (April 1983).

PART TWO

RETHINKING SOME BASIC ASSUMPTIONS

CHAPTER 4

Rethinking "Security"

Before World War II, U.S. diplomacy rested for the most part on two fundamental principles: isolation from the day-to-day entanglements of European politics, and neutrality in conflicts between foreign states. Shielded by the Atlantic, Pacific, and Arctic oceans, bordered by states lacking powerful military establishments, and therefore remarkably free of the threat of foreign intervention or invasion, the United States was not compelled to rationalize its security and survival primarily in terms of military power. Great Britain bore the brunt of world "peacekeeping" responsibilities, and thus the United States required only modest military means to safeguard national defense and hemispheric security.

All this changed, however, as of World War II and the years immediately following. The Spanish-American War, numerous armed interventions in Latin America after 1900, and ultimate United States involvement in World War I must be duly noted, of course. But it was not until World War II and the subsequent emergence of Soviet-U.S. tension that military strength to protect U.S. interests became for the United States the sine qua non of national security. As observed by U.S. Department of State historian David S. Patterson:

> The experience of total war and the perceived threat of worldwide Russian communist expansion produced a real revolution in U.S. foreign policy. The result was that by the late 1940s the United States had become organized for perpetual confrontation and war. Daniel Yergin, in his book *Shattered Peace: The Origins of the Cold War and the National Security State,* has appropriately labeled the unified pattern of attitudes, policies, and institutions by which these tasks were effected the "national security state"—in effect, a "state within a state," derived from anti-communism and a new doctrine of national security. U.S. policy makers . . . believed that the Soviet Union presented an immediate military threat to the United States. The result was an expansive interpretation of American security needs, involving a major redefinition of America's relationship to the rest of the world.[1]

In other words, perceiving a U.S.-defined world order precariously transformed and threatened by "godless Communism," United States policymakers came to conceive of national security almost exclusively in terms of the military instrument of state policy, characterized by the maintenance of large-scale conventional forces, the manufacture of nuclear arms, and the deployment of strategic weapon systems, all on a permanent basis.

In this regard, of course, the United States was not alone and still is not alone. In keeping with the geopolitical calculations that had dominated European politics for centuries, the USSR pursued the same course following World War II, and, like the United States, it continues to equate national security with military power. For almost four decades now, each country has sought to safeguard its vital interests and to ensure its national survival by underwriting the most powerful military establishments ever created in history.

Thus, it is small wonder that most who think and write about security in the international system assume arms and armies to be the true guardians of the national interest. Beginning, however, with the debacle of United States militarism in Indochina, and reinforced by a similar setback for the Soviet Union in Afghanistan, growing numbers of observers are questioning this traditional assumption. Also, there is the question of whether any major power, even with the help of its allies, can absorb the economic and political costs of maintaining a global military presence in a multipolar, mass-politicized world. Although the reality of competing socioeconomic and political systems cannot be denied, nor the potential for armed aggression underestimated, increasingly dependence on military power as the principle means of ensuring national and international security is coming under doubting scrutiny; increasingly the meaning of "security" is being reconsidered.

The readings in this chapter have been selected, first, to serve as helpful counterpoint to the standard approaches to national security policy, and second, to introduce alternative ways of conceptualizing and implementing national and international security (taken up in greater detail in Part Four). Because Soviet security thinking is more difficult to discern than is its superpower counterpart, however, and because this volume is intended primarily for U.S. audiences, the majority of the selections focus mainly upon U.S. security policy.

The brief contribution by Robert Luckham locates the meaning of "security" in contemporary usage and asks whether it has anything to do at all with the safety and well-being of the individual person. Richard Barnet's piece, written during the Vietnam conflict, then challenges the basic world views of military security that gave rise to U.S. intervention in Indochina and repudiates the utility of force in upheavals that adversely affect U.S. interests abroad. Finally, Lloyd Dumas and Richard Falk contend that nuclear weapons, which form the cornerstone of U.S. national security policy today, impose serious physical, economic, and political costs upon at least the U.S. polity.

NOTES

1. David S. Patterson, "A Historical View of American Security," in C. Stephenson, ed., *Alternative Methods for International Security* (Washington, DC: University Press of America, 1982), p. 41.

10. Myths and Realities of Security

Robin Luckham

"Security" is a nebulous word. Like patriotism and motherhood it is hard to be against. Yet it is as well to enquire into its history, meaning, and use, at least that made of it by politicians, the military establishment, and "security analysts." For up until the 1940s the term most in use was "defense." The "collective security" of nations was a term which came into use in the League of Nations following World War I, but fell into eclipse with the demise of the League and the outbreak of a second global conflict.

"Security" in the sense that it is now most commonly used is the brainchild of the Cold War. It is an ideology which legitimizes a number of crucial trends in the post–World War II world order.

Firstly the era of American imperialism. No longer is it a question merely of defending the United States or this or that European State from aggression. But it is the security of "the West" or more broadly still "the Free World"—i.e., of the international system of capitalism—which requires a worldwide American military presence and a global system of alliances. However, there is a deliberate and systematic conflation of national security (the protection of the power and resources of particular nation-states), international security (the protection of capitalism and the system of global alliances which protects it) and collective security (that of all States and through them, theoretically, of all mankind). For it is through the confusion of these levels of meaning that "security" obtains its ideological appeal.

Secondly, the transformation of international conflict into class war both between the capitalist West and the socialist East and between the industrial North and the developing South. The Cold War—the *real* Cold War—is directed almost as much against proletarian nations in the Third World as against the USSR, Eastern Europe, and China. Hence, for example, the growing popularity of the argument that Third World control over supplies and prices of energy and raw materials is a "threat" to Western security; and that the current economic crisis may be ushering us into an era of "resource wars," as General Alexander Haig has put it.

The association between international conflict and class war has also had profound effects on the internal structures of the nation-state. "National Security" requires that war be waged simultaneously upon the enemy within and upon the adversary abroad. Hence the construction of vast intelligence and security apparatuses in both East and West, their secrecy jealously protected from the inquisitive citizen even more than the prying foreign power. And hence, too, the transfer of the technology of repression to the national security bureaucracies that are being created in the Third World.

Finally, "security" is increasingly invoked in support of the notion that defense requires not just a permanent standing army, but a permanent mobilization of economic, social, and intellectual resources: higher peacetime military expenditures than ever before, a rapidly growing arms economy, massive investment in military R&D, and a large permanent military and security planning staff. National security doctrine, in sum, consecrates that tension-filled marriage between the economy, the military sector, and the State that is called the "military-industrial complex."

These, then, are the agenda contained in the word "security," of which one must at least be aware before one throws the word around too casually. To be sure one may argue that security, *real* security, should be something else. But in order to do so one must supply an alternative agenda. For without it, it is surely the Cold War definition of the situation that will prevail.

Moreover, if the character of security is doubtful, so too is that of those who are secured. The word is usually used with abstract qualifiers: "national security," "international security," or "regional security." But this does not at all settle the question of what it means to say a nation, an international system, or a region is secure. Who or what is it, actually, that is secure or insecure? If one pushes the question further it turns out that it is either particular States which are secure (usually against each other) or particular social classes (usually dominant or ruling classes; both against each other and against the people they govern).

However, security derives much of its ideological force from the myth that it is also the citizen who is secure (up there in the sky the pilot in his fighter-bomber makes sure we will all have our bread, petroleum, and TV sets tomorrow, that our women will not have children torn from their breasts by invaders and that we won't be blown to bits because goddamn it we can do the same to them). This has much visceral appeal, especially as it readily connects to nationalism. Yet it is problematic whether State or ruling-class security actually has anything at all to do with the safety and well-being of ordinary citizens. The latter indeed must be central to any critique of the official brand of security. What protection does the State in fact offer a worker, a farmer, or a housewife? Does it secure their moral and material well-being? Or does it put them increasingly at risk from war, economic crisis, and the activities of the national security bureaucracies which are supposed to protect them?

11. The Illusion of Security

Richard J. Barnet

The crisis of national security now faced by the United States stems, in my view, from a fundamental misconception of the nature of the problem. For [thirty-five] years we have been building a Maginot Line against the threats of the 1930s while the threats of the [1980s] are rapidly overwhelming us along with the rest of mankind.

United States national security policy is designed to deal with three classic threats. The first is a nuclear attack on the United States. In a world where nuclear weapons exist no one can say that such an attack could not happen. The question is whether American planners have (a) put that threat into proper perspective and (b) whether the strategy they have developed to deal with it has decreased or increased the threat. It seems likely that for much of the cold war period the United States has been running an arms race with itself. It was always *possible* that the Soviet Union would launch a nuclear attack on the United States, but everything we know about the nature of nuclear weapons, budgetary constraints, political pressures in the Soviet Union, and Communist ideology suggests that it was *highly unlikely.* The United States has had an enormous superiority in numbers of nuclear weapons, a fact that has neither made the people of the United States feel more secure, nor provided the "strength" to intimidate Communists to negotiate on our terms. Indeed, as one might have expected, the Soviets have seemed to be more willing to negotiate as they have approached nuclear parity with the United States. At the same time, the U.S. attempt to maintain superiority has encouraged the Soviet Union and China to develop their own nuclear capabilities and has given them greater power of life and death over the people and territory of the United States. In an arms race, neither side will permit the other to continue amassing an ever-widening lead.

The United States has believed that it could promote security by preserving the "option" to use nuclear weapons not only to retaliate for a nuclear attack, but also to protect "vital interests" of a lesser sort, primarily in Western Europe. The unwillingness to renounce the first use of nuclear weapons has thus led to less security, not more. We have communicated to all countries the fact that the greatest power in the world must rely on nuclear weapons to promote its foreign policy interests. Weaker countries, such as France, have taken this cue and have concluded that no country can be "sovereign" unless it, too, commands a powerful nuclear arsenal.

During the Cuban missile crisis President Kennedy said that the chances were at least one in three that nuclear weapons would be used by the United States and that if they had been used, at least 150 million people would have been killed. In a later speech he said that as many as 500 million would be killed in the opening hours of a nuclear conflict. Yet it was prestige, not military security, that was at stake in the Soviet-American confrontation of 1962. From a U.S. security standpoint, the resolution of the Cuba crisis was a disaster. Washington gave up everything it would have had to give in a negotiated settlement (Jupiter missiles in Turkey and Italy, and a pledge not to invade Cuba). And the 1962 humiliation of the Soviet Union led directly to a major rearmament program which has now made Moscow a far more formidable adversary than it was [twenty] years ago.

There is no objective, including the survival of the United States as a political entity, that merits destroying millions or jeopardizing the future of man. The pretense that it is legitimate to threaten nuclear war for political ends creates an international climate of fear in which Americans will continue to have less security, not more.

GUARDIANS AT THE GATE

National security planners have been reluctant to renounce the "option" to destroy millions of human beings in a nuclear "first strike" because of a mistaken analysis of the second threat to national security. This is the problem of aggression, its causes, and its cure. The official theory has been presented many times in Presidential speeches: we must assure peace by preparing for war and by making governments believe that we will do exactly what we say we will do to protect our positions of strength in the world, including our alliances. Thus we fight in small wars now to prevent fighting in larger wars later.

These ideas are not mere rhetoric. They are deeply held beliefs of a generation of National Security Managers for whom the decisive learning experience was the Second World War. Staggered by the apocalyptic events of the war, the demonic Hitlerian vision of a world order, the death camps, the fire bombings, the saturation raids, and the nuclear attacks, this generation has believed with the first Secretary of Defense, James Forrestal, that "the cornerstone in any plan which undertakes to rid us of the curse of war must be the armed might of the United States."[1] Despite the standard denial that the United States is not the "policeman of the world," which has been inserted in Presidential statements and State Department press releases since opposition developed to the Vietnam war, this is precisely the official image we have had of ourselves. "History and our own achievements have thrust upon us the principal responsibility for the protection of freedom on earth,"[2] President Johnson declared at a Lincoln Day dinner in 1965. Earlier, President Kennedy called our nation "the watchman on the wall of world freedom."[3] Both expressed their generation's judgment of America's security role. "We did not choose to be the guardians at the gate," Johnson declared, but "history" has "thrust" that "responsibility" upon us. Imperial nations always have a view of their own unique destiny.

In the early postwar period American planners had a self-conscious notion that they were playing out for their generation the particular imperial roles that England and France had played in the last—filling "power vacuums" and picking up "responsibilities" for keeping order. Unless the forces of international "stability," so the argument went, were always ready, and, most important, *willing* to use whatever force was necessary, aggressor nations would take over their weaker neighbors one by one. Unless nations with an impulse to upset the *status quo* were opposed at the outset, they would expand as far as their power permitted—even to the point of world domination. In this view of the world which has dominated American thinking on world affairs for a generation, there is an infinite supply of potential aggressors. Any "have-not" nation that can field an army will do. General Thomas Power of the Strategic Air Command, for example, warned in the mid-1960s of a possible "African Hitler" whom we might have to confront once we had disposed of the Communist threat.[4]

Because the principal threats to peace and security were foreign "aggressors" bent on world conquest, it was necessary for the United States as the world's most powerful country to attempt to organize an alliance of threatened nations to try to contain those threats. Postwar planners looked on their own time as a direct continuation of the pre-1945 period. The United States was spearheading a crusade against totalitarianism and militarism in behalf of a "free world" deemed to represent the forces of good, if only because of the evil of the Communist adversaries. Stalin was the postwar Hitler, the leader of an infinitely expansionist power who could be stopped only by the very show of strength England and France failed to make against Hitler. When President Truman enunciated the far-reaching doctrine that bears his name with its commitment to "support free peoples who are resisting attempted subjugation by armed minorities or by outside pressures," he defended this momentous change of policy as a protection of the investment already made in World War II.

MYTHS OF THE MANAGERS

A visitor from another planet in the early postwar days would have had a hard time reconciling the official American analogy, "Stalin is the Hitler of today," with the facts as they emerged. Indeed, the naive visitor might well have concluded that the problem of military aggression in the postwar period had its source in the United States. Soviet armies stopped at the point of their farthest advance in World War II and withdrew from adjacent areas such as Czechoslovakia only to return when political domination threatened to fail. The United States retained the major bases it had acquired in World War II and acquired more. Within a few years the Soviet Union was surrounded by air and later missile bases from which devastating nuclear attacks could be launched— all at a time when the Soviet Union lacked a similar capacity to attack the United States. It has been the United States and not the Soviet Union that has stationed its military forces on every continent and spread nuclear weapons in the tens of thousands on the continents of Asia and Europe and on the high seas. It is the United States and not the Soviet Union that has intervened with its military and paramilitary forces almost every year since 1945 on the territory of other countries either to prevent local insurgent forces from taking power or displacing them from power.

Despite Stalin's monumental crimes against his own people, a kind of permanent internal war, Dean Acheson, along with most of the National Security Managers of his generation, now admits that the early postwar fears of a Soviet military invasion of Western Europe may have been exaggerated.[5] The problem of European security was whether the West European countries would move toward domestic Communism, not whether the Soviets would attack them. As in Vietnam almost twenty years later, the National Security Managers used military measures in an effort to give psychological support to allies facing domestic economic and political crises. In Europe the policy worked—but at the cost of perpetuating the myth of outside military aggression on which it was premised. A generation later, there is still no historical evidence that Stalin or his successors ever contemplated an invasion of West Germany, or that they were deterred, as Winston Churchill claimed in a speech at M.I.T. in 1950, only because of the American possession of the atomic bomb. Indeed, the Soviet Union in Stalin's day, as many historians now conclude, was following a highly cautious course, more conservative in most respects than that in the present "era of negotiations." Today's Soviet leaders play a more active and dangerous role in world affairs, for example in Cuba and the Middle East, than Stalin ever dared to do. Indeed, it is ironical that the strategy chosen by the U.S. to deal with the limited Soviet challenge to American supremacy may well have helped to create a Soviet Union with global interests and commitments.

Although there were very few objective reasons for believing that Stalin, with his country ruined, was about to embark on a campaign of Hitler-like aggression, U.S. National Security Managers did indeed feel insecure. It is important to try to understand the source of that insecurity, which still persists. The United States will not change its role in the world as long as the official belief continues that the United States can be safe in the world only by running as much of it as possible.

Despite its unparalleled monopoly of power it was not surprising that the United States felt insecure at the close of the Second World War. The managers of the Number One Nation always feel the insecurity that comes with winning and having to defend the crown. Moreover, the floodgates of technological and political change were opened by the war and America's leaders felt the anxiety of being swept by unfamiliar currents, particularly when, because of the atomic bomb, the stakes were supremely high. It was natural that the managers of the new American empire should construct an analysis that justified their power and sanctified its use.

Thus the political analysis of security threats took on the character of military contingency planning. Many of the contingencies on which policies have been constructed have been highly implausible. During the whole postwar period there have been very few cases of World War II type "aggression," i.e. invasion of one state by another for the purpose of occupying it or dominating it. It must be said that a high percentage of the invasions of the last generation have been carried out by the United States in its self-appointed role as "guardian at the gates." The closest analogy to Hitler-type aggression from the Communist side was the invasion of South Korea by North Korea and the Soviet invasion of [Hungary and] Czechoslovakia, neither of which was or looked like the first slice of a "salami" program of world conquest, or so U.S. intelligence agencies concluded at the time.* Other examples of old-fashioned "aggression" include the 1962 incursions of Communist China into India, the 1965 India-Pakistan war, and the 1967 Israeli invasions of Egypt and Syria which the United States did not oppose with military power.** Although the United States has sought to enlist many other countries in a network of alliances aimed at containing one or another "aggressive" or "expansionist" power, the nations whose security is much more directly threatened by such powers have tended to drag their feet. This is especially true in Southeast Asia where Thailand and the Philippines, supposedly among the next "dominoes" to fall, [refused] to give more than token cooperation in the Vietnam war and exacted major political and economic concessions for their participation. If they

---

*Since the first publication of this essay in 1971, several Communist states have resorted to use of force to achieve political gains, the most conspicuous recent example being the Soviet occupation of Afghanistan. Others have included the seizure of Laos and Cambodia by Vietnam following the defeat of the Saigon regime in 1975. In addition, Cuban armed forces have intervened in Angola and the Horn of Africa to affect the outcome of indigenous struggles for national power.—*Ed.*

**Additional well-known examples of "old-fashioned aggression" since the first publication of this essay in 1971 are the 1973 Arab-Israeli War, the Falkland (Malvinas) Islands War, the ongoing Iran-Iraq conflict, Israel's 1982 invasion and occupation of Lebanon, and the 1983 "invasion" of Grenada.—*Ed.*

accepted the American analysis of the security threat, they would act as if their own security was gravely threatened.

There are two principal reasons why the problem of war and violence in the postwar world does not resemble the prewar problem of aggression. First, the development of technology has made the acquisition of strategic real estate for powerful nations much less important. Big powers like the United States and the Soviet Union can now hit any part of the globe with missiles launched from their own territory. The United States can dispatch powerful military forces by air transport anywhere within a matter of days, and the Soviet Union is developing its capacity to do likewise. Thus the pressure to achieve security by invading other countries is less than it used to be. The arms race has reduced the tactical incentive of both major powers to resort to territorial aggression.

Second, despite technology, the extension of formal physical and juridical control by a great power over other countries has become much more difficult because of the development of the techniques of partisan and guerrilla warfare, the ideology of self-determination and nationalism, and the resulting politicization of formerly colonized populations. The history of the last decade makes it clear that the entry of new countries into the Communist bloc involves heavy costs as well as benefits for the Soviet Union. Indeed, the extension of Soviet power into Cuba appears to have complicated life for Moscow. It has been a financial burden for the Soviet Union, has posed risk of conflict with the United States, and has involved conflict with the Cubans themselves. The same might be said of the Middle East. It has become more and more difficult to manage empires or to derive the prestige traditionally associated with empires. That is one reason why the United States does not officially admit to being an empire and prefers to conduct so many of its activities abroad by covert means.

THE COUNTERREVOLUTIONARY IMPULSE

The third major security threat which, in my view, has been misperceived in the official U.S. world view is the problem that John Foster Dulles used to refer to as "indirect aggression." Most of the violence and instability in the postwar world has arisen not from confrontation between national states but from revolutions and internal insurgencies. Between 1958 and 1966, according to Robert McNamara, there were over 149 serious internal insurgencies.[6]

The counterrevolutionary impulse has been a cornerstone of American policy since the end of the Second World War. On an average of once every eighteen months the United States has sent its military or para-military forces into other countries either to crush a local revolution or to arrange a coup against a government which failed to acquire the State Department seal of approval.[7]

Why has this been thought necessary to make the world safe for the United States? There have been essentially two theories about the connection between indigenous revolutionary change and American security. In the early days of the cold war it was assumed that any Communist revolutionary was a Kremlin agent. Ho Chi Minh's independence movement, Ambassador William C. Bullitt explained in 1947, was designed to "add another finger to the hand that Stalin is closing around China."[8] According to Dean Rusk, in a speech made [thirty] years ago, Mao's regime was "a colonial Russian government."[9]

It is now generally accepted that Communism is no longer "monolithic." Of course it never was in the Rusk-Bullitt sense. Far from being planned and initiated by the Soviet Union, the revolutionary movements in China, Indo-China, Greece, Cuba, and elsewhere were often at the outset opposed and discouraged by the Kremlin as embarrassments to the diplomatic relationships the Soviet Union was pursuing as a Great Power. The Soviet Union has barely disguised its reluctance at being sucked into the Vietnam war to oppose American intervention, although, as in the Cuban case, it has given aid to counter American military attacks. For years after the Geneva settlement of 1954 the Soviet Union acquiesced in the maintenance of a U.S. protected anti-Communist South Vietnam, which was contrary to the spirit of the settlement. The Soviets proposed the admission of North and South Vietnam as separate members of the United Nations as late as 1959.

As long as the myth of "indirect aggression"—the transformation of local revolutions into Soviet invasions by Trojan Horse—was credible, a counterrevolutionary policy could be defended as traditional balance-of-power politics. Every revolution was part of a pattern of world conquest emanating from a rival center of power. Thus the situation was sufficiently like Hitler's expansionism to justify a similar military response.

The Soviet Union sought to dominate every nation into which its troops marched in the Second World War and to establish subservient "revolutionary" governments. But every revolutionary government that has come to power without the Red Army has turned out to be ambivalent, cool, or even hostile to the Soviet Union—Yugoslavia, Albania, North Vietnam, China, and Cuba. In each case the relationship is complex, but in none of them can it be said that the existence of the Communist regime necessarily makes the Soviet Union stronger or more threatening to the physical safety of the United States.

There is another connection between revolutionary change in other countries and American national security which is not military, but psychological. The United States has consciously sought to expand its system so that other countries will not only buy our products but accept our values. We have wanted to be accepted as the world's definition of the good society. To a considerable extent this has happened. Only a few revolutionary societies have held out a vision of the future different from the American model—what Walt Rostow called "the high mass consumption society." Even the Soviet Union has adopted as its goal the American model of the highly industrialized consumer society. Its brand of socialism is a means for "overtaking and surpassing the United States" on the way to the same Utopia.

"WE'RE NUMBER ONE?"

For [more than] fifty years, however, America has been experiencing a continuing national identity crisis. In the thirties, amidst depression, seemingly permanent unemployment, and great social unrest, there was a serious loss of faith in the American system as it then existed. The pretensions of the foreign "isms"—state capitalism, Communism, fascism, and others—that they, rather than "free enterprise America," represented the wave of the future caused shudders of doubt in the United States. Victory in the Second World War brought new confidence. Yet there was enough awareness that the war had transcended but had not solved the domestic crises of the thirties to make both managers and the public uneasy about the future at the very moment of America's supreme power. Thus the rhetorical claims of Communist ideologues that they were the new "wave of the future" struck a terror out of all proportion to the real strength of what the State Department called "international Communism."

Much of what the United States does in the name of national security is designed to allay the inner fears of America's leaders that the United States may be slipping from the pinnacle of power. They spend hundreds of billions of dollars and tens of thousands of lives to preserve their "credibility" for toughness so that no one would dare to think of the nation which they manage as a "pitiful, helpless, giant." The principal argument in the government for persisting in Vietnam despite the obvious catastrophic political, economic, military, and social consequences [was] based on reputation and prestige. It may have been an error to have made a commitment in Vietnam, but to back down would [have] put the nation in a bad light. Reputation, as Thomas Schelling has said, is one of the few things worth fighting for. "We are the Number One Nation," Lyndon Johnson told a National Foreign Policy Conference at the State Department less than a year before he left office, "and we are going to stay the Number One Nation."

Like many empires before us we have used reputation abroad as the criterion of national success and as a diversion from intractable domestic problems. As long as our criteria of "development" and "progress"— such as the ratio of cars to bicycles on the main street of the capital— were accepted by other nations, this amounted to a kind of validation for the American system at home. American scientific achievements, American books, American magazines, American educational materials, American business techniques appeared to be changing the face of the world, making it look like an extension of America and hence giving the illusion that the globe was becoming a friendlier and more manageable place.

It is as illusory, however, to measure national security by the willingness of elites in other nations to imitate the United States as it is to do so by counting nuclear warheads. Whether American methods work elsewhere will not help solve the pressing security problem of a society unable to deal with its own internal violence. Indeed, there is now strong evidence that the export of American consumption values and American technology creates long-term security problems for the United States by encouraging economies of waste in the Third World which add to the world pollution and resource allocation problems. It is in our own selfish interest, if we care about prolonging the life support systems of the planet, that the irrational and destructive patterns of development and consumption of resources that have evolved in the United States not be repeated elsewhere.

FACING THE REALITIES

The United States cannot achieve national security until we begin to accept certain realities of our age. The first is that poor countries will, and many probably must, experiment with revolution to solve political and economic problems fast enough to permit survival for their people. Whether a country in Asia, Africa, or Latin America chooses another political and economic system, whether it looks to another country as its model, does not threaten our national security unless we define such events (over which we have no effective control in any event) as "defeats."

Second, the United States must be prepared to live with a high degree of disorder and instability, which are characteristics of a world experiencing rapid political and technological change. To set as a national security goal the enforcement of "stability" in a world in convulsion, a world in which radical change is as inevitable as it is necessary, is as practical as King Canute's attempts to command the tides. Real stability can come only with the building of a legitimate international order which offers genuine hope for people, whatever their history and wherever they are located. That sort of stability requires change and not always the sort that can be easily controlled.

Third, it is in the real security interest of the United States to ease rather than complicate the life of people with whom we coexist on the planet, whatever the political ideology of their governments. It does not increase American national security, for example, for Castro to suffer economic reverses, whatever the U.S. may have done to help bring them about. The point would be equally true if Castro were a right wing military dictator. When governments oppress their own citizens, stepping up outside military pressure hardly creates a more liberal atmosphere.

There is no existing political solution to the major problems of human development that can be called "the wave of the future." The problems transcend all existing ideologies. It is in the interest of the people of the United States as a whole, although not in the short-term interest of those who fear change because it threatens privilege, to encourage a variety of experiments around the globe to find ways to solve the worldwide crisis of political order. Until Americans can begin to identify with the people of other countries as members of the same species with the same basic problems, we will continue to treat other countries as abstractions to be manipulated for our own psychological and political needs and will continue to build our power on their suffering. The attempt to isolate, contain, or overthrow revolutionary governments makes them more likely to resort to terror against their own people and to adopt a militant nationalism to protect themselves from American attack. No nation, including the United States, can enforce virtue, moderation, or justice in another country. Making war on Germany did not save the Jews. Indeed, the mass exterminations did not begin until the war was on. All a nation can do is to help create an international political environment that will encourage other governments to permit freedom and a decent life for their own citizens.

A national security policy for the United States which can minimize the resort to violence and promote an international system for the resolution of the basic human problems of justice and order must see the United States not as the problem-solver of the world but as an integral part of the problem. America's extraordinarily disproportionate share of resources and power, which we have celebrated as proof of a messianic destiny, is itself a long-term threat to our national security. The United States will become increasingly isolated from the rest of humanity if we continue to set as a national security goal the preservation of present power and economic relationships in the world rather than the rapid evolution towards world community. The *status quo,* which we call "stable," will come to be seen by more and more other peoples as intolerable. Vietnam [showed] that despite the massive employment of military power the United States cannot always maintain positions of domination that it has acquired around the world. Perhaps in the short term the strategy that succeeded in Greece and the Dominican Republic and failed in Vietnam may succeed elsewhere. But it is clear that we need new criteria for defining "success." A military dictatorship that supports the United States in the United Nations and welcomes its military mission but uses American aid to hold down its population and to forestall institutional change contributes to the sum of repression, misuse of resources, and misery in the world. It should not be counted an American success.

SURVIVAL ISN'T GUARANTEED

American security is inextricably linked with the problem of global security. For this reason much of the debate in the United States about "neo-isolationism" seems Orwellian. Those who favor continuation of the policy of military intervention around the world whenever the United

States decides it is in America's interest to "project its power" advertise themselves as "internationalists." Those who wish to renounce the right to threaten nuclear war on behalf of American vital interests, to stop seeking American security by killing or assisting in the killing of Asians, Africans, and Latin Americans, are stigmatized as "isolationists."

The issue is not whether the United States should or can withdraw from the world but the character of American involvement. The development of technology and communication has multiplied international and transnational contacts of all kinds. Americans cannot and will not resign from the world. But they can renounce the myths on which their contact with the world has been so largely based: that the United States government can manage social and political change around the world; that it can police a stable system of order; that it can solve problems in other countries it has yet to solve for its own people; that there is no real conflict of interest between the people of the United States, with their high standard of living, and people in Asia, Africa, or Latin America, who make less than $100 a year; that the United States government, unlike all other governments, is capable of true philanthropy.

The United States cannot develop a national security policy that will improve the prospects for global survival until we seriously examine the extent to which a new foreign policy requires domestic changes. How much, for example, can we change America's present destructive definition of national security without dismantling the bureaucratic structures which promote a militarist definition of the national interest? Can we still have a military establishment anything like the present one without continuing to have an interventionist policy? I am virtually certain that the answer is no. Can we have relations with Third World countries that will close instead of further widen the gap between rich and poor countries without making major changes in the patterns of consumption in the United States and basic structural changes in the economy? On this question I am less clear. Both Marxists and the National Association of Manufacturers appear convinced that the standard of living cannot be maintained in the U.S. except through the continuation of imperialist policies. It is crucial to the building of a real national security policy to determine whether they are right or wrong. If they are right, then it is a prime security task to change consumption patterns in the United States. The alternative would be a global class war.

No national security problem can ultimately be solved except within the context of planetary security. The overshadowing risk to mankind is the destruction of the earth through nuclear war or the collapse of life support systems as a consequence of pollution and maldistribution of resources. The policy of seeking national security through permanent war preparation and intermittent wars directly contributes to the crisis of planetary survival in a variety of specific ways. Military establishments preempt resources. They produce waste. They generate an atmosphere of conflict and competition in which the minimal measures of cooperation necessary to insure planetary survival become impossible.

There is nothing to suggest that achieving security in the final [quarter] of the twentieth century will be easy, or even that the survival of civilization is guaranteed. No one has yet developed a global security system that works.

But we do know what does not work.

NOTES

1. Quoted in Arnold Rogow, *James Forrestal* (New York: Boulevard, 1963), p. 125.

2. Address of Lyndon B. Johnson, Feb. 12, 1965, quoted in the *New York Times,* Feb. 13, 1965.

3. Quoted in Ronald Steel, *Pax Americana* (New York: Viking Press, 1967), p. 3.

4. Thomas S. Power, *Design for Survival* (New York: Coward-McCann, 1964), p. 216

5. Dean Acheson, *Present at the Creation* (New York: W. W. Norton, 1969), p. 753.

6. Robert S. McNamara, Address to the American Society of Newspaper Editors, Montreal, Canada, May 8, 1966.

7. A few of the examples: Greece (1948), Iran (1953), Guatemala (1954), Indonesia (1958), Lebanon (1958), Congo (1964), British Guiana (1964), Cuba (1961), Dominican Republic (1965), Vietnam (1954–).

8. Quoted in Carl Oglesby and Richard Shaull, *Containment and Change* (New York: Macmillan, 1967), p. 30.

9. Quoted in Ronald Steel, op. cit., p. 129.

12. Military Spending and Economic Decay

Lloyd J. Dumas

INTRODUCTION

The terrible social and economic trauma of the Great Depression and the prolonged boom during and after the Second World War that finally laid it to rest, deeply imbedded an economic lesson in the American psyche: military spending stimulates production, creates employment, and generally brings prosperity. The problem with this well-learned lesson is that it is based on a combination of shoddy empiricism and poor economics, and more importantly, it is absolutely untrue.

Ultimately, the degree of material well-being generated by any economy depends not only on its ability to fully employ the productive resources (labor, capital, materials, energy, etc.) available to it, but also on its ability to employ them in ways that contribute to the societal standard of living. The production of ordinary consumer goods and services, such as food, clothing, housecleaning, barbering, etc. clearly add directly to the present material living standard. The production of producer goods and associated services, such as industrial machinery, rail transportation systems, factory buildings, supporting engineering consulting services, etc. is also contributive, but through a less direct route. This class of goods and services expands an economy's ability to produce, and by so doing enhances the supply of consumer-oriented output in the future. Hence it contributes not to the present, but to the future standard of living. There are also categories of mixed goods, i.e., both consumer and producer goods combined, the most prominent examples of which are probably education and health care. Resource use for the supply of mixed goods as well must therefore be considered productive since they augment both the present and the future standard of living.

Military-oriented production, however, falls into a wholly different category. It does not add to the supply of consumer goods or to the supply of producer goods, and so contributes to neither the present nor future material standard of living. Resources put to this use can then be said to have been diverted, i.e., channeled away from ordinary contributive use. They are not, in and of themselves, adding to material well-being.

When resources which have been idle are put to work, whether or not that work is useful, unemployment will be reduced, income will be distributed and at least the short-run appearance of prosperity will be achieved. But if those resources have been used unproductively, they will in the long term be a drain on the society. Because resources are being wasted, things which need doing will not be done, and so the economy and the wider society will suffer.

The issue of the use to which resources are put is so fundamental and so overriding in its impact on the ability of an economy to efficiently generate economically useful goods and services that economic systems as distinct as those of capitalism and communism experience similar structural problems when resources are diverted from contributive use. This is particularly true over the long run.

During the half decade or so of heavy World War II military spending in the U.S., neglect of the renewal of various types of civilian-oriented equipment and facilities (e.g. railroads, mass transit systems, industrial equipment), and neglect of civilian-oriented technological development did not create major problems. Such capital equipment is long-lived, and sizable technological leads do not typically disappear quickly. But as the substantial diversion of productive resources stretched from half a decade to three decades, severe strains and stresses did occur. And we see the effects of this sapping of our economic vitality all around us.

Neither capitalist nor socialist economies are capable of overriding negative economic effects of persistently high military spending. Differences in economic systems and circumstance, however, can and do influence the way in which the economic distress surfaces.

As will be discussed, the economic damage done by the military burden in the U.S. has surfaced mainly in the form of simultaneously high inflation and high unemployment, through the intervening variable of deteriorating productivity. In contrast, in the USSR, the damage has surfaced mainly in the form of chronic problems of supplying sufficient quantity and quality of goods and services—particularly consumer goods and services. There are two main reasons for these differences.

First, the military economy of the U.S. developed, post World War II, alongside a well-developed and booming civilian economy. In fact, the U.S. was the only major industrial nation in the world not devastated by the horrors of that war. The Soviet military economy, on the other hand, developed alongside a civilian economy massively damaged by that conflict and itself struggling hard to develop. Thus, the Soviet civilian economy was never able to work on breaking its chronic supply problems with a major, systematic, and sustained effort. On the contrary, shortages were continually made more severe by the demands of the military economy under the impetus of an escalating superpower arms race.

Second, the differences between the capitalist and communist economic systems make it easier for the latter to prevent unemployment and cope with inflation. A capitalist economy must rely on the voluntary actions of individuals seeking private economic gain (in present forms, with more or less government intervention) in order to provide employment, while relying on such private decisions, along with the impersonal mechanism of competition and governmental control of the money supply to control inflation; a communist economy, on the other hand, features direct government control of both employment opportunities and prices (though the latter tends to be somewhat more subject to external influence through rising import costs). On the other hand, incentive problems, along with ponderous bureaucratic and informational difficulties, tend to make adequate supply and coordination of supply with demand more difficult for a communist economy than for one operated by capitalist principles.

But doesn't the military contribute to the standard of living by protecting the nation and its people, i.e., by providing the consumption good "security"? Does it not therefore constitute a contributive resource use?

In the first place, the definition of "security" as a consumer good to be lumped in with all other consumer goods is yet another example of the tendency of economists to end run around sticky analytic problems by definitional manipulation, not unlike defining goods of differing quality to be different goods in order to avoid facing the difficult issues of quality measurement and competition. Security is, of course, necessary, but its production does not contribute to the material standard of living in quite the same way as does the production of cars, TVs, furniture, housing, machine tools, trucks, etc. It is, in a sense, a "necessary evil" type of activity, and as such is most usefully viewed as a burden on the directly and indirectly contributive elements of the economy. And since it is an economically painful activity, common sense would indicate that it needs to be constantly scrutinized and reviewed with an eye toward keeping it as small as possible, consistent with real security needs.

Secondly, it is not difficult to demonstrate that the stockpiling and expansion of military forces is an extremely costly and inefficient means of generating "security" at best. The lengthy U.S. experience in the Vietnam War, the ineffectiveness of military force or threat of force in countering the vast international redistribution of income and economic power from the industrialized world to the nations of OPEC, the inability of the extremely well-financed and well-supplied army of the Shah of Iran to prevail over an aroused population armed with "sticks and stones"—all of these and more should have by now taught us something about the limits of military power in protecting security interests (rightly or wrongly perceived) abroad. Furthermore, it is an undeniable fact of the nuclear age that there is not a thing the U.S. or Soviet militaries can do to protect their countries against being turned into smoldering radioactive wastelands within a couple of hours if either launches an all-out nuclear attack against the other. Is this security?

Finally, as I have argued in some detail elsewhere, the nuclear and associated forces beyond those necessary to constitute a minimal deterrent are not merely useless, but for military and technical reasons tend to substantially degrade security.[1] This is chiefly due to reliability problems interacting with excessive weaponry and associated systems to exacerbate problems of nuclear weapons accidents, accidental war, theft of weapons by hostile forces (including terrorists) and so on. Incorporating these effects into a theoretical arms race model centered on the desire of participants to maximize security further elaborates the security-reducing character of an interactive arms race.[2] This view is corroborated by the observation and arguments of such participants in the dynamics of the real world arms race as Herbert F. York, former Director of Defense Research and Engineering in the Department of Defense, and of Livermore Laboratories.[3]

But the main focus of this present analysis is not on the issue of security per se, but rather on the particular economic effects of military expenditure. And it is that question to which attention is now directed.

The fullest explication of these effects will be in the U.S. context, not because the damage is greater there or more easily understood, but simply because the relative availability of data and analysis is presently so much greater than for the USSR. Some of the analysis, however, is fairly easily translatable into the Soviet situation.

There are essentially four reasons why the maintenance of high levels of military expenditure in the U.S. during the post–World War II period has massively contributed to the generation of both inflation and unemployment. These are: (1) the economic nature of military goods; (2) the way in which military procurement has been conducted; (3) effects on the international balance of payments; and (4) effects on civilian technological progress. Each of these is now considered in turn.

THE ECONOMIC NATURE
OF MILITARY GOODS

Military goods are those products purchased by the military which are to some degree specialized to military use. Thus, tanks, rifles, bombs, fighter planes, etc. are military goods, while milk, meat, detergents, etc. purchased by the armed forces are not.

Despite the fact that military goods do not produce economic value in the sense of contribution to the material standard of living, as has been discussed, they do require valuable economic resources for their production, and therefore impose a real cost on society. This cost is best measured not purely in terms of money, but rather in terms of the sacrifice of the economically and socially useful goods and services that could have been produced with the labor, materials, energy, machinery, etc. which were instead devoted to military production.

Now, the money that flows to producers of military goods in exchange for their products is spent by the firms primarily on producer goods and by their work forces primarily on consumer goods. Thus these funds injected into the economy by the government call forth increased demand for consumer and producer goods without a corresponding increase in supply of either consumer or producer goods. The excess demand that tends to result, or put simply the situation of too many dollars chasing after too few goods, is a classic economic prescription for inflation. For example, during nearly all of the latter part of the decade of the 1960s, when the U.S. involvement in the Vietnam War was intensifying, the unemployment rate was under 4%.[4] Military spending was not offset, and between 1965 and 1969, the rate of inflation more than tripled.[5]

There were and are clearly no purely economic reasons for failing to offset expansions in military spending with higher taxation. Nor can this failure be explained by ignorance of the probably inflationary effects of failing to do so, since existing well-accepted macroeconomic theory would predict this part of the inflationary effect. Rather, this policy (or lack thereof) seems more readily attributable to a political calculation that raising taxes for the express purpose of supporting increased military activity might have quickened and heightened public opposition, particularly during Vietnam, since the economic costs of this activity would be made more explicit. So a political sleight-of-hand approach was adopted, making the public pay through increased inflation that eroded their purchasing power, rather than through direct taxation. It was a strategy that relied upon the unlikelihood that the public would directly connect the war and subsequent military expansion with the growing inflation about which they grew more and more concerned. And by all appearances, this strategy has been and still appears to be politically effective.

MILITARY PROCUREMENT PRACTICES

Care has been taken, over the years, to develop a variety of payment formulas for military contracts to provide strong incentives for military industrial firms to produce efficiently, that is, to produce products meeting the agreed upon performance specifications, adhere to agreed delivery schedules and hold costs down to a minimum. However, none of these payment formulas work. In practice, whatever the formulas formally written into major military procurement contracts, the contracts are effectively performed on a "cost plus" basis.[6]

A detailed analysis of this problem seems inappropriate here, but in essence there appear to be two main reasons why this is so. One seems to be in the fact that the formulas are designed to provide appropriate incentives for efficiency on the assumption that the firm involved is interested in maximizing profits. The incentives collapse to an essentially cost-plus situation in the case of a sales-maximizing firm. The other reason seems to be a plain and simple failure of the government to enforce the terms of the contract, an explanation that admittedly raises more questions than it answers.[7]

In any case, operating under an effectively cost-plus system, the producing firm is paid an amount equal to its total cost of production (whatever that eventually turns out to be) plus a guaranteed profit. Thus, the firm involved not only has no risk, but also has no incentive to hold its costs down. In fact, to the extent that the firm wants to increase its sales revenue, it will have a very powerful incentive to run its costs up in order to achieve the highest possible payment for its product.

Combining this incentive system with the very large amounts of money made available for military procurement year after year by the Congress has created a situation in which military industry can and does pay whatever is necessary and then some for whatever resources it needs or wants. As a result, it has bid up the price of those resources—resources like machine tools, engineers and scientists, skilled machinists, etc. To the extent that other industries require these same resources, they now face increased costs and hence feel pressed to raise their prices. Thus a cost-push inflationary pressure is fed throughout not only the military sector, but the entire economy.

Aside from its direct inflationary effects on resource costs, the purchasing power of defense firms, backed by their rich customer (the Federal Government), has completely preempted a substantial amount of some of these resources, with serious long-term effects on the health of the civilian economy.

For example, by crude and conservative estimate nearly one-third of all the engineers and scientists in the United States have been engaged in defense-related work (discussed below). This can be taken as a lower limit on the true figure. It seems more likely that the figure is higher, perhaps as high as one-half. Whether the actual figure is one-third or one-half, the crucial point is that a great deal of the nation's technological talent has been diverted to the development of military and military-related technology. The pre-emption by the military of such a large fraction of what we will subsequently see is a critical resource in a modern industrial society cannot fail to have significant effects on the functioning of that part of the economy that produces goods and services which, unlike military goods, do contribute to the standard of living and the quality of life. Furthermore, it is important to understand that this magnitude of preemption of technological resources has been maintained for two to three decades or more. But full discussion of the implications of this preemption will be deferred for now.

Thus directly through its effects on bidding up certain resource costs and less directly though more powerfully by its preemption of key resources from the civilian economy, the free-spending procurement practices of military industry have contributed importantly to the ongoing inflation.

INTERNATIONAL
BALANCE-OF-PAYMENTS EFFECTS

From 1893 through 1970, year by year the U.S. had a *balance of trade* surplus, i.e. the U.S. exported a greater value of goods and services than it imported. Since exports bring foreign currency into the U.S., while imports send U.S. dollars abroad, if this had been the only aspect of the U.S. international transactions, there would have been a considerable accumulation of foreign currencies (or gold) in the U.S., and comparative shortage of U.S. dollars abroad. Consequently, by 1971 the U.S. dollar would have been one of the strongest (if not the strongest) currencies in the world. Instead, in 1971 the U.S. dollar was officially devalued, in formal recognition of its declining worth relative to key foreign currencies. How could this seeming paradox occur?

The *balance of payments,* the total net figure of international currency flows, includes not only money flows related to trade, but all other international money flows as well (e.g. foreign investments in the U.S., profits flowing from U.S. subsidiaries abroad into the U.S., foreign aid, etc.). And the U.S. balance of payments has been in continuous deficit for decades now.

What role has U.S. military expenditure played in this situation? It has affected the U.S. international economic position directly through outflows of dollars for defense expenditures abroad, and indirectly through its effects on the balance of trade, chiefly via its influence on the competitiveness of U.S. civilian industries in domestic and foreign markets. This latter effect is extremely important and will be discussed in detail subsequently.

Table 1 presents some basic U.S. Department of Commerce data which bear on the direct effects of military expenditures abroad and on the U.S. international financial situation. We note that the entire cumulative balance-of-payments deficit for the period 1969–1970 (inclusive) was $35 billion, whereas over the same period, total direct defense expenditures (net after military sales abroad) were more than $30 billion. Hence, *U.S. military expenditures abroad accounted for 86.6% of the entire U.S. balance-of-payments deficit during that period.*

During the years 1955–1970 (inclusive) there was a huge inflow of foreign currencies into the U.S., represented by a cumulative balance of trade surplus of nearly $62 billion. But during those same years, net military expenditures abroad were responsible for an outflow of dollars from the U.S. amounting to more than $43 billion. *The outflow of U.S. currency owing to military spending abroad thus wiped out 69.9% of the balance-of-trade surplus, 1955–1970.*

These comparisons greatly understate the magnitude of U.S. defense expenditures abroad, because they do not include outright U.S. grants of military goods and services. Since they involve no international flows of currency, these gifts of military equipment and services are not involved in the balance of money flows. However, if included, the total of almost $34 billion worth of such grants recorded during the years 1960–1974 would increase the military expenditure figures given for that period by more than 80%.

It is clear from these data that direct outflows of dollars in the form of U.S. military expenditures abroad played a major role in destroying the favorable balance-of-trade surplus, and contributed to the severe weakening of the U.S. dollar. This substantially raised the price of imported goods (including oil) upon which the nation's business and consumers have become increasingly dependent in the past few years. Even when an imported product has not had a price increase in terms of its native currency, the declining value of the dollar relative to that currency will result in a rising dollar price. Insofar as consumer goods are directly imported then from countries against whose currency the dollar is weakening, this will contribute straightforwardly to domestic inflation. When industrial goods and resources are imported the effect of a failing dollar in raising their prices will result in a broad cost-push pressure on all U.S. industries using these goods and resources (and there are many, many such industries). To the extent that this pressure cannot be offset (a phenomenon that will be discussed shortly), rising prices of these domestically produced goods will result, further exacerbating inflation. Thus, the massive outflow of military spending abroad has directly and substantially contributed to the generation of inflation within the domestic U.S. economy.

But what of the huge increases in international oil prices in recent years? Has this, rather than the military, not been the major cause of

Table 1. U.S. military expenditures abroad and the inter-national balance of payments.

Year[1]	Balance of Trade[2] ($millions)	Balance of Payments[3] ($millions)	Net Direct Defense Expenditures Abroad[4] ($millions)
1955	2,897	--	2,501
1956	4,753	--	2,627
1957	6,271	--	2,466
1958	3,462	--	2,835
1959	1,148	--	2,503
1960	4,892	-3,667	2,752
1961	5,571	-2,252	2,596
1962	4,521	-2,864	2,449
1963	5,224	-2,713	2,304
1964	6,801	-2,696	2,133
1965	4,951	-2,478	2,122
1966	3,817	-2,151	2,935
1967	3,800	-4,683	3,226
1968	635	-1,611	3,143
1969	607	-6,081	3,328
1970	2,603	-3,851	3,354
1971	-2,268	-21,965	2,893
1972	-6,409	-13,829	3,621
1973	955	-7,651	2,316
1974	-5,528	-19,043	2,159
TOTAL	48,703		54,263

Notes: 1. Problems of data availability and comparability complicate a more complete analysis over the entire post World War II period.
2. Exports-imports, merchandise, adjusted excluding military (minus implies deficit).
3. Net liquidity balance (minus implies deficit).
4. Direct defense expenditures - military sales (does not include military grants of goods and services).

Sources: Bureau of Economic Analysis, U.S. Department of Commerce, Business Statistics (1973), pp. 13-14, and Survey of Current Business (June 1975), pp. 26, 30.

the international weakening of the dollar and its corresponding inflationary effects?

A simple look at the sequence of events is sufficient to demonstrate that neither the international breaking of the value of the dollar nor the high inflation/high unemployment economy of the U.S. could have been initiated by the actions of the Organization of Petroleum Exporting Countries (OPEC). In the first place, the U.S. has been suffering from unprecedented simultaneous high inflation/high unemployment every year since 1969. Secondly, the dollar was officially devalued for the first time in modern U.S. history in 1971. But the OPEC oil embargo and the subsequent huge increases in oil prices did not even occur until late 1973!

That is not to say that the OPEC oil price escalation has not contributed significantly to the piling up of dollars abroad and to the U.S. general economic woes. Certainly, it has had an important exacerbating effect, particularly in conjunction with the progressive loss of cost-offsetting capability by U.S. industries, a phenomenon clearly and importantly related to the military drain on the nation's civilian economy (as will be discussed in detail). But the chronology makes it obvious that it could not have been the fundamental cause of these problems.

IMPACT OF MILITARY SPENDING
ON CIVILIAN TECHNOLOGY
AND THE IMPLICATIONS THEREOF

Allocation of Scientific and Engineering Resources to Military-Oriented Activity. Since the beginning of the Second World War and with substantially more force since the latter half of the 1950s, the United States has channeled a large fraction of the nation's engineering and scientific resources into military-related research. Some of this has been direct, through priority allocation of Federal Government grants for these purposes; and some has been indirect, through the utilization of a considerable portion of the annual discretionary federal budget for purchase of increasingly technologically sophisticated weapons and related systems whose research, development, and production required military industrial firms to hire large quantities of technologists.

According to National Science Foundation (NSF) data, over the entire decade of the 1970s, the fraction of yearly Federal budget obligations for research and development going to the military and space programs averaged more than two-thirds of the total. More than half of this money was channeled to the military alone.[8] Looked at from another angle, as of the mid-1970s, 77% of the nation's research and development engineers and scientists (excluding social scientists) who received Federal support received it from the Department of Defense (DOD), National Aeronautics and Space Administration (NASA) and the Atomic Energy Commission (AEC)—again more than 50% from the DOD alone.[9] Nearly three-quarters of the engineers and scientists employed by business and industry who received federal support in that year received it from the same three agencies.[10]

Estimation of the fraction of the nation's total engineering and scientific talent engaged in military-related research is quite a bit more tortuous a task than it should be, primarily because publicly available data are not categorized in such a manner as to expedite this effort. For instance, published NSF data on characteristics of the nation's engineering and scientific employment for 1974 contains a table entitled, "Number of Scientists and Engineers by Field, Highest Degree and Critical National Interest."[11]

Though some ten categories of "critical national interest" are listed, ranging from "health," "food," "housing," etc. to "space," military work or its standard euphemism "national defense" is *not* one of them. Apparently, the NSF does not consider national defense a "critical national interest." Not surprisingly, the two miscellaneous categories in the table, labeled "does not apply" and "no report," which must therefore contain the bulk of the military-related engineers and scientists, constitute more than 57% of the total.

While the making of an accurate, up-to-date estimate of the military sector preemption of scientific and engineering talent, given this obfuscation, would be an involved and arduous task without access to primary data, it is possible to produce reasonable and fairly conservative rough estimates by manipulating some of the published data for the mid-1970s (most recent, at this writing). For example, if one assumes that only half of the engineers and scientists falling into the two miscellaneous categories of the NSF's "critical national interest" table just discussed are engaged in military work (n.b. ten major categories of national interest have already been explicitly subtracted), an estimate just under 30% of the total national pool of engineers and scientists results, whether the calculation is done with or without social scientists, and whether or not personnel with less than a bachelor's degree are included. Adding in the numbers explicitly listed for "space" research raises the fraction to just above 33%.

The estimate can be approached from another angle by extracting the numbers of full-time equivalent R&D scientists and engineers for three major military-oriented industry categories "electrical equipment and communication," "aircraft and missiles" and "machinery" from NSF data for 1967.[12] Assuming that roughly two-thirds of the R&D engineers and scientists in the first two industries and only one-quarter of those in the third industry are engaged in military-related work, and *ignoring all* other industries completely (industries *ignored* would include tank production, ordinance, nuclear submarines, etc.) results in an estimate of just under 33% for military-oriented engineering and scientific industrial R&D employment.

Though it is inappropriate to rely heavily on the accuracy of estimates so crudely developed, it would appear likely that an important fraction of the engineering and scientific personnel in the U.S. have been devoting their talents to the development of military-oriented technology, and unlikely that the fraction would be substantially less than one-third. In all probability, it is far higher. And in any case, it is important to remember that this magnitude of preemption of technological resources has been maintained for two to three decades or more.

Impact on Civilian-Oriented Technological Development. The kind of new technological knowledge that will ultimately emerge from any given research or development project will, of course, not be wholly predictable in advance. By definition, the researchers are engaged in a quest for new knowledge, and such explorations of the unknown and untried must always involve uncertainty and a degree of unpredictability. However, even while not wholly determinate, the kind of new technical knowledge developed is very strongly conditioned by the nature of the problems being studied and the type of solutions being sought. Since one-third or more of the nation's engineers and scientists have been seeking military-oriented solutions to military-oriented problems for the past several decades, it should be no surprise that the development of military technology has proceeded at a rapid pace in the U.S.—or that the development of civilian-oriented technology has become severely retarded here. How could it have been otherwise?

The much vaunted "spinoff" or "spillover" argument that military-oriented technological development produces massive improvements in areas of civilian application and thus does not retard civilian technological progress, makes very little conceptual sense, and more to the point, is massively contradicted by straightforward empirical observation. Of course, some transferability of technical knowledge between military and civilian application would be expected (in both directions), but conceptually it is difficult to see how directing attention to one area of technical research would routinely produce an *efficient* generation of knowledge pertaining to a completely different area.

On the empirical side, a 1974 report of a committee of the National Academy of Engineering stated:

With a few exceptions the vast technology developed by Federally funded programs since World War II has not resulted in widespread "spinoffs" of secondary or additional applications of practical products, processes and services that have made an impact on the nation's economic growth, industrial productivity, employment gains and foreign trade.[13]

The seventh annual report of the National Science Board, governing body of the National Science Foundation (*Science Indicators: 1974*) expressed concern over the serious erosion of the U.S. predominance in science and technology. In several international comparisons the empirical indicators behind this concern were detailed:

The "patent balance" of the United States fell by about 30% between 1966 and 1973. . . . The decline was due to an increasing number of U.S. patents awarded to foreign countries and a decline (in 1973) in the number of foreign patents awarded to U.S. citizens. Overall, foreign patenting increased in the United States during the period by over 65%, and by 1973 represented more than 30% of all U.S. patents granted. This suggests that the number of patentable ideas of international merit has been growing at a greater rate in other countries than in the United States.[14]

Further, the report describes the relative production of a total of 492 major innovations by the U.S., the U.K., Japan, West Germany, and France over the twenty-year period from 1953-1973:

The U.S. lead . . . declined steadily from the late 1950s to the mid-1960s, falling from 82 to 55% of the innovations. The slight upturn in later years represents a relative rather than an absolute gain, and results primarily from a decline in the proportion of innovations produced in the United Kingdom, rather than an increase in the number of U.S. innovations.[15]

More recently, the NSF's *Science Indicators: 1978* (National Science Board, 1979) points to a continuation of these downtrends, the foreign origin share of total U.S. patents having increased further from 30% in 1973 to 36% in 1977.[16] Furthermore, this high total share of foreign origin patents is clearly not the result of growing foreign success in only one or two areas. "Foreign patents account for between one-third and one-half of all U.S. patents across a wide spectrum of fields."[17] The NSF goes on to point out:

U.S. patenting has decreased abroad as well as at home. . . . From 1966 to 1976, U.S. patenting activity abroad declined almost 30% in ten industrialized countries. . . . The decline in U.S. patenting abroad could be attributable to a number of factors, including . . . a relative decline in the U.S. inventive activity.[18]

The relatively poor showing of the U.S. is even more remarkable considering that these data do not specifically exclude military-related technology and hence are biased in favor of the U.S. It is interesting to note that in these comparisons, Japan and West Germany did quite well.

Since 1963, inventors from West Germany have received the largest number of foreign origin U.S. patents (83,220). In fact, among U.S. foreign-origin patents, West Germany was first in 11 of the 15 major product fields and second in the remaining 4. . . .
   Japan ranks second in the number of total U.S. patents granted to foreign investors between 1963 and 1977 (61,510). Japan has the largest number of foreign patents in three product groups . . . and is second in an additional five categories. . . . Since 1970, Japan has dramatically increased its patent activity by over 100% in every product field except the two areas in which it already had a large concentration of patents. This finding is significant in that it seems

to dispute the widespread belief that Japanese R&D efforts are narrowly focused on specific technologies.[19]

Not so coincidentally, these two countries averaged about 4% (Japan, 1961–1975) and 20% (West Germany, 1961–1967) of government R&D expenditures on defense and space, as opposed to a U.S. average of about 70% (1961–1977).[20]

In a conceptually related comparison Michael Boretsky of the U.S. Department of Commerce presents data bearing on the relative civilian equivalent R&D effort (allowing for 10% spinoff from defense and space R&D) of the U.S., six European countries, Canada, and Japan in the 1960s.[21] In terms of R&D employment, Japan shows a civilian R&D effort nearly three times as intense as that for the U.S., and West Germany ranks some 60% higher than the U.S.; in fact, only Italy and Canada rank lower.

Furthermore, again using absolute numbers of patents granted as a measure of technological progress, and looking at the U.S. industrial technology situation overall, the NSF finds:

The total number of patents granted annually to U.S. inventors generally increased from 1960 to the early 1970s but showed a steady decline from 1971 to 1977. . . . Complex influences on the level of patenting make analysis of patent data difficult. . . . In the present case, since patenting has dropped in almost all product fields, the trends seem to indicate a real decline in the rate of production of inventions by U.S. industry from 1971 to 1977.[22]

Recognition of the serious retardation of civilian technological progress is also widespread in the nation's business community. In 1976 (February 26), *Business Week* ran an article entitled "The Breakdown of U.S. Innovation," the introduction of which included the phrase "from boardroom to research lab there is a growing sense that something has happened to U.S. innovation." Apparently that "sense" continued to grow, because by July 3, 1978, the story had made the cover of that journal. The article, entitled "Vanishing Innovation," began, "a grim mood prevails today among industrial research managers. America's vaunted technological superiority of the 1950s and 1960s is vanishing." The government also clearly recognized that a severe problem existed, as the Carter Administration ordered a massive, 18-month long, 28-agency domestic policy review of the influence of the government on industrial innovation.

Given the huge amounts of money and technical personnel which have indisputably been poured into military-related research over the past several decades in the U.S., the severity of the slowdown in civilian technological progress would not have occurred if the "spinoff" or "spillover" effects had been anything more than marginal. But if the transferability of invention and innovation was and is actually low, then the decades long diversion of at least a third of the engineers and scientists in the U.S. to military-related work would predictably have produced precisely the sort of civilian technological deterioration we have, in fact, experienced. Under conditions of low transferability it could not have failed to produce such a result.

Civilian Technological Progress and Productivity Growth. It is widely recognized that civilian technological progress is the keystone of productivity improvement and economic growth. As the National Science Board put it in their 1977 annual report (*Science Indicators: 1976*),

the contribution of R&D to economic growth and productivity is positive, significant and high, and that such innovation is an important factor—perhaps the most important factor—in the economic growth of the United States in this century.

According to Boretsky of the Commerce Department,

The most relevant historical evidence suggests that American technology reached parity with Europe by 1870 or thereabout . . . and by the end of World War II it had become a literal "wonder" to the rest of the world. . . . The present concern is not with the country's technology relevant to defense and the conquest of space which occupied the last two decades, but with technology relevant to the quality of life in society at large as well as more specifically, productivity and commercial markets at home and abroad.[23]

Civilian technological progress is that which is oriented to the development of knowledge leading to improved consumer and producer products and to more efficient ways of producing. These two aspects, new and better products and improved production methods, are not so distinct as it might seem, since a major source of increase in productive efficiency is the employment of new machinery and equipment embodying superior technology.

Civilian technological progress contributes to the growth of labor productivity by encouraging increases in the quantity of capital per worker and to the growth of both labor and capital productivity through the development of production techniques enabling the more efficient use of productive resources in general. Accordingly, as the development of civilian technology became increasingly retarded in the U.S., productivity growth began to collapse.

From 1947 to 1975, output per hour grew at an average annual rate of 3.3% in the nonfarm business sector of the U.S., according to the Council of Economic Advisors. From 1965 to 1978, that rate of labor productivity growth was cut in half, averaging 1.6% per year. In recent years the United States has had the lowest rate of productivity growth of any major noncommunist economy. Furthermore, the productivity growth collapse is accelerating. While the annual growth rate for 1965–1973 averaged 2.1%, from 1973–1978 it was 0.8%. In the first six months of

1979, output per labor-hour in the private business sector actually *fell* at an annual rate of 3.3%. During the second quarter of 1979, "productivity fell at an annual rate of 5.7%, the largest quarterly decline ever recorded in this series of statistics, which began in 1947."[24]

Boretsky presents an international comparison bearing on both capital and labor productivity growth among major industrial countries in two periods, 1955–1965 and 1965–1971. The results of his calculations are presented in Table 2. The performance of the U.S. is abysmal, both relative to its own historical performance, and relative to other nations. In the latter period, its labor productivity growth is the lowest of any nation compared, and only the United Kingdom shows a lower capital productivity growth ratio. Note particularly that the West German and Japanese performance is once again strong relative to the U.S. and other nations in the latter period, particularly in terms of labor productivity.

The fact of the productivity collapse is so overwhelming as to no longer be a matter of dispute. But its cause is still the source of much confusion and consternation. An article in the October 19, 1979, issue of *Science* by John Walsh bore witness to this situation. Its title and subtitle were: "Productivity Problems Trouble Economy—Everybody talks about the lag in the growth of productivity but nobody seems to know enough to do much about it." In the course of the article a number of candidates for cause of the productivity problem are cited: "Some economists assign major blame . . . to a shift to a 'service' economy"; "the recent rise in energy costs"; "the increase in government regulation"; "changing attitudes among workers . . . a new devotion to leisure and relaxation" (a euphemistic way of stating the lazy worker hypothesis); even sexist, "the labor force has become increasingly inexperienced because of an influx of women" and racist, "the transformation of the U.S. economy is proceeding in the direction taken by the British rather than the Japanese. Anglo-Saxon attitudes may produce a less pressured, less competitive way of life." All these explanations have been given some credence.

The service sector argument is easily dismissed by the fact that productivity growth in U.S. manufacturing (i.e., excluding services) has been undergoing a similar pattern of deterioration. From 1947 to 1964, the average annual rate of productivity increase in U.S. manufacturing was 4.1%; from 1965 to 1975 the average annual rate had dropped by more than half to under 1.7% per year. As cited in the Walsh article referred to above, Victor Fuchs of the National Bureau of Economic Research has estimated that the growth of the service sector contributed only about 0.1% to the decline in productivity from the 1960s to the 1970s. Fuchs further estimates a similar extremely small contribution to the influx of women.

Edward F. Denison, a senior fellow at the Brookings Institution and a noted authority on productivity and economic growth has examined in detail and rejected a whole series of commonly offered explanations

Table 2. International comparison relevant to labor and capital productivity performance, selected countries.

Country	Labor Productivity (% average annual growth in GNP per civilian employed)		Capital Productivity Ratio* (% average annual growth in GNP/year ÷ % average annual growth in fixed nonresidential investment)	
	1955-65	1965-71	1955-65 to 1953-63	1965-71 to 1963-69
United States	2.2	1.3	1.13	0.50
France	5.1	4.8	0.51	0.75
West Germany	4.5	4.3	0.56	0.80
Belgium-Luxembourg	2.7	3.7	0.59	0.85
Netherlands	3.1	4.3	0.62	0.63
Italy	5.6	5.5	0.63	4.42
United Kingdom	2.1	2.8	0.46	0.44
Canada	1.9	1.8	1.43	0.80
Japan	8.0	9.6	0.65	0.79
USSR	3.5	3.6	0.67	0.70

Source: Boretsky, M., "Trends in U.S. Technology: A Political Economist's View," *American Scientist* (January/February 1975), p. 72.

*Note: A two-year lag for the effects of new investment is assumed.

for the productivity problems as being responsible for too small a fraction of the decline to have real significance. These include stiffer environmental regulations, increased government paperwork, lazy workers, declining Yankee ingenuity, etc.[25]

On the matter of research and development, Walsh points out, "in the past, a belief that spending on R&D led to innovation was widely, rather uncritically held in the U.S. and used as blanket justification for government support of R&D. The view came to be considered as oversimplified both outside and inside government, and spending on R&D by government declined."[26] Denison argues that cuts in research and development spending are incapable of explaining the productivity drop. On the other hand, Edwin Mansfield of the University of Pennsylvania, another noted authority on productivity and in particular its relation to R&D has stated, reflecting on 20 years of economic studies, "Research and development seems to have had a very significant effect on the rate of productivity growth in the industries and time periods that have been studied."[27]

The fact is technological development does have an extremely important effect on productivity growth, *if* it is civilian technological development oriented to such a purpose. One cannot hope to see, and therefore cannot hope to understand, the fundamental role of failing technological progress in producing this present and ongoing productivity deterioration in the U.S. until a clear and precise distinction is made between civilian and military related technological development. For it is most assuredly not the failure of technology as a whole that has produced our present productivity problems—the U.S. scientific and engineering community is not becoming less ingenious or less productive. Rather the collapse is a direct, inevitable though long-term result of the decades-long diversion of a large fraction of the nation's critical scientific and engineering effort from productive civilian-oriented technological development.

Productivity Growth, Inflation, and Unemployment. The improvement in productivity plays a crucial role in the countering of inflationary pressures, for it is sustained productivity growth that offsets the effects of rising input costs. It is not the separate cost of labor, fuels, materials, and capital that is relevant to the determination of product price, but rather the combined cost of these productive resources *per unit* of product. Thus, the rise in labor costs, for example, might be at least partially offset by substituting cheaper capital for increasingly expensive labor, or by organizing production to use labor more efficiently, or both. As long as the net result is to produce more output per unit of input, rises in input costs need not be fully translated into rises in the cost per unit of product. Correspondingly, the upward "cost-push" pressures on price will be mitigated. But productivity is nothing more than a measure of output per unit input. Hence rising productivity permits absorption of rising prices of labor, fuels, etc. without full reflection of these resource cost increases in unit cost and thus in price.

It is therefore clear that the deterioration of productivity growth will substantially compromise this cost offsetting capability. In the absence of strong productivity improvement, rising costs of labor, fuels, etc. will be translated into rising product prices. As this occurs over a whole series of industries, a self-reinforcing rise in the general level of prices or "inflation" occurs.

The mid-1960s was the breakpoint for the growth of manufacturing productivity in the U.S. It should therefore also have been the point of shift for cost behavior in U.S. manufacturing industry from traditional "cost offsetting" or "cost minimizing" behavior to the sort of "cost pass-along" or "cost indifferent" behavior just described—behavior in which input cost increases are simply translated or "passed along" into product price increases. A first empirical investigation of the possibility of this shift in modal cost behavior was performed by Byung Hong, in doctoral research at Columbia University.[28] Hong developed a simple multiple regression model consisting of one price equation and one wage equation which he fit to quarterly data for U.S. manufacturing for two periods: 1948 (second quarter) to 1964 (fourth quarter) and 1965 (first quarter) to 1975 (second quarter).

In the price equation, the percentage change in wholesale prices was said to depend upon the percentage changes in wages and raw materials costs moderated by changes in productivity, the level of capacity utilization (as a measure of demand pressure) and profit rates. Under conditions of cost offsetting behavior, the change in productivity would be expected to have a strong negative effect, as pressure was applied to improve productive efficiency in response to rising input costs, whereas under cost pass-along, productivity growth would not be expected to have any significant impact on price increase. On the other hand, profit rate would have little effect on price under cost offsetting as compared to a clear positive effect under cost indifference, since profits are maintained or increased to a much greater extent by expansion of productivity in the former and by increase in price in the latter case. Furthermore, high capacity utilization would tend to lead to higher prices under cost offsetting ("demand pull") but *lower* prices under cost indifference because of lowered fixed cost per unit). Essentially all of the cost offset expectations are statistically supported in the earlier time period, and nearly all the expectations for cost indifference in the later time span.

In the wage equation, productivity change represents wage demand justification, past profits are wage demand targets, past consumer price inflation rates represent pressure for higher wages, and the unemployment rate is a kind of bargaining power variable. Under traditional cost offsetting behavior, the unemployment rate would be expected to have a significantly negative effect on wages, reflecting the Phillips curve type tradeoff, while no particular effect on wage increase would be expected under cost pass-along (since the source of inflation has nothing to do with demand pull pressures reflected in the unemployment rate). The consumer price variable would be stronger under cost pass-along than under cost offset as both rates of inflation and the price change expectations they generate are high and rising. All else held constant, a given increment in productivity growth might well have a larger effect on wage increase in a cost indifferent than in a cost offsetting environment because productivity growth would be so much weaker in such a period (a sort of decreasing marginal returns to productivity growth in terms of generating wage increases?). In any case, again nearly all of the expectations for cost offsetting behavior are statistically observed in the earlier period, and nearly all of the expectations for cost pass-along behavior are observed in the latter period, thus reinforcing the price equation results.

As the managements of U.S. industrial firms learned that cost indifference or pass-along was a viable behavior, the incentives for the kind of internal vigilance necessary for cutting edge cost minimization were mitigated. And so, the decline of productivity growth was further exacerbated, reinforcing the shift to cost pass-along.

The implications of the productivity induced shift of modal cost behavior for stagflation are straightforward. As cost indifference became the order of the day, input cost increases were more and more rapidly and strongly translated into output price increases. And of course, via the usual wage price spiral augmented by external input cost increases (e.g. OPEC oil price actions) themselves perhaps partly engendered by output inflation, the process was made more severe. This has been a powerful inflationary engine. But the same mechanism has also generated unemployment.

As the prices of U.S.-produced goods rose higher and higher, the nation's industry became less and less competitive vis-à-vis foreign competition. Overseas markets were lost and the U.S. export position weakened. Domestic markets were lost to foreign production and the U.S. import position worsened. The progressive loss of markets induced cutbacks in U.S.-based production with high unemployment rates the result. And this problem was exacerbated by the flight of U.S.-owned production facilities to cheap labor havens abroad, as one logical response to the inability to offset higher costs in the U.S. because of the productivity failure. It is thus preeminently the declining competitiveness of U.S. industry resulting from decreasing productivity growth that has generated unemployment even in the face of high product demand.

Productivity growth thus is "the economic linchpin of the 1980s," as the Joint Economic Committee of the Congress described it in its mid-1979 analysis of prospects for the economy. Its warning that, as the *New York Times* put it, "The average American is likely to see his standard of living drastically reduced in the 1980s unless productivity growth is accelerated"[29] is precisely correct.

During the entire decade of the 1970s the dynamic process of deterioration which has been described here has produced the unprecedented simultaneous high inflation/high unemployment that has become a fact of our economic life. For an entire decade, the inflation rate has averaged near 7% at the same time the unemployment rate has averaged more than 6%.

The current military buildup being proposed by the Reagan Administration is, as Lester Thurow has pointed out, three times as large as that which took place during the Vietnam War. And it is taking place in a context of a much weaker domestic economy than that of the 1960s, counterposed against the economic strength of our chief economic adversaries (who are at the same time our military allies). In Thurow's words,

> When a nation such as the U.S. sharply increases its military forces, it generally does so at a time when its industrial competitors are also attempting to increase their own military establishments, and are experiencing comparable economic strains. But the Reagan buildup is to take place in a time when our allies are not raising their military expenditures at anything like our pace.... This difference poses the problem of how the U.S. can maintain the industrial strength to compete with other countries in civilian production and sales.[30]

The economic prognosis for the coming decade is not good. If the arms race continues unabated, and we somehow manage to survive, these rates of inflation and unemployment—rates that were viewed as horrific at the beginning of the 1970s—may well look like economic good times compared to what will be commonplace by the end of the 1980s.

As damaging as the persistence of high levels of military spending has been to the domestic economy, and as dependent economic revitalization might be on a reversal of this situation, it is nevertheless true that the process of transition to a more fully civilian-oriented economy must be handled carefully. Producing a smooth economic conversion requires a clear understanding of the nature of the multifaceted transition problem. The solution to that problem lies at the core of the political economic strategy that is a key prerequisite to the linked process of reversing the present economic decay, particularly in the U.S. and USSR, and achieving real, meaningful arms reduction.

NOTES

1. Lloyd J. Dumas, "National Insecurity in the Nuclear Age," *Bulletin of the Atomic Scientists* (May 1976), and "Human Fallibility and Weapons," *Bulletin of the Atomic Scientists* (November 1980).

2. Lloyd J. Dumas, "Armament, Disarmament and National Security: A Theoretical Duopoly Model of the Arms Race," *Journal of Economic Studies* (May 1979).

3. Herbert F. York, *Race to Oblivion: A Participant's View of the Arms Race* (New York: Simon & Schuster, 1970). See especially Chapter 12.

4. Bureau of Economic Analysis, U.S. Department of Commerce, *Business Statistics* (1973), p. 69.

5. Ibid., p. 40.

6. For example, the Air Force's C5A transport plane, which experienced a $2 billion cost overrun (i.e., excess of actual cost over original cost estimates) was produced under a firm "fixed price" contract. Payment was simply adjusted upward to cover the overrun. Thus, the fixed price was fixed in name only. A number of fascinating "insider's" accounts of the operation of military procurement are available that document in detail these practices. Two such accounts are: *The High Priests of Waste* (New York: W. W. Norton, 1972) by A. Ernest Fitzgerald, former Air Force Deputy for Management Systems in the Pentagon (this includes much detail on the C5A); and *Arming America: How the U.S. Buys Weapons* (Boston: Harvard University Press, 1974) by J. Ronald Fox, former Assistant Secretary of the Army (for procurement).

7. Lloyd J. Dumas, "Payment Functions and the Productive Efficiency of Military Industrial Firms," *Journal of Economic Issues* (June 1976).

8. National Science Board, National Science Foundation, *Science Indicators: 1978* (Washington, D.C.: Government Printing Office, 1979), p. 182.

9. National Science Foundation, Surveys of Science Resources Series, *Characteristics of the National Sample of Scientists and Engineers: 1974, Part 2: Employment,* Table B-16 (pp. 128-142).

10. Ibid., Table B-15 (pp. 113-127).

11. Ibid., Table B-10 (pp. 85-89).

12. National Science Foundation, "Full-Time Equivalent Number of R&D Scientists and Engineers, by Industry and Source of Funds for R&D Projects: January, 1975, and January, 1976" (Table 93).

13. National Academy of Engineering Committee on Technology Transfer and Utilization, "Technology Transfer and Utilization, Recommendations for Reducing the Emphasis and Correcting the Imbalance" (Washington, D.C.: National Academy, 1974), p. i.

14. National Science Board, National Science Foundation, *Science Indicators: 1974* (Washington, D.C.: Government Printing Office, 1976), p. 17.

15. Ibid., p. 19.

16. NSF, *Science Indicators: 1978,* p. 2.

17. Ibid., p. 18.

18. Ibid., pp. 20-21.

19. Ibid., pp. 19-20.

20. Ibid., pp. 146-147.

21. Michael Boretsky, "Trends in U.S. Technology: A Political Economist's View," *American Scientist* (Janurary/February 1975), p. 76.

22. NSF, *Science Indicators: 1978,* pp. 78-79.

23. Boretsky, p. 70.

24. Clyde H. Farnsworth, "Lag in Productivity Called Major Peril to Living Standard," *New York Times,* August 13, 1979.

25. Edward F. Denison, *Accounting for Slower Economic Growth: The U.S. in the 1970's* (Washington, D.C.: Brookings Institution, 1979).

26. John Walsh, "Productivity Problems Trouble Economy," *Science* (October 19, 1979), p. 311.

27. Ibid.

28. Byung Hong, *Inflation Under Cost Pass-Along Management* (New York: Praeger, 1979).

29. Farnsworth, op. cit.

30. Lester Thurow, "How to Wreck the Economy," *New York Review of Books* (May 14, 1981).

13. Nuclear Weapons and the End of Democracy

Richard A. Falk

In this essay, my concern is with the *structural relevance* of nuclear weaponry and strategy to the future of democracy. The central contention is that the existence of nuclear weapons, even without any occurrence of nuclear war, interferes with democratic governance in fundamental ways. In other words, we don't have to wait for Armageddon to begin paying the price, as measured by the quality of democracy, for a system of international security constructed around the central imagery of nuclear deterrence. To presume this relevance of nuclear armaments and doctrines to democracy is itself somewhat unusual. For instance, one searches in vain the pages of the Trilateral Commission's notorious study, *The Crisis of Democracy,* for any reference to the erosion of democratic governance as a consequence of "the nuclear revolution"; the Trilateralists' idea of "crisis" is based on the alleged erosion of authority and stability through the undisciplined tactics of social movements demanding reform that surfaced in the late 1960s, a phenomenon described elsewhere in positive terms as the beginnings of a participatory model of democratic revitalization.[1] In the background, of course, is a concern about the preconditions for capitalist efficiency under contemporary conditions, including a fear that the work ethic, achievement syndrome, and greed impulse are being drained away by cultural developments, including a substantially alienated intelligentsia in so-called mature capitalist countries.[2]

The nuclear weapons question is inserted on the orthodox agenda of liberal democracy in a dramatically perverse way by David Gompert, overseer of an influential study, *Nuclear Weapons and World Politics,* a product of the 1980s Project of the Council on Foreign Relations. Gompert writes:

In the long run, the existence of nuclear weapons could fundamentally alter government-citizen relations. If, over time, the need of governments to field expansive deterrent forces is not appreciated by citizens who no longer sense a real nuclear threat, popular support for the maintenance of forces could fade— *and governments might feel themselves compelled to provide for deterrence without the consent of the governed.*[3]

Evident in this remarkable passage of unsurpassed reification, is a presumed priority being accorded "the government" on nuclear military policy over and against the possible opposition of "the citizenry." Democracy is turned on its head, not out of any alleged emergency that prevents either consultation or the participation of representative institutions, but because the perceptions of "the rulers" are favored over the adverse will of "the people" in an area of disagreement. Such a realistic vision of what has already become standard operating procedure throughout the nuclear age raises to the level of explicit ideology the dire impact of nuclear weaponry upon democratic governance.

Daniel Ellsberg, a former government official with responsibility in the nuclear policy area, confirms the extent to which American presidents were prepared to use nuclear weapons in non-defensive roles and far beyond what the American people were ever allowed to understand. He writes:

When I did most of my working plans in '59, '60, and '61, . . . I assumed that I was reading basically retaliatory plans. . . . The generals knew better. They knew that these plans were not at all for retaliation because, on the contrary, the Russians had no ability to strike first. So all these plans were really initiative plans, first-strike plans.

And, then, more concretely:

What I discovered, going back to Truman who made such threats in 1950, is that every team of every president has seen the serious recommendation by the Joint Chiefs of Staff of plans involving the initiation of nuclear warfare under certain circumstances. More significantly, at least four Presidents have secretly authorized advanced preparations for such first-use, or have actually threatened adversaries with U.S. first-use in an ongoing crisis.[4]

Ellsberg has documented these assertions thereby suggesting that political leaders in the United States have failed throughout the nuclear age to consult with, or disclose to, the public the occasions on which the use of nuclear weapons was seriously contemplated. In this sense, the government's refusal to accept notions of public accountability in the nuclear domain has been consistent and bipartisan.

In one of the few attempts at a systematic discussion of the relevance of nuclear weapons to the constitutional processes of the United States, Michael Mandlebaum considers their impact largely as a matter of adding an "enormous responsibility" to the presidency and of producing an unavoidable increase in governmental "power."[5] Mandlebaum even hazards the view that "Perhaps the reason for delegating nuclear authority to the President is similar to the role that anthropologists have assigned to divine kingship: a means of coping with forces that seem beyond human powers of understanding and control."[6] Of course, the view of "delegation" here is very strained, as the Congress, let alone the public at large, are ill-informed about the nature of presidential authority with regard to nuclear weapons. In a formal sense it is true that this grant of authority seems consistent with the underlying constitutional conception of the President as commander-in-chief of the armed forces.[7] Yet more substantively, the actuality of nuclear weaponry is such, with its requirement of constant readiness, as to defy the moral constitutional expectation that the President must have the unchallenged authority to make battlefield decisions in wartime, an authority conceived of as pertaining only to that special circumstance of emergency and national unity that is presumed to exist during a properly declared war. As is obvious, and will be discussed later in this essay, nuclear weapons, by their very existence, forever obliterate the occasion of "peace," thereby, in my judgement, depriving a democratic polity of one of its most essential preconditions. Even those optimistic about the capacity of the modern state to uphold democratic values generally concede that governing procedures for accountability by leaders and participation of citizens are substantially abridged in the context of "war." Thus, a permanent state of war, not by the nature of political will or the character of international antagonisms, but as a structural reflection of the nature of modern weaponry, casts a dark shadow across the very possibility of a democratic polity. Citizens of secondary nuclear and non-nuclear democracies, at least to the extent that their governments take part in the geopolitics of alignment via alliance relations, have "delegated" this awesome authority over the deployment and use of nuclear weaponry to leaders of another state! Here, again, such a delegation may conform to the formal logic of constitutionalism, but it shreds the fabric of democratic substance seemingly beyond repair.

More substantively, this new grant of powers to a particular leader does entrust an awesome actual capability to a fallible, flawed human being or, at most, to a small, often hidden, inner group of advisors. Traditionally, divine right prerogatives even if pathologically abused could only produce limited damage, although of a severe sort for a given time and place. Increasingly, the leadership of the main nuclear powers possesses a capacity for destruction commensurate with what traditional religions attributed to the divine, a capacity to cause in the fullest sense a global or human apocalypse. Authority and power to inflict such results by a single process of decision suggests the extent to which the citizenry is inevitably and permanently excluded from determinations that decisively shape societal destiny.

But it is not only the upholders of constitutional legitimacy that overlook the relevance of the nuclear weapons dimension. Sheldon Wolin, in an eloquent introductory editorial to his new journal of progressive opinion, pointedly titled *Democracy,* nowhere indicates that nuclear weapons may foreclose democratizing prospects in unsuspected, unacknowledged, and crucial respects. His emphasis is on "the steady transformation of America into an anti-democratic society" as a consequence of the increasingly authoritarian character "of the country's primary institutions." Similarly, Alan Wolfe in his excellent book, *The Limits of Legitimacy,* devoted to an assessment of anti-democratic pressures on the liberal state, neglects even to mention the relevance of nuclear weaponry.[8] Both Wolin and Wolfe are fully aware, of course, that nuclear weapons are crucial political "facts" that are reshaping the modern state, but they interpret political reality on the basis of traditions of political thought oblivious to the reality of nuclear weapons.[9]

Perhaps, the failure to emphasize nuclear issues partly reflects an attitude that their relevance is so manifest as to be taken for granted or so "structured" into our world context as to be beyond the domain of practical politics, however radical their intention. In either event, I believe the failure to address the issue of nuclear relevance is an important omission for any serious reflections on the current democratic prospect.

André Glucksmann writes that "Everything subtle, profound, definitive and rigorous that has been said about nuclear weapons—which means not much—was said already a century before."[10] By this provocative assertion, Glucksmann is arguing that antecedent acquiescence in "totalist thought" had completely vested in the state ample authority and modalities to subordinate ethics to considerations of state power—"The nascent order of reciprocal terror was a feature of Western culture long before the invention of nuclear weapons."[11] And, of course, such an observation is pertinent. The moral ease, for instance, with which American decision-makers adopted atomic tactics in World War II was definitely "facilitated" by belligerent policies already routinized, especially terror bombing of civilian centers of population.[12] This striving for nuclear rectitude was, in a sense, reinforced by the Nuremberg Judgment that imposed criminal punishments for the "immoral" political behavior of the defeated leaders of Germany and Japan, but neglected "the wrongs" of the victorious powers.

Taking at face value Glucksmann's contention that the secular triumph of totalist ideology had already destroyed the moral foundations of state power long before Hiroshima, I find myself unable to go along with the postulate of continuity as a way of avoiding the need for specific analysis and commentary on the distinctive relevance of nuclearism. In this regard, I agree with the important recent assessments of nuclear relevance by E. P. Thompson and Robert Jay Lifton, as well as the earlier wide-ranging analysis of Karl Japsers.[13] Thompson, in an indictment of left/Marxist thought for its failure to highlight the nuclear issue, analyzes the contemporary political situation beneath the overarching, trans-ideological category of "exterminism," that is, as underscored in his own title, "the last stage of civilization." As is now widely known, Thompson's special concern is centered on the particular victimization of Europe as a potential " 'theater' of apocalypse" in a struggle waged by the superpowers who, in effect, seek to maintain their homelands as "sanctuaries," that is, as "off-limits" in the event of a nuclear exchange.[14] Thompson notes in passing that "a prior condition for the extermination of European peoples is the extermination of open democratic process." Underneath this assertion is the conviction that citizens would never knowingly give their assent to such a suicidal arrangement, and that therefore their rulers (not any longer mere leaders) must impair their access to knowledge and their rights to act on what they know. Repression at home, preferably by anodyne means designed to induce apathy, becomes a necessity of governance if security is to be premised, directly or indirectly, on the logic of exterminism. Again nuclearism and democracy collide in a specific, concrete manner.

Robert Lifton, whose writings probe the psychological and cultural significance of nuclear weaponry, reaches conclusions startlingly similar to those of Thompson. As he puts his emphasis, the new capacity for totalist destruction "changes everything (fundamentally alters our ultimate and immediate relationships . . .) and seems to change nothing (it is apparently ignored by much of the human race, which goes about business as usual)."[15] Note that for Lifton, the element of continuity is maintained not by the antecedent terrorism of state power, as alleged by Glucksmann, but by the failure of most people, including leaders, to grasp the radical novelty of nuclear weaponry. This novelty centers upon the sheer magnitude of potential destruction, giving secular reality to what had previously been a largely symbolic reality associated with the apocalyptic premonitions of religious tradition.

As Lifton goes on to suggest, the special aura of urgency in the United States around atomic espionage issues during the 1950s, culminating in the incredible ritual of capital punishment enacted in response to "the crimes" of Ethel and Julius Rosenberg, was associated with guarding the unprecedented power and with anxiety about the potential vulnerability created by nuclear weaponry.[16] The full absurdity of the security pretext for internal repression became evident only two decades later when bomb designs were written up as undergraduate student exercises, and do-it-yourself bomb-producing technology became the subject matter of monthly magazine articles. What is not absurd, however, is the governmental need to frighten its own citizenry into subservience by insisting that no one challenge the awesome authority of the government to engage fully and secretly in the apocalyptic endgame of exterminism. We note the recent reflex outburst by Ronald Reagan's first National Security Advisor, Richard Allen, in reaction to the European grassroots movement against nuclear weaponry. In a rare post-1945 breakdown of Atlanticist decorum, Allen publicly castigated the emergent European mood, saying that "outright pacifist sentiments are surfacing abroad. One recent incident of concern is the split in the British Labor Party. Right now the second largest party in Great Britain has adopted as part of its official platform the renunciation of nuclear weapons. We are even hearing, in other countries, the contemptible 'better red than dead' slogan of a generation ago."[17] Allen's words lend substance to Lifton's fear of "the particularly dangerous radical right embrace of *American* nuclear weapons" that "might well lead one to seek nuclear Armageddon as a way of achieving total purification."[18] The animus of the revival of anti-Soviet, anti-Communist hatred, the resumption of the Cold War and arms race, marks the current period as a peculiarly dangerous phase within the wider context of nuclearism.[19] As such, we can expect an intensification of anti-democratic institutional initiatives. Such an expectation was confirmed in the early months of the Reagan presidency by such steps as an upgrading of the CIA, a renewed stress on the linkage between national security and broad governmental prerogatives of official secrecy and surveillance procedures, an attack on the Freedom of Information Act, and an impending proposal to reinstate capital punishment in relation to the federal crime of espionage.

A concrete instance of this attitude of sufferance toward the citizenry occurred on September 19, 1980, when a monkey wrench was dropped in a Titan II silo located near Damascus, Arkansas, producing a large explosion.[20] Local residents were naturally anxious to discover whether large amounts of radiation had been released. Astonishingly, the Pentagon took the incredibly arrogant position that it would neither confirm nor deny the reports that a nuclear explosion had occurred, or that there was a fallout danger. And more astonishingly, the public generally acquiesced in this display of official arrogance. Incidents of this sort, inherently revealing, are also indicative of a process whereby the citizenry is throroughly demoralized with respect to citizen rights and duties, being subjected to an experience of learned helplessness.

One scarcely noticed dimension of nuclearism is the dubious legality of nuclear weapons.[21] In fact, the entire edifice of the law of war rests upon the central prohibition of indiscriminate killing of innocent civilians and includes separate prohibitions for weapons that cause victims "unnecessary suffering" or disproportionate damage.[22] It hardly requires a learned disquisition to comprehend the radical inconsistency between the minimum reading of the law of war and the insistence on national discretion to threaten and use nuclear weaponry. Such an inconsistency is peculiarly significant for democratic polities as their deepest pledge is to govern within a framework of law (a government of laws, not men). Furthermore, all "mature democracies" insist that every political entity claiming sovereign rights accept the obligations of the international legal order, virtually as evidence of its intention to participate as a state in international life. The hue and cry directed at the Iranian governing authorities for their failure to uphold the immunity of American diplomats and embassy premises during the 1979–1981 Teheran hostage crisis was based on the apparent rejection by the Khomeini leadership of this behavioral standard.

The claims of international law in the war/peace area are particularly strong in relation to the U.S. conception of political legitimacy. It was, after all, the United States that had taken the lead throughout the century to circumscribe sovereign discretion in relation to force and had, after World War II, insisted on criminal liability for political leaders who commit war crimes.

Some apologists for nuclearism contend lamely that under international law the sovereign is permitted to do everything that has not been expressly prohibited. There is some basis for such a contention in relation to certain subject matter, but it hardly seems applicable to nuclear weaponry. In this setting, law follows closely the minimum imperatives of morality; international law has since the seventeenth century been an uneasy blend of governmental consent for contrived rules and procedures and the natural law postulate. In our time, conventional moral outrage is concentrated upon "terrorism," the victimization of the innocent for the sake of ulterior political motives. It hardly takes a master moralist to reach the conclusion that nuclear weaponry and strategy represents terrorist logic on the grandest scale imaginable, yet the popular discussion of terrorism usually exempts nuclear weapons despite the currency of such phrases as "the balance of terror." The point here is that law and morality converge to condemn nuclearism, an acknowledgment increasingly being made by religious and cultural leaders of independence and stature.[23]

To suggest that nuclear weapons are illegal and immoral, and that leaders who threaten or contemplate their use are guilty of crimes of state, is to raise core questions about the legitimacy of *any* governance structure. Reliance on nuclear weapons is not just one of many governmental functions, it is in many ways the decisive undertaking of national political leadership, the one upon which, almost everyone agrees, all else hinges. If that undertaking is perceived by a substantial fragment of the citizenry as a criminal enterprise, then it will be impossible for political leaders to achieve legitimate authority. Deception, secrecy, and coercion will become increasingly indispensable instruments of governance, not to handle anti-social deviants, but to prevent citizens of the highest moral authority from challenging the absolutism of the state. Criminal prosecutions of those who dare expose this state secret of illegitimacy disclose the inevitable dilemma of "democratic" governments that embrace nuclearism.[24] Either the government ignores such protests and acts of resistance despite the loss of legitimacy, or it prosecutes its clearest moral voices despite the loss of legitimacy. There is no way for a democratic political leadership to retain its legitimacy in the eyes of its citizenry for very long if a sustained campaign around the legal and moral status of nuclear weapons is mounted. Some overarching questions emerge. Can democratic forms retain even provisional vitality when their substance is so deeply perverted? Or do these forms become atrophied rituals that disguise the passing of democracy from the scene? Can the nuclear question be kept cordoned off from the overall, routine administration of state power? Responses to these questions vary from country to country and depend on the consciousness of the citizenry and the perceptions of national leaders, as well as upon the tension level of international relations. In general the higher the tension level, the greater the anti-democratizing impact of the legitimacy dilemma arising from the existence of nuclear weaponry.

The focus on the United States is not meant to exempt the Soviet Union from scrutiny, but since the Soviet system seems procedurally anti-democratic in its essence it falls outside the strict scope of this inquiry. To the extent that the Soviet political leadership relies on nuclear weaponry, a crucial dimension of authoritarian governance is added. By now, whatever may be said about its earlier ambivalence, the Soviet Union seems to be fully committed to a reliance on nuclear weapons as a means of upholding its interests.[25] Because secrecy and public participation are so curtailed in the Soviet political system, there seems to be little opportunity for citizen opposition to nuclearism, while at the same time, reliance on nuclear weapons places formidable, rarely acknowledged constraints on the possibilities of democratizing reform taking hold within Soviet society.[26]

Of course, I am not arguing that nuclear weapons nullify all democratizing impulses at the state level. It is certainly possible to alter government/citizenry relations in a democratizing direction despite a reliance, directly or indirectly, upon nuclear weapons. It is rather a matter of structural constraint that bears on the most essential issue of state power in a manner that is anti-democratic in an extreme sense (here, democracy refers not only to the consent of the governed, but also to the idea of a government of laws, not men, which given shared human vulnerability has to include policies at the state level bearing on war/peace, resource use, and environmental protection).[27]

The broad implications of this analysis are twofold: the restoration of democratizing potential at the state level depends on the downgrading and eventual elimination of nuclear weapons as an element of international political life; secondly, normative opposition to nuclear weapons or doctrines inevitably draws into question the legitimacy of state power and is, therefore, more threatening to governmental process than a mere debate about the propriety of nuclear weapons as instruments of statecraft. The Machiavellian question is foremost: can a system of sovereign states ever manage to get rid of a decisive weapon by which an unscrupulous leader might impose his will? The course of international history strongly supports a negative reply. In effect, democracy, as a political framework, seems to be a permanent casualty of the nuclear age, although democratic forms, as an increasingly empty shell, can persist, disguising for some time the actuality of their inner collapse. The trend toward authoritarian governance, although prompted mainly by other factors, may also be, in part, a consequence of the anti-democratic influences of totalist attitudes and capabilities operative even in non-nuclear states (often reinforced by way of alliance or acceptance of "a nuclear umbrella").

Of course, there is an apparent paradox present. The erosion of democracy by way of nuclearism is, at the same time as the European movement suggests, a stimulus to democracy. It may yet be possible for citizens to organize in such a way as to exert some measure of democratic control over nuclear weaponry short of achieving its total elimination. Advocacy of a no first-use declaration and posture could provide a realistic goal for democratic movements seeking to restore balance in the relationship between government and citizenry and sanity to the quest for international security.[28]

The future of democracy then is at one with two intertwined explorations: the possibility of a post-Machiavellian international political order[29] and of a post-nuclear world.[30] In central respects, safeguarding and restoring the democratic prospect for mature cpaitalist polities depends on a comprehensive world order solution. The beginning of such a solution may involve delegitimizing the state in the area of national security. For this reason the religious, medical, and legal campaign against nuclearism seems of vital relevance to the very possibility of a democratic revival.

NOTES

1. For a depiction of "participatory democracy" see C. B. Macpherson, *The Life and Times of Liberal Democracy* (Oxford, 1977), pp. 93–115.

2. Michael J. Crozier, Samuel P. Huntington, and Joji Watanuki, *The Crisis of Democracy: Report on the Governability of Democracies to the Trilateral Commission* (New York, 1975); Daniel Bell, *The Cultural Contradictions of Capitalism* (New York, 1976).

3. David C. Gompert and others, *Nuclear Weapons and World Politics* (New York, 1977), pp. 4–5 (emphasis added).

4. "Nuclear Armament: An Interview," pamphlet of the Conservation Press, pp. 1, 3, undated.

5. For discussion see Michael Mandlebaum, *The Nuclear Revolution* (Cambridge, 1981), pp. 177–183.

6. Ibid., p. 183.

7. Ibid., p. 182.

8. Alan Wolfe, *The Limits of Legitimacy* (New York, 1977).

9. It seems significant to note that Wolfe fails to enlarge the agenda even in the course of his otherwise devastating critique of the Trilateral Commission report. Wolfe, op. cit., pp. 325–330.

10. André Glucksmann, *The Master Thinkers* (New York, 1980), p. 151.

11. Ibid., p. 150. Simone Weil and Stanley Diamond push the argument back further, maintaining that the fundamentally coercive nature of the state has been the ground for all subsequent modes of official violence. For a brief discussion of their views see Falk, *Human Rights and State Sovereignty* (New York, 1981), pp. 128–131.

12. See a careful interpretation of the decision to use atomic bombs in Robert Jay Lifton, *The Broken Connection* (New York, 1979), pp. 369–381, including consideration of the "moral" interposition by Henry Stimson, then Secretary

of War, of reasons why Kyoto, because of its cultural stature, should be "spared," that is, taken off the list of approved targets.

13. See Karl Jaspers, *The Future of Mankind* (Chicago, 1961).

14. Edward Thompson, "Notes on Exterminism, the Last Stage of Civilization," *New Left Review,* No. 121, May-June 1980, pp. 3-31, at pp. 10-14.

15. Lifton, op. cit., p. 335.

16. Ibid., pp. 354-356.

17. Text of "Remarks by Richard V. Allen Before the Conservative Political Action Conference 1981," Washington, D.C., March 21, 1981, p. 10.

18. Lifton, op. cit., p. 359.

19. This danger is heightened by adoption of first-strike strategic thinking, by new weapons innovations, and by conflicts and instabilities that threaten hegemonic patterns of Western influence over resource-producing countries in the Persian Gulf and southern African regions.

20. See report of "U.S. Nuclear Weapons Accidents," *Defence Monitor,* Vol. 10, No. 5, 1981, p. 11.

21. Typical of this discussion is the assumption that international law currently imposes no restraints on the discretion of governments to use nuclear weapons. See, for example, Michael Mandlebaum, "International Stability and Nuclear Order: The First Nuclear Regime," in Gompert, op. cit., pp. 23-24, where such discretion is connected with the absence of express treaty restrictions and the general unenforceability of international law. For a refutation see Richard Falk, Lee Meyrowitz, and Jack Sanderson, "Nuclear Weapons and International Law" (unpublished paper, February 1981).

22. For a comprehensive treatment of this and related issues see Falk, Meyrowitz, and Sanderson, op. cit.

23. See, for example, James W. Douglass, *Lightning East to West* (Portland, Oregon, 1980); see also Delhi Declaration on the Prohibition of Nuclear Weapons (1978).

24. A notable instance of such civilian resistance has involved Catholic activists associated with Rev. Daniel P. Berrigan and his brother, Philip Berrigan. Their most recent undertaking involved entering a General Electric plant in King of Prussia, Pennsylvania, and damaging two nosecones intended for Mark 12A missiles. The eight individuals involved, known as the Plowshares 8, were prosecuted, convicted, and sentenced in a trial conducted in a highly emotional atmosphere in which the defendants were determined to center the case on their claim that nuclear weapons were illegal and immoral, and the judge was equally determined to rule such considerations out of order. For a brief evaluation see Falk, "Shield for Civil Disobedience—International Law—a Counterforce Weapon Against Nuclear War," Pacific News Service, August 1981.

25. See Mandlebaum, op. cit., pp. 202-203, for comments on the Soviet approach to nuclear weapons.

26. Jean-François Revel, for instance, reports that efforts by European anti-nuclear protesters to march from Copenhagen to Moscow, as well as Copenhagen to Paris, were refused, while at the same time the anti-nuclear protest was given Brezhnev's explicit blessing. Revel, "The Strange Nuclear Diplomacy of Willy Brandt," *Wall Street Journal,* August 19, 1981, p. 29.

27. For my world order analysis of these issues see Richard A. Falk, *A Study of Future Worlds* (New York, Free Press, 1975).

28. I owe the impetus for this paragraph to Robert C. Tucker, long a forceful advocate of no-first-use thinking. For Tucker's views on this prospect along

with the position of other commentators on international affairs, see Robert C. Tucker, Klaus Knorr, Richard A. Falk, and Hedley Bull, "Proposal for No First Use of Nuclear Weapons: Pros and Cons," Policy Memorandum No. 28, Center of International Studies, Princeton University, 1963; and Richard A. Falk, Robert C. Tucker, and Oran R. Young, "On Minimizing the Use of Nuclear Weapons," Research Monograph No. 23, Center of International Studies, Princeton University, March 1, 1966.

29. Cf. Ferenc Feher, "Toward A Post-Machiavellian Politics," *Telos,* No. 42, Winter 1979-80, pp. 56–64; see also Stanley Hoffman, *Duties Beyond Borders* (Syracuse, New York, 1981).

30. The main focus of a book to be written jointly by Robert Jay Lifton and myself, bearing the tentative title *Indefensible Weapons: A Political and Psychological Account of Nuclearism.*

———— Questions for Reflection and Discussion ————

1. What is national security? Historically, how has it been defined? What factors traditionally have been taken into consideration? Have some been overlooked? If so, which ones? What factors would you include? Exclude?

2. Are national security interests and foreign policy interests coextensive? Are there some foreign policy problems that do not implicate national security? Should all challenges to national interests abroad be viewed as national security threats?

3. What, if any, foreign policy interests merit protection through reliance upon military power? Why? Are there some foreign policy problems that are not amenable to military solution? Which? Why?

4. What national security interests are served by nuclear weapons? How well are they served? In what ways do nuclear weapons detract from national security? What have been the domestic socioeconomic and political consequences of national reliance upon nuclear weapons?

5. Does current national security thinking need revision from the standpoint of maximizing the physical and social well-being of the individual citizen? Is the current focus on external military threat appropriately responsive to the full range of threats to personal security?

6. Do you think there is a difference between the security needs of ruling elites and those of the people? Do armaments represent the best means for providing people's security?

Selected Bibliography

Barnet, Richard J. *Real Security: Restoring American Power in a Dangerous Decade.* New York: Simon and Schuster, 1981.

Beres, Louis René. *Terrorism and Global Security: The Nuclear Threat.* Boulder, CO: Westview Press, 1979.

Bezdek, Roger H. "The 1980 Economic Impact—Regional and Occupational— of Compensated Shifts in Defense Spending." *Journal of Regional Science,* Vol. 15, No. 2 (1975), pp. 183–198.

Borosage, Robert. "The Making of the National Security State." In *The Pentagon Watchers: Students Report on the National Security State,* ed. Leonard S. Rodberg and Derek Shearer. Garden City, NY: Doubleday, 1970.

Brodie, Bernard, Michael D. Intriligator, and Roman Kolkowicz, eds. *National Security and International Stability,* Cambridge, MA: Oelgeschlager, Gunn and Hain, 1983.

Brown, Harold. *Thinking About National Security.* Boulder, CO: Westview Press, 1983.

Brown, Lester R. *Redefining National Security.* Worldwatch Paper No. 14. Washington, DC: Worldwatch Institute, 1977.

Brown, Seyom. "The Changing Essence of Power." *Foreign Affairs,* Vol. 51, No. 2 (Jan. 1973), pp. 286–299.

Duedney, Daniel. "Whole Earth Security: A Geopolitics of Peace." Worldwatch Paper No. 55. Washington, DC: Worldwatch Institute, July 1983.

Enthoven, Alain C., and K. Wayne Smith. *How Much Is Enough?* New York: Harper & Row, 1971.

Fallows, James. *National Defense.* New York: Random House, 1981.

Frei, Daniel. *Risks of Unintentional Nuclear War.* New York: United Nations Publication, 1982.

Fuller, John G. *We Almost Lost Detroit.* New York: Reader's Digest Press, 1975.

Green, Christopher. "Economics of the Arms Race." *McGill Law Journal,* Vol. 28, No. 3 (July 1983), pp. 651–683.

Hermann, Charles F. "Defining National Security." In *American Defense Policy,* ed. John F. Reichart and Steven R. Sturm. 5th ed. Baltimore and London: Johns Hopkins University Press, 1982.

Huntington, Samuel P. *The Strategic Imperative: New Policies for American Security.* Cambridge, MA: Ballinger Publishing Co., 1982.

Johansen, Robert C. *The National Interest and the Human Interest: An Analysis of U.S. Foreign Policy.* Princeton: Princeton University Press, 1980.

Jordan, Amos A., and William J. Taylor, Jr. *American National Security: Policy and Process.* Baltimore: Johns Hopkins University Press, 1981.

Kaldor, Mary. *The Baroque Arsenal.* New York: Hill and Wang, 1982.

Lifton, Robert Jay, and Richard Falk. *Indefensible Weapons: The Political and Psychological Case Against Nuclearism.* New York: Basic Books, 1982.

Lovins, Amory B., and L. Hunter Lovins. *Brittle Power: Energy Strategy of National Security.* Andover, MA: Brick House Publishing Co., 1982.

Medvedev, Zhores A. *Nuclear Disaster in the Urals.* New York: Vintage Books, 1979.

Melman, Seymour. *The Permanent War Economy: American Capitalism in Decline.* New York: Simon and Schuster, 1974.

Pranger, Robert J., and Robert P. Labrie, eds. *Nuclear Strategy and National Security: Points of View.* Washington, DC: American Enterprise Institute, 1977.

Randle, Michael. "Militarism and Repression." *Alternatives: A Journal of World Policy,* Vol. 7, No. 1 (Summer 1981), pp. 61–144.

Raskin, Marcus G. *The Politics of National Security.* New Brunswick, NJ: Transaction Books, 1979.

Richardson, Lewis F. *Arms and Insecurity.* Pittsburgh: Boxwood Press, 1980.

Sajoo, Amynmohamed B. "Human Rights Perspectives on the Arms Race." *McGill Law Journal,* Vol. 28, No. 3 (July 1983), pp. 628–650.

Sivard, Ruth Leger. *World Military and Social Expenditures.* Leesburg, VA: WMSE Publications, 1983.

Snyder, Glenn H. *Deterrence and Defense: Toward a Theory of National Security.* Princeton, NJ: Princeton University Press, 1961.

Steinbruner, John D. "National Security and the Concept of Strategic Stability." *Journal of Conflict Resolution,* Vol. 22, No. 3 (Sept. 1978), pp. 411–428.

Syzmarski, Albert. "Military Spending and Economic Stagnation." *American Journal of Sociology,* Vol. 79, No. 1 (July 1973), pp. 1–14.

Tucker, Robert W. *The Purposes of American Power: An Essay on National Security.* New York: Praeger Press, 1981.

Tuomi, Helena, and Raimo Vayrynen, eds. *Militarization and Arms Production.* New York: St. Martin's Press, 1983.

"U.S. Nuclear Weapons Accidents: Danger in Our Midst." *The Defense Monitor,* Vol. 10, No. 5. Washington, DC: Center for Defense Information, 1981.

Wolfers, Arnold. "'National Security' as an Ambiguous Symbol." *Political Science Quarterly,* Vol. 67, No. 4 (Dec. 1952), pp. 481–502.

Yergin, Daniel. *Shattered Peace: The Origins of the Cold War and the National Security State.* Boston: Houghton Mifflin, 1977.

CHAPTER 5

Rethinking "Deterrence"

The concept "deterrence"—the restraining of an adversary's conduct by maintaining independent means sufficiently credible to render the conduct unacceptably costly or irrational—is nothing new. The strategies that have emerged under its banner since the Second World War are barely distinguishable from the strategies of coercive threat and counter-threat that previously characterized international politics at least as far back as the Congress of Vienna. What is new, of course, is the vastly more destructive power with which the concept has become associated. Today, nuclear weapons form the foundation of NATO and Warsaw Pact deterrence strategy.

To say that the concept "deterrence" is not new, however, is not to say that the doctrines and policies advanced in its name have been constant or uniform. On the contrary, the past three decades reveal numerous variations on the theme, some reflecting technological break-throughs, others representing shifts in geopolitical assessment and outlook. The history of U.S. strategic thought, with an equivalent history on the Soviet side, is illustrative.

In 1954, under President Eisenhower, the United States proclaimed the policy of "massive retaliation": any act of Communist aggression would trigger a full-scale nuclear air strike against the Soviet Union. Recognizing this policy's low credibility when applied to limited military incursions, however, and cognizant as well of the Soviet Union's then rapidly developing intercontinental bomber fleet, the Eisenhower administration added the notion of "graduated deterrence." In essence, the United States would allow the scope of the aggressive act to determine the intensity of the nuclear retaliation, a policy of proportionality that was further refined during the administration of John F. Kennedy when the notion of "flexible response" was adopted. By indicating a willingness to use nuclear weapons at any level of hostilities, but limiting their use to the area of conflict, the United States enhanced the credibility of its nuclear threat.

The Kennedy administration also articulated the strategic doctrine that was to remain at the center of U.S. deterrence strategy through the White House years of Lyndon Johnson, Richard Nixon, Gerald Ford, and Jimmy Carter: the doctrine of "mutual assured destruction" (or MAD), i.e., the ability to inflict an "unacceptable" amount of damage upon an enemy *after* withstanding a first nuclear strike. In strategic terms, this translates into the possession of a secure second-strike countervalue capability. In lay terms, it refers to the ability to withstand a nuclear assault and then to launch a devastating retaliatory blow against an adversary's cities and key economic and military assets. Theorists sympathetic to MAD thus envision security through the establishment of a mutual hostage relationship, maintaining that the perpetrator will be deterred from striking first if it is perceived that the recipient has the ability to strike back with equal or greater force.

In 1974, during the administration of President Richard M. Nixon, Secretary of Defense James R. Schlesinger further modified U.S. strategic nuclear doctrine by introducing the concept of "limited nuclear options," a strategy that called for the creation of contingency plans involving a mixture of military and urban-industrial targeting to mitigate the amount of indiscriminate killing. The assumption was that the greater the capacity of the United States to inflict discriminate destruction, the greater would be the belief on the part of the Soviet Union that the United States would resort to nuclear weapons if its interests were threatened.

Also in 1974, Secretary Schlesinger asserted that the United States should never have a strategic intercontinental capability inferior to that of the Soviet Union. This assertion became known as the doctrine of "essential equivalence," and in 1981 Secretary of Defense Harold Brown further refined the doctrine in terms of the following four conditions: (1) Soviet strategic forces should never become usable instruments of political leverage; (2) nuclear stability should be maintained at all times; (3) all advantages in Soviet strategic force should be offset by U.S. advantages; and (4) U.S. strategic posture must never be perceived as— nor in fact be—inferior in performance to that of the Soviet Union. As long as these four conditions are satisfied, "essential equivalence" will remain a basic component of United States strategic policy.

Finally, in 1980, President Jimmy Carter signed Presidential Directive 59, described by Secretary Brown as a "codification of our evolving strategic doctrine." PD 59 has since become known as the "countervailing nuclear strategy," which provides that U.S. strategic planning necessarily consider the widest range of options available to it, including especially the capacity to launch a continuum of counterforce strikes so as to provide the greatest flexibility possible. Current U.S. strategy under President Ronald Reagan continues to emphasize counterforce targeting (i.e., the power to destroy an adversary's nuclear forces, hence its first- *and* second-strike nuclear capabilities) as well as countervalue targeting, and in addition stresses "comprehensive deterrence" in the form of "escalation dominance" at all levels and nuclear war-fighting capability.

The readings selected for this chapter are meant to afford a detailed analytical exploration of these key manifestations of deterrence theory.

The article by Allan Krass pinpoints the basic fallacies of MAD. The extract by Louis René Beres outlines the current nuclear strategy of the United States and finds it fundamentally flawed in its technical and political assumptions. Finally, Hedley Bull examines the prospects for continued reliance on strategic, theater-level, and extended deterrence in the context of the ongoing horizontal proliferation of nuclear-weapon states. Individually and in combination, these selections reflect a new-found interest in bringing deterrence theory and practice out of the shadows of traditional official thinking into the daylight of widespread public scrutiny and reassessment.

14. Deterrence and Its Contradictions

Allan Krass

A strategic policy of deterrence is one of hindering or discouraging other nations by means of credible threats.

The popular conception of deterrence remains fundamentally defensive in character. It has been reinforced in many ways by many writers, but one statement of the doctrine stands out as historically significant:

> The way to deter aggression is for the free community to be willing and able to respond vigorously at places and with means of its own choosing. . . . to depend primarily on a great capacity to retaliate instantly, by means and at places of our choosing.[1]

This statement implies a defensive posture, based on threats of retaliation and punishment. In modern systems jargon it specifies a way of ensuring that the enemy's cost-benefit analysis always comes out negative when he considers an aggressive move. It is not difficult to find similar statements on the Soviet side: "If, however, the aggressive circles, relying on atomic weapons, should decide on madness and seek to test the strength and might of the Soviet Union, then it cannot be doubted that the aggressor would be crushed by that very weapon."[2]

These statements leave no doubt that deterrence is a system based on threat. But to understand what has happened to the concept of deterrence since Dulles and Malenkov made these statements in 1954, it is essential to understand the dual nature of threats. Threat can be used for both defensive and offensive purposes; it can be deterrent or coercive.

The ambiguities and intricacies of this connection, and the ramifications of a strategy based on threats, have been thoroughly explored by Thomas Schelling. He points out that "violence is most purposive and most successful when it is threatened and not used."[3] And to make a threat effective "one needs to know what the adversary treasures and what scares him and one needs the adversary to understand what behavior of his will cause the violence to be inflicted and what will cause it to be withheld."[4]

It is in this context that the modern concept of deterrence must be understood. The development of modern nuclear weapons and the systems needed to deliver them cannot be explained if one insists on defining deterrence in an essentially defensive and reactive form. Instead, the modern concept of deterrence has evolved into something much closer to the traditional understanding of the role of military force in the pursuit of national objectives. Deterrence is now seen as "flexible" or "extended," and a "second-strike counterforce" capability is defended as part of a deterrent on the grounds that a credible (i.e., non-suicidal) response must be available if deterrence fails.

The word "deterrence" survives even though (or perhaps because) it obscures more than it clarifies. Consider, for example, the following definition:

it is a fairly safe prediction that from now on neither side will be able seriously convincingly to use for political ends threats of strategic nuclear attack, or anything that in scale is even close to it. What one *can* threaten are lesser actions that *could* start events moving in that direction. The opponent cannot at any stage be deprived of the choice within his capabilities, of making the situation more dangerous or less so; but we can reasonably hope and expect to influence his choices appropriately. This is what we must henceforth mean by deterrence, or by containing aggression militarily.[5]

The following authors are willing to go even further, and in their words can be heard the echoes of Schelling's prescriptions reverberating without inhibition:

the West needs to devise ways in which it can employ strategic nuclear forces coercively, while minimizing the potentially paralyzing impact of self-deterrence. U.S. strategic planning should exploit Soviet fears insofar as is feasible from the Soviet perspective.[6]

One final example will serve to illustrate just how broad the spectrum of definitions of deterrence has become:

The political power of nuclear weapons is based on:

- the yield
- the number available
- the number of launch vehicles and the certainty of their availability
- hit and kill probabilities
- the credibility of their use.

As long as *superiority* really exists in all the parameters, the risk for the user is small and the *deterrent* concept is credible, as was demonstrated with Hiroshima and Nagasaki.[7]

These quotes represent U.S. interpretations of deterrence. Soviet views are more difficult to ascertain, but they seem to have been much more consistent and much less ambiguous (at least on the surface) than U.S. views. A wide range of interpreters of Soviet nuclear doctrines seem to be in essential agreement that the USSR has never made much of an intellectual effort to distinguish between the concepts of deterrence and war fighting. The Soviet Union has certainly recognized the deterrent value of its military power, but has appeared to assume that the power to deter arises ultimately out of the power to fight and win wars. Whether a Western intepreter chooses to focus on the deterrent aspect of the war-fighting aspect seems to depend more on the political preferences of the observer than on any inherent doctrinal distinction or preference in Soviet thinking. In summary, whatever meaning the concept of deterrence may once have had in the minds of the public has been stretched beyond any recognition by the technological and doctrinal evolution of the past 20 years, most dramatically in the past 10. This raises the question of why a doctrine which seemed at one time to be the only viable solution to living with nuclear weapons in a divided world did not survive.

Pure deterrence has never been practised, so in analysing its short-comings it is necessary to deal with abstractions. The closest either the United States or the USSR ever came to adopting a pure deterrent posture occurred in the 1950s when the economic, political, and technological problems associated with counterforce strategies seemed to many people to be insurmountable. This was the period in the United States during which the doctrine of massive retaliation was formulated by the Eisenhower Administration. During the same period the Soviet leadership which emerged after the death of Josef Stalin attempted to rationalize a shift in emphasis from military to civilian production by a reliance on nuclear deterrence and the mutually suicidal nature of nuclear war. The attacks which were made on these doctrines by proponents of counterforce strategies exposed many of the contradictions of deterrence, and the attacks from the other side advocating total nuclear disarmament exposed the rest.

Two of the deepest contradictions in a deterrent strategy have already been suggested by quotes in the previous section. One is the essentially defensive or reactive character of a deterrent posture, a strategy that leaves all the initiative to the adversary. It is this posture which results in the loss of any real political value in the possession of nuclear weapons; in a purely deterrent posture, nuclear weapons become useless as coercive implements.

In the United States, this criticism was well known to President Eisenhower and to Secretary of State Dulles, and it had already been the subject of much analysis and argument by the time massive retaliation was publicly enunciated. Indeed, in the very same speech, Dulles took pains to reassure his audience that the new doctrine did not abandon the initiative to the enemy:

Now the Department of Defense and the Joint Chiefs of Staff can shape our military establishment to fit . . . *our* policy, instead of having to try to be ready to meet the enemy's many choices. That permits . . . a selection of military means instead of a multiplication of means.[8]

But these reassurances were not convincing, ultimately even to Dulles himself, who changed his position substantially in 1957:

the resourcefulness of those who serve our nation in the field of science and weapon engineering now shows that it is possible to alter the character of nuclear weapons. It now seems that their use need not involve vast destruction and widespread harm to humanity. Recent tests point to the possibility of possessing nuclear weapons, the destructiveness and radiation effects of which can be substantially confined to predetermined targets.[9]

A second contradiction inherent in deterrence was suggested by the requirement that, to be deterred, the enemy must "understand what behavior of his will cause the violence to be inflicted and what will cause it to be withheld."[10] In other words a deterrent threat must be both unambiguous and credible. But by being explicit about just what is being deterred, and by committing himself irrevocably to carrying out the threat, a national leader has totally lost his *flexibility,* a position in which no political leader will ever willingly place himself.

The credibility criterion proved too full of logical flaws to survive analysis. Simply stated, the problem is how a nation credibly commits itself to retaliation by suicide. Attempts to resolve this problem led to some of the more bizarre proposals of the 1950s in the form of "doomsday machines" or the holding of hostage cities in such a way that the attacked party would have no choice but to carry out the retaliation it was committed to. Early on it was recognized that by assigning the retaliatory task to computers the unpredictable factors of human fear, remorse, or compassion could be eliminated.

Such proposals, by carrying the concept of deterrence to its full technological and logical implications, exposed a third contradiction in the theory: its utter moral repugnance. Naturally this contradiction was exposed more often in the beginning by advocates of disarmament than by advocates of counterforce, but the latter also have often relied on moral objections to the holding of hostages and mass murder to support their arguments for a counterforce strategy. It is a measure of the degree to which the entire spectrum of debate has shifted that advocates of disarmament now find themselves forced to defend on practical political grounds a strategy of minimal deterrence which conflicts fundamentally with their own moral convictions.

A fourth contradiction of deterrence is its effect on the morale of the political leadership, the military establishment, and the civilian population. The morale of political leaders cannot help but be reduced by a policy which puts the vital issues of national security effectively beyond their control, and the morale of the civilian population must certainly be undermined by the constant threat of massive destruction against which no defence is possible—or even desirable if the doctrine is taken seriously. But equally important would be the effect on military morale, which no political leader can take lightly.

A posture of minimal deterrence would put the military into an impossible position. It would recognize the possibility of war; indeed it postulates the predilection of one's adversary toward aggression. But it also leaves all the initiative to the adversary in deciding when, where, and how the war will be fought. The doctrine would deny the possibility of defence against nuclear attack and, in effect, say to military officers: you must sit and wait for the enemy to attack first. Then you must stand by and watch while his missiles destroy your planes, ships, missiles, communications facilities, and so on. Then you must gather together what is left and send them off to kill as many defenceless civilians in his country as you can.

If one believes that there is any dignity at all in the military profession, and there certainly is a great deal, then one cannot ask a military officer to carry out such a strategy. The good ones will not do it and the incompetent and unprincipled ones will do it badly.

It is important to emphasize in this context the very real differences between a deterrent and a defensive posture. Many countries are able to maintain a credible military posture and high military morale with a strategy based entirely on the defence of the homeland against attack: Sweden, Switzerland, and Japan come to mind as examples. But in these countries the soldiers know that they will be fighting other soldiers and that they will in truth be defending themselves and their country. Nuclear deterrence does not admit the possibility of defence and directs its destructive power against civilians rather than soldiers.

There is good evidence that these arguments about the impact of deterrence on military and civilian morale were instrumental in Nikita Khrushchev's successful efforts to oust Premier Malenkov and head off a Soviet minimal deterrence strategy. Khrushchev argued forcefully, and with the full support of the Soviet Army, that such a strategy would lead to "complacence" and "defeatism" and that it was essential to future Soviet foreign policy to maintain the idea that not only was defence possible but that it was also possible to win a nuclear war. But Khrushchev's early commitment to these notions was quickly followed by a return to his own version of deterrence. It cannot be determined whether this was a genuine attempt on his part to establish the doctrine or a concession to Soviet technological limitations.[11]

The final contradiction in a strategy of deterrence is its instability with regard to technological advance. A credible deterrent requires an invulnerable retaliatory striking force which can inflict "unacceptable" damage upon an attacker even after absorbing a full first strike, whose primary purpose can only be the total destruction of the deterrent. If the attacker has also deployed active and passive defences, then the remaining retaliatory force must be large enough to carry out its mission even though further degraded by the defences.

This statement of the deterrent mission raises many more questions than it answers. What level of damage is unacceptable? How does one estimate one's own invulnerability? How effective are the enemy's defences? How big should the margin of safety be? Should a launch-on-warning option be maintained as a hedge against miscalculation? Each of these questions may have an acceptable answer at any given time, but technological advances constantly render old answers obsolete and demand new ones. The submarine deterrent which was thought to be totally invulnerable for many years now seems to be losing this invulnerability. Doubts about the survivability of communications engendered by anti-satellite technologies and the ability to make selective attacks on C^3I facilities raise questions about being able even to order, much less plan and coordinate, a second strike. Each new technological advance by the offence demands a response by the deterrent, so there seems to be no fixed answer to the now famous question: How much is enough?[12]

These contradictions constitute a powerful indictment against a strategy of nuclear deterrence. But if the arguments of this section are correct and deterrence is unworkable, then what are the alternatives? They are clearly either nuclear disarmament or preparation for nuclear warfare. There can be little doubt about which course the major powers of the world have chosen.

NOTES

1. R. G. Head and E. J. Rokke, eds., *American Defense Policy* (Johns Hopkins University Press, Baltimore, 1973), reprint of speech by J. F. Dulles before the Council on Foreign Relations, 12 January 1954, p. 63.

2. H. Dinerstein, *War and the Soviet Union* (Praeger, New York, 1962), quoting G. M. Malenkov, Chairman of the Council of Ministers of the USSR, 27 April 1954, p. 74.

3. T. Schelling, *Arms and Influence* (Yale University Press, New Haven, 1966), p. 10.

4. Ibid., p. 2.

5. B. Brodie, *Escalation and the Nuclear Option* (Princeton University Press, Princeton, 1966), p. 101.

6. K. S. Gray and K. Paine, "Victory is Possible," *Foreign Policy,* No. 39, Summer 1980, p. 14.

7. Lt. Gen. N. Hanning (ret.), "Essential Equivalence: The End of the Nuclear Deterrent Myth," *International Defense Review,* Vol. 12, No. 2, 4 April 1979, p. 179 (emphasis added).
8. Head and Rokke, op. cit., p. 63.
9. W. W. Kaufmann, *The McNamara Strategy* (Harper & Row, New York, 1964), p. 26.
10. Schell, op. cit., p. 10.
11. Dinerstein, op. cit., Chapter 3.
12. A. C. Enthover and K. W. Smith, *How Much is Enough?* (Harper & Row, New York, 1971).

15. Nuclear Strategy and World Order: The United States Imperative

Louis René Beres

INTRODUCTION

The principal goal of U.S. nuclear strategy since the beginning of the Atomic Age has been to deter nuclear war. Over the years, however, the policies designed to implement this goal have changed significantly. Today, there is cause for concern that current strategic nuclear policy, as embodied in Presidential Directive 59 and as reflected in the Reagan administration's strategic program,[1] may actually hasten the arrival of nuclear war. This is the case because such policy creates the impression that the United States is moving toward an eventual first-strike against the Soviet Union.

Current U.S. nuclear strategy goes beyond the legitimate objective of survivable strategic forces to active preparation for nuclear war-fighting. Although U.S. nuclear weapon targeting has been primarily counterforce since 1960, the present administration's rejection of minimum deterrence is coupled with preparations for a nuclear war that might be protracted and controlled. Accepting the position that the function of strategic forces may not be limited to prevention of a nuclear war, President Reagan's nuclear strategy reflects the understanding that a combination of counterforce targeting, crisis relocation of urban populations, and ballistic missile defense could make nuclear war purposeful and tolerable. In the words of Leon Sloss, who directed this country's nuclear targeting policy review for the Department of Defense in 1978, "The emphasis has shifted from the *survivability* necessary to assure that we can launch a single preplanned strike to the *endurance* necessary to actually fight a war that may extend over some period of time and involve a series of nuclear exchanges."[2]

From its very beginning, the Reagan administration has worked to implement this provocative new form of a counterforce nuclear strategy.

The main feature of President Reagan's strategic deterrent program, announced on October 2, 1981, was to go ahead with the production and deployment of the MX (missile experimental). Since the announced basing mode chosen for the MX will have no effect on the much talked about "window of vulnerability," the MX's only remaining purpose will be to fulfill distinctive counterforce mission objectives. The President's parallel plans for ballistic missile defense of the MX, new anti-satellite weapons, continuing expansion of countersilo capabilities with Trident II and MK-12A RV weapons and further identification of intermediate retaliatory options confirm the Reagan administration's commitment to a nuclear war-fighting doctrine. Although the President's four-point arms control program (November 18, 1981) and the beginning of START were intended to communicate the administration's sincerity in seeking arms control measures, it did nothing to repudiate this commitment. Indeed, several weeks before the onset of START, Secretary of Defense Weinberger acknowledged that the Reagan administration had adopted a formal strategy for fighting a prolonged nuclear war with the Soviet Union.

President Reagan's nuclear strategy represents the latest retreat from the doctrine of "massive retaliation" first defined by John Foster Dulles in January 1954.[3] Designed to fulfill military tasks at a level far exceeding the requirements of "mutual assured destruction,"[4] its counterforce targeting plan envisions a broad array of possible nuclear responses within a carefully defined "spectrum of deterrence." Former Secretary of Defense Harold Brown has stated that,

deterrence remains, as it has been historically, our fundamental strategic objective. But deterrence must restrain a far wider range of threats than just massive attacks on U.S. cities. We seek to deter any adversary from any course of action that could lead to general nuclear war. Our strategic forces must also deter nuclear attacks on smaller sets of targets in the U.S. or on U.S. military forces, and be a wall against nuclear coercion of, or attack on, our friends and allies. And strategic forces, in conjunction with theater nuclear forces, must contribute to deterrence of conventional aggression as well.[5]

In essence, this counterforce strategy stresses the capacity to employ strategic nuclear forces "selectively." Anticipating intermediate levels of Soviet aggression, it was designed to impress on Soviet leaders the fact that the United States has both the will and the means to make such aggression irrational. It does this by operationalizing an incremental policy of strategic response that will allegedly make Soviet leaders less adventurous.

Former Secretary Brown stated on several occasions that this is not an altogether new strategic posture. P.D. 59 codifies a series of doctrinal modifications that have been underway for at least 25 years. In the Secretary's words,

The U.S. has never had a doctrine based simply and solely on reflexive, massive attacks on Soviet cities. Instead, we have always planned both more selectively (options limiting urban-industrial damage) and more comprehensively (a range of military targets). Previous Administrations, going back well into the 1960s, recognized the inadequacy of a strategic doctrine that would give us too narrow a range of options. The fundamental premises of our countervailing strategy are a natural evolution of the conceptual foundations built over the course of a generation by, for example, Secretaries McNamara and Schlesinger, to name only two of my predecessors who have been most identified with the development of our nuclear doctrine.[6]

The basic shape of the counterforce strategy was outlined by Secretary Brown in his Annual Report to the Congress for FY 1981. There he developed the argument that large-scale countervalue attacks may not be appropriate to deter the full range of potential Soviet threats. Faced with what he saw as a need for deterring Soviet attacks of "less than all-out scale," he proposed options to attack Soviet military and political targets while holding back a significant reserve. Such a strategy, he argued, could preclude an intolerable choice between no effective military response and all-out nuclear war. Instead, we could attack "in a selective and measured way, a range of military, industrial, and political control targets, while retaining an assured destruction capacity in reserve."[7]

Such a strategy may at first appear sound and prudent. Upon close examination, however, it becomes apparent that a policy of calibrating U.S. nuclear retaliation to the particular provocation (especially as this policy has been refined by the Reagan administration) does not support the overall objective of strategic deterrence. Indeed, careful scrutiny of the policy's underlying principles reveals that it actually encourages nuclear war because it is founded upon an implausible set of assumptions and upon a misunderstanding of interactive effects. These unwarranted assumptions include the notions: (1) that the Soviet Union might decide to launch a limited first strike on the United States or its allies; (2) that the Soviet Union is more likely to be deterred by the threat of limited American counterforce reprisals than by the threat of over-whelming, total nuclear retaliation; (3) that victory is possible in a superpower nuclear war; (4) that a counterforce nuclear strategy can be undertaken without compromising the prospects for vertical and horizontal arms control; and (5) that nuclear deterrence can work forever.

This paper examines each of these assumptions, and then proposes an alternative strategy for improving the likelihood of nuclear disarmament and nuclear war avoidance.

LIMITED NUCLEAR WAR

Perhaps the most curious assumption of current U.S. nuclear strategy is that the Soviets might decide to launch a limited first strike on the United States or its allies. Since America's developing counterforce capability is allegedly only for second-strike purposes, its rationale is necessarily based on the belief that a Soviet first strike might be limited. In the absence of such belief, the commitment to damage-limiting retaliation would make no sense since this country's second-strike strategic forces would be expected to hit only empty silos.

But why would the Soviets ever calculate that they have something to gain by launching a limited first strike? We have long known that the Soviets do not share our view of controlled nuclear conflict and that there is no reason for them to believe our declared commitment to proportionate retaliation. Faced with great uncertainty about the nature of a U.S. strategic response, Soviet leaders could not possibly make a rational decision to strike first in a limited mode. This is not to suggest that they would necessarily choose rationally to initiate total nuclear war with the United States, but only that once they had decided upon striking first they would be compelled to adopt a strategy of all-out assault rather than one of restraint.

These current U.S. views of nuclear strategy have their roots in the continuing search for a more credible policy of nuclear deterrence, one that would preserve a broad array of nuclear retaliatory options. Since such a policy, as indicated earlier, is founded on the notion of a "spectrum of deterrence," it led almost immediately to some tentative formulations of the idea of "limited nuclear war." Ultimately, many of these formulations found their way into the policies of the "McNamara Strategy" of the 1960s and the successor strategies of James Schlesinger, Donald Rumsfeld, Harold Brown, and Caspar Weinberger.

A full eighteen years before Presidential Directive 59 (and twenty years before the announcement of Secretary Weinberger's five-year "defense guidance" plan), Secretary McNamara, in a speech at the University of Michigan, described a strategy that went beyond the requirements of "minimum deterrence" and that included both counterforce and countervalue retaliatory options. Then as now, the argument was advanced that credible nuclear deterrence mandates a strategy that allows for intermediate levels of military response, a second-strike counterforce strategy. Many elements of this strategy had been articulated several years earlier, in 1957, by Henry Kissinger in his book, *Nuclear Weapons and Foreign Policy.* Confronting what he called "the basic challenge to United States strategy," Kissinger wrote:

We cannot base all our plans on the assumption that war, if it comes, will inevitably be all-out. We must strive for a strategic doctrine which gives our diplomacy the greatest freedom of action and which addresses itself to the question of whether the nuclear age presents only risks or whether it does not also offer opportunities.[8]

The precise nature of Kissinger's preferred "strategic doctrine" here is preparation for limited nuclear war. While recognizing that the arguments against limited nuclear war are "persuasive," he insisted—

in what must now be seen as a bellwether of current policy—that nuclear war need not be apocalyptic. Consequently, said the future Secretary of State, "Limited nuclear war represents our most effective strategy against nuclear powers or against a major power which is capable of substituting manpower for technology."[9]

These ideas of a limited nuclear war—of a strategy of controlled annihilation—were also widely accepted by James Schlesinger during his tenure as Secretary of Defense. On March 4, 1974, Schlesinger testified before Congress in support of U.S. capability of reacting to a limited nuclear attack with selected counterforce strikes. According to his testimony, such strikes could greatly reduce the chances for escalation into all-out strategic exchanges, thereby producing fewer civilian casualties.

Mr. Schlesinger's strategic doctrine, like that of his doctrinal forbears and successors, left many questions unanswered: What are the probable effects of a limited nuclear war? What sorts of casualties might be expected in the wake of counterforce attacks against military targets envisioned in this plan for flexible response? Would the costs of a limited nuclear war really be "limited," or would they be as overwhelming as the expected consequences of all-out, "spasm" nuclear conflict?

In his 1974 Annual Report as Secretary of Defense, Schlesinger remarked that nuclear attacks against U.S. military installations might result in "relatively few civilian casualties." Subsequently, on September 11, 1974, he told the Subcommittee on Arms Control of the Senate Committee on Foreign Relations that as few as 800,000 casualties could result from an attack on U.S. ICBM silos. This remarkably sanguine view was based on the assumptions of: (1) a Soviet attack on all U.S. Minuteman and Titan ICBMs with one single-megaton warhead targeted on each silo, and (2) extensive civil defense protection.

Since Schlesinger's conclusions generated considerable skepticism among several senators, the Office of Technology Assessment of the U.S. Congress was asked to evaluate the Department of Defense calculations. In response, the OTA convened an ad hoc panel of experts, chaired by Dr. Jerome Wiesner. The Panel "concluded that the casualties calculated were substantially too low for the attacks in question as a result of a lack of attention to intermediate and long-term effects." The Panel also concluded that the DOD studies "did not adequately reflect the large uncertainties inherent in any attempt to determine the civilian damage which might result from a nuclear attack."[10]

Even more significantly, perhaps, the panel could not determine from DOD testimony any consistent set of hypothetical Soviet objectives in the assumed nuclear strikes. While the panel acknowledged that the Soviets could detonate a small number of nuclear weapons over isolated areas in the United States without producing significant civilian damage, it could not understand how they might possibly benefit from such an attack.

Accordingly, the Ad Hoc Panel on Nuclear Effects insisted that any analysis of proposed changes in U.S. target strategy should be conducted within a larger set of considerations affecting policy in this area. Such considerations, it believed, must include the extent to which new strategies could be executed without escalation to general nuclear war; the effects of nuclear war on deterrence; the degree to which such policy increases or decreases our reliance on nuclear weapons; the extent to which it raises or lowers the threshold of nuclear first use; and the effect on our allies' perception of the credibility of the U.S. commitment to their security. The panel recommended, therefore, "that the Foreign Relations Committee ask for the additional analysis of casualties outlined in the following section only if it intends to engage in a discussion of these other issues."[11]

Ultimately, the Department of Defense completed new calculations which show that under certain conditions, an attack upon U.S. ICBM silos could result in casualties of between 3 and 22 million as opposed to the 800,000 to 6.7 million previously cited by Schlesinger.[12] Regrettably, however, the discussion of "other issues" called for by the Ad Hoc Panel on Nuclear Effects has yet to take place. As in the case of its doctrinal antecedents, current U.S. strategic policy is premised on an inherently flawed assumption—that is, the military reasonableness of a limited nuclear attack.

Even if such attacks might hold out the "promise" of *relatively* low casualty levels, there is little reason to believe that anything short of an all-out nuclear assault would make military sense to the Soviets. According to Dr. Sidney Drell's testimony before the Senate Subcommittee on Arms Control, in order to carry out a militarily effective attack against U.S. ICBMs, one that would destroy about 800 out of 1,054, or 80 percent, the Soviets would have to unleash an attack which would engender approximately 18.3 million American fatalities. And even so extensive a counterforce assault would not be entirely disabling, since the remaining U.S. ICBMs would still constitute a "healthy robust retaliatory force."[13]

What has been developing over a period of many years in U.S. strategic planning circles, then, is a counterforce doctrine that both understates the effects of limited nuclear war and ignores the primary fact that such a war makes no military sense. Moreover, nothing in our current strategy suggests a plausible connection between nuclear war and politics. Why, exactly, are the Soviets getting ready to "fight and win"[14] a nuclear war with the United States? What conceivable postwar prospect can be associated with alleged Soviet plans for a first-strike against the United States? Why should the Soviets be expected to disregard the Clausewitzian principle that war should always be conducted with a view to sustaining the overriding "political object"?[15]

The dangers of assessing Soviet nuclear intentions *in vacuo* are considerable. By assuming that their Staatspolitik offers no homage to plausible relationships between nuclear war and national political goals, our own nuclear policy creates a bewildering expectation of first-strike scenarios that in turn produces a staggering array of provocative tactics and deployments. The combined effect of such U.S. strategic thinking is a heightened prospect of escalation and irrevocable collision.

Reflecting Clausewitz's framework for reconciling military strategy with political objectives, Michael Howard, Regius Professor of Modern History at Oxford University, recently raised important questions about this country's penchant for identifying Soviet intentions with capabilities:

When I read the flood of scenarios in strategic journals about first-strike capabilities, counterforce or countervailing strategies, flexible response, escalation dominance and the rest of the postulates of nuclear theology, I ask myself in bewilderment: this war they are describing, *what is it about?* The defense of Western Europe? Access to the Gulf? The protection of Japan? If so, why is this goal not mentioned, and why is the strategy not related to the progress of the conflict in these regions? But if it is not related to this kind of specific object, what are we talking about? Has not the bulk of American thinking been exactly what Clausewitz described—something that, because it is divorced from any political context, is "pointless and devoid of sense"?[16]

There is, in fact, no clear picture of what the Soviet Union might hope to gain from the kinds of limited counterforce attacks that determine the direction of current U.S. strategic policy. Indeed, everything that we know about Soviet military strategy indicates that it has no place whatsoever for the idea of limited nuclear war. In the Soviet view, all nuclear conflict would necessarily be total.

Once the nuclear firebreak has been crossed, it is most unlikely that conflict could remain limited. Ironically, this point was hinted at by Henry Kissinger, when in 1965 he wrote: "No one knows how governments or people will react to a nuclear explosion under conditions where both sides possess vast arsenals."[17] And it was understood by the four prominent authors of the article on "Nuclear Weapons and the Atlantic Alliance" in the Spring 1982 issue of *Foreign Affairs:*

It is time to recognize that no one has ever succeeded in advancing any persuasive reason to believe that any use of nuclear weapons, even on the smallest scale, could reliably be expected to remain limited. Every serious analysis and every military exercise, for over 25 years, has demonstrated that even the most restrained battlefield use would be enormously destructive to civilian life and property. There is no way for anyone to have any confidence that such a nuclear action will not lead to further and more devastating exchanges. Any use of nuclear weapons in Europe, by the Alliance or against it, carries with it a high and inescapable risk of escalation into the general nuclear war which would bring ruin to all and victory to none.[18]

While the prudent course would be to assume that any onset of a nuclear exchange must be avoided lest it become total, current U.S.

strategic policy underscores expanded counterforce targeting and its corollary recognition of limited nuclear war-fighting. Although it is clear that once a nuclear exchange has begun it would become impossible to verify yields, sizes, numbers, and types of nuclear weapons employed, current policy reaffirms the notion of limited exchanges conducted in deliberate and controlled fashion. In his Annual Defense Department Report for 1978, former Secretary of Defense Donald Rumsfeld insistently defended the idea that a full-scale strategic response *would be* distinguishable from attacks on military targets, and that counterforce nuclear exchanges between the superpowers need not escalate to all-out attacks on cities. According to Rumsfeld:

In every case considered, both the short-term and the longer-run collateral damage from attacks on a comprehensive list of military targets (including ICBM silos) has been dramatically lower than the fatalities from direct attacks on population targets. It must be emphasized, however, that the results, even in limited and controlled exchanges, could be appalling. They could involve the potential for millions of fatalities, even though the distinction between 10 million and 100 million fatalities is great and worth preserving.[19]

What Rumsfeld failed to consider, however, is that not only would ten million fatalities be outside the normal boundaries of "acceptable damage," but that it is also a figure suggested by a strategic doctrine that is totally alien to the Soviet Union.

A counterforce capability can serve only the nation that strikes first. Used in retaliation, counterforce-targeted warheads would hit only empty silos. Indeed, a second-strike counterforce strategy is simply a contradiction in terms. We should not be surprised, therefore, when Soviet spokesmen continue to characterize America's nuclear strategy as a provocative move toward an eventual U.S. first strike.[20] In their view, this assessment is supported by this country's planned deployment of new medium-range missiles in Western Europe, a plan they say is designed to draw Soviet retaliation away from the United States in the aftermath of the American first strike.

The Soviet assessment of aggressive U.S. designs is also supported, in their view, by this country's plan to place Soviet civilian and military leaders in jeopardy and by various, overwhelming technological difficulties associated with counterforce doctrines of retaliation. While the essential rationale of a limited and controlled nuclear conflict requires the *preservation* of adversary leadership once a war has begun, America's current nuclear strategy is geared toward destruction of the Soviet ruling elite at the outset. Such a strategy can only contribute to unlimited, uncontrolled nuclear war; indeed, the provocative targeting of Soviet leaders actually increases the likelihood of a Soviet first strike in the near term.

Even if there were reason for pursuing a second-strike counterforce strategy, such a strategy is called into question by the absence of appropriate supporting weapons systems. In a letter written in April 1979 to then Secretary of Defense Harold Brown, General Richard H. Ellis, Commander-in-Chief of the Strategic Air Command, indicated that United States strategic nuclear forces were incapable of carrying out a selective counterforce targeting strategy and would be in this handicapped position until 1986.[21] Similar concerns have been expressed by Colin Gray, one of the most ardent supporters of a countervailing American nuclear strategy.[22] For the most part, these reservations about strategic force capabilities needed to support a second-strike counterforce strategy center on the alleged vulnerability of America's silo-housed ICBM force. To reduce such perceived vulnerability during the next few years, the United States may move toward launch-on-warning (sometimes called launch under confirmed attack) targeting policies.[23] While such policies might help to secure U.S. Titan, Minuteman, and silo-housed MX missiles against surprise attack if adequate information were immediately accessible to our National Command Authorities (the President, the Secretary of Defense, and their duly deputized alternates or successors), they would portend an expanded risk of accidental nuclear war and consequently also of Soviet preemption.

Launch-on-warning policies would also depend upon the successful functioning of the U.S. alert apparatus. Should this apparatus fail to function for any reason, including Soviet preemption, chances are that no decision to launch could be made or implemented in the few minutes available. At this time, the Soviet Union already has operational a high-energy laser weapon capable of destroying U.S. satellites in low earth orbit. According to a recent report in *Aviation Week and Space Technology*, U.S. intelligence analysts believe that the Soviet high-energy laser weapon is capable of damaging subsystems and sensors on U.S. satellites at 100 km, and that the Soviets are working on more powerful laser weapons that will be able to damage optical sensors on U.S. early warning and reconnaissance satellites at altitudes up to 49,000 km.[24] Moreover, even if the Soviets were unable to jeopardize the U.S. warning sytems, it is virtually certain that their first strike would entirely disable this country's guidance and communications systems with killer satellites. Since an effective damage-limiting counterforce retaliation at Soviet hard targets would require ultraprecise satellite guidance, this Soviet capability precludes such a retaliation.

Reservations about the strategic force capabilities needed to support a second-strike counterforce strategy also center on the alleged need for weapons that are engineered with a view to neutralizing time-sensitive, hardened point targets. But, the search for requisite combinations of accuracy, payload, yield, and responsiveness to create single-shot hard target kill capabilities is seriously misconceived, since it mistakenly presumes that a Soviet first strike would be executed with substantial forces held in reserve. Since such a search increases Soviet fears of U.S. first strike, it also heightens the probability of Soviet preemption.

Soviet fears of a U.S. first strike might also have a self-fulfilling effect. Such fears might occasion their own adoption of launch-on-warning strategies, expanding the risk not only of accidental nuclear war, but also of preemption by the United States. Once again, the synergistic effects of America's current nuclear strategy are at variance with the objectives sought by that strategy. Rather than strengthen nuclear deterrence, the U.S. search for a countervailing strategy will inevitably increase the likelihood of nuclear war with the Soviet Union. This is the case because such a search will inevitably generate an escalatory cycle of move and countermove with unforeseen interactive effects.

When the superpowers become engaged in the uncertain dynamics of escalation (including both threats and possible armed conflict), they will find themselves in the precarious situation of trying to steer a steady course between the sheer rock of Scylla and the whirlpool of Charybdis. Should one side or the other back down out of fear, the retreat would probably be costly in terms of future global influence and power. Should both sides continue to exploit the presumed advantages of a committal strategy, the resulting escalation could well produce nuclear holocaust.

Herman Kahn has tried to identify some of the apparent dangers that lurk in the hideously complex dynamics of escalation by likening these dynamics to the game of "chicken" as it is played by two drivers on a road with a white line drawn down the middle. According to Kahn:

Both cars straddle the white line and drive toward each other at top speed. The first driver to lose his nerve and swerve into his own lane is "chicken"— an object of contempt and scorn—and he loses the game. The game is played among teenagers for prestige, for girls, for leadership of a gang, and for safety (i.e., to prevent other challenges and confrontations).[25]

But, since the actual processes of escalation are much more complicated than this game, Kahn suggests that "chicken" would present a more accurate analogy if

it were played with two cars starting an unknown distance apart, traveling toward each other at unknown speeds, and on roads with several forks so that the opposing sides are not certain that they are even on the same road. Both drivers should be giving and receiving threats and promises while they approach each other, and tearful mothers and stern fathers should be lining the sides of the roads urging, respectively, caution and manliness.[26]

The second analogy is hardly more reassuring than the first. Whichever way the game is played, the prospect of ultimate collision is unacceptably high. However much care is exercised, the fact that the game is being played by imperfect and vulnerable human beings underscores an inescapable truth: the process of superpower escalation is the start of a lethal partnership. Ultimately, the partners—and perhaps a substantial number of bystanders as well—must suffer irreversible consequences.

But the game goes on. In the United States our national leaders continue to develop a nuclear strategy based on the prospect of limited nuclear war. Unaware that the interactive effects of such a strategy encourage brinksmanship, these policymakers, ironically called "realists," are doing their best to hasten the unthinkable.

IMPROVED NUCLEAR DETERRENCE

Current U.S. nuclear strategy is also founded on the curious assumption that the Soviet Union is more likely to be deterred by the threat of limited U.S. counterforce reprisals than by the threat of overwhelming, total nuclear retaliation. Closely related to the assumption that a Soviet first strike might be limited, this assumption expands the U.S. commitment to limited nuclear war as a plausible strategic option. Anticipating the prospect of limited levels of Soviet aggression, U.S. nuclear strategy, as indicated above, has operationalized a policy of incremental strategic response. Such a policy, says Edward Rowny, chief START negotiator, "is a more realistic and effective way to deter the Soviet Union, which has been inexorably building its military capabilities for the last 15 years."[27]

What this idea ignores, however, is the stated Soviet unwillingness to play by U.S. strategic rules. Since the Soviet Union continues to threaten the United States with all-out nuclear war once the nuclear threshold has been crossed, the credibility of the U.S. commitment to selective counterforce strikes must appear very doubtful. Once again, the asymmetry in U.S. and Soviet strategic doctrines on the plausibility of limited nuclear war impairs the credibility of America's nuclear strategy. There is now every reason to believe that the Soviet response to "limited" U.S. counterstrikes would be just as overwhelming as it would be to a massive U.S. countervalue strike. It follows that the alleged flexibility of our nuclear strategy is illusory, offering no deterrence advantages over a strategy of unlimited reprisals.

These flaws in U.S. nuclear strategy are aggravated further by this country's own published doubts concerning controlled nuclear conflict. In the words of Harold Brown:

In adopting and implementing this policy (the countervailing strategy) we have no more illusions than our predecessors that a nuclear war could be closely and surgically controlled. There are, of course, great uncertainties about what would happen if nuclear weapons were ever again used. These uncertainties, combined with the catastrophic results sure to follow from a maximum escalation of the exchange, are an essential element of deterrence.[28]

This argument is seriously confused. Rather than functioning as "an essential element of deterrence," the uncertainties to which Brown refers undermine the credibility of a U.S. threat to employ a "measured" strategy of annihilation. And their effect is made all the more worrisome by virtue of their open expression. After all, Soviet perceptions of U.S. strategic self-doubt can only reinforce their rejection of graduated nuclear conflict.

Similarly, the uncertainties that would surround the response to any U.S. use of nuclear weapons undermine this country's reliance on theater nuclear forces. In view of the enormously high probability of Soviet nuclear counterretaliation and the terrible destruction that would be visited upon allies "in order to save them" Soviet strategists cannot possibly accept claims of U.S. willingness to use theater nuclear forces. Indeed, in the aftermath of an overwhelming Soviet conventional assault against American allies, it could conceivably be more rational for this country's national command authority to bypass theater nuclear forces altogether, urging instead the immediate resort to a strategic strike.

The credibility of the U.S. threat to use theater nuclear forces on behalf of allies would be further eroded by the still-possible deployment of a new generation of intermediate-range ballistic missiles. Since these missiles, unlike existing theater forces, would pose a major threat to the Soviet homeland, their retaliatory capability would carry a perceptively higher risk of escalation than existing forces. In fact, there is every reason to believe that these weapons would carry the same escalatory risk as strategic nuclear forces.

Although unlikely that he was motivated by an understanding of these deficiencies, President Reagan, on November 18, 1981, proposed cancelling plans to deploy new U.S. intermediate-range missiles in Europe in return for the dismantling of comparable Soviet forces. In setting the stage for the Soviet-American talks on limiting intermediate range weapons begun in Geneva on November 30, 1981, the President announced this country's willingness to forego IRBM deployment in exchange for Soviet elimination of SS-4, SS-5, and SS-20 missiles. Regrettably, the President's offer may have been more an attempt to blunt the antinuclear movement in Western Europe than a realistic starting point for meaningful negotiations. As the Soviets indicated almost immediately, the President's proposal deliberately overlooked United States submarine-based missiles, forward based weapons borne by bombers located in Western Europe or on carriers off Europe, as well as French and British nuclear weapons. Unless the United States displays flexibility in moving beyond its primary proposal, the current talks at Geneva could fail to halt the deployment of new U.S. missiles in Western Europe in 1983 and 1984.

In conducting its negotiations, the United States must keep in mind the probable implications of failure. As in the case of other elements of this country's nuclear strategy, the NATO plan to deploy 572 advanced nuclear-armed missiles (108 Pershing II extended-range battlefield-support ballistic missiles and 464 ground-launched cruise missiles) would undermine deterrence and generate new Soviet incentives to preempt. As the first new U.S. land-based missiles in Europe in two decades that would have the capability of reaching targets in the USSR, they would offer no revolution in weapons design or operational role. Rather, they would seek to establish a "Euro-strategic" balance by neutralizing the threat of recently upgraded Russian intermediate-range nuclear weapons.

Yet, there is no deterrence role for the two U.S. missiles that could not be satisfied by existing or improved U.S. strategic systems. For one reason or another, U.S thinking on the new intermediate-range forces is governed by the assumption that the Soviets are particularly sensitive to the warhead launching sites, and that they would be less apt to engage in no-holds-barred nuclear war if an attack were launched from European bases. Regrettably, Soviet military doctrine has always regarded such fine U.S. distinctions as artificial and pointless.[29]

From the viewpoint of the Soviet Union, it would make little difference if an attack on its territory were from a U.S.-based ICBM or from a Europe-based Pershing II or ground-launched cruise missiles (GLCM). Nevertheless, U.S. nuclear policy in this area is founded upon the myth that Pershing II and GLCM deployments will create an "escalatory ladder that provides a variety of response options below the strategic level and helps to insure the linkage between lower response options and the strategic nuclear forces."[30] Such deployments are apt to produce not an "escalatory ladder" but *escalation.* As the U.S. Arms Control and Disarmament Agency points out, "the versatility of a mix of long-range theater nuclear systems could cause Soviet leaders to perceive themselves confronted with the potential at some future time for large-scale increase in the U.S. arsenal capable of striking the USSR. . . . These perceptions could lead to expanded deployments of Soviet systems such as the SS-20 as a counter to any perceived strengthening of NATO's position vis-à-vis the Warsaw Pact."[31]

A similarly misconceived rationale surrounds the U.S. decision to proceed with full production of neutron weapons. While enhanced-radiation weapons would not constitute a threat to the Soviet homeland, and while they would reduce damage, in comparison to existing tactical nuclear weapons, to friendly forces, civilians, and structures, these miniature thermonuclear warheads would not enhance the credibility of this country's nuclear commitment to NATO. This is the case because such weapons would still represent a crossing of the critical "firebreak" between conventional and nuclear weapons. Hence, in view of current Soviet policy to respond to any such crossing with unlimited retaliation, the use of the neutron bomb would carry an intolerably high risk of escalation to strategic nuclear war.

Whether the first nuclear weapons used between NATO and the Warsaw Pact were neutron bombs or tactical forces, escalation to unlimited nuclear war would be very likely. This reality would obtain since any nuclear exchange would lead each side to press ahead with its entire arsenal. To do otherwise amidst the momentum of military operations, fear, anger, and uncertainty would be decidedly irrational. It is most likely his understanding of this fact that led President Carter, on April 7, 1978, to defer (but not discount) production of enhanced radiation weapons. It is the Reagan administration's misunderstanding of this fact that has occasioned its decision to go ahead with the neutron bomb.

Even demonstrations of automatic reaction for alliance guarantees of nuclear retaliation cannot ensure the perception of willingness to retaliate. No matter how high a value the United States might place on "protection" of various allies (the term "protection" is somewhat ironic here, since execution of the nuclear retaliatory threat would most likely hasten the destruction of the ally to be protected), it can never be as high as the value that it places upon its own security. No matter how often or how vehemently the United States claims that an attack on our NATO allies would be tantamount to an attack on the United States itself, it is apt to be viewed as an incredible claim. Hence, no level of commitment by rational decision makers which involves a high probability of nuclear counter-retaliation will be seen as irrevocable. While the use of tactical nuclear weapons may not involve any greater destruction than the use of massive conventional firepower, the truly critical threshold or "fire-break" exists between conventional and nuclear weapons (including enhanced-radiation weapons) rather than between different forms of nuclear weapons. This is the case because of the clear and verifiable distinction that exists between nuclear and non-nuclear weapons, and because of the symbolic and psychological implications that accompany nuclear combat in any form. Nuclear weapons *are* different because they are widely *believed* to be different. It is now altogether likely that tactical nuclear retaliation (or, as we have already seen, retaliation with the neutron bomb) would be perceived as the beginning of a genuinely no-holds-barred situation.

President Kennedy certainly understood this when he stated that "inevitably the use of small nuclear armaments will lead to larger and larger nuclear armaments on both sides, until the worldwide holocaust has begun."[32] This view is supported by *The Defense Monitor,* a publication of the highly regarded Center for Defense Information:

Once the nuclear threshold has been broken it is highly likely that the nuclear exchanges would escalate. Radio, radar, and other communications would be disrupted or cut. The pressures to destroy the adversary's nuclear force before they land a killing blow would lead to preemptive attacks. In the confusion, subtle peacetime distinctions between lower level tactical nuclear war and higher level tactical nuclear war, and all-out spasm nuclear war would vanish.[33]

In spite of this argument, American NATO policy continues to emphasize the special role of theater nuclear forces as a deterrent to conventional as well as theater nuclear attacks. What is most peculiar about this emphasis is that it is coupled with the understanding that operational Soviet military doctrine does not subscribe to a strategy of graduated nuclear response and that the limited use of nuclear weapons is fraught with the danger of escalation. With such an understanding, it is difficult to believe that the United States would actually be willing to make good on its theater nuclear commitments to NATO allies, and thus these commitments begin to lose their deterrent value.

This difficulty is underscored by the effects that theater nuclear forces would have on the countries being protected. A recent study by the Center for Defense Information reveals that the use of only 10 percent of the roughly 7000 tactical nuclear weapons which the United States maintains in Europe would destroy the entire area where these exchanges took place.[34] This situation would not be altered by deployment of the neutron bomb, since—as we have already noted—the expected Warsaw Pact counter-retaliation would be devastating and unlimited.

The argument that current nuclear strategy enhances deterrence has been cast in terms of an illusory "spectrum of deterrence" that would offer the president a set of flexible options in crisis situations. It is now being suggested in certain quarters[35] that this flexibility can be made more effective by emphasizing the U.S. capacity and willingness for nuclear war-fighting. As expressed by former Secretary of Defense Brown:

In our analysis and planning, we are necessarily giving greater attention to how a nuclear war would actually be fought by both sides if deterrence fails. There is no contradiction between this focus on how a war would be fought and what its results would be, *and* our purpose of insuring continued peace through mutual deterrence. Indeed, this focus helps us achieve deterrence and peace, by ensuring that our ability to retaliate is fully credible.[36]

In this context, Brown's meaning was unambiguous. An "ability to retaliate [that] is fully credible" is an ability to fight a nuclear war. And the need to acquire such an ability is based on the premise that the Soviet Union is preparing to fight and win a nuclear war. Ironically, this premise is at odds with another assumption of current U.S. nuclear strategy—that the Soviets might launch a limited nuclear first strike and subsequently cooperate in a limited nuclear war with the United States.

Leaving aside these contradictory assumptions, the alleged linkage between nuclear war-fighting capacity and credible deterrence is inherently ill-founded. The Soviet Union is no more likely to be deterred by an adversary that has announced its intention to dominate escalation processes during a nuclear war than by one that remains content with the capacity for assured destruction.[37] This is the case because the Soviets (given their views about the implausibility of limited nuclear war) already calculate on the basis of total nuclear effort by both sides.

As with certain other aspects of current U.S. nuclear strategy, the emphasis on creating a nuclear war-fighting potential is entirely counterproductive to this country's security. Such an emphasis goes well beyond the reasonable requirements of an assured destruction capability to a provocative demonstration of first-strike intentions. Whether or not such intentions are genuine (and I seriously doubt that they are), all that matters are Soviet *perceptions*. The logic of deterrence requires a demonstrated willingness and capacity to deliver an unacceptably damaging retaliation after absorbing a first strike, but where such demonstrations are supplanted by bellicose counterforce posturing, incentives are created for a rational adversary to preempt. In the words of Messrs. Bundy, Kennan, McNamara, and Smith, whose Spring 1982 piece in *Foreign Affairs* captured headlines throughout the world, it is time "to recognize that in the age of massive thermonuclear overkill it no longer makes sense—if it ever did—to hold these nuclear weapons for any other purpose than the prevention of their use."[38]

This is perhaps the central flaw in current U.S. nuclear strategy. Virtually all of the essential elements of this strategy occasion doubts among Soviet leaders about this country's alleged rejection of a nuclear first strike.[39] Rather than reinforce U.S. security by projecting the image of survivable nuclear forces that we are prepared to use in retaliation, this strategy undermines U.S. security by fostering the impression of first-strike inclinations. By encouraging a climate of strategic interaction in which the Soviet Union must exist in a continual and increasing expectation of imminent attack, the United States compels its adversary to take steps to strike first itself. Naturally, these steps are perceived as aggressive in turn, and in "reaction" to apparent Soviet designs, an unstoppable cycle of move and countermove is initiated. The net effect, of course, is insecurity for all concerned.

Ironically, therefore, current U.S. nuclear strategy increases rather than reduces the likelihood of nuclear war with the Soviet Union. Even if the Soviets would prefer a condition of protracted enmity with the United States to a superpower nuclear war, the expectation of a U.S. first strike will encourage them to strike first themselves. This is the case because they recognize the damage-limiting benefits that would accrue to the country that strikes first. Of course, they would anticipate extraordinary levels of destruction for themselves, and would prefer non-war to relative strategic advantage *if they had the choice.* But faced with a situation that is perceived to omit peace as an option, they would be compelled to choose preemption as the rational course.

It follows from this analysis that U.S. nuclear strategy is seriously flawed in creating the impression of preferring relative victory to non-war. Even if this impression is erroneous, all that matters is that it is perceived as genuine in Soviet strategic calculations. Regrettably, everything about current U.S. nuclear strategy encourages such a perception. To reverse such a dangerous perception while there is still time, this strategy must seek to communicate a different set of expectations to the Soviet Union, one that clarifies this country's distinct preference for non-war over any conceivable outcome of nuclear conflict. With such clarification the Soviet Union would be less inclined to calculate that rationality requires preemption, and the United States would be in a position to progressively implement parallel processes of *de-escalation*.[40]

To give meaningful content to such clarification, the United States should give immediate attention to various offensive qualities of the MX missile. Not only will the newly announced MX basing mode fail to reduce the widely alleged vulnerability of the ICBM leg of the triad, the MX's preemptive attack qualities will also detract from stable deterrence. Designed to deliver its enormously destructive load within 100 meters of target, the MX seeks to fulfill a destabilizing U.S. search for a high single-shot kill probability against hard targets (silos, submarine pens, nuclear storage sites, and command bunkers).

Supporters of the MX counterforce targeting qualities argue that there is no reason to make such Soviet targets safe from U.S. ICBMs when comparable targets in this country are at risk from Soviet ICBMs. But this argument is based entirely on the confusion of survivability and targeting objectives, and substitutes "monkey-see-monkey-do" logic for a well-reasoned de-escalation of strategic competition. Indeed, considered together with the U.S. failure to ratify SALT II, its continuing failure to seek strategic arms control with the Soviet Union, its continuing reliance on a policy of nuclear first use, its program to modernize long-range theater nuclear forces, and its renewed commitments to ballistic missile defense (BMD) and civil defense, the MX's potential for placing Soviet strategic forces in jeopardy naturally provides the Soviet Union with a greater incentive to strike first.

The destabilizing aspects of the MX are paralleled by other U.S. strategic force developments. The Trident II missile and warhead programs are designed to provide U.S. countersilo capabilities that could put a large portion of Soviet fixed ICBMs at risk. Although Trident II's potential hard-target kill capabilities are intended to provide a hedge against catastrophic failure of the other legs of the triad, it will almost certainly stimulate the Soviets to increase the number of attacking reentry vehicles (RVs). Similarly, the MK12A reentry vehicle is now being acquired to replace the MK-12 RV on 300 of the 550 Minuteman III missiles currently deployed. Since the essential rationale of this planned deployment is to expand the ICBM force's counterforce capability, the MK-12A RV will also heighten Soviet fears of U.S. preemption.[41]

Moreover, what is our purpose in placing Soviet military and civilian leaders in particular jeopardy? Is it, as one strategic analyst suggested recently, "to destroy the ability of the Soviet leadership to continue to exercise political control over its domestic and 'colonial' territory—either by killing the leadership itself, making it impossible for the leadership to communicate with its subordinates, or destroying the means (people and facilities) by which the leadership's orders are carried out"?[42] If this *is* the purpose, then it is clearly contrary to the essential rationale of a countervailing nuclear strategy: that is, preserving the prospects for limited, controlled nuclear conflict. Indeed, in view of this country's current inability to support its countervailing strategy with advanced weapons systems,[43] the enhanced targeting of Soviet leaders actually increases the likelihood of a Soviet first strike in the near term.

But what about the Soviets? Aren't *their* current deployments and capabilities provocative and destabilizing? Aren't *they* continuing to strive for nuclear superiority that is oriented toward a "win the war" potential and that is augmented by a far-reaching civil defense effort? Haven't they been developing precision guidance for their heavy MIRVed ICBMs, the SS-18 and SS-19, with a view to threatening the survival of U.S. ICBM forces?

The evidence is hardly encouraging. The steady growth of Soviet military power has fostered legitimate questions over Soviet strategic objectives. It may even be true, as the so-called "Team B" appraisal of five years ago concluded, that Moscow's buildup stems from patently aggressive designs. But it is *not* true, even if our "worst case" assumptions are correct, that U.S. security is best served by acting in an equally provocative or more provocative manner.

In developing a long-term defense program vis-à-vis the Soviet Union, the Reagan administration should be guided exclusively by a careful comparison of the costs and benefits of alternative courses of action. Such a comparison must take careful note of expected Soviet reactions to U.S. military developments and of the long-range *cumulative effects* of these developments. It will make precious little sense, for example, to substantially increase funding for BMD research and development since the Soviets can be expected to offset the ICBM survivability benefits with a refined offensive strategic capability.

Until measures are found to replace deterrence with a saner security system, improving the survivability of the U.S. strategic triad must continue to be an overriding goal of this country's defense posture. But it is altogether clear that this goal will not be served by the planned MX system and its associated counterforce weapons systems and doctrines. Again, Soviet countermoves must be anticipated. It is likely that the search for hard-target kill capacity will do more to undermine deterrence than to provide safety. That the Soviets are already engaged in such a search in no way suggests the rationality of U.S. imitation.

A similar argument must be made concerning renewed U.S. interest in civil defense. In what is likely to become the *reductio ad absurdum* of U.S. mimicry, the Reagan administration has begun to call for funding to implement a "Crisis Relocation Plan." Were it to be subjected to careful scrutiny in terms of expected costs and benefits, CRP would be revealed as immensely impractical and needlessly provocative. Even if it were assumed that large-scale U.S. civilian evacuation plans were workable, and that a government-directed civilian exodus several days before a nuclear war would not degenerate into chaos, a Soviet nuclear attack could still doom virtually every American. According to Irwin Redlener, M.D., who has studied CRP for Physicians for Social Responsibility, civil defense calculations by U.S. authorities are "based on little hard data." Ignoring the many important differences that exist between a city being evacuated in the face of a hurricane and one being flattened by a nuclear bomb, says Dr. Redlener, CRP rests on highly questionable analogies rather than upon well-reasoned analysis. Furthermore, Redlener notes that "CRP makes the basic assumption that a warning time of one week is essential to effect any reasonable degree of evacuation and protection. This discounts any possibility of a surprise attack. The elimination of a presumptive attack scenario makes little sense even to traditional military planners."[44]

Moreover, rather than strengthening deterrence by demonstrating this country's war preparedness (a demonstration that the Soviets seem no longer to need), plans for crisis relocation would underscore Soviet fears of a U.S. first strike. As Dr. Redlener points out, "evacuating U.S. counterforce and other target sites carries the distinct possibility of provoking the war it claims it will protect us from. How would an adversary interpret such an evacuation? Could this mean the U.S. was preparing to deploy its first-strike weapons? If so, would not the Soviets feel the need to strike first? Such considerations are logical, lethal, and apparently disregarded by current civil defense planners."[45]

VICTORY IS POSSIBLE

The third major assumption of current U.S. nuclear strategy is that victory is possible in a superpower nuclear war. Closely related to the other flawed assumptions concerning limited nuclear war and improved nuclear deterrence, this assumption makes nuclear war more likely by creating the impression that such a war might be profitably sustained. Contrary to all of the recent findings of the medical and scientific communities,[46] this assumption rejects the informed understanding that nuclear war would be uniquely and unavoidably catastrophic. According to Colin Gray and Keith Payne, "Recognition that war at any level can be won or lost, and that the distinction between winning and losing would not be trivial, is essential for intelligent defense planning. . . . If American nuclear power is to support U.S. foreign policy objectives, the United States must possess the ability to wage nuclear war rationally."[47]

Nuclear war, we are told, can be waged "rationally." Hence, the United States is urged to achieve strategic superiority—the "ability to wage a nuclear war at any level of violence with a reasonable prospect of defeating the Soviet Union and of recovering sufficiently to insure a satisfactory postwar world order."[48] And in a burst of uninformed optimism, these two strategic planners tell us: "A combination of counterforce offensive targeting, civil defense, and ballistic missile and air defense should hold U.S. casualties down to a level compatible with national survival and recovery."[49]

In considering these suggestions, one must ask whether these armchair strategists have even taken the trouble to look at the available scientific literature on nuclear war. If they *have,* how can they explain their own sweeping dissent? If they haven't, perhaps they should take a moment to pause and reflect upon an open letter to former President Carter and Chairman Brezhnev from a respected organization of 1,600 physicians, Physicians For Social Responsibility:

As physicians, scientists, and concerned citizens, alarmed by an international political climate that increasingly presents nuclear war as a "rational" possibility, we are impelled to renew a warning, based on medical and scientific analyses, that:

1. Nuclear war, even a "limited" one, would result in death, injury and disease on a scale that has no precedent in the history of human existence;
2. Medical "disaster planning" for a nuclear war is meaningless. There is no possible effective medical response. Most hospitals would be destroyed, most medical personnel dead or injured, most supplies unavailable. Most "survivors" would die;
3. There is no effective civil defense. The blast, thermal and radiation effects would kill even those in shelters, and the fallout would reach those who had been evacuated;
4. Recovery from nuclear war would be impossible. The economic, ecologic, and social fabric on which human life depends would be destroyed in the U.S., the USSR, and much of the rest of the world;
5. In sum, there can be no winners in a nuclear war. Worldwide fallout would contaminate much of the globe for generations and atmospheric effects would severely damage all living things.[50]

For anyone who had known or studied the effects of the atomic bombings of Hiroshima and Nagasaki, it is clear that a superpower nuclear war would bring not only death, but incoherence. In the words of Robert Jay Lifton: "The ultimate threat posed by nuclear weapons is not only death, but meaninglessness: an unknown death by an unimaginable weapon. War with such weapons is no longer heroic; death from such weapons is without valor."[51] Such meaninglessness would be accentuated by the impairment of symbolic immortality, a process by which human beings ordinarily feel that they can "live on" through their posterity. Since the occasion of superpower nuclear war would represent an assault on the very idea of posterity for millions of people, death would take place without rebirth, and the continuity of life would give way to authentic feelings of disintegration, separation, and stasis.

[The author next summarizes the leading non-classified studies on the immediate and long-term effects of nuclear war, the same studies upon which the essays in Chapter 1 ("Facing Up to Nuclear Extinction") are premised. The author then resumes his repudiation of the concept of nuclear victory.]

The idea that the concept of "victory" has no place in a nuclear war is as old as the Atomic Age. In one of the first major theoretical treatments of the subject of nuclear war, Bernard Brodie wrote:

The first and most vital step in any American security program for the age of atomic bombs is to take measures to guarantee to ourselves in case of attack the possibility of retaliation in kind. The writer in making this statement is not for the moment concerned about who will *win* the next war in which atomic bombs have been used. Thus far the chief purpose of our military establishment has been to win wars. From now on its chief purpose must be to avert them. It can have no other useful purpose.[52]

Even long before the Atomic Age, philosophers and military strategists probed the idea of victory with reasoned sensitivity. Machiavelli, for example, recognized the principle of an "economy of violence"[53] which distinguishes between creativity and destruction: "For it is the man who uses violence to spoil things, not the man who uses it to mend them, that is blameworthy."[54] With respect to war, Machiavelli counseled that victory need not be in the best interests of the prince, and that it might even produce an overall weakening of a state's position in international affairs.[55]

Unlike proponents of the "victory is possible" school, Machiavelli understood the difference between violence and power. More recently, Hannah Arendt has reflected on this distinction, elucidating a situation wherein the technical development of the implements of violence has now outstripped any rational justifications for their use in armed conflict. Hence, war is no longer the *ultima ratio* in world politics, the merciless final arbiter in international disputes, but rather an apocalyptic chess game that bears no resemblance to earlier games of power and domination. In such a game, if either "wins" both lose.[56]

Hannah Arendt's speculations on violence and power raise still another problem with the idea of "victory" in a nuclear war. This is the problem of arbitrariness or unpredictability intrinsic to all violence. Contrary to the anesthetized expectations of strategic thinkers who anticipate near-perfect symmetry between human behavior and their own rarified strategic plans, violence harbors within itself an ineradicable element of the unexpected:

. . . nowhere does Fortuna, good or ill luck, play a more fateful role in human affairs than on the battlefield, and this intrusion of the utterly unexpected does not disappear when people call it a "random event" and find it scientifically suspect; nor can it be eliminated by simulations, scenarios, game theories, and the like. There is no certainty in these matters, not even an ultimate certainty of mutual destruction under certain calculated circumstances. The very fact that those engaged in the perfection of the means of destruction have finally reached a level of technical development where their aim, namely warfare, is on the point of disappearing altogether by virtue of the means of its disposal is like an ironical reminder of this all-pervading unpredictability, which we encounter the moment we approach the realm of violence.[57]

In this connection, Arendt's concern for the uncertainties of violence stands in marked opposition to the ranks of all passionate systematizers who deny the essential irregularity of battlefield activity. In the fashion of modern historians who seek "laws" to explain and predict the vagaries of human conduct on a global scale, the strategic mythmakers transform imperfect mosaics of military behavior into a structured "logic of events." Entangled in false assumptions and ignored interactions, the proponents of victory display a singular failure to understand the non-rational springs of action and feeling, and an unreasonable degree of faith in game-theoretic systems of rational explanation. If only these strategic mythmakers could learn to appreciate how little humankind can control amidst the disorderly multitude of factors involved in war. If only they could learn to understand what presumptuous hazards are associated with a strategy that seeks to impose order on what must inevitably be a heightened form of chaos.

Rejecting the strategic mythmakers, students of world affairs must learn to disassociate the idea of "victory" from considerations of nuclear war. Even Clausewitz understood that war must be conducted with a view to post-war benefit and that the principle of "utmost force" must always be qualified by reference to "the political object." This view is seconded even by Henry Kissinger: "In the nuclear age, victory has lost its traditional significance. The outbreak of war is increasingly considered the worst catastrophe. Henceforth, the adequacy of any military establishment will be tested by its ability to preserve the peace."[58]

For this country's nuclear strategy to contribute effectively to the avoidance of nuclear war, it will have to emphasize the understanding that victory is not possible. Although Secretary of Defense Weinberger seems to have moved toward such an understanding with his speech at the U.S. Army War College on 3 June 1982 (a speech which asserted that nowhere in President Reagan's $180 billion program to "revitalize" the nuclear deterrent "do we mean to imply that nuclear war is winnable"), the elements of this speech stand in marked contrast with his defense guidance document (on strategy for fighting a "protracted nuclear war"). While this document was conceived with a view to avoiding nuclear war by strengthening deterrence, this view is founded upon the presumed advantages of a strategy of "escalation dominance"—the ability to "*prevail*" under conditions of a protracted nuclear war. As we have already seen, however, there is no reason to believe that such an ability would place additional constraints on any Soviet incentives to strike first, but there is reason to believe that it might *remove existing constraints* by signaling renewed American provocativeness. And there is reason to believe that the repeated emphasis on American nuclear capabilities that can "prevail" reflects no more than a semantic departure from earlier references to "victory."

ARMS CONTROL IS POSSIBLE

The fourth principal assumption of current U.S. nuclear strategy is that such a strategy can be undertaken without compromising the prospects for vertical and horizontal arms control. Yet, it is clear that the countervailing nuclear strategy requires supporting strategic weapons systems which must preclude any Soviet-American START accord. And since such an accord and progress beyond is essential to the success of the nonproliferation regime, this strategy also contributes to the spread of nuclear weapons to other countries.

According to the terms of the Treaty on the Nonproliferation of Nuclear Weapons, the superpowers are obligated to move expeditiously toward meaningful arms control and disarmament. In the words of Article VI:

Each of the Parties to the Treaty undertakes to pursue negotiations in good faith on effective measures relating to cessation of the nuclear arms race at an early date and to nuclear disarmament, and on a treaty on general and complete disarmament under strict and effective international control.

In the absence of U.S. compliance with Article VI, it is difficult to imagine that non-nuclear weapon states will continue their restricted condition indefinitely. This point is supported by the results of the latest NPT review conference, which ended in September 1980 after developing countries accused the superpowers of failing to reduce their strategic arsenals.[59] Should the United States proceed with its countervailing nuclear strategy, the prospects for negotiated arms limitation with the Soviet Union would be greatly diminished. The resultant increase in nuclear weapon states would not only create new opportunities for nuclear conflict, but would also heighten the probability of a Soviet-American nuclear war. This is the case because of the increased likelihood of catalytic war (war provoked by a new nuclear power), war between new nuclear powers with alliance or interest ties to the superpowers, and nuclear terrorism.

On July 16, 1981, President Reagan formally announced his administration's policy on limiting the spread of nuclear weapons.[60] While designed to correct the "false impression" that the Reagan administration is not strongly committed to nonproliferation objectives, the statement did nothing to indicate U.S. support for Article VI of the NPT. Indeed, the President's stated commitment to "Strive to reduce the motivation for acquiring nuclear explosives by working to improve regional and global stability and to promote understanding of the legitimate security concerns of other states" could be read as a thinly-veiled reaffirmation of U.S. reliance on theater nuclear forces. Such reliance, of course, is not only needlessly provocative to the Soviet Union, it is fundamentally inconsistent with the requirements of superpower arms control.

Without a serious and explicit commitment to the imperatives of Article VI, the Reagan administration's policy on nonproliferation is destined to fail. To create such a commitment, there must take place a basic transformation of the flawed notion that arms control is tied to the administration's definition of "parity." Hopefully, this transformation has already been set into motion by the commencement of START.

The underlying rationale of current U.S. nuclear strategy can be summed up as follows: In a world system that lacks government, right is coincident with power. Therefore, each state must do what it can to strengthen its relative power position. Indeed, in a world situation of "all against all," each state is obligated to pursue national goals on a competitive basis and to continually strive for maximum strength and influence.

The problem with this "realist" kind of thinking (an international relations legacy from Thucydides to Morgenthau and beyond) is that it is strikingly unrealistic. It generates a spiraling pattern of fear and mistrust which progressively inhibits opportunities for general cooperation, freezes hostilities into fixed and intransigent camps, and ultimately explodes into general warfare. At the same time, this fear and mistrust "feeds back" to world leaders and reinforces the commitment to a "get what you can" philosophy of international conduct. All in all, "realism" is an uncanny formula for global catastrophe.

The militaristic nations in world politics coexist in the manner of a group of herdsmen who share a common pasture and who feel it advantageous to increase the size of their respective herds. Although these herdsmen have calculated that it is in their own best interests to continuously enlarge their herds, they have calculated incorrectly. They have done so because they have failed to consider the *cumulative effect* of their calculations which is an overgrazed commons and economic ruin.

In the fashion of the herdsmen in this analogy, the Reagan administration continues to act as if the security of the United States is coincident with continued increases in strategic military forces. Like the herdsmen, the failure of the administration to understand the cumulative effects of its reasoning leads this country farther and farther away from the intended condition (in this case, of real security). Its search for an improved strategic power position vis-à-vis the Soviet Union will inevitably generate Soviet countermoves that nullify any force "improvements," and inhibit any remaining opportunities for essential cooperation. Since the Soviet Union will never "stand still" for the United States and allow it to achieve its current strategic objectives, the Reagan administration will *never* be prepared for genuine arms reductions. By arming for arms control, the United States will inevitably make arms control impossible.

Before current U.S. nuclear strategy can be rendered compatible with the imperatives of superpower arms control and nonproliferation, the Reagan administration must abandon its planned deployment of strategic weapons with hard-target kill capabilities. As has already been noted, Trident II and MX could put a large portion of Soviet fixed ICBMs at risk. According to the U.S. Arms Control and Disarmament Agency, "This could have significant destabilizing effects, and thus a potential negative arms control impact."[61]

Moreover, the administration must carefully avoid taking any measures that could lead to renunciation of the ABM Treaty. In this connection, there is a real danger that the United States may seek to protect its MX forces by the deployment of a Ballistic Missile Defense System. Should such deployment take place, the resultant ABM Treaty termination would be widely interpreted as U.S. violation of Article VI of the NPT. It follows that such deployment would be injurious to a sound U.S. nonproliferation policy.

Such deployment would also degrade the stability of deterrence between the superpowers by generating a parallel Soviet deployment of BMD systems. This would in turn generate a mutual search for new offensive missile capabilities. Taken together, such developments would heighten each side's fear of a first strike by the other, and would undermine any remaining prospects for the negotiation of a strategic arms control agreement.

The failure of the Reagan administration to seriously pursue the START process would have additional corrosive effects on superpower arms control efforts. One such effect might be the end of negotiations on long-range theater nuclear forces in Europe. As a recently issued report by the Committee for National Security points out, "The abandonment of this process would make it impossible to proceed with such negotiations. There is no purpose in trying to negotiate limits on Soviet medium and intermediate range missiles if the Soviets are free to deploy as many ICBMs as they wish and target them against Western Europe."[62]

Another such effect would be the end of negotiations to bar testing and deployment of antisatellite weapons systems. Without a new START agreement, ASAT competition would undoubtedly continue, thereby heightening tensions and first-strike fears. The resultant space weapons race would produce increased temptations to each side to preempt since destruction of certain satellite capabilities would leave the victim nation "blind."

At the time of the beginning of START negotiations, the administration had already abandoned the search for an agreement with the Soviet Union to prohibit antisatellite weapons. Notwithstanding President Reagan's expressed concern (May 9, 1982) for the "growing instability of the nuclear balance," Secretary of Defense Weinberger—in early June 1982—directed the Air Force to deploy antisatellite weapons within five years. It follows that the President's idea for "deep cuts" has been subordinated to his comprehensive program to "revitalize" the United States nuclear deterrent.[63]

As we have seen, current U.S. nuclear strategy cannot be reconciled with the requirements of strategic arms control and nonproliferation. To satisfy these requirements, thereby enhancing the prospects of nuclear war avoidance, the Reagan administration must take immediate steps to forswear nuclear weapons programs and associated policies that generate fear and insecurity in the Soviet Union and elsewhere. Concurrent with these steps, the administration should begin a process of restoring the entire arms control agenda to a serious position of primacy in superpower strategic relations.[64] For this process to transpire, Mr. Reagan should begin to recognize that the adversary relationship between the United States and the Soviet Union must not be modeled after the conflict between the archangels Michael and Lucifer. Rather than continue to base U.S. foreign policy on a Manichean view of good versus evil, the administration must learn to build upon the understanding that the adversaries share a joint and irreversible commitment to the avoidance of nuclear war.

NUCLEAR DETERRENCE CAN WORK FOREVER

The fifth major assumption of current U.S. nuclear strategy is that peace can be maintained indefinitely via nuclear deterrence. Lacking any really insightful plan for more enduring patterns of world order reform, this strategy is content with perpetuating a system of "deadly logic" that cannot possibly last out the century. At one time or another, in one way or another, the manifestly catastrophic possibilities that now lie latent in nuclear weapons are almost certain to occur, either by design or by accident, by misinformation or miscalculation, by lapse from rational decision or by unauthorized decision. Such an occurrence cannot be prevented merely by the kind of strategic fine-tuning described in President Reagan's arms control proposals to the Soviet Union.

Despite the successful workings of nuclear deterrence thus far,[65] a nuclear war between the superpowers could come to pass in several ways. It might come about inadvertently through the outcome of competition in risk-taking. It might begin by the seizure of nuclear weapons by allied countries. It might be provoked by a smaller power (catalytic war) or by war between smaller powers.

Or it might take place because of errors in calculating the outcomes of various anticipated courses of action. It might even take place as a consequence of irrationality, through use by unauthorized personnel, or by mechanical/electrical/computer malfunction. This last possibility is especially disturbing. Several false alarms of Soviet nuclear attack have in fact already occurred over the past few years as a result of mechanical errors. After one of these occasions, on November 9, 1979, the official Soviet press agency, Tass, criticized the error and warned that another such episode could have "irreparable consequences for the whole world."[66]

The Soviets may have good reason to be concerned. In the United States, the record of publicly reported false warnings spans at least two decades.[67] In addition, Pentagon tests of its multi-billion dollar World Wide Military Command and Control System—the computer nerve center of the entire United States military apparatus—indicate intolerable shortcomings. A recent test of WWMCCS in Spring 1977, called PRIME TARGET, linked up computers in the U.S. Atlantic Command (LANTCOM), European Command (EUCOM), Readiness Command (REDCOM), Tactical Air Command (TAC), and the National Military Command Center. Overall, the computers failed 62 percent of the time.[68]

It should not be assumed that only the United States is subject to false warnings and communications failures that might lead to nuclear war. The Soviets, too, depend upon highly complex warning systems and command and control systems that are subject to failure. It is very likely that their systems have experienced the same sorts of breakdowns over the years as our own. The difference is that we do not learn of their problems in the newspapers.

The idea that a nuclear war might begin by accident has been with us for some time. In the popular novel and movie, *Fail Safe,* a U.S. nuclear attack on the Soviet Union is triggered by a "statistically impossible" double mechanical failure that sends this country's bombers to Moscow. While the story does play fast and loose with the actual facts of U.S. command and control, it does point correctly to the inherent and unavoidable risks involved in mechanical and electronic systems—risks that may be heightened rather than lowered by the piling of one system upon another. (At least one NORAD false warning was allegedly set off by the deterioration of a forty-seven-cent computer chip.)

The malfunction of nuclear weapons systems must also be considered from the standpoint of nuclear weapon accidents which, although they have no bearing upon the problem of accidental nuclear war between the superpowers, may nonetheless have catastrophic effects. In this connection, one must look at the U.S. record of accidents involving nuclear weapons, at least as far as that record is known. According to the Department of Defense: "There has been a total of 33 accidents involving U.S. nuclear weapons throughout the period that the U.S. has had these weapons," although none has resulted in a nuclear detonation.[69]

The Center for Defense Information, a respected research institute in Washington, D.C., however, reports that there is evidence of many other nuclear weapon accidents that have gone unreported or unconfirmed. In the words of the Center publication, *The Defense Monitor,* "Serious students of the problem estimate that an average of one U.S. nuclear accident has occurred every year since 1945, with some estimating as many as thirty major nuclear accidents and 250 'minor' nuclear accidents during that time."[70]

Yet, this does not suggest that each of the superpowers is failing to take precautions against the accidental use of nuclear weapons. While very little is known about the Soviet Union in this regard, the United States Department of Defense has adopted measures to avert the accidental use of nuclear weapons by U.S. forces.[71] The principal steps taken include strict custodial control of these weapons and a considerable array of redundant safety features. These features are incorporated into the chain of command and into the weapons themselves. Where they concern the chain of command, these features are highlighted by the so-called "Two Man Concept," whereby no single individual has the ability to fire nuclear weapons; by a control system whereby each individual with a nuclear weapons responsibility has been formally certified under the "Human Reliability Program"; and by the use of "secure codes."

Where they concern the weapons themselves, these features emphasize "highly secure coded locking devices." Moreover, although the exact release procedures for nuclear weapons are highly classified, it is known that safeguards against accidental nuclear firings do vary somewhat from one weapon system to another. For example, all tactical nuclear weapons that are deployed overseas include mechanical or electrical devices which prevent their firing in the absence of a specially coded signal issued by higher command. Strategic nuclear weapons under U.S. Air Force jurisdiction incorporate somewhat different sorts of command/control devices that nonetheless serve the same purpose as those associated with tactical nuclear forces. Additionally, all U.S. nuclear weapons—tactical and strategic—incorporate some sort of "environmental sensing device" that is designed to prevent unwanted detonations. These include switches that respond to acceleration, deceleration, altitude, spin, gravity, and thermal forces.

While the weapons engineers and the military authorities must be commended for the fact that none of the nuclear weapon accidents has produced a nuclear explosion, it would be the height of folly to assume that we can avoid accidental nuclear war or nuclear weapon accidents indefinitely. This is to say nothing of the Soviet system of "positive control" or the Soviet system of safeguards about which we know so little. For example, exactly how strict and how reliable is the Soviet system of codes and communications? What sorts of safety devices are built into the Soviet weapons themselves? What kind of "Human Reliability Program" is operative among Soviet personnel who deal with nuclear weapons? What sorts of redundancies are built into Soviet command/control procedures for nuclear weapons expenditure? Do these procedures include an alternative national military command center as well as a network of airborne command posts to provide reliability? What is the Soviet safety record concerning accidents involving nuclear weapons?

The threat of accidental nuclear war between the United States and the Soviet Union is aggravated by the command and control systems of other nuclear powers, both those systems already in existence (especially

China and India) and those systems of countries soon to join the "nuclear club." Since other nuclear powers will have great difficulty in protecting their nuclear forces from first-strike attack, they will almost certainly turn to the deployment of nuclear weapons with automatic systems of nuclear retaliation (based upon the processing of electronic warnings by computer) and to the pre-delegation of launch authority. The resultant conditions are certain to pose grave hazards to everyone.

The spread of such conditions would affect the likelihood of nuclear war between the United States and the Soviet Union. There are at least two reasons for this: First, the generally greater likelihood of nuclear war associated with relaxed command and control over nuclear weapons implies a general increase in the number of conflicts which might involve superpower participation. This is especially true if the initial nuclear conflict were to involve an ally of one or both of the superpowers. Second, with the steady increase in the number of nuclear powers, it is conceivable that a new nuclear power could launch its nuclear weapons against one or the other superpower without the victim knowing for certain where the attack originated. In the event that the victim were to conclude that the attack came from the other superpower, a full-scale nuclear war between the United States and the Soviet Union might ensue. In such a case, the new nuclear power—possibly as a result of its own inadequate system of command and control—will have "catalyzed" nuclear war between the superpowers.

Regrettably, little can be done about the flaws in the systems of command and control of nuclear weapons. The essential "fault" lies not with these systems, but with the underlying strategy of peace through nuclear deterrence. The implementation of even more stringent measures to prevent the accidental use of nuclear weapons would in most cases impair the credibility of a country's nuclear deterrence position. As long as nations continue to base their hopes for peace and security on the ability to deliver overwhelming nuclear destruction to an aggressor, the risk of accidental nuclear war and of other nuclear weapon accidents will simply have to be endured.

The ingredients of a credible deterrence posture are exceedingly complex. Such a posture requires a state to successfully persuade would-be aggressors that it possesses the ability and the resolve to respond with unacceptably damaging retaliation. This is no mean feat. In terms of *ability,* it means being judged capable of withstanding a first-strike attack and of penetrating the would-be attacker's active defenses with unacceptable levels of destruction. In terms of *resolve,* it means being judged willing to actually deliver the promised reprisal. There is little reason to believe that all states are likely to meet these requirements even in the short run, let alone indefinitely.

Moreover, the presumed rationality upon which deterrence rests is itself very doubtful. The actual behavior of national decision makers is obviously not always rational. Even if we could believe that it is, this would say nothing about the accuracy of the information used in rational calculations. Rationality refers only to the intention of maximizing specified values or preferences. It does not tell us anything about whether the information used is correct or incorrect. Hence, rational actors may make errors in calculation which lead them to nuclear war and destruction.

It is also worth noting that the ability to make rational decisions in world politics is frequently undercut by the consequences of crisis and stress. Even national leaders who deliberately gear their decisions toward the preservation of the state may actually precipitate contrary effects. This might be the result of errors in information or faulty calculations engendered by stress-warping of perception and alertness. In the post-Watergate era in U.S. politics, one can only speculate how close a President of the United States may have already come to experiencing the level of emotional strain required to upset rational decision making in world politics.

The myth that nuclear deterrence can work indefinitely between the superpowers also contributes to the proliferation of nuclear weapons to other countries. Consequently, as long as this myth is sustained by current U.S. nuclear strategy, this country's security will be further eroded by the additional dangers of nuclear weapons spread. By failing to live up to the requirements of Article VI of the NPT, the United States will encourage the appearance of new nuclear weapons states that will quickly engage in qualitative and quantitative nuclear arms races of their own. The net effect of such arms races can only be a greatly heightened risk of nuclear war, for the superpowers and for every other state.

NOTES

1. PD 59 was signed by President Carter on July 25, 1980, and was then clarified by former Secretary of Defense Harold Brown in a speech at the Naval War College on August 20, 1980. The Reagan administration's "countervailing" nuclear strategy actually goes beyond PD 59 principles in its advocacy of "atomic superiority" and its overriding commitment to build a capacity to fight nuclear wars at any level. At present, the essential elements of this strategy are embedded in Secretary of Defense Weinberger's "comprehensive proposal" to expand United States strategic nuclear forces so that they might meet the requirements of nuclear war-fighting, . . . and in Weinberger's new five-year defense plan. In May 1982, a five-year defense plan, initiated by Secretary Weinberger, was leaked to the press. This plan would have American military leaders prepare for nuclear counterattacks against the Soviet Union "over a protracted period." Acknowledged by Secretary Weinberger in an address at the U.S. Army War College in Carlisle Barracks, Pennsylvania, on June 3, 1982, this plan would allegedly give the President a variety of options to prevent the Soviet Union from imposing nuclear blackmail. According to the New York Times, the defense guidance plan states: "The United States nuclear capability must prevail even under the conditions of a prolonged war. . . . The armed forces must have enough offensive

nuclear ability so that the United States would never emerge from a nuclear war without nuclear weapons while still threatened by enemy nuclear weapons." Reflecting the strategic mythmakers' notion of "escalation dominance," the document goes on to say that American nuclear forces "must prevail and be able to force the Soviet Union to seek earliest termination of hostilities on terms favorable to the United States." (See Richard Halloran, "New Atom War Strategy Confirmed," *New York Times,* June 4, 1982, p. 7.)

2. Sloss, "Carter's Nuclear Policy: Going From Mad to Worse? No: It's Evolutionary, Not Revolutionary, and Aims to Strengthen Deterrence," *Los Angeles Times,* August 31, 1980, p. 3 (emphasis in original).

3. See *New York Times,* January 13, 1954, p. 2.

4. Mutual Assured Destruction (MAD) is a condition in which each adversary possesses the ability to inflict an unacceptable degree of damage upon the other after absorbing a first strike.

5. See Harold Brown, Remarks Delivered at the Convocation Ceremonies for the 97th Naval War College Class, Naval War College, Newport, Rhode Island, August 20, 1980, p. 6.

6. Ibid., p. 7.

7. *Department of Defense Annual Report for FY 1981* (Washington, D.C.: 1980), p. 66.

8. See Henry Kissinger, *Nuclear Weapons and Foreign Policy* (Garden City, N.Y.: Doubleday and Co., 1957), p. 15.

9. Ibid., p. 166.

10. See *Analyses of Effects of Limited Nuclear Warfare,* a report prepared for the Subcommittee on Arms Control, International Organizations, and Security Agreements of the Committee on Foreign Relations, U.S. Senate, September 1975, p. 4.

11. Ibid., p. 5.

12. See Opening Statement by Senator Case to Hearing before the Subcommittee on Arms Control, International Organizations, and Security Agreements of the Committee on Foreign Relations, United States Senate, on "Possible Effects on U.S. Society of Nuclear Attacks Against U.S. Military Installations," September 18, 1975, p. 3.

13. See Dr. Drell's testimony of September 18, 1975, at Hearing, ibid., p. 21.

14. This assessment, which was endorsed by Vice President Bush during the presidential election campaign and is now embedded in Secretary Weinberger's "comprehensive proposal," is now seen almost regularly in the journal and popular literature. See, for example, Leon Sloss' comment that, "All the evidence suggests that we confront an adversary who appears to believe it is possible to fight and win a nuclear war." (Commentary on article by this writer, "Presidential Directive 59: A Critical Assessment," *Parameters,* Vol. 11, No. 1, March 1981, pp. 19–28, appearing in *Parameters,* Vol. 11, No. 2, June 1981, p. 90. Mr. Sloss, now with SRI International, directed the nuclear targeting policy review for the Department of Defense in 1978.) See also Richard Pipes, "Why the Soviet Union Thinks It Could Fight and Win a Nuclear War," *Commentary,* Vol. 64, No. 1, July 1977; and Gray and Payne, "Victory Is Possible," *Foreign Policy,* No. 39, Summer 1980, pp. 14–27. Yet, Soviet spokesmen reflect the understanding that any nuclear war would be intolerable and that there would be no purpose to "fight and win" such a war. In a speech before the 26th Congress of the Soviet Communist Party on February 23, 1981, Leonid Brezhnev said: "To try

and outstrip each other in the arms race, or to expect to win a nuclear war, is dangerous madness." In a speech at a Kremlin rally on November 6, 1981, Marshal Dmitri F. Ustinov, Minister of Defense, stated: "Western politicians and strategists stubbornly push the thesis that Soviet military doctrine allegedly assumes the possibility of an 'initial disarming strike,' of survival, and even of victory, in a nuclear war. All this is a deliberate lie." And in an address at a Soviet-American seminar in Washington on January 12, 1982, Nikolai N. Inozemtsev, Director of the Soviet Institute of World Economy and International Relations, observed: "Political and military doctrines have been changed. This has been reflected in our internal life. There is new determination to seek sharp reductions."

15. See Carl von Clausewitz, *On War,* Book 8, Chapter 6B, "War Is An Instrument of Policy" (Princeton: Princeton University Press, 1976).

16. See Michael E. Howard, "On Fighting a Nuclear War," *International Security,* Vol. 5, No. 4, Spring 1981, p. 9.

17. See Kissinger's introduction to his edited book of readings, *Problems of National Strategy* (New York: Praeger, 1965), p. 6.

18. See McGeorge Bundy, George F. Kennan, Robert S. McNamara, and Gerard Smith, "Nuclear Weapons and the Atlantic Alliance," *Foreign Affairs,* Spring 1982, p. 9.

19. See Rumsfeld, *Annual Report of the Department of Defense for 1978,* U.S. Government, Washington, D.C., p. 73.

20. See, for example, "Soviet Charges Reiterated," *New York Times,* August 21, 1980, p. A8.

21. Little has happened since General Ellis's statement to suggest pertinent force improvements. See Drew Middleton, "SAC Chief is Critical of Carter's New Nuclear Plan," *New York Times,* September 7, 1980, p. 19.

22. Writing in response to an article by this writer in a recent issue of *Parameters: The Journal of the U.S. Army War College* ("Presidential Directive 59: A Critical Assessment," note 14), Gray observed: "So far as physical assets are concerned, PD 59 cannot be implemented with current forces and C³I capabilities. Even if there were no reason to question the merit of the strategic vision in PD 59, the fact remains that the United States is the better part of a decade away from a matching force posture."

23. U.S. launch-under-attack policies appear to be taken very seriously by the Reagan administration. Earlier receptivity to such policies was announced by former Defense Secretary Brown: "The question is, would you launch land-based missiles before explosion of nuclear weapons on the United States? It is not our doctrine to do so—neither is it our doctrine that under no circumstances would we ever do so." See Brown, "Launch on Warning or Launch Under Attack?" *Defense/Space Daily,* November 11, 1977, p. 68; cited by John M. Collins, *U.S.-Soviet Military Balance: Concepts and Capabilities 1960–1980.* (New York: McGraw Hill, 1980), p. 129n.

24. See *Aviation Week and Space Technology,* Vol. 112, No. 24, June 16, 1980, pp. 60–61.

25. See Herman Kahn, *On Escalation: Metaphors and Scenarios* (New York: Praeger, 1965), p. 10.

26. Ibid., p. 12.

27. See Edward Rowny, "That 'New' Nuclear Strategy," *Washington Post,* August 25, 1980, p. 19.

28. See Brown, *Annual Report of the Department of Defense for FY 1981,* U.S. Government, Washington, D.C., p. 67.

29. For a sound, critical analysis of the planned NATO deployment of intermediate-range nuclear weapons, see Kevin N. Lewis, "Intermediate Range Nuclear Weapons," *Scientific American,* Vol. 243, No. 6, December 1980, pp. 63–73.

30. See "Long-Range Theater Nuclear Missile Systems and the Sea-Launched Cruise Missile," in *Fiscal Year 1982 Arms Control Impact Statements.* Submitted to the Congress by the President, U.S. Government, Washington, D.C., February 1981, pp. 200–238. Statements prepared by the U.S. Arms Control and Disarmament Agency.

31. Ibid., p. 230. The ACDA report also points out that a hazard of planned deployments includes a negative impact on the prospects for arms control.

32. See John F. Kennedy, *The Strategy of Peace* (New York: Harper & Row, 1960), p. 185.

33. See the *Defense Monitor,* Vol. 4, No. 2, February 1975, p. 3.

34. Ibid.

35. See, for example, the previously cited writings of Gray and Payne, Sloss, and Pipes as well as the recently articulated policies of Eugene Rostow at ACDA and Caspar Weinberger at Defense.

36. See Brown, Remarks at the Naval War College, note 5, p. 6.

37. See the previously cited reactions of Colin Gray and Leon Sloss to this writer's article on PD 59 in *Parameters.*

38. See Bundy et al., op. cit., "Nuclear Weapons and the Atlantic Alliance," p. 768.

39. In this connection, it should be understood that Soviet images of the U.S. as a nuclear adversary have long been founded on the plausibility of an American first strike. For examples of such images, see V. D. Sokolovsky, ed., *Soviet Military Strategy,* 3rd ed., ed. H. F. Scott (New York: Crane, Russak, 1968), pp. 56–57; A. Grechko, "V. I. Lenin i stroitel'stvo sovetskikh vooruzhennykh sil," *Kommunist,* No. 3, February 1969, pp. 15–26; and William D. Jackson, "Soviet Images of the U.S. As Nuclear Adversary 1969–1979," *World Politics,* Vol. 33, No. 4, July 1981, pp. 614–638. Nonetheless, since late 1979 the Soviet leadership has expressed *heightened* alarm over the U.S. quest for strategic counterforce planning and theater nuclear force improvements.

40. In this connection, special attention should be given to Charles E. Osgood's very promising GRIT (Graduated and Reciprocated Initiatives in Tension-Reduction) strategy. For information on this strategy, see Osgood's "Psycho-Social Dynamics and the Prospects for Mankind," presented to the Peace Science Society (International) in 1977 and to a UN Colloquium in 1978; and "The GRIT Strategy," *Bulletin of the Atomic Scientists,* Vol. 36, No. 5, May 1980, pp. 58–60.

41. According to an assessment offered by the U.S. Arms Control and Disarmament Agency: "The MK-12A RV was designed to be employed against the total spectrum of targets but increasingly has been planned for employment against a growing Soviet hardened target system, where its combination of yield and accuracy could be used to military advantage. Although the MM III in its current configuration is effective to some degree against hard targets, improved accuracies which may accrue as a result of the guidance improvement program and the higher yield of the MK-12A (W78) warhead would increase this capacity." See *Fiscal Year 1982 Arms Control Impact Statements,* February 1981, p. 3.

42. See Jeffrey T. Richelson, "The Dilemmas of Counterpower Targeting," *Comparative Strategy,* Vol. 2, No. 3, 1980, pp. 226–227.

43. See, for example, the published concerns of CINCSAC General Richard Ellis, in Drew Middleton, "SAC Chief is Critical of Carter's New Nuclear Plan," *New York Times,* September 7, 1980, p. 19.

44. See Physicians for Social Responsibility, *PSR Newsletter,* Vol. 2, No. 2, Summer 1981, p. 2.

45. Ibid.

46. See for example, *Hiroshima and Nagasaki: The Physical, Medical, and Social Effects of the Atomic Bombings,* by the Committee for the Compilation of Materials on Damage Caused by the Atomic Bombs in Hiroshima and Nagasaki (New York: Basic Books, 1981, 706 pp.); Ruth Adams and Susan Cullen, eds., *The Final Epidemic: Physicians and Scientists on Nuclear War* (Chicago: Educational Foundation for Nuclear Science, Inc., 1981); Arthur M. Katz, *Life After Nuclear War* (Cambridge, Mass.: Ballinger, 1981, 452 pp.); "The First Nuclear War Conference," December 7, 1978, a special report of the *Bulletin of the Atomic Scientists* (Chicago, 1979, 43 pp.); *Analyses of Effects of Limited Nuclear Warfare,* a report prepared for the Subcommittee on Arms Control, International Organizations, and Security Agreements of the Committee on Foreign Relations, United States Senate, September 1975, 156 pp.; *Worldwide Effects of Nuclear War . . . Some Perspectives,* a report of the U.S. Arms Control and Disarmament Agency (not dated, but produced after 1975), 24 pp.; *Long-Term Worldwide Effects of Multiple Nuclear-Weapons Detonations,* a report by the Committee to Study the Long-Term Worldwide Effects of Multiple Nuclear-Weapons Detonations, National Academy of Sciences, Washington, D.C., 1975, 212 pp.; *The Effects of Nuclear War,* a report by the Office of Technology Assessment, U.S. Congress, Washington, D.C., May 1979, 151 pp.; *Economic and Social Consequences of Nuclear Attacks on the United States,* a study prepared for the Joint Committee on Defense Production, Congress of the United States, published by the Committee on Banking, Housing, and Urban Affairs, United States Senate, Washington, D.C., March 1979, 150 pp.; Kevin N. Lewis, "The Prompt and Delayed Effects of Nuclear War," *Scientific American,* Vol. 241, No. 1, July 1979, pp. 35–47; Bernard Feld, "The Consequences of Nuclear War," *Bulletin of the Atomic Scientists,* Vol. 32, No. 6, June 1976, pp. 10–13; Louis René Beres, *Apocalypse; Nuclear Catastrophe in World Politics* (Chicago and London: University of Chicago Press, 1980, 315 pp.); *The Effects of Nuclear War,* a report by the U.S. Arms Control and Disarmament Agency, Washington, D.C., April 1979, 26 pp.; Bennett Ramberg, *Destruction of Nuclear Energy Facilities in War* (Lexington, Mass.: Lexington Books, 1980, 203 pp.); Michael E. Howard, "On Fighting a Nuclear War," *International Security,* Vol. 5, No. 4, Spring 1981, pp. 3–17; Ruth Leger Sivard, *World Military and Social Expenditures 1980* (Leesburg, Va.: Arms Control Association et al., 1980, 35 pp.); Franklyn Griffiths and John C. Polanyi, eds., *The Dangers of Nuclear War* (Toronto: University of Toronto Press, 1979, 197 pp.); *U.S. Urban Population Vulnerability,* a report by the U.S. Arms Control and Disarmament Agency, Washington, D.C., August 1979, 50 pp.; Sidney D. Drell, "The Effect of Nuclear Weapons and Nuclear War on Civilians," a talk presented at the Symposium on the Effects of Nuclear War sponsored by the Physicians for Social Responsibility and the Council for a Livable World, Herbst Theater, San Francisco, November 17, 1980, 12 pp.; E. P. Thompson, "A Letter to America," *Nation,* Vol. 232, No. 3, January 24, 1981, pp. 68–93; Kevin N. Lewis, "Intermediate-Range

Nuclear Weapons," *Scientific American,* Vol. 243, No. 6, December 1980, pp. 63–73; George B. Kistiakowsky, *Can a Limited Nuclear War be Won? The Defense Monitor,* Center for Defense Information, Vol. 10, No. 2, Washington, D.C., 1979, 8 pp.; *The Race to Nuclear War: Three Statements, The Defense Monitor,* Vol. 9, No. 6, Washington, D.C., 1980, 8 pp.; *War Without Winners, The Defense Monitor,* Vol. 8, No. 2, Washington, D.C., 1979, 8 pp.; and the several conferences sponsored by Physicians for Social Responsibility on *The Medical Consequences of Nuclear Weapons and Nuclear War.* A full report of the physicians' campaign to prevent nuclear war is contained in the *Bulletin of the Atomic Scientists,* Vol. 37, No. 6, June/July 1981, 65 pp.

47. See Gray and Payne, "Victory Is Possible," *Foreign Policy,* No. 39, Summer 1980, p. 14.

48. Ibid., p. 19. This search for strategic superiority is, of course, an integral part of the Reagan administration's nuclear strategy.

49. Ibid., p. 25.

50. See "An Open Letter to President Carter and Chairman Brezhnev," Physicians for Social Responsibility, *PSR Newsletter,* Vol. 1, No. 2, April 1980, p. 1. This letter is a summary for informed laypersons of more technical studies undertaken by Physicians For Social Responsibility. These studies are the product of a series of symposia sponsored by PSR and affiliated groups on the subject of "The Medical Consequences of Nuclear Weapons and Nuclear War." Recent symposia were held in San Francisco (November 17–18 1980) and Chicago (June 19–20 1981). Similarly, scholarly studies of the effects of nuclear war have been undertaken by International Physicians For The Prevention of Nuclear War, a group of prominent physicians modeled after the Pugwash Movement. The June/July 1981 issue of the *Bulletin of Atomic Scientists* (Vol. 37, No. 6) is dedicated entirely to the writings of the international community of physicians on nuclear war, the ultimate medical emergency. See also Ruth Adams and Susan Cullen, eds., *The Final Epidemic: Physicians and Scientists on Nuclear War* (Chicago, Educational Foundation for Nuclear Science, 1981).

51. Robert J. Lifton and Eric Olson, *Living and Dying* (New York: Praeger, 1974), p. 129.

52. See Bernard Brodie, ed., *The Absolute Weapon* (New York: Harcourt, Brace, 1946), p. 76.

53. See the discussion of this principle in Sheldon S. Wolin, *Politics and Vision: Continuity and Innovation in Western Political Thought* (Boston: Little, Brown, 1960), pp. 195–238.

54. See *Discourses,* I, cited by Wolin, note 65, p. 221.

55. See *Discourses,* II, cited by Wolin, note 65, p. 222.

56. See Hannah Arendt, *On Violence* (New York: Harcourt, Brace, 1970), p. 3.

57. Ibid., pp. 4–5.

58. See Henry Kissinger, *The Necessity for Choice: Prospects of American Foreign Policy* (Garden City, N.Y.: Doubleday, Anchor, 1962), p. 12.

59. See "1980 Review Conference of the Treaty on the Non-Proliferation of Nuclear Weapons," ACDA Special Report, November 1980, 14 pp.

60. See "Reagan's Statement on Nuclear Weapons," *New York Times,* July 17, 1981, p. 6.

61. See *Fiscal Year 1982 Arms Control Impact Statements,* note 32, p. VIII.

62. See *An Arms Control Agenda For The Eighties,* The Committee for National Security, 1742 N Street, N.W., Washington, D.C., June 30, 1981, p. 10. This writer is one of the authors of the CNS report.

63. A secret five-year "defense guidance" document, signed by Secretary Weinberger in March 1982, instructs the services to build prototypes of space-based weapons to "be prepared to deploy fully developed and operationally ready systems should their use prove to be in our national interest." The Department of Defense has long been at work on space-based laser technology, and the Defense Advanced Research Projects Agency (DARPA) has spent considerable sums on space-related high-energy laser research.

64. In this connection, a clear difference in priorities is evident between the Carter and Reagan administrations. The difference is elucidated by a comparison of the positions of former Secretary of State Muskie and Secretary Haig. Speaking before the Senate Foreign Relations Committee on September 16, 1980, on "U.S. Nuclear Strategy," Muskie emphasized that "American nuclear strategy should be fully consistent with our arms control objectives, so that we preserve the opportunities to strengthen security and stability by means of equitable and verifiable arms control agreements." (See U.S. Department of State, Bureau of Public Affairs, *Current Policy,* No. 219, p. 1.) More recently, in an address before the Foreign Policy Association in New York on July 14, 1981, Secretary Haig stated, "arms control can only be one element in a comprehensive structure of defense and foreign policy designed to reduce the risks of war. It cannot be the political centerpiece or the crucial barometer of U.S.-Soviet relationships. . . . Arms control proposals should be designed in the context of the security situation we face, our military needs, and our defense strategy. Arms control should complement military programs in meeting these needs." (See U.S. Department of State, Bureau of Public Affairs, "Arms Control for the 1980's: An American Policy," *Current Policy,* No. 292, p. 2.)

65. In this connection, "successful" is defined very narrowly in terms of the avoidance of nuclear war. Where the workings of nuclear deterrence are considered more broadly in terms of effects on day-to-day life under the threat of nuclear annihilation, however, they can hardly be termed "successful." For example, the prevailing system of "deadly logic" has had terribly corrosive effects on ordinary human feelings of care and compassion. In the United States, small but growing bands of Americans dubbed "survivalists" are arming themselves and learning how to kill in a post-apocalypse milieu. Going far beyond the self-help aspect of the bomb shelter movement of the 1950s and 1960s, this retreat to medieval thinking entails a heightened form of social Darwinism, a generally accepted willingness to kill neighbors to survive. As one survivalist in northern Georgia put it recently, "If there is a nuclear war, I hope everyone in the cities is killed. I don't want them coming out afterwards expecting me to feed them or to take what I've got."

Another frequently overlooked cost of nuclear deterrence is the accumulation of vast quantities of nuclear waste. Up till now, 99 percent by volume of all high-level nuclear wastes (the most radioactive) in the United States has come from military activities. Since nuclear wastes can be dangerous to humans not only through direct contact, but also by getting into water supplies or the food chain of plants and animals that we eat, this cost of nuclear deterrence cannot be taken lightly. Indeed, even if all nuclear reactors were shut down today and not another hydrogen bomb produced, we would still have a mountain of nuclear wastes that could seriously imperil future generations. (See "Military Nuclear

Wastes: The Hidden Burden of the Nuclear Arms Race," *Defense Monitor,* Center For Defense Information, Washington, D.C., Vol. 10, No. 1, 1981.)

A far more widely understood cost of nuclear deterrence is, of course, the economic deterioration and social unrest brought by steadily rising military expenditures. Most importantly, perhaps, military spending is uniquely inflationary. While the Reagan administration's widely touted budget cuts are intended to create expectations of success in fighting inflation, its expanded military spending will overheat the economy by generating more spendable income than good and services to absorb it. This spending will also have a depressing effect on investment, which will in turn thwart economic growth and prolong inflationary pressures. Moreover, it will create a distinct government-dependent sector characterized by rapid obsolescence and product change, unstable markets, excessive waste endemic to large bureaucracies beyond public control, cost-plus pricing and reduced pressures for management efficiency.

In the final analysis, the essential human costs of military spending associated with the dead-end search for protracted nuclear deterrence are vast unmet needs for income, education, health, nutrition, and housing. In the words of the distinguished economist, Ruth Leger Sivard, "In short, what the arms race means in human terms is that more people are condemned to die of hunger and of foul water; children to grow up retarded in body and mind; the special needs of the elderly to be neglected; people to live out their lives in fear and with hate." (See *World Military and Social Expenditures 1980,* World Priorities, Leesburg, Virginia, 1980, p. 18.) For more information on the debilitating economic effects of the arms race, see John Kenneth Galbraith, "The Economics of the Arms Race and After," *East/West Outlook,* American Committee on East-West Accord, Vol. 4, No. 2, May-June 1981; Admiral Gene R. LaRocque, "We Spend Too Much on Defense," *New York Times,* February 1, 1981, p. F3; Wassily Leontief, "Big Boosts in Defense Risk 'Economic Calamity,'" an interview with the Nobel Prize winning economist in *U.S. News and World Report,* 1981, reprinted by the Committee for National Security; and Seymour Melman, "Beating 'Swords' Into Subways," *New York Times Magazine,* November 19, 1978, p. 43.

66. In this connection, we might note that the recent Titan missile accident in the United States can hardly be reassuring to the Soviets.

67. See Lloyd J. Dumas, "National Insecurity in the Nuclear Age," *Bulletin of the Atomic Scientists,* Vol. 32, No. 5, May 1976, pp. 28-29.

68. See this writer's article prepared for the Independent News Alliance (INA) in July 1980, "Flaws in Systems of Command and Control: Nuclear War by Accident."

69. From U.S. Department of Defense undated press release sent to the author by W. Y. Smith, Lieutenant General, USAF, and Assistant to the Chairman, Joint Chiefs of Staff, June 16, 1976.

70. See *The Defense Monitor,* Vol. 4, No. 2, February 1975, p. 9.

71. See U.S. Department of Defense, Directive No. 5030.15, *Safety Studies and Reviews of Nuclear Weapons System,* August 8, 1974, pp. 3-4.

16. The Prospects for Deterrence

Hedley Bull

Deterrence has been the leading strategic idea of our times, at least in the Western world. Along with the idea of limited war, it has enabled us to persuade ourselves that force can still be used as an instrument of state policy, even while recognizing that the outbreak of an unlimited nuclear war would represent the breakdown of policy. Around the idea of mutual nuclear deterrence we have built our hopes of avoiding such a war.

*   *   *

As we contemplate the period from now until the end of the century, it is appropriate that we should ask ourselves the following questions:

- To what extent, in thinking about peace and security in the future, should we continue to rely upon concepts of strategic deterrence, and especially upon the notion of a stable relationship of mutual nuclear deterrence? How valid are the old premises?
- To the extent that we *do* continue to rely upon these notions, how will our efforts be affected by the political and technological conditions likely to prevail between now and the year 2000? What are the future prospects for strategic nuclear deterrence?
- Should arms control continue to be directed towards the stability of mutual nuclear deterrence, and if so, what can arms control do to promote it?*

THE VALIDITY OF OLD PREMISES

The first of these questions is the most important. There is a great danger in this kind of discussion that we may consider merely how to promote deterrence, and not also whether this is what we should be promoting.

On the evidence so far, the system of mutual deterrence is fulfilling its promise. There has been no nuclear war, nor war of any kind between the superpowers or between the European alliances built around them, nor indeed any war between fully industrialized powers. The limited conflicts in Europe, which Kissinger and others in the late 1950s believed to have been made more likely by the rise of mutual deterrence at the strategic nuclear level, have not materialized. Furthermore, by contrast

---

*Hedley Bull's treatment of this question has been deleted in this extract.—*Ed.*

with the anxieties manifest during the second Berlin and Cuban missile crises, there is a strong public feeling of security over the issue of nuclear war—so much so that the phrase "balance of *terror*" is something of a misnomer when applied to the present time.

* * *

Our starting point, then, has to be the recognition that the doctrine of the pacific effects of mutual nuclear deterrence between the superpowers is, to say the least, not yet confounded. Nevertheless, it appears that those in the Western countries who plan strategic and arms-control policies are unduly reliant upon ideas of deterrence and mutual deterrence, and feel too comfortable about the bases of their own position. As we contemplate the future, it is important that we ask not simply how strategic deterrence can be preserved against the dangers that menace it but also how far peace and security can be provided in this way. Some of the limitations of the doctrine of peace through mutual nuclear deterrence are the following.

First, mutual nuclear deterrence provides at best an incomplete formula for dealing with even the immediate military dangers of the Soviet-American confrontation. For as long as it "works," what the relationship of mutual nuclear deterrence accomplishes is the avoidance of the outbreak of war by a deliberate or calculated attack. As critics of "deterrence only" policies pointed out almost from the beginning, this leaves unanswered the question of what happens if war nevertheless breaks out. The doctrines and weapons most suitable for maximizing deterrence are not necessarily those most suitable for the rational conduct of a war or for survival in one, and to the extent that the former requirement is in conflict with the latter, some balance between the two has been struck. It also leaves unanswered the question of how we are to avoid the outbreak of war by accident or miscalculation. The frontiers between war by calculation and war by miscalculation are not easily defined, but there is undoubtedly a distinction between seeing clearly that the course one has embarked upon will lead certainly to the destruction of one's country and failing to do so.

All this is familiar: the need to think beyond "deterrence only" so as to plan rational conduct in the event that deterrence fails and the need to cope with the danger of war by accident or miscalculation, especially by seeking to avoid or control crises, are well understood. The point is that the existence of a relationship of mutual nuclear deterrence, even one that is "stable" in the sense that it has a built-in tendency to persist, does not in itself provide solutions to these problems (a point often obscured by loose use of the term "stability," which can refer to the stability of the peace or of the "arms race" as well as to that of mutual deterrence).

Second, deterrence is a technique, the art of finding the means to a given end, in this case that of causing a potentially hostile opponent to desist from resorting to an attack. Within the framework of deterrence policy what we discuss is the means by which we can best achieve this goal: with this or that mix of forces, targeting doctrine, or device for demonstrating commitment or resolve. In deterring wars (as in fighting them) the tendency of the experts or professionals is to become absorbed in the choice of means and to lose sight of the choice of ends—the more so in this area because of the scope it provides for elegant analysis and quantification.

But we cannot afford to lose sight of the choice of proper ends, which are likely to be too complex and subtle to be accommodated in a conception as wooden as that of "deterring the opponent." Peace and security may require efforts not so much to respond to an enemy's hostility as to attempt to make the enemy less hostile—as George and Smoke argue in their admirable study, *Deterrence in American Foreign Policy;* such efforts may be served less well by threats of punishment than by the prospect of rewards for willingness to compromise, by diplomacy rather than deterrence—and this will require willingness to modify our own objectives as well as encouraging an enemy to modify his.[1] A preoccupation with deterrence, especially when it becomes a self-contained devotion to the choice of technique, will direct us away from these wider dimensions of the problem.

Deterrence (and mutual deterrence) theory was formulated in the setting of the Cold War and reflects the assumptions that there are two actors, that these actors are roughly comparable, and that they are very hostile to one another yet have certain common conceptions of what constitutes "rational action." The theory does not tell us what modifications have to be made if one or more of these assumptions cannot be made—if, for example, there are three or more actors, if the actors are radically different kinds of power, if the hostility between them is much less (or much greater) than it was between America and the Soviet Union in the Cold War, or if there are not shared beliefs about "rational" behavior. George and Smoke have criticized the attempt to translate the theory of deterrence into the context of limited war and sub-limited war. There are similar problems about the transposition of it from the Cold War to the détente to the post-détente phases of Soviet-American relations, and about its applicability to other pairs of nuclear and potentially nuclear antagonists and to conflicts in which more than two actors are involved.

Some time ago I pointed out that underlying contemporary Western strategic analysis there is a conception of "strategic man," a cousin of the "economic man" whose existence is assumed in classical economic theory, and that like his cousin, "strategic man" does not provide the key to human behavior at all times and in all places.[2] If we are to apply deterrence theory to a host of international political situations other than that of the Soviet-American conflict at the time of the Cold War, we have either to develop a conception of a genuinely universal "strategic man" or to abandon the concept.

Third, the doctrine of peace through mutual deterrence assumes that those who have the capacity to initiate nuclear warfare will act "rationally," at least in the sense that they will act in ways that are both consistent internally and with the principle of not deliberately willing the destruction of their own society.[3] This is the cardinal weakness of the doctrine, the reason why our hopes for peace cannot be allowed to rest permanently upon it. We can say that nuclear decision makers have so far acted "rationally" in this sense. But history gives us no reason to expect that present nuclear decision makers, the decision makers from other states, and perhaps non-state groups that will join them, and the succesors of all these throughout the ages can be relied on to act as the theory requires them to.

Fourth, underlying all Western (and, in so far as it exists, Soviet) thinking about mutual nuclear deterrence there is a glaring inconsistency. This is the inconsistency between the view we hold that mutual nuclear deterrence is a source of security in the relationship between the United States and the Soviet Union and our rejection of the view that it might also be a source of security in the relations of other antagonistic powers that are at present non-nuclear. As the nuclear "have-nots" never weary of pointing out, the doctrine that nuclear proliferation is good for ourselves but bad for others rationalizes the existing distribution of power. Of course, many arguments can be adduced to show that nuclear weapons in the hands of possible newcomers to the nuclear club would be likely to be more dangerous than those that are at the disposal of the present custodians. Some of these arguments have a good deal of force, but there is no way in which the present nuclear powers can convince the rest of international society that the logic of mutual nuclear deterrence applies only to themselves. While it is true that much of the impetus towards nuclear proliferation derives from conflicts among nuclear "have-nots" rather than from rivalries of the latter with the "haves," our attitude to mutual nuclear deterrence has to be determined not simply by its place in Soviet-American or East-West relations but by its meaning for the international political system as a whole. In the long run, the best course is to work against all nuclear proliferation, that which has already taken place as well as that which may occur in future, however difficult this may be. This requires us to take every opportunity to push nuclear weapons—and the doctrines and practices of nuclear deterrence associated with them—as far into the background of international political relationships as possible. The inconsistency to which I refer is a genuine one, and we should resolve it not by concluding that mutual nuclear deterrence can bring peace and security to all relationships of conflict in world politics but by questioning the assumption that it has brought peace and security in the conflict between the superpowers.

Fifth, all policies of nuclear deterrence, unilateral or bilateral, are morally disreputable. The deliberate slaughtering of millions of innocent people, for whatever reason, is wicked. So is threatening to do so, if this means that we actually intend to carry out the threat (as, according to official Western and Soviet doctrines, we do).

There are mitigating circumstances. The end which our deterrence policies serve—the preservation of our security and independence—has a high moral value for us, as the preservation of Soviet security and independence has for citizens of the Soviet Union. The alternative policy (that of relaxing nuclear deterrence to the point of jeopardizing our security) is also morally disreputable. There are moral difficulties, moreover, in the position of those individuals who elect to withdraw into a world of private moral rectitude and disavow responsibility. In this area there are no courses of action open to us that are free of moral difficulty, although this does not mean that any course of action is as morally good or bad as any other, or that the moral arguments for different policies all cancel one another out and can therefore be disregarded.[4]

If we are to persist in policies of nuclear deterrence, it is important to recognize that they do involve us in wickedness, and we must remain clear-sighted about what we are doing, whatever the efforts of the experts and the bureaucrats to obscure our vision. This awareness of the true moral character of our policies may not cause us to abandon them, but it will prevent us from being fully reconciled to them and will alert us to seize whatever opportunities may arise for improvements at the margin.

THE PROSPECTS
FOR STRATEGIC DETERRENCE

A review of the old premises, then, suggests that we ought to seek ways of making ourselves less dependent upon the concept and practice of strategic nuclear deterrence. We can agree with McGeorge Bundy, quoting Bernard Brodie, that deterrence should not be depreciated in order to improve the chances of "winning."[5] But it is important not to make a fetish of deterrence. We must break out of the intellectual straitjacket imposed by the professionals' attempt to make deterrence a technique and recognize that deterrence is not a sufficient goal of policy in itself. In the long run it does not provide a sound basis for peace and security.

However, the opportunities that seem likely to arise between now and the end of the century for making ourselves less dependent on strategic deterrence do not appear great. There is today in the Western world a widespread, and by no means unjustified, expectation of what David Gompert has called "strategic deterioration."[6] On the one hand, we are not going to be able to do without strategic deterrence, and on the other, the political and technological conditions for maintaining it seem likely to be less favorable in the next two or three decades than in the last.

The Central Balance

Are we likely to witness a decline in the stability of the Soviet-American relationship of mutual nuclear deterrence as a consequence of the acquisition by one side or both of a disarming capacity or an effective population defense? Are there signs that the growing vulnerability of American land-based strategic missile forces, about which we hear so much, will be seriously destabilizing? And what about the greater threat to the Soviet Union's deterrent presented by vulnerability of her (proportionately greater) land-based forces? Will the alleged "relative vulnerability" of strategic bomber and submarine-based forces, and the possible conjunction with these developments of some kind of breakthrough in defense against missile attack, make a substantial difference?

Twenty years is a long time, but all this is difficult to believe. At present the invulnerability of strategic forces other than the land-based missile forces is not in doubt. If it were, countermeasures would be taken that would be likely to restore their invulnerability or provide substitutes, as is happening now in the case of the land-based forces. More fundamentally, mutual nuclear deterrence does not necessarily require the invulnerability of land-based forces: at all events, even if it does as a matter of sound policy, it does not as a matter of logic. Richard Garwin has recently argued that even a Minuteman force that is entirely vulnerable has some deterrent value.[7] The point could be generalized. A potential attacker is deterred when his leaders are in a certain state of mind. Their state of mind, even when advised that the opposing retaliatory forces can be eliminated with near certainty, is still likely to include feelings of uncertainty about weapons that have not been tried in battle. It may also include uncertainty about the gains that can be expected from going ahead with the attack, even if they could rely on the weapons to do the job: the deliberate unleashing of war with a great power is a momentous action, setting in motion a chain of events the ultimate outcome of which cannot be foreseen. This does not mean that, in a desperate situation, such a decision will not be taken: war by miscalculation is an ever-present possibility, and the decisions that do set off such chains of events are sometimes taken without much thought being given to consequences other than the most immediate ones. Nevertheless, the essential conditions of mutual deterrence are subjective or psychological, and these conditions may in principle be satisfied even in the absence of totally invulnerable retaliatory forces.

Still less does mutual nuclear deterrence necessarily require what is called Mutual Assured Destruction, a concept which implies not only that retaliatory forces must be able to survive attack but also that they must be able to penetrate to targets to bring about a given level of damage or dislocation. Neither disarming forces nor (as Don Brennan has long argued) population defenses are in principle incompatible with mutual nuclear deterrence. The Wohlstetter thesis of the "delicate balance of terror" set out the technological requirements for maximizing deterrence but omitted the psychological and political dimension, which when inserted, helps to explain why, as Robert Jervis has said, "deterrence seems easier than the theory implies."[8] This is not to deny that steps should now be taken to restore the invulnerability of land-based missile forces or to find substitutes for them: no one, I think, would argue that the vulnerability of retaliatory forces is actually good for mutual deterrence. But the stability of mutual nuclear deterrence is less sensitive to degrees of force vulnerability than is presupposed in much of the recent argument.

The stability of the Soviet-American relationship of mutual nuclear deterrence is not called into question by recent developments. What is subject to debate is the state of the overall strategic balance between the United States and the Soviet Union. The achievement by the Soviet Union of rough strategic "parity," the impression of superiority in some dimensions and the evident improvement of the Soviet Union's capacity for "crisis bargaining," taken in conjunction with the growth of the Soviet Union's conventional forces and of her capacity for global intervention, have led to an understandable feeling in the West that the balance is shifting against it. We should notice, however, that the feeling that the balance is shifting towards the opponent is also evident in the Soviet Union, where the recent moves in the United States, Western Europe, and Japan to draw closer to China raise the specter of a Soviet Union isolated and encircled by a grand alliance of all the other great industrial powers. We should also consider that the fears on each side may be in some measure mutually reinforcing and that a situation in which each side believes that the balance is shifting against it may be one in which the danger of miscalculation is considerable.

Peace will depend, as much or more than it does on mutual deterrence, on the ability of the superpowers to avoid or control crises, for although these are liable to occur whatever the state of the strategic balance, they are more likely to occur when the balance appears to be shifting. Until recently the superpowers appeared to be strengthening their capacity to avoid or control crises by agreeing on the rules of the game and, more generally, through developing structures of arms control and comprehensive détente. It is clear that the momentum behind these efforts has now slackened—and, indeed, that the existing structures of superpower understanding are in danger of crumbling.

Strategic Deterrence and General Deterrence

Strategic deterrence (that is, deterrence of strategic nuclear attacks by threat of strategic nuclear retaliation) is only a particular case of general deterrence, which includes deterrence of other kinds of attack and deterrence by other kinds of response. An important issue is whether strategic nuclear weapons should and will be used only to deter the use of other nuclear weapons or whether they should also be used to deter other kinds of threat.

The prime concern of all the present nuclear powers is the deterrence of nuclear attack, but they have pointedly refused to cut the links between nuclear deterrence and general deterrence. The NATO powers are committed to the first use of nuclear weapons against conventional attack, and the Soviet Union maintains a similar policy vis-à-vis China. In cases where what is at stake is a possible conventional attack on the home territory of a nuclear state rather than on that of its allies, it is difficult to imagine that the government of the state concerned could make any distinction between nuclear deterrence and general deterrence—or be believed if it did.

Yet there is a strong prima facie argument for sharpening the distinction between nuclear deterrence and general deterrence and for cutting the link between the two wherever possible. A regime in which nuclear weapons are viewed as having the function only of deterring the use of other nuclear weapons might be thought to be a considerable advance upon the regime which exists at present.[9] Policies that help to cut the link (declarations of no first use of nuclear weapons are an example) might be thought to help push nuclear weapons into the background of world politics, to facilitate control of these weapons by nuclear powers, and to remove an incentive to proliferation. Some elements of a regime of this sort already exist: the explicit nuclear threats made by both the United States and the Soviet Union against certain non-nuclear states in the 1950s, for example, have not been repeated since that time.

At present, however, the prospects for further separating nuclear from general deterrence are not favorable. In the case of the Western powers, the persistence of Soviet conventional superiority, the growing importance of West Germany in the context of the European Community and of NATO, and the demand for a European-based response to the Soviet missile threat against Western Europe all militate against it. It is notable that in the Western world discussion of the longstanding question of how to balance preponderant Soviet conventional forces in Europe centers upon the choice between various means of introducing a nuclear threat (the threat to initiate tactical nuclear warfare, threats from European-controlled nuclear forces, or the threat of a United States counterforce strike) and pays little attention to the attempt to match conventional force with conventional force. Richard Garwin's proposal to remove tactical nuclear weapons and Forward Based Systems (FBS) from Western Europe and to rely upon conventionally armed cruise missiles and European access to a portion of the American strategic force (his proposal is not directed towards a NATO no first use position but is intended to help reduce the role of nuclear weapons) does not seem to take sufficient account of the psychological need felt in Western Europe for some locally based nuclear weapons.[10]

Strategic Deterrence and Extended Deterrence

In the past the superpowers have been prepared to extend nuclear deterrence to provide protection to other states, not only against nuclear but also in some cases against non-nuclear threats. Such protection has been extended to allies but also, at least on an informal or implicit basis, to other powers (for example, by both superpowers and by a Britain rediscovering her Himalayan frontiers in the early 1960s), and there have also been joint guarantees (of a not very serious kind) offered both separately and jointly to non-nuclear weapon states as inducements to adhere to the Non-Proliferation Treaty (NPT).

Such extended deterrence has already long been in decline as a consequence of the contraction of the two alliance systems and the disenchantment of Third World states with practices suggestive of superpower condominium or hierarchy. Will the "extended deterrence" provided by the superpowers continue to contract? Will new nuclear powers enter into the business of "extending" deterrence—China, perhaps, to Cambodia? Britain and France to the rest of Western Europe? A nuclear Japan to Korea or Australia? Or will "extended deterrence" eventually disappear completely, as every part of the world comes to be consolidated within one or another nuclear power, none of which looks beyond itself for deterrent support?

It seems unlikely that more will be heard of "joint guarantees" extended by the superpowers. ("Joint guarantees" here implies "positive" guarantees, or undertakings to come to the assistance of non-nuclear states; "negative" guarantees, or undertakings not to attack them with nuclear weapons still have a role, but these are not a form of deterrence.) Nor do we have any reason to expect a reversal of the decline of American "extended deterrence." The credibility of threats to use nuclear weapons on behalf of third parties depends less on "commitments" ritually affirmed, or on demonstrations of willingness to fulfil them, than it does on the interest the deterrer is judged to have in carrying out the threats. When American interest in doing so is evidently very strong, as it is in relation to Western Europe, "extended deterrence" may still have a long life, even though here also there are signs that the protected are growing dissatisfied with present arrangements. In Asia and the Pacific, perhaps, the strength of American interest is less clear. The achievement by the Soviet Union of nuclear parity, the progress of nuclear proliferation, and the continuing fragmentation of the alliance systems all make it less likely that there will be a strong American interest in extending nuclear guarantees to other powers.

Will the superpowers be willing to "extend deterrence" so as to stabilize regional balances in which nuclear weapons have become a factor, or will their impulse be to disengage and insulate themselves from the attendant dangers? In the event that Israel, Iran, South Korea, South Africa, or Pakistan were to demonstrate possession of nuclear weapons and seek to exploit them in local conflicts, the superpowers might experience both impulses—on the one hand, to seek to control events by "extending deterrence" to locally threatened parties; on the other hand, also to seek to avoid the dangers of involvement by cutting existing commitments to local parties and seeking safety through dis-engagement.

In the event that nuclear weapons fell into the hands of a so-called "crazy state" or came to be possessed by a non-state group that seemed likely to use them, a Hobbesian instinct for survival might surface in the superpowers that might lead them to set aside all niceties and to intervene directly and at once to disarm the state or group concerned. Such a crisis, posing a direct threat to the survival of the superpowers, might also reveal in them a common interest in preserving a minimum of security in world affairs which up to that point had been lost to sight.

Strategic Deterrence and Proliferation

Further nuclear proliferation is widely anticipated between now and the end of the century, partly because of the spread of the capacity to acquire nuclear weapons and partly because the motives to do so in some cases appear strong. These include prestige in the case of Brazil, the "Islamic bomb," and the desire for security in the case of expendable clients of the West such as Israel, South Africa, South Korea, or Taiwan. We cannot know at what pace this proliferation will occur, nor even be sure that it will occur at all. Moreover, the idea that further proliferation is inevitable is potentially self-fulfilling and therefore irresponsible. But how will strategic deterrence and proliferation affect each other?

There are two competing doctrines about the relation between the strategic deterrence policies of the superpowers and nuclear proliferation. According to the first, or "high posture," doctrine, the superpowers can best discourage proliferation by maintaining a wide margin in military nuclear capacity between themselves and other competitors. This will enable them to convince would-be entrants to the nuclear club that it is beyond their reach and will also allow them to "extend" strategic deterrence to third parties (West Germany and Japan are the classic examples) who might otherwise be forced to acquire nuclear weapons of their own. Underlying this doctrine is the belief that the hierarchical structure of power in the world today, at least in the realm of military nuclear affairs, can be maintained indefinitely. According to the second, or "low posture," view, the superpowers are more likely to stem the tide of proliferation if they seek to play down the role of nuclear weapons in their own policies and thus help to undermine the argument that nuclear weapons are a necessary status symbol or source of security. This points to the severing of links between nuclear and "general" deterrence, to the termination of "extended deterrence," and, ultimately, to the abandonment of nuclear deterrence itself and to nuclear disar-mament. It is, of course, the logic of Article VI of the Non-Proliferation Treaty, and it implies acceptance of a less hierarchical distribution of power.

Looking to the future, it is clear that powerful forces are working against the "high posture" doctrine. The United States and the facilities will not maintain their ascendancy in military technology indefinitely; even now they enjoy it not because of any inherent technological superiority over the powers of Western Europe and East Asia but because the latter have chosen not to devote their resources to this end. Nuclear guarantees to potential nuclear powers, even though the most crucial of them are still in good standing, have shown a steady decline, as we have seen. A large part of the world is in revolt against the hierarchical assumptions behind this doctrine: the discussion of the possible "widening" of SALT III to include European participation and the declining authority of the NPT regime are symptoms of its decline.

Nor does the future look bright for the "low posture" doctrine. The massive superpower rearmament that has been dramatized and partly generated by SALT does not augur well for the presentation of SALT process as the run-up to nuclear disarmament. The superpowers do not appear to be contemplating the adoption of no first use positions or other steps to qualify their reliance on nuclear deterrence. The prospect for the 1980s and 1990s is that the stability of the "balance of terror" will depend chiefly on unilateral measures taken by both sides and that force levels will remain high. The argument, moreover, that relatively high force levels enhance the stability of the mutual deterrence relationship is a powerful one.[11] Nuclear proliferation is in any case being generated by conflicts among the non-nuclear (but potential nuclear) powers themselves. There is little reason to expect that the passing of superpower hierarchy will usher in a new and more tranquil era of world politics in which the time will be ripe for a further downgrading of the role of nuclear weapons, for among the powers that are united against hierarchy there is no agreement as to what new distribution of power should replace it.

*   *   *

As proliferation takes place, it will highlight increasingly the inadequacies of our present deterrence theory. This assumes a two-power confrontation, whereas in future there will be greater need to consider deterrence in the context of several or many nuclear powers. It assumes that between the powers deterring one another there is a level of hostility above which deterrence would be impossible and beneath which it would be unnecessary. In the world of many nuclear powers that is approaching, there will be greater need to consider what a meaning deterrence might have in relationships which exhibit a greater or a lesser degree of hostility than the received theory assumes. The theory assumes, moreover, that both sides in a relationship of mutual deterrence share a conception of rational action. It is easy to conceive of situations of nuclear confrontation in the future in which states, divided not only politically and ideologically but also culturally, do not share a conception of rational action to the extent to which the superpowers have done in the past. Professor Dror's argument about the difficulty of applying "deterrence rationality" in a Third World context bears on this point.[12] We need to recognize that our present theory of deterrence is a "special theory" and that there is a need to proceed to a "general theory" that will be based not on the ideas of rational action that are unique to Western industrialized society but on those that are the common property of the many different kinds of society that exist in the world today.

NOTES

1. A. George and R. Smoke, *Deterrence in American Foreign Policy: Theory and Practice* (New York: Columbia University Press, 1974). I have also been helped by Robert Jervis's analysis in "Deterrence Theory Revisited," *World Politics* 31, no. 2 (January 1979): 289–324.

2. Hedley Bull, *The Control of the Arms Race* (London: Weidenfeld and Nicolson, 1961), p. 48.

3. Jervis, "Deterrence Theory Revisited," argues that rationality is neither necessary nor sufficient for deterrence and might even undermine it. But he does not say what rationality is. I do not think there is any such thing as "objective" rationality which can only be defined in relation to given goals.

4. To this extent I agree with R. B. Midgley's strictures on the "morality of antinomies and paradoxes" in contemporary writing about international relations (see his *The Natural Law Tradition and the Theory of International Relations* [London: Elek, 1975] and my "Natural Law and International Relations," *British Journal of International Studies* 5, no. 2 [July 1979]: 171–81).

5. See Bernard Brodie, *Strategy in the Missile Age* (Princeton: Princeton University Press, 1959), pp. 408–409.

6. See David C. Gompert et al., *Nuclear Weapons and World Politics*, 1980s Project, Council on Foreign Relations (New York: McGraw Hill, 1977).

7. See Richard Garwin, *Testimony to the Committee on Armed Services, U.S. House of Representatives, February 7, 1979* (Washington, D.C.: Government Printing Office, 1979). Garwin argues here that even a vulnerable Minuteman force, if it is part of a wider complex of retaliatory forces of which some are invulnerable, has deterrent value.

8. Jervis, "Deterrence Theory Revisited," p. 303.

9. On this point, see Richard Garwin's contribution to Gompert et al., *Nuclear Weapons and World Politics*, pp. 83–147.

10. Ibid.

11. See Michael Mandelbaum's discussion, "The First Nuclear Regime," in Gompert et al., *Nuclear Weapons and World Politics*, pp. 15–80.

12. See Yehezkel Dror, "Nuclear Weapons in Third World Conflict," in *The Future of Strategic Deterrence, Part II*, Adelphi Paper 161 (London: International Institute for Strategic Studies, 1980).

———— Questions for Reflection and Discussion ————

1. What are the basic elements of deterrence? What are the differences between retaliatory deterrence and war-fighting deterrence? What actions are each likely to deter? Which is said to deter more levels of military aggression? What forces are needed if deterrence fails?

2. What are the central dilemmas of a *countervalue* deterrence posture? How, if at all, does the adoption of *counterforce* doctrine overcome these dilemmas? What new dilemmas are posed by counterforce deterrence? Is either strategy of nuclear deterrence capable of averting nuclear war indefinitely? What factors render both strategies inherently unstable?

3. How viable is "extended deterrence"? Should the superpowers extend their nuclear umbrellas beyond current commitments?

4. It seems increasingly the case that nuclear deterrence cannot last forever. What alternatives are available to preserve the peace without submitting to an adversary? Should the nuclear-weapon states focus on developing the means to thwart a nuclear attack, e.g., an effective antiballistic missile system, rather than continuing to upgrade their offensive nuclear capabilities? Why? Why not? Are there other options available to them? Is a nondeterrence strategy of peace possible?

5. Can a democracy maintain a willingness to accept millions of deaths to assure political leverage in world affairs? To assure the security of its allies? To assure its own security? Can it do anything else?

Selected Bibliography

Aldridge, Robert C. *The Counterforce Syndrome: A Guide to U.S. Nuclear Weapons and Strategic Doctrine.* 2d ed. Washington, DC: Institute for Policy Studies, 1979.

_____. *First Strike: The Pentagon's Strategy for Nuclear War.* Boston: Southend Press, 1983.

Beres, Louis René. *Mimicking Sisyphus: America's Countervailing Nuclear Strategy.* Lexington, MA: Lexington Books, 1983.

Blechman, Barry M., ed. *Rethinking the U.S. Strategic Posture.* Cambridge, MA: Ballinger Publishing Co., 1982.

Bohn, Lewis C. "Is Nuclear Deterrence *Really* Necessary?" *War/Peace Report,* Vol. 12, No. 1 (Nov.-Dec. 1972), pp. 3–9.

Boserup, Anders. "Deterrence and Defense." *Bulletin of the Atomic Scientists,* Vol. 37 (December 1981), pp. 11–13.

Freedman, Lawrence. *The Evolution of Nuclear Strategy.* New York: St. Martin's Press, 1981.

Gaddis, John Lewis. *Strategies of Containment: A Critical Appraisal of Postwar American National Security Policy.* New York: Oxford University Press, 1982.

George, Alexander L., and Richard Srooke. *Deterrence in American Foreign Policy: Theory and Practice.* New York: Columbia University Press, 1974.

Gray, Colin S. "Nuclear Strategy: The Case for a Theory of Victory." *International Security,* Vol. 4, No. 1 (Summer 1979), pp. 54–87.

Green, Philip. *The Deadly Logic: The Theory of Nuclear Deterrence.* New York: Schocken Books, 1968.

Jervis, Robert. "Why Nuclear Superiority Doesn't Matter." *Political Science Quarterly,* Vol. 94 (Winter 1979/80), pp. 617–633.

Kahn, Herman. *On Thermonuclear War.* Westport, CT: Greenwood Press, 1978 (1961).

Kaplan, Fred. *The Wizards of Armageddon.* New York: Simon and Schuster, 1983.

Keeny, Spurgeon M., Jr., and Wolfgang K. H. Panofsky. "MAD Versus NUTS." *Foreign Affairs,* Vol. 60, No. 2 (Winter 1981/82), pp. 287–304.

Kissinger, Henry. *Nuclear Weapons and Foreign Policy.* New York: W. W. Norton, 1969.

Lodal, Jan M., "Deterrence and Nuclear Strategy." *Daedalus,* Vol. 109, No. 4 (Fall 1981), pp. 155–175.

Lowe, George E. *The Age of Deterrence.* Boston and Toronto: Little, Brown and Co., 1964.

Mandelbaum, Michael. *The Nuclear Question.* New York: Cambridge University Press, 1979.

Martin, Laurence, ed. *Strategic Thought in the Nuclear Age.* Baltimore: Johns Hopkins University Press, 1980.

Morgan, Patrick. *Deterrence: A Conceptual Analysis.* Beverly Hills, CA: Sage Publications, 1977.

Nitze, Paul H. "Strategy in the Decade of the 1980s." *Foreign Affairs,* Vol. 59, No. 1 (Fall 1980), pp. 82–101.

Payne, Keith B. *Nuclear Deterrence in U.S.-Soviet Relations.* Boulder, CO: Westview Press, 1983.

Pipes, Richard. "Why the Soviet Union Thinks It Could Fight and Win a Nuclear War." *Commentary,* Vol. 64, No. 1 (July 1977), pp. 21–34.

_____ . "Soviet Global Strategy." *Commentary,* Vol. 69, No. 4 (April 1980), pp. 31–39.

Pranger, Robert J., and Robert P. Labrie, eds. *Nuclear Strategy and National Security: Points of View.* Washington, DC: American Enterprise Institute, 1977.

Rothschild, Emma. "Delusions of Deterrence." *New York Review of Books,* Vol. 30, No. 6 (April 14, 1983), pp. 40–50.

Russett, Bruce. "The Calculus of Deterrence," *Journal of Conflict Resolution,* Vol. 7, No. 2 (June 1963), pp. 97–109.

Scheer, Robert. *With Enough Shovels: Reagan, Bush and Nuclear War.* New York: Random House, 1982.

Schelling, Thomas C. *The Strategy of Conflict.* New York: Oxford University Press, 1963.

_____ . *Arms and Influence.* New Haven, CT: Yale University Press, 1966.

Snow, Donald M. *Nuclear Strategy in a Dynamic World: American Policy in the 1980s.* University, AL: University of Alabama Press, 1981.

_____ . *The Nuclear Future: Toward a Strategy of Uncertainty.* University, AL: University of Alabama Press, 1983.

Snyder, Glenn H. *Deterrence and Defense: Toward a Theory of National Security.* Princeton, NJ: Princeton University Press, 1961.

The Future of Strategic Deterrence. Adelphi Papers Nos. 160 and 161. London: International Institute for Strategic Studies, 1979.

Wells, Samuel F., Jr., "The Origins of Massive Retaliation." *Political Science Quarterly,* Vol. 96 (Spring 1981), pp. 31–52.

Young, Oran R. *The Politics of Force.* Princeton, NJ: Princeton University Press, 1968.

CHAPTER 6

Rethinking "The Enemy"

A "mere" continental power thirty to forty years ago, the USSR is a formidable global adversary today. The considerable socioeconomic and political problems it faces internally simply cannot belie the large military advances it has made in the past three decades. Now, the Soviet Union is indisputably one of the globe's two superpowers, virtually coequal with the United States in the critical dimension of military power.

What has fueled this awesome rise in Soviet military capability? Through the tangled web of different interpretations, two basic views stand out. One is that the buildup is compelling evidence of Soviet plans to pursue an expansionist, aggressive foreign policy inimical to the historical preeminence and vitality of the Western democracies. The other is that Soviet military programs represent less a purposeful threat to the West than a reflection of Soviet conservatism, bureaucratic inertia, and a deeply engrained sense of vulnerability to external intervention or invasion, validated by centuries of deprivation and plunder at the hands of hostile foreign powers. The differences between these two interpretations are of course fundamental. Whereas the first tends to commit the West to a path of permanent military competition and confrontation, the second holds forth the possibility of Soviet tractability, ergo the potential for negotiation and compromise over the tensions that divide East and West.

For the most part, even during the days of détente, the United States and to some extent its allies may be seen to have adopted more the first tha~ ~~~~~~~1 of these views. And not without some justification. ~ssed goals of the Reagan administration, and in e deprivations suffered during the First and Second ver to defend the homeland aggressively and not iate has long been a central objective of post–World policy; and Soviet weapons and weapon systems nd deployed in ways that clearly reflect this fact. rthur Gladstone in a seminal essay published in including psychologically complex, reasons that ption of the Soviet Union as intractable and aggressive. Having the Soviet Union as an enemy, he observed, makes for several "advantages" and "satisfactions":

We have the very considerable stimulation to our economic system provided by the manufacture of armaments and preparations for war in general. . . . We are provided with a satisfying explanation for many conditions and events that displease us. Politicians are provided with a sure-fire campaign issue and vote-getter. The rest of us are provided with a crusade in which all can participate. Let us not underestimate the great psychological satisfactions provided by a crusade. There is the smug satisfaction arising from the recognition that we are morally superior to the Russians. There is the self-respecting satisfaction arising from the feeling of being needed by the cause, of being able to make a social contribution. And there is the red-blooded satisfaction of being able to hate and to prepare to kill and destroy without feeling qualms of conscience.[1]

And to this, he adds, "similarly, the Russians derive great advantages from having the United States as an enemy."

In this chapter, mindful that neither Western views of the Soviet Union nor Soviet views of the West have freed the world of burdensome armaments expenditures and the constant threat of hemispheric—potentially global—devastation, we consider the possibility of perceptual exaggeration and mistake. The opening selection, a memorandum distributed by the United States International Communications Agency (USICA), presents an American critique of Soviet perceptions of the United States, and the second, by Central Committee member Georgi Arbatov, presents a Soviet critique of American perceptions of Soviet society and processes. The third selection, by George Kennan, contradicts the mainstream notion of Soviet leadership as aggressive and expansionist, and contends that the USSR is conservative in world view but cognizant of the possibilities for a less threatening modus vivendi with the West. The fourth essay, by Robert H. Donaldson, develops the theme of national security as perceived by a Soviet planner, emphasizing the traditional Russian obsession with large military forces to protect the physical security of the Soviet state. The final selection, by Fred Kaplan, attempts a realistic appraisal of the true power of the Soviet military, arguing that its capabilities often are overstated, especially during U.S. budgetary debates on defense. In sum, this chapter considers the possibility that there really does exist a Soviet willingness to pursue meaningful negotiations to overcome continued geopolitical struggle and to reduce the attendant threat of nuclear war.

NOTES

1. Arthur Gladstone, "The Conception of the Enemy," *Journal of Conflict Resolution,* Vol. 3, No. 2 (1959), pp. 132–133.

17. Soviet Perceptions of the U.S.— Results of a Surrogate Interview Project

Office of Research,
U.S. International Communications Agency

THE SOVIET-AMERICAN RELATIONSHIP

General Observations

Soviets at all levels[1] see Soviet-American relations as their most critical international relationship. This perception appears to be shared by both those who hope for a cooperative relationship and those who fear or desire a confrontational relationship.

In general, Soviets believe that the U.S. does not attach as great a significance to the relationship as they do. They are disappointed that the perceived mutual benefits of détente were never realized, but they see this as the fault of the American side. Even before Afghanistan they felt that little more could be lost in the relationship, because they were convinced that the U.S. was not going to deliver its share of the bargain. This attitude makes it possible to fit almost any American action into a pattern of anti-Soviet behavior, and greatly blurs the perception of linkages between Soviet and American behavior.

The present crisis has not greatly diminished the traditional and widely held perception of the U.S. and the USSR as natural allies— which may arise from a desire to be associated with the industrial West as well as from a visceral intolerance of non-whites.

At the same time, elements hostile to a cooperative relationship with the U.S. have emerged from hiding with what is basically an "I told you so" message. Those who have staked their professional careers and reputations on a cooperative relationship with the U.S. appear to be taking a more defensive position and modifying some of their earlier views—at least for public consumption. For example, leading Americanists have taken the opportunity to point out to American contacts the basic hostility of the U.S. toward the Soviet experiment even from its beginning.

Rarely if ever do Soviets see their own actions as precipitants of U.S. action. Soviet foreign policy remains a sacred cow internally. Given their history, Soviets find it difficult to believe that they would take offensive actions, but are inclined to view each action as defensive in a hostile world. This unwillingness to be critical of their own actions makes it very difficult for them to understand other countries' actions which are predicated on a view that the Soviet Union is a military threat to their security.

Power Politics

Ideology clearly plays a role in Soviet views of the U.S. Yet, when Soviets discuss the relationship with Americans, the terms are usually non-ideological and framed much more within the context of power politics. Soviets say that world peace ultimately depends on the U.S. and the Soviet Union working together. They appear to desire the establishment of a Soviet-American co-dominion to stabilize a frightening world and avoid what is most feared: a third-party problem escalating into a superpower confrontation.

Soviets believe that a superpower has and should have the right to act in areas of its perceived national interest. While Soviets express a willingness to recognize that the U.S. has this right, they feel that the U.S. is unwilling to reciprocate. They are quick to draw a distinction between verbal abuse for a particular action—which they see as a normal part of the game—and actual retaliatory measures.

Nonetheless, Soviets still speak of the U.S. as a potential, if erratic, "partner" in resolving the problems of world peace. They believe that they have a longer-term view of the problems besetting the relationship and hope that American leaders will recognize its true importance. There is a strong feeling that the continuity in Soviet leadership requires of them a patient policy of educating each successive American administration to the real significance of the relationship.

The Question of Equality

Coupled with a feeling that world peace rests on the ability of the U.S. and the Soviet Union to work together, there is considerable sentiment that the U.S. is unwilling to recognize the legitimate place of the Soviet Union in the world of nations. For the most part Soviets see the U.S. as unwilling to acknowledge its loss of economic and political pre-eminence, and unable to accept the ascendance of the Soviet Union. The desire for U.S. recognition of Soviet equality and legitimacy is palpable in most conversations with Soviets.

Consonant with the official line, there is a strong feeling that the Soviet Union as a superpower must be involved in the resolution of any major international issue. Soviet isolation from the Middle East peace process is seen as evidence of American unwillingness to accord the Soviets their rightful status.

Soviets want American recognition of their equality on the international scene, but barring that recognition they appear willing to demonstrate this equality through unilateral action. Even those who are skeptical about the wisdom of the Afghanistan venture seem, nonetheless, pleased that the USSR acted as they perceive a superpower ought to act.

Many Soviets believe that the U.S., in failing to accept their equality and legitimacy, focuses in communication with the Soviet Union only on the negative and does not place disagreements in an "appropriate" context of mutual respect and recognition.

American Foreign Policy

There are some consistent strains in Soviet views of recent U.S. foreign policy, even though the the level of sophistication and information is quite varied. Ideological jargon and categories are used significantly less than one might assume in discussions of American foreign policy.

They see recent American foreign policy as inconsistent and, as they like to say, "zig-zaggy."[2] They claim to find the U.S. unpredictable and unreliable. To the extent that they see consistency, they see it as anti-Soviet. The wellsprings of this "anti-Sovietism" are seen variously as the President and his administration, the pressure of the "military-industrial complex," the imperatives of domestic politics, and/or the need for distractions from American foreign policy failures elsewhere.

Most Soviets believe that over the past few years there have been diminishing returns from the Soviet-American relationship, for which they blame the U.S. They see the U.S. backing away from earlier promises. For example, many who know the inner workings of the Soviet system argue that it was an uphill fight to increase emigration, but they did it, perceiving it to be a quid pro quo for better relations. But, they found that rather than receiving MFN and increased trade, their efforts went unappreciated.

Similarly they see SALT II as another instance of U.S. reluctance to enter fully into the relationship. It is commonly believed that the President had retreated from his initial support of the treaty—further evidence of a perceived unwillingness to treat the Soviet Union as an equal. They see this treaty as a benefit to both countries and the cause of world peace, as well as recognition of the military parity that the Soviet Union has achieved. They feel that the U.S. thought it was doing the Soviet Union a favor by signing the agreement. On those terms, American discussion of the treaty was perceived as offensive.

The Carrot-and-Stick Hypothesis

If asked in late fall 1979 what the Soviet Union had to lose in the Soviet-American relationship if it undertook an adventurist act, a Soviet would probably have responded: "Very little." In addition, given their views of the importance of a workable American relationship, probably most would have concluded that after a period of invective, things would return to where they had been.

There is considerable evidence that the Soviets miscalculated the vehemence and scope of American reactions and still tend not to credit it as reaction per se. We are dealing with attitudes and perceptions, not actions. We cannot conclude that if Soviets had perceived a higher payoff to the American relationship based on more restrained Soviet behavior, their actions would have been more constrained. Nonetheless, it seems clear that Soviets do not believe that the "carrot-stick hypothesis" has been tested yet. They believe that they have seen many sticks but few carrots.

To the extent that Americans believe that the hypothesis has been tested, there exists a fundamental perceptions gap. If we assume that the Soviets were willing to sacrifice major gains in the American relationship by invading Afghanistan, our understanding will sharply diverge from that of the Soviets.

American Military Power and Political Resolve

Soviets at most levels have a very healthy regard for American military strength. Recent American debates concerning military weakness are viewed as a pretext for reasserting American military superiority. Their views of the military balance are made more salient by an overwhelming preoccupation with the issue of war and peace.

While some Soviets believe that they have achieved military equality, most face the future with ambivalence. They, including the military, view American technology with awe, fearing that the U.S. could, if it chooses, unleash its productive capacity and eliminate the Soviets' hard-earned relative gains. This attitude is reenforced by other considerations.

First, most Soviets are convinced that they would not be the first to attack, but that their actions are defensive in nature. They find it difficult to believe that the U.S. sees the Soviet Union as a threat. But, they fear that the U.S., untempered by the horrors of war on its own territory, might be tempted to attack or that war might arise out of a third-country conflict.

Second, they view the U.S. as "trigger happy" and erratic, willing to commit its military strength much more readily than the Soviet Union—this even after Afghanistan. Such "militarism" is even more dangerous in Soviet eyes if the U.S. perceives itself to be losing preeminence around the world.

Third, even those insulated from economic sacrifices by virtue of their own privileged positions are aware of the society's vulnerabilities, especially economic. They fear that a new arms race will be severely detrimental to their own society and that they may not be able to keep up with the U.S.

These feelings are somewhat balanced by a view that they are more disciplined and willing to sacrifice for a perceived national interest than are Americans. Nonetheless, the situation is perceived as very dangerous. Soviets talk about the possibility of war with visceral emotion. While clearly they will continue to probe American strength and resolve, direct confrontation appears to be an unthinkable thought.

The Actors in the Foreign Policy Process

The Soviets have poured major resources into studying the various perceived actors in the policy process, ranging from the Congress and the "military-industrial complex" to public opinion. While appreciation of the importance of each of these factors has certainly grown, there are still fundamental misperceptions.

A year ago, Grigorii Romanov, Politburo member and head of the Leningrad Party organization, met with the Congressional delegation (Codel) led by Senator Ribicoff. After listening impatiently to a long discussion about the problems of SALT II and the role of the Congress, Romanov finally said that if the President really wanted SALT II why didn't he simply discipline the members of his party. There are really two separate but not necessarily mutually exclusive messages here. First, the Soviets intend to deal with only one U.S. Government, even if they do perceive the importance and role of other groups. Second, their misperceptions about the American system are basic.

Romanov's notions seem to be shared quite widely even among the best-informed Soviets. To the extent that they understand Western governments, they see them as various forms of parliamentary government based on the British model.

Even the Soviet Americanists do not have a "feel" for the workings of the U.S. system. A young researcher at the USA Institute, specializing in local politics, regaled an American with data on local elections which even the American, a resident of the state, did not know. But when the conversation shifted to national politics, the young man wondered why the President didn't simply crack the whip in Congress and get SALT ratified.

Specialists on the Congress seem to have come to grips with some of the interaction between the Hill and the White House, but do not understand the Congressman's links with his constituency. (A year ago the Embassy proposed the exchange of Codels with the intention of getting Soviets to spend time both in Washington and in the home district of a particular Congressman.)

Soviets have perhaps the greatest difficulty in appreciating the multiplicity of political and economic power bases in the U.S. They have focused on Washington and New York, failing to pay sufficient attention to both the nature of constituency politics and the autonomy of state and local governments. The role of the judiciary also seems to elude them. They have concentrated on understanding the White House, the Congress, "big" businessmen and labor "bosses"—all seen as components of the stereotypical "military-industrial complex." This approach has so permeated Soviet thinking that even those best informed about the U.S. retreat to clichés when confronted by the complexity and dynamism of the American political system.

Even specialists are frustrated in trying to understand U.S. public opinion, let alone its place in the policy process. An Americanist throws up his hands when he discusses a poll showing that 85 percent of the public favors arms-control agreements, but 83 percent doesn't trust the Soviet Union to honor agreements.

To exacerbate Soviet frustration, they have on occasion bet on the "wrong horses" in domestic American foreign policy debates. Major studies of industrialists have been undertaken on the assumption that they were primary actors in foreign policy concerns, but recent events suggest to them that the Rockefellers and Fords are not decisive in American foreign policy formation.

Much of the effort that has gone into studying the U.S. political system has been put on the back burner as the focus of contemporary discussion has centered increasingly on the personalities of the President and Dr. Brzezinski. Soviet frustration in dealing with the complexity of American society may have created a situation where simpler explanations for American actions have become more acceptable. It may also be that all of the work of the Americanists has not been perceived as useful in the short term in improving relations or in predicting American behavior.

AMERICAN SOCIETY

Curiosity, Envy, and Assertions of Moral Superiority

The insatiable Soviet curiosity about the U.S. stems from two factors. First, the U.S. represents an exotic forbidden fruit—hard to travel to and surrounded by mythology. Second, the U.S. is the only real standard of comparison for Soviets. Without doubt, Soviets perceive the standard of living and particularly the availability of services as much higher in the West than in the Soviet Union. If anything, Soviets tend to err on the side of assuming even greater wealth and ease in the West than in fact exist. Even those who are hostile to the U.S. see it as their standard of comparison. For many, the U.S. is in several respects the model of the future, particularly in the adaptation of technology to economic processes. Apparently, if the American dream is still believed anywhere, it is in the Soviet Union.

They are fascinated by the material products of American society. There has been for years a virtual Western craze in the Soviet Union. Western products are widely sought and assumed to be better than their Soviet counterparts, if any exist. Americans who deal with Soviets are continually impressed by this desire which extends even into the upper ranks, where professional travel is prized in large part because it provides a unique shopping opportunity.

Soviets feel inferior to the West in terms of economic development and standard of living. At the same time, they believe that they have achieved impressive economic gains which are not recognized. Quite the contrary, there is increasing feeling that the U.S. gloats without *sochuvstvie* (sympathy) over Soviet shortcomings. This sentiment does not extend to the cultural sphere, where, despite the fascination with modern America, Soviets are extremely proud of their own culture, believing it superior to the American.

Soviets feel that their deep, if not always well-informed, interest in the U.S. is not reciprocated by Americans. They appear disappointed when Americans, especially officials, seem either uninterested or ill-informed about Soviet culture and history. Moreover, they are particularly confused by a pervasive perception that America's Sovietologists are in the main unsympathetic to the Soviet Union. They cannot understand how people who devote their lives to the study of a country don't love its culture and its people.

There are a number of views of the U.S. held by individual Soviets which are not easy to reconcile and often appear to be mutually contradictory. Aspects of American society may simultaneously attract and repel Soviets. This phenomenon appears to bother the Western observer more than it does the Soviet who clings to these views. At the same time, there also lurks in the minds of many a basic dichotomy in which it is hard to believe that the country that produces rock music, jeans, and other goods is the same one that offers crime in the streets, unemployment, and "democracy" (Soviets read "anarchy").

Sorting through the conflicting views is difficult, but the overriding view is of America the land of plenty. Soviets tend to assume that they would somehow be in the "have" category if they were in the U.S. To some extent the image of the U.S. has been oversold, and American interlocutors often find themselves trying to explain that certain economic problems do in fact worry most Americans.

Soviets hold different views simultaneously: they assume that the average American is wealthy and has little material need; however, they perceive the U.S. to have endemic unemployment, inflation, and exploitation. They are comforted by the perceived economic security of their own system, tending to regard the American economy as benefiting only one group.

Perhaps in this area more than others, available information and Soviet media emphasis on U.S. economic problems bedevil Soviet attempts to understand America. Almost universally, they are ignorant of how Americans actually live. Few even know that such programs exist as unemployment compensation, medical insurance, and social security.

Although Soviets are awed by American economic and technological capacity, they see their own system's strength in its emphasis on economic rights and the security this implies. This view is broadly held even though there is general recognition (and perhaps acceptance) of a highly stratified distribution system. It is held even by people who complain about inefficiency of the system and the pervasiveness of *blat.*

While Soviets admit that the U.S. is economically productive in a manner that has eluded them, they quickly point out that the U.S. has not suffered the horrors of war as they have. They usually explain

Western material advancement in terms that are the basis for asserting Soviet moral superiority. The most visceral rationale is still the impact of World War II. The war explains everything—even for those too young to remember the experience themselves. There are some signs that this line is wearing thin, but it remains potent. It explains everything from the shortage of goods to the fundamental belief that the USSR must defend itself and could never commit aggression for it knows better than anyone else the consequences of war.

Searching for the Key to the American System

Soviet attitudes toward commercial aspects of the U.S. relationship mirror their political attitudes. Business deals are probably determined by strictly economic considerations. Yet, the Soviet desire to trade with the U.S. exceeds pure economic rationality and appears to be tied up with the prestige and legitimacy presumed to accrue from an association with the other great superpower.

Soviet interest in trade and other economic relations with the U.S. often appears to have little to do with the specific economic product, for they have access to finished Western goods through a variety of channels. There is, however, a continuing fascination with finding the "key" to American economic success. It may thus be that understanding the process, not obtaining the product, is the goal. While joint economic ventures are important, continuing contact may well serve a major function for the Soviets even if not translated into sales contracts.

Soviets who study the U.S. have long assumed that hidden somewhere in the economic system is the key to American success, and that there must be a planning mechanism for the American private sector. It is suspected that the existence of this mechanism is a U.S. state secret. Even experts on American management and industry seem puzzled that the private sector has no apparent planning center. They know that the system works but are puzzled how. The great efforts to establish the International Institute for Applied Systems Analysis[3] were based largely on the assumption that with greater study the key could be found.

Even the most astute observers remain baffled, continuing to assert that somewhere in the system is a planning apparatus. They are more comfortable and adept in dealing with the American public sector than in analyzing the private sector. Specialists express surprise when told that industrial production quota systems and price-fixing are considered illegal. They have just assumed that these arrangements had to exist for the economy to function.

Clearly, Soviets have a deep and abiding fascination with the U.S. They are keenly interested in down-to-earth details—how Americans live, what their houses are like, how much they earn, etc. Americans, as symbols of affluence and potential suppliers, may misinterpret Soviet interest in material goods and living standards as simply materialism. But, it is more than this.

While convinced that the U.S. is a very wealthy and productive society, they find it almost hopelessly confusing as a system. Everything in their own experience suggests that if the American system is what Americans say it is, then it ought to collapse of its own weight or fly apart from the centrifugal forces. Part of this is the mirror-image problem. Americans are often faced with Soviets who really wish to believe what they hear about the U.S., but have nothing in their own experience that helps them make sense of the processes in the U.S.

A system which functions without apparent rigid discipline or enforced order is difficult to comprehend. Even Soviet specialists, well-informed but lacking a fundamental grasp of the social/political dynamism of American society, continue to search for the "real" center(s) of control within the society.

Attraction and Fear

Soviets may accumulate Western consumer goods for use or status, but absorb none of the values of the system which created the goods. They may be no more materialistic than any other people; it is simply that the shortage of goods makes acquisition a much more convoluted process, requiring much time, effort, and concentration.

Soviets are ambivalent toward many aspects of the American system. Many seem not to share Americans' high value for political freedoms, generally placing a higher premium on economic rights, perhaps sensing that acceptance of one must be at the expense of the other. Many seem to regard the American exercise of political rights as license, not freedom, considering the exercise as a manifestation of weakness, not strength. Despite these negative views, however, Soviets are often intrigued by— and would like to share—some of the freedoms they perceive in U.S. society. There appears in particular to be high interest in the greater freedom to travel and thus the possibility of seeing the outside world with one's own eyes. In addition, while political freedoms may not rank high on their list of priorities, greater value appears to be placed on the diversity of cultural expression available in the outside world— particularly in the U.S.

The system grants privileged Soviets access to Western society without making it available more generally. Foreign travel remains a valued perquisite of "deserving" citizens. Internal access to Western publications, films, and goods is made possible primarily, although no longer exclusively, by position and privilege. Although information about the American political system is more available to Soviet professionals, serious problems of misunderstanding still persist.

Soviets do distinguish between product and process. They may be attracted to certain aspects of American society, but worry about their applicability to Soviet society. For example, they may wish greater access to information or travel, but believe that similar access by the Soviet *narod* would unbalance the society. They may want to see the flashy side of American life, but not wish to have it in their own country. Thus, a curious love-hate relationship emerges in the attitudes of many Soviets about the U.S.

Even if personally interested in greater political/individual freedom and intrigued by the American system, many hold the elitist view that while they and their peers could cope, widespread freedoms would lead to chaos in society and perhaps undermine their own positions. Thus, while privileged Soviets may desire personal freedoms for themselves, their fear of introducing Western values into Soviet society helps moderate their fascination with the outside world.

NOTES

1. Although the study focuses on elites, respondents mentioned that some specific views seemed to be shared by all of their contacts. In the report these views are indicated by a phrase such as "Soviets at all levels."

2. There is a striking congruence between the views discussed here and the Soviet official line as expressed publicly and privately.

3. This Institute, located near Vienna, was established in 1972. The current Chairman of the Board, Dzherman Gvishiani, was active in its establishment. Seventeen countries, including the United States, are active sponsors of the Institute.

18. Relations Between the United States and the Soviet Union—Accuracy of U.S. Perceptions

Georgi A. Arbatov

*1. Does the American public have
an accurate perception of the Soviet Union,
its people, and its leaders?*

I think it does not—even on the problems which are of high importance to the U.S. itself, its national interests and the formulation of its foreign policy. Inaccuracy of many American perceptions of the Soviet Union is hardly surprising given the fact there may be no other country in the world the U.S. perceptions of which have for such a long time been formed on the basis of so one-sided and distorted information. That is why they are so tinted with strong bias and prejudices.

Due to détente in Soviet-U.S. relations and the increase in contacts, exchanges and tourism that accompanied the process since early 1970 there were signs of change for the better in this field. Of late, however, one sees in the United States intensified efforts not only to slow down this process but also to reverse it.

2. On the basis of what information and as a result of what psychological, social, and political forces is American public opinion toward the Soviet Union formed?

The bulk of information the Americans get about the Soviet Union is secondhand, being delivered to the American public through American intermediaries (journalists, experts, politicians, reports by the CIA and other governmental and private organizations). To a certain extent this is probably the case with any other country. But in informing the U.S. public about the Soviet Union, these American intermediaries display very often a particular bias. This is the result of personal ideological prejudices characteristic of many of them and of direct or indirect pressure of the forces that have vested interests in creating a distorted picture of the Soviet Union.

I have in mind first and foremost the economic forces. The biggest business in the U.S. is military business. For the past several decades, together with the entire military establishment, this business has been thriving in the climate of distorted ideas about the Soviet Union, artificially bloated fears of the "Soviet military threat" and continuously fanned animosity and distrust toward the USSR. It is common knowledge that blatant disinformation is being fed to the American public (as well as to the lawmakers) in the interests of these forces, but the existing norms of American politics for some reason make a serious discussion of this (e.g. in U.S. Congress) look almost indecent.

The U.S. is hardly comparable to any other country in the world in terms of the extent to which special interests affect national policy and the concepts that underlie it. Among those vitally interested in the distortion of the American perception of the USSR are the military-industrial complex, the ultraconservative elements, groups benefitting from the cold war, organizations representing anti-Communist emigration from Eastern Europe, the Israeli lobby, and others. In fact, it is hardly necessary to tell the U.S. Senators about this influence on the American public opinion and even on the opinions of the U.S. legislators on issues regarding the Soviet Union.

What ideological and psychological patterns of American thinking are being used to achieve this end? First of all, one should mention anti-Communism which has been cultivated for a long time as well as fears generated by it. With some it is fear of Communism itself, with others, fear of seeming "soft on Communism."

A major psychological role is played by an inertia of thinking and by a difficult problem of adjusting to new realities of the time, and more specifically, of shaking off the burden of the old perceptions inherited from the "cold war."

The strength of these perceptions lies in their simplicity and easiness to comprehend—there is a concrete enemy who is the source of all evils; there is a clear aim—to fight this enemy with all available means; and there are well-established and tested methods of such a fight. It is easy, within the framework of these perceptions, to stir emotions deeply rooted in the psychology of many people—the feeling of national superiority, jingoism, suspicion and hostility towards everything unusual or strange. These perceptions also tend to shape specific norms of political behavior which identifies political courage with "toughness" and intolerance, political wisdom—with the skill to overwhelm the opponent in the dangerous game of who chickens out first.

The philosophy of détente, of peaceful coexistence, is much more sophisticated. It deals with coexistence, establishing good relations and cooperation between the states that truly differ in their social systems, political institutions, values, sympathies, and antipathies. It is not so easy to realize that relations between them are not a "zero sum game" in which one side gains exactly what the other loses, that notwithstanding all the differences and contradictions they might have common interests, that irrespective of their sympathies and antipathies they have to live together on one planet. It is even more difficult to understand that the source of troubles could be not only the actions of the other side but also miscalculations and mistakes in one's own policy, saying nothing of objective processes taking place in the world. It is not very easy to realize that under present conditions restraint, moderation and willingness to compromise take not only more wisdom, but more political courage, than "tough play." The accommodation to these new and much more complicated realities and perceptions is a serious and, as L. I. Brezhnev once said, difficult process.

The negative role of the inertia of thinking reveals itself in other problems as well. Americans, for instance, have grown accustomed to a sense of almost national security. Over the centuries this has been instilled in them by the almost insurmountable barriers of the two oceans, and in the first post-war decades by their confidence in the overwhelming U.S. military supremacy. Now the situation has changed, and America finds herself not only at a rough parity with the USSR militarily but absolutely equal with other countries in terms of her own vulnerability to a holocaust should a war break out. This is a new situation for Americans. It is undoubtedly not easy to get used to it, not easy to get along with it. It nurtures not only a climate for more panicking about the "Soviet threat" but also a permanent temptation to follow those who promise an act of magic—a return to past invulnerability if only a sufficient amount of dollars is allocated and an adequate number of weapons systems are produced.

What makes Americans susceptible to one-sided, simplified, and just incorrect perceptions of the world at large (USSR included) are in my opinion certain other peculiarities of their history and traditions. One may take, for instance, the very fact of the U.S. remoteness, almost complete self-sufficiency and isolation that for a long time did not encourage much interest in the outside world but resulted instead in a particular concentration of things domestic. That is why Americans are not particularly prone to scrutinize the intricacies of international scene, and that is why foreign policy so often falls a prey to domestic politicking. There is also a firm belief characteristic of many Americans dating back to the Pilgrims that it was in their country that a new civilization was born bearing closest resemblance to the Promised Land, free from the sins that had engulfed the Old World. Lately, this belief and the resulting messianism together with the faith in America's "Manifest Destiny," her right and even an obligation to carry the light of truth and American values to other countries, have been badly shattered.

But the underlying sentiments have not vanished. Facts show that they can be quite easily stirred, given the double standards brought to life by messianism and the traditional inability (and, at times, plain unwillingness) to understand a different country, a different nation, to realize that it may have her own values and ideals and to imagine how the other side feels about a given issue. Evidence of this is provided not only by the human rights campaign but also by many American interpretations of the security problem.

Currently, for instance, concern is often expressed in the United States that the Soviet military might exceeds the "legitimate defense needs." But has any American, while gauging these needs, attempted to position himself in our place and to realize that the USSR has to simultaneously confront a potential threat from the three largest military capabilities of the world: those of the U.S., Western Europe, and China?

I could continue citing all the forces and factors which prevent Americans from getting a correct perception of the Soviet Union, its people, its leaders, and its policies. They are quite formidable and if there were nothing to resist them, there would not be much hope left for normal relations between our two countries. Fortunately, this does not seem to be the case. On many issues of the U.S. policy toward the Soviet Union a majority of Americans voice sound, realistic judgments. They favor an improvement in Soviet-American relations, détente, arms limitation agreements, and development of trade. In any case this is borne out by U.S. public opinion polls.

This is probably explained by accurate American perceptions—but not so much of the Soviet Union as of the U.S. own interests—by common sense akin to Americans, their healthy instincts, their ability to draw the right conclusions from past experiences. One more aspect seems important to me in this regard. The Americans who realistically appraise Soviet-American relations are much more vocal these days in the U.S. than was the case 10 or 20 years ago. These Americans include those who far from being sympathetic with Communism or Soviet domestic ways take real American national interests close to heart.

*3. To what extent does American public opinion
affect official policy and attitudes toward
the Soviet Union, and to what extent do
official policy and attitudes affect American public opinion
about the Soviet Union?*

Without doubt American public opinion affects official policy. This influence at certain periods of time and under specific circumstances (on the eve of elections, for instance) can be substantial indeed. However, in my opinion, normally the Executive and the Congress tend to respond not so much to the public opinion as to the sentiments of well-organized pressure groups. Apart from that, in many instances, instead of echoing public sentiments the U.S. Government and groups wishing to influence its policies may attempt to attune those sentiments of the public, and change them in a desired fashion.

Official policy undoubtedly has a vast potential for influencing the public opinion. Unfortunately, so far in questions pertaining to the Soviet Union, this potential has been mostly used in a negative way (one may recall the human rights campaign, the "Soviet military threat" issue, etc.). However, on certain important issues it is impossible to properly shape public opinion without an active, clear-cut, and honest position of an administration and particularly of the White House. This is true, in particular, of the SALT treaty. No answer to the opponents of the treaty could be better and more authoritative than the one coming from the administration. Only the government can prove to the public that the USSR has no military supremacy over the U.S. whatsoever and does not seek one, that a genuine threat to the U.S. security comes not from the Soviet Union, but from an uncontrolled arms race. The U.S. Government better than anybody else could enlighten the public on the real situation in the sphere of Soviet-American trade and other major issues.

*4. Does American public opinion differ significantly
from the views of U.S. experts regarding the Soviet Union?*

It probably does, but one should bear in mind that there are great differences in the opinions of U.S. experts themselves. For a long time the majority of them adopted a position of utmost hostility to the Soviet Union. This is probably accounted for by the fact that the Soviet studies flourished in the time of the cold war the needs of which many of those experts served. A disproportionately high share of émigrés from Eastern Europe among the U.S. experts on the Soviet Union was also a factor. Their attitudes toward the Soviet Union and the changes that took place in their countries after World War II might be tainted by highly negative personal emotions.

The situation has been changing over the past few years. The U.S. has produced a "national cadre" of experts on the Soviet Union, differing widely in their political outlook, nevertheless reflecting the whole spectrum of American political opinion. However, policymakers can still find in this spectrum a confirmation of any desired viewpoint.

The above said is not meant as a call to distrust American experts on the Soviet Union. I only think that, first, even with the experts available, personal competence of the political leaders is essential, and, second, those who are inclined to rely on the advice of these experts should first of all become experts themselves—as to which of the experts on the USSR are likely to provide an objective and thorough analysis.

The latter is very important too. Here I would like to quote one of the most authoritative American experts on the Soviet Union— Ambassador George Kennan. Expressing regret over the fact that new data on the Soviet Union, "given the rather low state of Soviet studies in our country, has scarcely been digested by the scholars, much less by the policymakers, the critics, and the old-timers in this field of expertise," he argues that much in the field of Soviet studies has to be comprehended anew. Mentioning his 50-year experience in Soviet studies, Ambassador Kennan writes further: "Because of this long preoccupation with the subject—not despite it, mark you, but precisely because of it—it is time that my ideas, too, were taken thoroughly apart and put together again with relation, this time, to the present scene."

5. Does American public opinion of the USSR
differ significantly from that held, for example,
by the people of Canada, France, or Japan?

If we proceed from the assumption that the American people want peace and normal relations with the USSR—I do not see any reasons for other nations to think differently from the Americans on this issue. I believe such sentiments to be even more widespread there.

Canada is not influenced by militarism so much as the U.S., and she has never had any global ambitions. As for Japan and France (as well as the whole of Western Europe)—they better than the U.S. know from their recent past what suffering and devastation war means. This is why these nations are more likely to treasure détente and to realize that there is no reasonable alternative to good-neighbor relations with the USSR. Besides, these countries are more interested in developing trade and economic relations with the Soviet Union and the Eastern European countries.

19. Two Views of the Soviet Problem

George F. Kennan

Looking back over the whole course of the differences between my own view of East-West relations and the views of my various critics and opponents in recent years, I have to conclude that the differences have been, essentially, not ones of interpretation of phenomena whose reality we all agree on but, rather, differences over the nature and significance of the observable phenomena themselves—in other words, differences not about the meaning of what we see but, rather, about what it is that we see in the first place.

Let me illustrate this first with the example of our differing views of the nature of the Soviet regime.

My opponents, if I do not misinterpret their position, see the Soviet leaders as a group of men animated primarily by a desire to achieve further expansion of their effective power, and this at the expense of the independence and the liberties of other people—at the expense of the stability, and perhaps the peace, of international life. They see these men as pursuing a reckless and gigantic buildup of their own armed forces—a buildup of such dimensions that it cannot be explained by defensive considerations alone and must therefore, it is reasoned, reflect aggressive ones. They see them as eager to bring other countries, in the Third World and elsewhere, under their domination, in order to use those countries as pawns against the United States and other nations of the Western alliance; and they see the situations existing today in such places as Angola and Ethiopia and Afghanistan as examples of the dangerous success of these endeavors. My opponents reject the suggestion that Soviet policy might be motivated in any important degree by defensive considerations. In their view, the Soviet leaders do not feel politically encircled or in any other way significantly threatened. And though it is recognized that Moscow faces serious internal problems, it is not thought that these problems impose any very serious limitations on the freedom of the regime to pursue aggressive external intentions. What emerges from this vision is, of course, an image of the Soviet regime not greatly different from the image of the Nazi regime as it existed shortly before the outbreak of the Second World War. This being the case, it is not surprising that the conclusion should be drawn that the main task for Western statesmanship at this time must be to avoid what are now generally regarded as the great mistakes of the Western powers in the late 1930s; that is, to avoid what is called appeasement, to give a low priority to the possibilities for negotiations and accommodation, and to concentrate on the building up of a military posture so imposing and forbidding, and a Western unity so unshakable, that the Soviet leaders will perceive the futility and the danger of their aggressive plans, and will accept the necessity of learning to live side by side with other nations on a basis compatible with the security of those other nations and with the general requirements of world stability and peace. I do not question the good faith of American governmental personalities when they say that once this new relationship of military and political power has been established they will be prepared to sit down with their Soviet counterparts and discuss with them the prerequisites for a safer world; but I fear that they see the success of any such discussions as something to which the Soviet leaders could be brought only reluctantly, with gnashing of teeth, and this seems to me to be a poor augury for the lasting quality of any results that might be achieved. Now, all this, as I say, is what I believe my opponents see when they turn their eyes in the direction of the Kremlin. What I see is something quite different. I see a group of troubled men—elderly men, for the most part—whose choices and possibilities are severely constrained. I see these men as prisoners of many circumstances: prisoners of their own past and their country's past; prisoners of the antiquated ideology to which their extreme sense of orthodoxy binds them; prisoners of the rigid system of power that has given them their authority; but prisoners, too, of certain ingrained peculiarities of the Russian statesmanship of earlier ages—the congenital sense of insecurity, the lack of inner self-confidence, the distrust of the foreigner and the foreigner's world, the passion for secrecy, the neurotic fear of penetration by other powers into areas close to their borders, and a persistent tendency, resulting from all these other factors, to overdo the creation of military strength. I see here men deeply preoccupied, as were their Czarist Russian predecessors, with questions of prestige—preoccupied more, in many instances, with the appearances than with the realities. I do not see them as men anxious to expand their power by the direct use of their armed forces, although they could easily be frightened into taking actions that would seem to have this aim. I see them as indeed concerned—and rather naturally concerned—to increase their influence among Third World countries. This neither surprises me nor alarms me. Most great powers have similar desires. And the methods adopted by the Soviet Union are not very different from those adopted by some of the others. Besides, what has distinguished these Soviet efforts, historically viewed, seems to be not their success but precisely their lack of it. I see no recent Soviet achievements in this direction which would remotely outweigh the great failures of the postwar period: in Yugoslavia, in China, and in Egypt.

But, beyond that, a wish to expand one's *influence* is not the same thing as a wish to expand the formal limits of one's power and responsibility. This I do not think the Soviet leaders at all wish to do. Specifically, I have seen no evidence that they are at all disposed to invade Western Europe and thereby to take any further parts of it formally under their authority. They are having trouble enough with the responsibilities they have already undertaken in Eastern Europe. They have no reason to wish to increase these burdens. I can conceive that there might be certain European regions, outside the limits of their present hegemony, where they would be happy, for defensive purposes, to have some sort of military control, if such control could be acquired safely and easily, without severe disruption of international stability; but it is a far cry from this to the assumption that they would be disposed to invade any of these areas out of the blue, in peacetime, at the cost of unleashing another world war.

It is my belief that these men do indeed consider the Soviet Union to have been increasingly isolated and in danger of encirclement by hostile powers in recent years. I do not see how they could otherwise interpret the American military relationship with Iran in the time of the Shah or the more recent American military relationships with Pakistan and China. And these, I believe, are not the only considerations that would limit the freedom of the Soviet leaders to indulge themselves in dreams of external expansion, even if they were inclined toward such dreams. They are obviously very conscious of the dangers of a disintegration of their dominant position in Eastern Europe, and particularly in Poland; and this not because they have any conscious desire to mistreat or oppress the peoples involved but because they see any further deterioration of the situation there as a threat to their political and strategic interests in Germany—interests that are unquestionably highly defensive in origin.

I believe, too, that internal developments in the Soviet Union present a heavy claim on the attention and the priorities of the Soviet leaders. They are deeply committed to the completion of their existing programs for the economic and social development of the Soviet peoples, and I am sure that they are very seriously concerned over the numerous problems that have recently been impeding that completion: the perennial agricultural failures; the many signs of public apathy, demoralization, drunkenness, and labor absenteeism; the imbalance in population growth between the Russian center and the non-Russian periphery; the increasing shortage of skilled labor; and the widespread economic corruption and indiscipline. They may differ among themselves as to how these problems should be approached, but I doubt whether there are any of them who think that the problems could be solved by the unleashing of another world war. I emphatically reject the primitive thesis, drawn largely from misleading and outdated nineteenth-century examples, that the Kremlin might be inclined to resort to war as a means of resolving its internal difficulties. Nothing in Russian history or psychology supports such a thesis.

In saying these things, I do not mean to deny that there exist, interwoven with the rest of the pattern of Soviet diplomacy, certain disquieting tendencies, which oblige Western policymakers to exercise a sharp vigilance even as they pursue their efforts toward peace. I believe that these tendencies reflect not so much any thirst for direct aggression as an oversuspiciousness, a fear of being tricked or outsmarted, an exaggerated sense of prestige, and an interpretation of Russia's defensive needs so extreme—so extravagant and so far-reaching—that it becomes in itself a threat, or an apparent threat, to the security of other nations. While these weaknesses probably affect all Soviet statesmen to one extent or another, the evidence suggests to me that they are concentrated particularly in specific elements of the Soviet power structure—notably, in the military and naval commands, in the vast policy establishment, and in certain sections of the Party apparatus. So far, these tendencies do not seem to me to have dominated Soviet policy, except in the case of the decision to intervene in Afghanistan—a decision that was taken in somewhat abnormal circumstances and is now, I believe, largely recognized, even in Moscow, as a mistake. But there will soon have to be extensive changes in the occupancy of the senior political positions in Moscow, and Western policymakers should consider that a Western policy that offers no encouragement to the more moderate elements in the Soviet hierarchy must inevitably strengthen the hand, and the political position, of those who are not moderate at all.

So much, then, for our differences of view with respect to the Soviet regime. It is not unnatural that anyone who sees the phenomenon of Soviet power so differently from certain others should also differ from those others in his view of the best response to it. It is clear that my opponents see the Soviet regime primarily as a great, immediate, and growing military danger, and that this conditions their idea of the best response. I have no argument with them about the existence of a great danger. I do differ from them with regard to the *causes* of this danger. I see these causes not in the supposed "aggressiveness" of either side but in the weapons race itself. I see it in the compulsions that this, like any other weapons race between sovereign powers, engenders within all the participants. I see it in the terrible militarization of outlook to which this sort of competition conduces: a species of obsession which causes those who have succumbed to it to direct their vision and their efforts exclusively to the hopeless contingencies of military conflict, to ignore the more hopeful ones of communication and accommodation, and in this way to enhance the very dangers against which they fancy themselves to be working.

Leaving aside for the moment the problems of nuclear weaponry, I shall say a word about the military balance in conventional weapons. An impression has been created that there has recently been a new and enormous buildup of Soviet conventional strength on the European continent, changing the balance of forces in this respect strongly to the disadvantage of the West. This view has found expression in the statements of a number of distinguished Western personalities. I cannot flatly deny the correctness of this thesis. I am only a private citizen. I do not have access to all the information at the disposition of the governments. But, with all respect for the sincerity and good faith of those who advance this view, I am disinclined to accept it just on the basis of their say-so. I am so disinclined because I think I have made a reasonable effort, in these last few years, to follow such information as appears in the press and the other media about the military balance and I find this body of information confused, contradictory, statistically questionable, and often misleading. Most of it seems to derive from data leaked to the media by one or another of the Western military-intelligence services, and one cannot avoid the impression that it reflects a tendency to paint an exaggerated and frightening picture of Soviet capacities and intentions—a so-called worst-case image. This is done, no doubt, partly out of an excessive professional prudence but partly, too, I am afraid, with an eye to the reactions of various Western parliamentary bodies, which require to be frightened (or so it is believed) before they will make reasonable appropriations for defense. I can only say that if the NATO governments really wish us, the public, to believe in the reality of a recent dramatic increase in the Soviet conventional threat to Western Europe they will have to place before us a more consistent and plausible statistical basis for that view than anything they have given us to date. In terms neither of the number of divisions nor of total manpower nor of any of the other major indicators does the information now available to the ordinary newspaper reader prove that the balance of conventional military strength in Central Europe is significantly less favorable to the Western side than it was ten or twenty years ago.

To say this is not to claim that the present balance is satisfactory. That is not my contention. Of course there is a preponderance of strength on the Soviet side. Such a preponderance has existed since the Second World War. Of course it is not desirable. I myself favor a strengthening of NATO's conventional capacities, particularly if the strengthening be taken to mean an improvement of morale, of discipline, of training and alertness, and not just a heaping up of fancy and expensive new equipment that we do not have the manpower to operate or the money to maintain. But if this strengthening is to be effected I think it should be presented and defended to the public as a normal policy of prudence—a reasonable long-term precaution in a troubled time—and not as something responding to any specific threat from any specific quarter. The Western governments, in particular, should not try to gain support for such a program by painting on the wall an exaggerated and unnecessarily alarming image of Soviet intentions and capacities. This procedure represents, in my view, an abuse of public confidence, and one that, in the end, is invariably revenged.

So much for the conventional weapons. Now—with a sigh and a sinking of the heart—for the nuclear ones. Here, I am sorry to say, I have differences with every single one of the premises on which our government and some of the other NATO governments seem to act in designing their policies in this field. First of all, my opponents seem to see the nuclear explosive as just a weapon like any other weapon, only more destructive; and they think that because it is more destructive it is a better and more powerful weapon. I deny that the nuclear explosive is a proper weapon. It conforms, in my view, to none of the criteria traditionally applied to conventional weapons. It can serve no useful purpose. It cannot be used without bringing disaster upon everyone concerned. I regard it as the reflection of a vast misunderstanding of the true purposes of warfare and the true usefulness of weaponry.

My opponents see the Soviet Union as having sought and achieved some sort of statistical superiority over the NATO powers in this kind of weaponry. I myself have not seen the evidence that it has achieved that sort of superiority; nor do I see any reason to assume that that is what it would like to do. The evidence seems to me to suggest that it is striving for what it would view as equivalence, in the statistical sense—not for superiority. My opponents believe that differences of superiority or inferiority, in the statistical sense, have meaning: that if you have more of these weapons than your adversary has, you are in a stronger position to stand up against intimidation or against an actual attack. I challenge that view. I submit that if you are talking, as all of us are talking today, about what are in reality grotesque quantities of overkill—arsenals so excessive that they would suffice to destroy the adversary's homeland many times over—statistical disparities between the arsenals on the two sides are quite meaningless. But precisely that— the absurd excessiveness of the existing nuclear arsenals—is the situation we have before us.

My opponents maintain that the reason we must have the nuclear weapons is that in a conflict we would not be able to match the Soviet Union with the conventional ones. I would say: If this is true, let us correct the situation at once. Neither in respect to manpower nor in respect to industrial potential are we lacking in the means to put up conventional forces fully as strong as those deployed against us in Europe.

My opponents say: We must have these weapons for purposes of deterrence. The use of this term carries two implications: first, that it is the Russians who have taken the lead in the development of these weapons, and that we are only reacting to what they have done; and, secondly, that the Russians are such monsters that unless they are deterred they would assuredly launch upon us a nuclear attack, with all the horrors and sufferings that that would bring. I question both these implications; and I question in particular the wisdom of suggesting the latter implication thousands of times a year to the general public, thus schooling the public mind to believe that our Soviet adversary has lost every semblance of humanity and is concerned only with wreaking unlimited destruction for destruction's sake. I am not sure, furthermore, that the stationing of these weapons on one's territory is not more of a provocation of their use by others than a means of dissuading others from using them. I have never been an advocate of unilateral disarmament, and I see no necessity for anything of that sort today. But I must say that if we Americans had no nuclear weapons whatsoever on our soil instead of the tens of thousands of nuclear warheads we are now said to have deployed, I would feel the future of my children and grandchildren to be far safer than I do at this moment; for if there is any incentive for the Russians to use such weapons against us, it surely comes in overwhelming degree—probably, in fact, entirely—from our own enormous deployment of them.

Finally, there are many people who consider it useless, or even undesirable, to try to get rid of these weapons entirely, and believe that a satisfactory solution can somehow be found by halfway measures of one sort or another—agreements that would limit their numbers or their destructiveness or the areas of their deployment. Such speculations come particularly easily to a government such as our own, which has long regarded nuclear weapons as essential to its defensive posture and has not been willing to contemplate a future without them. I have no confidence in any of these schemes. I see the danger not in the number or quality of the weapons or in the intentions of those who hold them but in the very existence of weapons of this nature, regardless of whose hands they are in. I believe that until we consent to recognize that the nuclear weapons we hold in our own hands are as much a danger to us as those that repose in the hands of our supposed adversaries there will be no escape from the confusions and dilemmas to which such weapons have now brought us, and must bring us increasingly as time goes on. For this reason, I see no solution to the problem other than the complete elimination of these and all other weapons of mass destruction from national arsenals; and the sooner we move toward that solution, and the greater courage we show in doing so, the safer we will be.

20. Soviet Conceptions of "Security"

Robert H. Donaldson

To assert . . . that there is no single Soviet world view—and, by implication, no single conception in the USSR of the meaning and requirements of "national security"—challenges the hoary but still popular assumption that there is a certain distinctive set of values and beliefs that is founded in Leninist ideology and Russian culture and that has persisted virtually unchanged and unchallenged from the days of the original Bolsheviks to the present. This notion of an alien and monolithic "Bolshevik" world view is most fully developed in Nathan Leites' concept of the "operational code" as presented in his monumental work, *A Study of Bolshevism.*

As described by Leites, the Bolshevik image of politics is founded on a profound insecurity that was perhaps appropriate to the leaders of an upstart revolutionary regime taking power in a war-torn country and facing civil war and military intervention by ideological enemies. In this political universe of acute and irreconcilable conflict, the fundamental question is *kto-kavo*—who (will destroy) whom? No security can be found in compromises or the search for stable intermediate positions in such a world; the alternatives are limited to total world hegemony or total annihilation. Constant vigilance, obsessive attention to maximizing power, readiness to counterattack or even to retreat at a moment's notice—these traits are essential to the very survival of the Bolshevik politician.[1]

The image of a Soviet political elite plagued by a paranoiac insecurity, fundamentally inimical toward the existing international system, and finding safety and respite only at the expense of the autonomy of others became the keystone of the American postwar policy of containment. The thesis of an unceasing Soviet search for absolute security dominated George Kennan's classic 1947 exposition of the "sources of Soviet conduct." Stalin and his lieutenants were depicted as too insecure to tolerate the existence of rival political forces either at home or in satellite countries. A fierce and jealous fanaticism, untempered by a tradition of political compromise and fueled by a doctrinaire ideology, drove them to subjugate or destroy all competing power. In the search for their own security, Kennan argued, the Soviet leaders would accept no restraints, for they were convinced by their ideology of the implacable hostility of the outside world and of the utter necessity to overthrow its existing order.[2]

Although Kennan's description seemed to be a close fit to Stalin's own personality and methods of rule, he stated unequivocally that these characteristics applied to the regime itself and not simply to the style of one dictator. Certain attributes—secretiveness, duplicity, suspiciousness—were said by Kennan to be characteristic of Soviet policy and basic to the very nature of Soviet power.[3]

Both Leites and Kennan penned their gloomy thoughts about Soviet insecurity during the last years of Stalin's reign, when the dictator's paranoia and xenophobia were at their height and the monotonous rigidity of Soviet society was unsurpassed. And yet it is not at all uncommon to find almost identical descriptions of the Soviet world view propagated 30 years later, in the midst of the U.S. national debate about Soviet strategic intentions and capabilities. One prominent figure in that debate, Richard Pipes, has likened the world view of the present Soviet elite to that of the Russian peasant. This orientation, he maintains, is better understood from a knowledge of Russian proverbs than from the basic tenets of Marxism-Leninism. The peasant proverbs teach that life is hard, that one's survival depends on one's own resources rather than on others, and that force rather than decency is the surest means of getting one's way. The Russian peasant, Pipes contends, sees the world as an arena for ruthless combat, "where one either eats others or is eaten by them, where one plays either the pike or the carp." Out of this history comes a special mentality stressing slyness, self-reliance, manipulative skill, reliance on force, and contempt for the weak. As Pipes sees it, Marxism-Leninism, though it exerts through its theories only minor influence on Soviet behavior, does serve to reinforce these predispositions in the Russian national character.[4]

Colin Gray, arguing from the standpoint of the geopolitician rather than from that of the student of Russian history and national character, arrives at essentially the same conclusion. Soviet paranoia, Gray contends, is manifested in a search for "*absolute* security" that inevitably leads the USSR on the path of world conquest. "Expansion is the Russian/ Soviet 'way': the Pacific Ocean has been reached, but not (yet) the Atlantic." In Gray's estimate, Soviet officials are extremely unlikely to settle for anything less than complete control of "the entire World-Island of Eurasia-Africa."[5]

Dimitri Simes, formerly a researcher at the Soviet Institute of World Economy and International Relations, uses language somewhat less apocalyptic to reach much the same judgment: the Soviet leadership has an "absolutist" definition of security, founded on a "traditional respect for power" and contempt for being "weak and kindly." Like the Tsars, the present Soviet leaders seek to erect an adequate shield against all conceivable threats, even if this means that "all rivals are left without many teeth with which to defend their vital interests." In Simes' view, Henry Kissinger's condemnation of the search for "absolute security" for one superpower on the grounds that it means "equal insecurity for another" would evoke little sympathy from the present Soviet leadership.[6]

Thus, the Pipes-Gray-Simes thesis asserts the existence of a single-minded and persisting Soviet conception of national security threats and requirements that is essentially unchanged from the Leites-Kennan image of 30 years ago (the "Bolshevik" conception) of paranoiac insecurity and irreconcilable hostility. The burden of the argument of this paper is that this image is a serious distortion and oversimplification of the current Soviet view (or views) of security. Not only is it inaccurate to posit a monolithic and unchanging "Soviet world view," but it is also wrong to suggest even that the *dominant* Soviet conception is one founded on the quest for absolute security and a fundamental enmity to the existing international system. On the contrary, a moderated variant of the "Bolshevik" image persists as a *minority* view in the Soviet elite, but it has been overshadowed for several years by an image of security that is far more confident of Soviet strength and more reconciled to the present international order.

THE GROWTH OF SOVIET CONFIDENCE

The basic error of Pipes and Gray—one also committed by Leites and Kennan three decades ago—is the assumption that the views of the Soviet leaders are so rooted in an unchanging ideology and "national character" that they are entirely resistant to change. As important studies by William Zimmerman[7] and Jan Triska and David Finley[8] have documented in detail, perceptions of international events and of the changing international system have had an impact in modifying (and "softening") the *Weltanschauungen* of Soviet officials and scholars—and particularly of those who have carried major operational responsibilities for the conduct of foreign policy. As Zimmerman concludes from his study of a decade's work by Soviet scholars in the major foreign policy institutes, these experts "no longer let Lenin do their thinking," though they continue to use Lenin to legitimize their arguments.[9]

The lessened relevance of Leninism and the "Bolshevik" image of the world is in large part a result of the shift in what the Soviets term the "correlation of forces." The "operational code" of which Leites wrote was forged in an environment of Bolshevik weakness, in which the enemies of the Party and the Soviet state called the tune. But, as Politburo member and close Brezhnev associate Konstantin Chernenko recently put it, "the times of imperialism's omnipotence in international relations, when it could unceremoniously and with impunity throw its weight around in the world . . . have receded irretrievably."[10] As "imperialism" has been tamed, the USSR's sense of threat and alienation from the international system has lessened considerably.

The contrast between the early postrevolutionary period, in which it could truly be said that the Russian working class had "nothing to lose but its chains," and the present position of the USSR in the world is graphically depicted in a leading Soviet textbook. The book recalls the long and difficult road traversed by Soviet foreign policy, from its beginnings in a land torn by war and famine and encircled by hostile capitalist states, to its achievement of the status of the world's second-largest industrial power, embarking on the building of communism and leading an entire community of Socialist states. In sum, "it is one of the world's leading powers without whose participation no international problems can be settled."[11]

This statement—and especially the last sentence, which Foreign Minister Gromyko repeats at every opportunity—reflects an attitude of pride and confidence that is quite different from the earlier aura of hostility and suspicion. As the USSR's stake in the international order has increased, its unwillingness to mount a risk-laden challenge to the status quo has been reflected in a marked loss of revolutionary fervor. The Soviets have long claimed that their chief internationalist duty is not the export of revolution abroad, but the building of communism at home. Patriotism and emphasis on defense of the national state, once considered a bourgeois deviation from proletarian internationalism, have become the hallmark of Communist rhetoric. "As long as national statehood remains a political form of social development, patriotism, loyalty to one's homeland, and concern for the welfare of one's people will remain *the major principle* of the Communist doctrine."[12]

World War II—the great "patriotic" war—not only helped to weaken the "imperialist system," but it also left the Soviet Union with frontiers more defensible than even the Tsars had dreamed possible. From the perspective of the mid-1970s, the officially sanctioned history of Soviet foreign policy could present a relatively "satisfied" view of the outcome of World War II and the shape of the postwar world:

The victory led to the establishment of *just Western and Eastern frontiers* ensuring the Soviet Union's security. The capitalist encirclement . . . was thus broken. An end was put, *once and for all,* to the attempts of the imperialists to isolate the Soviet Union geographically by creating along its frontiers the infamous 'cordon sanitaire.'[13]

Events of recent decades have thus helped shape the perceptions held by Soviet leaders in the direction of greater confidence and patriotic pride and a lessened sense of insecurity about frontiers. But to argue this is not to suggest that the men in the Kremlin are therefore completely satisfied with the international order or complacent about the USSR's position in it. Nothing said above is meant to deny that the Soviet leadership regards itself as still locked in a highly competitive relationship with the United States, engaged in a struggle for greater influence in far-flung areas of the globe. Indeed, as Robert Legvold has put it, what we have seen in recent years is a "shift in the Soviet preoccupation from the struggle to secure Soviet power against the external world to a quest for a larger place in it."[14] But, to say that the Soviet Union is engaged globally in a competition for influence is not at all to conclude that its vital security interests are everywhere involved, much less to assert that some sense of omnipresent threat and possible annihilation is driving the Soviet Union toward world domination. Global involvement has created for the Soviet Union—as for the United States—a far more complex security situation, requiring a more precise assessment of threat and a more careful specification of just which interests are truly vital to its security. And it is on the basis of this assessment that the USSR will formulate its estimate of defense requirements.

THE SOVIET ASSESSMENT OF THREAT

In neither of the superpowers have political leaders and defense analysts avoided the temptation to specify how much in the way of military capabilities the *other* side "legitimately needs" to protect its vital security interests. Our own estimate of the threat we and its other adversaries pose to the Soviet Union is necessarily lower than the Soviets' own estimate will be. Each side plans its defense on the basis of a "worst case" analysis of threat. And since perception of threat rather than "actual threat" is the foundation of defense planning, a security problem exists for a country where its own leaders feel it to exist.[15] The prominent Soviet "Americanologist" Georgi Arbatov recently elaborated on this point:

the arguments about what defense needs are legitimate in another country are dubious. No country has the moral or political right to determine what another country's defense needs really are. Each country must do this for itself. The Soviet Union is forced to think seriously about its security and defense in order to meet the challenge by the military potential of the United States and Western Europe and . . . China. . . . It would be interesting to see how those who criticize the Soviet Union would talk about legitimate defense needs if they were in this country's position.[16]

While Arbatov's assessment of the USSR's "legitimate defense needs" is understandably focused on the miliary threat, there is another sort of challenge to the security of the Soviet regime that the Soviets seem to regard with equal seriousness. "A guarantee of the national security of a state implies, first and foremost, protection of its independence, sovereignty, territorial integrity, inviolability of its frontiers, and non-interference in its internal affairs on whatever pretext."[17] This latter phrase is a euphemism encompassing the fear of subversion, of infiltration of alien bourgeois ideas, of "softening up," and ideological infection. It is probably their acute awareness of the very attractiveness of Western culture and ideas—and of the corresponding unattractiveness in the West of Soviet ideology and society, which deprives them of a coun-terthreat—that has made the Soviets so sensitive to the subversive potential of "Basket III" or the "human rights campaign." For these campaigns challenge the very *legitimacy* of the regimes both in Eastern Europe and in the USSR itself, and their effectiveness as a threat is heightened by the fact that relative economic and political backwardness make the European Communist regimes so vulnerable. Indeed, it was the perceived subversive campaign from outside married with the resurgence of "counter-revolutionary elements" within that led to the Warsaw Pact invasion of Dubcek's Czechoslovakia in 1968. In pro-claiming the "Brezhnev Doctrine," Soviet authorities left no doubt that they regarded such developments as a serious threat to vital interests in a "core" security area.[18]

The importance to the Soviet Union of the long campaign for a Conference on European Security and Cooperation was precisely in its objective of shoring up the legitimacy of Socialist Europe by extracting from the West a recognition of the territorial and political *status quo* of divided Europe. And although the Helsinki conference did go far toward achieving this goal, it threatened to backfire on the Soviets by simultaneously legitimizing the "subversive" Basket III concern with the free flow of peoples, ideas, and information.

In suggesting the dominant Soviet perception of "legitimate defense needs," the above emphasis on the dual political-military and ideological threat perceived in Europe must be matched with a stress on the same sort of multidimensional threat that Soviet leaders see in China. The very existence of the threat of a two-front conflict vastly complicates Soviet defense planning. It was this phenomenon to which Gromyko was probably referring when he wrote: "Naturally, in assessing the defense needs of the USSR, we should take into account the geographical position of our country."[19] The salience of the "China factor," and in particular of the nightmare of an active Sino-U.S. combination against Soviet interests, was evident in the round of election speeches delivered by the members of the Soviet Politburo in February and March, 1979. Not one of the leaders failed to deplore in the strongest terms the growing threat posed by the Chinese leaders and certain unnamed "imperialists" who were said to be teaming up with them.

Indeed, a "worst-case analysis" by a Soviet politician or planner looking at the potential threat facing his country would have to include the possibility of an increased danger of confrontation with the United States. A Sino-American alignment is only one possible increment to the threat from the United States; to it could be added the possibility of leadership paralysis or change in Washington giving rise to a loss of power by the "more sober representatives of the bourgeoisie," or the possibility of rapid development of new strategic weapons and additional conventional fighting forces deployed against the USSR.

THE SOVIET DEFENSE DEBATE

In the light of such a perceived present and possible future threat, Soviet leaders have taken and will undoubtedly continue to take great pains to ensure the adequacy of their military capabilities. But how much is enough for "adequate" defense? Have the Soviets not themselves provoked a reluctant military buildup from the West precisely in response to their own rapid arms buildup? In thinking about these questions, it is helpful not only to recall Spykman's aphorism ("There is security only in being a little stronger"), but also to reflect on the likely Soviet perspective on the issue of which side is "building up" and which side is "responding" in the arms race of the past decade. In fact, a series of high-level Soviet statements in recent years have sought to underline the USSR's determination to be adequately defended, while denouncing the West's "myth of the Soviet menace" and denying any ambitions for a military superiority that allows first-strike capability. Brezhnev's January 1977 speech at Tula was one such statement:

Of course, comrades, we are improving our defenses. It cannot be otherwise. We have never neglected the security of our country and the security of our allies, and we shall never neglect it. But the allegations that the Soviet Union is going beyond what is sufficient for defense, that it is striving for superiority in armaments with the aim of delivering a 'first strike' are absurd and utterly unfounded . . . the Soviet Union has always been and continues to be a staunch opponent of such concepts. . . . Not a course aimed at superiority in armaments but a course aimed at their reduction, at lessening nuclear confrontation—that is our policy. On behalf of the Party and the entire people, I declare that our country will never embark on the path of aggression and will never lift its sword against other peoples.[20]

Although Brezhnev's statement probably had the approval of a majority of the Politburo, there have been signs for several years of top-level Soviet disagreement over defense policy. While it has been more obscured from public view than its American counterpart, an intense debate has been conducted in the USSR over such issues as how much defensive capability constitutes an "adequate" level, how grave is the threat facing the USSR and how immediate the danger of war, and how reliable and mutually beneficial is the path of détente in advancing Soviet foreign policy interests?

Some of the participants in this debate have approached it from an image of the world approximating the "Bolshevik" image described by Leites and Kennan (and put forward by Pipes and Gray as the prevailing Soviet view). The contemporary Politburo-level Soviet leader whose speeches and writings most nearly approached the "Bolshevik" conception of security was the late Marshal Grechko, Minister of Defense until his death in April 1976. His pronouncements tended to stress the dangers facing the USSR, the aggressive and untrustworthy nature of her adversaries, and the buildup of strong military forces as the only reliable guarantee of Soviet security.[21] Marshal Grechko's successor, Dimitri Ustinov, has not tended to indulge in rhetoric as hot or estimates as pessimistic, and he frequently has positive things to say about Brezhnev's détente policies.

An intensive reading of Supreme Soviet campaign speeches delivered in February and March of 1979 by the members of the Politburo shows that the "Bolshevik" image of Soviet security requirements has largely disappeared from such public pronouncements of the leadership.[22]

The speechmaking ritual at the time of the Supreme Soviet elections provides analysts with the rare opportunity to study views of individual leaders on a variety of issues within a constricted time frame. Although the 1979 election speeches reflect in some respects the specific domestic and foreign context of a particular period of time, both the individual perspectives and the collective profile of views do not differ significantly from other leadership pronouncements of the late 1970s. . . . Key phrases on major issues of détente and defense from each of the Politburo members' speeches, . . . [viewed together with] the relative positions of the thirteen Politburo voting members on the "détente" and "defense" axes . . . shows [a] relatively high consensus in the Soviet leadership on major foreign policy issues. That consensus supports a view most fully articulated by Brezhnev himself and most closely echoed by Konstantin Chernenko and Andrei Gromyko. A cluster of leaders, including Arvid Pelshe, Grigory Romanov, Andrei Kirilenko, and Dinmukhamed Kunayev, expressed themselves in far less detail on international issues, but what they did say was essentially supportive of Brezhnev's relatively confident assessment of the prospects for advancing détente and arms control. Party ideologist Mikhail Suslov, Defense Minister Dimitri Ustinov, and [former] KGB Chairman Yuri Andropov reflected their institutional interests in the relative emphasis they gave to defense and the need for vigilance against the imperialist threat, but even they were not in basic disagreement (as Ukrainian party secretary Vldimir Shcherbitskiy was) with the thrust of Brezhnev's assessment.

THE DOMINANT VIEW:
"SECURITY THROUGH COEXISTENCE"

The currently dominant Soviet conception, which might be labeled "security through coexistence," is far more confident of the USSR's relative security and international standing, as well as of its ability to achieve its interests through further pursuit of détente and arms control. While it does not deny the need for strong military capabilities and the existence of certain forces that are striving for a resumption of the cold war and an unrestrained arms race, this view emphasizes the adequacy of Soviet defenses and the sobriety of leading statesmen of the "imperialist" camp and it asserts that both sides can advance their legitimate interests through the moderation of their rivalry. Brezhnev described his understanding of the meaning of the détente concept in his speech at Tula:

What is detente, or the easing of tension? What meaning do we attach to this concept? Above all, detente signifies the overcoming of the cold war and a transition to normal, equable relations between states. Detente means a willingness to resolve differences and disputes not by force, not by threats and saber-rattling, but by peaceful means, at the negotiating table. Detente means a certain trust and the ability to take one another's legitimate interests into account.[23]

In other pronouncements Brezhnev has been careful to remind his listeners that not only does détente not imply the cessation of political and ideological struggle with the West, but that it in fact creates even more favorable conditions for the pursuit of Soviet objectives. These specifically include the promotion of "national liberation movements" in the Third World and the struggle for "social progress" in the capitalist world. Just as they have reaffirmed their own objectives, the Soviet leaders have also expressed confidence that Western politicians will continue to pursue conflicting goals, including a sharpened effort to spread ideological subversion in the Socialist camp.

As Brezhnev and his allies have expressed it, then, détente implies a continuation of a limited-adversary relationship with the United States. It brings both sides the benefits of a reduced level of tension and a diminished threat of nuclear war, and it holds out the promise of mutually beneficial commercial ties. For the United States it signifies a forced recognition of a shift in the correlation of forces and of the bankruptcy of its former role as "world policeman." And for the USSR it symbolizes attainment of a status of nuclear and diplomatic equality, it increases access to Western credits and technology, and it preserves

Moscow's opportunities to prevent collusion between the United States and China.

More pointedly, the proponents of this view argue that not only does détente bring more reliable security than the arms race, but that the quest for military superiority actually squanders resources while *lessening* security. One Soviet civilian analyst recently described the concept of military security as the "antipode" of the principle of undiminished security. The arms race and a policy based on armed force cannot ensure security; rather, he said, each new advance in weapons technology brings further instability and danger of war. "The national security of states can best be ensured through peace and detente."[24] A prominent military writer agreed, noting that a new spiral in the arms race, far from ensuring security, "can only lead to the squandering of national resources, and that means the lessening of national security." He too professed to see the path to strengthened security in the development of mutually advantageous cooperation and further limitation of the arms race.[25]

In its ostensible rejection of the path of resumption of the arms race and its advocacy of further progress toward arms control, the prevailing Soviet conception of security stresses the principle of "the undiminished national security" of both sides. Brezhnev recently said of the SALT II treaty that "it can be said definitely that its implementation will not inflict any damage to the security of the Soviet Union, or to the security of the United States for that matter. On the whole, I would say, it will be advantageous to both countries."[26]

Both by implication, as in this pronouncement, and in explicit statements, some Soviet leaders and analysts have renounced the "zero-sum game" image of international politics. Georgi Arbatov, for example, has written that international politics "is not like reckless gambling, in which one player wins the same amount the other player loses. Completely different situations are possible here, situations in which all sides are winners."[27] Through such statements, these officials have moved—in their public position, at least—far from the *kto-kavo* imagery of the "Bolshevik" conception of security. Even beyond the change of imagery, however, some Soviet analysts have begun to employ the argument that the security of each superpower is inextricably bound up with the other— that in order for one to be secure, the other must be also. According to [an] article in *New Times,* enormous nuclear overkill capacity means that "the national security of some countries is inseparable from that of others. . . . Security has ceased to be a purely national problem." Like peace, universal security is indivisible, and only peaceful coexistence, arms reduction, and the promotion of mutual trust and cooperation can effectively ensure national security.[28]

Indeed, there appear to be some officials in the USSR who have progressed beyond the view of "security through coexistence" to a stance of "security through cooperation"—a conception that minimizes the importance of national military power and stresses the need for conscious efforts to increase international cooperation, on the assumption that the security of one nation can increase only if the security of all nations increases. Dzhermen Gvishiani, deputy chairman of the USSR State Committee on Science and Technology, is one of the few Soviet officials who has voiced such a "globalist" perspective:

> The interdependence of nations and continents is an obvious fact from which one cannot escape. In this respect, the entire humanity has a common fate. All of us, if one may say so, are aboard the same spaceship which, by the way, does not have any exhaust pipes.[29]

Even Gvishiani's father-in-law, Prime Minister Alexei Kosygin, utilized some of the globalist rhetoric in his recent election speech. Referring to certain "global problems"—preventing war, supplying adequate energy and food, and protecting the environment—Kosygin declared that they could be solved only through international cooperation and "the collective efforts of the peoples."[30]

THE IMPACT OF U.S. POLICIES

This final conception of security through cooperation is by no means dominant among Soviet officialdom. Yet it is important for us to be aware that such views exist in the USSR, if only to realize that a return to the "Bolshevik" image of security through confrontation is not the only alternative to the currently dominant conception of security through coexistence. It is also important for Western officials and other participants in foreign and defense policy decisionmaking to realize that the debate over security options in the USSR is by no means over. Western rhetoric and especially Western actions are one of the subjects of controversy, and a change in their content can have an impact on the outcome of the Soviet debate. A Western policy of détente that is pursued antagonistically, with the avowed object of weakening Soviet influence in Eastern Europe or promoting the spread of "human rights" dissidence in the USSR, will be interpreted by the adherents of the "Bolshevik" image as evidence that détente, by spreading ideological infection, actually lessens Soviet security. Similarly, Senate rejection of the SALT II treaty or U.S. action taken in an effort to regain a clear margin of strategic superiority may also weaken the hand of Soviet officials who are arguing against continued pursuit of the arms race. This is not to argue that the United States should make such decisions solely on the basis of their likely impact on the Soviet debate; rather, it is simply a plea for awareness that such decisions will necessarily have such consequences in the USSR.

This study has shown that today's dominant Soviet image of security requirements is not markedly different from perceptions that U.S. leaders . . . have of America's security requirements. In each case, "security" means far more than simple physical survival, but also includes elements of economic well-being and internal political stability, as well as the preservation of fundamental alliances. While détente policies are recognized in both countries as promoting the relaxation of international tension, bringing benefits of mutual trade and economic progress, and reducing the dangers of war, they are simultaneously seen as raising new challenges to internal political consensus and bloc solidarity. Détente's promised vision of greater mutual security is thus accompanied by the large dose of uncertainty and complexity along the way. To recall Henry Kissinger's phrase of several years ago, it is not yet certain that either the United States or the USSR will be willing to come to terms with their mutual vulnerabilities and ultimately to abandon the quest for an "absolute security" that is founded on an equal insecurity for the other power.

NOTES

1. Nathan Leites, *A Study of Bolshevism*, pp. 24–25, 29.
2. "X" (George F. Kennan), "The Sources of Soviet Conduct," *Foreign Affairs*, July 1947, pp. 568–569.
3. Ibid., p. 572.
4. Richard Pipes, "Detente: Moscow's View," in *Soviet Strategy in Europe*, edited by Richard Pipes, pp. 11–12.
5. Colin Gray, *The Geopolitics of the Nuclear Era: Heartland, Rimlands, and the Technological Revolution*, pp. 35, 38.
6. Dimitri K. Simes, in *Perceptions: Relations Between the United States and the Soviet Union*, p. 94. See also the contribution to this volume by Edward Luttwak, who contrasts (pp. 340–341) Western "defensive" views of security with Soviet "imperial security."
7. William Zimmerman, *Soviet Perspectives on International Relations 1956–1967*.
8. Jan Triska and David Finley, *Soviet Foreign Policy*, especially Chapters 3–4.
9. Zimmerman, *Soviet Perspectives on International Relations 1956–1967*, p. 287.
10. Konstantin Chernenko, "Constantly Strengthening the Ties with the Masses," *Sovetskaia Moldaviia*, February 27, 1979, pp. 1–3, in Foreign Broadcast Information Service, *Daily Report: Soviet Union* (hereafter *FBIS*), Supplement, March 20, 1979, p. 71.
11. Boris Ponomarev, *History of Soviet Foreign Policy 1945–70* (Moscow: Progress Publishers, 1974), pp. 547–548.
12. G. Shakhnayarov, "Effective Factors of International Relations," *International Affairs*, February 1977, p. 86. Emphasis supplied.
13. Ponomarev et al., p. 11. Emphasis supplied.
14. Robert Legvold, "The Nature of Soviet Power," *Foreign Affairs*, October 1977, pp. 68–69.
15. For an interesting discussion of this point in the East European context, see Peter Bender, *East Europe in Search of Security*, pp. 1–9.
16. Georgi Arbatov, Radio Moscow, July 5, 1978, *FBIS*, July 6, 1978, p. B1.

17. V. Levonov, "Disarmament and International Security," *International Affairs*, July 1978, p. 79.

18. Sergei Kovalev, "Sovereignty and the Internationalist Obligations of Socialist Countries," *Pravda*, September 26, 1968.

19. Andrei A. Gromyko, "The Foreign Policy of the Soviet State—A Powerful Tool of the Communist Party in the Struggle for Peace and Social Progress," *Novaia i noveishaia*, No. 5, 1978, in *JPRS*, No. 72269, p. 12.

20. *Pravda*, January 19, 1977, pp. 1–2.

21. Andrei A. Grechko, *The Armed Forces of the Soviet Union*, p. 12.

22. Indeed, on this occasion the most noticeable emphasis on the threats facing the USSR and the need for greater vigilance came from Vladimir Shcherbitskiy, the Ukrainian first secretary. Long thought to be a protégé of Brezhnev's, Shcherbitskiy has recently been the object of ceremonial slights in status. (Since the top leaders usually deliver their speeches in inverse order of their political standing at the time of the election—with Brezhnev's own speech coming on the very eve of the election—the fact that Shcherbitskiy's was the second earliest confirms his present low standing in the hierarchy.) The flavor of his utterance on foreign affairs is suggested by the following excerpts:

one must not overlook the noticeable invigoration of reactionary imperialist forces. . . . In inflating the war psychosis, in instigating the arms race and in foreign political adventures, imperialist forces are obviously trying to find a way out of unsettled internal difficulties . . . reactionary circles [give] open support to fascist, revanchist and other reactionary regimes and forces. The ruling circles in NATO countries are directly responsible for creating hotbeds of dangerous tension. . . . The attempts by the most thick-headed imperialist circles to play the "China card" and to profit by militant Chinese chauvinism represents a serious danger to the cause of peace.

(V. V. Shcherbitskiy, Electoral Speech, *Pravda Ukrainy* [Kiev], February 16, 1979, pp. 1–2, in *FBIS*, February 27, 1979, p. 29.)

23. *Pravda*, January 19, 1977, pp. 1–2.

24. Levonov, pp. 82–85.

25. M. Milshteyn, "Where American Missiles Are Targeted," *Izvestiia*, July 19, 1978, p. 3, in *FBIS*, July 26, 1978, p. B6.

26. *FBIS*, March 5, 1979, pp. R6–R7.

27. *Izvestiia*, June 22, 1972, pp. 3–4. See also N. Lebedev, "Socialism and the Restructuring of International Relations," *International Affairs*, No. 2, 1978, p. 9.

28. Vyacheslav Boikov, "On the Pretext of Security," *New Times*, No. 48, 1977, p. 17. Emphasis added.

29. Quoted in Walter C. Clemens, *The USSR and Global Interdependence: Alternative Futures*, p. 24. Clemens' monograph is a provocative study of alternative Soviet stances in the coming era of international relations; it is extremely useful reading for anyone interested in Soviet images of the world—including conceptions of security.

30. *FBIS*, March 2, 1979, p. R12.

21. Dubious Specter: A Skeptical Look at the Soviet Nuclear Threat

Fred M. Kaplan

Renewed fears of Soviet strategic capabilities began to surface in the winter of 1976–77, when the conclusions of "Team B" were leaked to the press. Team B was the ad hoc panel chosen by President Ford's Foreign Intelligence Advisory Board to examine whether the CIA was systematically underestimating Soviet military strength. Their answer: Absolutely yes. Largely ignored in the reportage of the Team B hullabaloo was the genesis of the panel. The Ford Administration had deliberately decided to bring in a collection of frankly right-wing Russophobes, headed by Harvard historian Richard Pipes, an expert on prerevolutionary Russia, just to see if they could take CIA data and come to conclusions quite different from those reached by the in-house analysts. It was an experiment in intelligence analysis, and there was no pretense of objectivity in the selection of Team B members. Yet from the initial press acounts, it appeared that this was just a solid, bipartisan mix of experts who objectively came to some rather frightening conclusions about the Soviets.[1]

At about the same time, the Committee on the Present Danger was formed, with Paul Nitze serving as Policy Director. Nitze was ideal for the job: former Policy Planning Director at State under Dean Acheson, former Secretary of the Navy, former director of International Security Affairs at Defense, former SALT negotiator, a man who had sat on nearly every blue-ribbon panel over the last 25 years that had something hair-raising to say about the impending Soviet threat and the coming years of "maximum danger."[2]

The Team B leak also coincided with the retirement of General George Keegan from the directorate of Air Force Intelligence, consistently the most pessimistic of the intelligence agencies in the U.S. Government. Keegan held press conferences and travelled the speakers' circuit, leaking sensitive intelligence data (but only selectively) and lashing out at the pusillanimity and cowardice that the government was displaying in the face of Soviet military might.[3]

Throughout all this, the Soviets truly were strengthening their forces—no big crash buildup, but undeniably a determined, steady effort to whip their defense posture into something resembling that of a superpower. They began deploying MIRVed ICBMs in a fairly big way, and they improved their missile accuracy. Both actions were quite predictable, but occurred often more quickly than anticipated and were guaranteed to raise enormous fears on the other side of the globe.

Meanwhile, the Pentagon's open-faced counterforce doctrine bloomed. Defense Secretaries Schlesinger, Rumsfeld and Brown all decided to get frank about it. The time, after all, was ripe. With talk of the Soviet threat appearing with increasing frequency in the conversation of officialdom, in Congressional debates, and on the leading editorial pages across the land, talk of blasting away Soviet missile silos and engaging the Russians in "tit-for-tat" games of limited nuclear warfare seemed less provocative and bloodcurdling than it had just a few years ago.

Yet it was the Team B, Nitze and his Maximum Danger squad, and Keegan who attracted the most attention. These men and their many followers base their conclusions on published Soviet doctrine, recent Soviet capabilities, and current trends in the U.S.-Soviet military balance. The assumptions on which they base their conclusions, the evidence they muster to support their findings, and their positions generally are the topics of this essay. First, we will take a close look at the allegedly threatening Soviet military literature; then, at allegedly threatening developments in Soviet nuclear weapons procurement; and finally, at what the future brings in new technologies, developments in strategy, and prospects for serious arms control.

SOVIET MILITARY DOCTRINE

The published theoretical writings of several Soviet military officers have alarmed many Western analysts. According to these observers, the writings emphasize nuclear "war-fighting" rather than "war-deterring."

Two things need to be said about these publications. First, such sources are dubious footholds for conclusions as far-reaching as many that have been so unequivocally presented to the public. The published ideas of a particular group of military officers, in *any* country, do not necessarily reflect the actual convictions of the political leaders. Second, a careful reading of many Soviet military sources reveals that some American analysts, such as Pipes, Nitze, and others, have seriously misread or distorted their contents.

For example, many U.S. analysts have reported with horror that the Soviets still find the writings of Karl von Clausewitz relevant—Clausewitz, the nineteenth century philosopher-warrior whose masterpiece, *On War,* proclaimed that "war is the continuation of policy by other means." Several cite the late Marshal V. D. Sokolovskiy's statement in his seminal work, *Military Strategy:* "The essential nature of war as a continuation of politics does not change with changing technology and armaments."[4] Some also point out that many Soviet military theorists ridicule—as "idealism" and "metaphysics"—the American notion that nuclear war is fundamentally different from other types of warfare. Some American Sovietologists claim that the Clausewitzian attitudes held by the Russian High Command intrinsically endanger the United States. Professor Pipes goes so far as to contend that "as long as the Soviets persist in adhering to the Clausewitzian maxim of the function of war, mutual deterrence does not really exist."[5]

Such sweeping statements reveal a misunderstanding both of Clausewitz and of Soviet military doctrine. It is true that Marxists who study war tend to be quite taken with Clausewitz. Marx and Engels admired his wisdom and keen political perceptions; Lenin filled the margins of his copy of *On War* with annotations and enthusiastic jottings of approval; contemporary Soviet strategists cite him repeatedly, if somewhat simplistically. And true, it was Clausewitz who stressed, among other things, the importance of destroying "the enemy's [armed] power" as the means to attain the object of combat[6]—a sentiment that translates into counterforce in the nuclear age.

However, those who make much of the Clausewitz connection miss his central point:

Since war is not an act of senseless passion but is controlled by its political object, the value of this object must determine the sacrifices to be made for it in magnitude and also in duration. Once the expenditure of effort exceeds the value of the political object, the object must be renounced and peace must follow.[7]

The authors of one official Soviet document echo this theme: "The scale and intensity of wars are determined first of all by the political aims."[8]

Yet nobody—including those who dwell on Clausewitz and his lineage of contemporary Soviet war planners—has conceived of a credible scenario in which the Soviet leadership would risk a chance of nuclear attack on the Motherland; no one has thought of a political goal whose gain would be worth the sacrifice of possible American nuclear retaliation. In this sense, the Soviets' resolute political perspective of war should be not frightening, but rather somewhat reassuring.

The perspective found in Soviet military writings, too, is not, in the main, the stuff of nightmares. The connection that the Soviets perceive beween war and politics—Clausewitz with a Leninist twist—is summed up in the fifth edition (1972) of *Marxism-Leninism On War & Army,* an official book written by a group of top Soviet military officers and scholars: "Politics will determine when the armed struggle is to be started and what means [are] to be employed. Nuclear war cannot emerge from nowhere, out of a vacuum, by itself." In general,

war cannot be understood without first understanding its connection with the policies preceding it. . . . The political interests of the classes at war and of their conditions determine the war aims, while armed struggle is the means of achieving these aims . . . [W]ar is the continuation of the politics of definite classes and conditions by violent means.[9]

The point is that wars grow out of certain sociopolitical conflicts, and are the products of certain self-interested policies pursued by certain powers (or, in a Marxist-Leninist framework, classes). There is surely nothing so provocative about all this.

Soviet criticism of American nuclear war doctrine covers similar ground. According to Marxist-Leninist doctrine, modern war is the product of "the aggressive forces of imperialism," i.e., the United States and its allies. Wars, from this viewpoint, are rooted in capitalism, its position as a declining force in the world, and its leaders' desperate attempts to retain unchallenged "world domination." Thus, write the authors of *Marxism-Leninism On War & Army:*

The bourgeois ideologists do all they can to confuse and distort the question about the sources of wars, their nature, social and class essence. . . . By their arguments, the bourgeois theoreticians, consciously or unconsciously, attempt to divorce the nuclear missile war under preparation from the aggressive policies of imperialism. . . . [They] conceal who is responsible for imperialist aggression.[10]

Thus, much Soviet criticism of American defense doctrine does not substantively attack notions of deterrence, but rather aims to highlight what the Soviets see as the underlying political foundations of a future nuclear war, and to expose abstract, theoretical discourse on the matter by American technocrats as subterfuge diversions from these fundamental political issues.

Moreover, the historical context of Soviet military writings must be taken into account. Many Soviet articles proclaiming the feasibility of winning a nuclear war were—as pointed out by Harriet Fast Scott, American translator of Sokolovskiy's *magnum opus*—"prompted by Chinese accusations of revisionism."[11] Throughout the late 1950s and early 1960s, when many of the first Soviet theoretical documents on nuclear strategy were composed, the Kremlin was continuously under attack from the Maoists for indulging in "revisionism" in its relations with the capitalist camp. At this time, the Sino-Soviet competition for exclusive legitimacy as leaders of the Communist World was an immensely important matter to Soviet leaders, who sought above all else to maintain their control over their geographic sphere of influence and Communist Parties elsewhere.

Comments about winning a nuclear war must also be read in the historical context of post-Khrushchev military affairs. Khrushchev relied almost exclusively on a military strategy of nuclear "minimum deterrence," with the single option of massively retaliating against an attack by the United States. He articulated and implemented this philosophy at the expense, and over the virulent objections, of many military strategists. The succeeding Brezhnev-Kosygin regime stuck with Khrushchev's basic tenets of avoiding general nuclear war and maintaining deterrence; but they agreed with many factions of the military that nuclear war *was* possible (particularly, it could be ideologically justified, so long as imperialism exists) and that, therefore, preparations and contingencies should be developed for meeting this possibility, should it arise. In this sense, Soviet military planning, from 1965 to 1967, underwent a transformation similar to the U.S. Defense Department's transition from "massive retaliation" to "flexible options" in the early 1960s.[12] And the Soviets have, indeed, devoted considerable attention to problems of how to fight a nuclear war, maintaining secure command-and-control, and so forth. However, the temptation to identify a strict dichotomy between "deterrence" and "war-fighting," as many American academics do, should be resisted. According to Soviet philosophy, deterrence resides in the ability to fight a war if need be. This view is not so different from that of Harold Brown [Secretary of Defense during the Carter Administration], as stated in his FY 1981 posture statement:

There is no contradiction between this attention to the militarily effective targeting of the large and flexible forces we increasingly possess—to how we could fight a war, if need be—and our primary and overriding policy of deterrence.

Indeed, Brown explicitly notes:

To recognize that strong war-winning views are held in some Soviet circles . . . is not necessarily to cast any accusation of special malevolence, for these are traditional military perspectives by no means unreflected even in current Western discussion of these matters.[13]

Finally, these writings must be seen in the context of Communist ideology. During the late 1960s, an extensive debate was held in the pages of *Voyennaya mysl'* [Military Thought] on whether nuclear war would cause the end of civilization. *Military Thought* is circulated confidentially and exclusively within the Soviet military; it is not meant for a civilian or a Western audience; one should not mistake its articles for those in some Soviet publications designed to propagandize the West. The most eloquent and elaborate refutation to the end-of-civilization line was penned by General K. Bochkarev, Deputy Commandant of the General Staff Academy. He stressed that while nuclear war is "unquestionably . . . an adventuristic gamble," still "there is no serious proof that it has already been discarded by the general staffs of the Western powers, and above all by the Pentagon"; that "it is absolutely obvious" that "one cannot take at their face value" denials of aggressiveness by Western military men." Finally, he gets to the real point: that if military strategy and military victory are deemed fictitious in the nuclear age, then

the armed forces of the socialist states . . . will not be able to set for themselves the goal of defeating imperialism and the global nuclear war which it unleashes and the mission of attaining victory in it, and our military science should not even work out a strategy for the conduct of war since the latter has lost its meaning and its significance. . . . *In this case, the very call to raise the combat readiness of our armed forces and improve their capability to defeat any aggressor is senseless.*[14]

In short, "The morale-combat qualities of Soviet soldiers are moulded on the basis of the ideology of Marxism-Leninism which . . . instills in them unflagging confidence in the indestructability and final triumph of the forces of socialism."[15] Therefore, if all this talk about no-win scenarios gains much currency, the entire rationale of constant military preparedness and a hefty military buildup will be undermined, as will the role of the Communist Party and the Soviet State as the supreme protector of the people in case of imperialist aggression. In other words, the Soviet military, the Party, and the state all have a stake in insisting that nuclear war is winnable and that socialism can triumph from its ashes.

In fact, however, articles, many of them appearing in *Military Thought,* consider the prospect of nuclear war with no less horror or gravity than do Americans.[16]

The writings of Soviet strategists, taken in their full context, surely do not suggest nuclear warmongering. In fact, much evidence suggests that the Soviets seem driven, almost obsessively, often unreasonably, by the idea that the "Western imperialists" might attack the USSR or its socialist allies; Russia has, after all, been invaded three times in this century. As former CIA Director William Colby testified before the Senate Foreign Relations Committee:

You will find a concern, even a paranoia, over their own security. You will find the determination that they shall never again be invaded and put through the kinds of turmoil that they have been under many different invasions. . . . I think that they . . . want to overprotect themselves to make certain that that does not happen, and they are less concerned about the image that that presents to their neighbors, thinking that their motives are really defensive and pure and therefore other people should not be suspicious of them.[17]

In fact, the Soviet view of the interrelationship between war and politics is integrally linked with the fear of a possible attack. In a critique of Soviet columnist Aleksandr Bovin, who argued that nuclear war cannot serve as a political instrument, Soviet Col. Ye. Rybkin wrote:

While correctly asserting that a total nuclear war is not acceptable as a means of achieving a political goal, A. Bovin at the same time makes a noticeable methodological mistake . . . [N]either the nature of the modern era nor nuclear weapons have changed the position that *nuclear war, if the imperialists were able to unleash one, would be an extension of policy.* Those individuals who deny this are confusing the causes, essence, and social nature of the phenomenon with the expediency of using it as a means of achieving a political goal.

So long as there exist the economic bases for wars and a policy which is capable of generating a war, we cannot abandon a class evaluation of the functions of such a war, even though it exists only as a possibility. The great threat of a nuclear war on the part of anti-socialist, primarily anti-Soviet, forces is an extension of reactionary imperialist policy and a war would be an extension of this policy, if a nuclear conflict were to break out. . . . *From this point of view,* no principal changes in the interrelationship between war and policy have occurred.[18]

At the same time, Rybkin quotes the Communist Party of the Soviet Union as declaring that an all-out nuclear war "cannot and must not serve as a means of solving international disputes."[19]

Thus, if Richard Pipes and others are correct in insisting that we should take Soviet military writings seriously, Rybkin's article—and much of Sokolovskiy and what is published in confidential journals such as *Military Thought*—seems to suggest that the Soviets will *not* use nuclear weapons for political gain, but that they suspect the United States might and that therefore the Soviet camp must be prepared to make the best of things if war does erupt.

Some American analysts insist, nevertheless, that the Soviets would not mind suffering a retaliatory blow delivered by the United States if they could accomplish vast political gains (though they never specify what these might be) in the process. T. K. Jones—Paul Nitze's private systems analyst—has asserted in Congressional testimony, "I firmly believe that the present Soviet leadership would have no qualms in risking the loss of 20 million or so of its population."[20] Richard Pipes reckons that they would probably not mind losing 30 million; after all, they lost a similar percentage of their population during World War II.[21] Leaving aside for a moment the fact that 20 or 30 million certainly underestimates Soviet losses in a nuclear war, several points must be made here.

First, the Soviets did not enter World War II knowing that 20 million Russians would die in battle. Second, the deaths and all the assorted injuries were spread out over four years, not thirty minutes or so, as would be the case in a nuclear catastrophe. Third, the Soviet decision to go to war was an act of self-defense in the face of impending Nazi conquest—not, as would be the case in the launching or provocation of nuclear war, a display of suicidal adventurism. Fourth, the Soviets were able to save much of their industrial base by transporting it eastward by rail as the Nazis started plowing through Russian territory from the west; in a nuclear war, for which there would be little warning and during which targets all across the country could be blasted, they would have no such assurances in advance.

Still, according to some hardliners, a nuclear war might not be so devastating. After all, some trains in Hiroshima were running 48 hours after the blast; many buildings were left standing; and—as Professor Pipes cites British physicist P.M.S. Blackett's observation in the latter's

1949 book, *Fear, War and the Bomb*—Germany was hit with the blast equivalent of 400 Hiroshimas in the course of World War II and was still able to fight.[22] This is all highly misleading. First, Blackett changed his views on the military implications of nuclear weaponry after the first successful explosion of the hydrogen bomb, which proved that explosive yields of weapons could be theoretically limitless. Second, comparing nuclear with conventional blasts ignores the effects of radiation, fallout, thermal heat, electromagnetic pulse and other effects of nuclear weapons.[23] Third, the Hiroshima bomb was 14 kilotons, the equivalent of a 14,000-ton dynamite blast. About one-third of Hiroshima was directly hit. The smallest weapon in the U.S. strategic arsenal today is the Poseidon with 40 kilotons. And just one-sixth of the U.S. nuclear-missile submarine force alone—seven or eight subs, each loaded with 160 nuclear warheads—could thoroughly devastate all 220 Soviet cities with populations greater than 100,000.[24]

At the 30th Anniversary Celebration of the Great Patriotic War Victory, otherwise an occasion for Soviet self-glorification, Leonid Brezhnev declared that "the starting of a nuclear missile war would spell inevitable annihilation for the aggressor himself, to say nothing of the vast losses for many other countries perhaps not even formally involved in the war."[25] The same sentiment is expressed by various authors writing in *Military Thought,* by Marshal Sokolovskiy, by the authors of *Marxism-Leninism On War & Army.* Furthermore, in the first business meeting of the two SALT delegations in Helsinki, on November 18, 1969, the Soviet Delegation, in a little-known prepared statement, cleared by the highest political and military leaders, noted:

Even in the event that one of the sides were the first to be subjected to attack, it would undoubtedly retain the ability to inflict a retaliatory strike of crushing power. Thus, evidently, we all agree that war between our two countries would be disastrous for both sides. And it would be tantamount to suicide for the ones who decided to start such a war.[26]

A closer look at much of Soviet military literature, in short, reveals a picture quite different from that which Professor Pipes and others paint. The Soviets have obviously been influenced by Clausewitz; but this means only that they see the nature and intensity of war as being determined by political factors, and since nobody has figured out any political goal for which the Soviets might be willing to risk nuclear holocaust, the Clausewitz connection can hardly be seen as horrifying or as inimical to the prospects of deterrence. Soviet military literature does emphasize what happens after nuclear war begins more than American literature does; but this concern seems to grow out of a genuine fear of an attack on the Soviet Union by the United States or its allies; this fear has historical basis. In any event, the Soviets have not apparently worked out a decent operational definition of "winning" a nuclear war, or how to get there from here. Finally, the Soviets seem just as horrified about the prospects and consequences of nuclear war as anybody.

In short, very little in Soviet military doctrine lends credence to the proposition that, in Richard Pipes' words, "the Soviet Union thinks it can fight and win a nuclear war."

SOVIET MILITARY CAPABILITIES

Doctrine, of course, is one thing; action, quite another. Many Western analysts see trends in Soviet military developments that support their thesis that the Soviets are acquiring "strategic superiority." These analyses often point to various indices of this superiority: (1) rising military expenditures, especially for investment in strategic arms; (2) numerical superiority in missiles; (3) development of "heavy missiles," high in both throw-weight and megatonnage; (4) extensive civil defense planning; (5) new anti-ballistic missile developments, especially in charged-particle-beam technology; and (6) deployment of large numbers of highly accurate warheads, theoretically capable of knocking out 90 percent of American land-based missiles by the early- to mid-1980s. But what do all these things say, and what do they mean?

[In the immediately ensuing pages, the author proceeds to assess the strategic and political ramifications associated with the aforementioned aspects of Soviet military capabilities. He then summarizes his conclusions. —*Ed.*]

There is no doubt that the Soviets are increasing their strategic power. They spend more than the United States does, they have more missiles than we do, their missiles are heavier than ours, they seem to spend and write more on civil defense, and their ICBM warheads are growing in number and accuracy to the point that our own ICBMs will, at least theoretically, become vulnerable by the early to mid-1980s. Nevertheless, the question must be asked: How significant are these trends? Will the United States still, for the foreseeable future, be able to carry out its strategic missions and to deter Soviet attack?

Measuring Soviet military expenditures in dollars carries a strong upward bias, as the CIA readily admits; measuring them in Russian rubles makes spending levels appear much more equal. Further, Soviet strategic programs are far more inefficient than U.S. programs; indeed, our expenditures in nuclear weapons over the past decade have been about five times as cost-effective as Soviet spending.

Those pointing to Soviet numerical superiority in missiles and bombers point only at the irrelevant. The United States has 50 percent more warheads and bombs (the things that actually kill people and demolish targets); and in any event, both sides have more than enough to deter the other from nuclear adventurism.

True, Soviet missiles are heavier than American ones, but Soviet missile design is far less efficient; compared with the USSR, it takes far fewer pounds of payload for the United States to get equal explosive yield. Soviet missiles also have more megatons than American missiles; but megatonnage (or equivalent megatonnage) is only a good measure for destruction of area, whereas both sides' targeting strategies aim to destroy individual military or industrial facilities, rather than to bust up cities or do indiscriminate damage to territory. As missiles become increasingly accurate, explosive yield has increasingly diminishing impact on determining whether the warhead will destroy its intended target.

Some believe that a Soviet civil defense program will radically reduce the damage done to the USSR's economy, but there is no evidence supporting this claim and much evidence to refute it. The supreme difficulties of planning a mass evacuation and sheltering program—as well as the insurmountable contradiction between the industrial dispersion and protection needed for an effective civil defense program on the one hand, and the heavily bottlenecked, concentrated, and centralized Soviet economy on the other hand—make it a remarkably unreliable hedge on which an aggressive Soviet leader could depend for protection against an American retaliatory nuclear strike.

Finally, while calculations suggest that American ICBMs will be vulnerable to a Soviet first strike by the early to mid-1980s, the model on which these calculations are based is highly abstract, divorced from the numerous uncertainties facing any military planner in real life. Even if the missiles were truly vulnerable, this fact is not very significant: land-based missiles constitute only 22 percent of the U.S. strategic arsenal; the thousands of other SLBM warheads, gravity bombs, and cruise missiles could devastate Soviet society or, if the President chose, could respond to Soviet limited attacks with deliberate flexibility and selectivity. And if one is still worried about ICBM vulnerability after considering all this, the best solution may be to phase out the land-based missile force altogether and to make improvements in the other two "legs" of the Strategic Triad. In any event, moving toward a multiple-shelter system on land—such as the "race-track" basing scheme proposed for the MX missile—is the wrong way to go for a variety of reasons.

In short, there are few grounds for complacency about the Soviets; they are improving their forces more, and more quickly, than intelligence analysts had predicted just a few years ago. However, neither are there grounds for panic. The American deterrent force remains secure and strong; notions of impending Soviet "strategic superiority" have no operational meaning. We are still able to carry out our strategic missions, we can still deter the Soviets from attacking, and we can respond in limited fashion to limited strikes. As long as this is so, there is a "strategic balance."

THE SOVIET VIEW: AN AMERICAN THREAT?

The Threat game is one that thrives on both sides, making it, however elusive, a political fact of life. From the Soviet viewpoint, a glance at official U.S. literature and at various weapons systems under development could reveal signs of U.S. "superiority seeking" as well. When asked if he could make the United States seem a threatening aggressor were he working for the Kremlin High Command, one Pentagon planner responded, "Oh sure, I could paint a pretty scary picture."

The new Mark-12A warhead, three of which will be placed on each of 300 Minuteman III ICBMs over the next two years, will have an 83 percent chance of destroying a Soviet missile silo in a single shot by the mid-1980s—the same "kill-probability" assigned to the most advanced Soviet ICBM warheads of that time.[27] The MX, to be deployed in 1986, with the Mark-12A and an Advanced Inertial Reference Sphere (AIRS) inertial guidance system—allowing accuracies of 300 feet—will have a 97 percent single-shot kill-probability against Soviet silos.[28] The air-launched cruise missile will destroy anything it is fired at with virtual certainty, no matter how blast-resistant the target. And the Trident II missile, coming along in the late 1980s, with 14 warheads of roughly 150 kilotons and very good accuracy, will be highly capable against Soviet silos as well.[29]

U.S. Defense Department officials deny that these weapons give the United States anything like "strategic superiority," or that the Soviets should look at highly accurate U.S. warheads as "destabilizing," because, after all, the Soviet Union would still have its submarine missiles and bombers that could wipe out the American industrial base.[30]

These officials may be right, but if that argument applies to America's counterforce capability, why should it not also apply to Soviet counterforce weapons? Indeed, *the Soviets have more reason to fear ICBM vulnerability,* since more than 70 percent of its warheads are on ICBMs, compared with 22 percent of American strategic nuclear warheads. Given the pace of Soviet MIRVed ICBM programs, this percentage will certainly increase for the USSR—whereas, given cruise missiles and Trident submarines, it will certainly decrease for the U.S. Improvements in missile accuracy, in other words, endanger a much larger proportion of Soviet forces compared with the danger to American forces.

Recent reports released by the U.S. Defense Advanced Research Projects Agency (DARPA) would not assure the Russians much, either. DARPA, whose sole mission is to devise technological breakthroughs and to seek military applications for their scientific wonders, is coming up with some marvelous devices, particularly in the area of anti-submarine warfare (ASW). The authors of its annual report excitedly invite the reader to "ponder the consequences of an ability to not only detect but to localize and track quiet submarines at long range." They state: "As long as a large portion of the SSBN [nuclear ballistic-missile submarine] force can avoid continuous surveillance, a successful preemptive strike is not possible." This is certainly correct. They then proceed to describe their plans to make continuous surveillance—and presumably a "successful preemptive strike"—possible.[31]

The Soviets obviously spend much time and money on ASW projects as well. But U.S. intelligence analysts report that the Soviets have not been successful on a single ASW project—at least on any wide-ocean application of ASW technology. Even if the Soviets did latch on to the right technology, geography would be a monumental restriction to their successful operations.[32] This geographic disadvantage is exacerbated by American deployment of the Trident I missile, which will replace older missiles in 12 of the 31 Poseidon submarines over the next two years, and be fitted into the 24 tubes on each Trident submarine. The Trident I has a range of 4000 nautical miles, compared with the 2600 nautical-mile range of the Poseidon. This extra range expands the area of ocean from which U.S. submarines can operate and still hit their targets in the Soviet Union by 10 to 20 times.[33]

It should be pointed out that the scientists at DARPA do not always reflect consensus thinking at the top; but all of DARPA's work is approved by the top, and a Soviet military planner reading the reports coming from the agency would not be unreasonably "paranoid" for concluding that at least some high-ranking Defense Department officials are aiming for a first-strike capability against the Soviet Union.

As for civil defense, most America-watchers in the USSR must realize that a serious U.S. program does not really exist, just as most Russia-watchers in the U.S. realize that the Soviet program—though taken more seriously by more people—is a fatally flawed program for anything but marginal protection against a very limited (e.g., accidental or China-launched) attack. However, grounds exist for thinking otherwise. According to the U.S. Defense Civil Preparedness Agency, there are identified shelter spaces for 230 million Americans and existing plans to protect 85 percent of the population in case of nuclear attack. Civil defense manuals are in print for virtually every industrial sector in the economy.[34] Many private analysts with government contracts, such as Herman Kahn of the Hudson Institute (whom one Soviet publication describes as "an ideologue of U.S. imperialism," whose "morbid misanthropic books . . . have become manuals for Pentagon's military planning"), have spelled out the "feasibility and desirability of widespread evacuation and sheltering."[35] All of this may be nonsense—but grounds for Soviet anxiety nevertheless, just as much nonsense about Soviet civil defense has furnished grounds for some American anxiety.

Finally, the U.S. has several thousand theater nuclear weapons in Europe and on aircraft carriers that have the range necessary to strike Soviet territory.[36] The USSR has 3,500 theater nuclear weapons in Europe as well, but none of them can hit the United States. Furthermore, the United States now plans to upgrade its theater nuclear forces by deploying the Pershing II Extended Range missile and the Ground Launched Cruise Missile (GLCM)—with 1,000- and 1,500-kilometer ranges respectively, or enough to strike the Soviet Union from Western Europe. Pershing II and the GLCM are intended as responses to modern

Soviet theater weapons, particularly the SS-20 missile, launched from inside the USSR and intended to strike Western Europe; still, the SS-20 cannot hit the United States, and this "asymmetry" must surely be apparent to the Soviets.

None of this is to say that the United States will soon emerge with "strategic superiority," or that American attempts to launch a first strike would not fail as dismally as would Soviet attempts. The point is merely that the spiralling arms race is fueled by—and, in turn, promotes— *mutual* fear and uncertainty between the United States and the Soviet Union. Each new move by one side creates new fears and uncertainties on the other side. Moreover, it is worth noting that, while in some instances the Soviets have surpassed the United States in the number of some of these new systems, the United States has, often shortsightedly, been the side that has more often moved first in the deployment of new weapons and new military technologies.

NOTES

1. One notable exception was Murray Marder, "Carter to Inherit Intense Dispute on Soviet Intentions," *Washington Post,* January 2, 1977. For a critical analysis of Team B, see Senate Select Intelligence Committee, *The National Intelligence Estimates A-B Team Episodes Concerning Soviet Strategic Capability and Objectives* (February 1978).

2. Nitze directed or helped compose NSC-68 (the first study, written in April 1950, urging post-war American rearmament), the bomber-gap study, the Gaither Commission report (sounding the alarms for a missile gap), and others.

3. See especially Keegan's speech reprinted in *Aviation Week & Space Technology (AWST),* March 28, 1977.

4. V. D. Sokolovskiy, *Soviet Military Strategy,* 3rd ed., 1968, tr. by Harriet Fast Scott (New York: Crane Russak, 3rd ed., 1972), p. 15.

5. Richard Pipes, "Why the Soviet Union Thinks It Could Fight and Win a Nuclear War," *Commentary,* July 1977, p. 34.

6. Karl von Clausewitz, *On War,* ed. and trans. by Michael Howard and Peter Paret (Princeton: Princeton University Press, 1976), p. 95.

7. Ibid., p. 92.

8. Col. B. Byely et al., *Marxism-Leninism On War & Army* (Moscow: Progress Publishers, 1972), p. 44.

9. Ibid., pp. 44, 19.

10. Ibid., pp. 15, 43.

11. Editor's note in Sokolovskiy, p. 167.

12. See John Erickson, "Soviet Military Power," *Strategic Review,* Spring 1973, pp. 2-7.

13. Harold Brown, DOD, *Annual Report, FY 1981,* pp. 67, 83.

14. Lengthy excerpts from this article are reprinted and analyzed in Raymond L. Garthoff, "Mutual Deterrence and Strategic Arms Limitation in Soviet Policy," *International Security,* Summer 1978. Garthoff's article is a superb analysis of Soviet military doctrine.

15. Ibid.

16. See Garthoff, op. cit., for more examples.

17. William Colby, Hearings, Senate Foreign Relations Committee, *United States/Soviet Strategic Options* (January, March 1977), p. 142.

18. Col. Ye. Rybkin, "The Leninist Concept of War and the Present," *Communist of the Armed Forces,* October 1973.

19. Ibid.

20. T. K. Jones, Hearings, Joint Committee on Defense Production, *Defense Industrial Base: Industrial Preparedness and War Survival* (November 17, 1976), p. 185.

21. Pipes, op. cit., p. 34.

22. See T. K. Jones, Hearings, House Armed Services Committee, *Civil Defense Review* (February, March 1976); P.M.S. Blackett, *Fear, War and the Bomb* (New York: McGraw-Hill, 1949).

23. See Samuel Glasstone and Philip J. Dolan, eds., *The Effects of Nuclear Weapons* (Washington, D.C.: Departments of Defense and Energy, 3rd ed., 1977); U.S. Office of Technology Assessment, *The Effects of Nuclear War* (1979); *DCPA Attack Environmental Manual* (U.S. Defense Civil Preparedness Agency, 1973).

24. A 40-kiloton warhead has a "lethal area" of roughly 8 square miles. It would take 1,010 of these warheads to produce, on average, 5 pounds per square inch (psi) blast overpressure—enough to collapse most buildings—over the area encompassed by every Soviet city with populations greater than 100,000. There are 160 MIRV warheads in a Poseidon submarine. Assuming 90 percent reliability, seven subs could do the job; eight would be needed assuming 80 percent reliability. The U.S. has 31 Poseidon subs. [Calculated on basis of Glasstone and Dolan; and Geoffrey Kemp, "Nuclear Forces for Medium Powers," Adelphi Papers Nos. 105 and 106 (London: IISS, 1974).]

25. *Pravda,* May 9, 1975.

26. Cited in Garthoff, op. cit., p. 126.

27. See Les Aspin, "Are We Standing Still?" *Congressional Record,* July 9, 1979.

28. A. A. Tinajero, Congressional Research Service, *The MX Intercontinental Ballistic Missile Program* (Issue Brief 1B77080, July 27, 1977).

29. "New Propellant Evaluated for Trident Second Stage," *AWST,* October 13, 1975, pp. 16–17; Trident II will be a hard-target killer. (See Harold Brown, DOD, *Annual Report, FY 1979,* p. 114.)

30. For great double-talk on this, see Harold Brown, DOD, *Annual Report, FY 1980,* p. 77.

31. U.S. Defense Advanced Research Projects Agency, *FY 1978 Program for Research and Development,* February 1977, pp. I3.12–14, I122.30.

32. To get out into the Atlantic Ocean, the Soviet subs must traverse a fairly narrow gap of water between Greenland and Iceland and between Iceland and the United Kingdom (called G-I-UK Gap). The U.S. has sensors and ASW equipment all along this stretch of ocean. For material on overwhelming superiority of the U.S. in the area of anti-submarine warfare (ASW), see Senate Armed Services Committee, Authorization Hearings, FY 1979, Pt. 9, pp. 6662–6667; Ibid., Pt. 2, pp. 1038, 1041, 1121–1122; and Bruce Blair, "Arms Control Implications of Anti-submarine Warfare (ASW) Programs," in Congressional Research Service, *Evaluation of Fiscal Year 1979 Arms Control Impact Statements,* report to House International Relations Committee (January 3, 1979) pp. 103–119.

33. Senate Armed Services Committee, Authorization Hearings, FY 1980, Pt. 6, p. 2841.

34. See Hearings, House Armed Services Committee, *Civil Defense Review,* pp. 7–8, 60, 118, 290.

35. Byely et al., op. cit., p. 41.

36. See *The Military Balance, 1979–1980* (London: IISS, 1979), pp. 114–119.

──────── **Questions for Reflection and Discussion** ────────

1. What do you consider to be the root causes of Soviet-U.S. tension? Does mutual misperception add to the problem? If so, what are the misperceptions and the reasons for them? How might they be eliminated?

2. How do you react to Soviet perceptions of the United States? Have they any basis in reality? In what ways are they erroneous?

3. How does Georgi Arbatov react to American perceptions of the Soviet Union? What are his criticisms and do you find any of them valid? Is it possible that American perceptions are sometimes influenced by domestic budgetary politics?

4. The Soviet Union is widely characterized in the United States as an aggressive, expansionist state committed to global domination. What evidence supports this assertion? Is it possible that this same evidence represents a reasonable response to perceived external threats to the USSR? If you were responsible for Soviet national security policy, might you have a similar view of the United States, and, if so, would you seek to improve Soviet military capabilities in relation to U.S. power and influence?

5. Is Soviet commitment to overcoming strategic inferiority relative to the United States indicative of incessant hostility to Western values and interests? Should U.S. policymakers attempt to maintain a favorable balance of power or should they move toward genuine military parity? What are the likely consequences of each alternative?

Selected Bibliography

Alexander, George L. *Managing U.S.-Soviet Rivalry: Problems of Crisis Prevention.* Boulder, CO: Westview Press, 1983.

"American Strength, Soviet Weakness." *Defense Monitor,* Vol. 9, No. 5. Washington, DC: Center for Defense Information, 1980.

Arbatov, Georgi A., and Willem Oltmans. *The Soviet Viewpoint.* New York: Dodd, Mead and Co., 1983.

Barnet, Richard J. *The Giants: Russia and America.* New York: Simon and Schuster, 1977.

Berman, Robert P., and John C. Baker. *Soviet Strategic Forces: Requirements and Responses.* Washington, DC: Brookings Institution, 1982.

Bronfenbrenner, Urie. "The Mirror Image in Soviet-American Relations: A Social Psychologist's Report." *Journal of Social Issues,* Vol. 17, No. 3 (1961), pp. 45–56.

Cockburn, Andrew. *The Threat: Inside the Soviet Military Machine.* New York: Random House, 1983.

Cox, Arthur Macy. "The CIA's Tragic Error." *New York Review of Books,* Vol. 27, No. 17 (Nov. 6, 1980), pp. 21–24.

D'Encausse, Helene Carrere. *Confiscated Power: How Soviet Russia Really Works.* New York: Harper & Row, 1982.

Douglass, Joseph D., Jr., Amoretta M. Huber, and Richard Starr, eds. *Soviet Strategy for Nuclear War.* Stanford, CT: Hoover Institution Press, 1979.

Ermarth, Fritz W. "Contrasts in American and Soviet Strategic Thought." *International Security,* Vol. 3, No. 2 (Fall 1978), pp. 138–155.

Gladstone, Arthur. "The Conception of the Enemy." *Journal of Conflict Resolution,* Vol. 3, No. 2 (June 1959), pp. 132–137.

Holloway, David. "War, Militarism and the Soviet State." *Alternatives: A Journal of World Policy,* Vol. 6, No. 1 (March 1980), pp. 59–92.

_____. "Military Power and Political Purpose in Soviet Policy." *Daedalus,* Vol. 109, No. 4 (Fall 1980), pp. 13–30.

_____. *The Soviet Union and the Arms Race.* New Haven, CT: Yale University Press, 1982.

Jervis, Robert. *Perception and Misperception in International Politics.* Princeton, NJ: Princeton University Press, 1976.

Kanet, Roger E., ed. *Soviet Foreign Policy and East-West Relations.* Elmsford, NY: Pergamon Press, 1982.

Kennan, George F. *The Nuclear Delusion: Soviet-American Relations in the Atomic Age.* New York: Pantheon Books, 1982.

Laqueur, Walter. "Pity the Poor Russians?" *Commentary,* Vol. 71, No. 2 (Feb. 1981), pp. 32–41.

Leebaert, Derek, ed. *Soviet Military Thinking.* Winchester, MA: Allen and Unwin, 1981.

Medvedev, Roy A., and Zhores A. Medvedev. "A Nuclear *Samizdat* or America's Arms Race," *Nation,* Vol. 234, No. 2 (Jan. 16, 1982), pp. 38–50.

Nerlich, Uwe, ed. *Soviet Power and Western Negotiating Policies.* 2 vols. Cambridge, MA: Ballinger Publishing Co., 1983.

Perlo, Victor. "The Myth of Soviet Superiority." *Nation,* Vol. 231, No. 7 (Sept. 13, 1980), pp. 201, 214–218.

Prados, John. *The Soviet Estimate: U.S. Intelligence Analysis and Russian Military Strength.* New York: Dial Press, 1982.

Rosefielde, Steven. *False Science: Underestimating the Soviet Military Threat.* New Brunswick, NJ: Transaction Books, 1981.

Solzhenitsyn, Aleksandr. "Misconceptions About Russia Are a Threat to America." *Foreign Affairs,* Vol. 58, No. 4 (Spring 1980), pp. 744–834.

Somerville, John, ed. *Soviet Marxism and Nuclear War: An International Debate.* Westport, CT: Greenwood Press, 1982.

"Soviet Geopolitical Momentum: Myth or Menace?" *Defense Monitor,* Vol. 9, No. 1. Washington, DC: Center for Defense Information, 1980.

"Soviet Military Power: Questions and Answers." *Defense Monitor,* Vol. 11, No. 1. Washington, DC: Center for Defense Information, 1982.

Strategic Intentions of the Soviet Union: Fallacies in Western Assessments. London: Institute for the Study of Conflict, 1978.

"U.S.-Soviet Military Facts." *Defense Monitor,* Vol. 11, No. 6. Washington, DC: Center for Defense Information, 1982.

Wolfe, Alan. *The Rise and Fall of the "Soviet Threat": Domestic Sources of the Cold War Consensus.* Washington, DC: Institute for Policy Studies, 1979.

PART THREE

OPTING FOR NUCLEAR DISARMAMENT

CHAPTER 7

Overcoming
Distrust and Competition

Post–World War II relations between the Soviet Union and the United States have been marked by profound mutual distrust and potentially catastrophic rivalry. Both states have, for the most part, forsaken meaningful efforts to reduce the threat of war, choosing instead to augment their separate military means to defend and promote their respective (to large extent hegemonic) interests. Each, with the help of their allies, seeks to destabilize the geopolitical position of the other; each applies a wide array of overt and clandestine policies to keep the other in check—particularly in the Third World, where each, both intentionally and unintentionally, confuses genuine self-determinist movements with some conspiracy in support of the other.

There are, however, growing numbers of informed observers who believe that continuation of this pattern makes nuclear war a virtual certainty; that one day, because of mutual distrust and competition, a miscalculation or a megalomaniacal act will unleash upon both societies—and others far beyond—the apocalypse that all humanity hopes to avoid. These observers repudiate as impossible the superpowers' quests for global domination. They call out for them to construct a durable, stable relationship based on reciprocal forbearance and mutual tolerance, together with a joint commitment to the peaceful resolution of disputes when their national interests collide. But overcoming distrust and competition, a persistent challenge throughout history, is no easy matter. As long as states rely on independent military means and expansionist definitions of national security to protect their perceived self-interests, and so long as these means and definitions pose a threat of aggression to others, distrust and hostile competition will remain dominant features of the international system.

The core question, then, is whether humanity, and especially the Soviet Union and the United States, possesses the imagination and will to escape the distrustful competition that now threatens as never before in history, to realize that the benefits of a less militarized and less expansive conception of national self-interest far outweigh the risks to a complex, interdependent world. Over the years, insuffient attention has been given to this question. Governmental and academic analysts traditionally have focused on maintaining the balance of military power, and on questions concerning the "proper" role of force in global affairs. However, dissatisfaction with the current international security order, brought about by the high cost of continued militarism and the lack of effective controls on the sovereign use of force, has begun to generate among scholars and others a strong consensus that behavioral and systemic change must begin as soon as possible, and particularly between the Soviet Union and the United States. Especial attention has newly been given to what has come to be called "confidence-building measures" (CBMs): e.g., notification of military exercises and movements above a defined level; limitation of such exercises and movements to low tactical levels close to borders; limitation by duration and by prohibitions on live ammunition together with effective means of verification; exchange of observer personnel and liaison; and so forth. The growing potential for nuclear war renders it imperative that the policy elites of both countries overcome (or at least radically reduce) their mutual distrust and competition at the earliest possible moment, and that this effort be simultaneously accompanied by a similar yet deeper reorientation among their respective populations generally, who for decades have been nurtured to believe the worst about the other.

This chapter is devoted to a consideration of this increasing concern and to some of the more far-reaching confidence-building proposals that attend it. The Jerome Frank article sets forth certain of the psychoanalytic methods the two nations might consider to escape their dilemma. Charles Osgood posits a theory of disarmament that enables parties to reduce their nuclear arsenals confidently, without sacrifice to their national security. Walter Clemens argues for a multifaceted approach to assuring joint Soviet-U.S. security. Roger Fisher concludes by recommending a process of negotiation and more general dealing that can reduce competition and thereby facilitate the cooperation that is essential to avoid the confrontation no one desires.

22. Psychological Aspects of Disarmament and International Negotiations

Jerome D. Frank

Some years ago the UN General Assembly unanimously passed a resolution stating, "the question of complete disarmament is the most important one facing the world today." It is no news that progress toward this universally sought goal has been backward: far from being checked, the accelerating arms race is involving more and more countries; and the only favorable events have been the atmospheric nuclear test ban, which has perhaps slightly slowed research and development, and the United Nations resolution against sending armed satellites into space, which concerns future rather than existing arms. Nations, still committed to policies of self-help, still cling to their sovereignty and regard superior military power as the ultimate arbiter of international disputes. The halting of the arms race followed by disarmament is the most urgent and discouraging task confronting nations today.

To achieve lasting peace among nations requires substitution for armed might of peaceful ways of settling their disputes; and this depends in turn on the strengthening of methods for peaceful resolution of international conflicts and on developing more effective ones.

*   *   *

The most pervasive psychological obstacle to successful negotiations is mutual mistrust: each side fears that the other will cheat him in arriving at and carrying out agreements. A former high State Department official stated the American attitude well: "For Moscow to propose what we can accept seems to us even more sinister and dangerous than for it to propose what we cannot accept. Our instinct is to cast about for grounds on which to discredit the proposal instead of seizing it and making the most of it. Being distrustful of the Greeks bearing gifts, we are afraid of being tricked."[1] The Russians, no doubt, feel the same way about us.

Mistrust is aggravated by and contributes to difficulties in communication based on other grounds—negotiators often cannot make clear their own positions or hear accurately those of their adversaries, especially when they come from different societies which differ in certain attitudes, values, and habitual ways of thinking. Negotiations can also be impeded by certain aspects of the dynamics of conflicting groups and by features of the negotiating process itself.

PSYCHOLOGICAL PROBLEMS OF DISARMAMENT

It must be admitted that on this issue the mutual distrust of nations is justified. The troubles start with the paradox that each nation believes that successful negotiations are possible only if it is stronger, in effect taking the position that disarmament is eventually necessary, of course, but bitter experience has shown that the adversary cannot be trusted and understands only force; therefore, only by being strong can we hope to negotiate successfully with him. . . . [Thus] the very conditions regarded by one side as favorable for negotiations are regarded by the other as unfavorable.

Furthermore, because nations rely on arms for their security, none enters disarmament negotiations in good faith; their orientation is competitive rather than cooperative, and they bring to such negotiations the attitudes that led to the arms race initially. Each strives for an agreement that will increase its relative advantage at the adversary's expense rather than one that will lead to the greatest possible degree of mutual disarmament; and each wants to reserve the right to accumulate those weapons it believes to be most essential to its security and power. Hence, such negotiations in good faith as there are tend to be about relinquishing weapons that do not really matter, like obsolete bombers, and "disarmament turns out to be but one of the forms the armaments race can take."[2]

Negotiations will become genuinely cooperative only when nations accept the truth of President Kennedy's September, 1961, statement to the United Nations that "The risks inherent in disarmament pale in comparison to the risks inherent in an unlimited arms race."[3] If nations really believed this, they would be willing, in order to reach disarmament agreements, to run risks comparable to those run in pursuit of illusory security through arms, because disarmament negotiations can succeed only to the extent that participants are convinced that the risk of no agreement outweighs the risk of being cheated by the adversary.

*   *   *

Two types of activity might reduce mutual mistrust to the point where disarmament negotiations have some chance of success: inspection for concealed armaments and unilateral tension-reducing acts.

Problems of Inspection

If reliable methods of inspection for hidden arms could be devised, so that nations were reasonably sure the others were not cheating, prospects for agreements on arms control and disarmament would be enhanced.[4] Since Russia and the United States have actually been involuntarily submitting to rather extensive inspection by observation satellites for some time, they . . . have pinpointed each other's major military installations, and this [has] reduced the area of suspicion, thus improving chances for formal agreements. They cannot distinguish munitions factories from other types, of course, or detect stores of chemical, biological, or nuclear weapons.

All inspection agreements must rest on the assumptions that nations genuinely want to abide by them and prove to others that they are doing so, and that the main source of hesitancy is the fear that others will cheat. Inspection schemes have all concentrated on the detection of violations, but if inspection is seen as a means of promoting trust, its ability to enable each country to prove that it is not cheating would be as important as its ability to detect cheating. The crucial aspect— the main safeguard against a sudden flare-up of mutual suspicion that might precipitate a nuclear exchange—is the provision of a method by which a wrongly suspected nation could establish its innocence.

Inspection can increase as well as reduce tension—it is an incontrovertible fact that any inspection is a kind of spying and that mistrust is implied in a demand to inspect. . . . If inspection's main purpose were to establish innocence rather than detect guilt, its irritating aspect would be sharply reduced.

Inspection agreements would have to provide for continual adjudication of questions that arise in the course of carrying them out. Such provisions might be their most important feature because they would keep the parties in continuing contact, dispel unwarranted suspicion, and build up habits of resolving disagreements.

To get any inspection scheme into operation, participants would have to accept the fact that, human ingenuity what it is, any scheme involves some risk and no inspection scheme is absolute proof against cheating. With arms levels what they are today, however, it would take a lot of cheating to yield worthwhile advantages—one or two clandestine underground explosions (assuming extension of the test ban to include underground tests), for example, could not yield enough technological gain to be worth the risk that their discovery would wreck the inspection agreement. As disarmament progressed inspection would have to be increasingly rigorous, for with conventional weapons the lower the level of armaments, the more secure nations could feel; but with nuclear weapons the lower the general level, the greater the advantage of a slight preponderance. The country that had successfully concealed a few nuclear weapons while the rest of the world had totally disarmed could blackmail all the rest. This discouraging thought can be countered, however, by the encouraging one that disarmament can progress only as fast as international confidence grows, and that with increasing confidence would come increasing acceptance of inspection and familiarity with its procedures; thus total disarmament and inspection would probably become possible simultaneously.

Since the main danger of violations would come from clandestine disaffected groups within each country, the best place to start developing and testing inspection methods would be at home. Inspection games similar to war games could be devised in which one group would try to cheat and another to expose it; through such activities each nation would develop methods of inspection in which it had confidence, thereby increasing its willingness to use them and its ability to persuade other nations of their effectiveness.

Because weapons caches can be so easily concealed and even secretly manufactured, especially chemical and biological ones, inspection for weapons, however elaborate, will probably never be able to afford adequate assurance against cheating. But there would also be clues in arms budgets, personnel, and production records, and even the mass media to reveal, however indirectly, that weapons were being manufactured and stored on an appreciable scale.[5] And periodic systematic analysis of such records would, as an adjunct to direct inspection, increase its effectiveness. Governments would have to agree to make them available to each other, but this presents no greater obstacle than reaching agreement on any type of inspection. The facts that no weapon can be manufactured without many people knowing about it and that weapons are useless unless someone knows where they are and there is an organization trained to use them have led behavioral scientists to propose a variety of schemes for inspecting people rather than weapons.[6] Without an occasional on-the-spot check it would be impossible to be sure whether suspected violation of any scheme had in fact occurred, but knowledge inspection would greatly reduce the number needed.

One proposal, "inspection by the people," which would require laws in every country encouraging the populace to inform an international inspectorate of any known cheating, has been worked out in considerable detail, including methods of protecting informers and insuring free communication between the inspectorate and the citizens of the countries involved.[7] In public opinion polls in the United States, Western Europe, India, and Japan, 70 to 90 percent of respondents have indicated that they approve of such an inspection organization and that they themselves would report attempts to make forbidden weapons to a worldwide inspection agency.[8] Whether people would actually behave as they say they would is uncertain, but the polls at least suggest that the possibility of inspection by the people is not as fantastic as might appear at first glance. . . . Interest in it seems to have lapsed, but having received this much recognition, it should be easily revivable at an appropriate time.

The second approach to knowledge inspection is through direct interrogation of people who might know of violations. A scientist whose opinion must be respected believes that modern detection techniques using such physiological indices as changes in brain-wave patterns could be raised to a level of over 90-percent certainty; if so, this approach holds out substantial hope for checking the veracity of an official's public statements or statements to an adversary in negotiations.[9] He would have to submit to the tests, of course, but since this would be part of the overall agreement, refusal to be tested would be a virtual admission of lying. Furthermore, a leader who suspected that his nation was about to be falsely accused could volunteer to undergo the examinations.

Unilateral Moves to Reduce Mutual Mistrust

Inspection schemes would come into force only after negotiations had yielded agreements to disarm, but there is still the problem of how to reduce mutual mistrust to the point at which negotiations—confrontations bristling with mutual fears—have some chance of succeeding.

Because of their interdependence and the workings of the self-fulfilling prophecy, the range of alternatives for each modern nation is heavily restricted by the others' actions. Since each has some freedom of choice, however, and the more powerful the nation, the greater its freedom, nations might be able to act unilaterally to reverse the tension-armaments spiral. One psychologist has detailed this in a program termed Graduated Reciprocation in Tension Reductions, or GRIT.[10] One of the greatest hurdles for the nation taking the lead is that its actions would have to be calculated to diminish the apparent threat it poses to other nations but without frightening itself. Fortunately, the effect of a nation's actions on the international tension level is somewhat independent of their military significance: the Berlin Wall increased East-West tensions without affecting the balance of military power in the least.

* * *

On the other hand, if a major nation publicized detailed plans for converting its armaments industry to the manufacture of other products when a disarmament agreement was reached, the confidence of other nations in the sincerity of its desire to disarm would be increased. Such a unilateral step might improve the international atmosphere without incurring any risk at all.

Any conciliatory move by one nation would probably be regarded initially by the other as a ruse to get it to drop its guard. To have any hope of eliciting a reciprocal move, therefore, the initiating nation would have to take a big enough disarmament step to clearly weaken itself and persist in it despite a suspicious or hostile reception. But in the context of the universal reliance on force, such an act would tend to be viewed as surrender by both the sides, demoralizing the one that did it and perhaps tempting the adversary to attack while it saw an advantage. Since it would also be likely to be interpreted as a sign of weakness, it would have to be done purely voluntarily. . . .

An inconclusive but encouraging experiment with reciprocal unilateral initiatives—what Premier Khrushchev termed the policy of mutual example—began with President Kennedy's counciliatory speech at American University in June of 1962 in which he announced America's unilateral halting of atmospheric tests; widely publicized in Russia by newspapers and radio, it was soon followed by Khrushchev's announcement that Russia was halting production of bombers. At the United Nations other conciliatory gestures by both followed, and by August a ban on testing nuclear weapons in the atmosphere or outer space had been successfully negotiated.

Strangely enough, the Cuban missile crisis of October, 1962, interrupted conciliatory gestures only temporarily, and by giving leaders of both the United States and the Soviet Union a close view of the nuclear abyss into which mutual intransigency threatened to plunge their countries, it probably actually strengthened their incentives to find ways of reducing tension. In any case, subsequent agreements included the American wheat sale to Russia and the United Nations resolution against orbiting nuclear weapons. The initial steps were greeted with considerable ambivalence, as expected, but the decline of mutual distrust seemed to accelerate with time, and even the Vietnam war does not seem to have brought American-Soviet tensions back up to their pre-1963 pitch. The experience is inconclusive, however, for it did not lead to any major slowing of the arms race. Both countries' actions were essentially psychological gestures that had no significant effect on their actual relative power. Possibly a policy of "mutual example" cannot do more than start the ball rolling and its main effect is only to reduce the mutual fear and distrust of the citizenry of hostile nations, thereby giving the leaders more freedom of action.[11] Perhaps it can only be hoped that the limited success of this policy in 1963 will encourage national leaders to try it again.

*   *   *

EXPERIMENTAL STUDIES
OF NEGOTIATION AND BARGAINING

In addition to the empirical studies and observations that have contributed to the understanding of international negotiations, there is a growing body of experiments that cast light on some aspects of the process. Experimental studies fall into three broad groups—inter-nation simulation, the dynamics of groups in conflict, and mixed-motive or "prisoners' dilemma" games.

[The author next proceeds to consider briefly experimental studies on inter-nation simulation and on group dynamics in conflict situations. He then continues with the mixed-motive "prisoners' dilemma." —Ed.]

"Prisoners' Dilemma"

Whether the international power struggle is waged by warlike or peaceful means, it remains a mixed-motive [or variable-sum] game in which the participants have some common and some opposed interests.

*   *   *

In a variable-sum game the best solution would be that in which all players' sum is greatest, the worst the one in which all players' sum is least. The central feature of these games for our purposes is that the best outcome for both players can be obtained only if each takes the other's interests as well as his own into account; if each considers only his own interests, both wind up with an outcome that neither prefers.[12]

Consider the story of the prisoners' dilemma: a district attorney holds two suspects whom he does not have enough evidence to convict. So he goes to each and says that if he confesses and his partner does not, he will get off with a one-year sentence for turning state's evidence, but if he refuses to confess and his partner confesses, he will get the maximum penalty of ten years for his stubbornness; if both confess, each will get a five-year sentence, but if neither confesses, they will be convicted on a lesser charge and each will get two years. Each prisoner thinks to himself: "If I do not confess, I stand to get a two-year sentence (if I can trust my partner also not to confess) or a ten-year sentence if he confesses; but if I confess, the worst that can happen to me is a five-year sentence (if my partner confesses) and I may get off with one year if he does not; so it is to my advantage to confess, especially since my partner is going through the same calculation and will therefore probably confess." Both confess and get five years, whereas if they had trusted each other, they would have been given only two.

Nations would face an analogous problem with a test ban agreement that lacked a foolproof inspection system, so that cheating would be possible. Let us assume that two nations, Neptunia and Plutonia, have signed such an agreement: " 'If Plutonia does not cheat,' the Neptunian strategist reasons, 'then clearly it is in Neptunia's interest to cheat; for then we shall be ahead of Plutonia in our research on nuclear weapons. If, on the other hand, Plutonia does cheat, this is all the more reason why we should also cheat; for otherwise we let them get ahead. Consequently, regardless of whether Plutonia cheats or not, it is in our interest to cheat. We must therefore cheat in order to serve our national interest.'

"The Plutonian strategist, being in exactly the same position, reasons in exactly the same way and comes to the same conclusion. Consequently, both countries cheat and in doing so are both worse off than if they had not cheated, since otherwise there was no point to the agreement (which presumably conferred benefits on both countries)."[13]

The issue at stake in such games determines the size of the "payoffs" for the various possible outcomes, thereby influencing the relative strength of the players' motives to cooperate or defect. Regardless of the issue, however, the best outcome for both players will be reached if they trust each other. In Prisoners' Dilemma even the best outcome involves some loss for both, but in disarmament negotiations the cooperative solution would yield great rewards for all parties concerned.

The crucial feature of Prisoners' Dilemma is that it requires mutual trust while strongly tempting the players to try to double-cross each other: to reach the best outcome for both, each must trust the other in the very real sense of giving the other an opportunity to hurt him if he so chooses, but the game puts a premium on successful deceit. The best strategy for each contestant would be to convince his opponent that he will cooperate—so that the opponent will make a cooperative choice—and then defect. In the examples, Prisoner A would fare best if he could convince B that he (A) would never confess so that B would not do so; A could then confess and get a very light sentence at B's expense. In the international version, Plutonia would gain the greatest advantage if it could convince Neptunia that it would not cheat (so that Neptunia would not) and then cheat. Each contestant is torn between the contradictory goals of winning the other's trust and cheating him, and between his desire to trust the opponent and his fear of betrayal.

[Dr. Frank next points out how Prisoners' Dilemma readily lends itself to "experimentally minded social psychologists," observing that it can be quantified and computerized so that data can be easily obtained and analyzed. Then, after acknowledging that such experimental games produce ambiguous results, not least in relation to international negotiations, he notes the "promise" held out by two groups of experiments, the first concerning the role of communication in establishing mutual trust, and the second concerning the effect of introducing threats.]

Communication and Trust

An experiment explored the relationship between trust, trustworthiness, and amount of communication between the players.[14] Each player could choose one of two alternatives, and the payoffs were arranged to tempt each to make the non-cooperative choice, leading to lower payoffs for both than if they had cooperated; to enhance this temptation, each was told to try to win as much as possible for himself without regard to how his opponent fared. The second player was actually an accomplice who made a cooperative choice on the first trial (there were five) and then followed the subject, cooperating or defecting depending on what he had done on the previous trial.

Subjects were divided into several groups, and the amount of communication between them was systematically varied—some neither sent nor received written communications before each trial, some only received them, some only sent them, none did both. The communications contained four levels of information: intentions, expectations as to how the other should respond, what the penalty for defecting would be, and how the other could absolve himself in the next trial if he defected. Of the many measures made, the most interesting for our purposes were perceived trust and trustworthiness—"trust" was defined as the subject's expectation that his opponent would cooperate, as determined by his answer to a question to this effect before each trial, "trustworthiness" as making a cooperative choice. Both were greater, the more complete the communication sent or received: 80 percent of those who sent or received notes containing all four items of information expressed trust and made cooperative choices as compared to only 11 percent of those not allowed to communicate at all; of those who sent or received incomplete communications, the percentage who trusted and cooperated ranged between 30 and 60. This finding lends experimental support to two features of the GRIT proposal: nations should clearly announce their intentions in advance and invite the adversary to cooperate.

Of subsidiary interest is the finding that only 20 percent of the subjects were double-crossers who defected after perceiving that the opponent trusted them, and only a quarter of these had sent a message indicating that they were going to cooperate—committing themselves apparently helped to keep them trustworthy.

Communication and Threat

All negotiations include threats in some form, expressed or implied, and these often consist merely of one party's threat to prevent the other from achieving certain ends it desires, a type of threat that lends itself well to experimental study, since it is mild enough to be readily reproduced in the laboratory. The prototype for most such studies is a variable-sum game in which players pretend to operate rival trucking firms, and their earnings depend on being first to get their own trucks to a destination on a short road over which only one can pass at a time; either could use a longer road, which permits him to reach his goal independently of the other player's actions but which costs him money because of the time lost. In some variations one or both players control a gate that could deny the other's access to the short road—and this is the threat.[15] The players have a common interest in working out an arrangement for taking turns on the short road, since this would yield the highest total gain for both, but their interests conflict because the one who uses it first or more often (depending on the variation of the game being studied) profits more.

Three different instructions were used: cooperative—try to win as much for yourself as possible, but you want your opponent to come out ahead also; individualistic—try to do the best for yourself regardless of what happens to him; and competitive—try to come out as far ahead of him as you can. Since variations in instructions, kinds of communication permitted, the status or power of the players relative to each other, feelings of like or dislike, and schedules of costs and payoffs all have been found to affect players' choices, no general conclusions can safely be drawn from the findings. A few on the effects of communication and threat may be cited, however, as examples of the type of question that can be explored with this technique.

The more competitive the players' orientation, the less likely they were to avail themselves of opportunities to communicate. Communication helped improve both participants' outcomes only when they were required to communicate a fair proposal before each trial, one they would accept if it were offered them by the adversary. If their first trials had ended in deadlock and mutual loss, the tutoring was unnecessary—experience was, as usual, a good teacher.

With respect to the capacity to threaten, a repeated finding was that when both participants had control of a gate—when both had weapons, as it were—they did worse than when neither had a gate.

Apparently, when a player uses a gate, he implies by this use of threat that he feels himself in some sense superior to his opponent—perhaps more courageous, perhaps of higher status—so that it is his opponent's duty to defer to him. To allow oneself to be intimidated would therefore implicitly grant the other's right to demand submission— a humiliating posture—and the most effective way of rectifying this blow to self-esteem is to intimidate the threatener.[16] These psychological motivations may contribute to . . . examples . . . of counter-threat on the international scene.

The results in a modification of the trucking game, in which each subject could signal his intentions before each trial and also indicate what he thought the other would do, were shown to be strongly affected by whether the player intended to cooperate, to strive for precisely half the winnings, or to dominate. Cooperative pairs did much better than competitive pairs—hardly a startling finding—but in pairs in which one started with a cooperative and the other with a competitive attitude, both players fared badly in the long run. The cooperative partner's behavior apparently encouraged the competitive one to keep on pushing, until the former got angry and started to fight back, by which time it was too late. If the initially cooperative player immediately made a counter-threat, the players were much more likely to arrive at a cooperative agreement eventually.[17] The moral seems to be, Don't let your opponent think he can take advantage of you,[18] a finding that casts doubt on the effectiveness of turning the other cheek. To test this strategy further, the experimenters led subjects to think that their opponent refused to budge from a conciliatory strategy, even to the extent of accepting an electric shock each time his adversary blocked him. Since the "pacifist" was simulated by a computer, one cannot be sure how convincing he was, but a pacifist strategy did not in itself cause any player to change from a dominating to a cooperative strategy. In some runs, the "pacifist" explained the reason for his behavior, stressing his conciliatory intent, making fair demands, and emphasizing his refusal to use the shock and his intention to force the other to shock him if he were going to continue to be unfair. A small crumb of comfort for pacifists is that of the subjects who changed from dominating to cooperative, all were in the group receiving this communication— unfortunately, however, it reinforced other subjects in their dominating strategy because they saw the pacifist's tactics as efforts to trick them or make them feel guilty.[19]

As far as they go, these experiments confirm the general experience that the more bargainers communicate their intentions and expectations, the better (provided, of course, that the communications are genuinely intended to achieve the best outcome for both parties), and that threats are apt to impede negotiations. The best results for both parties were obtained when neither used threats, but if one player did make a threat, a prompt, firm counter-threat was more likely than a conciliatory initial response to facilitate an ultimately successful outcome. At least in one experimental situation, pacifist strategies do not work.

IMPLICATIONS FOR INTERNATIONAL
NEGOTIATIONS

Empirical and experimental studies of negotiations confirm the obvious fact that regardless of the issues, a successful outcome is impeded by the absence of mutual trust and lack of full and accurate communication. Their contribution lies in highlighting specific sources of difficulty that should concern all negotiators, and they also offer certain leads as to how negotiations could be improved.

In almost all international negotiations it is reasonable to assume some potential basis for mutual trust—even in war there are often tacit bargains between the combatants. The Prisoner's Dilemma depends on trust to the extent that both players must trust the person who sets the rules: if the prisoners did not trust the district attorney, there would be no dilemma, and each would simply refuse to confess and would take his chances. One important way of improving the chances for the successful outcome of negotiations, regardless of substantive issues, would thus be to pinpoint and combat sources of mutual mistrust. Participants in all negotiations could well make special efforts to get into the open the psychological sources of mutual misunderstanding and mistrust that operate out of awareness, including conflicting habits of thought and ways of proceeding, and above all, the universal difficulty in really hearing what the other fellow is saying—Adlai Stevenson's quip, "I sometimes think that what America needs more than anything else is a hearing aid,"[20] applies to all countries. If only it were enforceable, a splendid ground rule for all negotiations would be that there would be no bargaining until the parties could express each other's positions to their mutual satisfaction. . . .[21] To feel that a person is trying his best to understand you, especially someone you believe to be hostile or indifferent, creates a very favorable impression of his good sense, intelligence, and good will, and you are then in a much more receptive frame of mind for his ideas.[22]

From the organizational standpoint, the goal would be to set up conditions that foster in the negotiators a cooperative rather than a competitive stance. The aim would be to reduce the barriers between the groups by making each feel, at every step of the way, that they are working on a joint enterprise. Instead of negotiators being selected by each group separately, for example, they could be chosen jointly from a panel of names put up by each; this "criss-cross" panel would weaken the "traitor trap," because the negotiators would consider themselves representatives of both groups, who would have implicitly committed themselves in advance to accept the outcome of the bargaining.[23]

*   *   *

That such procedures are of more than theoretical importance is suggested by the finding that they improve outcomes of management-labor negotiations.

*   *   *

An important lesson to be learned from this review is that major psychological obstacles to successful international negotiations lie in the negotiating parties' attitudes. Procedural improvements can be of some help, but real progress depends on convincing nations that they have become geniunely interdependent. International negotiations, especially those involving armaments, have become prisoners' dilemmas in which all nations have more to gain by cooperating than by competing, and in which, in fact, persistence in competitive attitudes can bring all to disaster.

Day by day the advances in science, mass communication, and mass transportation are increasing this interdependence. The psychological problem is how to make all people aware that whether they like it or not, the earth is becoming a single community.

NOTES

1. L. J. Halle, "The Struggle Called 'Coexistence,' " *New York Times Magazine* (November 15, 1959), p. 110.

2. S. de Madariaga, "Disarmament? The Problem Lies Deeper," *New York Times Magazine* (October 11, 1959), p. 74.

3. J. F. Kennedy, quoted in *Science* 137 (August 24, 1962):591.

4. H. G. Kurtz and H. B. Kurtz, *War Safety Control Report* (Chappaqua, New York: War Control Planners, 1963). An ingenious suggestion for initiating disarmament, one that has been worked out in some detail, is "War Safety Control": nations would maintain their present arsenals but would devote present arms expenditures to perfecting worldwide electronic methods of detecting other nations' clandestine preparations for war; simultaneously, they would institute international institutions for nipping such activities in the bud. Only after all nations had achieved security by these means would disarmament be possible, but it should then proceed rapidly.

5. J. D. Singer, "Media Analysis in Inspection for Disarmament," *J. Arms Control* (July 1963):248–260.

6. L. C. Bohn, "Non-Physical Inspection Techniques," in D. G. Brennan, ed., *Arms Control, Disarmament and National Security* (New York: George Braziller, 1961) pp. 347–364. E. B. McNeil, "Psychological Inspection," *J. Arms Control* 1 (1963):124–138.

7. S. Melman, "Inspection by the People," in Q. Wright, W. M. Evan, and M. Deutsch, eds., *Preventing World War III: Some Proposals* (New York: Simon and Schuster, 1962), pp. 40–51.

8. W. M. Evan, "An International Public Opinion Poll of Disarmament and 'Inspection by the People': A Study in Supernationalism," in S. Melman, ed., *Inspection for Disarmament* (New York: Columbia University Press, 1958), pp. 231 ff.

9. R. W. Gerard, "Truth Detection," in Wright, Evan, and Deutsch, *Preventing World War III*, pp. 52–61.

10. C. E. Osgood, *An Alternative to War or Surrender* (Urbana, Ill.: University of Illinois Press, 1962). [For the GRIT proposal, see Reading 29, infra.—*Ed.*]

11. A. Etzioni, "The Kennedy Experiment," *Western Political Quarterly* 20 (June 1967):361–381.

12. A. Rapoport, *Fights, Games and Debates* (Ann Arbor: University of Michigan Press, 1960), pp. 71 ff.

13. A. Rapoport, "Research for Peace," *The Listener* (March 31, 1966):455.

14. J. L. Loomis, "Communication, the Development of Trust and Cooperative Behavior," *Human Relations* 12 (1959):305–315.

15. M. Deutsch, "Bargaining, Threat, and Communication: Some Experimental Studies," in K. Archibald, ed., *Strategic Interaction and Conflict* (Berkeley, Cal.: Institute for International Studies, University of California, 1966), pp. 19–41.

16. H. H. Kelley, "Experimental Studies of Threats in Interpersonal Negotiations," *J. Conflict Resolution* 9 (March 1965):79–105.

17. R. J. Meeker, G. H. Shure, and W. H. Moore, Jr., "Real-Time Computer Studies of Bargaining Behavior: The Effects of Threat upon Bargaining," *American Federation of Information Processing Societies Conference Proceedings* 25 (1964):115–123.

18. This can also be viewed as an example of the effect of disappointed expectations, like the finding that a friendly note following a hostile one elicits more friendliness than after a friendly one. . . . There are many real-life analogies—for example, the interrogation technique of suddenly showing consideration for a prisoner after treating him roughly, or the negotiating maneuver of unexpectedly making a concession after being adamant.

19. G. H. Shure, R. J. Meeker, and E. A. Hansford, "The Effectiveness of Pacifist Strategies in Bargaining Games," *J. Conflict Resolution* 9 (March 1965):106–117.

20. A. Stevenson, Godwin Lecture, Harvard University, 1955.

21. J. Cohen, "Reflections on the Resolution of Conflict in International Affairs," *Proceedings of the International Congress on Applied Psychology* 1 (Copenhagen: Munksgaard, 1962):59.

22. S. Hayakawa, "On Communication with the Soviet Union, Part I," *Etc.: A Review of General Semantics* 17 (1960):396–400.

23. R. R. Blake, "Psychology and the Crisis of Statesmanship," *American Psychologist* 14 (1959):90–93.

23. Disarmament Demands GRIT

Charles E. Osgood

"Calculated" escalation, described by Herman Kahn as "a competition in resolve" and "a competition in risk-taking,"[1] is a strategy that relies for its success upon the Neanderthal mode of thinking in humans, in high places as well as low. It is designed to push the villainous THEYs beyond their risk ceiling before the heroic WEs reach ours. This strategy has four salient features: first, the steps are unilaterally initiated (we did not negotiate with the North Vietnamese about increasing the tempo of our bombing or moving in closer to Hanoi; we just did it unilaterally). Second, each step propels the opponent into reciprocating if he can, with more aggressive steps of his own (our development of multiple nuclear warheads propels the Soviets into analogous developments). Third, such steps are necessarily graduated in nature—by the unpredictability of technological breakthroughs, by the limitations imposed by logistics, and by the oscillating level of perceived threat. But, fourth, calculated escalation is obviously a *tension-increasing* process, the termination of which is a *military* resolution (victory, defeat, or in our time even mutual annihilation). Now, if we change this last feature of calculated escalation and shift it from tension-induction to tension-reduction, we have the essence of a calculated de-escalation strategy in conflict situations. It is one in which nation *A* devises patterns of small steps, well within its own limits of security, designed to reduce tensions and induce reciprocating steps from nation *B*. If such unilateral initiatives are persistently applied and reciprocation is obtained, then the margin for risk-taking is widened and somewhat larger steps can be taken. Both sides, in effect, begin edging down the tension ladder, and both are moving—within what they perceive as reasonable limits of national security—toward a political rather than a military resolution. Needless to say, successful application of such a strategy assumes that both parties to a conflict have strong motives to get out of it.

GRIT IS THE APPROACH

The focus of my own long-term concern at the inter-nation level has been the rationalization of a strategy alternative whose technical name is "Graduated and Reciprocated Initiatives in Tension-reduction." While doodling at a conference in the early 1960s, I discovered that the initials of this mind-boggling phrase spelled out GRIT, and although I generally take a dim view of acronyms, this one was not only easy for people to remember, but also suggested the kind of determination and patience required to successfully apply it. One of the aims of GRIT is to reduce and control international tension levels. Another is to create an atmosphere of mutual trust within which negotiations on critical military and political issues can have a better chance of succeeding; in other words, GRIT is not a substitute for the more familiar process of negotiation, but rather a parallel process designed to enable a nation to take the initiative in a situation where a dangerous "balance" of mutual fear exists—and, to the degree successful, GRIT smooths the path of negotiation.

However, being unconventional in international affairs, the GRIT strategy is open to suspicion abroad and resistance at home. Therefore, it is necessary to spell out the ground rules under which this particular "game" should be played, to demonstrate how national security can be maintained during the process, how the likelihood of reciprocation can be maximized, and how the genuineness of initiations and reciprocations can be evaluated. These "rules" are spelled out in detail in my "basic" pocketbook, *An Alternative to War or Surrender. . . .*[2]

RULES FOR MAINTAINING SECURITY

Rule 1: *Unilateral initiatives must not reduce one's capacity to inflict unacceptable nuclear retaliation should one be attacked at that level.*

Nuclear capacity can serve rational foreign policy (a) if it is viewed not only as a deterrent, but also as a security base from which to take limited risks in the direction of reducing tensions; (b) if the retaliatory, second-strike nature of the capacity is made explicit; and (c) if only the minimum capacity required for effective deterrence is maintained and the arms race damped. Needless to say, none of these conditions have been met to date by the two nuclear superpowers. Not only are nuclear weapons ambiguous as to initiation or retaliation, but both strategic and tactical weapons are redundantly deployed and in oversupply as far as capacity for graded response to aggression is concerned. Therefore, at some stage in the GRIT process, graduated and reciprocated reductions in nuclear weapons, along with the men that are assigned to them, should be initiated.

Rule 2: *Unilateral initiatives must not cripple one's capacity to meet conventional aggression with appropriately graded conventional response.*

Conventional forces are the front line of deterrence, and they must be maintained at rough parity in regions of confrontation. But the absolute level at which the balance is maintained is variable. The general rule would be to initiate unilateral moves in the regions of least tension and gradually extend them to what were originally the most tense regions.

Rule 3: *Unilateral initiatives must be graduated in risk according to the degree of reciprocation obtained from an opponent.*

This is the self-regulating characteristic of GRIT that keeps the process within reasonable limits of security. If bona fide reciprocations of appropriate magnitude are obtained, the magnitude and significance of subsequent steps can be increased; if not, then the process continues with a diversity of steps of about the same magnitude of risk. The relative risk thus remains roughly constant throughout the process.

Rule 4: *Unilateral initiatives should be
diversified in nature, both as to sphere of action
and as to geographical locus of application.*

The reason for diversification is twofold. First, in maintaining security, diversification minimizes weakening one's position in any one sphere (such as in combat troops) or any one geographical locus. Second, in inducing reciprocation, diversification keeps applying the pressure of initiatives having a common tension-reducing intent (and, hopefully, effect), but does not "threaten" the opponent by pushing steadily in the same sphere or locus and thereby limiting his options in reciprocating.

RULES FOR INDUCING RECIPROCATION

Rule 5: *Unilateral initiatives must be designed
and communicated so as to emphasize
a sincere intent to reduce tensions.*

Escalation and de-escalation strategies cannot be "mixed" in the sense that military men talk about the "optimum mix" of weapon systems. The reason is psychological: reactions to threats (aggressive impulses) are incompatible with reactions to promises (conciliatory impulses); each strategy thus destroys the credibility of the other. It is therefore essential that a complete shift in basic policy be clearly signaled at the beginning. The top leadership of the initiating power must establish the right atmosphere by stating the overall nature of the new policy and by emphasizing its tension-reducing intent. Early initiatives must be clearly perceived as tension reducing by the opponents in conflict situations, must be of such significance that they cannot be easily discounted as "propaganda," and they must be readily verifiable. To avoid "self-sabotage," it must be kept in mind that *all* actions of one's government's with respect to another have the function of communicating intent. Control over de-escalation strategies must be just as tight and pervasive as control over war-waging strategies, if actions implying incompatible intents are not to intrude and disrupt the process.

Rule 6: *Unilateral initiatives should be
publicly announced at some reasonable interval
prior to their execution and identified as part
of a deliberate policy of reducing tensions.*

Prior announcements minimize the potentially unstabilizing effect of unilateral acts and their identification with total GRIT strategy helps shape the opponent's interpretation of them. However, the GRIT process cannot *begin* with a large, precipitate, and potentially destabilizing unilateral action. It is this characteristic of Senator Mansfield's proposal in May of 1971 (to cut by about half the United States forces permanently stationed in Europe in one fell swoop) that would have been most likely to destabilize NATO/Warsaw Pact relations, to threaten our allies, and possibly encourage Soviet politico-military probes.

Rule 7: *Unilateral initiatives should include in their announcement an explicit invitation to reciprocation in some form.*

The purpose of this "rule" is to increase pressure on an opponent by making it clear that reciprocation of appropriate form and magnitude is essential to the momentum of GRIT, and to bring to bear pressures of world opinion. However, exactly specifying the form or magnitude of reciprocation has several drawbacks: having the tone of a demand rather than an invitation, it carries an implied threat of retaliation if the demand is not met; furthermore, the specific reciprocation requested may be based on faulty perceptions of the other's situation and this may be the reason for failure to get reciprocation. It is the occurrence of reciprocation in any form, yet having the same tension-reducing intent, that is critical. Again speaking psychologically, the greatest conciliatory impact on an opponent in a conflict situation is produced by his own, voluntary act of reciprocating. Such behavior is incompatible with his Neanderthal beliefs about the unalterable hostility and aggressiveness of the initiators, and once he *has* committed a reciprocating action, all of the cognitive pressure is on modifying these beliefs.

RULES FOR DEMONSTRATING THE GENUINENESS OF INITIATIVES AND RECIPROCATIONS

Rule 8: *Unilateral initiatives that have been announced must be executed on schedule regardless of any prior commitments to reciprocate by the opponent.*

This is the best indication of the firmness and bona fides of one's own intent to reduce tensions. The control over what and how much is committed is the graduated nature of the process; at the point when each initiative is announced, the calculation has been made in terms of prior-reciprocation history that this step can be taken within reasonable limits of security. Failure to execute an announced step, however, would be a clear sign of ambivalence in intent. This is particularly important in the early stages, when announced initiatives are liable to the charge of "propaganda."

Rule 9: *Unilateral initiatives should be continued over a considerable period, regardless of the degree or even absence of reciprocation.*

Like the steady pounding on a nail, pressure toward reciprocating builds up as one announced act follows another announced act of a tension-reducing nature, even though the individual acts may be small in significance. It is this characteristic of GRIT which at once justifies the use of the acronym and which raises the hackles of most military men. But the essence of this strategy is the calculated manipulation of the intent component of the "perceived-threat-equals-capability-times-intent" equation. It is always difficult to read the intentions of an opponent in a conflict situation and they are usually very complex. In such a situation, GRIT can be applied to consistently encourage conciliatory intents and interpretations at the expense of aggressive ones.

Rule 10: *Unilateral initiatives must be*
as unambiguous and as susceptible to
verification as possible.

Although actions do speak louder than words, even overt deeds are liable to misinterpretation. Inviting opponent verification via direct, on-the-spot observation or via indirect media observation (such as televising the act in question), along with requested reciprocation in the verification of his actions, is ideal; what little might be lost in the way of secrecy by both sides might be more than made up in a reduced need for secrecy on both sides. However, both the United States and the USSR have long exhibited intense suspicion of each other and placed a heavy emphasis upon secrecy. This poses serious questions for the criteria for unambiguousness of unilateral initiatives and verifiability of reciprocations. However, the strategy of GRIT can be directly applied to this problem. Particularly in the early stages, when the risk potentials are small, observers could be publicly invited to guarantee the verifiability of doing what was announced, and although entirely *without* explicit insistence on reciprocation by the opponent, the implication would be strong indeed. Initiatives whose validities are apparently very high should be designed (for example, initial pullbacks of forces from border confrontations), and they can operate to gradually reduce suspicion and resistance to verification procedures. This should accelerate as the GRIT process continues.

APPLICATIONS OF GRIT STRATEGY

Over the past fifteen years or so there has been considerable experimentation with the GRIT strategy, but mostly in the laboratory.[3] There have been sporadic GRIT-like moves in the real world; for example, the graduated and reciprocated pullback of American and Soviet tanks that had been lined up practically snout-to-snout at the height of the Berlin Crisis. But for the most part in recent history, these have been one-shot affairs, always tentatively made and never reflecting any genuine change in basic strategy.

The one exception to this dictum was "the Kennedy experiment," as documented in a significant paper by Amitai Etzioni.[4] The real-world test of a strategy of calculated de-escalation was conducted in the period from June [1962] to November of 1963. The first step was President Kennedy's speech at the American University on June 10, in which he outlined what he called "a strategy of peace," praised the Russians for their accomplishments, noted that "our problems are man-made . . . and can be solved by man," and then announced the first unilateral initiative: the United States was stopping all nuclear tests in the atmosphere, and would not resume them unless another country did. Kennedy's speech was published *in full* in both *Izvestia* and *Pravda,* with a combined circulation of 10 million. On June 15 Premier Khrushchev reciprocated with a speech welcoming the U.S. initiative, and he announced that he had ordered the production of strategic bombers to be halted.

The next step was a symbolic reduction in the trade barriers between East and West. On October 9, President Kennedy approved the sale of $250 million worth of wheat to the Soviet Union. Although the United States had proposed a direct America-Russia communication link (the "hot line") in 1962, it was not until June 20, 1963—after the "Kennedy experiment" had begun—that the Soviets agreed to this measure. Conclusion of a test-ban treaty, long stalled, was apparently the main goal of the experiment. Multilateral negotiators began in earnest in July, and on August 5, 1963, the test-ban treaty was signed. The Kennedy experiment slowed down with the deepened involvement in Vietnam, and it came to an abrupt end in Dallas.

Had this real-world experiment in calculated de-escalation been a success? To most of the initiatives taken by either side, the other reciprocated, and the reciprocations were roughly proportional in significance. What about psychological impact? I do not think that anyone who lived through that period will deny that there was a definite warming of American attitudes toward Russians, and the same is reported for Russian attitudes toward Americans. The Russians even coined their own name for the new strategy, "the policy of mutual example."

The novelty of GRIT raises shrieks of incredulity from hawks and clucks of worry even from doves. The question I am most often asked is this: Doesn't any novel approach like this involve too much risk? Anything we do in the nuclear age means taking risks. To escalate conflicts that involve another nuclear power unquestionably carries the greatest risk. Simply doing nothing—remaining frozen in a status quo that is already at much too high a level of force and tension—is certainly not without risk over the long run. GRIT also involves risk. But the risking comes in small packages. Looked at in a broad perspective, the superpower confrontation has many positive elements in it and many motivations on both sides that favor détente. It therefore offers itself as a potential proving ground for a strategy that is novel but yet appropriate to the nuclear age in which we are trying to survive. The assumption behind nuclear deterrence—that we can go spinning forever into eternity, poised for mutual annihilation and kept from it only by fragile bonds of mutual fear—is untenable. The ultimate goal must be to get out from under the nuclear sword of Damocles by eliminating such weapons from the human scene.

NOTES

1. Herman Kahn, *On Escalation: Metaphors and Scenarios* (New York: Praeger, 1965).
2. Charles E. Osgood, *An Alternative to War or Surrender* (Urbana, Illinois: University of Illinois Press, 1962).
3. For an excellent interpretive review of this research in relation to the "rules" of GRIT strategy, see Svenn Lindskold, "Trust Development, the GRIT Proposal, and the Effects of Conciliatory Acts on Conflict and Cooperation," *Psychological Bulletin* 85 (1978):772–793.
4. Amitai Etzioni, "The Kennedy Experiment," *Western Political Quarterly* 20 (1967):361–380.

24. National Security and U.S.-Soviet Relations

Walter C. Clemens, Jr.

INTRODUCTION

The Soviets want much the same things in life that we do. They also have much the same problems, only worse.

Imagine that our two giant neighbors, Mexico and Canada, are both hostile to the United States. Not only are they hostile, but teeming with people, ideas, and inventions hostile to our way of life. Imagine also that their cause is supported by our main adversary in world affairs, the Soviet Union, which has deployed a ring of listening devices, air fields, and other military bases just beyond Mexico and Canada.

This is roughly the kind of challenge which Poland and Afghanistan present to the Soviet Union. But Moscow's troubles extend far beyond these two countries, for the Soviet Union is a country surrounded by hostile neighbors, most of them Communist. The Soviet border with most of these countries is under dispute, openly or covertly, because it resulted from Soviet expansion in World War II. The Kremlin is afraid to give an inch, even to Japan, whose technology Moscow dearly wants, lest the Soviet Union be asked to give thousands of miles to its other neighbors, from China to Czechoslovakia.

The challenge presented by China to the Soviet Union is beyond any comparison with the problems of the United States with its neighbors. To find an analogy we would have to imagine that Canada has the world's largest population, presently confined to a few river beds and barren deserts; is angry about hundreds of years of exploitation by our imperialist policies; is filled with an anti-American ideology and backed by the other superpower which provides it with new technologies that promise over time to make it a modern military power.

The Soviet Union's geographical problems go on and on. Imagine that our navy could pass onto the high seas only by exiting narrow waterways that are closely patrolled, observed, and guarded by our foes (for the Soviet Union this means Turkey, Norway, Japan—all cooperating with the United States), and that many of our ports are ice-bound most of the year.

Imagine also that instead of the world's most dynamic agricultural system we depended for our daily bread upon relatively poor soil, frozen or rain-starved by a hostile continental climate that gets colder as it moves east and drier as it extends south, leaving us with very unfavorable growing conditions two out of every five or six years. To make matters worse we have committed ourselves to expanded meat production and to depending upon grain shipped by our major adversary and its allies.

We have many problems the outer world hears even less about. Our health standards seem to be falling: infant mortality has increased in recent years. Air and water purity standards are more and more difficult to maintain. Birth rates are declining especially among the better-educated, European portions of the population. It will become more and more difficult to maintain our large armed forces unless we cut deeply into the labor force pool. Because of increased tensions with China, Eastern Europe, and our operations in Afghanistan, our need for active armed forces grows all the time, but it is increasingly difficult to sustain existing numbers—especially the highly trained personnel needed to operate modern weapons.

After a few years of quiescence our major adversary and its allies are arming once again. They are not satisfied to have nearly twice the number of strategic nuclear warheads that we do; numbers of men under arms comparable to ours (with fewer foes to deal with); naval forces whose tonnage is twice ours; a monopoly on aircraft carriers; and marines over ten times more numerous than ours. On the soil of our neighbors they will now put large numbers of cruise and modern Pershing missiles capable not only of tactical combat but of striking our cities.

The Soviet Politburo may well reason that experience is on its side. Western governments change every few years, while Brezhnev . . . reigned since 1964, backed by associates whose technical responsibilities extend back for decades. Foreign Minister Gromyko was ambassador to the United States during World War II; Defence Minister Ustinov has been charged with weapons development and production since before World War II. The most senior Soviet leaders are in their seventies and have cause to be worn out, not like President Reagan whose life has been almost carefree by comparison with those of men who had to cope with Stalin, Hitler, Khrushchev, and the vicissitudes of running a very creaking and complex industrial corporation.

SUPERPOWER POLITICS:
NEITHER POKER NOR A GAME OF ANGELS

Neither side can compel the other to alter its system or withdraw from the world arena. Nor can either side hope to destroy the other's retaliatory instruments in a surprise attack. Given the present political and military realities, our only alternative is to work out a *modus vivendi* that limits prospects of a military confrontation and enhances joint interests in survival, economic well-being, environmental protection, and other matters of common concerrn.

Indeed, the security needs of the superpowers in dealing with each other remain, as they have since the mid-1950s, to diminish the chances of war; to curtail the costs of arms competition; and to limit the damage produced in any military confrontation that might occur. Beyond these survival requirements, each may prefer to alter the other's system; but this goal is a will-o'-the-wisp and could jeopardize the *sine qua non* of national survival. Indeed, as Moscow prepares for leadership succession and copes with mounting centrifugal forces in Eastern Europe, Washington should gear its security policies toward accords not threatening to Soviet domestic tranquility. We must be careful not to goad those within the Soviet Union who may want East-West confrontations so as to justify more repression at home and in Eastern Europe.

The superpower engagement is no poker game. It is a variable-sum, not a zero-sum relationship. Soviet suffering is not necessarily a plus for the West. On the other hand, the relationship is not necessarily a positive sum where one's gain is automatically a benefit to the other as well. The relationship is more complex—and frustrating. It remains one in which we have some interests in common and some in conflict. A wise strategy will seek to develop joint interests while controlling or diminishing those in conflict.

*   *   *

FLEXIBILITY AND FIRMNESS

In a variable-sum framework U.S. policy must flow from a judicious mixture of firmness and flexibility, of restraints and incentives. A wise policy must always be on guard lest the adversary exploit a temporary advantage in ways that might do us serious harm. At a minimum we must be sure that we maintain a deterrent sufficient to persuade any rational adversary that attack on the United States or our allies would generate unacceptable damage to the assailant. But we must also have the means to dissuade the Soviets or others from expanding in the Third World or Europe in ways that jeopardize world peace or U.S. interests. These goals probably require that we maintain rough parity with the Soviet Union in strategic and theatre weapons in Europe and that we maintain powerful conventional forces which, in conjunction with our allies, will deter Soviet aggression in Europe or the Third World. This task is not overwhelming or infeasible, for Moscow will be absorbed for some time with digestive problems in Afghanistan and regurgitation problems in Eastern Europe—all of which could reinforce pressures upon the Kremlin to quiet the Soviet Union's western front.

While arms have their role in containment, it is also vital—and perhaps more difficult—to cultivate a sense of solidarity between the United States and our allies and friends along the Soviet periphery. To revitalize our working relationships around the world we must consult, not dictate; show imaginative leadership, not play the blind zig-zagging in the dark; provide optimal levels of military and economic aid; and avoid moral exhortations which prove almost impossible to exact in an imperfect world.

The most powerful inducement to Soviet restraint may be carefully articulated strategy of interdependence. This strategy would make it worth Moscow's while to forgo short-term gains to develop a long-term relationship of mutual advantage with the Western countries and, ideally, a positive role in North-South collaboration as well. This strategy would be rooted in the awareness that the survival of civilization depends upon avoidance of nuclear war by the superpowers and others. It recognizes that all nations have pressing domestic needs which present the most immediate threats to their security. Malnourishment, poor housing, air and water pollution, erosion of top soil, social and racial conflict—these are among the clear and present dangers to the security and well-being of the United States and the Soviet Union. Despite ideological differences and imperial rivalries in such outposts as Somalia and Ethiopia, there are few real conflicts of vital interests between the superpowers. If each kept its troops and KGB/CIA agents at home, both countries could better attend their urgent domestic needs to universal advantage. Even the spectre of a superpower struggle for Middle Eastern oil could be eliminated in a climate of détente and reduced arms spending. In this climate both countries would have more funds and scientific personnel to devote to harnessing fusion, solar, and other power sources. Meanwhile, the Soviet Union could freely purchase U.S. drilling equipment, and U.S. technology could focus on enhanced oil recovery and other technologies to exploit energy resources available within the United States.

REVERSING THE CONFLICT SPIRAL

How then to move again toward improving U.S.-Soviet relations? How do we make the most of our interdependence? The strategy of GRIT (Graduated Reciprocated Initiatives in Tension-reduction) provides key insights about how to move from a conflict spiral to sustained relaxation and improvement of mutual relations.

The approach of GRIT proved useful both in the early 1960s and again in the early 1970s. It could also prove efficacious in the 1980s.

It requires that one side, probably the stronger party (on balance, the United States), announce a long-term plan to improve relations and that it spell out what steps it plans to improve relations with the other side. The first steps can be symbolic initiatives to reduce tensions (e.g., lowering some trade barriers); if these are reciprocated, further reaching steps will be taken. With reciprocity these moves build a momentum which could take us from symbolic to truly significant actions. But time and persistence are demanded. And both sides must be careful not to permit their tension-reducing strategy to be disrupted by hawks at home, in their alliances, or by peripheral troubles in the Third World.

We can only hint at the character of this strategy, but it would entail movement in many arenas of East-West relations. Just as the cold war ranges the globe and involves competition on many fronts, so a pattern of tension-reduction can and must be multidimensional. Indeed, its multidimensionality makes it easier to select moves that sustain momentum and show good faith.

One first step has already been taken, reducing restrictions on Soviet grain purchases in this country. Rather than making such moves as a response to domestic American issues (the farm lobby, campaign promises), it would be wiser to link them to sought-for Soviet policies.

Barriers to scientific and cultural exchange should be dropped, perhaps in tandem with Soviet moves to permit emigration by dissident scientists.

Before even symbolic steps proceed very far, however, ways must be found to reduce the Soviet involvement in Afghanistan. This is the Soviet Union's albatross, as ours was Vietnam. A multilateral pledge of meaningful détente, arms control, and trade could be part of a package to induce Soviet acceptance of a "Finnish" or "Austrian" status for Afghanistan. Though Moscow rejected in July 1981 a European plan for a two-stage conference on Afghanistan, the basis for a multilateral solution may still be found. Just as Dr. Kissinger insisted on Vietnam accords that gave the Saigon regime a chance to survive, so the Soviets will insist on a package with some hope of maintaining their friends in Kabul. But the Kremlin's willingness to accept a face-saving mechanism for Soviet withdrawal will probably be heightened if the Soviet Union is assured of improved trade and credit relations with Western trading partners. Another inducement would be a cutback in the pace of Sino-American military cooperation (which has been spurred in part by the goal of throttling Soviet intervention in Afghanistan).

Obstacles to free trade should be reduced, and the carrots of most-favored-nations treatment and long-term credits be raised as rewards for specified acts such as withdrawal from Afghanistan.

While enhanced trade between the superpowers would not guarantee world peace, normalization in this arena—as in others—would probably help in establishing bases for a less precarious peace. And while we should continue to make known our abhorrence of human rights abuses in the Soviet Union, we should not cut off our nose to spite our face by drastically curtailing cultural and other exchanges. While the human factor cannot be readily measured, its impact can be portentious—whether at summit meetings, in the exchanges of trade or scientific delegations, or in the programs worked out by [private] groups.

The anti-Soviet decibel level of administration language should also be lowered because it offends Moscow gratuitously and grates on our allies. Indeed, public name calling offends many Americans who believe it lowers their own country's dignity. In any event it agitates Kremlin emotions to no useful end. Soviet leaders seem to feel deeply about how outsiders talk about them. Lenin advised Foreign Commissar Chicherin before he departed for the 1922 Genoa Economic Conference: "Avoid biting words." We should do the same, even if Communist propaganda does not immediately reciprocate.

We should avoid fanning unnecessarily the flames of cold war rhetoric. Both Washington and Moscow should refrain from pronouncements implying that they are considering a first strike or that they believe nuclear war could be "winnable." While a few generals and marshals on each side plan how to prevail in a nuclear war, the top political leaders—probably since the mid-1950s—have understood that nuclear war would envelop or destroy all sides. This point should be reiterated, rather than casting doubt on the motives of the top leaders on either side. We should also avoid statements magnifying Soviet military capabilities, if only because this demeans our own assets and influence. Manipulation of Soviet budget data to show that the Kremlin is outspending America in defense is nonscientific and misleading. No matter how much the Kremlin spends, an amount that we do not know and cannot comparatively assess, U.S. defense spending should be based on perceived threat, as rooted in weapons systems, not in fanciful calculations.

LET US NOT FEAR TO NEGOTIATE

The admixture of firmness and flexibility utilized by the Eisenhower and Nixon administrations proved particularly efficacious in dealing with the Soviet Union, but President Kennedy also left us a valuable legacy of foreign policy wisdom, even though he did not live the years needed to implement it. On June 10, 1963, he delivered an address, "Toward a Strategy of Peace," which took note of the Soviet Union's heavy casualties in World War II and the valuable role played by the Soviet Union in defeating our common foe. His were not "biting words" but conciliatory ones recalling years when collaboration prevailed over conflict in U.S.-Soviet relations. They elicited a quick and positive response from Moscow, one that helped set the stage for a successful conclusion of the nuclear test ban negotiations.

The importance of serious dialogue between adversaries is summed up in Kennedy's words: "Let us never negotiate out of fear. But let us never fear to negotiate."

Obvious? Yes, one would think that the wisdom of this epigram is almost self-evident. Yet, the United States and other Western governments have often spurned Soviet proposals to negotiate or work together for common goals.

Most historians concede that the West missed a good bet in not taking up Moscow's call for collective security arrangements against Hitler in the 1930s. Many feel that we should have explored more seriously the Kremlin's proposals in the 1950s to create a unified but nonaligned Germany. By the same token most observers are pleased with the outcome of one set of negotiations where both sides took each other seriously—the European security arrangements of the early and mid-1970s. In that case the West gained much and lost little except the hypothetical option of changing Europe's postwar frontiers by force.

Today the Kremlin reiterates its willingness to negotiate on a host of issues: strategic nuclear arms, theatre weapons, the Persian Gulf, Afghanistan (perhaps in tandem with the Gulf), and other problems. An article by a Soviet writer in *Foreign Affairs* emphasizes that the Soviet Union is "very flexible in its approach to these problems because it really wants to abolish today's conflicts and sources of tension, and to prevent new ones from arising."[1]

What is to be lost if we take the Kremlin at its word and pursue negotiations again on a wide array of common problems? Surely we need not wait until we have somehow ratcheted the balance of power a bit more to our advantage. Indeed, history suggests that negotiations are more feasible from positions of parity than from superiority.

Surely negotiations with the present generation of Soviet leaders are more feasible than they were with Stalin or even with Khrushchev. And it may be vitally important to demonstrate to the next generation of Soviet leaders that the Western governments can be reliable partners in the quest for a more peaceful and prosperous world.

Trofimenko's *Foreign Affairs* article reveals many Soviet sensitivities. [Washington], the author complains:

- Listed the Soviet Union almost last in ranking of U.S. foreign policy priorities.
- Refused to carry on a constructive dialogue except on strategic arms.
- Sought to remove the Soviet Union from negotiations on the peaceful settlement of conflict situations, even in regions lying within the immediate vicinity of its borders (thereby ignoring the commitment made in the Joint Soviet-American Statement on the Middle East of October 2, 1977).
- Dragged on ratification of SALT II while actively modernizing U.S. and NATO arms.
- Tried to use the China card.
- Intensified the buildup of the U.S. naval presence near the Soviet Union's southern borders.

All these factors affected "Soviet assessments of the strategic situation" and the context in which Moscow responded to the request for assistance from the "revolutionary regime" in Afghanistan.[2] Put into plain English, the author seems to say that Washington gave little inducement to Moscow not to intervene in Kabul.

In the 1980s, as in earlier years, Soviet proposals are meant to advance Kremlin objectives. They proceed from an amalgam of both strength and weakness. Now, as in earlier decades, the question is whether there exist bases for agreement that may be advantageous on both sides. Soviet overtures may or may not be made in good faith, but we will never know unless we explore them. If they are hypocritical, this fact will become manifest. If there is room for a compromise accord, we may purchase more opportunities in which to move from cold and hot war toward policies premised on our mutual vulnerability in a world of escalating interdependencies.

THE SUPERPOWERS AND THE THIRD WORLD

Trofimenko, with other Soviet spokesmen, contends that the Soviet Union does not want or need the oil resources of the Persian Gulf; even if it did, the Kremlin knows that this could mean war with the West and would therefore avoid any scheme to cut off oil supplies to the West. Ferment in the Third World is due mainly to the processes of national development and liberation, and not to agitation or support from the Soviet Union. Attempts to stabilize the Third World by injecting a large American military presence will not provide any "final solution" to the problems created by revolutionary movements.[3] This appraisal, I submit, is basically correct.

The root problem is that though both superpowers have recognized many parallel interests in East-West affairs, they have tended to see the Third World as an arena of zero-sum competition. So long as zero-sum expectations prevail, conflicts in the Third World are likely to prevent the normalization of East-West relations. It is therefore vitally important to regulate Soviet-U.S. competition and cultivate areas of complementary interests in the Third World.

Though not immediately apparent, Moscow and the West have many common interests in the Third World. The first is to avoid conflicts that could entangle the superpowers or their allies in confrontations, and escalate into regional or extra-regional warfare. Both superpowers have on occasion attempted to rein in Third World clients whose actions threatened regional and even global peace. Moscow even risked its Egyptian connection by refusing President Sadat certain offensive arms in 1971–1972. Washington has endeavored to stay Israel's penchant for preventive and preemptive blows, albeit with little success in recent years.

Even when one superpower seems to have gained the upper hand with some new regime, the door need not be shut to advantageous forms of East-West cooperation. Thus, although the Soviet Union and Cuba won out over the United States and South Africa in Angola in the 1970s, Gulf Oil has continued operations there—with security provided in part by Cuban troops. Since Third World nations often alter their orientations quickly, it is not unthinkable that today's foe may be tomorrow's associate.

These thoughts lead to a larger thesis: Superpower gains in the Third World have generally been ephemeral, especially when weighed against *costs* and, more importantly, the *risks* of competing for influence there. Both superpowers—not to speak of the Third World nations themselves—would be better off if modes of peaceful cooperation could be worked out to supplant cold world rivalries extended to steaming jungles or barren highlands.

Perhaps some "rules of the game" can still be worked out to regulate competition: agreements not to inject outside military forces where they do not now exist; areas of abstention; limits on arms transfers. But such rules tend to collapse when one side or the other sees a major opportunity and believes the other is not able or willing to thwart a move exploiting the evolving situation.

A more useful approach would be to identify and develop areas of mutually advantageous cooperation between Moscow, the West, and Third World countries. Iran, surprisingly, provided an example of such cooperation under the Shah. Western capital and steel were used to build gas pipelines that took Iranian gas to the Soviet Union and other pipelines that took Soviet gas to Western Europe. This was a complementary relationship in which one side put up capital and steel; one party put up gas and territory; the third party put up technicians, gas, and territory. Were we to look carefully at the globe in non-zero-sum terms, perhaps we could find other arenas in which Western, Communist, and Third World countries might find positive outcomes in multilateral cooperation.

Though the Iranian case has been eclipsed by political turmoil (turmoil disadvantageous and dangerous for the West and for the Soviet Union as well as for most Iranians), it suggests the elements of a major trade-off: peace for energy, energy for peace. The Soviet Union desperately needs Western capital and technology to fulfill the gas and other energy goals of the new Five-Year Plan adopted in 1981. The West is reluctant to make this capital or technology available unless assured that the Soviet Union will not threaten the West or its energy supplies in the Third World. We are all mutually vulnerable: Our problems can best be solved by cooperative behavior.

The United States and Soviet Union have worked along parallel lines for certain mutual interests in the Third World. Since the late 1960s both Moscow and Washington have supported the Nuclear Non-Proliferation Treaty and attempted to make it viable, though with different tactics. The Carter administration leaned toward heavy pressure and open diplomacy to curb potential nuclear military developments in Pakistan, Brazil, South Korea, India, and other countries. Moscow has engaged in more quiet methods, e.g., in pressuring India to accede to safeguards in exchange for heavy water supplies. The Kremlin can point to the example of its regional fuel cycle system for members of the Council for Mutual Economic Assistance with processing facilities located in the Soviet Union.[4] The Kremlin, though less outspoken in its concern about nuclear proliferation, may feel itself even more threatened than the United States, in part because it is geographically closer to the Middle East and the Indian subcontinent. Thus, though U.S. and Soviet methods and perceptions have differed, both superpowers have worked for similar goals.

Both superpowers also worked to help bring about an accord in the Law of the Sea negotiations. Despite the temptation to mobilize Third World nations against each other, Soviet and U.S. representatives cooperated with diplomats representing many large and small states to reach a compromise agreement regulating commercial, navigational, fishing, and security objectives. This agreement should be quickly endorsed by the Reagan administration lest a remarkable achievement be subverted.

We should build upon these examples of positive East-West cooperation and seek to broaden them rather than attempting to exclude the Soviet Union or downgrade the Kremlin as weak merely because it has shown restraint.

The Kremlin operates at a disadvantage in the Third World, a disadvantage that serves both as an obstacle and as an inducement to Soviet participation in programs of "North-South" cooperation and conflict resolution. The Soviet Union's major vehicle for influencing the Third World has been military assistance, a very narrow option by comparison with the wide array of economic, cultural, and other instruments available to the United States and its allies. The Kremlin is therefore uneasy lest its weaknesses be underscored by collaborative actions undertaken with the West. It worries also lest the Soviet Union be tarred with the same image of "imperialism" or "neo-imperialism" with which Soviet propaganda has attacked the West. More fundamentally, the Kremlin is anxious that peaceful resolution of some Third World conflict may leave the Soviet Union with less influence than a festering no war/no peace situation. To make matters worse, Washington has generally practiced what George W. Breslauer aptly terms "exclusionary diplomacy,"[5] attempting to create a U.S. monopoly on peacemaking if not kingmaking in the Middle East and other regions.

Why, the exclusionists ask, should Washington permit the Soviet Union to take part in peace negotiations if it can be excluded? Why should we risk Soviet involvement when the Kremlin may merely torpedo the deliberations? Why give the Soviet Union any more standing and prestige than it has won by its own efforts?

First of all, the long-term reality is that East-West relations can never be put on a stable footing so long as each superpower sees the Third World as an arena for zero-sum competition. American diplomacy has helped foster conditions where the only way the Kremlin can penetrate the Third World is by means inimical to East-West détente. We should encourage the Soviet Union to become a partner in peacemaking, trade, and development in the Third World no less than in East-West affairs. We should help the Kremlin to develop a stake in positive North-South collaboration rather than endless conflict.

A second reality is that we may not be able to resolve regional disputes without Soviet cooperation. If the Kremlin feels excluded, it can easily keep Palestinian or Syrian tempers on edge; what is difficult is to calm emotions and to find compromise solutions that leave each party relatively satisfied.

Third, excluded from peacemaking and legitimate diplomatic activity, the Kremlin will be more prone toward the very military and subversive actions that unsettle East-West as well as regional peace. One of the few prospects we have for curbing Soviet military and KGB expansion is by showing the Politburo that some of its objectives can be enhanced by peaceful cooperation.

If we treat the Kremlin as an international outlaw, we help promote a self-fulfilling prophecy. The Soviets will have little reason not to pursue their aims by the very instruments we would have them eschew.

Fourth, increased Soviet prestige and legitimate diplomatic activity will hardly transfer automatically into a swing by Third World regimes toward Moscow.[6] Most of these ruling elites prefer the higher quality goods and services available in the West. The more peaceful their circumstances, the more they can buy from the West, and the more they can export (oil, coffee, tin, etc.). The more turbulent their region, the more they will consider buying arms and, contrary to their own religious inclinations, permit penetration by representatives of an atheistic regime.

Fifth, the more peaceful Third World regions become, the less need for scenarios in which U.S. expeditionary forces are dispatched to take on the difficult, if not impossible, tasks of guarding pipelines, tanker routes, and fragile regimes from anti-Western forces, whether indigenous or Soviet backed.

Sixth, Soviet participation in peacemaking should facilitate ideas and actions that utilize interdependence to mutual advantage, trading on common needs for energy, development, and peace.

Meanwhile, as superpower competition continues, we should guard against overreacting to Third World developments in which Soviet or Cuban activities are suspected or affirmed. If we believe that a prospective Soviet intervention in the Third World poses a serious threat to Western interests, we should make this clear before the Kremlin goes too far to halt or retreat. Before we charge other governments with meddling, we must also ask whether our accusations are factual; whether the alleged meddling is in areas salient to our interests; whether it has been invited by local governments; and how it compares with U.S. interventions, past or present, in similar situations. Private or low-key communications are in any case more likely to resolve such situations than public chest thumping if we find that Soviet behavior is indeed a breach of what we regard as legitimate conduct.

Finally, we should bear in mind the adage, "An ounce of prevention is worth a pound of cure." Prevention of conflicts, though difficult, is more feasible than therapy after they break out into a small or larger war. And surely preventative diplomacy will be easier with Moscow's cooperation than without it.

Alleviation of the social distress that breeds conflict and war would be the cheapest and most humane approach to the problems of the Third World. Here too we should seek Moscow's participation. With or without Soviet cooperation, however, the task of helping developing nations to help themselves is one that we cannot shirk.[7]

CAPPING THE VOLCANO

Like it or not, linkage exists between superpower activities in the Third World and efforts to cap the volcano of U.S.-Soviet arms competition. In principle this should not be the case. The survival requirements of each country ought to outweigh any displeasure experienced over the actions of its rival in some remote region. But there is also psychological truth in Maxim Litvinov's argument in the 1930s: peace is indivisible. From Washington's standpoint Angola derailed détente and Afghanistan killed SALT II. Americans view Soviet actions in the Third World as a litmus indicator of the extent to which the Kremlin can be trusted in arms control.

Americans, unfortunately, tend to be self-righteous and employ a double standard in judging their behavior and that of their rivals. We may seek to exclude the Soviet Union from Middle East negotiations but fret if Moscow gains the upper hand in Ethiopia. We can expand the numbers and improve accuracies of our warheads but denounce the Soviets for seeking superiority if they move in the same direction.

We have created many of our supposed strategic problems by our deeds, our omissions, our words, and our interpretation of the world about us. Why is there no SALT II treaty in place? Because the Carter team jettisoned for a time the understandings already reached between the Ford administration and Brezhnev and pursued "deep cuts" instead. Because later, when SALT II was finally signed in 1979, congressional critics seized on every possible loophole to attack a balanced compromise agreement. Afghanistan served them well as a pretext for a *coup de grâce.*

Why are Minutemen missles said to be vulnerable to a Soviet preemptive strike in the mid-1980s? Their theoretical vulnerability stems from the fact that we developed a hydra-headed monster, multiple warheads, in the 1960s and deployed them beginning in 1970, without waiting to see whether they might be banned altogether in SALT I. After all, we had a substantial headstart in this domain. Within a few years, however, the Soviets started MIRVing their large missles. With ten warheads spitting from its nose cone, each attacking missile might knock out several retaliatory missiles. This situation now drives us to look for ways to eschew the dangers our own technological genius has spawned.

Still, the capacity of Soviet MIRVs (multiple independently targetable reentry vehicles) to destroy most of the Minutemen force in a first strike is more a matter of pencil and paper calculations than material or psychological reality.[8] Neither Soviet nor U.S. missiles have been test fired in a North-South axis. Their accuracies and general reliability in wartime conditions are likely to be far inferior to those generated in idyllic peacetime tests. Neither Soviet nor U.S. leaders are inclined to risk their country's safety on such slender reeds as a theoretical potential for a knockout blow. Moscow has attacked weak neighbors—usually to reimpose friendly regimes—but never a major power, unless one includes tottering Japan in 1945. Each alternative proposal to deal with the supposed window of Minuteman vulnerability in the 1980s has serious drawbacks.[9] None eliminates the *theoretical* possibility that Moscow could destroy a large part of America's land-based missile forces. Each proposed solution is horrendously expensive. And most of the proposals call for weapons systems which Moscow must perceive as enhancing America's capacity for a preemptive strike against Soviet missiles— even more concentrated on land than the U.S. triad. Last, but not least, each alternative would make it more difficult to maintain the force ceilings and ABM limits already agreed to in SALT I and II. Many of the proposals call for land-mobile systems raising major problems of verification. Were the Soviets to emulate the American plans for mobility and deception, our national means of verification would be hard pressed to ensure that the Kremlin was not deploying more missiles than present or future treaties may permit.

The MX and most of the alternative plans make our problems worse rather than better. Not only are these plans expensive and likely to generate unpleasant countermoves from Moscow, but they are not needed. In short, they are neither sufficient nor necessary. Assuming that the Soviet Union needs to be deterred from attacking the United States, the Minutemen, bombers, and submarine-based missiles that would survive even a Soviet first strike are more than enough to stay any rational foe. If the Soviet leaders are madmen, they will hardly be more deterred by MX or its variants than by the existing American triad. Indeed, if the Soviets are paranoid, the defense schemes emanating from

Washington in recent years might lead them to strike sooner rather than wait until the United States' latest missile plans are implemented.

Why not recognize these facts and return once more to serious arms limitation talks? The reality is that both superpowers are hostage to one another and there is little either can do to alter the situation. The danger is not so much that a rational Soviet government will scheme to strike first; the greater danger is that both superpowers will become engaged in such a tense, conflictual relationship that confrontations may escalate. What we need is not more arms and tension, but arms control and détente—the easing of tension.

Though the United States has invented much of the present arms dilemma, including nonratification of SALT II, the Kremlin also bears a heavy share of the responsibility. While the Kremlin says it has merely been catching up with the West, the rate of Soviet weapons production and deployment has raised the possibility that Moscow seeks not just parity but a war-winning capacity. Both sides have been shortsighted in failing to contemplate the impact that their words and deeds have on the rival.

Still, history books do not credit statesmen who merely cried out, "Don't blame us; it's not our fault." They value leaders who rose above circumstances, adopted a long view, assayed goals others said were impossible, and achieved them—at least partially. Skeptics could, and did, easily contend that the Marshall Plan for European Recovery and the Fulbright-Hays exchange programs would never be passed by a penurious Congress or accepted by suspicious foreign governments. By dint of statesmanship—abroad and on Capitol Hill—both programs got under way, producing what may have been America's greatest peacetime achievements in foreign policy. As a result, George Marshall will probably be remembered more as secretary of state than for his roles as a five-star general or secretary of defense.

Power connotes responsibility. Leaders of the most powerful nation on earth have a profound responsibility to exert the kinds of statesmanship that will lead us from the dead-end prospects of a perpetual arms race. While Americans rightly worry about gains in Soviet military capability, the fact remains that we possess the margins of power and the climate of free thought that make creative initiatives much more feasible for us than for the Soviet leadership.

President Nixon's opening to China and his participation in the 1972–1974 summits with General Secretary Brezhnev demonstrated that staunch anti-Communist credentials need not preclude significant diplomatic relations with Communist powers. Though President Reagan has been quite outspoken in denouncing Soviet theory and practice, his actions have not been so provocative as Nixon's bombing of Hanoi and Haiphong on the eve of his Moscow visit. Though the Kremlin has parried Reagan's verbal assaults, there is little doubt that the Brezhnev Politburo would welcome serious efforts to cap the arms volcano by negotiation.

NOTES

1. Henry Trofimenko, "America, Russia, and the Third World," *Foreign Affairs*, 59, 5 (Summer 1981):1040.
2. Ibid., pp. 1031–1032.
3. Ibid., pp. 1035–1039.
4. See Gloria Duffy, "The Soviet Union and Nuclear Drift," in W. Raymond Duncan, ed., *Soviet Policy in the Third World* (New York: Pergamon Press, 1980), pp. 35–37.
5. George W. Breslauer, "Why Detente Failed," Berkeley, California, manuscript, May 1981.
6. See also Walter C. Clemens Jr., "Independence and/or Security: Dilemmas for the Kremlin, the White House and Whitehall," in *1977: The Caribbean Yearbook of International Relations* (Alphen aan den Rijn: Sithoff & Noordhoff, 1980), pp. 27–58.
7. For elaboration, see Walter C. Clemens Jr., *The USSR and Global Interdependence* (Washington, DC: American Enterprise Institute, 1978).
8. See, e.g., William H. Kincade, "Missile Vulnerability Reconsidered," and Kosta Tsipis, "Precision and Accuracy," in *Arms Control Today* (Washington, DC) 11, 5 (May 1981); also Council on Economic Priorities, "Misguided Expenditure: An Analysis of the Proposed MX Missile System," New York, mimeo., July 6, 1981.
9. See the conflicting views of the Charles H. Townes Committee established by the Pentagon to review the problem, reported, e.g., in the *Los Angeles Times*, July 6, 1981, pp. 1, 6.

25. Getting to "Yes" in the Nuclear Age

Roger Fisher

The political and military intentions of the Soviet Union are of utmost concern to American officials. Since World War II, a central task of United States foreign policy has been to influence Soviet decisionmaking. To this end the United States has employed a variety of approaches, ranging from arms limitation agreements and the expansion of East-West trade, to economic sanctions, geopolitical confrontations, and the pursuit of nuclear superiority.

Recently, the United States has been looking especially hard to do something. Faced with a continuous Soviet arms buildup, the military domination of Afghanistan, the presence of Cuban and East German forces in Africa, the potential invasion of Poland, and Soviet failures to comply with the human rights provisions of the Helsinki Accords, Washington has taken a decidedly military approach toward influencing the Soviet Union. Strategic and theatre-level nuclear forces have been upgraded toward a first-strike capability; "rapid deployment" forces have been expanded; overall military spending has been vastly increased. There also has been tough talk about American resolve and willingness to fight a nuclear war, variously accompanied by public denunciations, a boycott of the Olympics, and on-again/off-again grain embargoes. And all too often, Washington has placed tight restrictions on communication. We have tended not only to hang up the phone, but to cut the line. For nine months the United States had no ambassador in Moscow. At every level, contacts with Soviet officials have tended to be stiff, peremptory, and minimal.

The underlying assumption is clear enough: the way to make the Soviets more peaceful is for the United States to behave more belligerently. The idea is that by engaging in a massive military buildup, and threatening to use it, we will scare the Soviet Union into being more peaceful.

But let us stop and think. How do we react when the Soviets build more weapons and threaten us? Do we ask ourselves whether U.S. policies have looked unduly aggressive? Do officials suggest that we show restraint by slowing down our military spending and behaving in more peaceful ways? No. When the Soviets build SS-20 missiles by the score, we become more bellicose. And we step up our military spending.

Knowing how we react, common sense tells us how the Soviet Union will react to our bellicosity. We react belligerently to the fact that the Soviets outspent the United States during the past decade by some $300 billion for military purposes. We should well understand why the Soviet Union reacts similarly to the fact (equally true) that during that same decade we *and* our NATO allies outspent the Soviets and their allies by some $280 billion for military purposes.

Of course, throwing our arms away cannot be expected to cause the Soviets to lie down like lambs, no more than the United States would do so were the Soviet Union to pursue the same course. But now that each of us has more than enough military hardware to serve as a deterrent, now that both sides have roughly comparable military forces (all the talk about a "missile gap" or a "window of vulnerability" to the contrary notwithstanding), more U.S. weapons will hardly cause the Soviets to produce less.

In sum, the suggestion that being more belligerent will cause the Soviets to behave less belligerently is contrary to both experience and common sense. And the companion notion that we make the world safer for the United States by acquiring weapons that make it more dangerous for the Soviet Union is far worse. So far as nuclear war is concerned, we are in the same boat. We cannot make our end of the boat safer by making the Soviet end more likely to tip over. And to diminish Soviet confidence in the physical security of their nuclear forces only increases the pressure to use them.

Thus, while the original international problem for which we got our nuclear weapons was fear of aggression by another Hitler, the cure has now become more dangerous than the disease. Like drugs to which we have become addicted, our nuclear weapons have become habit-forming and dangerous. Designed to protect us from other countries that legitimately give us cause for concern, they themselves have become a threat to national survival; and a failure to appreciate this blunt fact indicates a failure to comprehend the radical change from the days when there were only conventional weapons available. We can boldly say: "Better dead than Red." But, honestly, each of us would prefer to have our children in Havana, Belgrade, Beijing, Warsaw, or Leningrad today than in Hiroshima or Nagasaki when the nuclear bombs went off. A general nuclear war would be far more damaging to our national interest than even the most outrageous political domination.

I

Before World War II, superior military force was persuasive indeed. Defensively, if a country had the clear physical ability to protect itself, then others could be persuaded not to attack: since an attack would fail, why try? Offensively too, if a country had the clear ability physically to impose its will and to produce the result it desired, then why resist? In an era which considered both colonialism and war legitimate, the political cost of imposing a desired result was likely to be modest. The power to bring about a result by self-help if negotiations should fail made it far more likely that a weaker country would agree to the result requested by a stronger country. A country that could not prevent a given result by fighting might just as well agree without a fight. Political power was directly related to military power.

Despite our nuclear age, some military weapons still do enhance the power to persuade. Having enough "smart" anti-tank weapons helps persuade an adversary not to launch a tank attack. A strong physical barrier, a mine field, an anti-submarine net, or anti-aircraft batteries may effectively persuade an opposing country not to attempt a particular military action. Such weapons deter action because they have the power to prevent it. Offensively, too, where the desired result is to occupy and maintain control over nearby territory, the physical power to do so greatly enhances a State's negotiating power. The situation of Israel and the Golan Heights is a case in point.

But in the world today, most foreign policy objectives—particularly those of the United States and the Soviet Union toward one another— cannot be accomplished by military means. There is no way we can physically impose freedom upon the Soviet Union, and no way they can physically impose their values upon us. We cannot physically impose self-government on some country that does not have it. The United States has found that its possession of vast military forces has not given it the power to persuade Vietnam, Libya, South Africa, Syria, or Iran to make the decisions we want them to make. And the Soviet Union has discovered that the billions of rubles it has spent on arms have not

TABLE 1.
Today's Context: Where Military Power Is Not the Power to Persuade

---

QUESTION: SHALL WE, THE SOVIET UNION, PRESS FOR THE END OF MARTIAL LAW IN POLAND?

If "Yes"	If "No"
− We accept full responsibility for the mess in Poland	+ We limit our responsibility for Poland
− We risk instability in Eastern Europe	+ Eastern Europe is likely to remain stable
− We antagonize Poland nationalists of all kinds in the military, in Solidarity, in the Church, and in the Party	+ We buy time + We stand up to the United States
− Both the economy and the political situation are likely to become worse	+ The Polish Army may bring the situation under control
− We look weak in backing down to a US demand	+ We limit our confrontation with the Poles
	+ We keep our options open (we can always do something later if it appears desirable)

---

given it the power to influence others either. Ten years ago, Egypt had 17,000 Soviet troops. Today those troops have been expelled and American and Egyptian troops conduct joint maneuvers.

This point—that the power to persuade and military power are no longer necessarily synonymous or coextensive—is especially important in the context of nuclear confrontation. The consequences of a nuclear war would be catastrophic. And they would be worse for some countries than for others. But unless a real prospect of nuclear war appears on one side of the choice a country faces, the consequences of a nuclear war are irrelevant to that choice. For example, as we press the Soviet Union to bring about an end to martial law in Poland, the Soviet Union might see their choice as depicted in Table 1. If this is the way the Soviet Union sees its choice, our military weapons, including our nuclear weapons, are irrelevant to their decision. Equally so our nuclear superiority has been irrelevant to our negotiations with Iran over the hostages, to our efforts to persuade Israel to stop building settlements in the West Bank, to our efforts to moderate Libya's behavior, or to persuade our European allies to support sanctions against the Soviet Union.

True, our nuclear weapons do serve one important function. They make it extremely dangerous for the Soviet Union to do outrageous things such as bomb Pearl Harbor or New York, or land forces in Florida or Britain, or try a blitzkrieg attack across Western Europe. But once we have enough strategic forces to make any such action extremely risky, additional nuclear forces do not improve our negotiating position on the daily problems we have with the Soviet Union and with other governments of the world. If having a superior power to destroy gave one the power to persuade, then the Soviet Union—and the rest of the world, for that matter—would have been dancing to our tune for the last 30 years.

In sum, diplomatic success today depends less upon what can be produced by physical means than upon what takes place in somebody else's head; "our" success depends upon "their" decision. An in all such cases the critical balance is not the balance of destructive power, but, rather, the balance sheet of the presently perceived choice: how do the consequences of "their" deciding as "we" wish compare in their minds with the consequences of not doing so? The critical balance, in other words, is not that between our military force and the force on the other side, but the balance between the consequences they see of saying "yes" and the consequences they see of saying "no."

Of course, beyond an analysis of Soviet decisionmaking, we can see that *our* choice also is subject to influence. Indeed, the major case for an enormous strategic weapons buildup rests on the premise that those weapons will protect us against a Soviet demand that is backed up with a nuclear threat. But just as a large number of nuclear weapons provide no protection against attempted extortion by a lone terrorist, they cannot protect us from attempted extortion by a Soviet leader who might be equally indifferent to the fate of others. The outcome of such attempted blackmail is not determined by counting potential casualties; the numbers are all but irrelevant. In such an exchange of unprincipled threats, the advantage goes to the leader who is least concerned with human life, is more ruthless, is more willing to gamble for high stakes, is less vulnerable to criticism by a free press, and has fewer constituents to whom he must later answer. But there is no way in which our acquiring additional nuclear warheads will make it wise policy for an American President to compete in ruthlessness with a leader of the Soviet Union.

Our ability to influence the Soviet Union depends, then, upon our ability to affect the way they see a future choice, independent of the nuclear threat; and this is as true in the realm of arms control and disarmament as it is in any other. To persuade the Soviet Union to agree to meaningful arms limitation and reduction proposals, we need to formulate and present a series of choices where each time the consequences of deciding as we would like are more attractive to them as well as to us than their proceeding down the road toward a deteriorating relationship.

II

Of the many variables that enhance such negotiating power, one of the most important is *effective two-way communication.* If we are to change Soviet minds, we need to know what is on those minds; we need to listen. Whatever Soviet officials may try to conceal, the more extensive our discussions, the more we can listen "between the lines," the better will be the intelligence we can glean.

There are those who favor breaking or reducing diplomatic relations as a response to outrageous conduct. They suggest that talking under such circumstances looks "soft," that it implies approval, and that actions speak louder than words. Actions do speak loudly. But our purpose is not simply to express ourselves. It is to affect Soviet behavior, and to this end communication is more powerful if it is two-way, precise, and continuous. To close down the Soviet purchasing office, to suspend talks on wheat sales and merchant marine matters, or to reduce scientific exchange, tends to *decrease* our ability to influence the Soviet Union, not increase it. Such actions suggest that we are enemies no matter what the other side does, thus eliminating any incentive for change. With continuous talks, however, we learn more and there is more time for good ideas to prevail. We also avoid the unfortunate result that if stopping talks is used to signal disapproval, then resuming talks—as we did over wheat sales—implies approval, it implies for instance, that Soviet conduct, even in Afghanistan, is not so bad after all.

The model for good communication is not a "high-noon" confrontation between gunslingers, but the kind of intensive talks that produced the treaty banning atmospheric nuclear tests. We exert influence most effectively when the other side knows exactly what is expected, why it is legitimate, and what we will do next. These are conditions that are hard to meet without talking extensively and in detail. We can be just as firm in a meeting as elsewhere—and a great deal clearer. Our negotiating power is enhanced by maintaining the maximum amount of two-way communication at all levels. Without effective two-way communication there is no successful negotiation.

III

Another key variable to successful negotiation is *how we negotiate.* Our purpose is to work out with the Soviet Union a way to live together on this precarious globe. We want to clarify existing restraints and develop additional ones because it is in our mutual interest to do so. But to increase the chance of our devising wise restraints in time to avoid disaster, we should stop bargaining over positions as though haggling over the price of a rug; we should use a method more likely to serve our shared interests. The process of negotiation itself is critical.

The traditional mode of conducting a two-party international conference is well illustrated by the SALT—now START—process, and has three key features:

Decide first, talk later. Each side unilaterally develops and decides upon its proposed solution before talking with the other side.

Argue about positions. Most of the discussion among negotiators is devoted to explaining and defending one's own one-sided position and attacking that of the other side.

Make concessions slowly. As time goes by, one side or the other reluctantly makes a small concession to keep the talks from breaking down.

This is a poor method of negotiating.

First, this approach is unlikely to produce optimal results: with it more time is spent arguing over extreme positions than in trying to develop creative solutions. When negotiators bargain over positions, they tend to lock themselves into those positions. The more often they restate a position and defend it against attack, the more committed they become to it. The more they try to convince the other side of the impossibility of changing their opening position, the more difficult it becomes to do so. Egos become identified with positions. There develops a new interest in "saving face"—in reconciling future action with past positions. This process makes it less and less likely that any agreement will wisely reconcile the parties' original concerns.

The danger that positional bargaining will impede a negotiation was well illustrated by the breakdown of talks under President Kennedy for a comprehensive ban on nuclear testing. A critical question arose: how many on-site inspections per year should the Soviet Union and the United States be permitted to make within the other's territory to investigate suspicious seismic events? The Soviet Union finally agreed to three inspections. The United States insisted on no less than ten. And there the talks broke down—over positions—despite the fact that no one understood whether an "inspection" would involve one person looking around for one day, or a hundred people prying indiscriminately for a month. The parties had made little attempt to design an inspection procedure that would reconcile the United States's interest in verification with the desire of both countries for minimal intrusion.

As more attention is paid to positions, less attention is devoted to meeting the underlying concerns of the parties. Agreement becomes less likely. Any agreement reached may reflect a mechanical splitting of the difference between stated positions rather than a solution carefully crafted to meet the legitimate interests of the parties. The result is frequently an agreement less than satisfactory to each side than it could have been.

Second, this "bazaar" or "haggling" approach to negotiation tends to be extremely inefficient; it takes a lot of time. The United States devoted a full year to producing preliminary agreement among Army, Navy, Air Force, State Department, Arms Control Agency, and White House officials, as well as our NATO allies, merely on an opening SALT/START position—which everyone knew had no chance of being accepted by the Soviet Union. Now, over the months and years ahead, we will have to get similar agreement on each of many concessions arising from this maximum position.

Bargaining over positions creates incentives that stall settlement. In positional bargaining we try to improve the chance that any settlement reached be favorable to us by starting with an extreme position, by stubbornly holding to it, by deceiving the other party as to our true views, and by making small concessions only as necessary to keep the negotiation going. The same is true for the other side. Each of those factors tends to interfere with reaching a settlement promptly. The more extreme the opening positions and the smaller the concessions, the more time and effort it will take to discover whether or not agreement is possible.

The standard minuet also requires a large number of individual decisions as each negotiator decides what to offer, what to reject, and how much of a concession to make. Decisionmaking in this fashion is difficult and time-consuming at best. Where each decision not only involves yielding to the other side but the possibility of having to yield further, a negotiator has little incentive to move quickly. Dragging one's feet, threatening to walk out, stonewalling, and other such tactics become commonplace. They all increase the time and costs of reaching agreement as well as the risk that no agreement will be reached at all.

Finally, in addition to producing unwise agreements and to being time-consuming, positional bargaining is politically costly, endangering ongoing relationships. During the entire process there is an incentive for everyone to be stubborn, hoping that someone else will yield first. In the East-West context, the contest of will that this process involves can be expected to exacerbate relations not only with the Soviet Union but among our allies as well.

Each negotiator asserts what he will and won't do. The task of jointly devising an acceptable solution becomes a battle. Each side tries through sheer will power to force the other to change its position. "We're not going to give in. If you want to limit or reduce arms, it's our way or nothing." Anger and resentment often result as one side sees itself bending to the rigid will of the other while its own legitimate concerns go unaddressed.

Positional bargaining thus strains and sometimes shatters the relationship between the parties. This has happened between the United States and the Soviet Union on numerous occasions, and the world is not a safer place for it.

TABLE 2.

PROBLEM

Positional Bargaining: Which Game Should You Play?

SOFT	HARD
Participants are friends.	Participants are adversaries.
The goal is agreement.	The goal is victory.
Make concessions to cultivate the relationship.	Demand concessions as a condition of the relationship.
Be soft on the people and the problem.	Be hard on the problem and the people.
Trust others.	Distrust others.
Change your position easily.	Dig in to your position.
Make offers.	Make threats.
Disclose your bottom line.	Mislead as to your bottom line.
Accept one-sided losses to reach agreement.	Demand one-sided gains as the price of agreement.
Search for the single answer: the one *they* will accept.	Search for the single answer: the one *you* will accept.
Insist on agreement.	Insist on your position.
Try to avoid a contest of will.	Try to win a contest of will.
Yield to pressure.	Apply pressure.

On the other hand, being "nice" is no answer either. Many people recognize the high costs of hard positional bargaining, particularly on the parties and their relationship. They hope to avoid them by following a more gentle style of negotiation. Instead of seeing the other side as adversaries, they prefer to see them as friends. Rather than emphasizing a goal of victory, they emphasize the necessity of reaching agreement. In a soft negotiating game the standard moves are to make offers and concessions, to trust the other side, to be friendly, and to yield as necessary to avoid confrontation.

Table 2 illustrates two styles of positional bargaining: soft and hard. Most people see their choice of negotiating strategies as between these two styles. Looking at the table as presenting a choice, should the United States or the Soviet Union be a soft or a hard positional bargainer?

The soft negotiating game emphasizes the importance of building and maintaining a relationship. Within families and among friends much negotiation takes place in this way. The process tends to be efficient, at least to the extent of producing results quickly. As each party competes with the other in being more generous and more forthcoming, an agreement becomes highly likely. But the agreement may not be wise. Any negotiation primarily concerned with the relationship runs the risk of producing a sloppy agreement.

Further, pursuing a soft form of positional bargaining makes us vulnerable to someone who plays a hard game of positional bargaining. In positional bargaining, a hard game dominates a soft one. If the hard bargainer insists on his position while the soft bargainer insists on agreement, the negotiating game is biased in favor of the hard player. Any agreement reached will be more favorable to the hard positional bargainer than to the soft one.

IV

Fortunately, the "bazaar" approach to negotiation is not the only way to seek agreement. If we do not like the choice between hard and soft positional bargaining, we can change the game.

A more efficient and effective approach to negotiation, a method explicitly designed to produce wise outcomes efficiently and amicably, is called *principled negotiation* or *negotiation on the merits*. Based on the principle of talking first and deciding later, it can be boiled down to four basic points.

These four points define a straightforward method of negotiation that can be used under almost any circumstance. Each point deals with a basic element of negotiation, and suggests what you should do about it.

People: Separate the people from the problem.
Interests: Focus on interests, not positions.
Options: Generate a variety of possibilities before deciding what to do.
Criteria: Insist that the result be based on some objective standard.

The first point responds to the fact that human beings, including representatives of national governments, are not computers. We are creatures of strong emotions who often have radically different perceptions and have difficulty communicating clearly. Emotions typically become entangled with the objective merits of the problem. Taking positions just makes this worse because people's egos become identified with their positions. Hence, before working on the substantive problem, the "people problem" should be disentangled from it and dealt with separately. Figuratively if not literally, the participants should come to see themselves as working side by side attacking the problem, not each other. Hence the first proposition: *Separate the people from the problem.*

The second point is designed to overcome the drawback of focusing on stated positions when the object of a negotiation is to satisfy underlying interests. Since any norm we might later agree upon must be in the interests of the Soviet Union and the United States, we should learn as much as possible about Soviet needs and wants, and we should make sure that Moscow is equally clear about ours. We should ignore any declared position except as evidence of some underlying interest. Compromising between positions is unlikely to produce an agreement which will effectively take care of the human needs that lead people to adopt those positions. The second basic element of the method thus is: *Focus on interests, not positions.*

The third point responds to the difficulty of designing optimal solutions while under pressure. Trying to decide in the presence of an adversary narrows one's vision. Having a lot at stake inhibits creativity. So does searching for the one right solution. A major aim, therefore, is to invent, without commitment, different ways of possibly reconciling conflicting interests. We can offset the constraints of pressured circumstance by setting aside designated occasions within which to think up a wide range of possible solutions that advance shared interests and creatively reconcile differing interests. During the SALT I talks, two members of each delegation (called "the wizards" by the Russians) used to meet for the purpose of creative brainstorming, understood to be without commitment on behalf of either government. Some such process is extremely valuable, permitting the Soviet Union and the United States to devise norms of behavior, both for weapons and for military-political activity, that are in the interest of each country to respect so long as the other is demonstrably doing so. Hence the third basic point: Before trying to reach agreement, *invent options for mutual gain.*

Some negotiators obtain a favorable result simply by being stubborn. To allow that to happen rewards intransigence and produces arbitrary results. It is possible to counter such a negotiator by insisting that his single say-so is not enough and that any agreement must reflect some fair standard independent of the naked will of either side. This does not mean insisting that the terms be based on the standard we select, but only that some fair standard determine the outcome. In negotiating arms limitations, there are many possible objective standards to assure fairness or rough equivalence in arms reductions, in force levels, or in military vulnerability. By discussing such criteria rather than what the parties are willing or unwilling to do, neither party need give in to the other; both can defer to a fair solution. Hence the fourth basic point: *Insist on using objective criteria.*

The method of principled negotiation is contrasted with hard and soft positional bargaining in Table 3, which shows the four basic points of the method in boldface type. With a good understanding of each other's interests, with multiple options that have been designed to meet them, and with the principle of reciprocity as a guide, there is an optimal chance that negotiators can produce recommendations for official decision.

It is important to note also that the four basic propositions of principled negotiation are relevant from the time one begins to think

TABLE 3.

PROBLEM		SOLUTION
Positional Bargaining: Which Game Should You Play?		Change the Game — Negotiate on the Merits
SOFT	**HARD**	**PRINCIPLED**
Participants are friends.	Participants are adversaries.	Participants are problem-solvers.
The goal is agreement.	The goal is victory.	The goal is a wise outcome reached efficiently and amicably.
Make concessions to cultivate the relationship.	Demand concessions as a condition of the relationship.	**Separate the people from the problem.**
Be soft on the people and the problem.	Be hard on the problem and the people.	Be soft on the people, hard on the problem.
Trust others.	Distrust others.	Proceed independent of trust.
Change your position easily.	Dig in to your position.	**Focus on interests, not positions.**
Make offers.	Make threats.	Explore interests.
Disclose your bottom line.	Mislead as to your bottom line.	Avoid having a bottom line.
Accept one-sided losses to reach agreement.	Demand one-sided gains as the price of agreement.	**Invent options for mutual gain.**
Search for the single answer: the one *they* will accept.	Search for the single answer: the one *you* will accept.	Develop multiple options to choose from; decide later.
Insist on agreement.	Insist on your position.	**Insist on objective criteria.**
Try to avoid a contest of will.	Try to win a contest of will.	Try to reach a result based on standards independent of will.
Yield to pressure.	Apply pressure.	Reason and be open to reasons; yield to principle, not pressure.

about negotiating until the time either an agreement is reached or a decision is made to break off the effort. That period can be divided into three stages: analysis, planning, and discussion.

During the *analysis* stage one is simply trying to diagnose the situation—to gather information, organize it, and think about it. Negotiators will want to consider the people problems of partisan perceptions, hostile emotions, and unclear communication, as well as to identify their interests and those of the other side. They will want to note options already on the table and identify any criteria already suggested as a basis for agreement.

During the *planning* stage negotiators deal with the same four elements a second time, both generating ideas and deciding what to do. How do they propose to handle the people problems? Of their interests, which are most important? And what are some realistic objectives? They will want to generate additional options and additional criteria for deciding among them.

Again during the *discussion* stage, when the parties communicate back and forth, looking toward agreement, the same four elements are the best subjects to discuss. Differences in perception, feelings of frustration and anger, and difficulties in communication can be acknowledged and addressed. Each side should come to understand the interests of the other. Both can then jointly generate options that are mutually advantageous and seek agreement on objective standards for resolving opposed interests.

To sum up, in contrast to positional bargaining, the principled negotiation method of focusing on basic interests, mutually satisfying options, and fair standards typically results in a *wise* agreement. The method permits reaching a gradual consensus on a joint decision *efficiently* without all the transactional costs of digging in to positions only to have to dig out of them. And separating the people from the problem allows dealing directly and empathetically with the other negotiator as a human being, thus making possible an *amicable* agreement. If all this is possible, an actual commitment becomes less important. The provisions of SALT I have expired and those of SALT II never have come in to effect. Yet, except for the dismantling provisions, both the Soviet Union and the United States are respecting those terms. Even nonbinding norms can establish a modus vivendi. As with an unmarried couple sharing an apartment, it may be easier for both countries to live together than to enter into major commitments.

*   *   *

We and the Soviet Union have good reason to be skeptical about each other's intentions. Yet however high our level of mutual distrust, we share an enormous interest in avoiding a calamitous collision. On the high seas the danger of ships colliding is reduced through international agreement on a system of signals and evasive turns. What matters is not that the signals are legally binding but that they have been worked out in advance and have become well understood.

The danger of a military collision between the Soviet Union and the United States is both far more dangerous and far more difficult to avoid. The fact that we distrust each other makes joint planning for crisis management both more important and more urgent. As disastrous as any nuclear war would be, it would be tragic indeed to have a nuclear war which both sides wanted at the last minute to avoid, but didn't know how. Maintaining effective two-way communication and adopting techniques of principled negotiation in the pursuit of common interests are among the first prerequisites for overcoming mutual distrust and avoiding such a calamity.

——— Questions for Reflection and Discussion ———

1. What are the material and psychological barriers to a de-escalation of superpower confrontation? To arms control and disarmament? What incentives do the two governments share to overcome their mutual distrust and competition? What disincentives?

2. Does GRIT represent a viable approach to arms control and disarmament? Upon what assumptions concerning the political utility of military—especially nuclear—power is GRIT premised? What methods are available to assure compliance with GRIT reductions? Why hasn't GRIT been utilized to overcome Soviet-U.S. arms competition?

3. What are the opportunities for Soviet-U.S. cooperation in the realm of military affairs? What are confidence-building measures (CBMs) and how might they be used to reduce superpower tensions at points of direct military confrontation? What types of CBMs are already being implemented? What other types might be used to reduce the possibility of strategic surprise, conventional or nuclear?

4. What long-term strategy might the superpowers implement in relation to one another to overcome the mutual threat of war? What immediate steps would you take to reduce Soviet-U.S. competition? What unilateral steps would you take? When would you demand reciprocity?

5. Should arms control and disarmament efforts between the Soviet Union and the United States be made to depend on the international conduct of the other or should such linkage be eschewed? What should be the scope of Soviet-U.S. political and economic contacts? How might trade expansion be utilized to create a greater set of common interests? Can expanded economic ties be exploited to reduce military tensions?

6. Why has "bargaining-chip" diplomacy been the prevalent approach in U.S.-USSR negotiations? In what ways has this approach impeded progress toward arms control and disarmament? What other negotiating styles are available? Would you advise your government to test Fisher's theories on negotiation in the context of nuclear weapons reductions?

Selected Bibliography

Alford, Jonathan. *The Future of Arms Control: Confidence-Building Measures.* Adelphi Paper No. 149. London: International Institute for Strategic Studies, 1979.

Barnet, Richard J., and Richard A. Falk, eds. *Security in Disarmament.* Princeton, N.J.: Princeton University Press, 1965.

Bertram, Christoph. "Rethinking Arms Control." *Foreign Affairs,* Vol. 59, No. 2 (Winter 1980/81), pp. 352–365.

Birnbaum, Karl E., ed. *The Politics of East-West Communication in Europe.* Westmead, UK: Saxon House, 1979.

Butterworth, Robert L. *Managing Interstate Conflict, 1945–74: Data with Synopses.* Pittsburgh: University of Pittsburgh Center for International Studies, 1976.

Cox, Arthur Macy. *Russian Roulette: The Superpower Game.* New York: Times Books, 1982.

Czempiel, Ernst-Otto. "Peace as a Strategy for Systemic Change." *Bulletin of Peace Proposals,* Vol. 10, No. 1 (1979), pp. 79–90.

Deutsch, Morton. "Trust and Suspicion." *Journal of Conflict Resolution,* Vol. 2 (1958), pp. 258–279.

Disarmament Study Group, International Peace Research Association. "Building Confidence in Europe: An Analytical and Action-Oriented Study." *Bulletin of Peace Proposals,* Vol. 11, No. 2 (June 1980), pp. 150–166.

Fisher, Roger, and William Ury. *Getting to Yes: Negotiating Agreement Without Giving In.* Boston: Houghton Mifflin, 1981.

Galtung, Johan. "Why Do Disarmament Negotiations Fail?" *Gandhi Marg,* Vol. 4, Nos. 2–3 (May–June 1982), pp. 298–307.

Goldman, Ralph M. *Arms Control and Peacekeeping.* New York: Random House, 1982.

Iklé, Fred C. *How Nations Negotiate.* New York: Harper & Row, 1964.

Janis, Irving L. *Victims of Groupthink: A Psychological Study of Foreign-Policy Decisions and Fiascoes.* Boston: Houghton Mifflin, 1972.

Jervis, Robert. "Cooperation Under the Security Dilemma," *World Politics,* Vol. 30, No. 2 (Jan. 1978), pp. 167–214.

Kelman, Herbert C., ed. *International Behavior: A Social-Psychological Analysis.* New York: Holt, Reinhart and Winston, 1965.

Nerlich, Uwe, ed. *Soviet Power and Western Negotiating Policies.* 2 vols. Cambridge, MA: Ballinger Publishing Co., 1983.

Newcombe, Alan, ed. "GRIT 1." *Peace Research Reviews,* Vol. 8, No. 1 (Jan. 1979), pp. 1–89.

————. "GRIT 2." *Peace Research Reviews,* Vol. 8, No. 2 (Feb. 1979), pp. 1–104.

Orlick, Terry. *Winning Through Cooperation.* Washington, DC: Aeropolis Books, 1978.

Osgood, Charles E. *An Alternative to War or Surrender.* Urbana, IL: University of Illinois Press, 1962.

Stockholm International Peace Research Institute. *Strategic Disarmament Verification and National Security.* New York: Crane, Russak and Co., 1977.

Tefft, Stanton K., ed. *Secrecy: A Cross-Cultural Perspective.* New York: Human Sciences Press, 1980.

CHAPTER 8

Breaking the Momentum Toward Nuclear War

Soviet-U.S. relations, although barely positive at any time, have deteriorated substantially in the last few years, and consequently the possibility of nuclear war has been heightened. In the 1970s, there was widespread hope that continued mutual commitment to détente would lead to a genuine reduction in superpower tensions, but the gains won from expanded Soviet-U.S. cooperation appear now to have been sacrificed upon the altar of mounting geopolitical competition. As the global capabilities of each of the two superpowers have grown, the possibility of direct military confrontation between them has become more likely.

Worse, current "war-fighting" trends in military doctrine and nuclear weapons technology make it highly probable that such a confrontation would involve the purposeful use of nuclear weapons. The development and deployment of nuclear weapon systems possessing the speed and accuracy required to deliver a preemptive or disarming first strike has naturally provoked a keen sense of vulnerability that places strategic forces ever more on alert, prepared to launch upon warning rather than, as before, upon attack. Hence the anxious perception by more and more people throughout the world that among official circles nuclear war has become an increasingly admissible policy option. Hence, at least in part, the Soviet pledge, "solemnly" declared before the United Nations Second Special Session on Disarmament, on June 15, 1982, "not to be the first to use nuclear weapons."

The readings in this chapter represent some of the leading policy recommendations that hold out the potential for halting the gathering momentum towards nuclear war, for building trust and channeling political will to start down the road toward genuine disarmament. The first article, much celebrated in the media because of the prominence of its authors, argues that nuclear weapons serve no useful objective beyond deterrence of a nuclear attack, and that the refusal by NATO to commit to a no-first-use policy entails political costs that heavily outweigh the benefits of maintaining a first-strike option. The second selection, by peace activist Randall Forsberg, is a detailed presentation of the most significant arms control proposal so far to have captured the public imagination, espousing the immediate desirability *and possibility* of a mutual and verifiable freeze on both the quantitative and qualitative dimensions of the superpowers' nuclear arms race. The next two essays recommend substantial mutual reductions in the nuclear weapons inventories of both the Soviet Union and the United States, with Ambassador George Kennan, in the first article, examining the political potential that attends such cuts, and Admiral Noel Gayler, in the second article, surveying the military ramifications of substantial nuclear arms reductions. The final piece, from the 1982 Palme Commission Report, sets forth a series of steps available to the Soviet Union and the United States to reduce military tensions along the interface of direct nuclear and other armed confrontation.

26. Nuclear Weapons and the Atlantic Alliance

McGeorge Bundy, George F. Kennan,
Robert S. McNamara, and Gerard Smith

We are four Americans who have been concerned over many years with the relation between nuclear weapons and the peace and freedom of the members of the Atlantic Alliance. Having learned that each of us separately has been coming to hold new views on this hard but vital question, we decided to see how far our thoughts, and the lessons of our varied experiences, could be put together; the essay that follows is the result. It argues that a new policy can bring great benefits, but it aims to start a discussion, not to end it.

*   *   *

It is time to recognize that no one has ever succeeded in advancing any persuasive reason to believe that any use of nuclear weapons, even on the smallest scale, could reliably be expected to remain limited. Every serious analysis and every military exercise, for over 25 years, has demonstrated that even the most restrained battlefield use would be enormously destructive to civilian life and property. There is no way for anyone to have any confidence that such a nuclear action will not lead to further and more devastating exchanges. Any use of nuclear weapons in Europe, by the Alliance or against it, carries with it a high and inescapable risk of escalation into the general nuclear war which would bring ruin to all and victory to none.

The one clearly definable firebreak against the worldwide disaster of general nuclear war is the one that stands between all other kinds of conflict and any use whatsoever of nuclear weapons. To keep that firebreak wide and strong is in the deepest interest of all mankind. In retrospect, indeed, it is remarkable that this country has not responded to this reality more quickly. Given the appalling consequences of even the most limited use of nuclear weapons and the total impossibility for both sides of any guarantee against unlimited escalation, there must be the gravest doubt about the wisdom of a policy which asserts the effectiveness of any first use of nuclear weapons by either side. So it seems timely to consider the possibilities, the requirements, the difficulties, and the advantages of a policy of no-first-use.

I

The largest question presented by any proposal for an Allied policy of no-first-use is that of its impact on the effectiveness of NATO's deterrent posture on the central front. In spite of the doubts that are created by any honest look at the probable consequences of resort to a first nuclear strike of any kind, it should be remembered that there were strong reasons for the creation of the American nuclear umbrella over NATO. The original American pledge, expressed in Article 5 of the Treaty, was understood to be a nuclear guarantee. It was extended at a time when only a conventional Soviet threat existed, so a readiness for first use was plainly implied from the beginning. To modify that guarantee now, even in the light of all that has happened since, would be a major change in the assumptions of the Alliance, and no such change should be made without the most careful exploration of its implications.

In such an exploration the role of the Federal Republic of Germany must be central. Americans too easily forget what the people of the Federal Republic never can: that their position is triply exposed in a fashion unique among the large industrial democracies. They do not have nuclear weapons; they share a long common boundary with the Soviet empire; in any conflict on the central front their land would be the first battleground. None of these conditions can be changed, and together they present a formidable challenge.

Having decisively rejected a policy of neutrality, the Federal Republic has necessarily relied on the nuclear protection of the United States, and we Americans should recognize that this relationship is not a favor we are doing our German friends, but the best available solution of a common problem. Both nations believe that the Federal Republic must be defended; both believe that the Federal Republic must not have nuclear weapons of its own; both believe that nuclear guarantees *of some sort* are essential; and both believe that only the United States can provide those guarantees in persuasively deterrent peacekeeping form.

The uniqueness of the West German position can be readily demonstrated by comparing it with those of France and the United Kingdom. These two nations have distance, and in one case water, between them and the armies of the Soviet Union; they also have nuclear weapons. While those weapons may contribute something to the common strength of the Alliance, their main role is to underpin a residual national self-reliance, expressed in different ways at different times by different governments, which sets both Britain and France apart from the Federal Republic. They are set apart from the United States too, in that no other nation depends on them to use their nuclear weapons otherwise than in their own ultimate self-defense.

The quite special character of the nuclear relationship between the Federal Republic and the United States is a most powerful reason for defining that relationship with great care. It is rare for one major nation to depend entirely on another for a form of strength that is vital to its survival. It is unprecedented for any nation, however powerful, to pledge itself to a course of action, in defense of another, that might entail its own nuclear devastation. A policy of no-first-use would not and should not imply an abandonment of this extraordinary guarantee—only its redefinition. It would still be necessary to be ready to reply with American nuclear weapons to any nuclear attack on the Federal Republic, and this commitment would in itself be sufficiently demanding to constitute a powerful demonstration that a policy of no-first-use would represent no abandonment of our German ally.

The German right to a voice in this question is not merely a matter of location, or even of dependence on an American nuclear guarantee. The people of the Federal Republic have demonstrated a steadfast dedication to peace, to collective defense, and to domestic political decency. The study here proposed should be responsive to their basic desires. It seems probable that they are like the rest of us in wishing most of all to have no war of any kind, but also to be able to defend the peace by forces that do not require the dreadful choice of nuclear escalation.

II

While we believe that careful study will lead to a firm conclusion that it is time to move decisively toward a policy of no-first-use, it is obvious that any such policy would require a strengthened confidence in the adequacy of the conventional forces of the Alliance, above all the forces in place on the central front and those available for prompt reinforcement. It seems clear that the nations of the Alliance together can provide whatever forces are needed, and within realistic budgetary constraints, but it is a quite different question whether they can summon the necessary political will. Evidence from the history of the Alliance is mixed. There has been great progress in the conventional defenses of

NATO in the 30 years since the 1952 Lisbon communiqué, but there have also been failures to meet force goals all along the way.

In each of the four nations which account for more than 90 percent of NATO's collective defense and a still higher proportion of its strength on the central front, there remain major unresolved political issues that critically affect contributions to conventional deterrence: for example, it can be asked what priority the United Kingdom gives to the British Army of the Rhine, what level of NATO-connected deployment can be accepted by France, what degree of German relative strength is acceptable to the Allies and fair to the Federal Republic itself, and whether we Americans have a durable and effective answer to our military manpower needs in the present all-volunteer active and reserve forces. These are the kinds of questions—and there are many more—that would require review and resolution in the course of reaching any final decision to move to a responsible policy of no-first-use.

There should also be an examination of the ways in which the concept of early use of nuclear weapons may have been built into existing forces, tactics, and general military expectations. To the degree that has happened, there could be a dangerous gap right now between real capabilities and those which political leaders might wish to have in a time of crisis. Conversely there should be careful study of what a policy of no-first-use would require in those same terms. It seems more than likely that once the military leaders of the Alliance have learned to think and act steadily on this "conventional" assumption, their forces will be better instruments for stability in crises and for general deterrence, as well as for the maintenance of the nuclear firebreak so vital to us all.

No one should underestimate either the difficulty or the importance of the shift in military attitudes implied by a no-first-use policy. Although military commanders are well aware of the terrible dangers in any exchange of nuclear weapons, it is a strong military tradition to maintain that aggressive war, not the use of any one weapon, is the central evil. Many officers will be initially unenthusiastic about any formal policy that puts limits on their recourse to a weapon of apparently decisive power. Yet the basic argument for a no-first-use policy can be stated in strictly military terms: that any other course involves unacceptable risks to the national life that military forces exist to defend. The military officers of the Alliance can be expected to understand the force of this proposition, even if many of them do not initially agree with it. Moreover, there is every reason for confidence that they will loyally accept any policy that has the support of their governments and the peoples behind them, just as they have fully accepted the present arrangements under which the use of nuclear weapons, even in retaliation for a nuclear attack, requires advance and specific approval by the head of government.

An Allied posture of no-first-use would have one special effect that can be set forth in advance: it would draw new attention to the importance of maintaining and improving the specifically American conventional forces in Europe. The principal political difficulty in a policy of no-first-use is that it may be taken in Europe, and especially in the Federal Republic, as evidence of a reduced American interest in the Alliance and in effective overall deterrence. The argument here is exactly the opposite: that such a policy is the best one available for keeping the Alliance united and effective. Nonetheless the psychological realities of the relation between the Federal Republic and the United States are such that the only way to prevent corrosive German suspicion of American intentions, under a no-first-use regime, will be for Americans to accept for themselves an appropriate share in any new level of conventional effort that the policy may require.

Yet it would be wrong to make any hasty judgment that those new levels of effort must be excessively high. The subject is complex, and the more so because both technology and politics are changing. Precision-guided munitions, in technology, and the visible weakening of the military solidity of the Warsaw Pact, in politics, are only two examples of changes working to the advantage of the Alliance. Moreover there has been some tendency, over many years, to exaggerate the relative conventional strength of the USSR and to underestimate Soviet awareness of the enormous costs and risks of any form of aggression against NATO.

Today there is literally no one who really knows what would be needed. Most of the measures routinely used in both official and private analyses are static and fragmentary. An especially arbitrary, if obviously convenient, measure of progress is that of spending levels. But it is political will, not budgetary pressure, that will be decisive. The value of greater safety from both nuclear and conventional danger is so great that even if careful analysis showed that the necessary conventional posture would require funding larger than the three-percent real increase that has been the common target of recent years, it would be the best bargain ever offered to the members of the Alliance.

Yet there is no need for the crash programs, which always bring extra costs. The direction of the Allied effort will be more important than its velocity. The final establishment of a firm policy of no-first-use, in any case, will obviously require time. What is important today is to begin to move in this direction.

III

The concept of renouncing any first use of nuclear weapons should also be tested by careful review of the value of existing NATO plans for selective and limited use of nuclear weapons. While many scenarios for nuclear war-fighting are nonsensical, it must be recognized that cautious and sober senior officers have found it prudent to ask themselves what alternatives to defeat they could propose to their civilian superiors if a massive conventional Soviet attack seemed about to make a decisive breakthrough. This question has generated contingency plans for battlefield uses of small numbers of nuclear weapons which might prevent that particular disaster. It is hard to see how any such action could be taken without the most enormous risk of rapid and catastrophic escalation, but it is a fair challenge to a policy of no-first-use that it should be accompanied by a level of conventional strength that would make such plans unnecessary.

In the light of this difficulty it would be prudent to consider whether there is any acceptable policy short of no-first-use. One possible example is what might be called "no-*early*-first-use;" such a policy might leave open the option of some limited nuclear action to fend off a final large-scale conventional defeat, and by renunciation of any immediate first use and increased emphasis on conventional capabilities it might be thought to help somewhat in reducing current fears.

But the value of a clear and simple position would be great, especially in its effect on ourselves and our Allies. One trouble with exceptions is that they easily become rules. It seems much better than even the most responsible choice of even the most limited nuclear actions to prevent even the most imminent conventional disaster should be left out of authorized policy. What the Alliance needs most today is not the refinement of its nuclear options, but a clear-cut decision to avoid them as long as others do.

IV

Who should make the examination here proposed? The present American Administration has so far shown little interest in questions of this sort, and indeed a seeming callousness in some quarters in Washington toward nuclear dangers may be partly responsible for some of the recent unrest in Europe. But each of the four of us has served in Administrations which revised their early thought on nuclear weapons policy. James Byrnes learned the need to seek international control; John Foster Dulles stepped back somewhat from his early belief in massive retaliation; Dwight Eisenhower came to believe in the effort to ban nuclear tests which he first thought dangerous; the Administration of John F. Kennedy (in which we all served) modified its early views on targeting doctrine; Lyndon Johnson shelved the proposed MLF when he decided it was causing more trouble than it was worth; and Richard Nixon agreed to narrow limits on anti-ballistic missiles whose large-scale deployment he had once thought indispensable. There were changes also in the Ford and Carter Administrations, and President Reagan has already adjusted his views on the usefulness of early arms control negotiations, even though we remain in a time of general stress between Washington and Moscow. No Administration should be held, and none should hold itself, to inflexible first positions on these extraordinarily difficult matters.

Nor does this question need to wait upon governments for study. The day is long past when public awe and governmental secrecy made nuclear policy a matter for only the most private executive determination. The question presented by a policy of no-first-use must indeed be decided by governments, but they can and should be considered by citizens. In recent months strong private voices have been raised on both sides of the Atlantic on behalf of strengthened conventional forces. When this cause is argued by such men as Christoph Bertram, Field Marshal Lord Carver, Admiral Noel Gayler, Porfessor Michael Howard, Henry Kissinger, François de Rose, Theo Sommer, and General Maxwell Taylor, to name only a few, it is fair to conclude that at least in its general direction the present argument is not outside the mainstream of thinking within the Alliance. Indeed there is evidence of renewed concern for conventional forces in governments too.

What should be added, in both public and private sectors, is a fresh, sustained, and careful consideration of the requirements and the benefits of deciding that the policy of the Atlantic Alliance should be to keep its nuclear weapons unused as long as others do the same. Our own belief, though we do not here assert it as proven, is that when this possibility is fully explored it will be evident that the advantages of the policy far outweigh its costs, and that this demonstration will help the peoples and governments of the Alliance to find the political will to move in this direction. In this spirit we go on to sketch the benefits that could come from such a change.

V

The first possible advantage of a policy of no-first-use is in the management of the nuclear deterrent forces that would still be necessary. Once we escape from the need to plan for a first use that is credible, we can escape also from many of the complex arguments that have led to assertions that all sort of new nuclear capabilities are necessary to create or restore a capability for something called "escalation dominance"—a capability to fight and "win" a nuclear war at any level. What would be needed, under no-first-use, is a set of capabilities we already have in overflowing measure—capabilities for appropriate retaliation to any kind of Soviet nuclear attack which would leave the Soviet Union in no doubt that it too should adhere to a policy of no-first-use. The Soviet government is already aware of the awful risk inherent in any use of these weapons, and there is no current or prospective Soviet "superiority" that would tempt anyone in Moscow toward nuclear adventurism. (All four of us are wholly unpersuaded by the argument advanced in recent years that the Soviet Union could ever rationally expect to gain from such a wild effort as a massive first strike on land-based American strategic missiles.)

Once it is clear that the only nuclear need of the Alliance is for adequately survivable and varied *second-strike* forces, requirements for the modernization of major nuclear systems will become more modest than has been assumed. In particular we can escape from the notion that we must somehow match everything the rocket commanders in the Soviet Union extract from their government. It seems doubtful, also, that under such a policy it would be necessary or desirable to deploy neutron bombs. The savings permitted by more modest programs could go toward meeting the financial costs of our contribution to conventional forces.

It is important to avoid misunderstanding here. In the conditions of the 1980s, and in the absence of agreement on both sides to proceed to very large-scale reductions in nuclear forces, it is clear that large, varied, and survivable nuclear forces will still be necessary for nuclear deterrence. The point is not that we Americans should move unilaterally to some "minimum" force of a few tens or even hundreds of missiles, but rather that once we escape from the pressure to seem willing and able to use these weapons first, we shall find that our requirements are much less massive than is now widely supposed.

A posture of no-first-use should also go far to meet the understandable anxieties that underlie much of the new interest in nuclear disarmament, both in Europe and in our own country. Some of the proposals generated by this new interest may lack practicability for the present. For example, proposals to make "all" of Europe—from Portugal to Poland—a nuclear-free zone do not seem to take full account of the reality that thousands of long-range weapons deep in the Soviet Union will still be able to target Western Europe. But a policy of no-first-use, with its accompaniment of a reduced requirement for new Allied nuclear systems, should allow a considerable reduction in fears of all sorts. Certainly such a new policy would neutralize the highly disruptive argument currently put about in Europe: that plans for theater nuclear modernization reflect an American hope to fight a nuclear war limited to Europe. Such modernization might or might not be needed under a policy of no-first-use; that question, given the size and versatility of other existing and prospective American forces, would be a matter primarily for European decision (as it is today).

An effective policy of no-first-use will also reduce the risk of conventional aggression in Europe. That risk has never been as great as prophets of doom have claimed and has always lain primarily in the possibility that Soviet leaders might think thay could achieve some quick and limited gain that would be accepted because no defense or reply could be concerted. That temptation has been much reduced by the Allied conventional deployments achieved in the last 20 years, and it would be reduced still further by the additional shift in the balance of Allied effort that a no-first-use policy would both permit and require. The risk that an adventurist Soviet leader might take the terrible gamble of conventional aggression was greater in the past than it is today, and is greater today than it would be under no-first-use, backed up by an effective conventional defense.

VI

We have been discussing a problem of military policy, but our interest is also political. The principal immediate danger in the current military posture of the Alliance is not that it will lead to large-scale war, conventional or nuclear. The balance of terror, and the caution of both sides, appear strong enough today to prevent such a catastrophe, at least in the absence of some deeply destabilizing political change which might lead to panic or adventurism on either side. But the present unbalanced reliance on nuclear weapons, if long continued, might produce exactly such political change. The events of the last year have shown that differing perceptions of the role of nuclear weapons can lead to destructive recriminations, and when these differences are compounded by understandable disagreements on other matters such as Poland and the Middle East, the possibilities for trouble among Allies are evident.

The political coherence of the Alliance, especially in times of stress, is at least as important as the military strength required to maintain credible deterrence. Indeed the political requirement has, if anything, an even higher priority. Soviet leaders would be most pleased to help the Alliance fall into total disarray, and would much prefer such a development to the inescapable uncertainties of open conflict. Conversely, if consensus is reestablished on a military policy that the peoples and governments of the Alliance can believe in, both political will and deterrent credibility will be reinforced. Plenty of hard questions will remain, but both fear and mistrust will be reduced, and they are the most immediate enemies.

There remains one underlying reality which could not be removed by even the most explicit declaratory policy of no-first-use. Even if the nuclear powers of the Alliance should join, with the support of other Allies, in a policy of no-first-use, and even if that decision should lead to a common declaration of such policy by these powers and the Soviet Union, no one on either side could guarantee beyond all possible doubt that if conventional warfare broke out on a large scale there would in fact be no use of nuclear weapons. We could not make that assumption about the Soviet Union, and we must recognize that Soviet leaders could not make it about us. As long as the weapons themselves exist, the possibility of their use will remain.

But this inescapable reality does not undercut the value of a no-first-use policy. That value is first of all for the internal health of the Western Alliance itself. A posture of effective conventional balance and survivable second-strike nuclear strength is vastly better for our own peoples and governments, in a deep sense more civilized, than one that forces the serious contemplation of "limited" nuclear scenarios that are at once terrifying and implausible.

There is strong reason to believe that no-first-use can also help in our relations with the Soviet Union. The Soviet government has repeatedly offered to join the West in declaring such a policy, and while such declarations may have only limited reliability, it would be wrong to disregard the real value to both sides of a jointly declared adherence to this policy. To renounce the first use of nuclear weapons is to accept an enormous burden of responsibility for any later violation. The existence of such a clearly declared common pledge would increase the cost and risk of any sudden use of nuclear weapons by either side and correspondingly reduce the political force of spoken or unspoken threats of such use.

A posture and policy of no-first-use also could help to open the path toward serious reduction of nuclear armaments on both sides. The nuclear decades have shown how hard it is to get agreements that really do constrain these weapons, and no one can say with assurance that any one step can make a decisive difference. But just as a policy of no-first-use should reduce the pressures on our side for massive new nuclear forces, it should help to increase the international incentives for the Soviet Union to show some restraint of its own. It is important not to exaggerate here, and certainly Soviet policies on procurement are not merely delayed mirror-images of ours. Nonetheless there are connections between what is said and what is done even in the Soviet Union, and there are incentives for moderation, even there, that could be strengthened by a jointly declared policy of renouncing first use. At a minimum such a declaration would give both sides additional reason to seek for agreements that would prevent a vastly expensive and potentially destabilizing contest for some kind of strategic advantage in outer space.

Finally, and in sum, we think a policy of no-first-use, especially if shared with the Soviet Union, would bring new hope to everyone in every country whose life is shadowed by the hideous possibility of a third great twentieth-century conflict in Europe—conventional or nuclear. It seems timely and even urgent to begin the careful study of a policy that could help to sweep this threat clean off the board of international affairs.

VII

We recognize that we have only opened this large question, that we have exhausted no aspect of it, and that we may have omitted important elements. We know that NATO is much more than its four strongest military members; we know that a policy of no-first-use in the Alliance would at once raise questions about America's stance in Korea and indeed other parts of Asia. We have chosen deliberately to focus on the central front of our central alliance, believing that a right choice there can only help toward right choices elsewhere.

What we dare to hope for is the kind of new and widespread consideration of the policy we have outlined that helped us 15 years ago toward SALT I, 25 years ago toward the Limited Test Ban, and 35 years ago toward the Alliance itself. Such consideration can be made all the more earnest and hopeful by keeping in mind one simple and frequently neglected reality: there has been no first use of nuclear weapons since 1945, and no one in any country regrets that fact. The right way to maintain this record is to recognize that in the age of massive thermonuclear overkill it no longer makes sense—if it ever did—to hold these weapons for any other purpose than the prevention of their use.

27. Call to Halt the Nuclear Arms Race— Proposal for a Mutual U.S.-Soviet Nuclear-Weapon Freeze

Randall Forsberg

STATEMENT OF THE PROPOSAL

To improve national and international security, the United States and the Soviet Union should stop the nuclear arms race. Specifically, they should adopt a mutual freeze on the testing, production and deployment of nuclear weapons and of missiles and new aircraft designed primarily to deliver nuclear weapons. This is an essential, verifiable first step toward lessening the risk of nuclear war and reducing the nuclear arsenals.

The horror of a nuclear holocaust is universally acknowledged. Today, the United States and the Soviet Union possess 50,000 nuclear weapons. In half an hour, a fraction of these weapons can destroy all cities in the northern hemisphere. Yet over the next decade, the U.S. and USSR plan to build over 20,000 more nuclear warheads, along with a new generation of nuclear missiles and aircraft.

The weapon programs of the next decade, if not stopped, will pull the nuclear tripwire tighter. Counterforce and other "nuclear war-fighting" systems will improve the ability of the U.S. and the USSR to attack the opponent's nuclear forces and other military targets. This will increase the pressure on both sides to use their nuclear weapons in a crisis, rather than risk losing them in a first strike.

Such developments will increase hairtrigger readiness for massive nuclear exchange at a time when economic difficulties, political dissension, revolution, and competition for energy supplies may be rising worldwide. At the same time, more countries may acquire nuclear weapons. Unless we change this combination of trends, the danger of nuclear war will be greater in the late 1980s and 1990s than ever before.

Rather than permit this dangerous future to evolve, the United States and the Soviet Union should stop the nuclear arms race.

A freeze on nuclear missiles and aircraft can be verified by existing national means. A total freeze can be verified more easily than the complex SALT I and II agreements. The freeze on warhead production could be verified by the Safeguards of the International Atomic Energy Agency. Stopping the production of nuclear weapons and weapon-grade material and applying the Safeguards to U.S. and Soviet nuclear programs would increase the incentive of other countries to adhere to the Non-proliferation Treaty, renouncing acquisition of their own nuclear weapons, and to accept the same Safeguards.

A freeze would hold constant the existing nuclear parity between the United States and the Soviet Union. By precluding production of counterforce weaponry on either side, it would eliminate excuses for further arming on both sides. Later, following the immediate adoption of the freeze, its terms should be negotiated into the more durable form of a treaty.

A nuclear-weapon freeze, accompanied by government-aided conversion of nuclear industries, would save at least $100 billion each in U.S. and Soviet military spending (at today's prices) in 1981–1990. This would reduce inflation. The savings could be applied to balance the budget, reduce taxes, improve services, subsidize renewable energy, or increase aid to poverty-stricken Third World regions. By shifting personnel to more labor-intensive civilian jobs, a nuclear-weapon freeze would also raise employment.

Stopping the U.S.-Soviet nuclear arms race is the single most useful step that can be taken now to reduce the likelihood of nuclear war and to prevent the spread of nuclear weapons to more countries. This step is a necessary prelude to creating international conditions in which:

- further steps can be taken toward a stable, peaceful international order;
- the threat of first use of nuclear weaponry can be ended;
- the freeze can be extended to other nations; and
- the nuclear arsenals on all sides can be drastically reduced or eliminated, making the world truly safe from nuclear destruction.

SCOPE OF THE FREEZE

(1) Underground nuclear tests should be suspended, pending final agreement on a comprehensive test ban treaty.
(2) There should be a freeze on testing, production, and deployment of all missiles and new aircraft which have nuclear weapons as their sole or main payload. This includes:

U.S. DELIVERY VEHICLES
In Production:
Improved Minutemen ICBM

Trident 1 SLBM
Air-launched cruise missle (ALCM)
In Development:
MX ICBM
Trident II SLBM
Long-range ground- and sea-launched cruise missiles (GLCM,
SLCM)
Pershing II IRBM
New Bomber

SOVIET DELIVERY VEHICLES
In Production
SS-19 ICBM
SS-N-18 SLBM
SS-20 IRBM
Backfire bomber
In Development:
SS-17, SS-18, SS-19 ICBM improvements
New ICBM
New SLBM (SS-N-20).

(3) The number of land- and submarine-based launch tubes for nuclear
missiles should be frozen. Replacement subs could be built to keep
the force constant, but with no net increase in SLBM tubes and
no new missiles.
(4) No further MIRVing or other changes to existing missiles or bomber
loads would be permitted.

All of the above measures can be verified by existing national means
of verification with high confidence.

The following measures cannot be verified nationally with the same
confidence, but an effort should be made to include them:

(5) Production of fissionable material (enriched uranium and plutonium)
for weapon purposes should be halted.
(6) Production of nuclear weapons (bombs) should be halted.

There are two arguments for attempting to include these somewhat
less verifiable steps. First, with a halt to additional and new delivery
vehicles, there will be no need for additional bombs. Thus, production
of weapon-grade fissionable material and bombs would probably stop
in any event. Second, the establishment of a *universal* ban on production
of weapon-grade fissionable material and nuclear bombs, verified by
international inspection as established now for non-nuclear-weapon states
under the Non-proliferation Treaty and the International Atomic Energy
Agency, would greatly strengthen that Treaty and improve the prospects
for halting the spread of nuclear weapons.

THE AGREEMENT TO FREEZE

The U.S. and Soviet governments should announce a moratorium on all further testing, production, and deployment of nuclear weapons and nuclear delivery vehicles, to be verified by national means. The freeze would be followed by negotiations to incorporate the moratorium in a treaty. The negotiations would cover supplementary verification measures, such as IAEA inspections; and possible desirable exceptions from the freeze, such as an occasional confidence test.

This procedure follows the precedent of the 1958–1961 nuclear-weapon test moratorium, in which testing was suspended while the U.S., USSR, and UK negotiated a partial test ban treaty.

RELATION TO SALT NEGOTIATIONS

The bilateral freeze is aimed at being introduced in the early 1980s, as soon as sufficient popular and political support is developed to move the governments toward its adoption.

The freeze would prevent dangerous developments in the absence of a SALT treaty. It would preclude exploitation of loopholes in past treaties and, at the same time, satisfy critics who are concerned that the SALT process may not succeed in stopping the arms race.

The freeze does not replace the SALT negotiating process, but should supplement and strengthen it. The freeze could be adopted as a replacement for SALT II or as an immediate follow-on, with the task of putting the moratorium into treaty language the job of SALT III.

THE CASE FOR A NUCLEAR-WEAPON FREEZE

There are many reasons to support a halt to the nuclear arms race at this time:

Parity. There is widespread agreement that parity exists between U.S. and Soviet nuclear forces at present.

Avoiding "Nuclear War-fighting" Developments. The next generation U.S. and Soviet nuclear weapons improve "nuclear war-fighting" capabilities—that is, they improve the ability to knock out the enemy's forces in what is termed a "limited" nuclear exchange. Having such capabilities will undermine the sense of parity, spur further weapon developments, and increase the likelihood of nuclear war in a crisis, especially if conflict with conventional weapons has started. It is of overriding importance to stop these developments.

Stopping the MX and New Soviet ICBMs. Specifically, a freeze would prevent the deployment of new and improved Soviet ICBMs, which are expected to render U.S. ICBMs vulnerable to preemptive attack. This would obviate the need for the costly and environmentally-destructive U.S. mobile MX ICBM, with its counterforce capability against Soviet

ICBMs. That, in turn, would avoid the pressure for the USSR to deploy its own mobile ICBMs in the 1990s.

Stopping the Cruise Missile. The new U.S. cruise missile, just entering production in an air-launched version and still in development in ground- and sea-launched versions, threatens to make negotiated, nationally-verified nuclear arms control far more difficult. Modern, low-flying terrain-guided cruise missles are relatively small and cheap and can be deployed in large numbers on virtually any launching platform: not only bombers, but also tactical aircraft, surface ships, tactical submarines, and various ground vehicles. They are easy to conceal and, unlike ICBMs, their numbers cannot be observed from satellites. If the United States continues the development and production of cruise missiles, the USSR will be likely to follow suit in 5–10 years; and quantitative limits on the two sides will be impossible to verify. A freeze would preclude this development.

Preserving European Security. A freeze would also prevent a worsening of the nuclear balance in Europe. To date the USSR has replaced less than half of its medium-range nuclear missiles and bombers with the new SS-20 missile and Backfire bomber. The United States is planning to add hundreds of Pershing II and ground-launched cruise missiles of the forward-based nuclear systems in Europe, capable of reaching the USSR. Negotiations conducted *after* additional Soviet medium-range weapons are deployed are likely to leave Europe with more nuclear arms on both sides and with less security than it has today. It is important to freeze before the Soviet weapons grow to large numbers, increasing pressure for a U.S. response and committing both sides to permanently higher nuclear force levels.

Stopping the Spread of Nuclear Arms. There is a slim chance of stopping the spread of nuclear weapons if the two superpowers stop their major nuclear arms race. The freeze would help the U.S. and the USSR meet their legal and political obligations under the Non-proliferation Treaty. It would make the renunciation of nuclear weapons by other countries somewhat more equitable and politically feasible. In addition, a U.S.-Soviet freeze would encourage a halt in the nuclear weapon programs of other countries which are known or believed to have nuclear weapons or nuclear-weapon technology. These are Britain, France, and China, with publicly acknowledged nuclear weapon programs, and India, Israel, and South Africa, without acknowledged programs.

Timing. There is a unique opportunity to freeze U.S. and Soviet nuclear arms in the early 1980s. The planned new U.S. and Soviet ICBMs and the U.S. Pershing II and ground-launched cruise missile are not scheduled to enter production until 1983 or later. The Soviets have offered to negotiate the further deployment of their medium-range nuclear forces and submarine-based forces. Given the pressure to respond to new weapons on both sides and the existing nuclear parity, an equally opportune time for a freeze may not recur for many years.

Popular Appeal. Campaigns to stop individual weapon systems are sometimes treated as unilateral disarmament or circumvented by the development of alternative systems. The pros and cons of the SALT II Treaty are too technical for the patience of the average person. In contrast, an effort to stop the development and production of all U.S. and Soviet nuclear weapons is simple, straightforward, effective, and mutual; for all these reasons it is likely to have great popular appeal. This is essential for creating the scale of popular support that is needed to make nuclear arms control efforts successful.

Economic Benefits. Although nuclear forces take only a small part of U.S. and Soviet military spending, they do cost some tens of billions of dollars annually. About half of these funds go to existing nuclear forces, while half are budgeted for the testing, production, and deployment of new warheads and delivery systems. A nuclear-weapon freeze, accompanied by government-aided conversion of nuclear industries to civilian production, would yield several important economic benefits:

- About $100 billion each (at 1981 prices) would be saved by the United States and the Soviet Union over the period from 1981 to 1990 in unnecessary military spending.
- The savings could be applied to balance the budget; reduce taxes; improve services now being cut back; subsidize home and commercial conversion to safe, renewable energy resources; or increase economic aid to poverty-stricken Third World regions, thereby defusing some of the tinderboxes of international conflict.
- With the shift of personnel to more labor-intensive civilian jobs, employment would rise. At the same time, the highly inflationary pressure of military spending would be mitigated.

VERIFICATION

The comprehensive nature of a total freeze on nuclear weapon testing, production and deployment (and, by implication, development) would facilitate verification.

Long-range bomber and missile production would be proscribed. The letter of assurance attached to the draft SALT II Treaty that the USSR will not increase its rate of production of Backfire bombers indicates that not only *deployment* but also *production* of the relatively large aricraft and missiles in question can be observed with considerable confidence. While concealed production and stockpiling of aircraft and missiles is theoretically possible, it would be extraordinarily difficult to accomplish with no telltale construction or supply. Any attempt would require the building or modification of plants and the development of new transport lines that are not operational at present. It would also involve high risks of detection and high penalties in worsening relations without offering any significant strategic advantage.

Verification of a ban on *tests* of missiles designed to carry nuclear weapons can be provided with high confidence by existing satellite and other detections systems. Here, too, a comprehensive approach is easier to verify than a partial or limited one.

Verification of aircraft, missile, and submarine *deployments*, by specific quantity, is already provided under the terms of the SALT II and SALT I Treaty language. Verifying *no* additional deployments or major modifications will be considerably easier, in fact, than checking compliance with specific numerical ceilings in a continually changing environment.

Verification of a comprehensive nuclear *weapon test* ban, the subject of study and negotiation for many years, has been determined to be possible within the terms of the existing draft comprehensive test ban treaty.

INITIATIVES TOWARD THE FREEZE

Either the United States or the Soviet Union could initiate movement toward the freeze by taking modest, unilateral steps that would: demonstrate its good faith, start movement in the right direction, and make it easier for the other country to take a similar step.

For example, either country could:

1. Undertake a three-month moratorium on nuclear test explosions, to be extended if reciprocated.
2. Stop further deployment, for a specified period, of one new strategic weapon or improvement of an existing weapon.
3. Draw up and publish comprehensive conversion plans for the nuclear facilities and employment that would be affected by a freeze, as a sign of serious commitment to the goal.

28. A Modest Proposal

George F. Kennan

Adequate words are lacking to express the full seriousness of our present situation. It is not just that we are for the moment on a collision course politically with the Soviet Union, and that the process of rational communication between the two governments seems to have broken down completely; it is also—and even more importantly—the fact that the ultimate sanction behind the conflicting policies of these two governments is type and volume of weaponry which could not possibly be used without utter disaster for us all.

For over 30 years wise and far-seeing people have been warning us about the futility of any war fought with nuclear weapons and about the dangers involved in their cultivation. Some of the first of these voices to be raised were those of great scientists, including outstandingly that of Albert Einstein himself. But there has been no lack of others. Every president of this country, from Dwight Eisenhower to Jimmy Carter, has tried to remind us that there could be no such thing as victory in a war fought with such weapons. So have a great many other eminent persons.

When one looks back today over the history of these warnings, one has the impression that something has now been lost of the sense of urgency, the hopes, and the excitement that initially inspired them, so many years ago. One senses, even on the part of those who today most acutely perceive the problem and are inwardly most exercised about it, a certain discouragement, resignation, perhaps even despair, when it comes to the question of raising the subject again. The danger is so obvious. So much has already been said. What is to be gained by reiteration? What good would it now do?

Look at the record. Over all these years the competition in the development of nuclear weaponry has proceeded steadily, relentlessly, without the faintest regard for all these warning voices. We have gone on piling weapon upon weapon, missile upon missile, new levels of destructiveness upon old ones. We have done this helplessly, almost involuntarily: like the victims of some sort of hypnotism, like men in a dream, like lemmings heading for the sea, like the children of Hamlin marching blindly along behind their Pied Piper. And the result is that today we have achieved, we and the Russians together, in the creation of these devices and their means of delivery, levels of redundancy of such grotesque dimensions as to defy rational understanding.

I say redundancy. I know of no better way to describe it. But actually, the word is too mild. It implies that there could be levels of these weapons that would not be redundant. Personally, I doubt that there could. I question whether these devices are really weapons at all. A true weapon is at best something with which you endeavor to affect the behavior of another society by influencing the minds, the calculations, the intentions, of the men that control it; it is not something with which you destroy indiscriminately the lives, the substance, the hopes, the culture, the civilization, of another people.

What a confession of intellectual poverty it would be—what a bankruptcy of intelligent statesmanship—if we had to admit that such blind, senseless acts of destruction were the best use we could make of what we have come to view as the leading elements of our military strength!

To my mind, the nuclear bomb is the most useless weapon ever invented. It can be employed to no rational purpose. It is not even an effective defense against itself. It is only something with which, in a moment of petulance or panic, you commit such fearful acts of destruction as no sane person would ever wish to have upon his conscience.

There are those who will agree, with a sigh, to much of what I have just said, but will point to the need for something called deterrence.

This is, of course, a concept which attributes to others—to others who, like ourselves, were born of women, walk on two legs, and love their children, to human beings, in short—the most fiendish and inhuman of tendencies.

But all right: accepting for the sake of argument the profound iniquity of these adversaries, no one could deny, I think, that the present Soviet and American arsenals, presenting over a million times the destructive power of the Hiroshima bomb, are simply fantastically redundant to the purpose in question. If the same relative proportions were to be preserved, something well less than 20 percent of those stocks would surely suffice for the most sanguine concepts of deterrence, whether as between the two nuclear superpowers or with relation to any of those other governments that have been so ill-advised as to enter upon the nuclear path. Whatever their suspicions of each other, there can be no excuse on the part of these two governments for holding, poised against each other and poised in a sense against the whole northern hemisphere, quantities of these weapons so vastly in excess of any rational and demonstrable requirements.

How have we got ourselves into this dangerous mess?

Let us not confuse the question by blaming it all on our Soviet adversaries. They have, of course, their share of the blame, and not least in their cavalier dismissal of the Baruch Plan so many years ago. They too have made their mistakes; and I should be the last to deny it.

But we must remember that it has been we Americans who, at almost every step of the road, have taken the lead in the development of this sort of weaponry. It was we who first produced and tested such a device; we who were the first to raise its destructiveness to a new level with the hydrogen bomb; we who introduced the multiple warhead; we who have declined every proposal for the renunciation of the principle of "first use"; and we alone, so help us God, who have used the weapon in anger against others, and against tens of thousands of helpless non-combatants at that.

I know that reasons were offered for some of these things. I know that others might have taken this sort of a lead, had we not done so. But let us not, in the face of this record, so lose ourselves in self-righteousness and hypocrisy as to forget our own measure of complicity in creating the situation we face today.

What is it then, if not our own will, and if not the supposed wickedness of our opponents, that has brought us to this pass?

The answer, I think, is clear. It is primarily the inner momentum, the independent momentum, of the weapons race itself—the compulsions that arise and take charge of great powers when they enter upon a competition with each other in the building up of major armaments of any sort.

This is nothing new. I am a diplomatic historian. I see this same phenomenon playing its fateful part in the relations among the great

European powers as much as a century ago. I see this competitive buildup of armaments conceived initially as a means to an end but soon becoming the end itself. I see it taking possession of men's imagination and behavior, becoming a force in its own right, detaching itself from the political differences that initially inspired it, and then leading both parties, invariably and inexorably, to the war they no longer know how to avoid.

This is a species of fixation, brewed out of many components. There are fears, resentments, national pride, personal pride. There are misreadings of the adversary's intentions—sometimes even the refusal to consider them at all. There is the tendency of national communities to idealize themselves and to dehumanize the opponent. There is the blinkered, narrow vision of the professional military planner, and his tendency to make war inevitable by assuming its inevitability.

Tossed together, these components form a powerful brew. They guide the fears and the ambitions of men. They seize the policies of governments and whip them around like trees before the tempest.

Is it possible to break out of this charmed and vicious circle? It is sobering to recognize that no one, at least to my knowledge, has yet done so. But no one, for that matter, has ever been faced with such great catastrophe, such inalterable catastrophe, at the end of the line. Others, in earlier decades, could befuddle themselves with dreams of something called "victory." We, perhaps fortunately, are denied this seductive prospect. We have to break out of the circle. We have no other choice.

How are we to do it?

I must confess that I see no possibility of doing this by means of discussions along the lines of the negotiations that have been in progress, off and on, over this past decade, under the acronym of SALT. I regret, to be sure, that the most recent SALT agreement has not been ratified. I regret it, because if the benefits to be expected from that agreement were slight, its disadvantages were even slighter; and it had a symbolic value which should not have been so lightly sacrificed.

But I have, I repeat, no illusion that negotiations on the SALT pattern—negotiations, that is, in which each side is obsessed with the chimera of relative advantage and strives only to retain a maximum of the weaponry for itself while putting its opponent to the maximum disadvantage—I have no illusion that such negotiations could ever be adequate to get us out of this hole. They are not a way of escape from the weapons race; they are an integral part of it.

Whoever does not understand that when it comes to nuclear weapons the whole concept of relative advantage is illusory—whoever does not understand that when you are talking about absurd and preposterous quantities of overkill the relative sizes of arsenals have no serious meaning—whoever does not understand that the danger lies not in the possibility that someone else might have more missiles and warheads than we do but in the very existence of these unconscionable quantities of highly poisonous explosives, and their existence, above all, in hands as weak and shaky and undependable as those of ourselves or our adversaries or any other mere human beings: whoever does not understand these things is never going to guide us out of this increasingly dark and menacing forest of bewilderments into which we have all wandered.

I can see no way out of this dilemma other than by a bold and sweeping departure—a departure that would cut surgically through the exaggerated anxieties, the self-engendered nightmares, and the sophisticated mathematics of destruction, in which we have all been entangled over these recent years, and would permit us to move, with courage and decision, to the heart of the problem.

President Reagan recently said, and I think very wisely, that he would "negotiate as long as necessary to reduce the numbers of nuclear weapons to a point where neither side threatens the survival of the other."

Now that is, of course, precisely the thought to which these present observations of mine are addressed. But I wonder whether the negotiations would really have to be at such great length. What I would like to see the President do, after due consultation with the Congress, would be to propose to the Soviet government an immediate across-the-boards reduction by 50 percent of the nuclear arsenals now being maintained by the two superpowers—a reduction affecting in equal measure all forms of the weapon, strategic, medium-range, and tactical, as well as all means of their delivery—all this to be implemented at once and without further wrangling among the experts, and to be subject to such national means of verification as now lie at the disposal of the two powers.

Whether the balance of reduction would be precisely even—whether it could be construed to favor statistically one side or the other—would not be the question. Once we start thinking that way, we would be back on the same old fateful track that has brought us where we are today. Whatever the precise results of such a reduction, there would still be plenty of overkill left—so much so that if this first operation were successful, I would then like to see a second one put in hand to rid us of at least two-thirds of what would be left.

Now I have, of course, no idea of the scientific aspects of such an operation; but I can imagine that serious problems might be presented by the task of removing, and disposing safely of, the radioactive contents of the many thousands of warheads that would have to be dismantled. Should this be the case, I would like to see the President couple his appeal for a 50 percent reduction with the proposal that there be established a joint Soviet-American scientific committee, under the chairmanship of a distinguished neutral figure, to study jointly and in all humility the problem not only of the safe disposal of these wastes but also the question of how they could be utilized in such a way as to make a positive contribution to human life, either in the two countries themselves or—perhaps preferably—elsewhere. In such a joint scientific venture we might both atone for some of our past follies and lay the foundation for a more constructive relationship.

It will be said: this proposal, whatever its merits, deals with only a part of the problem. This is perfectly true. Behind it there would still lurk the serious political differences that now divide us from the Soviet government. Behind it would still lie the problems recently treated, and still to be treated, in the SALT forum. Behind it would still lie the great question of the acceptability of war itself, any war, even a conventional one, as a means of solving problems among great industrial powers in this age of high technology.

What has been suggested here would not prejudice the continued treatment of these questions just as they might be treated today, in whatever forums and under whatever safeguards the two powers find necessary. The conflicts and arguments over these questions could all still proceed to the heart's content of all those who view them with such passionate commitment. The stakes would simply be smaller; and that would be a great relief to all of us.

What I have suggested is, of course, only a beginning. But a beginning has to be made somewhere; and if it has to be made, is it not best that it should be made where the dangers are the greatest, and their necessity the least? If a step of this nature could be successfully taken, people might find the heart to tackle with greater confidence and determination the many problems that would still remain.

It will also be argued that there would be risks involved. Possibly so. I do not see them. I do not deny the possibility. But if there are, so what? Is it possible to conceive of any dangers greater than those that lie at the end of the collision course on which we are now embarked? And if not, why choose the greater—why choose, in fact, the greatest—of all risks, in the hopes of avoiding the lesser ones?

We are confronted here, my friends, with two courses. At the end of the one lies hope—faint hope, if you will—uncertain hope, hope surrounded with dangers, if you insist. At the end of the other lies, so far as I am able to see, no hope at all.

Can there be—in the light of our duty not just to ourselves (for we are all going to die sooner or later) but of our duty to our own kind, our duty to the continuity of the generations, our duty to the great experiment of civilized life on this rare and rich and marvelous planet—can there be, in the light of these claims on our loyalty, any question as to which course we should adopt?

In the final week of his life, Albert Einstein signed the last of the collective appeals against the development of nuclear weapons that he was ever to sign. He was dead before it appeared. It was an appeal drafted, I gather, by Bertrand Russell. I had my differences with Russell at the time as I do now in retrospect; but I would like to quote one sentence from the final paragraph of that statement, not only because it was the last one Einstein ever signed, but because it sums up, I think, all that I have to say on the subject. It reads as follows:

We appeal, as human beings to human beings: Remember your humanity, and forget the rest.

29. How to Break the Momentum of the Nuclear Arms Race

Noel Gayler

Everyone understands that nuclear weapons are the most deadly things ever invented by man. If they were ever to be used, the chances are overwhelming that they would be used in great numbers. And that would mean the slaughter of innocents in the hundreds of millions, the end of Western civilization, perhaps even the end of a livable world.

What many Americans do not understand is that there is no sensible military use for any of the three categories of nuclear weapons—strategic (of intercontinental range), theater (capable of reaching targets within one theater of military operations), or tactical (designed, like atomic cannon, for battlefield use). I say this as a military man, a former commander in chief of all United States forces in the Pacific, an aviator and mariner, soldier and intelligence officer of 46 years' experience.

In the battles I saw and the military strategy I helped carry out, the means employed bore a reasonable relation to the ends in view. But now the nuclear forces of the United States and of the Soviet Union have become so large and so threatening that there is no conceivable military objective worth the risk of nuclear war.

This truth offers us a way out. There are specific ways in which we and the Russians can reduce the now very real risk of nuclear conflict. We and they can renounce first use of nuclear weapons. We and they can redeploy tactical weapons beyond each other's range. Together, we can freeze nuclear-weapons activity just where it is, as a prelude to cutting back. Most especially, we and the Russians can agree on massive cuts in our nuclear arsenals.

There are fancy theories current about controlled nuclear exchanges and bloodless, chesslike calculations between opponents in the middle of nuclear war. People who think like that do not understand nuclear weapons, and they do not understand war. Real war is not like these complicated tit-for-tat imaginings. There is little knowledge of what is going on, and less communication. There is blood and terror and agony. We cannot deal with war a thousand times more terrible than any we have ever seen in some bloodless analytic fashion. To kiss off nuclear war in this abstract way makes it more likely, for we and the Russians may convince each other that we have aggressive plans that we do not in fact have.

Both the Soviet and the American governments have repeatedly expressed their wish to reach agreements reducing the risk of nuclear apocalypse. But President Reagan's campaign pledge to commence strategic arms limitations talks "immediately" upon taking office has not been honored. The pacific statements of the Soviet leader, Leonid I. Brezhnev, are compromised by the continuing buildup of Soviet nuclear arms and the not-so-veiled threats of Soviet counteraction if agreement is not reached. The only nuclear arms-control game in town now is the negotiation in Geneva on so-called medium-range weapons in the European theater. But the news from the negotiating table seems to rehearse the same tired old arguments that have gotten us nowhere in the past. What's the problem?

In all our negotiations, past and present, both we and the Russians have been hung up on the following three issues:

1. What is fair and equal? Neither side will stand still for unilateral disarmament, nor should it. But we Americans talk about equal effectiveness in terms of weapons systems, while the Russians talk about equal security, and the way they define their security needs is unacceptable to us.

2. What is verifiable? We are tremendously concerned about the potential for Russian cheating. They are equally concerned that our proposals for inspection inside the Soviet Union might be a cover for espionage.

3. How do you classify weapons, and what weapons do you count? For example, is the Russian Backfire bomber capable of intercontinental range, as our military contend, or is it a medium-range aircraft, as the Russians insist? Do you count as "strategic" those long-range weapons that cross oceans (our idea) or any weapons that can reach Soviet soil no matter where they start from (their idea)?

These built-in difficulties were the principal reasons the United States Senate refused to ratify the SALT II nuclear-arms limitation treaty signed by President Carter and Mr. Brezhnev in Vienna in June 1979. And they are still bedeviling the current talks in Geneva. What can we do to get negotiations moving again?

When I joined the Army as a kid, the old sarge had a hell of a time getting us slew-foot recruits to march in some decent semblance of order. Once in a while, when things got out of hand, he would order: "Fall out and fall in again!" That's what we have to do with arms-control talks. Time is running out. We need a fresh approach.

On the occasion of receiving the Albert Einstein Peace Prize in Washington in May of 1981, George F. Kennan, the distinguished Soviet-affairs scholar and former Ambassador to the Soviet Union, put forward a proposal that goes to the heart of the problem. Kennan proposed an immediate 50 percent across-the-board reduction in American and Soviet nuclear weapons, "without further wrangling among the experts." Eloquently, he spoke a simple and profound truth: "There is no issue at stake in our political relations with the Soviet Union, no hope, no fear, nothing to which we aspire, nothing we would like to avoid, which could conceivably be worth a nuclear war."

His suggestion has had a strong impact. A Gallup Poll last December showed three out of four Americans backing the idea. There is compelling evidence that public opinion in Western Europe and Japan is strongly in favor of such an approach, and the same appears to be true of public sentiment in the Third World. Yet our policymakers in Washington do not seem to have grasped the proposal's extraordinary promise. They tend to dismiss the notion as simplistic, or impractical, or impossible to negotiate. Some even see danger in any deep cuts, arguing that they might arouse false hopes, or offer opportunities for Soviet propaganda, or tend to destabilize the precarious balance. There is even some flavor of N.I.H. (Not Invented Here) that is many a bureaucrat's instinctive reaction to new ideas in his field.

Yet all these concerns are misplaced. Deep cuts are practical. They can be negotiated, simply because they are in the best interests of both parties. They can be designed to have a stabilizing effect and reduce the risk of nuclear war. Solutions are available to all obstacles, real or imaginary.

Einstein once said that "everything should be made as simple as possible, but not simpler." Kennan's proposal is pretty close to that ideal; the trick now is how to go about it. Let us take a leaf from Grover Cleveland, who said: "The way to begin is to begin." The way to get rid of nuclear weapons is to get rid of nuclear weapons.

Here is the idea. We look for a solution that is fair, that we can verify and that does not get us into fruitless arguments about how different kinds of weapons should be classified. To do this, we have to look at security requirements, the politics of negotiations and the nature of nuclear weapons. Taking these factors into consideration, we find there is a way to bring about arms reduction that satisfies essential concerns on all three counts.

Let each side turn in an equal number of explosive nuclear devices. Let each side choose the weapons it wishes to turn in, whether missile warheads, bombs, or artillery shells. Each weapon would count the same—as one device.

This proposal has some major advantages. A nuclear device is uniquely identifiable and can be counted without error when turned in; thus, there is full verification without intrusive inspection in either country. Since each side chooses the weapons it wishes to turn in, there can be no problem about what is fair. And since all explosive fission devices count equally, we have no arguments about how the weapons should be classified.

Self-interest will make each side turn in its more vulnerable weapons. This is good. As we now stand, both the United States and the Soviet Union have relatively vulnerable land-based strategic missiles, mounted in fixed silos. It would be logical for both sides to start giving up these weapons, while retaining their less vulnerable strategic bombers and virtually invulnerable nuclear-armed submarines. In this way, the temptation of either side to fire first in time of crisis, lest it lose its weapons to an enemy who attacks first, will be reduced. The "hair trigger" character of the nuclear forces, the most dangerous aspect of the present situation, will be eliminated.

Similarly, the missiles on each side that are the more threatening to the adversary's fixed silos—such as the highly accurate, high-yield, multiwarhead Soviet SS-18 and the equally formidable projected American MX—will tend to lose value. They will be deprived of their "counterforce" targets—the land-based strategic missile force of the other side, which they now threaten with destruction in a preemptive first strike. If deep enough cuts are made, the strategies of both sides are likely to revert to reliance on the relatively invulnerable components of their strategic forces. Crisis stability will be improved, and the chances of accidental or unauthorized firing will be greatly reduced.

To whom do we and the Russians hand over these weapons? Probably to a joint Soviet-American commission established for the purpose; perhaps a third party can be brought in as referee. What do you do with the devices? Convert them, under safeguard, to nuclear power for civilian purposes. Uranium 235, one of the elements of nuclear weaponry, can be diluted with the plentiful isotope uranium 238 to a level of concentration suitable for nuclear energy but not for bombs. Plutonium, another such element, can be burned directly in a nuclear power reactor.

We can start by each turning in a relatively small number of weapons— say 50—to test the system and establish confidence. From there, we should proceed on an agreed schedule of a very large reduction—say 10,000 devices each. Again, the idea is to compel each side to choose to retain only a small number of weapons in a strategic reserve.

How will this or some similar proposal satisfy the basic concerns enumerated above?

Let us look first at security. America's primary security need is that the United States, its allies, and the free world not be conquered, coerced, or threatened by the military forces of the Soviet Union and its proxies. Historically, we have relied partly on the deterrent role of nuclear weapons to contain aggression employing conventional arms. The military doctrines of the United States and the North Atlantic Treaty Organization still plug the usefulness of nuclear force against a conventional Soviet attack. But now, with the Soviet Union's strategic forces roughly equal to ours, these doctrines are obsolete. Kennan and three former senior

American officals—Robert S. McNamara, McGeorge Bundy and Gerard C. Smith—hit the nail on the head in their recent article in *Foreign Affairs* urging retreat from our strategy of defending Europe by first use of nuclear weapons: "Deterrence cannot be safely based forever on a doctrine which more and more looks to the people of the alliance like either a bluff or a suicide pact." There is growing recognition that the game is not worth the candle. The security of the United States and its allies must be protected in ways other than with nuclear weapons.

Yet our European allies are torn by conflicting impulses. Their governments, as well as important segments of the political opposition and of public opinion, want the United States to be married to the defense of Europe not only by conventional force but by the threat of nuclear retaliation. Hence the original demand by European leaders for the deployment of American medium-range weapons in Western Europe. At the same time, Europeans entertain the entirely reasonable wish not to be the nuclear battlefield of the giant powers. This wish finds expression in popular demonstrations against deployment of the new American missiles.

Current United States policy also has violently conflicting elements. On the one hand, Presidential Directive 59, issued by Jimmy Carter in 1980, still implies readiness to fight and win a limited nuclear war—as do many previous and subsequent official statements. There is still a green light—and an enormous appropriation—for development of the MX missile, even though the best brains in the country cannot figure out a sensible way to provide it with an invulnerable base. The B-1 bomber program bids fair to waste as much money on an obsolete means of weapons delivery as would be required to modernize, in many respects, the entire United States Army. And the so-called neutron weapon is still in the works, even though it is a battlefield weapon not so different from other nuclear weapons and is clearly regarded by the Russians as offensive and not defensive in nature.

On the other hand, President Reagan himself has expressed a desire for deep cuts. He has also proposed a "zero option" for Europe—no American medium-range weapons in Europe capable of reaching Soviet territory and no Soviet weapons aimed specifically at Western Europe. He has spoken of the overriding need for strategic nuclear talks, though at other times he and his aides have conditioned negotiations on better Soviet behavior.

In any event, the overwhelming logic of the situation, the political imperative being created by the growing revulsion against nuclear arms, dictates movement toward real and deep reductions. There are two major politcal problems yet to be overcome.

First, the primitives in American politics will not be satisfied with anything less than the unattainable—American nuclear "superiority." Why is this unattainable? In the real world, "superiority" has no meaning. We and Russia are like two riverboat gamblers sitting across a green table, each with a gun pointed at the other's belly and each gun on hair trigger. The size of the guns doesn't make much difference; if either weapon is used, both gamblers are dead. In the same way, the size of the nuclear forces makes little difference. States of readiness, targeting decisions, even which way the wind is blowing (carrying nuclear fallout), make a greater difference than a thousand extra missiles on either side.

Moreover, even if having more missiles than Moscow did give us "superiority," the Russians would not stand still for it. They have said they won't and we had better believe them, for in their controlled society they can put into weapons whatever resources they choose. So the argument that we have to attain "superiority" before we can negotiate—an argument still being made in some Administration circles—just won't wash. We are not "inferior" in any meaningful sense, and we are not going to become "superior," no matter how much we ratchet up the nuclear arms race.

The second major political problem in the United States is the notion that we can punish the Soviet Union for its misdeeds—many of them very real—by withholding nuclear arms talks. We cannot use nuclear arms talks as a stick or carrot to make Moscow behave. And if we wait for the Soviet regime to shape up, by our standards, before we engage in nuclear arms reductions, we will wait a long time indeed. The reverse is true: The more our relations turn sour, the more imperative it is to drive down the risk of nuclear war.

What about the Russians? They see themselves, however erroneously, as surrounded by hostile, nuclear-armed powers on their long borders. Their leaders are greatly concerned by any change that would threaten their power, the security of Mother Russia, or the control of the Communist Party. Yet they, too, understand the terrible dangers of nuclear war. Many an official pronouncement and many an unofficial approach testifies to their willingness, even eagerness, to entertain the idea of deep cuts in nuclear weapons.

Soviet spokesmen contend that Soviet doctrine on nuclear war has changed in the past five years, and radically so in the last two. This is what they are saying:

- "To try and outstrip each other in the arms race, or to expect to win a nuclear war is dangerous madness."—Leonid Brezhnev, in a speech before the 26th Congress of the Soviet Communist Party, Feb. 23, 1981.
- "Western politicians and strategists stubbornly push the thesis that Soviet military doctrine allegedly assumes the possibility of an 'initial disarming strike,' of survival, and even of victory, in a nuclear war. All this is a deliberate lie."—Marshal Dmitri F. Ustinov, Minister of Defense, in a speech at a Kremlin rally, Nov. 6, 1981.

- "Political and military doctrines have been changed. This has been reflected in our internal life. There is new determination to seek sharp reductions."—Nikolai N. Inozemtsev, director of the Soviet Institute of World Economy and International Relations, at a Soviet-American seminar in Washington, Jan. 12–14, 1982.

These and other similar statements are accompanied by the interesting assertion that the change of doctrine is recent, that it involved internal political struggle, and that it was resolved by Brezhnev himself. We in the West are invited to note that this change will find expression in Soviet military schools, in military training manuals and elsewhere.

How much can we trust these declarations? Are they not just propaganda, intended to put us to sleep? If I were planning a military campaign, or even betting on the stock market, I would evaluate the downside risk of any given course of action. If we treat these statements as sincere and the Russians are deceiving us, the worst that can happen is that we lose some propaganda points or get otherwise snookered in some inconsequential way during arms negotiations. For no matter what the Russians say, we would never accept an unequal treaty. But if we fail to take these statements seriously—and hence fail to negotiate on arms reductions—we risk getting our heads blown off. It will be little consolation that the Russians will lose theirs also.

But the most compelling reason to take the Soviet authorities seriously on this score has been given by W. Averell Harriman, President Roosevelt's Ambassador to Moscow and, like Kennan, a profound scholar of Soviet affairs: "You *can* trust the Russians—to act in the Russian interest." Our own best minds have come to the conclusion that nuclear war is unwinnable. It would be folly to assume that the Russians are too dumb to have reached the same judgment.

Thus, in measuring the deep-cuts proposal against the security interests of the United States, the West, and the Soviet Union, we find no major obstacles in the way.

Let us look next at whether deep cuts are negotiable—in other words, whether such reductions can be embodied in a treaty that (1) takes account of practical realities, and (2) can be sold to those elements within the American and Soviet societies that dominate the two countries' domestic politics. These are tough criteria, and they can be met only by a treaty that conforms to a strict set of principles.

An acceptable treaty must not only reduce the risk of nuclear war or nuclear blackmail but must be readily seen as achieving those ends. It must not only improve the security of both sides but must do so in ways that each side recognizes as valid for its own concerns. It must be equitable in mutually acceptable ways. The planned reductions must be such as to improve stability in a crisis by cutting down the advantage to be gained by striking first. Most especially, the negotiating parties must not be duplicitous, or strike phony poses, or arouse false hopes or unreasonable expectations.

Fortunately, these principles can be solidly based on the common interest. Neither superpower wishes to be destroyed. Neither wishes to be in the hands of a variety of small powers or terrorist groups. If these overriding concerns can be kept separate from all other issues between Washington and Moscow, fruitful negotiations are almost certain. It is essential, however, that each government give a clear political directive to its negotiators: "Find solutions that remove our joint peril and enhance the security of both."

The third factor—the physical technicalities of deep cuts—presents lesser difficulties. The essence of a nuclear weapon is its fissionable material. All else is mere supporting hardware—missile or cannon or airplane, guidance system or reentry shield or arming and fusing. Moreover, all nuclear weapons have roughly the same amount of fissionable material. In a "small" weapon, the fission element accounts for the weapon's entire explosive yield; in a megaton-range weapon, which depends on fusion, a similar quantity of fissionable material acts only as the spark for the enormously greater succeeding explosion.

Hence, in counting the weapons to be eliminated from the nuclear arsenals of both sides, all weapons can be treated alike. That provides a realistic basis for counting every weapon, no matter what its size, as one nuclear device, and for implementing the cuts by converting the fissionable material to nuclear energy. A desirable, though not essential, corollary to enhancing the effectiveness of weapons disposal would be an agreement to stop manufacturing weapons-grade fission material— both from reactors designed for that purpose and from the spent products of civilian power plants. A stop to production from weapons reactors can be verified by each side with current intelligence techniques. Diversion from nuclear-power reactors is more difficult to monitor, but not impossible.

The effect of deep cuts would be extraordinary. Reductions in the nuclear weaponry of the United States and the Soviet Union would prove the superpowers' willingness to bring the nuclear arms race to a halt. That would produce a much better climate for efforts to limit proliferation of nuclear weapons around the world. Major reductions in the more threatening or more vulnerable systems would enhance stability, thus reducing the probability of nuclear war. Weapons would no longer be available for "war-fighting" strategies, and greater validity would be given to the assurances of national leaders on both sides that their nuclear forces had no objective beyond deterrence. The chances of accidental or unauthorized firings would be greatly diminished.

In all of the above, several things stand clear. Deep cuts are practical. They will enhance the security of the United States, of NATO, of the Soviet Union, of the world. They can be equitable and verifiable. They can be negotiated by the great powers and sold domestically. And there is a straightforward way to begin.

No one can doubt the extreme peril that nuclear weapons pose to civilization on earth. Getting rid of a lot of weapons on both sides will reduce the peril immeasurably. In Leonid Brezhnev's astonishing phrase, "God will not forgive us" if we do not act.

30. Elements of a Programme for Arms Control and Disarmament: The Nuclear Challenge and East-West Relations

Independent Commission on Disarmament and Security Issues

There will be no winner in a nuclear war. The use of nuclear weapons would result in devastation and suffering of a magnitude which would render meaningless any notion of victory. The size of existing nuclear stockpiles and the near certainty of devastating retaliation make it futile and dangerous to consider nuclear war an instrument of national policy. Nuclear war would amount to an unprecedented catastrophe for humanity and suicide for those who resorted to it.

NO VICTORS IN A NUCLEAR WAR

Were they ever to cross the nuclear threshold, nations would be set on a course which does not lend itself to prediction. The very process of destruction would render prior calculations and attempts to exercise control fruitless. We reject any notion of "windows of opportunity" for nuclear war. Any doctrine based on the belief that it may be possible to wage a victorious nuclear war is a dangerous challenge to the prudence and responsibility which must inspire all approaches to international peace and security in the nuclear age. *We conclude that it is impossible to win a nuclear war and dangerous for states to pursue policies or strategies based on the fallacious assumption that a nuclear war might be won.*

NO LIMITED NUCLEAR WAR

The idea of fighting a limited nuclear war is dangerous. Nuclear weapons are not war-fighting weapons. Once the nuclear threshold had been crossed the dynamics of escalation would inexorably propel events towards catastrophe. Doctrines and strategies of limited nuclear war thus carry dangerous connotations. Their acceptance would diminish the fears and perceived risks of nuclear war and blur the distinction between nuclear and "conventional" armed conflict, thus lowering the nuclear threshold.

Even if it is understood that nuclear war cannot be controlled, nations would feel compelled to attempt to limit war should it begin. Paradoxically, preparations for such contingencies, manifested in the acquisition of certain weapons and control systems, can be dangerous to the extent that they may be interpreted as suggesting the possibility of fighting a limited nuclear war as a matter of deliberate policy.

Deterrence cannot be made foolproof. It could collapse in many different ways: because of a technical accident, a human error or miscalculation, the snowballing effect of a local conflict, among others. Nations must guard against these possibilities through cooperative agreements for emergency communications. But they also must abandon doctrines and preparations for fighting limited nuclear war as a matter of deliberate policy.

Nuclear deterrence cannot provide the long-term basis for peace, stability, and equity in international society. It must be replaced by the concept of common security.

The conclusion is therefore inevitably that nuclear weapons must be eliminated. We are fully aware, however, that this can only be achieved through a gradual process which must be initiated by concrete steps.

Reductions and Qualitative Limitations of Nuclear Forces

Nuclear weapons are part of the established reality. The nuclear arms race continues. In a very real sense a nuclear shadow hangs over all political and armed conflicts in the contemporary age. Most disturbing is the development and deployment of weapons which may lead to a lowering of the nuclear threshold with the attendant increased risk of nuclear war. The greatest danger would be for people anywhere to become so used to an open-ended nuclear arms race that they become complacent about the danger involved, or lose faith in their capacity to turn aside the tide. But nations are not condemned to live by the ugly dictates of nuclear weapons. They have the choice and indeed the responsibility to curb and eliminate the horrendous forces of destruction which nuclear weapons represent.

We believe that there is an urgent need for agreements specifying major reductions of nuclear weapons and restraints on their qualitative improvements, with a view to maintaining parity at the lowest possible level of forces. Stabilizing the nuclear arms race in this way could create a basis for further steps in the direction of stopping the production of nuclear weapons and reaching agreement on their eventual elimination. There is a need to create a downward momentum. Nations cannot confine their efforts to managing the existing high levels of armaments. Major reductions and constraints on qualitative "improvements" must be a dominant theme in future negotiations and agreements.

Reductions and Qualitative Limitations
in U.S. and Soviet Strategic Forces

Nuclear deterrence can be but a temporary expedient. It provides no permanent solution to international security. The consequences of failure are too terrifying to leave the system unchanged. The world must break with a system which equates the maintenance of peace with holding millions of human beings and the fruits of their labour as hostages for the good behaviour of the governments of the nuclear weapons states.

The process of strategic arms limitation therefore is indispensable. It is important, too, because it has become a key factor in the relations between the United States and the Soviet Union, affecting the very framework and climate of international relations. The 1972 and 1979 SALT agreements constitute an important beginning; they must be preserved and the process continued to provide a downward spiral in nuclear arms.

Negotiations must be resumed without precondition and further delay. The objective of the negotiations must be twofold: *First, the parties should reaffirm the important limitations and restraints that the SALT II Treaty provides, and agree on any necessary clarifications or adjustments of the treaty in that connection. Second, the parties should seek a follow-on treaty providing for major reductions and qualitative limitations resulting in essential parity at substantially lower and more stable levels of forces. Particular emphasis should be accorded to reductions and qualitative limitations that would reduce fears of a "first strike," an attempt to disarm an opponent or to forestall a possible attack by a preemptive surprise attack. Any new agreement should also contain provisions necessary to assure adequate verification of these reductions and qualitative limitations, and should prohibit deployment of weapon systems which would circumvent agreed limitations and reductions or render verification impossible.*

Successive agreements should point to the eventual elimination of strategic nuclear arms through interim stages that restrict the arsenals of the nuclear weapon states to small, secure strategic forces in consonance with the principle of equal security.

The Anti-Ballistic Missile Treaty Must Be Upheld

The 1972 Treaty Limiting Anti-Ballistic Missile Systems is an important agreement designed to lessen the chance of nuclear war and to constrain the strategic arms race from escalating into broader dimensions. It does not suggest that international peace and security should be based on the ability of the great powers to inflict unacceptable destruction on each other. It does reflect the fact that for the foreseeable future there are no effective means of defending against ballistic missiles. States must coexist, therefore, in a condition of mutual vulnerability, making the pursuit of common security a matter of survival for humanity.

The Anti-Ballistic Missile Treaty is a substantial and necessary building block in a viable system of common security. Abrogation of the Treaty would undermine the whole strategic arms limitation and reduction process. *The failure to uphold the Anti-Ballistic Missile Treaty could lead to a destabilization of the international situation and a greater risk of nuclear war. We urge that the treaty be upheld.*

Parity in Conventional Forces in Europe
Should Be Established at Lower Levels

The major military confrontation between East and West is in Europe and takes place between NATO and the Warsaw Pact. The concentration of military power assembled in Europe is the greatest in history. The Commission recognizes the complex interrelationships which exist among the various elements of the armed forces on both sides, nuclear and conventional, as well as between the force postures of the two alliances. A fair appraisal of the East-West balance of forces on the continent of Europe is extremely complicated. So many aspects of economy, geography, technology, traditions, military organization, and threat perceptions are involved. A comprehensive approach to arms limitation and reductions must be adopted in order to assure approximate military parity at substantially reduced levels and to reduce the risk of nuclear war.

We are convinced that a large-scale conventional war in densely populated Europe would be enormously destructive and in all likelihood would escalate to the nuclear level. It would affect not only the nuclear weapon states or allied states, but also neutral and non-aligned countries. War is not an acceptable option for the resolution of political conflict in the nuclear age. *The armies which are poised against each other in Europe today are much larger than would be necessitated by realistic appraisals of basic security needs. Common security would be enhanced by drastic mutual reductions.*

Since 1973 the two alliances in Europe have been negotiating in Vienna about an agreement on mutual force reductions in Central Europe. They have reached consensus on most of the basic principles that would govern an agreement. It would provide for reductions in two phases leading to equal collective ceilings of 900,000 men, a subceiling of 700,000 for land-force personnel in the reduction area, and associated measures designed to ensure compliance with the provisions of the agreement and to enhance both sides' confidence. The parties have still to agree on what is the number of troops in the reduction area at the present time, the details of the linkage between the two phases of reductions, and the scope of the associated measures. The Commission considers that the outstanding differences could be resolved satisfactorily provided there were the political will to do so. Continued stalemate will seriously diminish public confidence in negotiations for arms reductions. *We urge that the participating states convene a meeting of Foreign Ministers to resolve the differences and conclude an agreement before the end of 1982.*

An agreement specifying parity and reduction of conventional forces in Central Europe should be accompanied by commitments to abstain from moving arms and troops to areas where they would diminish the security of other countries in Europe. Agreement in Vienna on conventional forces in Central Europe would provide a basis for, and facilitate the negotiation of, agreements on withdrawal and reduction of nuclear weapons in Europe. A subsequent agreement on parity of conventional forces in Europe at substantially reduced levels could facilitate more far-reaching agreements on the withdrawal and reduction of nuclear weapons. Such agreements would be more likely if in the negotiations for conventional force reductions the parties were to emphasize reducing those elements of the two sides' military postures which the parties consider the most threatening.

Reducing the Nuclear Threat in Europe

The nuclear arsenals in Europe are awesome. Furthermore, the Commission is deeply concerned about those nuclear postures and doctrines which dangerously and erroneously suggest that it may be possible to fight and "win" a limited nuclear war. In the event of a crisis their effect could be to drive the contending forces across the threshold of a nuclear war. The Commission is convinced that there must be substantial reductions in the nuclear stockpile leading to denuclearization in Europe and eventually to a world free of nuclear weapons. A necessary precondition is a negotiated agreement on substantial mutual force reductions establishing and guaranteeing an approximate parity of conventional forces between the two major alliances.

Therefore, *the Commission supports a negotiated agreement for approximate parity in conventional forces between the two alliances. Such an agreement would facilitate reductions in nuclear weapons and a reordering of the priority now accorded to nuclear arms in military contingency planning.*

The Commission has devoted much time and effort to examining various alternative ways for bringing these changes about.[1] Among the alternatives studied was nuclear-weapon-free zones. It should be remembered in this connection that some countries in Europe do not belong to any of the military alliances and have renounced the acquisition of nuclear arms.

Here we propose a functional approach concentrating on specific weapons and classes of weapon. *Our proposal for the gradual removal of the nuclear threat posed to Europe includes establishment of a battlefield-nuclear-weapon-free zone and measures to strengthen the nuclear threshold and reduce pressures for the early use of nuclear weapons, and substantial reductions in all categories of intermediate- (medium-) and shorter-range nuclear weapons which threaten Europe.*

(a) A battlefield-nuclear-weapon-free zone in Europe. We call special attention to the dangers posed by those nuclear weapons whose delivery

systems are deployed in considerable numbers to forward positions in Europe. These are known as "battlefield" nuclear weapons. A large portion of NATO's and the Warsaw Pact's nuclear munitions in Europe are of this type. The weapons are designed and deployed to provide support to ground forces in direct contact with the forces of the opponent. Their delivery systems have ranges up to 150 kilometers, and are primarily short-range rockets, mines, and artillery. Most of the delivery systems are dual-capable, i.e. they can fire either conventional munitions or nuclear munitions.

Because of their deployment in forward areas battlefield nuclear weapons run the risk of being overrun early in an armed conflict. Maintaining command and control over such weapons in "the fog of war" would be difficult. Pressures for delegation of authority to use nuclear weapons to local commanders and for their early use would be strong. The danger of crossing the nuclear threshold and of further escalation could become acute. It should be remembered in this connection that the areas close to the East-West border in Central Europe are densely populated and contain large industrial concentrations.

The Commission recommends the establishment of a battlefield-nuclear-weapon-free zone, starting with Central Europe and extending ultimately from the northern to the southern flanks of the two alliances. This scheme would be implemented in the context of an agreement on parity and mutual force reductions in Central Europe. No nuclear munitions would be permitted in the zone.[2] Storage sites for nuclear munitions also would be prohibited. Manoeuvres simulating nuclear operations would not be allowed in the zone. Preparations for the emplacement of atomic demolition munitions and storage of such weapons would be prohibited.

There also should be rules governing the presence in the zone of artillery and short-range missiles that could be adapted for both nuclear and conventional use. The geographic definition of the zone should be determined through negotiations, taking into account the relevant circumstances in the areas involved, but for illustrative purposes, a width of 150 kilometres on both sides may be suggested (see Figure 1). Provisions for verifying compliance with these prohibitions would be negotiated. They would have to include a limited number of on-site inspections in the zone on a challenge basis.

The Commission recognizes that nuclear munitions may be brought back to the forward areas in wartime, and that nuclear weapons may be delivered by aircraft and other longer range systems. However, we consider the establishment of the proposed zone an important confidence-building measure which would raise the nuclear threshold and reduce some of the pressures for early use of nuclear weapons. It is consistent with our rejection of limited nuclear war as a matter of deliberate policy.

The agreement for withdrawal of "battlefield" nuclear weapons from the forward zone should be followed by substantial reductions in the

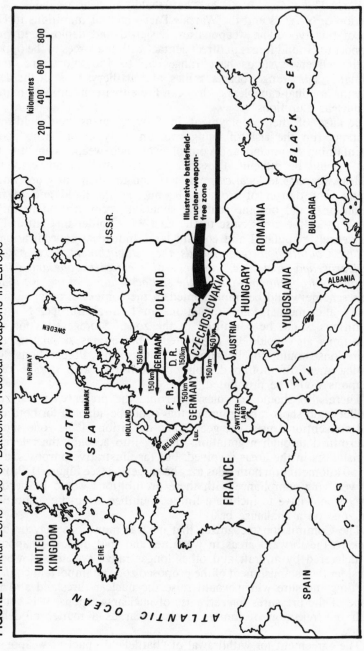

FIGURE 1. Initial Zone Free of Battlefield Nuclear Weapons in Europe

number of nuclear munitions in Europe with adequate measures of verification.

(b) Maintain a clear nuclear threshold. To contain and reduce the danger of nuclear confrontation in Europe it is important to maintain a clear distinction between nuclear and conventional weapons. We urge the nuclear weapon states to abstain from deploying weapons which blur the distinction by appearing to be more "useable." The so-called "mini-nukes" and enhanced radiation (neutron) weapons both fall into this category.[3]

(c) Reduction of intermediate- (medium-) range nuclear weapon systems. The Commission welcomes the opening of negotiations between the United States and the Soviet Union on intermediate-range nuclear weapons and urges the parties to give the search for agreement the highest priority. The competitive deployment of these weapons constitutes a serious blow to political and military stability between East and West, particularly in Europe. *Negotiations should reduce the number of all such weapons to essential parity at the lowest possible level, preferably at a level which would mean that NATO would forgo the introduction of a new generation of intermediate-range missiles in Europe. Furthermore, we call on the parties also to agree to a ban on deployment of new short-range nuclear weapon systems to areas from which they could threaten the same targets which are threatened by intermediate- (medium-) range nuclear weapons.*

In addition to an accord on intermediate-range nuclear weapons in Europe the parties should commit themselves to continue negotiations to limit all other nuclear forces which threaten Europe, including sea-based cruise missiles. All nuclear weapons which are deployed in or against Europe, including French and British forces, should be taken into consideration.[4]

A Chemical-Weapon-Free Zone in Europe

The world may be on the brink of a major new arms race in chemical weaponry. The Commission considers chemical weapons particularly abhorrent, and condemns any use of such inhumane weapons.

Chemical weapons (including contact gasses and nerve agents) fall between, and share some of the characteristics of, both conventional and nuclear warfare. They may be dispensed from munitions adaptable to most types of conventional weapon system. They have indiscriminate and unpredictable effects due to weather. Some can persist, poisoning the environment for a long time. It has been estimated that if chemical weapons were used in densely populated Europe, the ratio of non-combatant to combatant casualties could be as high as twenty to one. Moreover, the use of chemical weapons would blur the distinction between conventional and nuclear warfare. This would increase the danger of one sliding into the other.

Chemical weapon stockpiles include both bulk storage containers for chemical agents from which munitions can be charged, and such munitions as artillery shells, rocket warheads, aerial bombs, and mines already loaded with chemical agents. Since they are highly toxic, special safety precautions are needed during storage and handling. This is why it is generally assumed that chemical weapons are stored in a small number of central depots in Europe. Information about the possible distribution of chemical weapons to troops in the field is both uncertain and contradictory. The development of so-called "binary" munitions, however, could facilitate their distribution. These munitions are filled with two less toxic chemicals which are combined to create a lethal nerve gas only after the munition has been fired.

The Commission calls for the establishment of a chemical-weapon-free zone in Europe, beginning with Central Europe. The agreement would include a declaration of the whereabouts of existing depots and stockpiles in Europe, adequate means to verify their destruction, and procedures for monitoring compliance on a continuing basis, including a few on-site inspections on a challenge basis. The training of troops in the offensive use of chemical weapons also would be prohibited.

Confidence- and Security-Building Measures in Europe

The Commission considers the Final Act of the 1975 Helsinki Conference on Security and Cooperation in Europe and the follow-up process important to the evolution of the security arrangements in Europe. It points beyond confrontation to cooperation and the pursuit of common security. A system of confidence-building measures relating to military manoeuvres has been instituted and adhered to by the participating states. In the follow-up meeting in Madrid, which will reconvene in November 1982, the participating states are negotiating the mandate for a Conference on Disarmament and Confidence and Security Building Measures. *The first phase would be devoted to negotiating agreement on Confidence and Security Building Measures which would apply to all of Europe, contribute to military security, be verifiable, and constitute a binding and lasting commitment. The Commission considers this effort an important contribution to the growth of a system and practice of common security in Europe. The second phase should comprise negotiations for substantial disarmament in Europe.*

NOTES

1. They were the subject of a separate comment by Egon Bahr of the Federal Republic of Germany, omitted here.

2. Georgi Arbatov (USSR) expressed doubts about the arms control value of this proposal as nuclear munitions could be quickly reintroduced into the proscribed area. Such an agreement, which is of small military significance, would be difficult to negotiate, and could create an unfounded impression of enhanced security. In his opinion, other more effective measures are needed—radical reductions up to a complete ban of all medium-range and tactical nuclear weapons. This would amount to a genuine zero-option for Europe.

3. Robert Ford (Canada), David Owen (United Kingdom), and Cyrus Vance (United States) comment as follows on the Commission's recommendations on enhanced radiation weapons: We do not advocate the deployment of such weapons at this time. We consider, however, that both in their asserted benefits for military effectiveness and in their alleged adverse impact on the risk of nuclear war, any incremental effects of enhanced radiation weapons are relatively minor as compared to the basic problems raised by any nuclear weapon. A decision to initiate nuclear war, the most momentous decision any political leader would ever confront, would not be made more easily or more quickly because enhanced radiation weapons, rather than nuclear weapons of older design, were available for use.

4. Joop den Uyl (Netherlands) endorses the proposal of the Commission for the gradual removal of the nuclear threat to Europe. He maintains his conviction that an overall balance of nuclear arms does not require precise parity of nuclear weapons on every level and for every class of weapon. He reaffirms his opposition to the stationing of new nuclear weapon systems in NATO and Warsaw Pact countries.

–––––––– **Questions for Reflection and Discussion** ––––––––

1. Should NATO adopt a no-first-use pledge? Why? Why not? How might such a pledge contribute to a reduction in the threat of nuclear war? What measures to upgrade NATO's defenses might be necessary should NATO forego the first use of nuclear weapons? Would such measures be desirable? What might be their economic and political costs? Who would shoulder the burdens involved? The industrial North? The underdeveloped South?

2. What are the arguments supporting the bilateral freeze? What are the arguments opposing a nuclear freeze *at current force levels*? What are the merits of nuclear parity? What are its potential dangers? If a nuclear freeze were negotiated, how long would it likely withstand pressures generated by technologies offering strategic superiority? If you were a U.S. or Soviet policymaker, how would you verify compliance on the other side? Would you forego indefinitely the opportunity to gain superior military power?

3. Is it possible for the Soviet Union and the United States to make substantial reductions in their nuclear arsenals without jeopardizing their national security? What are Soviet incentives to agree to Kennan's 50 percent reduction proposal? U.S. incentives? What strategic weapon systems would you seek to retain? What are the ramifications of reducing sharply the number of launchers and warheads when counterforce technology is advancing rapidly?

Selected Bibliography

Epstein, William, and Lucy Webster. *We Can Avert A Nuclear War.* Cambridge, MA: Oelgeschlager, Gunn and Hain, 1983.

Ford, Daniel, Henry Kendall, and Steven Nadis, eds. *Beyond the Freeze: The Road to Nuclear Sanity.* Cambridge, MA: Union of Concerned Scientists, 1982.

Forsberg, Randall. "A Bilateral Nuclear-Weapon Freeze." *Scientific American,* Vol. 247, No. 5 (Nov. 1982), pp. 52–61.

Gore, Albert, Jr. "The Fork in the Road." *New Republic,* Vol. 186, No. 18 (May 5, 1982), pp. 13–16.

Johansen, Robert C. *The Disarmament Process: Where to Begin.* New York: Institute for World Order, 1977.

_____ . *Toward a Dependable Peace: A Proposal for an Appropriate Security System.* New York: Institute for World Order, 1978.

Lodal, Jan M. "Finishing Start." *Foreign Policy,* No. 48 (Fall 1982), pp. 66–81.

Noel-Baker, Philip. *The Arms Race: A Programme for World Disarmament.* London: John Calder, 1958.

Ravenal, Earl C. "No First Use: A View from the United States." *Bulletin of the Atomic Scientists,* Vol. 39, No. 4 (April 1983), pp. 11–16.

Sigal, Leon V. "Kennan's Cuts." *Foreign Policy,* No. 44 (Fall 1981), pp. 70–81.

CHAPTER 9

Curbing
the Nuclear Danger

In the preceding chapter, a series of proposals were put forward aimed at the immediate halt of the escalating nuclear weapons spiral. A pledge of no first use, a verifiable bilateral freeze on current nuclear capabilities and planned deployments, substantial reductions in standing nuclear weapons inventories, and significant modification of conventional force postures—these are among the solutions proposed to reverse the current gathering momentum towards nuclear war.

A basic obstacle to the implementation of even these essentially limited measures, however, is the inability of the United States and the USSR to establish a mutually acceptable method of controlling, with confidence, the qualitative—sometimes called "vertical"—aspects of their armaments competition. Under the logic of deterrence, neither super-power is willing to accept strategic vulnerability, neither is willing to forego unilaterally the deployment of weapons yielding a decisive military advantage. For both the Soviet Union and the United States, a secure deterrent posture means unceasing technological vigilance and inno-vation. Thus, finding the means to control military R&D presents a formidable challenge.

Another major dilemma created by nuclear technology—military *and* civilian—is horizontal nuclear proliferation. The worldwide expansion of nuclear power facilities yielding weapons-grade materials and in-creasing access to nuclear weapons technologies and delivery systems, firmly establish a growing potential for a nuclear war outside the superpower context. The number of confirmed nuclear-weapon states currently is small, it is true, but at least a dozen states are believed to possess or to be actively seeking nuclear weapons options at the present time. Regional adversaries, divided by chasmic conflicts of interest, tend to follow the examples set by their mentors, the existing nuclear-weapon states.

The writings in this chapter proceed on the assumption that significant change in the nuclear status quo will not be forthcoming in the absence of effective controls on both vertical and horizontal proliferation, and accordingly they present a number of possible solutions to the problems posed by the refinement and spread of nuclear capabilities. The article by Harvey Brooks begins by recommending a number of bilateral options available to the superpowers to constrain each other's nuclear R&D, to enable each to rely on existing weapons for deterrence purposes, and thus to establish a strategic stasis free of incentives to undertake a first use of nuclear weapons or to launch a first strike. The wide-ranging selection by William C. Potter then addresses the comparative utility of most of the proposed solutions to the accelerating problem of horizontal proliferation. Richard Falk argues that global security and survival cannot be assured without comprehensive—including civilian—denuclearization. And finally, another extract from the 1982 Palme Commission Report provides a broad overview of the measures believed necessary to halt at least the qualitative arms race and to assure worldwide confidence in arms control undertakings.

31. Potentials for Curbing the Qualitative Arms Race

Harvey Brooks

In the past it has often been assumed that limitation of progress in weapons technology was rendered impossible by the difficulties inherent in verifying such limitations, especially in the research and development stage. Thus, arms-control discussions have tended to concentrate on agreements for numerical limitations to the deployment of certain classes of weapons that can be verified with reasonable confidence through unilateral intelligence means. However, even the Partial Test Ban (PTB) was an attempt to limit technological progress in the sense that it was expected, through the prohibition of atmospheric tests, to inhibit the development of high-yield nuclear weapons and to make all weapons testing more costly and thus slow it up. In fact, the PTB did not prove to be as inhibiting as expected. Its main benefit was the reduction of atmospheric contamination. But driving tests underground made them publicly less visible, and thus reduced the pressure of world opinion for further damping the qualitative race in nuclear arms.

The SALT agreements did include a specific prohibition of the testing of certain kinds of ABM components of satellite-based ABM development. Less than complete confidence in verification was accepted in these agreements, which seem to have set a precedent for other possible limitations without insistence on verification. That verification is as much a political as a technical matter, that perfect verification is impossible, and that it is also unnecessary if there is some measure of political trust are also increasingly accepted ideas. The terms of an arms-control agreement are sufficiently interconnected to allow each element to affect the others, and hence not every element has to be verifiable with complete confidence so long as some parts of the agreement can be tested on a sample basis.

Obviously, the closer a weapons system is to deployment the more readily can its progress be verified. The final proof-testing of a weapon, necessary to demonstrate sufficient confidence in its reliability to warrant deployment, is a large, complex process, and it is difficult to conceal. On the other hand, once a weapon has reached that stage, bureaucratic vested interests have usually consolidated to insure its further development, so that ease of verification is offset by greater internal bureaucratic momentum. In what follows, we shall examine a series of proposals, starting with those that aim at inhibiting innovation nearest to the final deployment stage and ending with attempts to limit innovation at earlier stages of the process. The object of all these proposals is to prohibit or retard developments that are politically or militarily destabilizing or that simply add to the costs of maintaining a military posture on both sides without contributing to the security of either.

COMPREHENSIVE NUCLEAR TEST BAN (CTB)

The prohibition of all nuclear testing has been an important aim for arms control from the very beginning. Its importance derives from the belief that no nation will place a new type of weapon in inventory if its properties cannot be realistically tested or its reliability verified by proof testing. It is theoretically possible to develop and deploy a nuclear weapon on the basis of scaled laboratory tests alone, but confidence in the reliability and the characteristics of such a weapon would probably be too low for use in a crisis.

The past obstacles to conversion of the limited test ban treaty of 1963 into a permanent comprehensive test ban (CTB) have been American insistence on the need for on-site inspection for suspected underground nuclear tests and the alleged value of underground nuclear explosions for peaceful purposes, such as large earth works or the stimulation of natural gas sources. On the Soviet side, a desire not to subject itself to limitations not enforceable against the Chinese was probably also an important factor. More generally, neither side was prepared to accept constraints that would decisively impair its subsequent freedom of action. The PTB was acceptable precisely because it contained no real constraint on innovation in nuclear weapons or peaceful uses.

Since 1963, the technology of detection and identification of underground tests by unilateral means has advanced rapidly, more rapidly than most scientists then expected it could. It is now doubtful that significant weapons advances can be made using tests that are small enough to escape detection with certainty. Even if progress could be made with such small tests, reliable warheads would probably not be placed in inventory without conducting many proof and training tests, a few of which are likely to be detected and to provoke suspicions. The non-adherence of other powers to a CTB could be handled by an agreement of finite duration, subject to reopening if a universal ban were not achieved within a specified period of time. Such an interim agreement would probably increase the pressure on all nations to adhere formally to the ban. Unlike the situation in the non-proliferation treaty, the superpowers would be taking the lead in foregoing their freedom of action, as opposed to demanding a forebearance from others that they were unwilling to impose upon themselves.

There is, perhaps, a risk that significant new results achieved in the laboratory would become dammed up, as it were, behind the test ban, and that one power might then denounce the ban and launch an accelerated "testing race" to verify its laboratory findings, thus creating political tensions that might not otherwise have occurred. Such a risk seems worth taking in view of the political benefits of a CTB.

New weapons that might be developed clandestinely under a CTB would principally be very small pinpoint battlefield nuclear types. Indeed, with sufficient improvement in accuracy, such "mininukes" could be used in conjunction with MIRV to threaten land-based missiles and other military targets, with very little collateral civilian damage. On the battlefield, the use of such weapons would tend to blur the threshold between conventional and nuclear war and thus reduce inhibitions against crossing it; this might tend to make nuclear war more likely. The threat to land-based missiles would be similarly destabilizing. On the other hand, it is doubtful that such weapons could ever be decisive in providing military advantages to the side that developed them. Their destabilizing effects would outweigh any contribution they might make in terms of military advantage. Hence one could argue that, to the extent that a CTB made the development of such weapons more difficult and risky, it would be advantageous to world security, while, to the extent that it did not preclude such development, the security of one side or the other would not be seriously jeopardized. In sum, the possibility of the development of "mininukes" provides an additional argument in favor of a CTB.

LIMITATION ON THE NUMBER
OF MISSILE LAUNCHINGS

Experimental launchings are an essential part of missile development and are at the same time readily detectable by unilateral methods, using observation from satellites as well as electronic monitoring of communications and telemetering. In addition, training and confidence missile firings are necessary to keep a weapons inventory in readiness. Therefore, limitation of the number of test firings is a potential means for retarding innovations in missiles that can be verified unilaterally. The limitation that would be most practical to enforce would be one on the total annual number of firings, whether for research and development, proof testing, or training. The difficulty is that the number of launchings permitted would have to be sufficient to allow each side to retain confidence in the readiness of its deterrent, but that this number, if entirely diverted to research purposes, might permit one side to achieve a dangerous technological advantage. Separate limits on confidence firings and on research and development launches would be a preferable alternative, but they would be much harder to enforce because of the difficulties involved in distinguishing experimental from proof launches. For this reason, a limitation on total number of launches, combined either with agreements or with mutual declarations foregoing specific kinds of research, development, testing, and evaluation, would be more practicable.

RESTRICTIONS TO PERMIT INTERNATIONAL
OBSERVATION ON THE LOCATION OF TARGET AREAS

As pointed out by Herbert York,[1] the SALT agreements included a provision for restricting ABM tests to specified test ranges. This stipulation suggests an excellent precedent for a restriction on all kinds of missile testing to specified ranges and for a restriction on down-range impact areas to locations that can be fairly easily observed by other countries, for example, international waters, or land sites close to international boundaries, or coastlines. Such mutually agreed-upon restrictions would improve ability to distinguish between experimental and proof tests, and they might thus make separate limits on the number of such tests more feasible. Furthermore, the SALT agreements have established a precedent for prohibiting interference with unilateral means of observation, either directly or through attempted concealment of certain classes of activities, such as construction of missile silos. The reaffirmation of this concept in the case of missile testing would clearly be desirable.

SPECIFIC PROHIBITION OF POTENTIALLY
DESTABILIZING MISSILE IMPROVEMENTS

*   *   *

Improved missile accuracy is also a potentially destabilizing development which has recently been the subject of a great deal of discussion in the United States. While it would no doubt be desirable to inhibit such improvements, it is very hard to see how this could be done and still maintain confidence on either side that the prohibition is being observed. Improved accuracy is extremely difficult to verify in the observation of proof testing. On the other hand, given the size of present strategic forces, accuracy has no military value so long as the posture on both sides is truly confined to mutual assured destruction. The problem arises when more limited "counterforce" options are included into the overall deterrent posture. The United States is already ahead in this respect, and little would be lost by even an unverifiable agreement to forego further development in such technology.

In principle, mutual recognition of the impact of technological developments on the stability of deterrence might have considerable political value, even in the absence of verifiable restrictions. The major powers could declare their intent not to develop weapons threatening the survivability of the other side's invulnerable retaliatory capability. Such a public declaration by the United States and the Soviet Union could have the salutary effect of forcing communication within each government about every new weapons system and even some of the old ones. It would legitimize, at a very early stage, internal concern about the destabilizing effects of various potential weapons developments. Declarations of this sort would be no different in principle from the declaration of intent in the 1972 Moscow agreements to forego both interference with the unilateral intelligence means of the other side and concealment of strategic weapons. Such a declaration might become the basis, within this country at least, for requiring an "impact statement" for each new major weapons development, analyzing the impact of the proposed system on actual and perceived strategic stability and on international political stability generally.

RESTRICTIONS ON ASW RESEARCH AND DEVELOPMENT

. . . [S]trategic stability is especially sensitive to technological developments that tend to compromise the invulnerability of a sea-based deterrent. This suggests that possible limitations on ASW developments are of special importance in any attempt to inhibit the qualitative arms race. Unfortunately, it is very difficult in practice to distinguish between techniques that threaten the submarine deterrent and those directed at protecting sea communications generally from submarine attackers. In this respect there is a geographic imbalance between China and the Soviet Union, on the one hand, and the Western industrialized nations, on the other. The latter, including Japan, are much more dependent on sea communications, both economically and militarily. The maritime nations will, therefore, be unlikely to forego the development of any ASW technique that would offer protection against submarine attack on commercial shipping or naval forces. Even an ocean-wide surveillance system, designed primarily to monitor and track the opponent's deterrent fleet, would offer considerable incidental protection against submarines deployed to raid shipping. Since the main shipping lanes cover only a small fraction of the oceans over which a deterrent fleet might range, we might try confining surveillance to those vital lanes, leaving large areas of the ocean as "sanctuaries" for missile submarines. This would work most effectively if the surveillance systems were of the "distributed" rather than the "searchlight" type. By a distributed system, we mean an interconnected array of passive or active sonic detectors distributed very widely over the oceans, but with each individual sensor capable of detecting a submarine only within a relatively short range. By a "searchlight" system, we mean a much smaller number of highly sophisticated, directional, long-range sensors capable of detecting submarines and locating them over a very extended geographical area— hundreds or even thousands of miles distant from an individual sensor. The distributed system could be deliberately confined to major shipping lanes, or "corridors," and thus would not threaten the opponent's deterrent force, so long as it avoided those corridors. The searchlight system, however, would cover large sweeps of ocean, and it would thus inevitably detect the opponent's deterrent force as well as its attack submarines threatening the shipping lanes. The problem is that future developments in technology may make searchlight systems considerably less expensive than distributed systems for a given degree of coverage. In addition, all kinds of intermediate configurations between "pure" distributed and "pure" searchlight systems are possible. In practice, it may be difficult to make distinctions between the two kinds of sensor deployment sufficiently convincing to assure an opponent that his strategic forces are invulnerable, so long as they avoid well-defined geographical areas.

Techniques for continuous trailing of submarines might also threaten deterrent forces without being especially useful for the protection of naval or commercial shipping. This is because, in a campaign against attack submarines that threaten shipping, the primary objective is to destroy the submarine immediately after it is detected and located. Since hostilities would then already have begun, there would be no reason to withhold attack once the submarine is positively identified as hostile. But continuous trailing of such submarines without attacking does not add much to the protection of sea communications, and it is, therefore, probably not worth the extra cost. The only advantage of trailing might lie in more secure identification of submarines as hostile. But, for this and other reasons, maintaining the distinction between protection of shipping and threatening the opponent's deterrent forces may be harder to maintain in practice than in theory.

Nevertheless, a declaration foregoing the effort to develop a trailing capability may have considerable political value, especially if coupled with an agreement limiting the construction of attack submarines capable of interdicting sea communications. Such a *quid pro quo* would make for greater symmetry between the "heartland" powers and the maritime nations, and it would make limitations on ASW of a more fundamental sort worthy of serious consideration.[2]

Finally, more searching questions must be raised as to how realistic, under modern conditions, concern about sea communications really is.

The powerlessness of the non-Communist industrial nations in the face of the Arab oil embargo suggests that, in a world as interdependent industrially as ours, sea communications may no longer be the weakest link in maintaining war-fighting capability in a long-drawn-out conflict. At the very least, the traditional arguments for sea power and sea communications need to be carefully restudied in the light of a world economy now radically different in the extent of its interdependence from that which existed at the outbreak of World War II.

THE LIMITATION OF MILITARY BUDGETS

There are two main arguments for limiting military expenditures. The first is that it is the most direct means for slowing the arms race without having to conduct endless technical bargaining over the equivalence of specific weapons systems. The second is that the resources thus saved could then be devoted to the solution of other basic international problems. Indeed, to the extent that military expenditures divert the world's resources from economic development, they become major contributors to world political instability, quite apart from the more direct effects of the "toys" on which the money is spent.

Two ways of approaching reduction of military budgets are: (1) reduction of the total military budget by mutual agreement of the superpowers (with the intention also of constricting military research and development); or (2) direct reduction of military research and development budgets only. Either of these methods presents problems because a great deal of military-related research is supported from outside the formal military budget. In this country, the AEC and NASA budgets include a large military component, and some military research and development is probably hidden in other appropriations (*vide* recently highly publicized technological expenditures of the CIA). Early exploratory research is especially easy to bootleg under other categories of expenditure. In the Soviet Union a great deal of military research is apparently part of the "science budget," and it is not included in reports of military expenditure.

Another difficulty is that what we call "test and evaluation" and what the Russians call "assimilation into production" are excluded from research and development in the Soviet system, though included as such in American expenditures. On the other hand, a considerable amount of "independent R&D" by industry in this country is not treated as military, although it is indirectly financed out of military procurement appropriations. There are also important differences in the cost factors for military research and procurement between the United States and the Soviet Union, so that direct comparison of any military budget is exceedingly difficult. Although salaries of technical personnel are lower in the Soviet Union, the rate of "productivity" in technical work is almost certainly much lower as well. For example, the Russians lack a high quality instrument industry, with the result that much experimental equipment is made and maintained by individual scientists.

Nevertheless, even recognizing these difficulties, the possibilities of mutually agreed limitations in military budgets should not be dismissed completely, especially if they could be coupled with agreements to deploy the skilled manpower thus released for some more beneficial purpose, such as the development of new energy resources related to world development.

DEMOBILIZATION OF MANPOWER AND FACILITIES DEVOTED TO MILITARY RESEARCH AND DEVELOPMENT

[Herbert] York[3] has proposed a plan for the gradual removal of secrecy from research, so that scientific findings may ultimately be redirected to other purposes, and he cites the conversion of the Fort Detrick biological-warfare facility to cancer and related biological research as a precedent for what might be achieved on a larger scale in other areas of military-related technology. He proposes the annual transfer of five to ten percent of the people now working on secret projects to "non-secret projects conducted in open facilities." Since this would result in a much more rapid increase in non-secret publishable research than could be accomplished through the normal growth of the scientific community, the transfers could be readily monitored, especially if the United States and the Soviet Union would also agree to an exchange of statistics on scientific and technical personnel, including the occupations and organizational affiliations of new university graduates.

There is no question that secrecy in research has contributed greatly to the mutual suspicions and the apprehensions about "technological surprise" that have characterized so much Cold War thinking. The monitoring of the transfer proposed by York would be facilitated by the natural inclinations of scientists and engineers to disseminate their work among their peers and thus gain public credit for priority in discovery or invention. It might even be possible to organize official international meetings dealing with military technology, its progress, and the assessment of its broader effects and socio-political implications. Eventually an authoritative public literature on military technology might appear open to criticism and evaluation by the international technological community.[4]

This greater openness in military technology may not only reduce apprehensions about "technical surprise," but also make it more difficult for the "hawkish" experts in any country to use selective release of information about an opponent's technical capabilities as an argument for large new weapons programs. On the other hand, too much publicity may stimulate irresponsible "gadgeteering" and unreasonable public fears about weapons possibilities that are in fact impractical.

There are also those who would argue that secrecy encourages inefficiency and "boondoggling" with resources that might be used much more effectively if the public were really privy to what was going on. While this is certainly a possibility, we believe that the advantages of publicity and open criticism outweigh the dangers of accelerated progress in politically perilous directions.

UNILATERAL ACTION OF SCIENTISTS AS A WORLDWIDE COMMUNITY TO WITHHOLD THEIR SERVICES FROM MILITARY RESEARCH AND DEVELOPMENT

It has been argued that, were scientists simply to refuse to participate in military research, the qualitative arms race could be slowed and the "technological imperative," which drives advances in military technology, could be dampened. A frequent proposal has been for a kind of Hippocratic Oath of scientists (and presumably also engineers) not to engage knowingly in research whose purpose is to facilitate the destruction of human life or the injury of fellow human beings.[5] Another similar proposal is for a professional "codes of ethics" among scientists, which would be made prerequisite to membership in a professional society and would necessarily be combined with some licensing system. Sanctions could then be applied, after the manner of disbarment proceedings in medicine or law, which would effectively prevent individuals who violated the code from earning a living in their profession. Still other proposals have included forms of strike or boycott against organizations engaged in military research. These, however, are effective weapons only if the decision of a majority of members of an occupational group can be enforced on the entire membership. They are ineffective unless employment in a profession can be given some attribute that the entire group can benefit from collectively, or not at all.

Perhaps the most obvious point to be made in connection with all these suggestions is that, to be effective, they would have to involve sanctions against individuals that could reach across national lines. A code of ethics enforced effectively in one nation and not in another would not much inhibit military technological progress, and it could well lead to alterations in the military balance that would increase rather than decrease the likelihood of conflict. It would also be enforceable only in a world already largely disarmed, i.e., in which the overwhelming number of technical people were engaged in non-military research. At present, one quarter of all technologists derive some support for their work, if not their livelihood, from military research, and—in the absence of realistic employment alternatives for these people—the code-of-ethics idea does not appear very practical. A partial adoption of such a code would only tend to isolate military scientists from the moral climate of the majority of their fellow professionals, thus making military development less rather than more sensitive to broader human implications.

A second and perhaps more fundamental point is that the distinction between "good" and "bad" research is much more difficult to draw in practice than the simplifications required for collective action can accommodate. Except in the final stages of development, most technical progress has manifold implications. Furthermore, so long as the use of force or the threat of force is an accepted instrument of international politics or domestic security, the line between "good" and "bad" research will remain obscure. Is it evil to work on temporarily disabling chemicals when the alternative may be thoroughly lethal bullets? By what logic is tear gas a legitimate police weapon in domestic disorders, but an illegal weapon in international conflict? If the use of conventional air-dropped bombs is a legitimate form of warfare, is research directed toward improving their ability to discriminate more accurately between military and non-military targets to be regarded as aimed at the destruction of human life or at its protection? Is research directed at improving intelligence gathering about military matters stabilizing or destabilizing? Will research on body armor for infantry and police be condemned or condoned by a "Hippocratic oath"? What is the moral status of research directed at better care of war casualties? These examples just begin to indicate the complexity of the issues. Codes of ethics usually break down when applied to such complex moral questions, as we already know from modern medical practice.

One could, of course, take the position that any research whose results are likely to be used primarily in a military setting is morally suspect because its ultimate purpose is to facilitate the killing or injuring of fellow human beings. One could even argue in favor of allowing military action to become *more* lethal for the sake of making force ultimately less acceptable as a means for settling political conflict. Such subtleties, however, do not lend themselves to the kind of universal moral consensus essential to the enforcement of a professional code of ethics.

The final argument is essentially a political one. If the majority in a nation decides that a certain course of action is legitimate and desirable, does some small group have the right or duty to withhold its special skills as a means of enforcing its own political value judgments on the majority? Most of us would agree, I think, that the *individual* has the right and duty to follow the dictates of his own conscience, and that he should be afforded some protection by society in doing so. However, in an organization where the views of a majority are enforced on all members and in a situation where membership is a precondition for practicing one's profession, the problem becomes more complicated. For then one is opening up the possibility that national policy will be determined not by a majority of citizens, but by, for example, a majority of physicists or electrical engineers. Is this compatible with a democratic polity?

So long as war and preparation for the possibility of war are generally regarded as legitimate, if regrettable, national activities, it is difficult to see how collective unilateral action on the part of selected occupational groups can be either effective or politically legitimate. However, an entirely different situation would obtain with respect to activities that had been outlawed by mutual agreement of governments. Once agreements have been reached to prohibit or limit certain kinds of research, collective actions of scientists or engineers can become a legitimate and useful tool in enforcing their observation by organizations. Under such circumstances, it might even be legitimate for the majority in a professional group to enforce its views on a minority, if the action thus enforced prevents, for example, the violation of a treaty.

REORGANIZING RESEARCH AND DEVELOPMENT TO MINIMIZE THE "TECHNOLOGICAL IMPERATIVE"

It is frequently argued that the organization of military research in the United States creates irresistible pressures to get the resulting hardware into production, often without adequate public debate as to its full implications. (There are indications that similar kinds of pressures exist in the Soviet Union.) For one thing, the Congress is often reluctant to appropriate research funds without specific plans for a weapons system, thus precluding research to generate options from which to select. Too often development is treated as part of a rational process in which the final result should be fully defined in advance.[6] Research in industry is also funded with the strong expectation that the results will be converted into an operational weapons system. Furthermore, in a period when force levels are relatively stable, service technical organizations and their industrial clients can guarantee their own survival only by generating a continual stream of qualitative improvements to make existing deployments obsolete. This tends to be the case even though, in fact, the majority of systems undergo some development, but never reach operational deployment. The system also tends to favor "product differentiation" for its own sake, much as in other sectors of the industrial economy. Research and development that do not lead to a deployed system are looked upon as failures and a waste of resources; little value is attached in practice to the knowledge gained in a project, if there are no tangible results.

This process is driven by a "military requirements" system that is partly based on fiction. Experience has taught the military technical community that it is much easier to sell interesting research if it can be pushed as a fully conceptualized weapons system meeting a well-defined military requirement based on a well-established threat from a postulated opponent. In practice, both the threat and the requirement may have been invented to provide a rationale for a development program started for other reasons, such as to perpetuate existing organizations, or to exploit a "sweet" technical concept.

*   *   *

A system that has passed successfully through the advanced development stage is seldom canceled, at least overtly, through reconsideration of an established military requirement; it would be too great an admission of failure on the highest policy level. Therefore, the justification for cancellation or redirection or a large weapons system must appear to be made on technical or economic grounds. This does not mean that the history of military development is not strewn with the skeletons of canceled systems. . . . But the tragedy is that they were canceled for reasons that in most instances could have been foreseen when the original requirements were established, although the cancellation may have been publicly justified on other grounds. Still others were carried to the hardware stage, not because they were needed but simply because there was no valid cost overrun or technical justification for canceling them.

*   *   *

Military research also leads to premature and useless development of many components of a system. In the nuclear aircraft program, for example, a great deal of effort went into development and acquisition of non-nuclear and rather conventional hardware before sufficient research had been done to determine the feasibility of making a nuclear fuel element that would meet the original performance specifications. Many of these components had to be scrapped as the system specifications were progressively adjusted downward to meet the reduced capabilities of the feasible fuel element. The histories of TFX . . . and several other celebrated military white elephants provide similar examples. Yet development even of these less critical components created pressure to go forward with the entire system, even in the face of other technical failures or a reconsideration of policy.

*   *   *

Criticism of defense procurement tends to focus on the "military-industrial complex" and its dynamic role in generating "planned obsolescence" in weapons systems. Without question, the symbiosis between the technical bureaucracies in the Pentagon, contractor-technical personnel, and the Armed Services committees of the Congress (usually from districts heavily benefited by defense procurement) has been a factor in the continuing preference for new weapons. However, it is not so clear that the problem could be avoided by returning to the government arsenal system, or to the treatment of the defense industry as a regulated monopoly, as has sometimes been proposed. Recent attempts to shut down obsolete military bases suggest that it is considerably harder to close a purely governmental operation than it is to cancel a large contract with a private firm, even when equally large local labor forces are involved. Ownership or control of the military-industral complex does not in itself appear to be a crucial factor in making military development more responsive to broader policy guidance or to arms-control considerations.

CONCLUSION

To summarize, the most promising lines of action for controlling the qualitative arms race probably lie in mutually agreed limitations on testing, including limits on the number of permissible missile launches, and on a comprehensive nuclear-test ban. Agreements to refrain from research are often difficult to monitor, though they may have considerable value if accompanied by well-publicized commitments to refrain from actions that would jeopardize the stability of mutual deterrence. In fact, such general declarations may be more useful than attempts to negotiate highly detailed prohibitions, since they can shift the balance of the internal bureaucratic debate on whether to go forward with a given weapons development. The ban in the ABM treaty on the testing of exotic ABM techniques in space provided a precedent, though it fell short of clearly limiting research and development. Attempts at unilateral action by professional groups, such as "codes of ethics" forbidding participation in research aimed at injury to or destruction of human life, are likely to be ineffective because of the ambiguity and lack of consensus regarding what constitutes "good" and "bad" research. However, professional self-discipline that is legitimized by official mutual weapons-control declarations provides some hope.

NOTES

1. H. York, "Some Possible Measures for Slowing the Qualitative Arms Race," *Proceedings of the 22nd Pugwash Conference on Science and World Affairs*, Oxford, England, September 7–12, 1972 (Oxford, 1973), pp. 228–235.

2. H. Brooks, "The Political Interaction Between Tactical and Strategic ASW," C. Tsipis, A. H. Cahn, and B. T. Feld, eds., *The Future of the Sea-Based Deterrent* (Cambridge, Mass., 1973), pp. 79–86.

3. York, op. cit., p. 232.

4. An approach to what we have in mind is exemplified by D. G. Hoag, "Ballistic Missile Guidance," in Feld, Greenwood, Rathjens, and Wienberg, eds., *Impact of New Technologies on the Arms Race* (Cambridge, Mass., 1971), a reader/text that was the product of a privately sponsored international conference held at Wingspread, Wisconsin, on the implications of new technology for the future of the arms race.

5. *Physics Today*, March 1970, p. 67.

6. H. Brooks, "Applied Research: Definitions, Concepts, Themes," in *Applied Science and Technological Progress*, a report to the U.S. House of Representatives by the National Academy of Sciences (GPO, Washington, D.C., June 1967), pp. 21–56; also H. Brooks, *The Government of Science* (Cambridge, Mass., 1968), pp. 279–332.

32. Strategies for Control

William C. Potter

Many strategies have been proposed to deal with the phenomenon of nuclear proliferation. Most can be distinguished in terms of their emphasis on affecting the *demand* for versus the *supply* of weapons. Demand-oriented approaches are intended to reduce the incentives and strengthen the disincentives of a party to acquire nuclear weapons. They include such "political-fix" strategies as security and fuel supply guarantees, conventional arms transfers, and sanctions, and arms control measures such as nuclear-free zones and a comprehensive test ban. Supply-oriented approaches, on the other hand, are designed to make it more difficult for a party seeking nuclear weapons to obtain them. Representative of this approach to nonproliferation are "technological fixes" (including export restrictions on sensitive technologies and safer fuel cycles) and international and domestic safeguards.

The general characteristics and strengths and weaknesses of these approaches are discussed below. An effort is then made to assess their relative utility with respect to several possible proliferation developments.

DEMAND POLICIES

Reducing Incentives

International security concerns represent the principal nuclear incentives for many states. . . . Among the most frequently proposed strategies to reduce security incentives to acquire nuclear weapons are the provision of conventional arms substitutes and the extension of superpower security guarantees.

1. Arms Transfers. The proposal to use non-nuclear arms transfers as an instrument of nonproliferation policy is founded on the premise that states sufficiently equipped with conventional arms will gain confidence in their ability to defend themselves and will consequently have less reason to covet nuclear arms. Advocates of this approach can point to recent breakthroughs in conventional weapons technology providing increased accuracy and firepower which may enable advanced conventional weapons to assume certain military missions previously reserved for nuclear arms.[1]

The applicability of the arms transfer approach to nonproliferation to specific *N*th countries is the subject of considerable debate. Among the states most frequently mentioned as possible targets for a selective arms transfer strategy are Taiwan, South Korea, Pakistan, and Israel.[2]

For these and other countries, however, the goal of nonproliferation may come into conflict with other foreign policy objectives, including that of limiting regional arms races. The tension between the dual arms control goals of containing nuclear proliferation and slowing conventional arms transfers has been called the "dove's dilemma."[3]

The use of conventional arms as a nonproliferation tactic entails a number of risks. One of the most significant is the possibility that an influx of arms will increase regional instability by emboldening the recipient to assume a more belligerent posture and/or encouraging the recipient's adversary to escalate the arms race (perhaps even to the nuclear level) or to strike preemptively before the military balance has been changed.[4] Arms transfers also run the risk of exacerbating the supplier's relations with other countries in the region without necessarily satiating the recipient's appetite for nuclear arms.[5] This latter point is emphasized by Richard Betts, who argues that arms aid does not erase the attractiveness of nuclear weapons as an autonomous deterrent for a state with international security fears that is "dependent on foreign arms suppliers who retain leverage through the option to stop resupply in a crisis or embargo spare parts and cripple maintenance."[6] The possibility exists, moreover, that even if security pressures were reduced by arms transfers, other compelling proliferation incentives would remain.[7] There is also the risk that although the leaders of proliferation-prone countries may accept the logic of the arms transfers-nonproliferation linkage and the implied dependence, they may not be able to fulfill their end of the bargain because of domestic politics and intragovernmental opposition.[8]

Perhaps the most serious deficiency of most proposals to use arms transfers as an instrument of nonproliferation policy is the tendency to focus on narrow considerations of one Nth country's security dilemma in isolation from broader regional and international political issues. For example, as one perceptive analyst points out, "most of the restraints on the potential use of arms transfers to ease proliferation pressures in Taiwan, South Korea, Pakistan, and South Africa result from U.S. policy goals rather than a desire to limit arms sales or aid."[9] In Taiwan, this is a concern for normalization of relations with the PRC; in South Korea, this is (or at least was until recently) the desire for a general reduction in the American presence in Asia; in Pakistan, this is the desire to avoid upsetting the South Asian balance by estranging India, the preeminent power; and in South Africa, this is (or again, until recently, was) the U.S. commitment to support the international arms embargo and the search for better relations with the black African nations.[10]

The preceding discussion of the risks of transferring arms as an instrument of nonproliferation policy does not point to a resolution of the dove's dilemma. Although the risks associated with arms transfers are certainly great, they may still be preferable to the introduction of nuclear weapons into a conflict-prone region.[11] Before a determination of these relative risks can be made, it is essential, at a minimum, that an analysis is undertaken of: (1) the Nth country's security perceptions and incentives to go nuclear; (2) its conventional defense capabilities and the impact arms transfers will have on them; and (3) its near-term capabilities to acquire nuclear weapons.[12] Unless a judgment can be made that the Nth country's proliferation incentives are principally security-related, can be alleviated by the infusion of more arms, and can be translated into an operational nuclear weapons capability, an arms transfer nonproliferation strategy is apt to entail great risks but holds little prospect of success.

2. Security Guarantees. Another approach to reducing the security incentives of potential proliferators, often discussed in conjunction with the provision of arms transfers, is the extension of security guarantees by one or more of the nuclear weapons states. These guarantees may be in the form of the deployment in the Nth country of the guarantor's troops, military facilities, and weaponry (including nuclear arms and their delivery vehicles), formal alliances which provide explicit binding guarantees, or less formal commitments to ensure the territorial integrity of the Nth country.

Illustrative of the first form of security guarantee is the deployment in South Korea of U.S. troops and military facilities. These deployments are designed not only to bolster the host country's military capability, but to strengthen the credibility of the formal U.S. security commitment by providing a "tripwire" which increases the likelihood of American involvement should an attack occur. The extension of the American nuclear umbrella to Western Europe and Canada through NATO, the comparable Soviet nuclear guarantee to its Warsaw Pact allies, and the U.S. mutual assistance treaty with Japan are other examples of formal security assurances. A less formal but nevertheless firm pledge is the American commitment to the survival of Israel.[13]

The success of security guarantees, from a nonproliferation standpoint, has been mixed. On the one hand, security assurances from nuclear powers have been a prerequisite for the willingness of many states to adhere to the NPT and to justify their decisions in the face of domestic opposition.[14] Security guarantees appear to have been especially important for such isolated and insecure NPT parties as South Korea and Taiwan. Firm, if not formal, U.S. security assurances, on the other hand, have not kept Israel from moving to the threshold of nuclear weapons status. The formal American security commitment to Pakistan also has proved ineffective as a deterrent to the Pakistani quest for nuclear weapons.[15] American nuclear guarantees and the NATO umbrella, moreover, failed to deter Great Britain and France from developing their own nuclear arsenal.

Although the nonproliferation strategy of security guarantees may be successful in specific situations, the general applicability of the approach is constrained by a number of factors. Among the most important are the reluctance of potential guarantors to extend security guarantees that may entangle them in the Nth country's foreign and domestic policy problems and the unwillingness of many Nth countries to accept security guarantees if they entail the loss of control of certain aspects of their own domestic and external policies.[16] The utility of security guarantees may also be compromised if they are directed against other allies or states with whom the prospective guarantor seeks improved relations.[17] At the end of 1979, for example, the United States judged it necessary to terminate its defense treaty with the Republic of China in the interest of improving relations with Mainland China.

The difficulty of providing credible security guarantees should also be mentioned. Credibility is not something that can be produced by a treaty signature or solemn pledge. It results instead from past performance and the perception of strong and enduring common interests.[18]

Finally, the use of security guarantees as an instrument of nonproliferation policy is subject to two caveats made previously with respect to conventional arms transfers: (1) security-oriented approaches are irrelevant for Nth countries whose primary motives for acquiring nuclear weapons are international prestige, the assertion of autonomy and influence, technological momentum, or domestic politics; and (2) security guarantees must not be viewed in isolation from broader foreign policy objectives, some of which may be at odds with the extension of security commitments.

It occasionally has been proposed that the nuclear powers jointly guarantee the security of states which renounce nuclear weapons. Some non-nuclear countries, in fact, sought this kind of assurance during the negotiations preceding the NPT.[19] The most that has been achieved in the form of joint obligations, however, is very limited. It consists of the nonspecific reference in the NPT preamble to the obligation of states under the UN Charter to refrain from the threat or use of force and a security guarantee to non-nuclear weapon state parties to the NPT by the depository governments of the NPT (i.e., the U.S., the USSR, and the UK) in the form of UN Security Council Resolution 255.[20] This latter pledge is generally regarded as meaningless since it provides that assistance to any non-nuclear nation threatened with nuclear aggression will be given in accordance with the UN Charter, that is, through the Security Council where each of the guarantors, as well as France and China, has a veto.

3. Arms Control Measures. International and regional arms control measures represent another approach to reducing proliferation incentives. They tend to be directed at both the security and prestige motivations of potential proliferators and to emphasize the obligations of the nuclear powers under Article VI of the NPT to work for a cessation of the nuclear arms race at an early date and for nuclear disarmament.[21] Among

the more frequently proposed arms control measures are adoption of a comprehensive test ban and creation of nuclear-free zones.[22]

Proponents of a comprehensive test ban (CTB) cite both political and technical reasons why the complete cessation of nuclear weapons testing would serve the cause of nonproliferation.[23] Politically, they argue, a CTB would reduce the incentives for present non-nuclear weapons states to acquire nuclear weapons by demonstrating the nuclear powers' commitment to Article VI of the NPT (pursuit of "negotiations in good faith on effective measures relating to the cessation of the nuclear arms race at an early date"). Failure to make progress on the CTB front, it is argued, underscores the discriminatory aspect of the NPT and undermines the effectiveness of the nonproliferation regime.[24] The technical argument is more straightforward and simply notes that "non-nuclear nations could not with confidence develop a nuclear explosive without nuclear testing." A corollary of this technical argument is that in the absence of testing, design of an explosive would have to be more conservative and would require more fissionable material per weapon.[25]

Those who oppose a CTB generally maintain that there is little, if any, connection between the arms race behavior of the superpowers and nonproliferation; in addition, they cite a litany of perceived adverse effects likely to accompany a comprehensive test ban.[26] This list includes: difficulties in verifying Soviet compliance with a CTB; problems of assuring the reliability of existing nuclear weapons without an ongoing test program; the need to make weapons safer and more secure against accidents and misuse; the need to study the effects of nuclear explosives (e.g., in designing a ballistic missile defense system); the potential peaceful uses of nuclear explosives; the danger of losing trained personnel; and the problem of nuclear powers who refuse to take part in test ban negotiations.[27]

It is not possible here to examine in detail the competing charges of proponents and critics of a CTB. This task is performed admirably by Barry Blechman, Dan Caldwell, and Sidney Drell, who argue persuasively that many of the critics' charges are not well founded.[28] More relevant to our discussion is the fact that regardless of the merits of the critics' charges, few respond to the contentions of CTB proponents or pertain directly to the relationship of a CTB nonproliferation. Indeed, there is much to Dan Caldwell's observation that "neither the claims of the ardent proponents not the dire predictions of the hard-line opponents accurately depict the most likely effect that a comprehensive test ban would have on proliferation [i.e., very little.] In all probability the 'near nuclear states' would remain ambiguously non-nuclear."[29]

If one assumes that a CTB would not affect those near-nuclear states such as Israel, South Africa, and Pakistan, its major promise lies in making the superpowers' call for nuclear restraint more credible to other states, thereby reducing at least the political excuse, if not the primary incentive, for some nations to pursue a nuclear weapons program.[30] For those parties that signed, the CTB would also raise the political costs of "going nuclear."

Nuclear-free zones constitute another arms control approach to strengthening the NPT regime. Unlike the CTB negotiations that the superpowers dominated,[31] most nuclear-free zone proposals have been initiated by the non-nuclear weapon states of the region concerned. Although the immediate impetus for nuclear-free zone proposals vary from region to region, proposals tend to share the general objective of promoting regional peace and stability and the more specific goal of removing the region from the sphere of competition and confrontation between current nuclear weapon states.[32]

The idea of strengthening regional security by establishing geographical zones in which nuclear weapons would be prohibited grew out of the German question in the 1950s and first found formal expression in the so-called Rapacki Plan to denuclearize Central Europe.[33] Subsequent proposals have been made for the denuclearization of the Middle East, the Mediterranean, the Nordic countries, South Asia, Africa, the Balkans, and the Indian Ocean.[34] The approach was also reflected in the Antarctic Treaty of 1959, the Outer Space Treaty of 1967, and the Seabed Treaty of 1971.[35] The most significant nuclear-free zone in existence and the only one to affect a major inhabited region applies to Latin America under the Treaty for the Prohibition of Nuclear Weapons in Latin America, commonly known as the Treaty of Tlatelolco. The current status of the Tlatelolco regime and nonproliferation in Latin America illustrates both the potential and the problems of a nuclear-free zone approach to nonproliferation.

Under the terms of the Treaty of Tlatelolco, open for signature in 1967 and currently in force for twenty-two Latin American states, parties pledge to keep their territories entirely free of nuclear weapons. The treaty also established an international agency to ensure compliance with the accord and a control system that includes the application of IAEA safeguards to all nuclear activities of the contracting parties.[36] The significance of this nonproliferation measure, sometimes viewed as a model for other regions, is mainly diluted by the absence as full parties to the treaty of the two countries generally regarded as the region's prime proliferation candidates, Argentina and Brazil.[37] Their abstinence tends to obscure the presence of three full parties to the treaty who have not ratified the NPT (Columbia, Barbados, and Trinidad and Tobago).

The major problems which have prevented the Tlatelolco Treaty from fully achieving its nonproliferation objective involve the issue of peaceful nuclear explosions (PNEs) and superpower attitudes. The PNE issue is complicated by the ambiguous language of the treaty, which in Article 18 speaks favorably of PNEs but stipulates in Article 5 that such explosives "appropriate for use for warlike purposes" are prohibited. Although most Latin American states have interpreted the treaty as not permitting indigenously produced PNEs, this interpretation has not been shared by Argentina and Brazil and is advanced as a major justification for their failure to adhere to the treaty.[38] Although the Brazilian position on PNEs has recently become more flexible, that of Argentina remains unaltered and is founded on the argument that the key factor distinguishing a PNE from a weapon is the intent of the user.[39] Argentine officials, moreover, cite the PNE issue as a prime example of a modification of the rights of Tlatelolco parties by nuclear weapon states.[40]

The issue of superpower attitudes is highlighted by two protocols to the treaty which: (1) require states having territorial interests in the region affected by the treaty to keep their possessions free of nuclear weapons; and (2) seek pledges by nuclear weapon states "not to use or threaten to use nuclear weapons" against the full parties of the treaty. The United States, the Soviet Union, Great Britain, France, and China have ratified Protocol II dealing with the "no first-use" pledge.[41] The United States and France, however, have yet to ratify Protocol I.[42] U.S. failure to ratify the protocol appears to be due more to domestic political concerns (about the brouhaha which might result if U.S. nuclear prerogatives for Puerto Rico, the Virgin Islands, and Guantanamo were surrendered) than to international strategic considerations. It is therefore significant that in his first major statement on nonproliferation President Reagan announced that he would promptly seek the Senate's advice and consent to ratify Protocol I.[43]

It is difficult to judge the applicability of the Tlatelolco experience to other regions. Progress toward the Latin American nuclear-weapon-free zone was certainly facilitated by the coincidence of a number of circumstances. John Redick includes among these: (1) the establishment of a legal instrument in advance of military-technological momentum (i.e., nuclear technology was not well established in Latin America in the 1960s); (2) the strong leadership and tenacity of Mexican Under-Secretary Garcia Robles; (3) the stimulus of the Cuban missile crisis in October 1962 (at which time the initial proposal for the Latin American nuclear-free zone was introduced); (4) the shared cultural and legal traditions of the region, as well as commonly held perceptions of a regional identity; and (5) the relative absence of superpower competition in the region.[44]

It is unlikely that the entire set of circumstances noted by Redick will be duplicated, although a number of the conditions may be found elsewhere. Perhaps most difficult to obtain will be a region relatively free of superpower competition and confrontation. The slow but steady progress toward completion of the Treaty of Tlatelolco system, nevertheless, suggests the possibility of success for a nuclear-free zone if it enjoys the general support of the states in the region concerned, is based on a genuine search for a common interest, and does not significantly alter the regional balance of power.[45]

4. Fuel Supply Assurances. So far our discussion of "demand policies" and means to reduce proliferation incentives has focused on considerations of international security. Although insecurity appears to be the dominant motive for the majority of states intent on the acquisition of nuclear weapons, a number of nonproliferation approaches focus on alternative motivations. One that has received considerable attention (especially after the 1974 Indian nuclear explosion) and is designed primarily to reduce incentives for premature use of plutonium and the development of nationally controlled sensitive technologies is the provision of nuclear fuel supply assurances.

Although there is little evidence that considerations of fuel supply assurances have, to date, had much bearing on national decisions to go or to refrain from going nuclear, the concept of assured supply has been fundamental to the nonproliferation regime that has evolved since the mid-1950s. The logic underlying the strategy of assured supply is clearly presented in a recent report of the Atlantic Council's Nuclear Fuels Policy Working Group:

Supply alone, on an *ad hoc* basis, unaccompanied by assurances of its dependability on reasonable terms, would not have had the intended deterrent effect on the development of independent and potentially uncontrolled sources of nuclear materials and equipment. In normal markets, this assurance is supplied largely by the traditions of the market itself, and the self-interest of the supplier in maintaining his profitable supply arrangements. In the case of nuclear materials and equipment, the security sensitivity of the products, the absence of any orderly market tradition and the limited number of suppliers combined to make a new form of governmentally assured supply essential, if the objective of deterring independent sources was to be realized.[46]

This logic was endorsed by the International Nuclear Fuel Cycle Evaluation, which concluded that "assurance of supply and assurance of non-proliferation are . . . complementary and that greater assurance of supply can . . . contribute to non-proliferation objectives by reducing the pressures for a world-wide spread of enrichment and reprocessing facilities."[47]

Almost without exception, nuclear supplier and recipient states publicly acknowledge that because nuclear energy programs require enormous investments and long lead times, there must be reasonable assurances of supply of fuel, equipment, and services. The tensions between supplier and recipient states stem from past attempts by suppliers to use their leverage to encourage compliance with more stringent nonproliferation measures. Canada in 1977, for example, imposed an embargo on the sale of uranium to members of the European Atomic Energy Community and Japan while negotiations were under way to incorporate stricter nonproliferation provisions in their fuel supply agreements. The U.S. Nuclear Non-Proliferation Act (NNPA) of 1978, with its imposition of new conditions on existing supply agreements, is also widely viewed abroad as an unjustified, unilateral action which jeopardizes the energy security of America's trading partners.[48] Skepticism about the motives underlying U.S. fuel supply policy also has strained relations among supplier states, the 1974 U.S. decision to suspend the signing of new foreign contracts for uranium enrichment services often being cited as an example of arbitrary U.S. supply policy unrelated to nonproliferation objectives.[49]

A number of methods have been proposed to remove security of supply as a driving force for the acquisition of nationally controlled sensitive technologies. These include both market mechanism and governmental control measures and range from the removal of all political restrictions on purchases of enriched or natural uranium fuels and reliance on a competitive market for protection against interruptions of supply to bilateral and multinational fuel cycle arrangements in which accession to full-scope safeguards would be a precondition for fuel supply guarantees.[50]

One of the most frequent proposals involves multinational agreements, or cross-guarantees, among several suppliers and consumers that provide for emergency allocation of either natural or low-enriched uranium. This kind of multinational fuel assurance arrangement might be modeled after the past practice of utilities in Europe (on both a national and multinational level) of assisting each other in cases of supply interruptions by making available loans of fuel out of inventories for limited periods.[51] For this plan to work, the suppliers entering into the agreement would need to have the capacity to increase their exports to meet emergency demands.[52] The practicability of the approach also depends on the nations to be involved and the nonproliferation conditions attached to fuel supply assurances. Involvement of the United States in a cross-guarantees network, for example, would require revision of the 1978 Nuclear Non-Proliferation Act, which sets strict conditions on any export of nuclear materials.[53]

As an alternative to the assurance of fuel supplies through cross-guarantees backed by national stockpiles, an international nuclear fuel bank has been proposed.[54] This institution would most likely have assets of physical stocks of natural and enriched uranium as well as claims on fuel held by other governmental and private entities and could distribute fuel to nations suffering from fuel supply interruptions which were related to their nonproliferation obligations. Among the practical issues which might be contentious and would have to be resolved before an international fuel bank could be established are: Where should the bank be located? What assets should the bank hold? How should its operations be financed? What conditions should be attached to fuel supplies?[55]

The International Nuclear Fuel Cycle Evaluation noted both safety net arrangements such as cross-guarantees and an international nuclear fuel bank as possible short- to medium-term supply guarantee mechanisms. A competitive market, however, was identified as the preferred long-term solution to fuel supply problems.[56] A number of market-oriented approaches have received considerable attention recently.[57] Most approaches emphasizing market incentives, however, tend to be attuned more closely to supplier rather than consumer concerns.[58] In particular, they ignore consumers' fears that uranium supplies will be suspended for political reasons or that supply contracts will be unilaterally amended and new conditions applied retroactively.[59]

More generally, nonproliferation strategies which emphasize fuel supply assurances appear to be more appropriate for relatively low-risk Nth countries that may move unintentionally up the nuclear weapons capability ladder, than for states actively pursuing nuclear weapons because of international security considerations. This does not mean that efforts to establish reliable, long-term fuel supply assurances should be abandoned. Such assurances are probably both attainable and necessary for rebuilding international confidence in the nuclear nonproliferation regime. Measures that restore stability, predictability, and security to the fuel supply market, however, should not be regarded as treatment for the underlying causes of proliferation.

Strengthening Disincentives

To strengthen disincentives means to raise the perceived costs of acquiring nuclear weapons. A frequently proposed means to accomplish this task is to threaten to impose, and to impose, sanctions.

Sanctions can take a variety of forms; they range from low-level economic and political penalties such as the delay of economic assistance and diplomatic protest to the ultimate reprisal of the use of military force. Other sanctions often suggested include the termination of nuclear assistance and trade, imposition of a multilateral trade embargo, termination of military assistance and the supply of conventional arms, a ban on private investment in the country in question, and withdrawal of prior security gurarantees.[60]

The effectiveness of sanctions depends on the nature of the incentives for an Nth country to go nuclear, the economic and political vulnerability of the proliferator, and the degree of support from the international community for specific sanctions. The nature of the Nth country's proliferation motives are critical since some, such as perceived threats to national survival, may not be susceptible to influence by any form of sanction but might be reduced by security guarantees. Some domestic political and international prestige pressures to proliferate, moreover, might actually be intensified rather than reduced by the imposition of sanctions which would produce a nationalist reaction. While unilateral action by a great power may work well in selected cases where overwhelming leverage can be exerted (e.g., U.S. success in inducing South Korea to rescind its order for a French reprocessing plant),[61] unilateral sanctions against other Nth countries are apt to be futile. For countries such as Brazil, Argentina, and South Africa, for example, even multilateral sanctions involving both superpowers probably could only raise the cost but not prevent the implementation of a decision to produce nuclear weapons.[62]

Historically, there is little evidence that economic and political sanctions have been very effective, whether applied unilaterally (e.g., by the United States against North Vietnam and Cuba) or collectively (e.g., against Rhodesia after its declaration of independence).[63] As one study notes, "Belief in the efficacy of sanctions, both in terms of the probability of their application in the event of violation and their effectiveness when applied, . . . suffered a major setback as the result of the Indian nuclear explosion."[64] Not only was international reaction generally mild, but India made clear it was not prepared to surrender the right which it asserted to construct its first nuclear explosive.[65]

The case of India illustrates another important point with respect to the utility of sanctions: policies designed for discouraging proliferation may not be appropriate for encouraging moderation once the nuclear threshold has been breached. This dilemma is well expressed by George Quester, who points out that instead of "punishing India for its decision to acquire what amounts to a nuclear weapon or making a last-ditch attempt to induce New Delhi to surrender these weapons, the more pressing concern may be to keep India on a moderate course on whether it brandishes or tests such explosives and on whether it shares the technology with any other aspiring nuclear weapons state."[66] Despite the apparent cynicism of the policy shift, therefore, "the last culprit may have to be aided as much as punished."[67]

SUPPLY POLICIES

Supply-oriented approaches to nonproliferation are designed to limit the nuclear weapons capabilities of states that do not now have nuclear weapons. They tend to focus on means to prevent the misuse of civil nuclear energy facilities for military purposes.[68] One of the most widely discussed and controversial supply-oriented mechanisms is the system of international and domestic safeguards.

The Safeguards Approach

Since the outset of the nuclear age, arguments have been made that nuclear energy must be subject to safeguards to ensure that it be used exclusively for peaceful purposes. What constitutes "safeguards," however, has never been defined very precisely, and the term has been used to describe a wide range of national and international nonproliferation measures. They include the Baruch Plan's call for international ownership, management, and control of atomic energy, the system of worldwide IAEA nuclear facility inspection and reports, national measures to guard against the loss or diversion of nuclear material, and nuclear export regulations and restraints.[69]

Our discussion focuses primarily on international safeguards, used here to mean the system of measures applied by the International Atomic Energy Agency to detect and deter national governments' diversion of nuclear material from peaceful uses to military purposes. National safeguards, in contrast, refer to measures undertaken by national governments "to detect, deter, prevent, or respond to the unauthorized possession or use of significant quantities of nuclear materials through theft or diversion and sabotage of nuclear facilities."[70] They tend to emphasize the provision of physical security and are directed at nonstate actors.[71]

According to Article III, A, 5 of the statute of the IAEA, the agency is:

To establish and administer safeguards designed to ensure that special fissionable and other materials, services, equipment, facilities, and information made available by the Agency or at its request or under its supervision or control are not used in such a way as to further any military purpose; and to apply safeguards, at the request of the parties, to any bilateral or multilateral arrangement, or at the request of a State, to any of that State's activities in the field of atomic energy.[72]

No authority is granted the agency to recover diverted material or to provide physical security for nuclear materials or facilities. The IAEA Statute and its safeguards system, it should also be emphasized, do not prohibit states from acquiring fissile material or making nuclear weapons. India, for example, did not technically violate any IAEA safeguards agreement when it exploded a nuclear device. The safeguards are simply intended to ensure that specific facilities, projects, and nuclear material are not diverted from peaceful to military uses.[73]

Until the entry into force of the NPT in March 1970, the IAEA's safeguards system was based on the idea of safeguards for specific projects. If a nation, for example, sought to obtain agency assistance for the operation of a nuclear power reactor, it would apply for approval of that specific project and would have to accept agency safeguards for the nuclear facility. In addition, a state might unilaterally submit some or all of its nuclear energy activities to the agency's safeguard system. Thus, as William Epstein points out, "a state might have one facility under agency safeguards while retaining, unsafeguarded, all or part of a nuclear fuel cycle."[74] Under the NPT, however, this project-specific focus on safeguards shifted to one designed to apply to all peaceful nuclear activities within non-nuclear weapon states. Article III of the NPT, moreover, requires that the IAEA system of safeguards be accepted by all non-nuclear weapon parties to the treaty (within twenty-four months for the original parties and eighteen months for states acceding later). As of February 14, 1981, seventy-eight non-nuclear weapon states party to the NPT had negotiated safeguards agreements with the IAEA.[75] Two nuclear weapon state parties to the NPT, the United States and the United Kingdom, and the non-NPT nuclear weapon state, France, also have agreed voluntarily to submit those nuclear installations "not directly significant for their national security" to IAEA safeguards.[76] Thirty-two NPT parties, however, still had not concluded the required safeguard negotiations with the IAEA (see Appendix B for a list of NPT parties with safeguards in effect). Although most of these countries did not have extensive nuclear activities, six non-nuclear weapon states at the end of 1980 operated significant nuclear facilities not subject to IAEA or bilateral safeguards. These states and their relevant nuclear facilities are indicated in Table 1. Two nuclear weapon states, the Soviet Union and the PRC, also have refused, to date, to submit their nuclear installations to IAEA safeguards.

The effectiveness of international safeguards is a subject of considerable controversy. Critics of the existing safeguards system point, in particular, to the nonuniversal scope of the NPT and its safeguards requirements; provisions of the NPT which tend to discriminate against non-nuclear weapon states (NNWS) party to the treaty by requiring "full-scope" safeguards on exports to NNWS parties, but only "project specific" safeguards to nonparties; the IAEA's commitment to nonintrusive safeguards and its unwillingness to insist on strict safeguards compliance; and problems regarding the physical security of nuclear material which is left exclusively to individual states.[77] The point is also sometimes made that although the safeguards system is useful in helping to build confidence in the nonproliferation regime, it does not prevent nations from moving within days or less of having nuclear explosives without violating existing safeguards.[78] As Henry Rowen notes, "It is not a violation of the NPT to have possession of nuclear explosive materials nor is it a violation to do experiments on rapidly crushing materials at very high pressures, i.e., to build the non-nuclear components of nuclear explosives."[79] Because Article X.1 of the NPT gives parties the right to withdraw from the treaty upon serving three months notice, any state that is concerned that detection of safeguard violations is imminent can withdraw and refuse controls.[80]

During the Carter administration, the United States also raised two additional critiques of the international safeguards system. As discerned by Pierre Lellouche, this twofold challenge entailed: (1) the charge that it was no longer sufficient to rely on the voluntary character of safeguards (i.e., all recipients of nuclear exports should be obliged to submit to full-scope safeguards); and (2) the assertion that certain nuclear fuel cycle facilities were too dangerous and should be denied even with safeguards.[81] Consistent with the first charge was the provision of the Nuclear Non-Proliferation Act, which required a cutoff of all U.S. nuclear exports to non-nuclear weapon states lacking full-scope safeguards. Illustrative of the second assertion was the position taken by the Carter administration (but modified by President Reagan) that plutonium reprocessing and breeder reactor development should be curtailed.[82]

TABLE 1. INFCE Evaluation of Technical Measures to Reduce Proliferation Risk[a]

Alternative Technology	Proliferation Risk				Effect on IAEA Safeguards	Other Assessment Factors		Effort Needed to Bring to Industrial Scale
	No National Reprocessing/ Refabrication	Proliferation Under Safeguards	Proliferation Not Under Safeguards	Subnational Theft		Economic[c]	Environmental[d]	
Co-location	N/A	+	0	++	+	+	+	None
Storage/transport as MOX	N/A	+	0	++	0	−	0	Small
Co-processing	N/A	+	+	++	0	0	0	Moderate
Pre-irradiation	+	0	0	++	0	−−	−	Moderate
Spiking	+	0	0	++	−	−−	−	Large
Partial processing	+	+[b]	+[b]	++	−	−−	−	Large
Physical barriers	N/A	+	0	++	+	0	+	Moderate

Source: Reprocessing, Plutonium Handling, Recycle, Report of INFCE Working Group 4 (Vienna: IAEA, 1980), p. 144. For a similar evaluation see Nuclear Proliferation and Civilian Nuclear Power, Report of the Nonproliferation Alternative Systems Assessment Program (Washington, D.C., 1980), Vol. 1, p. 45.

[a] "+ indicates a net improvement or saving when compared with the reference technology; a large improvement is shown as ++. When there is a net deterioration or loss when compared with the reference technology this is shown as −; a large deterioration is indicated by ——. When there is little or no change when compared with the reference technology, the symbol 0 is used. N/A means "not applicable."

[b] Only for out-of-pile recycle times of up to two to three years.

[c] For a discussion of this issue see Reprocessing, Plutonium Handling, Recycle, pp. 91–110.

[d] For a discussion of this issue see Reprocessing, Plutonium Handling, Recycle, pp. 73–90.

Although much of the criticism of the existing safeguards system comes from those who believe it needs to be strengthened, one can also discern resistance to the upgrading of IAEA safeguards if that entails further spending by the agency. This resistance comes primarily from developing countries and involves the fundamental tension between Articles III and IV of the NPT and the difficulty of striking a balance between nuclear safeguards and the transfer of nuclear technology and peaceful purposes.[83] More specifically, a number of developing countries appear to worry that safeguards may come to dominate the IAEA's program to the detriment of the agency's technical assistance functions.[84]

There is widespread recognition among nonproliferation analysts that the international safeguards system is imperfect and needs improvement. Among the partial remedies often suggested are technological improvements such as advanced material accounting systems,[85] augmenting IAEA funding, staffing, and technical competence at a rate commensurate with the global expansion of civilian nuclear energy production,[86] closing the gap between the NPT and non-NPT safeguards regime (e.g., standardizing bilateral safeguard measures);[87] and moving toward compulsory full-scope and universal safeguards.[88] The last recommendation in the list is the most contentious and would require the greatest change in the existing safeguards system although steps in this direction have been taken by some members of the London Suppliers Group after 1975 and received considerable support among supplier states at the 1980 NPT Review Conference.[89] Both superpowers, significantly, have taken very similar positions on this issue.

One additional strategy for strengthening the nonproliferation regime, frequently discussed within the context of international safeguards, is the establishment of regional, multinational fuel cycle facilities (MFCFs) for uranium enrichment, fuel fabrication, reprocessing, spent fuel storage, and waste disposal.[90] From a nonproliferation standpoint, the primary intent of MFCFs is to remove sensitive fuel cycle facilities from national controls and to facilitate the safeguarding of nuclear material and sensitive technology.

The advantages usually attributed to MFCFs are: (1) the reduction of economic incentives and rationales for national facilities and the corresponding increase of political costs associated with a decision to develop national facilities; (2) the improvement of physical security and more effective safeguards against diversion of material, at lower cost; (3) movement away from the discriminatory nature of most nonproliferation measures by the participation of nuclear "have-nots"; and (4) a constructive approach to bridge considerations of nonproliferation, energy security, and international equity.[91] These possible advantages, however, may be offset by the potential of MFCFs to spread the disease they are designed to control (i.e., transfer sensitive technologies to nations which might not otherwise have obtained them) and to stimulate plutonium reprocessing and legitimize commerce in separated plutonium.[92] The criticism is also sometimes made that establishment of MFCFs would have no direct bearing on the problem of proliferation because the states intent on developing a nuclear weapons program would probably not forgo domestic facilities in order to participate in a MFCF.[93]

One cannot easily dismiss the arguments about the potential counterproductiveness of MFCFs. The critics' case, however, is much weaker for MFCFs devoted to certain fuel cycle activities than others and hinges, in part, on the philosophy guiding nonproliferation policy (i.e., technology denial or dissuasion). The establishment of multinational storage facilities for spent fuel, for example, would appear to avoid many of the disadvantages attributed to MFCFs generally and at the same time might provide a means of testing the viability of the MFCF concept.[94] This concept was endorsed by the INFCE Waste Management and Disposal Working Group, which concluded that "centralized facilities for the disposal of spent fuel and/or vitrified high-level waste would alleviate the concerns of countries with small nuclear power programs [and] could reduce the diversion risk."[95]

It is beyond the scope of this study to examine and assess the wide array of institutional arrangements for fuel cycle activities that have been described as multinational in conception. It is important to note, however, that a number of historical precedents exist for the establishment of multinational ventures in sensitive fuel cycle areas, although they have tended to involve technologically advanced states with common interests and have been primarily motivated by economic and technical considerations rather than nonproliferation concerns.[96] Principal ones include URENCO and EURODIF (uranium enrichment consortia) and EUROCHEMIC and United Reprocessors Group (spent fuel reprocessing and plutonium separation consortia).[97]

One can identify a number of practical problems with all multinational arrangements including such sensitive issues as membership, financing, voting arrangements, conditions of access, dispute settlement, and status of the host government. Agreement on the site for a MFCF is apt to be particularly troublesome since ideally it should be free of serious local or international political problems and in a host country (if a non-nuclear state) perceived as unlikely to seek nuclear weapons.[98] It may also be difficult to alleviate the suspicions of Third World countries that MFCFs will not be dominated by the industrialized nuclear supplier states. This problem will be accentuated if the principal criterion in selecting a MFCF site is one of safe and stable environment or, essentially, a Western industrial state.[99]

Despite these inherent difficulties, the concept of multinational fuel cycle arrangements has much merit, not as *the* solution to the problem of proliferation but as a means to bridge often competing nuclear considerations of nonproliferation, energy security, and nondiscrimination. The challenge, as Lawrence Scheinman points out, is to fashion "institutional arrangements so as to meet the political, economic, operational, and management concerns that inevitably will enter into any consideration of multinational activity and . . . to insure that multinationalism does not become a pretext or subterfuge for activities which could undermine the stability of the international nuclear regime."[100]

Export Controls

Export restrictions on sensitive technologies represent perhaps the most hotly disputed means of attempting to contain the spread of nuclear weapons. At the heart of the dispute are disagreements over the efficacy of technology denial measures and their justifiability under the terms of the NPT.

Proponents of export restraints on technologies such as enrichment and reprocessing plants generally do not regard controls as a potential solution to the problem of proliferation, but see them as a means to slow the spread of nuclear weapons capabilities and thereby buy time for the development of safer fuel cycle components and a stronger international nonproliferation regime. This perspective is well articulated by Joseph Nye, one of the architects of the Carter administration's nonproliferation policy:

We are sometimes told that the goal is hopeless because the nuclear "horse is out of the stable." But proliferation is a matter of degrees, not absolutes. Our policy can affect the number of horses, which horses, and when horses leave the barn.[101]

Underlying the nonproliferation strategy articulated by Nye and the measures taken by the United States in the form of the Nuclear Non-Proliferation Act is the subordination of Article IV of the NPT (dealing with the promotion of nuclear energy for peaceful purposes) to the principle that some sensitive nuclear technologies should be denied even under safeguards. As two high-ranking nonproliferation spokesmen in the Carter administration put it, "By the late 1970s, it appeared to many, including the U.S. government, that the nonproliferation treaty was inadequate even for parties to it, because inspection alone might not provide 'timely warning' of diversions for nuclear-weapons purposes."[102]

Outside of the U.S. Congress, it is difficult to find strong support today for the NNPA. Many of its critics, however, do not dispute the need for export restraints, but simply regard the rigidity of the 1978 act and its imposition of new conditions on most of America's nuclear trading partners (in some cases retroactively) as counterproductive.[103] U.S. attempts to gain nonproliferation leverage through the denial of nuclear materials, it is argued, "only tightens near-term supply conditions and increases uncertainties abroad, adding to the pressure to decide in favor of the very activities the United States is trying to restrain."[104] A nonproliferation strategy emphasizing technology denial, in other words, may reduce confidence among importing states about access to materials and technology and give impetus to nuclear autarky. "The result," it is maintained, "is likely to be a short-term reduction in proliferation risks—e.g., South Korea will not soon acquire reprocessing capability . . . —but an increase in such risks over the longer term."[105] The failure to consider nuclear export policy within a broader foreign policy context and the indiscriminate application of export controls, moreover, have aggravated U.S. relations with critical non-nuclear weapons states—many of whom have long had the technical capability to develop nuclear weapons but not the motivation to do so—without seriously affecting the weapons programs of overt nuclear aspirants.[106]

For other critics of the NNPA, opposition to nuclear export restraints is more fundamental. Many Third World states, for example, appear to regard U.S. export legislation, as well as the activities of the London Suppliers Group, as concerted efforts by the nuclear weapons states to flout the nuclear assistance provisions of the NPT. They are also inclined to view the restrictive measures taken by the nuclear supplier countries as serving the suppliers' economic interests rather than nonproliferation goals and protest that the technological restrictions introduced by the London Club were drawn up without consultation by other NPT parties.[107] At a more abstract level, Third World opposition to nuclear export controls sometimes also appears to be based on the premise that export restraints perpetuate the international nuclear status quo and the "have-not" status of most Third World countries.[108]

Efforts to regulate nuclear exports generally have been directed at two groups of industrialized states: the so-called "first-tier" nuclear suppliers capable of providing the entire range of advanced civilian nuclear technology, facilities, and services, and "second-tier" suppliers with a more limited range of nuclear exports. A "third-tier" of nuclear suppliers, however, has recently begun to emerge: developing states with advanced nuclear technologies. Argentina and India have alredy assumed the role of third-tier nuclear suppliers, and Brazil, Taiwan, Pakistan, and South Korea may well attempt to emulate their nuclear export programs in the future.[109] From a nonproliferation standpoint, this development is troubling since many of the third-tier suppliers are not NPT parties. The prospects for coopting third-tier suppliers into future nuclear supplier group arrangements, moreover, seems slim given the existing level of suspicion about export restraints by third-tier suppliers. India, for example, has expressed no interest in joining the suppliers group, although it has also taken the stance that it will not export sensitive technology.[110]

More generally, nonproliferation proposals involving supplier cooperation and coordination must overcome enormous political and economic obstacles. At a minimum, nuclear-exporting countries will have to perceive sufficient shared interests and dangers to overcome economic rivalries and the inclination to view nuclear exports as a source of political influence and prestige.[111] Export controls also must be sufficiently flexible and sensitive to consumer state concerns so as not to stimulate the development of national nuclear industries including enrichment and reprocessing facilities. In other words, not only must the opportunity costs of controls be perceived by the supplier states as equitably distributed, but the perception must also exist among importers that "controls do not unreasonably hinder diffusion of the benefits of civilian nuclear energy—either in terms of energy supply or cost."[112] These are difficult conditions to satisfy. As a consequence, as one U.S. government study points out, "the political viability of export controls for more than the short term is very much in doubt."[113]

Technical Measures

The potential impact of technical measures on proliferation is restricted by the widespread availability of the material and technical wherewithal to make nuclear weapons. The lack of a "technical fix" for the problem of proliferation is reflected in the findings of both the International Nuclear Fuel Cycle Evaluation (INFCE) and the U.S. Nonproliferation Alternative Systems Assessment Program (NASAP). Although these two massive studies differ substantially in their operating assumptions and specific recommendations, they generally agree that technical measures by themselves can have only a limited impact on the full range of proliferation risks, particularly those above the level of subnational seizure threats.[114] Nevertheless, many proliferation analysts continue to search for technical ways of increasing fuel cycle proliferation resistance.

Technical measures aimed at making it more difficult for national governments or subnational groups to divert nuclear material generally fall into one of three categories. They are: (1) measures to reduce the presence and quantities of pure plutonium or highly enriched uranium in the fuel cycle; (2) measures to use radioactivity to protect those materials from diversion; and (3) measures to guard the materials by means of physical barriers.[115]

Among the more frequently proposed technical measures to reduce the presence of plutonium in the fuel cycle in separated form are co-location of reprocessing and mixed-oxide (MOX) fuel-fabrication plants, the storage and transportation of plutonium in dilute MOX form, co-processing (i.e., managing the plutonium extraction system in a repro-cessing plant so that the product is a mixture of uranium and plutonium rather than just plutonium), and co-conversion (i.e., mixing the plutonium nitrate recovered during reprocessing with uranyl nitrate and co-con-verting them into mixed oxide).[116] Co-location is generally regarded as the simplest and most feasible of these measures and would have the unambiguously positive effect of reducing both the need for transport between sites and the resources necessary for effective physical protection, nuclear material accountancy, and the application of other international safeguards.[117] Elimination of the transport of concentrated plutonium could also be accomplished by physically blending the oxide powders of plutonium and uranium to form a MOX material. Although this "technical fix" would not pose a major obstacle to national governments intent on diversion, the increased quantity of material that would have to be diverted and the need to separate the plutonium might increase proliferation resistance for nonstate actors. The retention of a chemical dilution barrier by co-processing or co-conversion would also probably reduce the risk of diversion by subnational groups. Co-processing and co-conversion techniques, however, are much less relevant as a means of increasing resistance to national proliferation, especially for countries possessing facilities for separating plutonium oxide from mixed plutonium/uranium oxide fuel.[118]

A second category of technical measures relies on the introduction of a radiation barrier in order to deter diversion. Among the methods that have been proposed for introducing this radiation barrier are spiking of fresh fuel with a highly radioactive material such as cobalt-60; pre-irradiation, in which the mixed uranium/plutonium oxide fuel element is irradiated before shipment to the reactor site; and partial processing or decontamination, in which the reprocessing plant is designed so that a portion of the fission products always remains associated with the plutonium.[119]

Spiking can take several forms ranging from the addition of small quantities of radioactive isotopes as tracers to facilitate detection and material containment to the introduction of lethal amounts of radioactive material to fresh reactor fuel for the purpose of disabling a potential divertor. Most studies now discount the utility of massive spiking, in part because of the economic, environmental, and safeguards disadvantages associated with its employment,[120] and also because of its dubious effectiveness against any group competent to separate plutonium from uranium in mixed-oxide fuel. Both the INFCE and NASAP reports, for example, conclude that while spiking may have some effectiveness against theft by nonstate actors, it would prove generally ineffective against diversion by national governments.[121]

Pre-irradiation of fabricated MOX fuel would probably be accomplished in a specially constructed neutron irradiation facility. This facility might be a reactor designed for rapid on-line refueling that would provide a small but significant burnup to the fresh fuel elements. At such a low burnup, the NASAP study suggests, "the fuel would be radioactive enough that it would require, in effect, a dedicated, shielded, and remotely operated chemical separation facility to recover the plutonium."[122] The major difficulties with this approach are the economic costs involved and the potential for increased population exposure to radiation and environmental hazards. Like spiking, pre-irradiation also poses difficulties for existing methods of nuclear material accounting and other safeguards procedures.[123]

Partial processing is a further variation on co-processing and co-conversion whereby some of the radioactive fission products would be kept with the recovered uranium and plutonium, thereby creating a radiation barrier throughout the fuel cycle. Although the technique is less well developed than spiking and irradiation, the principal advantages and disadvantages appear to be similar.[124] One additional limitation of the technique, however, stems from the short-lived nature of the fission products. Because they are short-lived, the protection given by them will decrease after about two years from the time the spent fuel was originally discharged from the reactor.[125] Partial processing, like the other methods to retain a radiation barrier in recycle materials, would seem to offer somewhat greater potential for increasing proliferation resistance than does co-processing or co-conversion of uranium and plutonium because of its requirement of more elaborate facilities (e.g., shielding and remote controls) to recover plutonium from diverted material.[126]

The physical isolation of the reprocessing and/or MOX fuel-fabrication process by means of structural barriers represents yet another category of technical measures designed to decrease the opportunities for diversion. Proposed techniques to create physical barriers include automatically or remotely controlled systems that reduce accessibility to sensitive materials and security devices which shut down or disable equipment under specified conditions. France and West Germany have shown particular interest in developing physical barrier techniques, one of the more promising of which is known as Pipex.[127]

An overall evaluation of the diversion resistance of the alternative technical measures discussed above is provided in Table 2. This list of technical measures, it should be emphasized, is by no means exhaustive. One might also have included proposals to adopt entirely different fuel cycles (e.g., the denatured thorium-unraium cycle . . . , the so-called CIVEX method of reprocessing which combines a number of the "Category One" techniques in a single operation,[128] and the radical measure, articulated most forcefully by Amory Lovins et al., to abandon civilian nuclear power altogether.[129] What is most apparent from our survey is the much greater potential deterrent impact of technical measures on subnational groups than national governments. This finding suggests the hazard of relying extensively on technical approaches if it obscures what is generally regarded as the greater danger of national proliferation and the need to reduce the political and security pressures for acquisition of nuclear weapons.

MANAGING PROLIFERATION

The discussion in this chapter so far has focused on the assets and liabilities of alternative strategies for limiting the spread of nuclear weapons to additional parties. Notwithstanding the implementation of the best of these approaches, some further proliferation may well occur. It is therefore relevant to consider how this might come about, the

TABLE 2. Operating Nuclear Facilities Not Subject to IAEA or Bilateral Safeguards, as of 31 December 1980[a]

Country	Facility	Indigenous or Imported	First Year of Operation
Egypt	Inshas research reactor	Imported (USSR)[b]	1961
India	Apsara research reactor	Indigenous	1956
	Cirus research reactor	Imported (Canada/USA)[c]	1960
	Purnima research reactor	Indigenous	1972
	Fuel fabrication plant at Trombay	Indigenous	1960
	Fuel fabrication plant, CANDU-type of fuel elements, at the Nuclear Fuel Cycle complex, Hyderabad	Indigenous	1974
	Reprocessing plant at Trombay	Indigenous	1964
	Reprocessing plant at Tarapur	Indigenous	1977
Israel	Dimona research reactor	Imported (France/ Norway)[d]	1963
	Reprocessing plant at Dimona	Indigenous (in cooperation with France)[e]	
Pakistan	Fuel fabrication plant at Chashma	Indigenous (in cooperation with Belgium)[f]	1980
South Africa	Enrichment plant at Valindaba	Indigenous (in cooperation with FRG)[g]	1975
Spain	Vandellos power reactor	Operation in cooperation with France[h]	1972

Source: SIPRI, *World Armaments and Disarmament: SIPRI Yearbook 1981* (London: Taylor & Francis, and Cambridge, Mass: Oelgeschlager, Gunn & Hain, 1981), p. 310.

[a]Significant nuclear activities outside the five nuclear weapon states recognized by the NPT.

[b]Egypt also has a small-scale reprocessing facility not subject to safeguards. Operability and current status are unknown. In view of Egypt's recent adherence to the NPT, all its nuclear activities will have to be safeguarded by the IAEA.

[c]The reactor is of Canadian origin; some heavy water was supplied by the USA.

[d]French-supplied reactor running on heavy water from Norway.

[e]Assistance by Saint Gobain Techniques Nouvelles.

[f]Assistance at an early stage by Belgo-Nucleaire. In addition, Pakistan is about to establish significant reprocessing and enrichment capacities. The status of these programs is unknown.

[g]Cooperation between STEAG (FRG) and UCOR (South Africa).

[h]Negotiations with the IAEA on safeguarding of this reactor were being held.

kinds of problems it would pose, the utility of previously identified demand and supply measures to moderate these difficulties, and additional steps that could be taken to minimize the dangers of proliferation.

[Deleted is the author's discussion of how the "further proliferation" might occur and what problems it might pose. Mentioned in conclusion are the problems associated with the destruction of nuclear power plants in time of war, problems which he notes, have received "surprisingly little attention in the public literature."—*Ed.*]

The failure of most nonproliferation studies even to recognize the problem of the destruction of nuclear energy facilities in war, much less propose solutions, may be an atypical oversight and not a fair measure of the adequacy of existing nonproliferation strategies to cope with the problems of life in a world of continuing proliferation.[130] A legitimate criticism of most nonproliferation approaches, however, is their fixation on stopping additional states from "going nuclear" (defined as the detonation of a single nuclear device) to the neglect of possible methods for managing the proliferation process in order to moderate its most threatening characteristics.

It is, of course, much easier to note this deficiency of prior research than to remedy it. Some tentative conclusions regarding the utility of alternative demand and supply strategies for influencing the proliferation process, however, may be drawn from the preceding analysis.

The first point that can be made is that none of the nonproliferation strategies identified above can provide much assurance that "timely warning" will be given prior to the entry of a new nation into the nuclear weapons club. This is the case even though international safeguards are justified primarily as an alerting mechanism and even though some of the most frequently proposed approaches to control proliferation (e.g., sanctions) assume the need for adequate warning of movement toward a bomb in order to organize an effective international response.[131] The length of the warning period, moreover, continues to shrink with the global proliferation of plutonium separation and uranium enrichment facilities as well as research reactors using highly enriched uranium.[132] At best, improved safeguards and the convergence of international views on appropriate sanctions in anticipation of possible proliferation developments may make it more difficult for a prospective proliferator to count on announcing a *fait accompli* and thereby raise the political costs of embarking on a nuclear weapons program.

The traditional nonproliferation strategies discussed in this chapter, including both demand and supply approaches, also do not appear to be very helpful in reducing the risk of an inadvertent of unintended nuclear war intiated by a nuclear weapons novice. One alternative and controversial strategy that has been proposed to deal with this contingency is the provision by existing nuclear weapon states of technical assistance to *N*th countries, designed to influence the characteristics of their future nuclear forces and strategic doctrine.[133] Technical assistance, for example, could be provided to improve early warning system and command and control reliability, weapons safety, and force survivability.[134] The existing nuclear powers could also attempt to influence doctrine and reinforce the nuclear taboo by encouraging the assessment of nuclear war outcomes and the study of deterrence theory.

Unfortunately, although such assistance might promote development of a more secure *N*th country nuclear force and reduce the risk of war by accident, miscalculation, or unauthorized use, or as the result of preemption due to fear of strategic vulnerability, it might also have several counterproductive effects. Assistance which reduces the danger of preemptive attack by increasing force survivability, for example, might remove what otherwise would be a compelling proliferation disincentive. Efforts to improve weapons reliability and safety and command and control performance also run the risk of making nuclear forces more usable. An additional danger is that such assistance would be perceived by other potential *N*th countries as a reward for going nuclear.

The risks of attempting to influence *N*th country nuclear postures and policy to reduce the probability of inadvertent or unintended war illustrates the basic tension that exist between efforts to manage proliferation and attempts to retard it. The proper nonproliferation emphasis, moreover, is apt to vary from case to case and to depend on such factors as the anticipated proliferation impact of a given country, other national security policy objectives, the means available for retarding a particular *N*th country's movement toward nuclear weapons, and the means available for influencing the characteristics of that state's nuclear program at the margin.

Careful consideration of the means available for retarding or managing proliferation is itself a necessary first step toward adoption of an effective nonproliferation strategy. There is a need, in other words, to assess nonproliferation measures not only in terms of the extent to which they address the most important proliferation problems (however they are defined) but also with respect to their relevance for problems that are susceptible to manipulation, prevention, and cure. From this perspective, the source of recent U.S. nonproliferation policy difficulties is principally one of misconception, not implementation. Far too much emphasis was placed on supply-oriented approaches in pursuit of the improbable task of restructuring other countries' domestic nuclear energy programs. Inadequate attention, on the other hand, was given to the implementation of fuel supply assurances—a less pivotal factor with respect to nuclear weapons decision-making, but one over which the United States could have exercised significant influence.

Two additional proliferation problem areas appear to be susceptible to manipulation and treatment, if not prevention: nuclear theft and terrorism by nonstate actors and vertical proliferation. Most applicable to the former problem are domestic safeguards and more diversion-resistant fuel cycle technologies. The limited effectiveness of safeguards and so-called technological fixes with respect to national proliferation should not detract from their potential utility as means to curb subnational proliferation threats. Similarly, although superpower-initiated arms control measures such as a CTB may have only a limited direct impact on the decision-making calculus of potential Nth countries, this should not obscure their potential for moderating vertical proliferation and restoring the credibility and acceptability of other nonproliferation measures, some of which may be necessarily discriminatory in nature. A failure to moderate U.S.-Soviet arms competition and the postponement of serious strategic arms control negotiations, on the other hand, can only increase pressures in both the United States and the Soviet Union to subordinate nonproliferation policy objectives to other foreign policy goals defined more narrowly in East-West terms. One likely consequence of this kind of preoccupation is the reliance on security guarantees and conventional arms transfers not as measures to reduce proliferation incentives, but as enticements to resist the advances of the other superpower. Potential nonproliferation measures utilized in this fashion may whet rather than satiate the appetites of potential Nth countries for nuclear weapons by emphasizing security threats and the perceived utility of weapons.

CONCLUSION

It would be convenient to conclude this study by identifying a single culprit responsible for proliferation and a simple nonproliferation remedy in need only of faithful implementation. What is most apparent . . . , however, is the multicausal nature of the spread of nuclear weapons and the need to tailor nonproliferation measures to specific cases.

This does not mean that patterns of proliferation are nonexistent or that we should abandon efforts to model the proliferation process. Indeed, Stephen Meyer's careful application of quantitative methods to explore the correlates of proliferation is a useful reminder of an under-utilized approach to test contending proliferation hypotheses.[135] Particularly noteworthy is his demonstration of the inadequacy of the "technological imperative" model to account for the scope and pace of past proliferation. This conclusion is consistent with the findings from our survey of thirteen past and potential proliferators, which reveals the predominance of international political and security incentives for and constraints on proliferation.

One of the most disturbing findings of our study is the recurrent tension between nonproliferation objectives and other domestic and foreign policy goals and priorities. This policy dilemma is further complicated by the tendency for priorities in both foreign and domestic sectors to vary substantially across countries. Illustrative of this variation is the greater importance in recent years attached to energy independence in most West European states and Japan than in the United States and the resulting discrepancy in these countries' views toward plutonium reprocessing and early commercialization of the breeder. The attractiveness to different states of alternative nonproliferation measures such as nuclear export restraints, multinational fuel cycle facilities, fuel supply assurances, and diversion-resistant fuel cycle technologies also can be explained, in many instances, in terms of each country's individual energy demands and resources. Our survey of the economics of nuclear power and the politics of nonproliferation, however, cautions against automatically assuming the operation of economic rationality in nuclear decision-making and indicates the necessity of accounting for additional military, political, and psychological factors. An understanding of these variables, unfortunately, is more easily recommended than accomplished.

Much more attention could also profitably be given the study of competing international perspectives on nuclear power and nonproliferation. What is apparent from the brief examination undertaken in this study is the existence of profound differences which divide the international community on most of the major issues pertaining to nuclear energy and proliferation. The task of forging a consensus among nations about these nuclear issues or restoring a strong international nuclear nonproliferation regime would therefore appear to be enormous. The very different interpretations given to the conclusions of the International Nuclear Fuel Cycle Evaluation, released in 1980, reinforce this pessimistic interpretation.[136] The INFCE experience, moreover, seems to indicate that it is unlikely that any new nuclear consensus that may emerge will reflect fully or even in large part what has been the U.S. position for most of the last decade.[137] The objectives of future U.S. nonproliferation policy, therefore, may have to be redefined more modestly. This may mean shifting attention away from unilateral measures to deny sensitive nuclear material and technology to more cooperative efforts aimed at influencing at the margin the nuclear programs and ambitions of critical *N*th countries.

The relationship between the growth of nuclear power and nonproliferation is still evolving. Unfortunately, the relationship to date has been an antagonistic one. This has led even sophisticated observers sometimes to pose the necessity of choice between "the avoidance of nuclear weapons spread and the provision of additional energy sources."[138] To pose the dilemma in this fashion, however, is to exaggerate the technological component of the proliferation problem. More to the point is Richard Rosecrance's observation almost two decades ago that the dispersion of nuclear weapons is "eminently a problem in strategy and politics."[139] To this one might add that no nonproliferation policy is a substitute for a sound foreign policy and that major nonproliferation successes are probably attainable by the United States only at substantial cost to other domestic and foreign policy goals.

NOTES

1. See Richard Burt, "Nuclear Proliferation and Conventional Arms Transfers: The Missing Link," California Seminar on Arms Control and Foreign Policy, September 1977; James Digby, "Precision Guided Weapons," Adelphi Paper No. 118 (London: International Institute for Strategic Studies, 1975); and John Mearsheimer, "Precision-Guided Munitions and Conventional Deterence," *Survival* (March/April 1979), pp. 68–76.

2. See, for example, Lewis Dunn, "Some Reflections on the Dove's Dilemma," *International Organization* (Winter 1981), pp. 183–184; Ted Greenwood, "Discouraging Proliferation in the Next Decade and Beyond," in Ted Greenwood, Harold A. Feiveson, and Theodore B. Taylor, *Nuclear Proliferation: Motivations, Capabilities, and Strategies for Control* (New York: McGraw-Hill, 1977), p. 61; and Burt, pp. 23–24.

3. A particularly good discussion of the dilemma is provided by Jo Husbands, "Arms Transfers and Nuclear Proliferation: Policy Implication of the 'Dove's Dilemma' " (Paper delivered at the Annual Meeting of the International Studies Association, Los Angeles, March 19–22, 1980). See also Dunn.

4. See Dunn, pp. 185–186.

5. Ibid., p. 187.

6. Richard K. Betts, "Paranoids, Pygmies, Pariahs and Nonproliferation," *Foreign Policy* (Spring 1977), p. 177.

7. See Husbands, p. 39, and Dunn, p. 185. These other incentives may have been less visible while security concerns were paramount.

8. This point is discussed by Husbands, p. 35.

9. Ibid., p. 42.

10. Ibid.

11. See Dunn, p. 188, on this point.

12. Husbands, p. 37.

13. See Joseph A. Yager, ed., *Nonproliferation and U.S. Foreign Policy* (Washington, D.C.: Brookings Institution, 1980), p. 409. It should be noted that nuclear nonproliferation was not the original or primary objective of these guarantees.

14. This point is made by Philip J. Farley, "Nuclear Proliferation," in Henry Owen and Charles Schultze, eds., *Setting National Priorities: The Next Ten Years* (Washington, D.C.: Brookings Institution, 1976), p. 150.

15. The nonproliferation relevance of the U.S. security commitment to Pakistan, it should be noted, is diluted by the failure of the guarantee to apply to an attack by India.

16. See Greenwood, pp. 58–59.

17. Ibid., p. 58.

18. See, for example, Greenwood, p. 59, and Alan Dowty, *The Role of Great Power Guarantees in International Peace Agreements* (Hebrew University of Jerusalem, February 1974), p. 21.

19. Beverly Rowen and Henry Rowen, *In the Face of Nuclear Proliferation—An Assessment of Policy Options for the United States*, Report prepared for the U.S. Arms Control and Disarmament Agency (Los Angeles: Pan Heuristics, 1977), p. 12.

20. For a discussion of this resolution see William Epstein, *The Last Chance: Nuclear Proliferation and Arms Control* (New York: Free Press, 1976), pp.139–143,

and Stockholm International Peace Research Institute, *World Armaments and Disarmament: SIPRI Yearbook 1981* (London: Taylor & Francis and Cambridge, Mass.: Oelgeschlager, Gunn & Hain, 1981), p. 331.

21. See William Epstein, "NPT Article VI: How Have the Parties Met Their Obligations? (Including a List of Recommendations for Possible Amendments to the NPT or for Inclusion in a Declaration Signed to Strengthen the NPT)," in Anne W. Marks, ed., *NPT: Paradoxes and Problems* (Washington, D.C.: Arms Control Association and the Carnegie Endowment for International Peace, 1975), pp. 74–91.

22. Additional measures proposed to reduce the prestige attached to nuclear weapons and to strengthen the security of potential Nth countries are "no-first-use" declarations, curtailment of "vertical proliferation" (i.e., the further development, accumulation, and deployment of nuclear weapons), and a cessation of the production of fissionable material for weapons purposes. For a discussion of these measures, see the Office of Technology Assessment study, *Nuclear Proliferation and Safeguards* (New York: Praeger, 1977), pp. 63–65, and Epstein, *The Last Chance*, pp. 181–194.

23. Our discussion focuses on the effects of a CTB on horizontal proliferation (i.e., the spread of nuclear weapons to additional states). It does not address the effects that a CTB might have on the development of new nuclear weapons by existing nuclear weapon states.

24. See, for example, Gerard Smith and George Rathjens, "Reassessing Nuclear Nonproliferation Policy," *Foreign Affairs* (Spring 1981), p. 890; *Nuclear Power Issues and Choices* (Cambridge, Mass.: Ballinger, 1977), pp. 290–291; Barry M. Blechman, "The Comprehensive Test Ban Negotiations: Can They Be Revitalized?" *Arms Control Today* (June 1981), p. 3; Dan Caldwell, "CTB: An Effective SALT Substitute," *Bulletin of the Atomic Scientists* (December 1980), p. 31; Sidney D. Drell, "The Case for the Test Ban," *Washington Post* (July 4, 1978), and Herbert York and G. Greb, "The Comprehensive Nuclear Test Ban," California Seminar on Arms Control and Foreign Policy, June 1979, p. 12.

25. Wolfgang Panofsky, cited by York and Greb, p. 12.

26. A few go as far as to contend that the vertical-horizontal proliferation relationship is negative and that a CTB would be interpreted as a sign of weakness by the allies of the superpowers who would be encouraged to develop weapons of their own. See George Will, "The Test Ban Quest," *Washington Post* (June 4, 1978).

27. See, for example, Will, op. cit.; Donald G. Brennan, "A Comprehensive Test Ban: Everybody or Nobody," *International Security* (Summer 1976), pp. 92–117; and Michael May, "Do We Need a Nuclear Test Ban?" *Wall Street Journal* (June 28, 1976).

28. See Blechman; Caldwell; and Drell.

29. Caldwell, p. 31.

30. A number of near-nuclear powers (e.g., Brazil, Israel, and South Africa) which have refused to ratify the NPT are nevertheless parties to the Limited Test Ban Treaty whose preamble commits parties to subscribe to a CTB.

31. Negotiations for a CTB have taken place in various formats. The latest round of negotiations, initiated in 1977 and involving the United States, the Soviet Union, and Great Britain, was concluded in the fall of 1980 without producing an agreement. The next round of talks had yet to be scheduled as of mid-1981.

32. *Nuclear-Weapon-Free Zones* (Vantage Conference Report, Stanley Foundation, 1975), p. 26.

33. See Epstein, p. 55, and *Comprehensive Study of the Question of Nuclear-Weapon-Free Zones in All Its Aspects* (Special Report of the Conference on the Committee of Disarmament, United Nations, 1976), pp. 20–22.

34. See Epstein, pp. 207–220, and *Nuclear-Weapon-Free Zones.*

35. For texts of these treaties, see *Arms Control and Disarmament Agreements: Texts and History of Negotiations* (Washington, D.C.: U.S. Arms Control and Disarmament Agency, 1975).

36. *Comprehensive Study*, p. 13

37. Argentina has signed the treaty and announced its intention to ratify. Brazil has signed and ratified the agreement, but because of the treaty's complex implementation conditions is not yet a full party to the accord. For a discussion of the treaty and the provisions by which it can come into force, see John Redick, "The Tlatelolco Regime and Nonproliferation in Latin America," *International Organization* (Winter 1981), pp. 106–107.

38. *Nuclear-Weapon-Free Zones*, p. 13.

39. See George Quester, "Brazil and Latin American Nuclear Proliferation: An Optimistic View" (ACIS Working Paper No. 17, University of California, Los Angeles, 1979), p. 28, and Redick, p. 121.

40. Redick, p. 122.

41. Quester (p. 14) notes, however, that U.S. adherence to Protocol II was accompanied by an "interpretation" that leaves open the option of "transit" through the Canal Zone, an interpretation shared by France and Great Britain.

42. The two other countries affected by Protocol I, Great Britain and the Netherlands, have completed ratification.

43. "Reagan Statement on Spread of Atomic Arms," *New York Times* (July 17, 1981).

44. Redick, p. 111.

45. For a similar conclusion, see *Nuclear Proliferation and Safeguards*, p. 82.

46. *Nuclear Power and Nuclear Weapons Proliferation*, Report of the Atlantic Council's Nuclear Fuels Policy Working Group, Vol. 1 (Boulder, Co.: Westview Press, 1978), p. 82.

47. *INFCE Summary Volume* (Vienna: IAEA, 1980), p. 122. The objective of Working Group 3 of INFCE was "to assess alternatives for assuring reliable long-term supplies of the fuel, heavy water, reactors and services, and their related equipment and technology, which are needed to make nuclear energy widely available as a credible, long-term energy source in the interest of national needs, consistent with non-proliferation."

48. For a discussion of the new conditions imposed by the Nuclear Non-Proliferation Act, see Neff and Jacoby, "Nonproliferation Strategy in a Changing Nuclear Fuel Market," *Foreign Affairs* (Summer 1979), pp. 1127–1130.

49. See Nuclear Energy Policy Study Group, *Nuclear Power Issues and Choices* (Cambridge, Mass.: Ballinger, 1977), p. 373.

50. For a survey of alternative and governmental mechanism approaches, see *INFCE Summary Volume*, pp. 125–132, and *Nuclear Proliferation and Civilian Nuclear Power*, Report of the Nonproliferation Alternative Systems Assessment Program, (U.S. Department of Energy, June 1980), Vol. 7, pp. 2-7 to 2-22; and Joseph A. Yager, *International Cooperation in Nuclear Energy* (Washington, D.C.: Brookings Institution, 1981), pp. 41–82.

51. *Nuclear Proliferation and Civilian Nuclear Power*, p. 2-12.

52. For a discussion of the development of national stockpiles to make a system of cross-guarantees more effective, see Yager, pp. 58-59.

53. Ibid., p. 57.

54. A good discussion of this institutional alternative is provided by Yager, pp. 60-66. See also *Nuclear Proliferation and Civilian Nuclear Power*, pp. 2-12 to 2-13, and *The Nuclear Fuel Bank Issue as Seen by Uranium Producers and Consumers* (London: Uranium Institute, 1979).

55. These questions are addressed by Yager, pp. 61-66.

56. *INFCE Summary Volume*, p. 130. See also *Assurances of Long-Term Supply of Technology, Fuel and Heavy Water and Services in the Interest of National Needs, Consistent with Non-Proliferation*, Report of INFCE Working Group 3 (Vienna: IAEA, 1980).

57. See, for example, Ted Greenwood and Robert Haffa, Jr., "Supply-Side Non-Proliferation," *Foreign Policy* (Spring 1981), pp. 125–140; Steven J. Baker, "Why Not a Nuclear Fuel Cartel?" in William H. Kincade and Jeffrey D. Porro, eds., *Negotiating Security: An Arms Control Reader* (Washington, D.C.: Arms Control Association and the Carnegie Endowment for International Peace, 1979), pp. 152–156; and Amory Lovins, L. Hunter Lovins, and Leonard Ross, "Nuclear Power and Nuclear Bombs," *Foreign Affairs* (Summer 1980), pp. 1137–1177. Lovins et al. believe that reliance on the market mechanism would ultimately move nations away from nuclear power altogether.

58. Greenwood and Haffa recognize this problem, p. 138

59. See *Nuclear Proliferation and Civilian Nuclear Power*, pp. 2-20.

60. See, for example, *Nuclear Power and Nuclear Weapons Proliferation*, Report of the Atlantic Council's Nuclear Fuels Policy Working Group, Vol. 2 (Boulder, Co.: Westview Press, 1978), pp. 22–23; Ted Greenwood, "Discouraging Proliferation in the Next Decade and Beyond," in Ted Greenwood, Harold A. Feiveson, and Theodore B. Taylor, *Nuclear Proliferation: Motivations, Capabilities, and Strategies for Control* (New York: McGraw-Hill, 1977), pp. 78–79; *Nuclear Proliferation and Safeguards*, p. 67; and Rowen and Rowen, p. 37.

61. For a discussion of U.S. sanctions in this case, see Ernest W. Lefever, *Nuclear Arms in the Third World* (Washington, D.C.: Brookings Institution, 1979), p. 130, and Leslie Gelb, "Arms Sales," *Foreign Policy* (1977), pp. 11–13.

62. Combined U.S. and Soviet pressures on South Africa appear to have prevented that country, to date, from demonstrating a nuclear weapon but not from acquiring the capability. *Nuclear Power and Nuclear Weapons Proliferation*, Vol 2, p. 27. See also Ashok Kapur, *International Nuclear Proliferation* (New York: Praeger, 1979), pp. 233–272, and Richard Betts, "South Africa," in Yager, *Nonproliferation and U.S. Foreign Policy*, pp. 283–308.

63. *Nuclear Power and Nuclear Weapons Proliferation*, Vol. 2, p. 27.

64. Ibid., p. 23.

65. Ibid.

66. George Quester, "Introduction: In Defense of Some Optimism," *International Organization* (Winter 1981), p. 11.

67. Ibid. An alternative view is that the threat of strong sanctions kept India from exploding a second device. This interpretation was suggested to me by Thomas Graham in a personal communication.

68. As will be discussed below, an alternative focal point might be so-called dedicated facilities, i.e., plants designed specifically for the production of weapons-grade uranium or plutonium.

69. See Epstein, *The Last Chance*, p. 147, and *Nuclear Proliferation Factbook* 3rd edition (Washington, D.C.: Government Printing Office, September 1980), pp. 390–391.

70. *Nuclear Proliferation and Safeguards*, p. 194.

71. See ibid., p. 206, and Gene I. Rochlin, *Plutonium, Power and Politics* (Berkeley: University of California Press, 1979), p. 151. An excellent discussion of national safeguards is provided by Mason Willrich and Theodore Taylor in *Nuclear Theft: Risks and Safeguards* (Chambridge, Mass.: Ballinger, 1974).

72. Reprinted in Epstein, *The Last Chance*, pp. 148–149.

73. Ibid., p. 149. See also Ralph Mabry, "The Present International Nuclear Regime," in Yager, *International Cooperation*, pp. 145–171. For a discussion of the technical means used by the IAEA in implementing its safeguards system, see Kapur, pp. 125–133, and *Nuclear Proliferation and Safeguards*, pp. 205–211.

74. Epstein, *The Last Chance*, p. 151.

75. *IAEA Bulletin*, March 1981, p. 32.

76. SIPRI, *SIPRI YEARBOOK 1981*, p. 311.

77. See, for example, Rochlin, p. 145; Epstein, *The Last Chance*, p. 153; and *Nuclear Power Issues and Choices*, p. 292.

78. See Henry S. Rowen, "How to Develop Nuclear Power While Limiting Its Dangers: Proposed Changes in the International Nuclear System," Mimeo., August 23, 1977, pp. 5–6.

79. Ibid., p. 6.

80. See Mabry, p. 167, and Paul C. Szasz, "The Inadequacy of International Nuclear Safeguards," *Journal of International Law and Economics*, Vol. 10 (1975), p. 434.

81. Pierre Lellouche, "Internationalization of the Nuclear Fuel Cycle and Nonproliferation Strategy," (SJD Dissertation, Harvard Law School, 1979), pp. 182–187.

82. President Reagan, in his first major statement on nuclear proliferation, indicated that his administration would not "inhibit or set back civil reprocessing under breeder-reactor development abroad in nations with advanced nuclear power programs *where it does not constitute a proliferation risk*" (emphasis added). *New York Times* (July 17, 1981). The magnitude of change in U.S. policy is obscured by the last phrase.

83. Opposition to safeguards by states with large commercial nuclear activities on the grounds that they compromise industrial secrets and inflict commercial penalties is now rarely raised. (See SIPRI, *SIPRI Yearbook 1981*, p. 306.) For a discussion of French and German resistance to the principle of the automatic extension of full-scope safeguards to clients purchasing nuclear goods, see Lellouche, pp. 188–189.

84. Mabry, p. 171.

85. See Mabry, p. 171, and David Fischer, *International Safeguards 1979*, Working Paper of the International Consultative Group of Nuclear Energy (New York: Rockefeller Foundation and the Royal Institute of International Affairs, 1979), pp. 33–34. Mabry reports that the in-plant dynamics material control system (Dymac) currently being developed in the United States is expected to provide near real-time material control by performing nearly continuous measurements of all materials being stored, transferred, or processed.

86. *Nuclear Proliferation and Safeguards*, p. 80.

87. Mabry, p. 171; Fischer, p. 31; Feiveson and Taylor, p. 157; and *Nuclear Proliferation and Safeguards*, p. 80.

88. Epstein, *The Last Chance*, p. 160 and SIPRI, *SIPRI Yearbook 1981*, p. 309. For lists of additional measures to strengthen safeguards see *Nuclear Proliferation and Safeguards*, pp. 80–81; Epstein, *The Last Chance*, pp. 160–161; Rochlin, pp. 174–180; Fischer, pp. 31–35; and Feiveson and Taylor, pp. 155–158.

89. See Lellouche, p. 186, and SIPRI, *SIPRI Yearbook 1981*, pp. 307–308. At the conference, most opposition to the imposition of full-scope safeguards as a condition of supply to non-NPT parties came from the Group of 77, a body of principally developing and nonaligned states.

90. Excellent reviews of multinational institutional arrangements for non-proliferation are provided by Lellouche; Rochlin, pp. 189–308; Lawrence Scheinman, "Multinational Alternatives and Nuclear Proliferation," *International Organization* (Winter 1981), pp. 77–102; the collection of essays in Abram Chayes and W. Bennett Lewis, eds., *International Arrangements for Nuclear Fuel Reprocessing* (Cambridge, Mass.: Ballinger, 1977). The most comprehensive examination of the subject is the two-volume IAEA study, *Regional Nuclear Fuel Cycle Centres: 1977 Report of the IAEA Study Projects* (Vienna: IAEA, 1977).

91. See, for example, Michael Guhin, *Nuclear Paradox: Security Risks of the Peaceful Atom* (Washington, D.C.: American Enterprise Institute for Public Policy Research, 1976), pp. 48–49; Albert Wohlstetter et al., *Swords from Plowshares* (Chicago: University of Chicago Press, 1979), p. 31; *Nuclear Proliferation and Safeguards*, p. 219; and Scheinman, pp. 98–99. Economies of scale is another potential advantage not directly related to proliferation considerations often attributed to MFCFs.

92. Scheinman, p. 98.

93. *Nuclear Weapons Proliferation and the International Atomic Energy Agency* (Report prepared by the Congressional Research Service for the U.S. Senate Committee on Government Operations, March 1976), p. 127.

94. See Rochlin, pp. 315–328, for an attempt to assess the relative advantages and disadvantages of multinational centers for different fuel cycle activities and the relative difficulty of negotiating arrangements for them. See especially the summary chart on p. 323.

95. *INFCE Summary Volume*, p. 48.

96. Scheinman, pp. 82–83.

97. For a discussion of these multinational ventures as possible models for MFCFs, see Scheinman, pp. 82–92; Lellouche, pp. 402–417; and *Nuclear Power and Nuclear Weapons Proliferation*, Vol 1, pp. 98–110.

98. Mabry, pp. 125–126.

99. Scheinman, p. 97.

100. Ibid., p. 101. For two innovative proposals that attempt to meet this challenge, see Bennett Ramberg, "Preventative Medicine for Global Nuclear Energy Risks: A Proposal for an International Nuclear Export Review Board," Paper presented to the California Seminar on Arms Control and Foreign Policy, July 1979, and John H. Barton, ed., *Evaluation of an Integrated International Fuel Authority* (Institute for Energy Study, Stanford University, 1978).

101. Joseph S. Nye, "Nonproliferation: A Long-Term Strategy," *Foreign Affairs* (April 1978), p. 602.

102. Smith and Rathjens, p. 877.

103. See, for example, Neff and Jacoby, pp. 1141–1143.

104. Smith and Rathjens, p. 887.

105. Ibid.

106. Japan and West Germany are examples of the first category of states; Pakistan is the prime example of the second category.

107. See *SIPRI Yearbook 1981*, pp. 317–318, for a discussion of these and other complaints by Third World states raised at the Second NPT Review Conference.

108. For a discussion of these views, see Charles K. Ebinger, "International Politics of Nuclear Energy," *Washington Papers*, No. 57, pp. 82–83.

109. Useful discussions of possible third-tier suppliers are provided by Lewis A. Dunn, "After INFCE: Some Next Steps for Nonproliferation Policy," Hudson Institute Paper, October 22, 1969, pp. 11–13, and Henry Rowen and Richard Brody, "Nuclear Potential and Possible Contingencies," in Joseph Yager, ed., *Nonproliferation and U.S. Foreign Policy*, pp. 220–225.

110. See Kapur, p. 118. India has provided technical nuclear assistance and training to Egypt, Vietnam, Argentina, and Libya. See Dunn, p. 12.

111. This point is made in *Nuclear Proliferation and Safeguards*, p. 75.

112. Ibid.

113. Ibid., p. 76.

114. For a discussion of this point, see Scheinman, p. 79.

115. See *Reprocessing, Plutonium Handling, Recycle*, Report of INFCE Working Group 4 (Vienna: IAEA, 1980), p. 145.

116. For a discussion of those "Category One" technical measures, see *Reprocessing, Plutonium Handling, Recycle*, pp. 60–64 and 146; *Nuclear Proliferation and Safeguards*, pp. 200–201; and *Nuclear Proliferation and Civilian Nuclear Power*, Vol. 1, pp. 143–148, and Vol. 2, pp. 2-25 and 2-35.

117. *Reprocessing, Plutonium Handling, Recycle*, p. 60. For a less positive assessment, see *Nuclear Proliferation and Safeguards*, pp. 40 and 202.

118. See *Nuclear Proliferation and Civilian Nuclear Power*, Vol 2, p. 2-26, and *Reprocessing, Plutonium Handling, Recycle*, pp. 26 and 61–65.

119. Useful discussions of these techniques are provided in *Nuclear Proliferation and Civilian Nuclear Power*, Vol. 1, p. 42; Rochlin, pp. 215–216; *Nuclear Proliferation and Safeguards*, pp. 200–201; and *Reprocessing, Plutonium Handling, Recycle*, p. 147.

120. These difficulties are discussed in *Nuclear Proliferation and Civilian Nuclear Power*, Vol. 1, pp. 42 and 148.

121. See *Reprocessing, Plutonium Handling, Recycle*, p. 147, and *Nuclear Proliferation and Civilian Nuclear Power*, Vol. 2, p. 42.

122. *Nuclear Proliferation and Civilian Nuclear Power*, p. 144.

123. See ibid., pp. 146 and 148.

124. The INFCE report indicates that the effect of retaining the fission products in the fabrication process is not known and that "it is unlikely that partial processing could be developed to the point where it could be introduced into industrial plants until some time after the end of the century." *Reprocessing, Plutonium Handling, Recycle*, p. 66.

125. Ibid. See also *Nuclear Proliferation and Civilian Nuclear Power*, Vol. 1, p. 144.

126. See *Nuclear Proliferation and Civilian Nuclear Power*, Vol. 2, p. 2-27.

127. For a discussion of the Pipex concept, see *Reprocessing, Plutonium Handling, Recycle*, pp. 68–69, and IFCE/DEP/W64/64, "Pipex—A Model of Design Concept for Reprocessing Plants with Improved Containment and Surveillance Features," France/Federal Republic of Germany, March 15, 1979.

128. For a discussion of the CIVEX process, recently advanced as an alternative to the PUREX method of reprocessing, see Rochlin, pp. 218–219; *Nuclear News* (April 1978), pp. 31–37; and "Fuel Reprocessing Still the Focus of U.S. Nonproliferation Policy," *Science* (August 1978), p. 697.

129. See Lovins et al., pp. 1137–1177.

130. For a discussion of possible means to diminish the wartime vulnerability of nuclear energy facilities, see Bennett Ramberg, *Destruction of Nuclear Energy Facilities in War: The Problem and the Implications* (Lexington, Mass.: Lexington Books, 1980), pp. 113–160.

131. For a discussion of the concept of "timely warning," see Wohlstetter et al., pp. 24–25; *Nuclear Power and Nuclear Weapons Proliferation*, Vol. 2, pp. 20–22; Rochlin, pp. 146–149; and Mabry, pp. 167–168.

132. The Iraqi reactor bombed by the Israelis utilized 93 percent enriched uranium. The lesson of the Iraqi nuclear program for "timely warning" is mixed. Although the Israelis struck before Iraq had developed a bomb, post hoc analyses of the program reveal mixed intelligence estimates of the time Iraq required for construction of a nuclear explosive, no evidence of unambiguous Iraqi violations of IAEA safeguards, and few clues to how the United States or other Western nations would have responded had they been convinced, as were the Israelis, that Iraq would soon have begun the manufacture of nuclear weapons. See "Israeli Attack on Iraqi Nuclear Facilities," Hearings before the Committee on Foreign Affairs, U.S. House of Representatives, June 17 and 25, 1981.

133. See, for example, Lewis Dunn and Herman Kahn, *Trends in Nuclear Proliferation, 1975–1995* (Croton-on-Hudson, N.Y.: Hudson Institute, 1976), p. 144, and Harold W. Maynard, "In Case of Deluge: Where Nuclear Proliferation Meets Conventional Arms Sales," (Mimeo., USAF Academy, July 29, 1977). For a critique of this approach, see Thomas A. Halsted, "Nuclear Proliferation: How to Retard It, Live With It," a Workshop Report of the Aspen Institute for Humanistic Studies, 1977, pp. 19–20.

134. See Dunn and Kahn, pp. 89–94.

135. Stephen M. Meyer, "Probing the Causes of Nuclear Proliferation: An Empirical Analysis, 1940–1973" (Ph.D. Dissertation, University of Michigan, 1978).

136. For a much more optimistic outlook on nonproliferation, see George Quester, "Introduction: In Defense of Some Optimism," *International Organization* (Winter 1981), pp. 1–14.

137. This point is also made by Lewis A. Dunn, "The Proliferation Policy Agenda: Taking Stock," Report of the World Peace Foundation Conference on Managing in a Proliferation-Prone World (Dedham, Mass., December 9–11, 1977).

138. This is George Quester's formulation in "Nuclear Proliferation: Linkages and Solutions," *International Organization* (Autumn 1979), p. 566.

139. Richard Rosecrance, "International Stability and Nuclear Diffusion," in Rosecrance, ed., *The Dispersion of Nuclear Weapons* (New York: Columbia University Press, 1964), p. 314.

33. Nuclear Policy and World Order: Why Denuclearization?

Richard A. Falk

One line of attack on nonproliferation doctrine emerges from the bosom of the nuclear industry itself. Writing in *Fortune*, Tom Alexander (1975) declares that "it seems clear that we are sacrificing too much of our foreign policy on the altar of nonproliferation." In effect, Alexander is indicting U.S. foreign policy, not only because it is futile so far as nonproliferation is concerned, but also because it is self-defeating as well—merely shifting important shares of the export market to foreign competitors who have less concern for nonproliferation goals than we. It also saturates the export market with more proliferation-prone technology (e.g. Canada's CANDU reactor, whose wastes are fissionable without reprocessing). Given the logic of the competition, on the one hand, and the priority of security, on the other, American policy regarding international nuclear transactions is indeed implausible in a sense. Why shouldn't French and German competitors strive for a larger share of a lucrative market estimated to be worth $295 billion over the period 1971–1985? (Baker, 1975). Why shouldn't Brazil or South Africa acquire a nuclear option to satisfy the drive for a first-rank power status or as a hedge against future contingencies? Whether the issue be whales or nuclear bombs, all governments are primarily motivated by relatively short-term calculations of national economic and political self-interest. Their willingness to sacrifice any portion of that self-interest out of deference to the world-community well-being is purely rhetorical, if, and to the extent that, it exists at all. On nuclear policy specifically, America's apparently greater concern with nonproliferation does not display a more evolved world-community consciousness, but rather reflects its geopolitical position as a global security manager. As Hedley Bull (1975) puts it, implicit in the superpowers' choice "of proliferation as the danger to peace and security that must be curbed now—rather than, say, the danger inherent in the growth of their own weapons stockpiles—is the perception that curbs in this area will restrict others and not themselves." It is hegemony which is jeopardized by proliferation, because the spread of nuclear weapons makes it harder for the superpowers to control the boundaries and predict the outcome of regional conflicts in which they themselves have some involvement. In other words, both geopolitical control and bipolar stability are distinctively superpower preoccupations. Hence, it is not surprising that the United States aspires to reconcile its geopolitical and commercial goals at the altar of nonproliferation.

At the same time, I also agree with Richard Betts (1977) that "the full cost of preventing a country from going nuclear has to be weighed against contradictory goals. Senator Ribicoff to the contrary, strategy has to accommodate to the fact that the United States has other interests in foreign policy besides prevention of nuclear spread." One can add, of course, that so have other nuclear powers. These interests include export markets, political influence, regional balance, and great-power rivalry. There is simply no painless way for any of the nuclear supplier-states to implement a strategy of nonproliferation, and even American policymakers don't necessarily agree among themselves that nonproliferation deserves absolute priority over all other foreign policy goals. For instance, if key countries like Iran, Saudi Arabia, or Turkey credibly threatened to shift their geopolitical allegiance away from the West unless they were allowed to achieve nuclear status, American leaders would probably cease to insist on nonproliferation in strategically sensitive cases.

Nevertheless, if the nuclear suppliers can reach an agreement on common ground rules, then both the superpowers will be able to pursue their global geopolitical strategies without losing ground in the lucrative commercial market. Although the Soviet Union is more exclusively concerned with geopolitics than the United States, both countries seem to be moving toward a similar set of policies on nuclear issues (as was evident at the NPT review conference), and have even supported and taken part in the London supplier conferences. A common superpower position on nonproliferation seems to be emerging without any explicit concert of action.

An additional factor sets the nuclear superpowers apart from the other supplier-nations. The United States and the Soviet Union are both concerned with maintaining "first use options" in situations other than the ultimate self-defense of homeland. Consequently, nonproliferation goals provide a convenient means of protecting existing military advantages for the present owners of nuclear weapons. For example, by threatening to defend South Korea with nuclear weapons during the Kissinger era, American officials sought a cheap option (compared to that pursued in Vietnam) of intimidating a non-nuclear Third World country with the specter of nuclear devastation.

Of course, such diplomacy itself undermines efforts to curtail proliferation, by demonstrating how vulnerable non-nuclear states are to such one-sided blackmail. Precisely because such a menacing posture brings the inherent discrimination of the NPT system into the open, it is criticized by moderate arms controllers. Generally, "liberals" and "rationalists" understand that it could be costly to undermine the calculus of gains and losses associated with non-nuclear status.[1] However, the liberal critique is directed only to the excess of discrimination, not to its *existence*, not to its underlying structure.

According to a less sentimental perspective on proliferation policy, the discrimination issue is only a red herring, an illustration of "the moralist fallacy" which alleges that moral considerations have an important influence on behavior (in this instance, decisions to acquire nuclear capabilities), when the evidence seems to favor other explanations (namely, self-interest as related to fear and ambition). One analyst of this persuasion (Betts, 1977) contends that "Stressing the discriminatory immorality of Soviet and American maintenance of large nuclear arms capabilities is analytically wrong, prescriptively quixotic, and a dangerous misdirection of effort." Although its tone is strident, the statement does contain a grain of truth. Liberal attempts to blunt such "discriminatory immorality" do tend to underestimate the logic of self-interested behavior, which is, after all, the dominant feature of the statist system of world order.

At the same time, I strongly applaud all efforts to stress discrimination within the existing international order, if such efforts form part of an overall assault on the primacy of state interests and the war-based security system, on the hierarchical and hegemonical features of the state system, and on statist logic altogether. If our perspective is one of system-change rather than system-reform, then the acknowledged discrimination of nuclear-weapons distribution within the present system is both a mobilizing focus and a primary target. This emphasis is especially appropriate if our primary audiences are not policymaking elites, but more flexible and open-minded sectors of public opinion.

Even in the terms of statist logic, a geopolitical strategy that goes no farther than proliferation is questionable on both pragmatic and principled grounds. On pragmatic grounds, it is unlikely to work because there is no basic reason why those who want nuclear weapons should forego them, so long as some states insist upon their right to retain and develop weapons further. Moreover, so long as civilian nuclear power continues to expand, there can be no reliable assurance that any given state has not acquired a covert or latent nuclear-weapons capability. From a statist perspective, the most effective approach to nonproliferation would probably require a maximum extension of superpower roles. However, that outcome would itself conflict with the geopolitical goals held by the most intense advocates of nonproliferation. As Betts (1977) argues, "There is no free lunch in nonproliferation policy . . . the biggest price would be the reaffirmation or extension of protective alliances which would relieve the insecurities" of those states tempted by their national situation to acquire nuclear weapons. Betts specifies this price tag in suggestive ways. It is worth stationing American troops on Israeli soil to obtain Israeli adherence to the NPT, he argues; it is also worth acquiescing in South Korean repression; worth incurring India's displeasure by aiding Pakistan in non-nuclear respects; worth letting China choose whether it wants the U.S. to guarantee Taiwan against invasion or would rather risk having a nuclear Taiwan; and worth abandoning South Africa with the warning that the U.S. will support the armed struggle of black Africans if Pretoria ever threatens its adversaries with nuclear attack (Betts, 1977). What is evident, whether or not one goes along with these policy prescriptions, it that there is no way within the state system to reconcile nonproliferation goals with other widely endorsed world-order values such as nonintervention, human rights, and peace. It is self-deceiving to claim otherwise.

On principled grounds, the morality of the state system is built around the primacy of state interests as conceived by governmental leaders. It is instructive to recall how enthusiastic our highest officials became upon being told in July 1945 that the atomic bomb would soon be definitely available to the United States—as a weapon of war (against Japan) and as an instrument of diplomacy (against the Soviet Union, and to a far lesser extent, Great Britain).[2]

True, once the horrible effects of atomic power became clear, there was some attempt (whose seriousness and reasonableness still are difficult to assess) to rid the world of nuclear weapons for all time. Nevertheless, the main patterns of behavior suggest that the use, development, and role of nuclear arms have been almost entirely determined by considerations of state power. Hence, there is little reason to suppose that such considerations will not prevail in the future, as they have in the past, in determining whether additional governments will decide to develop, deploy, and use nuclear arms. Government leaders may pursue self-destructive policies based on the narrow interests of their ruling groups and may, further, be entrapped within horizons of time and security which are far too short even from the perspective of national well-being. Nevertheless, such leaders are the only effective policymakers on nuclear matters, given the structure and political realities of the state system. Furthermore, in a world system that has been victimized by imperial patterns of exploitation, there is little rational and even less emotional appeal in positions which are premised upon inherent discrimination between states which do and do not possess nuclear weapons at a given moment of time. The identity of "responsible states" and "terroristic elements" may seem crystal clear to George Ball and Henry Kissinger, but not at all so to the leaders of a wide variety of Third World nations, wherein more than two-thirds of humanity reside. Hence, a major conclusion of a world-order analysis guided by the values already enumerated is that nonproliferation goals can become persuasive ingredients of global policy only when they are integrated into a credible program of total denuclearization.

TOWARD MILITARY DENUCLEARIZATION

Military denuclearization means the process of progressively eliminating nuclear weapons. The goal is a non-nuclear world in which nuclear weapons are neither legitimate, nor possessed by any state. In the context of denuclearization, nonproliferation is obviously an integral but secondary goal. From this perspective, the gravest dangers are presented, not by those international actors who *may* acquire nuclear weapons, but by those who already possess them, who rely on their active role in a variety of security situations, and who have continued to deploy and "improve" upon nuclear weapon systems.[3]

In world order terms, the argument for denuclearization is again both pragmatic and principled. From a pragmatic perspective, denuclearization is the only way to overcome the inherent discrimination of the present world-order system and, in particular, the most extreme manifestation of that discrimination—namely, the capacity of nuclear states to decisively affect the security of non-nuclear and lesser nuclear states, under a wide variety of circumstances. Moreover, the state system derives its moral legitimacy from the juridical premise of sovereign equality. From a principled perspective, then, denuclearization would constitute a fuller realization of statist logic, which would in turn provide a positive basis for moving beyond the state system at some future time. Hence, whether the ultimate goal is to *reform* the state system or to actually *transform* that system, denuclearization would have a decisively beneficial effect. Nonproliferation divorced from denuclearization, by contrast, is at best ambiguous from both perspectives: it could possibly make the system more stable, but might well stabilize it in an imperial fashion.

Assuming, then, that denuclearization is a positive goal, is it also a feasible one? If so, to what extent? Even those who favor the approach disagree among themselves here. If denuclearization is to gain any momentum, far-reaching changes in the political climate must first take place within the leading nuclear nations. The prospects of denuclearization, at least in the decade ahead, will depend largely on domestic politics, and partly upon the interactive behavior and perceptions of the two superpowers. So long as the goal of genuine denuclearization lies outside the mainstream political debate in the United States and the Soviet Union, it has virtually no hope of getting started, at least this side of nuclear catastrophe.

Does the present atmosphere permit at least *modest* steps toward denuclearization? Unfortunately, even limited efforts in this direction are more problematical than is generally supposed. So long as the statist logic persists, government bureaucracies will be inherently incapable of endorsing policies which reject the endless search for military advantage. Hence, small steps like signing the ABM treaty or cancelling the B-1 program seem positive only when viewed in isolation, but not if evaluated in their full bureaucratic context. In such cases, as we have seen, alternative weapons systems at least as lethal are accelerated—"to fill the vacuum." This process is especially misleading to the general public. Encouraged to focus on dramatic and well-publicized concessions to "peace," most citizens can hardly help overlooking the technical diversion of funds to other weapons programs. Significantly, when President Carter vetoed the B-1 bomber, his explanation did not seem influenced at all by world-order goals.[4] Only a visionary leader willing to mobilize populist support could circumvent powerful special interests and the structures of bureaucratic politics. And then it is not evident whether such a leader could survive, physically or politically. Existing political elites seem genuinely entrapped, and cannot provide credible leadership to achieve even modest world-order goals.

Despite these caveats, several promising steps toward denuclearization could be taken right now. For instance, top government officials can and should repudiate the loose talk about using nuclear weapons in Third World contexts or against non-nuclear weapons states. Perhaps the main nuclear powers could even pledge never to use nuclear weapons first against a signatory of the NPT, or against non-nuclear powers. Such pledges might be reinforced and given credibility by shifting patterns of nuclear deployment (for example, nuclear weapons could be removed from Korea and from forward positions in Western Europe). However, such denuclearization steps, desirable as they are, might also be viewed as nothing more than attempts to restore the prospects of nonproliferation. In this respect, such forms of denuclearization are of a piece with various proposals designed to extend the so-called "nuclear shield" to non-nuclear states, or to work out contractual arrangements for peaceful nuclear explosions.[5] With all such proposals, nonproliferation is the essential goal and modest denuclearization is viewed—usually implicitly—as a tactic, virtually as "a bargaining chip."

In some instances, admittedly, denuclearization and nonproliferation appear to work at cross purposes. For example, in 1977 South Korea's President Park Chung Hee declared that his country would acquire its own nuclear arsenal, if the U.S. followed through President Carter's plan to remove nuclear weapons and American troops from South Korean territory.[6] How seriously should such a threat be taken?[7] Suppose South Korea does develop nuclear weapons in the wake of American withdrawal? Is the process of denuclearization worth the dangers of short-term proliferation? In another context, advocates of the neutron bomb (the so-called "enhanced radiation weapon") contend that its deployment in Europe will enhance NATO's credibility and make the outbreak of nuclear war less likely (Weinraub, 1977). In the short run, the logic of strategic thinking cuts deeply into arguments for denuclearization.

A comprehensive test ban (CTB) would represent a more momentous step down the denuclearization path, because it could substantially inhibit further nuclear weapons innovations—provided, of course, that it was imposed before accuracy, reliability, and throw-weight goals had been already attained. Here again, CBT is generally viewed as an element of reciprocity required to make nonproliferation credible in a world of self-assertive states. However, its implications could be more systemic—especially if linked to shared commitments by Moscow and Washington, first, to renounce limited nuclear war options, and, second, to limit the role of nuclear weapons to mutual deterrence of nuclear aggression.

A comprehensive no-first-use pledge would be another constructive step. Such a declaratory measure could provide important symbolic acknowledgement that nuclear weapons are illegitimate weapons of war, much as poison gas or biological weapons. To be credible, a no-first-use pledge would have to be coordinated with programs to redeploy nuclear weapons away from frontiers, and to augment conventional capacities, thereby signaling specific second-use intentions for nuclear weapons. Such a no-first-use declaration, if solemnly made and implemented, would have immense value as an educational experience that would, in turn, seem to support more drastic forms of denuclearization. Ironically, in the present world setting, it is not the superpowers but the pariah states vulnerable to armed attack who may prove the most reluctant to make such declarations. These pariah states are the only ones who face a severe security threat, but who do not seem capable of evolving any substitute for nuclear weapons.[8] Nevertheless, even if pariah states should remain outside the no-first-use orbit, the step would be a promising one, as it touches upon the geopolitical nexus of the existing system.

If we are to move beyond these secondary declaratory steps, however, the continental divide which separates nonproliferation thinking from denuclearization thinking must sooner or later be crossed.[9] Up to this point, the two perspectives overlap and conflicting interpretations are plausible for any given step. As suggested already, unambiguous denuclearization presupposes a domestic political shift of values and priorities within the principal nuclear states. It is difficult to depict the precise character of this value shift, but it would almost certainly have to involve a societal commitment to the pursuit of drastic global change, based on the sort of world-order values outlined above.[10] This shift need not entail a commitment to world government nor to any other specific structure. In fact, I personally favor world-order solutions based on political and economic decentralization combined with functional centralization.

A value shift would finally clear the path for genuine nuclear disarmament, to be accompanied at later stages by conventional disarmament as well (beginning with high-technology weapons like precision-guided munitions). Nevertheless, even after genuine nuclear disarmament becomes an accepted goal, the traditional bureaucratic consensus is likely to make sure that each step toward denuclearization and disarmament is followed—and perhaps even more than offset—by compensatory moves which augment conventional weapons both quantitatively and qualitatively. In other words, even if the denuclearization divide has been clearly crossed, the disarmament divide will still remain. In time, the value shift needed to cross the first may also generate sufficient momentum to carry the political process across the second as well. However, this optimistic possibility is by no means assured. So long as policymaking elites in powerful states adhere to conventional notions of national security, the outlook for disarmament is bleak indeed.[11]

During the transitional periods when each of these major divides are being traversed—from nonproliferation to denuclearization and finally to general disarmament—political leaders are bound to feel that their national security is being eroded. Coping with these fears and with the counterproductive behavior they may incite will present critical challenges to advocates of drastic global change. The problem can hardly be solved until new concepts of national security and positive visions of comprehensive change find their way into the ruling circles of major powers.

When the governments of the world at last begin to lay down their nuclear arms and then their conventional weapons as well, it will probably be useful to establish a supranational police/military capability to serve on both regional and global levels. An institution of this kind could help enforce the disarming process, and could also play a transitional role as supranational "manager" for maintaining global peace.[12] To prevent new incarnations of the war system from emerging, an appropriate constitutional framework will also be needed, with particular emphasis on checks and balances, separation of powers, compromises between efficiency and accountability, and, most of all, a new image of national security that does not depend on military might.[13] Deep in such a disarming process lies the question of whether a supranational security agency should itself possess nuclear weapons as a residual deterrent against cheating, nuclear rearmament, terrorism, and the like. If and when the time comes, this will be an extremely vexing issue, but it is not one which can be predetermined in the present global setting. (Even should a supranational security agency be armed with nuclear weapons, presumably that decision would be a conditional and temporary one hedged by elaborate constraints.)

IS MILITARY DENUCLEARIZATION ENOUGH?
A CASE FOR CIVILIAN DENUCLEARIZATION

The history of civilian nuclear power is a twisted one. It is closely associated with the sense of guilt felt by those who first developed the atomic bomb, and who subsequently tried to make partial atonement by putting the atom to constructive use. Their hope was that the civilian nuclear spin-offs, once perfected, could be lifted from their military context, put to good domestic use, and then transferred abroad through the Non-Proliferation Treaty—which would yield lucrative foreign markets for U.S. industry in the process. However, the hope that atomic power could serve peace without being tarnished by the horror of Hiroshima fostered an artificial separation between the military and civilian nuclear programs. The catch, and it is a catch-22, is that there is no way to spread nuclear technology around without inevitably spreading the weapons capability right along with it.[14] It took India's nuclear explosion to bring this reality home. Until then, nations with civilian nuclear programs were indiscriminately put in the category of non-nuclear states, for military and international-legal purposes, unless they had actually tested a nuclear bomb. This view reinforced the illusion that only military proliferation as such was evil, but that civilian nuclear spread was beneficial (or at least neutral) from the perspective of international stability.

In recent years, however, far more sophisticated measures of nuclear capability have emerged. They include the possession of basic nuclear knowledge, the number and kind of fuel-cycle facilities, access to fissionable material, the extent of technological engineering and managerial know-how, and so forth (Dunn and Overhold, 1976). More generally speaking, the link between civilian nuclear proliferation and the proliferation of nuclear weapons has now passed into conventional wisdom.

Three major strategies have evolved in response to this new insight, but all with only the limited goal of halting the spread of nuclear arms. In other words, the principal lines of thought all represent extensions of the nonproliferation approach to international security. The first such strategy involves a moratorium or even an outright ban on commercial nuclear power. In part, this approach is an offshoot of the general Western anxiety about nuclear weapons falling into "wrong" hands (Yergin, 1977a). Responding to "the terrifying prospects of atomic bombs almost everywhere," Daniel Yergin cites the abandonment of civil nuclear power as possibly "the decisive step" in the struggle against proliferation. In view of his overall assessment of nuclear power, including its declining commercial appeal, Yergin calls for an American moratorium on "the new development of conventional fission nuclear power."[15] In several major countries there is already growing support for this approach,[16] motivated largely by the belief that civilian nuclear power facilities simply cannot be safeguarded well enough to permanently deter or foil nuclear theft. Lovins, an antinuclear spokesman, explains: "The fundamental reason that nuclear theft cannot be prevented is that people and human institutions are imperfect. No arrangement, however good it looks on paper, and however competently and devotedly it is established, is proof against boredom, laxity, or corruption."

Those who adhere to an opposing line of thought insist that it is misleading to lump all civilian nuclear technologies together. They point out that there are, in fact, several distinct variants already in being and even more are in the offing. Therefore, this approach to nonproliferation is to discourage the most proliferation-prone technologies (those having to do with breeder reactors and plutonium recycle), and to encourage those that are most resistant to use for weapons production.[17] This camp has always found fusion technology especially attractive, since it produces no weapons-grade material as a by-product, and the attendant problems of accident, radioactive hazard, and waste disposal seem smaller than in the case of fission. However, certain serious environmental and security problems do exist. Moreover, fusion reactors require astronomical capital outlays that would centralize energy production to an even greater degree than a large-scale fission program. It has been estimated that $20 billion would be needed in the research and development phase "before commercial use could be contemplated."[18] Moreover, the technical obstacles to commercial nuclear fusion remain so formidable that they may well prove impossible to overcome. At best, it seems implausible to expect fusion technology to be available until well into the next century, if at all (Kenward, 1976, Lovins, 1975, Miller, Jr., 1975). Finally, the most probable line of fusion development would embody the worst features of breeder technology, including its susceptibility to proliferation. For technical and economic reasons, "the first generation of fusion reactors would consist of fusion-fission hybrids designed to breed plutonium" (Hayes, 1976). Hence, all things considered, nuclear fusion appears to be an impossibly difficult or at best an exceedingly long-term and costly energy option which, in all probability, would not even achieve the goal of curbing weapons proliferation.

Up to now, the United States has been pursuing a third strategy: attempting to strike a compromise between nonproliferation objectives and economic/energy goals. This official approach centers on internationalizing those elements of the fuel cycle most susceptible to illicit diversion.[19] Its essence, however, is to regard inherent discrimination as a permanent feature of international relations, and to assume that the global spread of civilian nuclear power facilities is inevitable and irreversible. For this reason, the prevailing goals, as expressed in nonproliferation terms, are to bring the pace of nuclear spread into line with "realistic" expectations. The most we can hope for, in this view, is to avoid the emergence of 20 to 50 nuclear powers by the year 2000; and to prevent illicit acquisition altogether. For example, the Aspen group's positive image is a world with no more than ten nuclear powers by 2020; George Quester (1975) suggests that one more nuclear power each decade would be acceptable.

Perhaps the most notable aspect of the twin debates over civilian nuclear spread and over nuclear proliferation in the military realm is their relative isolation from one another. So far, domestic discussions of nuclear power have largely ignored international security questions, focusing instead on matters of safety, health, environmental quality, political centralization, and civil liberties (Falk, 1976, and Hayes, 1976). Failure to link these two sets of issues seems foolishly shortsighted, because both the capital requirements and the lead times needed to readjust energy systems make civilian nuclear power a world-order issue of first magnitude. To be more specific, the heavy investments demanded by a large-scale nuclear energy program would set critical—even though not yet generally evident—limits on the prospects for realizing world-order values.

This paper, however, limits itself to exploring whether meaningful and permanent denuclearization can be achieved in the military sphere as long as governments continue to pursue the civilian nuclear energy option. In other words, if we are to rid the world of atomic weapons forever, must we repudiate the "peaceful atom" as well? The answer seems clear, given the impact of a global civilian nuclear power program. First of all, the rapid spread of reactors (SIPRI estimates a fourfold growth from 99 reactors in 15 countries in 1970 to 405 reactors in 28 countries by 1980) in the years ahead vastly increases the global potential for weapons proliferation.[20] If that potential should be rapidly translated into weapons capability, then the movement toward denuclearization is likely to be thwarted and perhaps irreversibly so. The mere attempt to discourage the surreptitious manufacture of nuclear weapons would require significant degrees of surveillance and intrusive inspection, as well as changes in export policies of all nuclear suppliers. Surely, the prospects for denuclearization, already doubtful in a world of persisting inequality and conflict, would be even more vulnerable to disruption at an increasing number of points in a world of ubiquitous nuclear power plants. Clearly, there is something incoherent about trying to get rid of nuclear weapons while simultaneously disseminating the techniques and materials that make their acquisition even easier.[21] More important still, the prospects for denuclearization presuppose broad social movements within many societies, around a series of interrelated value goals. These goals include some loosening of centralized political controls over national populations, but that possibility is virtually precluded by civilian nuclear power—with its terrorist potential, its high degree of energy centralization and its concomitant need for equally centralized political control.

All nuclear facilities, whether civilian or military, must be vigilantly guarded. Recent studies in the United States and elsewhere emphasize the vulnerability of these facilities, especially in view of the inadequacy of present security standards (Lovins, 1977). Better protection, extending to lines of supply, shipments of nuclear fuel and, possibly, spent fuel and wastes requires a virtual paramilitary capability with extensive authority to handle suspects and threats. Democratic procedures and associated civil and political rights are too fragile to withstand such intense security pressures (Ayres, 1975). Given a world-order perspective that emphasizes the interrelations of values, it is important to assess energy and security policy choices with reference to their impacts on prospects for humane governance. On this basis alone, nuclear power appears unacceptable.

Symbolically and psychologically, the movement against nuclear power must be comprehensive, encompassing its military and civilian dimensions alike, if it is to achieve real mobilizing power. Lovins (1975) puts this well in arguing that the combination of elements in the overall denuclearization process produces "a psychological synergism that is essential to their success." In effect, the linkage between nuclear weapons and nuclear power produces mutually reinforcing patterns of support, as the coherent possibility of life-affirming alternative approaches to security and energy become more credible. A comprehensive antinuclear movement draws upon the vital energies of peoples devoted to keeping the earth safe and secure for future generations. To repudiate nuclear technology in all its forms would be to withdraw from a nuclear bargain that should never have been struck in the first place. The human species is not so constituted that it can achieve the infallibility and societal performance that nuclear safety presupposes, just as it isn't able to achieve the perfect rationality presupposed by deterrence-based security programs.

Is it feasible to eliminate commercial nuclear power from the world scene? Current trends certainly lead in the opposite direction, and to reverse them would require at least momentous decisions by the United States and other advanced industrial countries. In the short run, while alternative energy sources and decentralized social systems are being developed and deployed, some oil-dependent, balance-of-payment deficit countries may feel that they are locked into the nuclear option. However, recent research shows that even nations as dependent on imported energy as Japan could actually become energy independent, through a combination of rigorous conservation measures and the use of renewable, decentralized fuels (Lovins, 1976).

In view of the costs and dangers of nuclear energy, soft-energy alternatives, whose viability has been sufficiently demonstrated, deserve serious commitment. Even the prestigious Ford Foundation study of 1977 concludes, despite its acceptance of the inevitability of nuclear power, that "there is enough solar energy to meet any foreseeable needs for electrical energy. The question is one of price." Essentially because of this "question of price," the study concludes that solar energy "may provide a significant fraction of energy in the United States, but not until rather far into the twenty-first century, and with a price premium over nuclear or coal power."[22] Other assessments of solar potential are far more encouraging in respect of both time and cost. For instance, Feiveson and Taylor (1977) contend that "the prospects are excellent that solar energy can be developed and implemented on a large scale in a period of time comparable to that required to develop fully-safeguarded breeder systems."[23] Even a government-sponsored study of solar energy, which shares the conventional wisdom about high energy requirements, concludes that "Solar energy is not a cure-all for our energy problems; but combined with a larger strategy that includes energy conservation, cascading, and some sacrifice of convenience, solar energy does offer the option of a society based upon a renewable source of energy."[24]

In a sense, these assessments of solar potential are only minimal statements, based on technical and economic considerations. More positive and ambitious scenarios for the energy future of the world are now being projected. Writes Denis Hayes (1977a):

About one-fifth of all energy used around the world comes from solar resources: wind power, water power, biomass, and direct sunlight. By the year 2000, such renewable energy sources could provide 40 percent of the global energy budget; by 2025, humanity could obtain 75 percent of its energy from solar sources. Such a transition would not be cheap or easy, but its benefits would far outweigh the costs and difficulties.

During the period of transition, coal and conservation techniques (in building codes, automobile designs, and many industrial processes) could play an enormously constructive role in assisting us to move from our current reliance on finite reserves of oil and natural gas, to renewable energy sources. Lovins (1975) envisions an "energy income economy by 2025" (that is, one based on renewable resources) and argues that this goal can be implemented without great strain if "the sophisticated use of coal, chiefly at the modest scale" is encouraged to relieve the pressure on oil and gas during the transition period. Full-scale arguments on the viability of renewable fuels and possible transition strategies are enormously complex, of course, and are not all equally convincing. Nevertheless, authors like Hayes and Lovins have effectively shifted the balance of persuasion to those who persist in their belief that nuclear power is necessary and/or inevitable.

The changing economic realities pertaining to nuclear power, too, make its elimination more feasible than is generally supposed. The original case for peaceful nuclear power was based on the extravagant claim that it would be "too cheap to meter." But recent trends reveal a steadily increasing price per nuclear kilowatt hour, as well as a deteriorating cost picture relative to other energy sources. A careful analysis of U.S. fuel costs shows that in all regions of the country, coal is now cheaper than nuclear power, although the degree varies from 2% less in the northeast, to 49% in the Mountain Pacific northwest region.[25] Although nuclear power is often justified on economic grounds by those who believe we cannot afford to forego its cost advantages while basic needs go unmet around the world, the reality of rising nuclear costs undermines the validity of such economic rationale for proceeding down the nuclear path.

It is necessary to consider briefly the impact of these proposals on the economic prospects for poor Third World countries. Of course, the renewable energy potential of a given country varies according to geographical location, wind and geothermal resources, and hydroelectric potential. On the whole, however, Hayes (1977a) maintains that "In the Third World, enormous strides can be made with relatively modest investment if those investments are made wisely. For example, 2 percent of the world military budget for just one year could provide every rural Third World family with an efficient stove—doubling overnight the amount of useful work obtained from fuel wood, and reducing the pressure on the world's forests accordingly. On the other hand, to the extent that Third World development is culturally or economically tied to energy strategies in the industrial world, the pressure to import nuclear technology will remain strong." At one stage, renewable energy systems were viewed as "second-rate" solutions that no self-respecting Third World country would adopt. More recently, however, especially in the wake of the OPEC experience of 1973-74, Third World countries have shown a great deal more interest in evolving indigenous capabilities for energy production. As Hayes notes, these "indigenous technologies born of the new capability may prove to be more compatible with world needs than borrowed machines and methods." He goes on to point out that "Brazil's large methanol program, India's gobar gas plants, and the Middle East's growing fascination with solar electric technologies can all be read as signs of an interest in renewable energy resources that bodes well for the future."

Furthermore, renewable energy systems tend to be far more labor-intensive and decentralized, thereby encouraging productive use of the labor surplus which characterizes most poor countries, and also disengaging the economies of these countries from their expensive dependence on imported energy, capital, and technology. In this regard, goals of equity and self-reliance associated with world-order values seem to be tangibly facilitated by soft energy options.

Finally, even double denuclearization—eliminating nuclear weapons and civilian nuclear power—will not be enough to assure the success of the wider program of global changes envisioned here. The process of getting the nuclear genie back in the bottle must be associated with and sustained by a social movement organized around the interrelated pursuit of peace, economic well-being, social and political justice, and ecological balance, held together by an emergent sense of human community and planetary identity.[26] Such a movement need not be dedicated to global federalism. However, I personally hope that it would emphasize the deconcentration of wealth and the dispersal of authority at the national level. Presumably, some modes of central guidance will be required, but the preferable organizational dynamic would be dialectical, weighted toward the greatest possible decentralization of societal functions which still allows for the satisfaction of basic human needs. Separate state sovereignties, although still often useful to redress grievances within the existing frame of world politics, cannot be trusted to protect long-run human or overall planetary interests. I do not suggest that the state as actor will *disappear*, but that it will be *displaced* to varying degrees on various issues in varying places, by functional arrangements (international and transnational actors) which augment the roles of individuals, groups, and international institutions.

NOTES

1. See criticisms by the Aspen group of "loose talk" by James Schlesinger (as Secretary of Defense) with respect to possible uses of nuclear weapons by the United States. As Michael Nacht puts the views of the conference participants (in note 1 on page 15 of the report), "the right person to speak on questions of nuclear weapon use is the President and the tone should be one of awe."

2. The news of the successful test explosion at Alamogordo came to American leaders as they were attending the Potsdam Conference on the settlement of World War II, along with Soviet and British heads of state. Churchill observed that the news cheered up Truman to such an extent that "He was a changed man." One interpreter of the period reports that "the reassuring news about the bomb brought a complete reversal of U.S. goals for the conference" (Yergin 1977b).

3. The R&D and innovations pursued especially by the superpowers have been undertaken in a competitive pursuit of "superiority" rather than to assure the stability of deterrence. In other words, one cannot even argue convincingly that existing nuclear powers behave "responsibly" within the framework of stable deterrence. In the current context of international relations, the nuclear arms race with only its few mutually agreed upon "constraints" such as arms control measures seems every bit as "irresponsible" as the acquisition of nuclear weapons by additional governments. In essence, there is no particular reason to believe that today's nuclear powers are any more reliable than future nuclear states (in the Third World or elsewhere) would be. The evidence suggests that virtually *all* states are highly irresponsible when it comes to issues of national security.

4. As Bernard Weinraub, Pentagon correspondent for the *New York Times*, concludes: "it is evident that Mr. Carter's impulses were based by and large on military considerations." See Weinraub's persuasive analysis of the B-1 decision in the *New York Times*, July 3, 1977.

5. I have in view the various proposals and incentives to forego nuclear weapons contained in articles by Bloomfield (1975) and Frye (1976) in this light.

6. President Park Chung Hee has warned of this consequence of U.S. troop withdrawals (Holloran 1976; Evans and Novak 1976).

7. Of course, the tendency toward self-nullifying actions should not be ignored. After President Carter declared that he was planning to remove nuclear weapons from South Korean soil, he reaffirmed their possible use by air or sea launch in the event of a Korean War (*New York Times*, May 30, 1977, p. 2). The result is the worst of both worlds: nuclear deterrence in Third World contexts is perpetuated, and South Korea is induced to acquire nuclear weapons of its own. In cases like this, liberal statists do more to subvert stability in the present world order system than do their more conservative counterparts. The most recent reports suggest that the Carter Administration may not, after all, remove nuclear weapons from Korea, or do so slowly and tentatively over a period of 4–5 years (Beecher 1977).

8. It is possible to imagine security guarantees that would substitute for the residual threat to use nuclear weapons. Such guarantees have been proposed in the United States on behalf of Israel. However, to guarantee the security of a pariah state means trying to freeze a status quo which seems unacceptable to most of the world. The very offer of a guarantee entails high social costs, and its controversial character probably makes the guarantee itself unreliable. The pariah state, sensing this unreliability, would still, I suspect, be hesitant to renounce an ultimate nuclear option even if it received a strong guarantee of its present borders. Similarly, in such contexts political compromises may not appear available to the parties, and hence there would be no alternative to armed struggle. In such a conflict, the parties will not often be prepared to renounce any weapon or tactic that might prove useful under some set of circumstances. But in such a case official renunciation would not seem reliable anyway.

9. For a world-order analysis of the Vladivostok Accord, see Johansen (1976).

10. For one concept of a transition process that aims to achieve total nuclear disarmament, see Falk (1975).

11. For a persuasive depiction of institutional barriers to disarmament on the national level, see Barnet (1972).

12. One proposal along these lines may be found in the WOMP II paper of Robert Johansen and Saul H. Mendlovitz, "Global Enforcement of Just Law: A Transnational Police Force."

13. For some creative research and analysis along these lines, see Roberts (1976).

14. For documentation, see Wohlsletter (1976-77).

15. The most effective discussion of these issues is to be found in Theodore B. Taylor and Mason Willrich (1974).

16. See Sweet (1977); see also the international opposition to nuclear power in Hayes (1976). See also Lovins (1977), who portrays the situation as follows: "Nuclear industrialization is all but halted by grass roots opposition in Japan and the Netherlands: has been severely impeded in West Germany, France, Switzerland, Italy, and Austria; has been slowed and may soon be stopped in Sweden; has been rejected in Norway and (so far) Australia and New Zealand, as well as in several Canadian provinces; faces an uncertain prospect in Denmark and many American states; has been widely questioned in Britain, Canada, and the USSR; and has been opposed in Spain, Brazil, India, Thailand, and elsewhere."

17. In this regard, see Feiveson and Taylor (1977), especially the discussion of the thorium option (generating power by using thorium as the basic fuel), which the authors allege is easier to safeguard against diversion than fission technology. But see Lovins (1977) for the contrary view that the thorium cycle uses a mixed oxide from which plutonium can easily be extracted.

18. *Nuclear Power Issues and Choices.* Report of the Nuclear Energy Policy Study Group, the Ford Foundation, Cambridge, Mass., 1977, p. 147.

19. See Baker (1975); see also Bloomfield (1975), who says: "Our puzzle is how to change the system enough to get a better political-psychological base under nonproliferation without having to work a total transformation in man or in the basic geometry of his political world." This basic geometry appears to include the retention, and even the continuing development, of nuclear weapons by the existing nuclear powers. See also a list of proposed steps to undergird NPT system in Nacht (1975); see also Wohlsletter (1976-77).

20. See *The Nuclear Age*, 1974, Stockholm International Peace Research Institute, Cambridge, Mass., MIT Press, p. 45.

21. As Wohlsletter (1976-77) notes, a nonnuclear recipient of nuclear technology can come to the very verge of weapons capability without violating any legal obligations under the NPT. He illustrates this with the startling assertion that a nonweapon state can come closer to a plutonium weapon today than was the United States in 1947 when the assembly of bombs required many hours for fusing and wiring components together.

22. The text goes on to argue that "the capital cost per kilowatt of peak capacity for most methods of converting solar energy to electricity in central-station facilities is estimated to be more than double that of nuclear power, a figure that must be multiplied by another factor for additional costs of energy storage" (p. 37). This cost assessment seems unduly pessimistic; it presupposes a continuing need for centralized electrical energy systems, and overlooks important cost savings (most obviously, of course, on fuel supplies and pollution

control). On the availability of solar energy, the figures thrown up in the study are reassuring: "The amount of solar energy falling on the United States is enormous: 44,000 quads per year. The present annual U.S. consumption of electrical energy could be supplied by 0.15 percent of this solar energy, if it could be used at 10 percent efficiency."

23. After considering the sort of economic obstacles which the Ford study finds decisive in the intermediate period, Feiveson and Taylor (1977) conclude, "We are more optimistic about solar energy than most people and are encouraged by the increasing rate at which promising new concepts are being proposed and assessed. The biggest uncertainty about solar energy, in our minds, is how long it will take to implement its use on a large scale. However, it is not at all clear that this time will be significantly longer than the time required to develop worldwide fission breeder reactor systems that are effectively safeguarded against diversion of nuclear materials to destructive purposes."

Note, also, that breeder technology is a virtually inevitable sequel if we opt to rely on fission power, because uranium is expected to run out by the end of the century. Of course, even if the U.S. doesn't resort to breeders, plutonium will be present in large quantities by the early 1980s in many other countries.

24. *Solar Energy in America's Future—A Preliminary Assessment*, Stanford Research Institute, Report for U.S. Energy and Research Development Administration, January 1977, p. XVII.

25. Testimony by Charles Komanoff on the costs of nuclear power before the House Subcommittee on Environment, Energy and Natural Resources, September 21, 1977 (mimeographed); see table on relative costs of coal and nuclear power in different regions of the United States, p. 1.

26. Amory Lovins advocates a three-part strategy for the United States: (1) abandoning nuclear power, (2) reallocating resources in the direction of making soft-energy paths based on solar, wind, and geothermal energy courses viable at home and abroad, and (3) treating nonproliferation, control of civilian nuclear technology, and strategic arms reduction "as interrelated parts of the same problem with intertwined solutions." He maintains that these three steps provide "a universal, nondiscriminatory package of policies" that "would be politically irresistible to North and South, East and West alike." This approach very closely parallels the argument of this paper, but with two significant differences. First, I believe that the total elimination of nuclear-weapons capabilities is essential to any process of strategic arms reduction. Secondly, I believe that denuclearization and energy policy must be related to the wider social and economic issues of global reform. Of course, there is a tactical advantage in presenting the smallest credible package in order to make the process of adjustment appear as manageable as possible. My own assessment, however, is that the package will not be credible unless it is enlarged in the ways I have indicated. Lovins's proposals are sufficiently integrated and bold to start us down the right path. Once firmly on this path, we may be able to widen it along the lines discussed above, but I am fearful of mounting a radical argument that is not convincing on its own terms.

REFERENCES

Alexander, Tom (1975). "Our Costly Losing Battle Against Nuclear Proliferation." *Fortune*, December, 143–150.
Ayres, R. (1975). *Harvard Civil Rights—Civil Liberties Law Review* 10:369–443.

Baker, Stephen J. (1975). "Commercial Nuclear Power and Nuclear Proliferation." Cornell University Peace Studies Program Occasional Paper No. 5, May, 1–66.

Barnet, Richard J. (1972). *Roots of War*. Atheneum: New York.

Beecher, William (1977). "Carter May Keep Tactical Nuclear Weapons in Korea." *Boston Globe*, July 10.

Betts, Richard K. (1977). "Paranoids, Pygmies, Pariahs, and Nonproliferation." *Foreign Policy* 26:157–183.

Bloomfield, Lincoln P. (1975). "Nuclear Spread and World Order." *Foreign Affairs* 54:743–755.

Bull, Hedley (1975). "Rethinking Non-Proliferation." *International Affairs* 51:175–189.

Dunn, Lewis S., and Overhold, William H. (1976). "The Next Phase in Nuclear Proliferation Research." *Orbis*, Summer, 497–524.

Evans, Rowland, and Novak, Robert (1976). "Korea: Park's Inflexibility." *Washington Post*, June 12, p. A19.

Falk, Richard A. (1975). *A Study of Future Worlds*. Free Press: New York, Chapter 1 and the General Introduction by Saul H. Mendlovitz, pp. xvii–xxvii.

Falk, Richard A. (1976). "A Non-Nuclear Future: Rejecting the Faustian Bargain." *Nation*, March 13, 301–305.

Feiveson, Harold, and Taylor, Theodore (1977). "Alternative Strategies for International Control of Nuclear Power." In T. Greenwood et al., *Nuclear Proliferation, 1980's Project*. McGraw-Hill: New York, 123–193.

Frye, Alton (1976). "How to Ban the Bomb: Sell It." *New York Times Magazine*, January 11, 11–12 and 76–79.

Halloran, Richard (1976). *New York Times*, November 1, p. 22.

Hayes, Denis (1976). "Nuclear Power: The Fifth Horseman." Worldwatch Paper No. 6, May 8–10.

Hayes, Denis (1977a). *Rays of Hope: The Transition to a Post-Petroleum World*. Norton: New York.

Hayes, Denis (1977b). "Energy for Development: Third World Options." Worldwatch Paper No. 15, December.

Johansen, Robert (1976). "The Vladivostok Accord: A Case Study of the Impact of U.S. Foreign Policy on the Prospects for World Order Reform." Center of International Studies, World Order Studies Program Occasional Paper No. 4, Princeton, March, 1–114.

Kenward, Michael (1976). *Potential Energy: An Analysis of World Energy Technology*, Cambridge University Press: Cambridge, 118–132.

Lovins, Amory B. (1975). *World Energy Strategies*, Friends of the Earth International: San Francisco, Calif., 74–76.

Lovins, Amory B. (1976). "Energy Strategy: The Road Not Taken?" *Foreign Affairs* 55:65–96.

Lovins, Amory B. (1977). *Soft Energy Paths: Toward A Durable Peace*. Ballinger: Cambridge, Mass.

Miller, Jr., Tyler (1975). *Living in the Environment: Concepts, Problems, and Alternatives*. Wordworth Publishing Co.: Belmount, Calif., E148–E150.

Nacht, Michael (1975). *Nuclear Energy and Nuclear Weapons*. Report of the 1975 Aspen Workshop on Arms Control, Aspen Institute for Humanistic Studies Occasional Paper 1-22.

Quester, George H. (1975). "What's New on Nuclear Proliferation?" Aspen Institute for Humanistic Studies Occasional Paper 1-23.

Roberts, Adam (1976). *Nations in Arms: The Theory and Practice of Territorial Defense.* Praeger: New York.

Roszak, Theodore (1975). *The Unfinished Animal.* Harper & Row: New York, 152–181.

Sweet, William (1977). "The Opposition to Nuclear Power in Europe." *Bulletin of the Atomic Scientist* 33 (December):40–47.

Taylor, Theodore B., and Willrich, Mason (1974). *Nuclear Theft: Risks and Safeguards.* Ballinger: Cambridge, Mass.

Wienraub, Bernard (1977). *New York Times.* July 8, p. A7.

Wohlsletter, Albert (1976-77). "Spreading the Bomb Without Breaking the Rules." *Foreign Policy,* Winter, 88–96.

Yergin, Daniel (1977a). "The Terrifying Prospect: Atomic Bombs Everywhere." *Atlantic,* April, 46–65.

Yergin, Daniel (1977b). *Shattered Peace: The Origins of the Cold War and the National Security State.* Houghton, Mifflin: Boston, 115–123.

34. Elements of a Programme for Arms Control and Disarmament: Curbing the Qualitative Arms Race and Assuring Confidence Among States

Independent Commission on Disarmament and Security Issues

CURBING THE QUALITATIVE ARMS COMPETITION

Competitions in armaments focus as much on the characteristics of the weapons being acquired as on their number. Contrary to the principles of common security, states have sought to guarantee their survival and enhance their influence by developing or purchasing weapons that are more effective and lethal. The nuclear-weapon states continue to develop new kinds of nuclear weapons and new means of delivering them. They are searching for new means of warfare in space and other frontiers of human exploration. At the same time, a growing number of other states are increasing their potential to develop nuclear weapons at some future time.

All these developments aggravate existing political tensions among nations and make more difficult the avoidance and resolution of conflicts. The appearance of new types of military capabilities, no less than the appearance of greater numbers of weapons, can contribute to regional instability, raise fears of war and suspicion of hostile intentions. If nations are to live in common security, qualitative aspects of the arms race, like its quantitative features, must be constrained.

Advances in military capabilities begin in the human mind, proceed in different strands in numerous offices and laboratories. Only when they are near completion do they coalesce in the concrete form of a new weapon. New applications of technology can sometimes be stabilizing, but more often they generate new instabilities and competitions. Large research and development establishments represent vested interests which generate pressures for further research and increased effort.

It is difficult to identify points in the process of military research and development at which nations could agree to exercise restraint and at which compliance with such agreements could be verified. The notable exception is the point at which prototypes of weapons are tested in the field. The possibility of restricting the development of new or improved weapon systems at this critical point should be utilized on a much more extensive scale. Indeed, agreements already have been reached which restrict qualitative aspects of arms competitions at the testing stage; the 1963 Partial Test Ban Treaty, the 1974 Threshold Test Ban Treaty, the 1972 Anti-Ballistic Missile Treaty, and the 1979 SALT II Treaty.

Moreover, just as in the case of quantitative limitations, nations are unlikely to be willing to exercise unreciprocated unilateral restraint for substantial periods. *The major nuclear-weapon states have a special responsibility, but all nations must seek qualitative restraints. Steps have to be taken in common by nuclear- and non-nuclear-weapon states, by arms exporters and arms purchasers, by East and West, by great powers and small states.*

A Comprehensive Test Ban Treaty

The conclusion of a treaty banning all nuclear tests would make the introduction of new weapon designs into the armories of the nuclear-weapon states much more difficult. It would be a major constraint on the qualitative development of more sophisticated nuclear weapons. It also could be an important contribution to limiting the improvement of the present stocks of nuclear weapons. Hence it would enhance the acceptability and credibility of the Non-Proliferation Treaty, which works to limit the spread of nuclear weapons.

The Commission considers that efforts should be concentrated on the negotiation of a treaty banning all nuclear tests. Such a treaty is needed in order to forestall a new round of nuclear weapon developments which could exacerbate East-West relations, reduce stability, and weaken the Non-Proliferation Treaty.

The Commission welcomes the decision of the Committee on Disarmament in April 1982 to establish an ad hoc working group on a nuclear test ban. The Commission trusts that it will soon be possible to negotiate and conclude the Comprehensive Test Ban Treaty which for more than a quarter of a century has been awaited in vain by peoples the world over.

In further support thereof, we urge that the trilateral negotiations between the United States, the Soviet Union, and the United Kingdom on a comprehensive test ban be resumed immediately in order to settle the still unresolved issues, including the question of verification. Political will is needed in order to transcend the remaining obstacles. The Commission is of the view that it is possible to establish an effective system of verification and confidence building by arrangements involving the International Seismic Data Exchange, agreed procedures for consultation and on-site inspection, and a network of national seismic stations.

During the period between completion of negotiations and formal ratification of the test ban treaty, all the nuclear powers should participate in a voluntary moratorium on all nuclear tests.

A Ban on Antisatellite Systems

Outer space has become an important part of the military competition between East and West. The military machines of the major powers have become increasingly dependent on space-based support. Satellite systems have opened up a wide range of possibilities for verification and warning, for command, control, and communications. If these satellites were threatened, it could result in a substantial expansion of the strategic arms race into outer space, as each side sought to protect its own system.

Between 1977 and 1979 the Soviet Union and the United States discussed a ban on antisatellite weapons. Time is running out. *The Commission recommends that these negotiations be reopened and that priority be given to a suspension and prohibition of the testing of antisatellite weapons. It is essential that such a ban go into effect before irreversible technological "progress" has been made. Negotiations also should aim at reaching agreement that would ban the deployment of antisatellite weapons and require the dismantling of existing systems.*

Further bans on weapons and activities in outer space will undoubtedly be needed. The exploitation of outer space raises a number of complex technical questions and judgments. *The Commission urges the major industrial powers to develop a dialogue with the aim of identifying and preventing military uses of outer space that might constitute threats to international peace and security. This dialogue should lead to negotiated bans and limits on specific weapon systems or entire areas of activity.*

A Chemical Weapon Disarmament Treaty

The existing chemical and biological arms control and disarmament agreements are among the few safeguards against the dangers of an expanded arms race. Use in war of both chemical and biological weapons is prohibited by the 1925 Geneva Protocol and its associated body of customary international law. Possession of biological weapons, including toxin weapons, is outlawed by the 1975 Biological Weapons convention.

But the possession of chemical weapons is not prohibited and a number of states have reserved the right to use them if they are attacked with chemical weapons. The majority of states are parties to these agreements and have under the 1975 convention committed themselves to continue negotiations "in good faith" to prohibit possession of chemical weapons.

Since the First World War, chemical weapons have only been used in conflicts in the developing world. All reports of alleged use also are limited to Third World countries. Thus a new arms race in chemical weapons poses worldwide dangers, in particular for the developing world.

Pressures to build up stocks of chemical weapons are in danger of subverting the existing accords. *It is vital to accelerate negotiations aimed at extending and strengthening existing agreements by the introduction of a comprehensive chemical weapon disarmament treaty banning such weapons altogether.* This requires resumption of the stalled bilateral talks between the United States and the Soviet Union. When these negotiations last were convened, in July 1980, there was agreement in principle on the use of on-site inspection as a verification technique. Bilateral talks do not, of course, substitute for renewed efforts within the Committee on Disarmament to negotiate agreement on a comprehensive chemical weapon disarmament treaty, but would strengthen those efforts.

The negotiations involve complex technical matters and sensitive political issues and will require time to conclude successfully. Therefore *we call in addition for agreement on consultative procedures so that problems arising under the Geneva Protocol and the Biological Warfare Convention can be resolved through international cooperation. Such procedures could include the option of consultative meetings being convened at the expert level under the auspices of the United Nations that would be open to all states.*

A chemical weapon disarmament treaty should contain provisions for a permanent consultative commission composed of all the parties to the treaty and served by a small technical staff. The commission should ensure implementation of the treaty and thereafter monitor continued compliance. It could also be charged with the establishment of an effective complaint procedure.

Appropriate verification must be agreed for each stage of implementation of a treaty on chemical weapon disarmament. Both the declaration and destruction of stockpiles and production facilities and subsequent monitoring of compliance with provisions for non-production of chemical weapons must be verified under adequate international control. Verification measures should include a combination of voluntary confidence-building measures, national verification measures, and agreed international means.

Developing countries have a special interest in ensuring compliance with a treaty banning stockpiles and production of chemical weapons. Since very few developing states have the technology to develop adequate national means of verification, international means are necessary also in order to protect their interest.

Over the past fifteen years scientific understanding of the molecular and cellular processes of life has grown enormously. So far there is no evidence of military exploitation of this knowledge. Should the biological sciences be tapped for military purposes, however, hideous new weapons could emerge. Our well-being and economic and social development could be drastically retarded. *The Commission calls for an international convention which would prohibit any secret development or experimentation in the military applications of molecular biology and its associated disciplines.*

Universal Adherence to the Non-Proliferation Treaty

Preventing the spread of nuclear weapons is a critical element in any international effort to halt and reverse the nuclear arms race and ensure the maintenance of international peace and security. Progress in this direction demands obligations and responsibilities on the part of both nuclear-weapon states and non-nuclear-weapon states.

The problem of proliferation has fallen into two sections, popularly termed "vertical" and "horizontal" proliferation. Vertical proliferation refers to the growth of the stockpiles of nuclear weapons held by existing nuclear-weapon states. Horizontal proliferation refers to the spreading of nuclear weaponry to new countries. Efforts to stop both kinds of proliferation resulted in the conclusion of the Non-Proliferation Treaty in 1970, which committed non-nuclear-weapon states to refrain from acquiring such weapons and the nuclear-weapon states to halting and reversing their processes of qualitative and quantitative growth of nuclear weapons.

The Non-Proliferation Treaty is the centerpiece of the widespread international interest in maintaining the presumption against proliferation. One hundred and eighteen states are now parties to the treaty. However, France and China, which are nuclear-weapon states, as well as a number of important countries on the threshold of being able to build nuclear weapons, have so far failed to sign and ratify the treaty. *The Commission urges all states to adhere to the Non-Proliferation Treaty.*

Some opponents of the treaty point to its discriminatory nature, accepting nuclear weapons for those five countries which already have them but forbidding others to develop similar capabilities. But, by its very nature, non-proliferation involves a degree of discrimination. The key issue is how this fact of life is handled. The Commission recognizes that the failure of the nuclear-weapon states to make progress towards nuclear disarmament, as promised in Article VI of the Non-Proliferation Treaty, affects the attitudes and commitments of others. The proposals we have made for a complete nuclear test ban, for the reduction and withdrawal of nuclear arms in Europe and in the Soviet and American stockpiles, are a reflection of our concern to strengthen the treaty's appeal. Failure to stop vertical proliferation will compromise the integrity of the Non-Proliferation Treaty.

Safeguarding the Nuclear Fuel Cycle

International cooperation is needed in order to reduce the danger that the development and application of peaceful uses of nuclear energy may lead to diversion of nuclear materials for military purposes. *Particularly sensitive parts of the nuclear fuel cycle should be placed under international authority. This could include the establishment of international fuel banks, an international plutonium storage scheme, and internationally managed sites for spent fuel storage.* Regional organizations can contribute significantly to such international arrangements, which should be drawn together by the International Atomic Agency through its Committee on Assurance of Supply.

Participants in the 1977–1980 International Fuel Cycle Evaluation acknowledged that fuels usable in weapons require special procedures. The Committee on Assurance of Supply of the International Atomic Energy Agency may be developed into a central negotiating and management forum comprising both suppliers and recipient countries. Such cooperation would conform with Article IV of the Non-Proliferation Treaty which underlines the need for equitable cooperation in the use of nuclear energy for peaceful purposes.

The Need to Limit Conventional Arms Transfers

The volume of arms transfers has more than doubled during the past decade. Deliveries are now close to $30 billion per annum and orders are substantially higher. More than three-quarters of all arms transfers go to the countries of the developing world.

In our view, there is an urgent need for a concerted effort to develop a fair system of guidelines and restraints covering arms exports, based on cooperation among recipient and supplier states.

Supplier states should open talks aimed at establishing criteria by which they could regulate arms transfers on an equitable basis. Restraints need to be defined in terms of quantities and qualities, geography and military circumstances. The guidelines for arms transfer should include such principles as

- No significant increase in the quantity of weapons which are transferred to a region.
- No first introduction of advanced weapons systems into a region which create new or significantly higher levels of combat capabilities.
- Special restrictions on the transfer of lethal weapons to warring parties, taking into account the inherent right of individual or collective self-defence.
- Adherence to the implementation of U.S. resolutions and sanctions.

- No transfer of particularly inhumane and indiscriminate weapons.
- Special precautions to be taken when transferring weapons, such as hand-held anti-aircraft weapons, which, if they fell into the hands of individuals or subnational groups, would be especially dangerous.

The United States and the Soviet Union held Conventional Arms Transfer talks in 1977–1980. The Commission endorses the resumption of such talks which should include also France, the United Kingdom, and other major supplier states. Another need is for talks between supplier states and recipients in regions where tensions are particularly severe. There is a need for multilateral restraints.

Recipient states should similarly undertake to develop guidelines and codes of conduct designed to curb the flow of arms and avoid arms races. An important beginning was made by eight Andean states in the Declaration of Ayacucho in 1974 in which they pledged to "create conditions which permit effective limitation of armaments and put an end to their acquisition for offensive warlike purposes in order to dedicate all possible resources to economic and social development." Regrettably, the discussion of specific restraints broke down. However, at a meeting in Mexico City in 1978, twenty Latin American and Caribbean states agreed to exchange information on weapon purchases and work towards a regime of restraints on arms transfers.

Recipient states may wish to bar or limit certain types of weapon. They may consider that if those weapons were used in their part of the world they would enhance offensive capacities and introduce incentives for rapid action in a crisis. They may wish, too, to outlaw weapons which are starkly inhumane in their effects. The "rules of the game" will need to be tailored to the specific circumstances of the area in question. Regional Conferences on Security and Cooperation could discuss general principles. States which are participating in zones of peace or similar groupings could decide on more specific guidelines. The latter would have to be adhered to also by the supplier states.

ASSURING CONFIDENCE AMONG STATES

Adequate verification is an important part of any agreement on arms limitation or reduction. States are loath to enter into such agreements on the basis of good faith alone. The development of the so-called national technical means gave the parties to arms control agreements confidence that they could monitor compliance with the provisions of treaties adequately. Technologies used to observe and monitor military activities have advanced impressively. Military secrecy still exists, however.

Consequently, monitoring compliance with treaty proscriptions remains an issue in negotiations. There should be a close link between the scope and design of treaties and the means prescribed for their verification. There are no all-purpose forms of verification. Requirements have to be determined in each specific instance. Verification requires cooperative arrangements and, in some instances, on-site inspection.

While the purpose of verification is to provide for timely detection of any illegal, surreptitious activity, it could hopefully also lead to improved confidence among treaty parties and promote compliance with treaty norms.

Confidence-Building Measures Relating to Military Expenditure, Research and Development

Satellites can only detect forces in being or in formation. However, it takes from seven to fifteen years for a modern weapon system to move through the various stages of research, development, testing and deployment. States hedge against the possible future results of decisions other states may have made today, assuming the worst about the decisions of the adversary. Confidence building is necessary if the spirals of suspicion and fear are to be broken.

The greater sharing of information about budgetary expenditure, for example, could enhance confidence. A standardized reporting system has been developed and tried out under the auspices of the United Nations. The 35th General Assembly of the United Nations urged all states to report information about their expenditure for military purposes in accordance with the system. *The Commission urges all states to comply with the resolution of the General Assembly.*[1]

In view of the momentum and vested interests which affect the process of military research and development, *the Commission urges the major industrial powers to conduct a dialogue about questions relating to research and development of all types of military forces.* This would provide an opportunity to voice concerns about the implications of actual and possible programmes, so that the response could be taken into account prior to national decisions about procurement and deployment. The danger of unintended destabilization and aggravated competition could thereby be reduced.

NOTES

1. Georgi Arbatov (USSR) called attention to the fact that from the Soviet point of view the whole problem is extremely complicated due to differences in military structures, salaries, prices, etc. This recommendation does not in his view provide an adequate basis for comparison and assessment. The Soviet Union consequently, together with twenty other states, abstained from voting on the resolution in question.

——— **Questions for Reflection and Discussion** ———

1. What basic methods are available for curbing the qualitative arms competition between the United States and the Soviet Union? What obstacles impede their application?

2. How would a comprehensive test ban treaty restrain military research in respect of nuclear weapons? What are the reasons for negotiating a ban on antisatellite systems? Why is a chemical and biological weapons ban an essential supplement to the meaningful control of nuclear weapons?

3. How might the nuclear fuel cycle be safeguarded from military diversion? Are these safeguards adequate to prevent weapons development by states possessing civilian nuclear energy facilities? Should national governments or international agencies have primary jurisdictional control over nuclear materials?

4. What are the major approaches to the control of horizontal proliferation? Do any of them offer a final guarantee of no additions to the number of nuclear-weapon states? Which nonproliferation policies would you support and in what contexts? What deficiencies in the NPT and other efforts would you seek to correct? How might multilateral agencies or supranational institutions play an effective role in the detection and control of horizontal proliferation?

5. Is comprehensive denuclearization achievable? Would you commit national resources and energies to this goal even though you might believe the objective to be beyond reach in the near future? If not, why not? In the end, is not Falk's position the only real guarantee of freedom from nuclear war? How would you design and implement a long-term strategy to achieve comprehensive denuclearization?

Selected Bibliography

Barton, John H., and Lawrence D. Weiler. *International Arms Control: Issues and Agreements.* Stanford, CA: Stanford University Press, 1976.

Beres, Louis René. "Steps Toward a New Planetary Identity." *Bulletin of the Atomic Scientists,* Vol. 37, No. 2 (Feb. 1981), pp. 43–47.

Birnbaum, Karl E. *Arms Control in Europe: Problems and Prospects.* Laxenburg Paper No. 1. Vienna: Austrian Institute for International Affairs, 1980.

Blechman, Barry M., and Mark R. Moore. "A Nuclear-Weapon-Free Zone in Europe." *Scientific American,* Vol. 248, No. 4 (April 1983), pp. 34–43.

Brito, Dogbert L., Michael D. Intriligator, and Adele Ernst Wick, eds. *Strategies for Managing Nuclear Proliferation: Economic and Political Issues.* Lexington, MA: Lexington Books, 1983.

Caldicott, Helen. *Nuclear Madness: What Can We Do?* Brookline, MA: Autumn Press, 1979.

DeVolpi, Alexander. *Proliferation, Plutonium and Policy: Institutional and Technological Impediments to Nuclear Weapons Propagation.* New York: Pergamon Press, 1979.

Dunn, Lewis A. *Controlling the Bomb: Nuclear Proliferation in the 1980s.* New Haven, CT: Yale University Press, 1982.

Epstein, William. *The Last Chance: Nuclear Proliferation and Arms Control.* New York: Free Press, 1976.

Ford, Daniel, Henry Kendall, and Steven Nadis, eds. *Beyond the Freeze: The Road to Nuclear Sanity.* Cambridge, MA: Union of Concerned Scientists, 1982.

Glodblat, Jozef. *Agreements for Arms Control: A Critical Survey.* London: Taylor & Francis, 1982.

Greenwood, Ted, Harold A. Feiveson, and Theodore B. Taylor. *Nuclear Proliferation: Motivations, Capabilities, and Strategies for Control.* New York: McGraw-Hill, 1977.

Heckrotte, W., and George C. Smith, eds. *Arms Control in Transition: Proceedings of the Livermore Arms Control Conference.* Boulder, CO: Westview Press, 1983.

Jones, Rodney W. *The Spread of Nuclear Weapons: Security Planning and American Foreign Policy.* Lexington, MA: Lexington Books, 1983.

Kaldor, Mary, and Dan Smith, eds. *Disarming Europe.* London: Merlin Press, 1982.

Kalydin, A. *Nuclear Energy and International Security.* Moscow: Novosti Press, 1970.

Kincade, William H., and Jeffrey D. Porro. *Negotiating Security: An Arms Control Reader.* Washington, D.C.: Carnegie Endowment for International Peace, 1979.

Krass, Allan S., Peter Boskma, Boelie Elzen, and Wim A. Smit. *Uranium Enrichment and Nuclear Weapon Proliferation.* London: Taylor & Francis, 1983.

Lovins, Amory B., and L. Hunter Lovins. *Energy/War: Breaking the Nuclear Link—A Prescription for Non-Proliferation.* New York: Harper & Row, 1981.

————. *Brittle Power: Energy Strategy for National Security.* Andover, MA: Brick House Publishing Co., 1982.

Lovins, Amory B., L. Hunter Lovins, and Leonard Ross. "Nuclear Power and Nuclear Bombs." *Foreign Affairs,* Vol. 58, No. 5 (Summer 1980), pp. 1137–1177.

Markey, Edward J. *Nuclear Peril: The Politics of Proliferation.* Cambridge, MA: Ballinger Publishing Co., 1982.

Meller, Eberhard, ed. *Internationalization: An Alternative to Nuclear Proliferation?* Cambridge, MA: Oelgeschlager, Gunn and Hain, 1980.

Myrdal, Alva. *The Game of Disarmament: How the United States and Russia Run the Arms Race.* Rev. Ed. New York: Pantheon, 1982.

Newhouse, John. *Cold Dawn: The Story of SALT.* New York: Holt, Rinehart and Winston, 1973.

Nye, Joseph S., Jr. "Restarting Arms Control." *Foreign Policy,* No. 47 (Summer 1982), pp. 98–113.

Panofsky, W.K.H. *Arms Control and SALT II.* Seattle and London: University of Washington Press, 1979.

Park, Jae Kyu, ed. *Nuclear Proliferation in Developing Countries.* Boulder, CO: Westview Press, 1983.

Quester, George H., ed. *Nuclear Proliferation: Breaking the Chain.* Madison, WI: University of Wisconsin Press, 1981.

Russett, Bruce M., and Bruce G. Blair, eds. *Progress in Arms Control? Readings from Scientific American.* San Francisco: W.H. Freeman and Co., 1979.

Smith, Gerard, and George Rathjens. "Reassessing Nuclear Nonproliferation Policy." *Foreign Affairs,* Vol. 59, No. 4 (Spring 1981), pp. 875–894.

Stockholm International Peace Research Institute. *Arms Control: A Survey and Appraisal of Multilateral Agreements.* London: Taylor & Francis, 1978.

_____. *Nuclear Energy and Nuclear Weapon Proliferation.* London: Taylor & Francis, 1979.

_____. *Postures for Non-Proliferation: Arms Limitation and Security Policies to Minimize Nuclear Proliferation.* New York: Crane, Russak and Co., 1979.

_____. *Internationalization to Prevent the Spread of Nuclear Weapons.* London: Taylor & Francis, 1980.

_____. *The NPT: The Main Political Barrier to Nuclear Weapon Proliferation.* New York: Crane, Russak and Co., 1980.

Talbott, Strobe. *Endgame: The Inside Story of SALT II.* New York: Harper & Row, 1979.

Williams, Frederick C., and David A. Reese, eds. *Nuclear Nonproliferation: The Spent Fuel Problem.* Elmsford, NY: Pergamon Press, 1980.

Willrich, Mason. *Civilian Nuclear Power and International Security.* New York: Praeger Publishers, 1971.

Wohlstetter, Albert, et al., eds. *Swords from Plowshares: The Military Potential of Civilian Nuclear Energy.* Chicago: University of Chicago Press, 1979.

PART FOUR

PURSUING ALTERNATIVE GLOBAL SECURITY

CHAPTER 10

Relying on Alternative Defense Strategies

The commitment of both East and West to nuclear deterrence as the cornerstone of national security policy has, together with the constant competition for global influence as well as other factors, led to an unending and costly armaments competition that threatens devastating nuclear war. With symptoms of malfunction breaking out on an unprecedented scale at virtually every level and dimension of planetary organization, it is fair to say that the world is undergoing at least the birthpangs of historic—fundamental—system change. Accordingly, the development of viable alternatives to current nuclear-based foreign policies and defense strategies seems imperative.

Reliance on conventional forces to deny an aggressor's political-military objectives, for example, is one option, but it surely must be viewed as only a first—and very limited—step toward a world secure from the threat of nuclear war. Though obviously preferable to reliance upon nuclear arms, and arguably necessary for transition to a genuinely denuclearized world, the fact is that conventional forces are by no means benign and clearly are capable of causing threatened states to resist the dismantling of their nuclear arsenals or to reinstate nuclear weapons they may previously have given up. Thus, a key task facing proponents of nuclear disarmament is to develop alternative defense strategies that, together with other measures such as those considered in the next two chapters, are simultaneously credible and capable of eliminating the temptations and minimizing the pressures to resort to nuclear warfare. The goal of nuclear disarmament would seem wholly unattainable in the absence of alternative strategies that can allow governing elites to back away from mutual nuclear threat without jeopardizing the physical security of their populations, their territories, the world.

The readings in this chapter thus represent the beginning of a search for methods that hold out the potential for allowing states to curb their reliance on nuclear weaponry, in whole or in part, without increasing the risks of foreign military intervention or aggression—methods that reduce the likelihood of foreign military action while preserving sovereign confidence in the national competence to deter and defend. The first essay by Jonathan Dean, for example, argues that nuclear parity between the NATO and Warsaw Pact (WTO) countries has rendered suspect the reliability of NATO's nuclear deterrent against Soviet conventional aggression. Dean argues that conventional rather than nuclear defense represents the most credible and least provocative deterrent posture because primary reliance on conventional defense would deter a Soviet offensive without reducing Soviet confidence in its own deterrence capabilities. The selection by Dietrich Fischer advocates a redirection of military security policy—predicated on Swiss defense strategy—toward the acquisition of defensive weapon systems that allow states to defend themselves without posing a menace to others, that allow each to create an essentially nonaggressive force structure capable of denying an adversary meaningful benefits from attack and conquest. Going further yet, the Alternative Defence Commission in Great Britain argues that the credible threat of indefinite civilian noncompliance with occupation forces, i.e., civilian-based defense, is sufficient to thwart most foreign aggression. The final selection, by Louis Kriesberg, stresses nonviolent inducements that make the benefits of peace more attractive than any possible gains from aggression, and recommends a potentially effective nonmilitary deterrence and defense strategy that would enable a nation to pursue its particular interests without jeopardizing world peace and security.

The reader is invited to consider these suggestions more in combination than separately, as a composite of policy options that jointly could define a comprehensive national defense posture free of nuclear weapons and the threat of nuclear war. One can envision a national defense posture that relies, for example, upon some blend of conventional defensive weapons, nonviolent civilian resistance, and a continuous use of nonmilitary inducements for peace and mutual well-being.

35. Beyond First Use

Jonathan Dean

Years of extensive discussion in the United States of the U.S.-Soviet nuclear balance have brought an inescapable message to the West European public: namely, that U.S. nuclear superiority, on which extended deterrence and the first use strategy have been based, no longer exists. Consequently, large segments of the public, in many cases for the first time, are now looking more closely at what would happen if war broke out in Europe and existing NATO strategy actually had to be applied. They do not like what they see. This reaction is particularly strong in

West Germany, where an exposed location and the searing experience of World War II combine to create understandable sensitivity in dealing with the implications of NATO strategy.

The frequently presented evidence that the USSR has achieved parity with the United States in nuclear armaments has increased the number of West Europeans who suspect that in the event of an overwhelming Soviet attack on Western Europe the U.S. president would decide not to use American nuclear weapons against the invading Soviet forces because the Soviets might retaliate with their strategic weapons directly against the United States. At the same time, evidence of Soviet nuclear equality has elicited increasing nervousness in different segments of the Western European public for another reason: They fear that if the West was losing in a conventional conflict, the U.S. president would in fact authorize use of American nuclear weapons, but against targets in Eastern Europe rather than in the Soviet Union, and that the Soviets for their own part would respond with nuclear weapons aimed at Western Europe. Thus each superpower would delay resorting to strategic attack on the other's home territory while Europe was devastated by the nuclear exchange.

The NATO decision of December 1979 to deploy modernized American Pershing II missiles and ground-launched cruise missiles in Western Europe was an effort to counter these concerns and to maintain the credibility of the American extended deterrent and of the strategy of flexible response. NATO governments argued that deployment of these missiles would establish a seamless deterrent linking tactical and intermediate-range nuclear armaments with U.S. strategic nuclear weapons. To many Western Europeans, however, the logic of the proposed remedy did not appear compelling. They feared that deployment would instead increase the risk of a U.S.-Soviet nuclear exchange in Europe. Rather than reassuring the population of Western Europe, the decision to deploy became a center of controversy, especially in the Northern Tier countries.

*   *   *

If the current level of abrasion and friction in Western European public opinion over NATO's nuclear deterrent strategy continues, the consequences can be serious. Both the willingness of the West European public to sustain large defense budgets and the resolve of West European leaders to resist possible Soviet pressures could decline. This damage to defense morale could in time outweigh whatever gain for the defense of Western Europe deterrence might provide. Already the controversy threatens to contribute to a destabilizing realignment of the West German political parties. And it could ultimately, through a cycle of action and reaction, result in serious pressure for withdrawal of American forces from Western Europe. Conversely, if well handled, the current dissatisfaction in Western Europe over nuclear deterrence could have a productive outcome: It could finally convince the West Europeans, especially the West Germans, to take conventional defense seriously.

[Thus, it seems clear that NATO's] real and continuing requirement is for a conventional force posture that makes attack by Warsaw Pact forces an irrational course and that, in the event of a Soviet miscalculation, could lead to defeat of the attacking forces. But after establishing their original ambitious conventional force goals in 1952, the NATO allies deliberately revised those goals and decided not to try to match estimated Warsaw Pact strength man for man, tank for tank, aircraft for aircraft. Instead, they placed primary reliance on U.S. superiority in nuclear weapons, with conventional forces playing a lesser role. The reasons for this decision were many, including distrust of excessively large West German forces and the sensitivity of West Germany to the idea of prolonged conventional warfare on its soil. But in large part, the decision reflected the belief of the NATO allies that Warsaw Pact conventional advantages were so great that NATO would find conventional parity too expensive in economic and political terms.

These were NATO's conclusions in the early 1950s. At that time, the Soviet Union did have a marked preponderance in conventional forces because of the postwar disbandment of West European and American forces and the disarmament of defeated Germany. But today such pessimistic conclusions may no longer be valid.

COMPARING THE ALLIANCES

Despite the concerns of recent years over trends in Soviet and Warsaw Pact forces, NATO forces in central Europe today have important advantages in specific areas. NATO air forces maintain an impressive edge over Pact air forces in many categories including payload. NATO pilots have logged more flying hours and are better trained. NATO has about twice as many modern fighter-bombers as the Warsaw Pact. NATO leads in antitank guided missiles and helicopters.

NATO possesses the important advantages of a force defending its own soil: prepared defensive positions, relatively favorable terrain, greater knowledge of its own area, and higher military morale. NATO also benefits from the general requirements that the potential attacker must have considerable overall superiority to insure success. An additional advantage would come from the supportive efforts of the West European civilian population, which in a war would cooperate fully with Western defense forces.

Facing Western forces would be Warsaw Pact troops with a manpower advantage in central Europe of about 175,000 in ground and air force personnel—a level that does not appear to have markedly increased since the 1968 Soviet invasion of Czechoslovakia. Although this margin has a different significance in an arms control context, it does not appear to create a decisive advantage for the Pact in conflict. It is true that Soviet ground forces in the western USSR could be used to reinforce Warsaw Pact troops already in central Europe, but this advantage is offset by the possibility of Western reinforcement by French ground forces in France. Moreover, according to figures published by the Defense Department, since 1972 the United States has increased its ground and air force manpower in West Germany by 38,000 men. It has also carried out a major reorganization of U.S. Army forces in central Europe to increase combat capability by reducing support forces.

NATO military commanders face problems regarding the quality of military manpower, but so do Soviet commanders. Soviet conscripts in general have a low level of education and mechanical aptitude, which decreases their usefulness in a highly mechanized force. And the pronounced centralism of the Soviet system creates difficulties in training the commanders of small units to show initiative. And some Soviet units in the area are not equipped with latest model armaments. Over half the Soviet units in central Europe are equipped with the older, less advanced T-62 tank. Western force analysts professionally avoid qualitative estimates. But it is probable that the quality of Soviet ground forces in central Europe, clearly the best in the Warsaw Pact, is considerably lower than that of West Germany's Bundeswehr.

Assessment of the military balance in central Europe must take into account the actual political situation in Europe today. In the 1950s a large portion of the Western European population was loyal to Communist parties subservient to Moscow. This loyalty posed a serious threat to Western defense in the event of conflict, as NATO commanders envisaged large-scale efforts at fifth-column activities. Today the situation is reversed. Following the 1956 Hungarian uprising, the 1968 reform movement in Czechoslovakia, and the 1980–1981 developments in Poland, the locus of political crisis in Europe has shifted form West to East. The Soviet Union faces a permanent political challenge in Eastern Europe. This challenge raises important questions both about the behavior of civilian populations in Eastern Europe during a conflict and about the military value to the Soviets of the armed forces of Warsaw Pact countries in the area.

The Czechoslovak army remains demoralized and of poor quality. Soviet commanders must have second thoughts about trusting East German conscripts in West Germany for any length of time. The loyalty of the Polish army to Soviet leadership is highly questionable. In the face of these problems, before launching an attack on the West the Soviet Union would probably have to assign a considerable number of its existing forces to insure its lines of communication through Eastern Europe. Militarily, in other words, the Soviet Union is largely on its own in Eastern Europe. Even in the early stages of conflict in Europe, the entire Soviet system in Eastern Europe might be at risk. Awareness of these dangers is itself an important deterrent to any Soviet decision to attack the West.

The most plausible scenario of a Soviet attack on Western Europe— perhaps the one most feared by NATO leaders—is an attack by Soviet forces already in central Europe, with minimum preparation of a week or less and without immediate reinforcement from the Soviet Union. For such an attack, the Soviets would have available 19 divisions in East Germany and perhaps 3 to 4 divisions in Czechoslovakia, or a total of about 23 divisions. This figure is far short of the 175 Pact divisions so often mentioned in popular discussion of the subject. Twenty-three Soviet divisions constitute a formidable force, but given the advantages of defense, NATO should be able to cope with them. Leaving out the three French divisions in West Germany, NATO has considerably more manpower in active duty combat units in central Europe than the Soviets have personnel in all their combat units in this area.

Attack by Soviet forces alone after limited preparation is not the only form that conflict in central Europe could take. Some part of non-Soviet Warsaw Pact forces might move forward, sandwiched between loyal Soviet forces to insure obedience. NATO commanders must take this possibility into account. But even in these circumstances, the value of the East European troops remains questionable. Apart from their uncertain morale and motivation, these troops possess inferior equipment. Nearly all their tanks are of a design more than 30 years old. They have only a handful of modern third generation fighter-bombers. The actual readiness level of many divisions usually counted among active duty forces is very low and it would take weeks to mobilize these divisions fully. In addition, mobilization of both Soviet and non-Soviet Warsaw Pact forces would be highly visible. Assuming the Western alliance would react accordingly, some 750,000 West German reservists and the reserves of other allies could reinforce active duty Western forces in the area. In short, the West can field a formidable force in central Europe, quite apart from American reinforcements. And the United States has pre-positioned enough equipment for four divisions in West Germany, thus enabling reinforcements to arrive rapidly by air.

This necessarily incomplete evaluation of the East-West military balance in central Europe does not suggest that NATO has no problems in the conventional defense of Western Europe. It does. But from some perspectives, the balance is decidedly less unfavorable for the West than is often assumed.

A NEW DEFENSIVE APPROACH

There remain two final objections to relinquishing NATO's no first use doctrine: First, an adequate conventional defense for Western Europe would be prohibitively expensive for the West. Second, even if the West were able to shoulder the burden, a conventional defense of Western Europe would result in destruction and loss of life, especially in West Germany, at a level approaching or equaling the carnage of World War II or even of a nuclear war.

Assessing the economic costs of an adequate conventional defense of Western Europe must rest in large part on an evaluation of the military balance in the area. But as argued above, evidence indicates the capabilities of Warsaw Pact forces in central Europe are not as great as often assumed. Therefore, if NATO countries achieved a 3 percent real increase in defense expenditures over a period of four or five years, the chances of a successful conventional Warsaw Pact attack could be made reassuringly low even under the most improbable, worst case scenarios.

In fact, in recent years NATO's logistics and defense preparations have improved considerably. Important programs for further improvements continue. They include NATO programs to facilitate rapid deployment of U.S. reinforcements by improving the host nations' support capabilities and by enhancing U.S. air transport. NATO is also proceeding with programs of aircraft modernization, with increases in stocks of ammunition and war materiel reserves, antitank guided missiles, and artillery, and with improvements in joint command and control.

All these actions are useful. But even more can be done if NATO is prepared to consider innovative approaches to conventional defense. Several such approaches are now under discussion. One idea was first discussed as the West German forces were being established in the mid-1950s: NATO can make more extensive use of prepared defensive positions in the forward area either with standing forces or with a home guard. This approach is relatively inexpensive. A second improvement calls for wider use of modern technology with precision-guided munitions designed to interdict possible Soviet reinforcement. Although more expensive, this approach could be implemented in stages.

An official statement by the government of France that, in the event of Soviet attack, French forces would come to the support of NATO forces would of itself do a great deal to invigorate NATO conventional defense. Such a statement would not require France to rejoin the NATO integrated command. Nor would it cost anything in economic terms. But it would enable NATO political and military leaders, and West European public opinion, to count on the French to help in the event of war rather than merely to hope that they will do so. France would guarantee use of its logistics, airfields, and mobile ground forces to help stop Warsaw Pact attackers after minimum penetration of West Germany. This assurance would make the prospects for successful conventional defense appear more solid to Western European public and political opinion.

NATO conventional defense could also be strengthened if a greater number of West Germany's ground force reserves were organized into combat units, creating a reserve division to match each of the present 12 West German divisions on active duty. Six brigades or the equivalent of 2 divisions of such forces already exist: The additional 10 reserve divisions, perhaps 5 armored and 5 light infantry, could have a cadre of 10 percent full-time active duty personnel and be equipped in part with used equipment from active duty divisions. If these divisions are added to West German forces at the rate of 2 a year over a period of five years or longer, West Germany could implement this program with a limited increase of its defense budget.

The present concept for conventional defense against Warsaw Pact attack, at least in its public versions, requires the front line of NATO conventional forces to stand firm and immobile under attack. It would not cede an inch. Nor would it move forward into enemy territory, lest NATO's defense posture be misread. Locked into position, NATO forces would absorb the entire impact of a Warsaw Pact attack. They would then have to bring it to a halt and defeat enemy units on the spot. Even with heavy numerical superiority, which NATO does not have, success in carrying out such a strategy would be difficult. The doctrine therefore contributes to the general belief that conventional defense of Western Europe is implausible. The stage is thus set for possible early use of nuclear weapons by the West.

A forward defense posture is politically vital and remains valid. The Federal Republic could not support an alliance whose strategy called for surrender of large portions of West German territory even temporarily. But although long-standing political reservations have prevented active consideration of defense through mobile counterattack, these should be overruled to permit study of the advantages and disadavantages of such a doctrine. Under this concept, NATO would hold its armored forces in reserve behind a screen of defensive forces. The screen would include the additional West German reserve divisions, as well as British, Belgian, Dutch, and U.S. units already in forward position. They would absorb the impact of a first Warsaw Pact attack. The mobile armored forces would then counterattack, carrying the conflict into enemy territory. The counterattack would have the limited objective of encircling and cutting off the attacking force from its reinforcements in order to bring about a negotiated end to the conflict.

Following this concept in the event of conflict would not involve the massive destruction and civilian casualties in West Germany that many envisage. Much of the combat action would take place in the border area between West and East Germany and would involve direct confrontation of mobile military units. Indeed, aerial bombing of cities caused most World War II civilian casualties in West Germany. The Soviet Union has inadequate aircraft and would in any event be unlikely to make such bombing part of a conventional attack designed to capture West Germany's industrial plant intact.

It is not the object of this description of alternative possibilities for improvement of NATO conventional forces to argue for a particular version. Rather it is simply to make the point that with a Warsaw Pact challenge of finite dimensions and with the large standing forces and resources already at its disposal, NATO should be able to develop an effective and credible strategy for conventional defense that will—and this is the central issue—permit decreased reliance on extended nuclear deterrence.

In June 1982 President Reagan urged renewed attention to the Mutual and Balanced Force Reduction (MBFR) talks in Vienna. And in July 1982 Western participants in the negotiations presented new proposals.

There are strong reasons for seeking an East-West agreement in Vienna apart from the favorable impact it would have on the direction of public opinion in Western Europe toward NATO defense. The East-West military balance in central Europe is the largest and most expensive peacetime confrontation of manpower and firepower in human history. A military confrontation of these dimensions, with about one million men on each side heavily armed with nearly the whole range of conventional and nuclear weapons, entails a considerable risk that conflict will erupt through misperception or miscalculation of the military activities of the potential adversary. It is therefore imperative to press for an East-West arms control agreement aimed at stabilizing and defusing this confrontation. An agreement in Vienna could bring the West an increment of security at no cost. It could reduce and limit Soviet forces in central Europe. Additional measures could commit each side to notify the other of force concentrations or of movements of large numbers of troops. The two sides could also establish an annual quota of ground and air inspections to verify adherence to manpower ceilings and to increase advance warning of possible preparation for attack.

In the context of the other approaches discussed, such an increment of security would legitimately make conventional defense appear more feasible to the West European public. In turn, public support for a continuing program to improve conventional forces in Western Europe might increase. An agreement along the lines foreseen by the NATO participants in the Vienna talks does not envisage reduction of armaments in an initial agreement. It would not prevent, therefore, continued improvement in NATO conventional forces. Nor is there anything inconsistent about simultaneously improving the equipment or logistical base of conventional forces while reducing the manpower of those forces through an arms control agreement with the Warsaw Pact states. The objective of both actions is to stabilize the East-West military confrontation in central Europe and to reduce the possibility that the confrontation could lead to war.

The two sides have already made considerable progress toward East-West agreement along these lines. The East earlier this year presented a draft agreement incorporating many of the Western proposals. Some important aspects of a possible agreement remain in dispute: The two sides have not agreed on the actual number of Warsaw Pact ground and air force personnel now in the central European area. The East has not yet accepted the Western proposal for an annual quota of inspections of forces of the opposite alliance. Yet if President Reagan and the leaders of the other NATO states participating maintain the interest and involvement they have recently shown in the MBFR talks, they should be able, with time, to elicit similar involvement on the part of the Soviet leadership. It should then be possible to solve the data problem and to move forward toward a first agreement in Vienna. Such an agreement would not represent a zero-sum game benefiting only the West. Both East and West would benefit from a reduction in the risk of war in Europe and in the connected risk of nuclear escalation.

CONCLUSION

As noted, the debate over the first use strategy is only one aspect of an underlying problem of NATO strategy—continued primary reliance on the American extended deterrent at a time when the United States has lost its nuclear superiority over the Soviet Union. In these circumstances, it is understandable that governments attempt to forestall change by trying to preserve appearances. But unless it is assumed that the United States can regain unmistakable and enduring strategic nuclear superiority over the Soviet Union, no amount of patching can restore the American nuclear deterrent to its former effectiveness or credibility. Attempts to do so primarily by improving NATO's nuclear arsenal in Western Europe do not have the right emphasis. They elicit controversy and compound the problem. The conclusion seems clear: The changed U.S.-Soviet nuclear relationship necessitates a change in NATO strategy, a shift away from primary reliance on nuclear deterrence to primary deterrence by conventional forces.

36. Invulnerability Without Threat: The Swiss Concept of General Defense

Dietrich Fischer

1. INTRODUCTION

With the ever-increasing destructiveness of modern weapons, especially nuclear, biological and chemical weapons, the world faces the danger that a future world war could bring an end to human civilization, or even human life. To prevent this is the most urgent task of all.

Most ordinary people want peace. But in the approaches to safe-guarding peace, people differ. Some seek "peace through strength," through overwhelming military superiority over their opponents. But if both pursue that goal, this only leads to an uncontrolled arms race and ultimate insecurity for all. Others advocate unilateral disarmament as a form of peace initiative. Yet history has shown that defenseless nations easily fall victim to aggressors, regardless of their proclaimed neutrality. Is there a way out of this dilemma?

One approach to international security is negotiated mutual disarmament. Unfortunately, the recent history of disarmament negotiations has proved this approach to be a failure, partly because of the lack of a supranational entity that can enforce agreements reached.[1] Yet there exists an alternative. Countries can maintain their own security, without contributing to an arms race, by concentrating on pure defense. This strengthens their own security, without posing any threat to others.

This paper will explore these concepts, and examine to what extent Switzerland's approach to national defense corresponds to them.[2] *Section 2* differentiates between the two components of the notion of "military strength": invulnerability and the capability to inflict harm on others. Whereas being invulnerable is a desirable attribute, posing a threat to others is seen as undesirable. The two are quite different, but they have long been confused, and this confusion, whether intended or accidental, has had dangerous consequences. *Section 3* discusses the distinction between offensive and defensive arms, with a number of examples. *Section 4* lists some non-military approaches to national defense which will be part of total defense. *Section 5* considers as an example the Swiss concept of general defense, and examines to what extent it corresponds to a desirable defense policy. *Section 6* offers some concluding remarks.

2. THREAT VS. INVULNERABILITY

Boulding (1978, p. 33) states that he uses "the word 'strength' not in the frequently accepted sense of the ability to create strain through, for instance, violence, but in terms of the ability to resist strain." He mentions that this ambiguity in language has created real difficulties in thought about these problems.

The confusion between the two meanings of strength or "military power" as the ability to inflict harm on others and the ability to resist harm intended by others can be observed in the call by certain military circles for the acquisition of offensive arms which threaten the security of other nations in the name of "defense." But even some members of the peace movement have fallen victim to this confusion if they advocate unilateral disarmament in order to reduce tension in the world. To demand that a nation be weak so as not to pose any threat to others is to confuse "posing no threat" with "being vulnerable."

To bring clarity into this confusion, a diagram adapted from Menger (1934) can help. He categorized people into those who tend to *hurt others* (*unhöflich,* meaning literally impolite or inconsiderate) and those who *don't hurt others* (*höflich,* i.e., polite, considerate). He further distinguished between those who are *easily hurt* (*empfindlich,* literally sensitive, in the meaning of being easily offended, intolerant) and those

FIGURE 1. Menger's Categorization of People's Character

	easily hurt	not easily hurt
hurting others	most difficult character	
not hurting others		most pleasant character

who are *not easily hurt* (*unempfindlich,* in the sense of being tolerant). This yields the four categories shown in Figure 1.

Menger then analyzes what types of people can get along with each other, and which cannot stand each other. He finds, among other things, that people who are considerate and tolerant can get along well with everybody. People who are inconsiderate and intolerant cannot even stand others of the same type, only people who are both considerate and tolerant.

Figure 2 shows a classification of nations, which is in a sense analogous to Menger's classification of individuals. It is to be seen as an isomorphism, not an anthropomorphism. I do not in any way imply that there are considerate or inconsiderate nations, only possibly their leaders.

A nation is invulnerable if it has both the capability *and* the will to defend itself against any potential threat. Neither of these two ingredients alone is sufficient. Similarly, a nation is aggressive only if it both possesses offensive arms and also has the intention of using them for aggressive purposes. But since intentions can change relatively quickly, and verbal proclamations of peaceful intentions are not always believed by an opponent (sometimes with good reason), the only safe way for

FIGURE 2. A Classification of Nations

	vulnerable	invulnerable
aggressive	unsafest posture, most likely to become involved in a war	
non-aggressive		safest posture, greatest contribution to international peace

a nation to show credibly that it is not aggressive may be not to acquire any offensive arms. More about the distinction between offensive and defensive arms will be said in the next section.

The most desirable characteristic of a nation in terms of contributing to international peace is not to be "militarily superior" over others, but to be strong in terms of defense, and weak in terms of offense. Nations that are vulnerable often see the need to make up for this deficiency by acquiring offensive arms with which to retaliate against a potential aggressor. If a nation is so vulnerable that it cannot afford to have any fighting take place inside its own borders, it may feel compelled to "defend" itself on the territory of others, preferably before it has been attacked. It may feel a strong temptation to launch a preemptive first strike.

A similar tendency can be observed in individuals. People with vulnerable spots tend to be more aggressive against others, as a "protective reaction." For example, teachers who are insecure about their knowledge typically tend to criticize students more severely, in a preemptive way, to give themselves an aura of superiority and to prevent them from asking questions. People who feel comfortable about their abilities can afford to be much more tolerant.

Invulnerability is composed of many forms of resistance against power exerted by others over oneself or one's nation. Galtung (1980) uses the classical distinction between three forms of power: punitive, remunerative, and normative. Military power is one form of punitive power. Remunerative power includes the offering of economic rewards to those who behave according to one's will. Normative or persuasive power includes, among other things, praise and criticism, propaganda, etc. To make oneself invulnerable against these various forms of power, there is a subjective and an objective component, as shown in Table 1.

For true resistance, both the subjective will to resist and the objective ability to resist are needed. Fearlessness may partially compensate for objective defenselessness, but not completely. Self-reliance is strengthened both by the objective ability to provide for oneself, and by subjective modesty or self-restraint, so as not to be attracted by unnecessary material rewards offered. Self-reliant in terms of food is someone who can either grow a lot, or survive on little, or preferably both. In order not to be influenced by others' value judgments a good portion of self-respect helps. But it is also useful to have more experience and objective knowledge than someone who tries to influence one.[3]

The six forms of ability to resist power mutually strengthen one another: Defensive capability enhances economic strength, and vice versa. Self-reliance and indomitability strengthen self-respect. Self-respect makes one less vulnerable to economic incentives, less fearful, etc. Together, all these forms of resistance against power constitute *invulnerability*.

508

TABLE 1. Forms of Resistance Against Power

form of power	resistance		
	subjective	objective	combined
punitive	fearlessness[a]	defensive capability	indomitability
remunerative	self-restraint (modesty of wants, voluntary simplicity)	economic strength[b]	self-reliance[a]
normative	self-respect,[a] self-conviction	knowledge	autonomy

[a] These terms are described in Galtung (1980). See also Galtung, O'Brien and Preiswerk, Eds. (1980).
[b] By this is meant the ability to provide for oneself without exploiting others or depending on the good will of others, through resources and/or knowledge, skill, ingenuity, etc.

A complete system of pure defense should seek to strengthen all six forms of resistance against foreign power, but should seek none of the three forms of power over others.

The next section takes a closer look at one form of power, military power over others which depends on offensive arms, and the objective ability to resist such power, provided in part by defensive arms.

3. OFFENSIVE VS. DEFENSIVE ARMS

The acquisition of armaments by a country usually has a dual effect: it increases its own national security,[4] and it reduces the national security of potential opponents. Arms that reduce the security of others without contributing to one's own security are called purely offensive. Arms that enhance one's own security without endangering others are called purely defensive. Most types of arms can serve offensive as well as defensive purposes, and would be classified somewhere along a continuous spectrum between these two pure cases.

In order to decide whether certain types of arms are offensive or defensive, it is essential to agree on what constitutes "national security." If that notion is taken to be as all-encompassing as to include "business interests abroad," "foreign raw material supplies," or the promotion of one's own religion or ideology abroad, then almost any weapons can be claimed to serve "defensive" purposes. This is clearly a position that is untenable, since it leads to incompatible claims between different nations. What is typically considered a legitimate object of defense is the national territory. If nations only defend the territory currently under their control, this does not lead to war. Another object of defense may be national political institutions, or, at a more advanced level, national self-determination, i.e., the right to choose one's own political institutions, without the imposition of force from outside. For a national security objective to be logically acceptable, it must not lead to incompatible claims if several nations have the same objective.[5]

In the following discussion the objective of defense considered is to keep hostile forces outside national borders and to protect the lives of the people living inside the national borders. "Interests abroad" are not considered as legitimate objectives of armed "defense." Each nation will, of course, seek to pursue its interests in the world through diplomtic negotiations, mutually advantageous trade, etc. But such efforts must be based on voluntary cooperation with other nations, whose benefits are *mutual.* They must not be obtained through coercion, through the use of military force abroad.

Under certain circumstances, there may be reasons for mutual defense treaties. These can help weaker nations to become better able to resist aggression, by forming an alliance with others. (Switzerland originated as such a defense alliance.) But such alliances must reflect the desire of the majority of the people in each participating nation. They must not be concluded with an unpopular minority that abuses them to keep itself in power. Neither must they serve the interests of one (dominant) nation at the expense of other members. Such alliances must serve purely defensive purposes, not any aggressive aims. One problem with such defense treaties is that they can draw *all* the members of an alliance into a war that was provoked by any *one* of them, usually the most adventurous member. In this way they can expand the scope of an otherwise limited war. They can even increase the probability of a war, if certain members feel encouraged by the protective umbrella of the alliance to engage in provocative steps that can lead to hostilities or even to commit outright aggression. Whether a defense alliance increases or reduces the probability and destructiveness of war depends to a great extent on the behavior of its members. It is not clear a priori.

To expect *every* nation to have only territorial defense as its objective would be utopian and unrealistic, at least in the short run. This paper does not necessarily postulate such an ideal state of the world. Rather, it seeks to outline a security strategy through which any nation that pursues it can live in peace, even if other nations have aggressive intentions.

Taking territorial defense as the objective, typical examples of purely defensive arms are passive obstacles, such as tank blockades or, in historical times, the Chinese Wall. Such immovable objects cannot be used directly to attack another country, they only impede a potential attack from outside. They do not in themselves threaten the security of any other country, but can improve the security of the country that builds them.

A typical example of a purely offensive weapon might be a gunboat that used to be stationed in front of the capital of a weak country, in order to extract concessions. It clearly reduced the security of the country threatened by it, but hardly increased the security of the country of origin, which could hardly have been attacked by the threatened country.[6]

Most arms that can potentially be used for offensive purposes, such as rifles, tanks, bombers, etc., can also be used in a defensive way, to attack an enemy after he has invaded one's own territory. Even nuclear missiles aimed at targets in an enemy's territory, which one would never want to use inside one's own territory, can potentially serve defensive purposes, if they are only to be used in retaliation against a first attack from outside. But it is not easy to convince a potential enemy that only defensive uses are intended as long as the objective potential for offense exists. On the other hand, defensive arms alone can never be used for offensive purposes.[7] Here lies a certain asymmetry.

Whether the acquisition of certain arms is perceived as defensive or offensive does not depend only on the arms themselves, but also on the past behavior of the country acquiring them. While some countries have not fought outside of their own borders for centuries, others keep intervening militarily abroad. Words alone proclaiming only peaceful intentions meet with understandable scepticism.

There exist also weapons systems that do not only reduce the security of potential opponents, but also the security of the nation acquiring them. For example, a highly sophisticated weapons system that is so delicate that it may fire accidentally *reduces* directly the security of the country possessing it, instead of increasing it.[8] Such weapons could be called "superoffensive."

On the other hand, there exist also "superdefensive" arms, which increase not only one's own security, but also that of an opponent. For example, a fence which is impenetrable from both sides, or a peacekeeping force from a neutral party that separates two warring parties, can increase the security of both. As another example, a country may reduce its vulnerability from dependence on foreign energy supplies by the discovery of energy conservation technologies or of safe new energy sources. If it makes such discoveries available to the whole world, it can help increase the energy security of all countries.

Yet another instrument that could increase the security of all nations would be a system of reliable early warning satellites that would provide all nations with accurate information about each other's military preparations, so as to prevent surprise attacks—as the French proposal before the UN.

The entire range from superoffensive to superdefensive measures can be represented in Figure 3.[9]

A somewhat different definition of what constitutes offensive or defensive arms has been proposed by Quester (1977). Offensive he calls those arms which give an advantage to the one side which initiates fighting, which strikes first, whereas defensive arms give an advantage to the side which responds to an attack and defends itself.

A typical example of a defensive arm in that sense is a machine-gun post inside a bunker. If two hostile posts are facing each other, whoever ventures out first from his safe environment makes himself vulnerable and is likely to lose. Such situations tend to lead to a stalemate (provided there are no other, offensive arms).

A typical example of offensive arms in that sense is a fleet of bombers on an open airfield. If two such hostile fleets face each other, whoever is up in the air first and can destroy the other fleet while it is still on the ground is likely to win. Whoever hesitates and waits to see what will happen takes a grave risk. Such arms tend to precipitate the outbreak of a war in a period of tension and uncertainty.[10]

In general, mobility favors the offense, whereas fixed emplacements favor the defense. For example, tanks are offensive arms, whereas tank barrages or antitank weapons are defensive. Bombers are offensive, whereas ground-to-air missiles are defensive.

In the present nuclear age, one of the most destabilizing and dangerous developments has been the increasing accuracy of missiles, and especially the invention of multiple independently targetable reentry vehicles (MIRVs). This has raised the specter of the unwanted outbreak of a

512

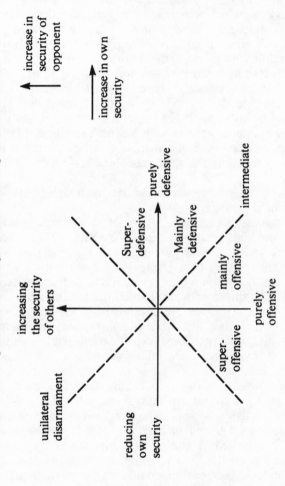

FIGURE 3. The Spectrum from Superoffensive to Superdefensive Arms

nuclear war. As long as each nuclear missile carried a single warhead, and both superpowers had approximately equal numbers of missiles, it was impossible for any side to destroy all the enemy's missiles in a first strike.[11] The remaining intact missiles would have inevitably been used for a devastating retaliatory second strike. This balance of mutual assured destruction, however tenuous and mad it was, provided at least some deterrence against the initiation of a nuclear war. Now that a typical missile can carry ten or more warheads, the probability that ten independently targeted nuclear bombs can destroy an enemy missile in its reinforced silo is close to certainty.[12] If there are no other weapons of significance, then in a period of high tension, there is an almost irresistible pressure on both sides to attack first, because to wait would be suicidal. Whoever strikes first has a chance to obliterate his opponent and survive, whereas the side that hesitates takes grave risks.

At the present moment, this extremely dangerous situation of a mutual first strike capability has not yet been reached, because both superpowers also have nuclear submarines, whose precise location it is not yet possible to detect. Any attacker would thus have to expect massive retaliation from submarine-launched missiles, and this not only deters a first strike, but also removes the pressure of either acting first or being left defenseless. But both superpowers, in an incomprehensible drift towards ultimate disaster, are now working feverishly on methods to make the oceans transparent. If submarines can be accurately located, and a single warhead can destroy a submarine that typically carries 160 nuclear warheads,[13] then the pressure on both sides not to wait under uncertainty becomes enormous.

What could provide a temporary measure of tenuous security would be large numbers of dispersed missiles with single warheads, either ocean or land-based (or better both), so that no first strike can destroy them all.[14] This may help steer the world away from a nuclear war for a little while longer. At the same time, efforts are needed to build workable and lasting international peace systems, which are not based on the threat of mutual annihilation. Little time is left to do something.[15]

The tragedy is that the victims of this madness would not only be those who perpetrate it, but many others as well, including neutral countries, who would be affected by radioactive fallout, even if they escape direct attack. Therefore, all have a right and a duty to warn against it and help in trying to prevent it.

Table 2 contrasts some offensive and defensive arms. The main distinguishing feature is that offensive arms pose a constant potential threat to others (at least in their own perception), whereas defensive arms cannot do any harm to others as long as they don't attack.

What is the result of combining defensive and offensive arms? Will the defensive or the offensive element prevail? When combined with offensive arms, even apparently purely defensive arms can become highly offensive. The result may be more offensive than either of the two components alone.

TABLE 2. Some Examples of Offensive and
Defensive Weapons

Offensive	Defensive
Tank	Tank barrage, anti-tank weapons
Bomber	Anti-aircraft weapons, bomb shelters, radar warning systems[a]
Nuclear missiles	Shelters, dispersal of population and industries, early warning satellites

[a] True warning systems must be distinguished from radar *guiding* systems that can direct missiles into an opponent's territory.

For example, we have seen that bomb shelters alone do not threaten anyone else. But if a country which already possesses nuclear missiles builds protective shelters for its population and industry, this can be seen by its adversaries as a preparation for a first strike.

A country that does not have shelters for its civilians would never want to use its missiles in a first strike, for fear of retaliation. The missiles would serve only as deterrent against an attack from outside. But if the population can be protected, the threat of retaliation is reduced, and a first strike becomes conceivable. These considerations apply to any defensive weapons, if they are combined with offensive forces.

It follows from this that one cannot look at individual weapons to judge whether they are offensive or defensive, but one must consider the entire combination of weapons and other defense preparations of a country, to decide whether the *whole system* is more offensive or defensive.

To conclude this section, the relationship between offensive or defensive arms and the dynamics of an arms race will be briefly discussed.[16]

Let us assume at first that two hostile countries, A and B, are concerned only with their own security, as governments typically claim they are, and have no aggressive intentions. If country A acquires offensive arms, allegedly only for self-defense, country B will see its national security endangered, and also build up its arms, to restore its own security.[17] If the predominant arms technology is offensive, B will need *more* arms than A to compensate for its loss of security, because offensive arms reduce mainly the security of others, and contribute little to one's own security. In response to that, country A will need even more arms to restore its security position, and so on. The only limit to the pace of such a mutually stimulated arms race is set by the two countries' economic capacity to produce or purchase arms. The arms race will put a heavy burden on their civilian economies, and reduce their economic growth.

Clearly, both countries could benefit from mutual disarmament. But in the absence of trust and enforceable agreements, none of them can afford to take a unilateral disarmament initiative without reducing its perceived security.

If the available arms technology were predominantly defensive, then the acquisition of arms by A would reduce the security of B only slightly. B would add to its arms to compensate for that, but less than A. This in turn would induce A to increase its armaments, but even less than B, etc. Soon this process would come to a halt.

How do countries choose between offensive or defensive arms? In the absence of any mutual agreement, each of them acquires the arms that are "cheapest," in the sense of adding most to its own security per monetary unit, regardless of the loss of security this inflicts on the other side. Under these assumptions, the discovery of cheap defensive arms could bring an end to an arms race.

To illustrate this, imagine someone develops a very cheap and accurate antitank missile. A country that wants to protect itself against a possible invasion with tanks will then find it in its own best interest to acquire such antitank missiles, rather than tanks of its own to fight off an attack. But these antitank missiles, if their action radius is sufficiently short, do not pose any threat to the other country, as long as it stays within its own borders. There is no need to match these antitank missiles either with tanks or with other antitank missiles to maintain one's own security.[18]

One of the reasons why there has been so much emphasis on offensive arms in recent history may be that with current technology offensive arms are generally much cheaper than equivalent defensive arms. For example, a single missile can threaten thousands of different targets, and protecting all of them with strong enough shelters can be very costly. Whereas an aggressor can choose the point of attack and concentrate all his forces on that point, a defender must be able to withstand an attack from everywhere. This explains the saying "offense is the best defense." But if one takes into account the *indirect* effects of an offensive "defense," namely the contribution to arms races and the increased danger of war, then it may well be that the added initial expenses for true, non-threatening defense are well worth it in the long run.

One result of this analysis is that it is much more profitable to export offensive arms, preferably to both parties in a conflict, because this will lead to an ever-growing demand. Supplying both sides with truly defensive arms would make them both secure, and soon lead to a drying up of the demand for further arms.

If two hostile countries are not only concerned with their own security, but both try to conquer each other, then they will not only be interested in acquiring arms to restore their own security, but also deliberately try to reduce the security of the other side as much as possible. In that case, even the discovery of cheap defensive arms will not bring an end to their mutual arms race.

However, it is sufficient that *one* of the two countries is interested only in its own defense, for an end to the arms race to be achievable with a corresponding technological breakthrough. For example, if someone could develop a cheap and effective method of destroying missiles in the air, then no government would continue to build nuclear missiles, no matter how aggressive its intentions were. It would only ruin its own economy, without achieving any of its aggressive objectives.

By shifting away from offensive to defensive arms, which do not pose any threat to a potential enemy, countries can make a unilateral contribution towards peace, without jeopardizing their own security. In taking such a step, a country does not have to wait for others to do the same, as is necessary in the case of mutual disarmament.

4. NON-MILITARY DEFENSE

Galtung (1968) has shown how a country can increase its national security against potential aggression through non-military means. His basic idea can be summarized as follows. A potential aggressor will have to consider what gains he expects from an attack, and what losses he may have to incur. (Gains and losses need not be in a material sense only. They will also include prestige or humiliation, and anything else that a decisionmaker values.) Similarly, he will evaluate the expected gains and losses if he does not attack.

Traditional armed defense concentrates exclusively on one of these four possibilities, namely on increasing as much as possible the losses of an aggressor through armed defense and retaliation (case 1 in Table 3). The other possibilities have been neglected.

One can reduce the gains of an enemy in case of an attack, if the population refuses to cooperate with a hostile occupation force, and offers non-violent resistance (case 2 in Table 3). Industrial plants can be constructed in such a way that the removal of a few essential components renders them useless to an enemy, without destroying them. Stocks of goods, bridges, etc. inside one's own territory can be destroyed in case of an enemy occupation. It is important to announce that such measures would be taken in case of an occupation, and make them credible. Automatic mechanisms, which would operate in case of an attack independent of anyone's control, would enhance the credibility of such measures.

The gains of a potential opponent in the case of his peaceful cooperation can be increased through scientific, technical, and cultural exchange, mutually beneficial trade, cooperation on joint projects, etc. (case 4 in Table 3).

The losses in case of no attack can be reduced if injustices are removed voluntarily, if one does not exploit other countries, and if one does not give them the impression that war is the only way out of an intolerable situation. One should never criticize others to such an extent that they

TABLE 3. Four Forms of Defense

Attack		
Increase losses	(1)	Armed defense or retaliation
Reduce gains	(2)	Non-violent resistance; industrial sabotage in occupied areas of one's own country

No Attack		
Reduce losses	(3)	No exploitation; no 'loss of face' for an opponent
Increase gains	(4)	Scientific, cultural, political and economic cooperation; trade, diplomatic services

believe that only a military confrontation can restore their prestige. Initiatives towards a compromise by an opponent should not be represented as weakness[19] (case 3 in Table 3).

These four possibilities are summarized below.

Among these four measures, military defense has the disadvantage that it leads to mutual fear and to an arms race, unless it is purely defensive. Up to now, almost all arms races have ended up in a war. In order to increase truly the security of one's country, more emphasis should be put on the three forms of non-military defense. These do not represent any threat to other countries, and do not increase one's own security at the expense of others, but increase the security and well-being of all. They can make a real contribution towards peace, without any sacrifice in one's own national security.

An important component of national defense without threat to others is to make oneself less vulnerable, and to become less dependent on others, i.e., more self-reliant. The storage of food reserves for periods of need and greater self-sufficiency in food production can reduce the potential suffering of the population if supplies from abroad are interrupted, and such measures do not threaten anyone else. If the population is widely dispersed and if a sufficient number of fall-out shelters are available, a country can be less exposed to nuclear blackmail. All these measures do not endanger anyone else.

There are four levels of defense, listed below in order of decreasing violence:

1. Threat of retaliation against the civilian population of an aggressor, possibly by means of mass destruction (nuclear, biological, chemical).
2. Conventional military defense inside one's own borders.
3. Guerrilla warfare in occupied territory. Harrassment of an occupation force by small, decentralized units with a high degree of autonomy.
4. Non-violent resistance and other forms of non-military defense.

The first of these options should be excluded, because mutual suicide leaves nothing worth being defended.

The most effective defense may be some combination of the remaining three forms of defense. Diversity is a general method to reduce vulnerability. If one component fails, others remain to continue resistance. A certain amount of duplication or redundance provides much greater resilience and may be well worth the effort.[20]

This principle also applies to forms of organization. In a strictly hierarchical command structure, it is sufficient to eliminate the top of the pyramid in order to make the entire organization leaderless and helpless. In a federal form of organization, which has not only vertical but also many horizontal channels of communication, it is much more difficult to create chaos.

Another reason for combining military and non-military forms of defense is to preserve a democratic social structure, which allows for a maximum amount of personal freedom and choice, where no group imposes its will on any other group. For this reason, conscientious objectors against violent forms of defense should be permitted to contribute to their country's security with non-violent methods, in which they believe. For the same reason, adherrents of non-violence should not impose their views on the rest of society, and should admit "conscientious objectors against non-military defense," who believe that only force can effectively deter an aggression. The two forms of defense should be closely coordinated and support each other, not work against each other.

The next section will briefly examine how the Swiss concept of general defense compares with the theoretical ideas outlined here.

5. THE SWISS CONCEPT OF GENERAL DEFENSE[21]

A good strategy should answer the question *who* should do *what, why, when, where,* and *how* (Galtung 1979), and one could add, *at whose expense.* For the Swiss defense strategy, these questions could be answered as follows:

What is to be defended is the right to *democratic self-determination,* the freedom of the people to choose and develop their own institutions, without the imposition of military force from outside.[22] This objective does not in any way infringe on the right of other nations to equal self-determination, and is thus a logically compatible, legitimate objective that does not lead to conflicts if other nations seek the same for themselves.

Why self-determination is to be defended is out of the conviction that it is the best prerequisite for *individual freedom, common welfare,* and the *possibility of further developing* the state and its institutions according to the people's wishes (13). It also enables the citizens themselves to develop as human beings. It does not mean defending any "anachronistic and obsolete concepts" (21).

Who is to defend it is *the entire population,* in various forms. The army is a militia army that consists of about 80 percent of the men between the age from 20 to 50 years, all those who are not physically or mentally impaired. They keep their personal arms, ammunition, and uniform at home, and most report for duty in case of an attack within a short distance from their home. The remaining population participates in civil defense, medical services, in keeping the economy operating at a necessary minimum, and in non-violent resistance if parts of the country should be occupied. "Keeping out of war through defense readiness (dissuasion) . . . is not uniquely a military task, but presupposes also a far-reaching capacity for endurance on the part of the population and the authorities" (423). "The close bonds between the army and the population are a great asset" (542). Since Switzerland does not have a small professional army isolated from the population, a military coup is almost unthinkable.

When should the country be defended? *Constantly,* but in various forms, depending on circumstances. In times of relative peace, the main emphasis is on diplomacy and the offering of good services in the international sphere. In the event of an armed attack from outside, the army would play the major role in defending the national territory. In the event of an enemy occupation of major portions of the country, guerrilla warfare, sabotage, and civil disobedience would keep harassing the enemy and prepare for ultimate liberation (544). In the event of an attack with means of mass destruction, the primary objective would be to ensure the survival of the population to the maximum feasible extent (23).

Where does the defense take place? Military efforts are *purely defensive* and the army prepares to fight "*only within its own territory*" (541). No retaliation against the civilian population of an aggressor is considered. "Switzerland takes all its general defense measures *in accordance* with the provisions of the law of war and international law. This entails the prohibition of any recourse to indiscriminate conduct of war against the population of the opponent, even though in the atomic age, *only* the threat of the destruction of the opponent's population seems to be an effective deterrent" (512). An active component of the security policy, aimed at the exterior, consists only of non-violent efforts "to contribute to the shaping and securing of a permanent peace within the international context" (13).

At what expense, to whom, does Switzerland defend itself? The burden is carried by the entire population, mostly through regular participation in defense exercises, within a comparatively moderate budget.[23] In safeguarding its own national security, Switzerland does not threaten any other nation, i.e. its defense efforts are *not at the expense of the security of anyone else.* Other countries may not like Switzerland, they may feel envious of its wealth, but at least no country has a reason to feel threatened by it.

The question still remains whether the current allocation of defense efforts and expenditures is the most effective one. Efforts in such areas of non-military defense as greater technical cooperation with poorer countries, on an equitable basis, and in conflict and peace research, might well contribute more significantly to Switzerland's national security than marginal additions to military hardware. Opportunity costs of present efforts must be considered.

The biggest question is *how* Switzerland is to defend itself. A discussion of this will constitute the remainder of this section.

The meaning of *general* defense is that it uses *all legitimate means against all forms of power* and all attempts at foreign domination. I will in turn compare Swiss defense policies with the four forms of defense, including non-military defense (Table 3) and the six forms of resistance to power (Table 1). A brief glance at the historical evolution of the principles governing Switzerland's defense policies will follow, and the section concludes with a list of problems with current defense policies.

The general principle guiding Swiss defense efforts is *"dissuasion,"* a form of inoffensive deterrence, which should make it clear to any potential aggressor that any possible gains from attacking Switzerland are not worth the costs. This means both that the costs to the enemy of an attack should be as high as possible, and the gains as low as possible. It also means that the gains from leaving Switzerland in peace should be as high as possible, and the losses as small as possible. These are also the four considerations underlying Galtung's principles of non-military as well as military defense.

To maximize the costs of an attack, Switzerland maintains a strong army compared to its population. It is also prepared for protracted war and guerrilla activities out of mountain sanctuaries with reserves of ammunition and food. If the regular army should be unable to function, an occupation force would continue to suffer attacks from guerrilla warfare. "The risks which a potential aggressor must be made to perceive consist in the *loss* of prestige, military forces, war-potential, and time, as well as in *running counter* to his ideological, political and economic interests" (423). "Unilateral disarmament, as it is sometimes also demanded of small states, would *not increase the general security, but would rather reduce it,* because demilitarized areas in strategically important zones have a way of attracting the interest of neighboring states" (3).

To minimize the gains of an enemy in case *of an attack,* preparations are made to make industrial plants useless to an occupation force, destroy goods in warehouses and stores that might fall into enemy hands (563), destroy bridges and railways in occupied territory, etc. The passive refusal of the population to cooperate with an enemy in occupied territory is also stated as an important factor of dissuasion (426).

To minimize the losses of a potential enemy *from not attacking* Switzerland, the main pillar is its neutrality policy, which guarantees that Switzerland will not attack another country out of treaty obligations with third powers, and will not fight unless it is attacked first. This means that no country takes any military risk from not occupying Switzerland and trying to eliminate its armed forces.

Switzerland also had a policy of refraining from praising and criticizing other countries or governments. Foreigners are prohibited from making public speeches in Switzerland which might offend a foreign power.[24] This is probably also the main reason why Switzerland has not yet joined the United Nations, because it prefers to avoid having to take a stand (even visible abstention from voting or non-participation in a particular vote) on controversial international issues, which would earn it hostility from one side or the other.

Another means by which Switzerland tries to minimize other countries' grievances against it in time of peace is by not exploiting any one country too visibly. Switzerland's economy does benefit substantially from the repatriation of profits from Swiss-owned enterprises in other countries, and from deposits of illegally gained money in secret Swiss bank accounts. But since these profits are spread thin over many countries, and Switzerland is of relatively small size, no country feels particularly oppressed by Switzerland.[25]

To *maximize the gains* of other countries if they leave Switzerland in *peace,* Switzerland offers its diplomatic services, e.g. as a channel of communication between states having no diplomatic ties, participates in humanitarian actions and disaster relief, works towards the extension of international arbitration, participates in international organizations, etc. (532). It also participates in technical cooperation with developing countries (although Switzerland's official development assistance is one of the lowest based on percent of GNP), and in mutually beneficial trade. Generally it seeks to show to a potential enemy the value to him of an intact Switzerland.

This means that Switzerland practices all forms of defense listed in Table 3 to some extent, both military and non-military.[26] Let us next examine what forms of resistance Switzerland uses not only against military (punitive) power, but also against economic (remunerative) and psychological (normative) power, on the basis of Table 1.

Switzerland tries to maintain "peace in liberty" through dissuasion of aggression, as just explained. At the same time, it attempts to minimize its own losses in case it is attacked, by making itself as invulnerable as possible. Besides the objective *ability* to defend itself, it also stresses the popular *will* to defend its independence. For the people to have the courage (or *fearlessness*) to defend their institutions, be it as members of the armed forces or as civilians enduring a hostile occupation and offering non-violent resistance, the people must have something worth defending. In this lies the importance of a *just social order,* the protection of *personal liberty* and *human dignity* (21).

To make itself as invulnerable as possible, even under the worst possible assumptions, Switzerland takes no chance. It has one of the most extensive programs of civil defense shelters.[27] "*Each inhabitant* of our country must have a chance to survive the war" (715). It stresses that "the employment of weapons of mass destruction (atomic, biological, and chemical weapons) in a conflict cannot be excluded as long as any power possesses these weapons" (314). It further recognizes that "the *danger* of a breach of international agreement is always present" (311), and that "espionage cases, acts of sabotage and terrorism, also against our country, leave no doubt that the effects of the world wide struggle, which always could lead to war, do not bypass a small neutral state like Switzerland" (32). Effective protection of the population also reduces its vulnerability against blackmail (315).

Other measures to make itself invulnerable, without threatening others, are passive obstacles against tanks, and other defensive weapons such as anti-aircraft missiles, radar warning systems, etc. It also possesses some arms that can potentially be used in an offensive way, such as tanks and fighter-planes. But it claims to use them only within its own borders, and past history makes this quite credible.

To make the structure of leadership as invulnerable as possible, it states that "our *federal* system with its tightly woven net of organizations and domains . . . overlapping in part, is here an element of strength . . . in the case of a falling-out of the top echelon of a certain domain, only a relatively small part of the whole domain will be without leadership. Those still functioning domains . . . may immediately step into the breach" (64).

In the field of transportation, "the great density of our networks offers . . . many *alternative routes*" (552), even when they come under constant attack.

To make itself less vulnerable against economic pressure and embargoes from abroad, Switzerland aims at economic *self-reliance* in all areas vital for the survival of the population and for defense (552). This consists both of a cutback of domestic demand (the subjective element) and of an increase of domestic supply when required (the objective element).

The plan for self-reliance in food, which was pioneered by Fritz Wahlen, may serve as a good illustration.[28] During peacetime, Switzerland produces only about 60 percent of its food consumption. In the event of a sudden and lasting forced interruption of food imports, four measures would be taken to insure self-sufficiency:

1. A reduction of daily calorie intake by about 30 percent;
2. A change in the composition of food consumption, reducing meat and sugar consumption to about one-third of peacetime use, and increasing potato consumption over five times, among other things;
3. A gradual increase in the area planted with food crops by ploughing more grassland, while the number of livestock would be reduced, over a period of three years;
4. Until the cultivated area has reached its maximum level, stocks of food reserves would be consumed to cover the difference (see Figure 4). Sufficient reserves of non-perishable food are kept in households (in civil defense shelters) and in mountain sanctuaries to supply the army.

Similar measures exist or are planned for other raw materials that are essential for survival and for supporting military defense. For example, underground reserves of oil and gas are being built up, and the sources of energy are being diversified.[29]

Should Switzerland strive for autarky in important domains of the economy even during peacetime? This would be uneconomical, as long as imported food and other raw materials are cheaper. It is also unnecessary, provided plans exist to increase domestic production in time, and fill the temporary gap with reserves.[30]

Such a policy of self-reliance makes Switzerland invulnerable against economic threats, and does not pose any danger to anyone else. In this way, Switzeland can make credible that it has no need to raid, for example, Northern Italy for food in case of a shortage, since it can show that it has other approaches to meet a potential food emergency, despite the fact of the vital importance of food and its heavy dependence on imports during peacetime.[31] It would be in the interest of peace if countries which depend, for example, on oil imports in peacetime would make similar plans for energy self-sufficiency when necessary, through reserves, plans for increases in domestic energy production, and for a reduction of inessential consumption. This would be a real contribution to their national security, unlike any thoughts of raiding the Persian Gulf for oil, if the flow should be interrupted. That provides a very dubious measure of security, and could escalate into a major war.[32]

No state has a right to force any other state into a trade relationship through the use of violence. Trade must be based on *voluntary,* mutually beneficial exchange. While some trade for mutual advantage is desirable, *dependence* on trade can become a source of war. Therefore *self-reliance promotes peace,* by reducing sources of conflict that might erupt in the outbreak of direct violence. At the same time, self-reliance is an aspect of peace, as the absence of exploitation, i.e., structural violence.

To make itself invulnerable against foreign propaganda and rumors (an objective form of resistance against "normative power" by an enemy, namely *knowledge*), Switzerland recognizes the need for a truthful and

FIGURE 4. Alimentation Plan 75: Expansion of cultivation, consumption reduction and utilization of stocks during the different cultivation expansion states

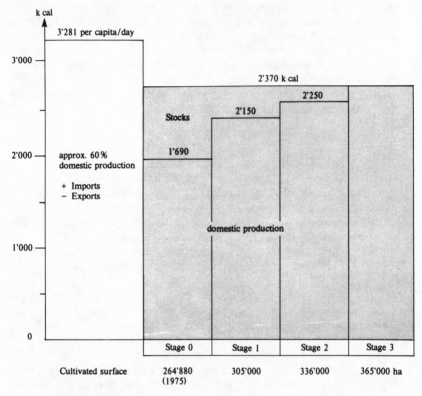

Stage = Cultivation expansion stage under wartime economic conditions of 12 months duration, beginning with fall planting. In order to reach self-sufficiency, cultivation must be expanded at the expense of live stock.

Stage 0 = Initial year according to the alimentation planning 1974/1975
1 cal   = 4.1897 joules (J)
1 kcal = 4189.7 joules

(Source: Zentralstelle für Gesamtverteidigung, 1979, p. 30)

honest national news service, particularly when being attacked. "Manipulated information which tries to keep setbacks and negative developments secret "may, after a while, have the opposite effect from that desired" (553). Also, a good general education for all is sought.

The subjective form of resistance against psychological influence from abroad is "*self-respect.*" The Swiss population is taught to feel pride in their institutions.[33]

Switzerland does not seek power over others, in any of the three forms. "Switzerland has renounced the use of force in backing its demands vis-à-vis other states" (423).[34] "To help prevent an automatic escalation through *appropriate, (not excessive*[35]) but *sufficient reactions* is one of the most important tasks if peace is to be kept in the atomic age" (412).

Switzerland does not use economic embargoes against other countries to put pressure on them, nor does it try to influence the internal affairs of other countries through propaganda.

How did this policy of armed neutrality evolve in Swiss history? Switzerland was founded in 1291 as a loose defense treaty between three localities (Uri, Schwyz and Unterwalden) against attempts at subjugation by the Hapsburgs. More localities, later called cantons, joined, and after having successfully fought against several expeditions by armies of the Hapsburgs, Switzerland entered a period of active foreign military policy, conquering some territory, particularly to control passes over the Alps. This period lasted about two centuries. In 1476, the Swiss defeated the army of Duke Charles of Burgundy, who had attempted to conquer parts of Switzerland. They could have annexed the whole of Burgundy, but refrained from doing so. In 1515, two Swiss mercenary armies, one in the service of the French king and another in the service of an Italian duke, fought each other at Marignano in Northern Italy, in a very long and bloody battle. This event created such an outrage in Switzerland that it brought about an end to the active period of Swiss military adventures abroad. Mercenaries kept serving abroad, but avoided fighting other Swiss, and Switzerland did not take sides in foreign wars as a nation. In 1847, during a civil war between protestants and Catholics, some Jesuits called on the Hapsburgs to intervene in favor of the Catholics. It never came to that, but the anger against calling on a foreign power to intervene in the internal affairs of Switzerland went so deep that the Jesuits have been banned from Switzerland until today, despite periodic referenda to lift the ban. Since Napoleon's armies swept through Europe around 1815, Switzerland has not been drawn into any international war. It was able to keep out of World Wars I and II. Its relatively strong army may have played some role, as well as the fact that it does not possess any raw materials of value, and has a difficult terrain to pass through. But probably most important was its successful "demonstration of the usefulness of an intact Switzerland to any potential aggressor," as a banking and information center, and through economic cooperation. Such a position will be called immoral by some, who maintain that there are situations where it is necessary to join the right cause and not to remain neutral. But it may be understandable from a small and weak country. Today there is a strict prohibition against service in any foreign army. Whoever violates this provision is jailed on return to Switzerland, or loses his Swiss citizenship.

So far, more or less everything seems fine with Switzerland's defense policy. There are, however, also a number of problems.

1. Switzerland does not permit conscientious objectors against the use of force to prepare for alternative forms of non-military defense,

or to do other forms of public service. The principle that liberal democracy should be defended in a compatible way with its principles (704) and that efforts should be made to overcome a "growing disenchantment with the state by *working together critically and constructively* to eliminate the causes of this malaise" (522) would lead one to expect a different treatment of conscientious objectors than giving them a mandatory jail sentence.

2. The command structure of the army is too hierarchical, despite theoretical emphasis on the value of *federal* structures and "tightly woven nets" of communication. The hierarchical structure of the army also duplicates to some extent civilian hierarchies, with the same people occupying top positions both in civilian and military life.

3. Switzerland exports arms, some of which are being used in combat. Although there is an official policy that prohibits the export of arms to countries at war, private firms sometimes find ways to circumvent this provision, for example by supplying third parties who then resell these arms.

4. Like probably every army, the Swiss army is plagued by cost overruns in procurements. People who do not spend their own money have a natural tendency to be less careful in what they pay. Most famous is the cost overrun that occurred in the purchase of Mirage fighter planes from France, which were modified at great and unforeseen costs at the request of the Swiss military.

5. Despite an extensive discussion of non-violent civil disobedience and other forms of non-military defense, no maneuvers are being regularly held for such forms of defense. How can people be credibly expected to practice them, if they have never prepared for such behavior?

6. The 1973 report stated explicitly that "Switzerland can make its contribution . . . to a decrease in tensions and to the peaceful settlement of conflicts and disputes. Peace and conflict research activities constitute a part of these efforts" (422). In spite of that, no funds whatsoever have been made available by the government so far for peace research as such. In 1980, the Geneva International Peace Research Institute (GIPRI) was founded on private initiative. But it depends so far mainly on voluntary contributions. In what a state would our military defense be, if it had to rely on voluntary donations? At the 1978 Special Session of the United Nations General Assembly, Secretary-General Waldheim appealed to all nations to make available one tenth of one percent of their military expenditures for research and education in the field of disarmament. It seems that such a sum would detract very little from our military efforts, and could possibly make a much more significant contribution to our security than military defense alone.[36] It could help find new ways to solve conflicts without resort to violence, and to eliminate the causes of war long before hostilities reach a state that is almost irreversible.

All of these shortcomings can and should be corrected. In spite of them, the Swiss defense policy, which tries to maintain peace and not to pose a threat to the security of any other country, seems overall quite desirable, at least when compared with some other current "defense" doctrines.

6. CONCLUSIONS

The main thrust of this paper has been to show that it is possible to make a contribution towards peace without sacrificing one's national security by

(a) increasing purely defensive arms and non-military defense efforts;
(b) reducing offensive arms, so as not to stimulate arms races and not to pose any real or imagined threat to others which would make them insecure and thus tempted to launch a preemptive strike;
(c) making the structure of the entire society as invulnerable as possible, through decentralized federal forms of organization, dispersal of population and industries, economic self-reliance at various levels, and by creating an equitable social order perceived as worth defending;
(d) undertaking peace initiatives by offering assistance to other nations when they need it, sharing useful information, strengthening just international law, etc. (Unjust international law may strengthen structural violence.)

The more nations take such a position, the safer the world is. Measures to strengthen one's defensive capability, while reducing any offensive threat to others, have the advantage that they can be taken unilaterally, without having to wait for reciprocal steps by other nations, and without endangering one's own national security.

To preserve peace and one's own security, it is necessary to make it clear that aggression can never succeed. But it is equally important to make it credible that one does not pose any threat to others as long as they leave one in peace. To threaten others, or even to allow them to wrongly believe they are threatened, can be suicidal in the nuclear age.

NOTES

1. The ability to enforce agreements is by no means a sufficient condition for success, but without it, the situation is very difficult. For example, what would be the value of domestic laws, if they could not be enforced?

2. The entire paper is limited to a discussion of the prevention of direct violence, i.e., the avoidance of war and peaceful resolution of conflicts. It does not deal with the prevention of structural violence, i.e., the avoidance of exploitation and the search for equitable cooperation. The latter is also a very important concern, but it is beyond the scope of the present paper.

3. For example, advertisement for baby milk powder found easy victims among mothers in the Third World with little education, who were misguided to substitute it for the much healthier mother's milk. The use of contaminated water has led to the death of many infants. Had the mothers been better informed about the health hazards involved, they could have formed their own independent judgment and would not have naively accepted the advertisements' claims.

4. This definition makes it necessary, of course, to define what is meant by national security. It may be difficult to measure "national security" in precise quantitative terms. It will be related to a country's ability to avoid a war, and to its citizens' probability of survival in case of war. It will also depend on people's ability to maintain their own way of life, free from foreign domination (otherwise living in a concentration camp would be compatible with national security). Even if the concept is somewhat vague, it is essential to deal with it, because it is so central to thinking about defense. The choice of concepts should be made on the basis of their relevance, not their elegance. Too often, intellectuals give in to the temptation of dealing with concepts for which statistical data are readily available or which permit sophisticated manipulations, but which have little to do with the fundamental problem to be addressed.

5. Unless there is agreement on legitimate goals of defense, the distinction between offensive and defensive arms becomes arbitrary. For example, as Patrick Healey has pointed out, if an imperial power wants to establish a colony to exploit cheap labor, and the indigenous population simply runs away without offering any resistance, this may be regarded as highly "offensive" by the colonizers who are deprived of cheap labor. The following quotation from Preiswerk (1980) also illustrates the confusion in certain people's minds about what is offensive and what is not. He writes: "Not to enter into trade relations has always been considered an offense. China had this experience in the 19th century. Samir Amin reports from the 1976 Nairobi Conference of UNCTAD: 'I have asked the representatives of the Soviet Union and the United States whether they considered the refusal by one country to entertain economic or commercial relations with other countries to be an "aggression." Both said: "Yes, it is intolerable!" The American explained that we are living in the same world and we all have to cooperate; the Soviet affirmed that to abandon international economic exchange would be a return to savagery. If one followed both, one would have to add to the Charter of the United Nations a new crime of aggression against civilization: "the refusal to trade." ' "

6. A modern successor to the gunboat is the aircraft carrier. It can only be deployed against weaker nations, who do not have the capability to sink it with a single missile.

7. However, certain defensive arms can be converted relatively easily into offensive arms, e.g., if a ground-to-air missile can be converted into a ground-to-ground missile. To have a defensive system that is convincingly threat-free, such convertibility must be avoided.

8. According to the *New York Times* of October 29, 1980, no less than 3,804 false alarms of a potential nuclear attack on the United States were generated by the NORAD computerized radar warning system during the 18 months from January 1, 1979, to June 30, 1980. So far, all of these alarms could be identified as errors in time, but 4 of them were serious enough that nuclear bomber and missile units were put on an increased state of alert. One of these false warnings occurred when a technician inadvertently inserted a training tape, simulating

a nuclear attack, into the live warning system. Other errors resulted from equipment malfunctions. If that system fails, it does not only threaten the security of the Soviet Union, but that of the United States as well.

The Reagan administration plans to improve the reliability of that system, so that "the President could order a retaliatory nuclear strike against the Soviet Union, without risking an accidental nuclear war, after ascertaining that Soviet missiles are definitely heading toward the United States" (*New York Times* of October 12, 1981). But how can anyone trust the absolute reliability of such a complex system that can never be fully tested in the real world?

9. The vertical axis to the top in Figure 3 would correspond to measures which increase the security of others, without having any effect on the security of one's own country, a form of "altruism." The horizontal axis to the left would correspond to measures which reduce one's own security, without affecting that of other countries, a sort of national "masochism." The top left region corresponds to certain unilateral disarmament measures that increase the security of others, but may reduce one's own security.

10. According to Quester, this model describes the outbreak of the 1967 Middle East war.

11. This would require near certainty that every missile fires, and the capability of hitting a small target with a reliability very close to 100 percent, which is almost impossible to achieve.

12. If the probability that one warhead comes close enough to its target is 0.5, then the probability that of 10 warheads all miss is $(0.5)^{10}$ or less than 0.001. If the probability of a hit is 0.9 for each warhead, the probability of 10 misses is $(0.1)^{10}$ or 10^{-10}. Even if several missiles fail to fire, cross-targeting still assures that all enemy missiles will be hit by at least one bomb.

13. A Polaris submarine carries 16 missiles with 10 independently targetable nuclear bombs each.

14. To prevent accidental misfirings from a widely dispersed missile force under decentralized control, a central location should constantly emit a secret code that physically prevents missiles from being fired. Only if that central unit is destroyed, would control pass over automatically to decentralized levels.

15. Kenneth Boulding has calculated that if the probability of a nuclear war is 2 percent per year, as some experts estimate, then the probability that there will be a nuclear war within 50 years is 64 percent, within 100 years 87 percent, within 200 years 98 percent, within 500 years 99.99 percent, and within 1000 years a virtual certainty.

16. A mathematical treatment of this problem can be found in Fischer (1981).

17. Fear of an opponent need not be the only cause of arms races. In some cases, the internal dynamics of a profit-seeking military industry, having close ties with the government officials who appropriate military contracts, can lead to a "self-stimulated" arms race. It is also possible that an unpopular power elite pursues an arms race and seeks an external confrontation to rally support from a dissatisfied population against an "external threat."

18. Similarly, if it were possible to develop a particle beam that could destroy missiles, this might bring a temporary halt to the competitive buildup of nuclear missiles. However, if such weapons were accessible exclusively to the superpowers, this would strengthen their dominance over the rest of the world.

As Galtung (1980, p. 190) has pointed out, the development of any new arms has a tendency to lead opponents to develop countermeasures, such as "anti-antitank weapons," etc. But these are not necessary for defense, only if the goal is aggression.

19. For example, an unnamed Eastern European diplomat said in 1946 that if Russia withdrew her troops from Austria, this had to be seen as a voluntary gesture, and should not be interpreted as a diplomatic defeat in face of the Anglo-Americans (Rauschensteiner 1979, p. 11). I am grateful to Erich Haager for this reference.

20. A good illustration of this principle was the Ho-Chi-Minh trail through which North Vietnam supplied the NLF during the war. It consisted of a very widespread and dense network of alternative paths, and thus it was not possible to interdict the flow of material even with very heavy bombing. If one path was destroyed, there were numerous alternatives to choose from.

21. This section is mainly based on two documents of the Swiss Government, edited by the Zentralstelle für Gesamtverteidigung (1973 and 1979), and on some personal experience. Numbers in parenthesis refer to sections in the 1973 statement on the Swiss concept of general defense. Both reports are available in Gemran, French, Italian and English from the Zentralstelle für Gesamtverteidigung, 3003 Bern, Switzerland. All emphasis is in the original.

22. No country can, of course, completely isolate itself from the impact of what is going on in the rest of the world. Growing economic interdependence has made most countries increasingly dependent on trends in the world economy. Nevertheless, one can seek to minimize one's vulnerability even to non-military forms of force, through greater economic self-reliance and political and cultural autonomy.

23. The direct financial military expenditures, 2.3 percent of GNP in 1979, are lower than the true costs to the economy because the government does not pay citizens during their military service. They remain on the payroll of their company. Also, such efforts as promoting food self-reliance for national security reasons, which represent a cost, are not included in the military budget.

Even so, the costs of a purely defensive, but effective military posture are not excessive, as it has sometimes been claimed, in order to justify an offensive posture. Indeed, these expenditures are relatively modest, as an international comparison shows. As a percentage of GNP, military expenditures in 1977 for a selection of countries were: Israel 26.6%, Egypt 25.1%, USSR 8%, Nigeria 7.3% (in 1975), Pakistan 5.8%, U.S. 5.3%, France 3.9%, India 3.4%, Norway 3.1%, Switzerland 2.1%, Brazil 1.2%, Japan 0.9%. The world average was 4.6% of GNP. Per capita military expenditures in 1977 (U.S. $) were approximately: Israel $1002, U.S. $466, France $287, Norway $285, USSR $270, Switzerland $206, Egypt $125, Japan $55, Nigeria $34, Brazil $16, Pakistan $12, India $5. The world average was $88 per capita. (Source: *SIPRI Yearbook 1979.* Population figures and world GNP were taken from the World Bank Atlas, 1979.)

24. This prohibition might well be lifted, since it should be clear that whatever any individual says on Swiss soil is not necessarily the position of the Swiss government.

25. Johan Galtung has compared Switzerland in this respect to a cat with 150 soft paws on 150 shoulders, whose weight nobody feels. If it had concentrated all its economic power on one country alone—for example, Austria—there would have been a liberation movement in Austria and a war with Switzerland long ago.

26. Suppose that before World War II Switzerland had made itself defenseless by letting its army dissolve itself; had prohibited the use of German in schools in German-speaking regions, causing internal disunity and making itself look

weak; had called on the German people through daily broadcasts to overthrow the murderous dictatorship of Hitler; and had taken hostage the diplomatic personnel of a superpower, isolating itself internationally and losing support. This would have violated all of the above principles of dissuasion. It is doubtful, to say the least, whether under such circumstances Switzerland would have been spared from a war. Clearly the moral blame for an attack on Switzerland would have rested on Hitler's Germany, but that would not have helped Switzerland much.

27. In 1979, there were modern ventilated shelters for 70 percent of the population and traditional shelters for another 20 percent, although they did not exactly match the population distribution (Zentralstelle für Gesamtverteidigung, 1979, p. 24). In 1974, at the peak, 748 million Swiss Francs were spent for civil defense, out of 3,530 million expenditures for general defense or 21.2 percent. Total defense expenditures represented 2.4 percent of GNP (ibid., pp. 50–52). Until 1980, 50 percent of the cost of shelters in private houses was covered by public funds provided by the communities. From 1981, house-owners will pay 100 percent of the cost of civil defense shelters. Every new house is required by law to have a ventilated shelter. (Private civil defense expenditures, which match those of the communities, but are not listed in the report, have been included in the above figures.) A substantial number of underground hospitals have also been built.

28. Zentralstelle für Gesamtverteidigung, 1979.

29. Such defense efforts, which do not pose any threat to others and are relatively invulnerable, need not be kept secret. On the contrary, they are publicly announced, and everybody is welcome to imitate them.

30. It is wise to keep some candles and matches at home, in case the electricity is interrupted. But it is not necessary to use only candles (or even to make them) for fear of an electricity cutoff. In this sense, economic self-reliance means the *potential for autarky* when necessary, not permanent autarky.

31. Even if Switzerland wanted to rely on getting food from other countries, if necessary by force, it is simply too weak to even conceive of such options, as superpowers may be tempted to do, and it may have made a virtue out of necessity.

32. Recently, a bomb was planted in a New York Railway Station by the Puerto Rican Liberation Front. Nobody was hurt, and little damage done, but soon it may be possible for terrorist organizations to plant nuclear bombs. The most effective delivery vehicle may not be a rocket but a suitcase.

33. Perhaps a little too much, and this paper may look like yet another example of this. The recent youth disturbances in Zürich have shown that not everyone in Switzerland is proud of all the present institutions.

34. "At the same time, *no doubt* has been left concerning Switzerland's determination and capability to defend itself." (423)

35. "Nicht überdimensioniert" in the German original. That expression was omitted in the official translation. (Author's note)

36. Even such a modest contribution would increase the efforts devoted to peace research and education by several hundred percent.

REFERENCES

Boulding, Kenneth, 1978. *Stable Peace.* Austin: University of Texas Press.
Fischer, Dietrich, 1981. "Dynamics of an Arms Race with Offensive or Defensive Arms." Discussion Paper No. 81-06, Starr Center for Applied Economics, New York University.

Galtung, Johan, 1968. "On the Strategy of Nonmilitary Defense: Some Proposals and Problems." In Bartels, ed., *Peace and Justice: Unity or Dilemma.* Institute of Peace Research, Catholic University of Nijmegen. Also in Galtung, Johan, 1976. *Essays in Peace Research,*Vol. 2. Copenhagen: Christian Ejlers.

Galtung, Johan, 1979. "What Is a Strategy?" International Federation of Development Alternatives, Dossier 6, April 1979, Nyon, Switzerland.

Galtung, Johan, 1980. *The True Worlds: A Transnational Perspective.* New York: Free Press.

Galtung, Johan, Peter O'Brien, and Roy Preiswerk, eds., 1980. *Self-Reliance: A Strategy for Development.* London: Bogle-L'Ouverture Publications Ltd.

Menger, Karl, 1934. *Moral, Wille und Weltgestaltung.* Wien: Springer-Verlag. Translated as *Morality, Decision and Social Organization.* Dordrecht, Holland: D. Reidel, 1974.

Preiswerk, Roy, 1980. "Source of Resistance to Self-Reliance." In Galtung, Johan, Peter O'Brien, and Roy Preiswerk, eds., *Self-Reliance: A Strategy for Development.* London: Bogle-L'Ouverture Publications Ltd.

Quester, George H., 1977. *Offense and Defense in the International System.* New York: Wiley and Sons.

Rauschensteiner, M., 1979. *Der Sonderfall—die Besatzungszeit in Oesterreich 1945-55.* Graz.

Stockholm International Peace Research Institute, 1979. *World Armaments and Disarmament. SIPRI Yearbook 1979.* New York: Crane Russak & Co., Inc.

World Bank Atlas, 179. Washington, D.C.: World Bank.

Zentralstelle für Gesamtverteidigung, 1973. "Report of the Federal Council to the Federal Assembly on the Security Policy of Switzerland (Concept of General Defense) (of June 27, 1973)," Bern.

Zentralstelle für Gesamtverteidigung, 1979. "Interim Report of the Federal Council to the Federal Assembly on the Security Policy of Switzerland (of December 3, 1979)." Bern.

37. Defence by Civil Resistance

Alternative Defence Commission

INTRODUCTION

[A] system of conventional military defence in the nuclear age would require a fall-back strategy to deal with the possibility of nuclear escalation or blackmail. If protracted guerrilla war could not be expected to play a major role . . . , the alternative—or additional—fall-back option is defence by civil, nonviolent, resistance.

There are, however, many other types of situation that might be best dealt with by a combination of political pressure and nonviolent resistance. A small country, for instance, threatened by an overwhelmingly stronger opponent—such as Czechoslovakia when it faced the Soviet and Warsaw Pact forces in 1968—might decide not to use the military forces at its disposal but to concentrate on nonviolent forms of resistance.

Similarly a country might decide to respond with nonviolent resistance to relatively marginal infringements of its territorial integrity rather than resorting to war. The notion of nonviolent defence in fact predates the nuclear age and has long been advocated by many of those who reject war as a matter of principle.

There are arguments in favour of shifting the emphasis of defence still further towards nonviolent methods. The ultimate vulnerability of conventional defence in face of a sufficiently ruthless nuclear opponent is seen by some as pointing in this direction, at least in the long term. There is also the consideration that a major war between modern industrial states would in any case be immensely destructive, and unlikely to be conducted with the discrimination enjoined by the concept of the just war. And if one side alone pursued a consistent policy of limiting itself to discriminate forms of warfare during a conflict it could put itself at a major disadvantage against a less scrupulous opponent, even if the latter did not use nuclear or chemical weapons. Finally, there is the urgent need to check the prodigious level of global military expenditure which is indirectly costing millions of lives because of the diversion of resources from economic and social development.

Britain and Western Europe do of course face a potential nuclear adversary, so the argument for preparing for nonviolent resistance, at least as a fall-back strategy, is a strong one. How central its place in an overall strategy should be depends in part on how likely one thinks it is that the Soviet Union would resort to the use of nuclear weapons, or would deliver a nuclear ultimatum in a war or major crisis, and the importance one attributes to the role of conventional defence in deterring a Soviet attack. Some of the advocates of defence by civil resistance argue that if one is going to place a considerable reliance on moral and political disincentives, these are more likely to prevent the Soviet Union from attacking a substantially disarmed Britain or Western Europe in the first place than to prevent the use of nuclear weapons (much less the indiscriminate use of conventional weapons) once war has started. They also argue that a country that has chosen to rely centrally on civil resistance has a better chance of being able to control the circumstances under which this resistance is conducted than one which has adopted it as a fall-back strategy; in the aftermath of a particularly destructive war, for instance, it might take some time before mass civil resistance could be initiated. There is also the risk of a conventional war escalating to the nuclear level before a fall-back strategy could be put into operation, since one has to allow for the irrational dynamic that can take control once war has started and thousands of people are being killed.

There are then four main ways in which civil resistance could contribute to defence. Firstly it could replace military preparations altogether, as many pacifists advocate. Secondly it could become the central element in a defence strategy, but with some military forces being retained for basically "policing" functions, to deal with limited threats, etc. Thirdly civil resistance, as we suggested above, could be seen as an option to be used in particular circumstances, or against particular types of threat. Finally it could be regarded solely as a fall-back option to be employed if one's armed forces met with defeat, or if the country had to capitulate in face of a nuclear ultimatum; in this case it might be accorded a rather marginal significance, or it could be given greater importance if the risk of occupation was thought to be substantial.

Examining the Concept

Civil resistance[1] is resistance by the civilian population in the form of strikes, boycotts, civil disobedience, mass non-cooperation—the methods that have played a central role in economic and social struggles, particularly since the nineteenth century, and have become increasingly important in political and liberation struggles in the present century. Examples of its role in the latter context are the Indian independence struggle, the resistance to the Kapp putsch in Germany in 1920 and to the Franco-Belgian occupation of the Ruhr in 1923–1925, much of the resistance in occupied Norway, Denmark, Holland, and other countries during World War II, Czechoslovak resistance to the Soviet and Warsaw Pact invasion of 1968, and the Solidarity movement in Poland.[2] The proposition examined in this chapter is that this form of resistance could be incorporated into the national system of deterrence and defence.

Defence by civil resistance rests on the proposition, discussed earlier in relation to guerrilla warfare, that states and governments rely upon the cooperation, or at least the compliance, of the majority of the population. Its aim is to deprive any illicit or occupation regime of this basis of social power, to encourage international sanctions against an aggressor, and to seek support among the population, or within particular circles, in the aggressor state. Advance preparation is central to the notion and a period of transition is normally envisaged during which there would be a gradual shift from reliance on military defence to defence by civil resistance.

The notion of relying on forms of civil resistance as an alternative to military defence has been strongly associated with pacifism and philosophical nonviolence.[3] However, the achievements of civil resistance, together with concern about weapons of mass destruction, have led to an interest in the idea among a much wider circle. In Britain the military historian Basil Liddell Hart and Sir Stephen King-Hall were interested in the possibilities of civilian resistance in the 1930s, and King-Hall advocated it in 1938 as a suitable response by the Danish government and people in the event of a Nazi occupation.[4] King-Hall also played a key role in the post-war revival of interest in the notion. The coming together in Britain during the early 1960s of people from a pacifist and peace movement background with historians, strategists, and political analysts can be said to have produced the first systematic studies.[5] During the 1960s and 1970s the notion has been further explored by analysts and research institutes in a number of countries. Several governments too have taken an interest in the notion and have commissioned studies and research projects into its possibilities.[6]

THE POLITICAL BASIS OF CIVIL RESISTANCE

Classic strategic theory maintains that the purpose of war is ultimately political—the "continuation of policy by other means" to quote Von Clausewitz.[7] Frequently the political objective will be achieved without the total military defeat of the opponent, for instance when military setbacks or stalemate coincide with rising social, economic, and political costs in continuing the war.

The political dimension of warfare has become increasingly important during the present century even in conventional war. It is particularly important in guerrilla warfare, but civil resistance shifts the struggle still more decisively to the political arena. It has been described as the political equivalent of war.[8] It cannot match conventional or guerrilla warfare with regard to certain tasks and objectives. Unlike conventional warfare, it cannot physically halt or destroy invading forces, and unlike guerrilla warfare, it cannot deplete them by the cumulative effect of many small engagements. It resembles guerrilla warfare, however, in that it is normally a form of protracted struggle, achieving its effects by gradually undermining the morale and confidence of the opponent, making their task increasingly difficult and costly.

Civil resistance can plausibly aim to:

(1) make governing a country difficult if not impossible. Sometimes it can thwart an attempted military takeover, as during the attempted Kapp putsch of 1920 in Berlin, and the Generals' Revolt in Algeria in 1961;
(2) maintain the values, institutions, and general culture of an occupied country;
(3) deny to the opponent many of the political and economic benefits that it might seek to gain from an occupation.

These are essentially defensive tasks. But the resistance must also aim to take the struggle into the opponent's camp, and inflict costs in its turn. Thus it can aim to:

(4) sow dissent and disaffection among the armed forces and officials entering the country, or carrying out the occupation. In Czecho-slovakia, for instance, there is evidence that some of the troops were nonplussed by demonstrations and passive resistance during the 1968 invasion;[9]

(5) disrupt economic and cultural exchanges that existed between the countries before an attack, so that the invasion not merely fails to bring advantages to the aggressor but brings tangible disadvantages. The Swiss threat to blow up certain tunnels through the Alps during the last war in the event of a German invasion is one illustration of this kind of sanction. In the East/West context, the aim would be to signal to the opponent that there was more to be gained economically and in other respects from continuing normal, peaceful trading relations, than from any attempt to seize assets by force;
(6) mobilize international opinion against the attacker, for instance through the United Nations, and various governmental and non-governmental bodies in other countries;
(7) work to bring about divisions, or widen existing divisions, within the opponent's forces and officials, and leaders in the opponent's own country, culminating in the extreme case in a change of government, or revolutionary upheaval.

The extent to which these objectives can be carried out will vary according to the circumstances, including the soundness of the tactics and strategy. Some observations on these are made later.

The support of the international community can be an important source of pressure on the opponent, and a country adopting a policy of defence by civil resistance would probably want to strengthen its international links and seek the maximum support, short of military action, in the event of an attack. There might be an agreement for instance that a variety of economic and diplomatic sanctions would be applied if an attack occurred. The notion of a general strike against war, across national boundaries, collapsed with the onset of World War I. It, or a partial strike, could be applied, however, in response to aggression against a state offering no armed resistance. Now that Solidarity has been suppressed in Poland, independent unions do not exist in the Soviet bloc, so here we are looking mainly to future possibilities, as far as East/West conflicts are concerned. Later we discuss novel forms of international direct action and the possibility of having a specially trained nonviolent action corps or "Peace Army" for such purposes.

If Vietnam provides the classic case of a successful guerrilla war in an anti-imperialist struggle, India provides the classic parallel for non-violent struggle. The campaigns of civil disobedience, non-cooperation, boycotts of British goods and other measures made British rule increasingly untenable. Moral and psychological pressure was exerted by the nonviolent discipline of the resistance, and anti-colonialist sentiment was mobilized within Britain (partly by Gandhi himself during his visit to Britain in 1931) and in other countries, notably the United States.

Gandhi was of course working under more favourable circumstances than countries under occupation from totalitarian regimes have experienced. Organizing resistance of any kind in such circumstances is difficult and hazardous and the problem of making contact with, let alone influencing, the population of the aggressor state is particularly acute. Yet there was resistance, both guerrilla and nonviolent, under Nazi occupation in Europe, and at certain levels at least the latter was effective. Severe repression has also failed in some cases to end civil resistance or to prevent it from achieving its objective, notably in the campaign in Iran in 1978–79 which brought down the Shah's regime. In Poland, the imposition of martial law in December 1981 has, for the time being at least, driven Solidarity underground. Nevertheless the methods of civil resistance, coupled in the early period particularly with a nonviolent discipline to prevent the authorities from having any reason or excuse for sending in the militia or armed forces, brought some of the most remarkable changes ever seen in a state within the Soviet bloc. We have not come to the end of the story and Poland is unlikely to go back to what it was before August 1980 when the movement was born.[10] These and other examples show that civil resistance is not some marginal phenomenon that can be effective only against relatively non-repressive regimes. Whether or not it is formally adopted by any country as part of its defence policy, the political importance of civil resistance is likely to grow and to play a role in the regulation of power within and between states.

However, when we come to consider its possible role in defence policy a number of questions arise:

(1) What types of action would be involved and what would be their function in the overall campaign?
(2) Can these actions be structured into a general strategy of civil resistance against occupation or other external and internal threats?
(3) Do plans for civil resistance have a credible deterrent value?
(4) Would civil resistance be effective against a dictatorial or repressive opponent?
(5) Could civil resistance constitute a defence strategy on its own?
(6) What are the possibilities of combining it with a military strategy?
(7) To what extent is it an option that would suit the strategic needs and social and political conditions of Britain?
(8) What measures of organization, training, and other preparations would be needed to facilitate effective resistance during an occupation?
(9) What international arrangements could be made to strengthen defence by civil resistance and provide an element of mutual security?

These questions are briefly surveyed in the rest of this chapter.

TYPES OF ACTION AND THEIR FUNCTION

Nonviolent action can be categorized in various ways. Here we group activities in terms of their function in the overall resistance. We suggest three broad categories of action, while recognizing that many actions perform several functions simultaneously.

Communication, Persuasion and Mobilization

Actions in this category would include marches, vigils, leafletting, painting slogans and symbols—like the V for Victory sign which appeared everywhere across Europe under German occupation—displaying national flags or colours, singing patriotic or resistance songs, and holding public fasts, or even token strikes.

The communication is aimed at the opponent, though more at the troops and functionaries than at a leadership which would probably be impervious to such appeals, at third parties (other governments and populations) and most crucially in the early stages at one's own population, especially elements who may be tempted to collaborate. Mobilizing the population and maintaining morale should be seen as the key defensive task, just as undermining the morale of the opponent is the key offensive task. So it is important to find the right words and actions that will strike a responsive chord among the population, appealing to shared experience, tradition, and values.

Action may be still more eloquent, and this is the key to understanding the importance of "symbolic" acts. Gandhi's Salt March in 1930 was in one sense no more than a defiant gesture. It was also an action that was understood right across the subcontinent, and a signal for tens of thousands to begin a campaign of defiance and non-cooperation.[11] In the context of a guerrilla war, Castro's attack on the Moncada barracks in 1953 had a similar symbolic yet mobilizing function. Thus symbolic action is not to be understood as merely token. At its most effective it can rouse a population to action, and mobilize international opinion in favour of the resistance.

Denial Actions

The objective here is to prevent the occupier or usurper from reaping the expected political, economic, and other advantages of their action. Strikes, boycotts, go-slows may prevent the production or flow of goods upon which the occupier was counting. During the winter of 1941/42 the Belgian government in exile could report a drop in Belgian coal production under German occupation of 36%.[12] Similar instances of strikes, go-slows and obstruction occurred throughout occupied Europe.

Obstruction and non-cooperation can also hamper or bring to a standstill the administration of an occupying or illicit regime. An occupying force might bring in its own administrators, but this is frequently not practicable. Historians of the German occupation of Europe have noted the German dependence on the national, regional, and local administrations of the countries they occupied, and the opportunities this provided for hampering and obstructing German plans.[13]

Non-cooperation does not have to take the form of outright defiance; forms of semi-resistance, such as go-slows or deliberately misunderstanding instructions, may be the predominant mode, particularly if repression is severe.

The denial of legitimacy to an occupying regime is another important aspect of this form of struggle. Governments in exile, provisional governments, alternative elected assemblies and other bodies may claim the allegiance of the population and so deny it to the opponent. Setting up provisional revolutionary governments and assemblies and other institutions at every level of society has occurred in a number of anti-colonial struggles, though usually in the context of guerrilla war.

Interventions, such as the occupation of buildings and worksites; obstruction, such as forming human barricades in front of tanks as happened in cities in Czechoslovakia in 1968; the selective destruction of property, like removing street signs; and possibly limited forms of sabotage that did not involve risk to human life, such as cutting power and telephone lines—all deny access to goods, services, and property as well as fulfilling in many cases important symbolic functions.

The denial of ideological objectives is a still more crucial objective. The refusal of churches, trade unions, teachers, and other organizations to cooperate with the plans of the Quisling regime in Norway to construct a corporate state on National Socialist lines was one of the outstanding successes of the civil resistance to the German occupation of Europe. The resistance to, and obstruction of, Nazi persecutions of Jews and others in occupied Europe is another example of an effort to deny the occupier important ideological and policy goals; the most notable success here was in Denmark where 95% of the Jewish population were smuggled to Sweden in October 1943.[14]

Undermining the Opponent

Undermining the opponent's sources of power and legitimacy represents the "offensive" element of civil resistance. In the case of an invasion and occupation, it includes putting pressure on soldiers and officials on the spot to refuse certain orders such as firing on unarmed strikers and demonstrators, to use go-slow or obstructive tactics, for instance turning a blind eye to resistance activities or collaborating with the resistance by giving it tip-offs when police or army raids are going to take place. This pressure would be exercised not only by written and broadcast appeals, but by actions designed to put the discipline of the opponent's forces to severe test, for instance disciplined symbolic protests where the clear rejection of the occupation is combined with the absence of any physical threat to the safety of soldiers or officials. Undercover support and help for a resistance from occupation personnel is not uncommon,[15] and the dynamic of a nonviolent opposition would tend to make it more likely to occur than if the resistance is violent.

The second aspect of the attempt to undermine the opponents' sources of power would be to take the political struggle back to their homeland.

We discuss later on the difficulties of achieving this against an aggressor state that does not allow free political association and discussion among its citizens. Sometimes even in such circumstances there may be divisions within the army or ruling group that can be exposed or that develop as a result of the failure to establish a credible client regime in the occupied state and a loss of face internationally; sometimes the weak link in the opponent's armour may be in other allied or subjugated states—in the case of the Soviet Union some of the countries of Eastern Europe. International pressure could be important here, in particular countries which had strong ties with the aggressor state but which were nevertheless prepared to put pressure upon it to withdraw; movements and parties aligned ideologically to the aggressor state may also be willing and able to exert pressure. A number of Western communist parties protested to no avail against the Soviet and Warsaw Pact invasion of Czechoslovakia in 1968, but the disunity of the international communist movement as a result of Soviet actions in Hungary, Czechoslovakia, and Afghanistan represents a net loss of Soviet power and influence. Possibly one of the factors inhibiting a direct Soviet intervention in Poland to crush the Solidarity movement is the likelihood that this would be the final blow to pro-Soviet sympathies among the majority of outside communist parties.

The morale and political will of the opponent is at the heart of their endeavour and is therefore the ultimate target of the offensive strategy of a resistance. Even where direct contact with the opponents' population or ruling elite is not possible, the goal of striking back at their base of power may still be achieved by thwarting political and economic goals in the occupied territory and by fomenting disaffection and a breakdown of discipline among the forces and officials who have been sent there. Such a failure is likely to have repercussions among the political and military leaders of the aggressor state and may even trigger off sweeping political changes.

THE STRATEGY OF CIVIL RESISTANCE

A detailed strategy for defence by civil resistance would have to relate to particular situations; here we want only to make some general observations.[16]

The problem can be stated in this way: given that quick victories in civil resistance cannot normally be expected, especially where resistance to a foreign occupation is concerned, what pattern of activity or plan of campaign is best calculated to sustain the momentum of opposition and lead to eventual success? Are there discernable stages in a campaign of resistance with activities appropriate to them?

It can be argued that the notion of an indefinite general strike in response to invasion is not realistic. It could probably not be sustained and, unless there was a plan for continued resistance, its collapse could bring demoralization and failure.

It seems too much to expect the majority of the population to be capable of a prolonged and heroic resistance. In the event of occupation, society is likely to divide into three groups; a small strong-willed and highly motivated minority would refuse allegiance to the conquerors; the majority would accommodate themselves to the situation, however unwillingly and resentfully; and another minority would actively and treasonably collaborate with the occupiers.[17] Can we devise a strategy that takes this likely pattern into account and still holds out the prospect of success?

There could be three principal stages in resistance to invasion or *coup d'état:* an initial phase of intensive resistance; a second phase of consolidation characterized mainly by selective, passive and "semi" resistance; and a third stage of counteroffensive and renewed mass action aimed at achieving a final victory.

There is an approximate correspondence here to the phases of military resistance envisaged by Mao and other writers on guerrilla and revolutionary war.

In the initial phase two main responses are possible. The first is all-out defiance and non-cooperation—what Gene Sharp calls "Nonviolent Blitzkrieg."[18] All-out defiance is appropriate where there is some possibility of a rapid victory, for instance where the attacker is perceived to be acting out of weakness, the defending society is confident and well-prepared, and the lineup of international forces is such as to make a quick success possible. However, even if a rapid victory is not possible, the all-out resistance policy can serve to mobilize the population for the longer-term resistance, and provide dramatic evidence to the outside world that aggression has taken place and that the population is determined to resist it.

The second possible immediate response of communication, mobilization, and warning differs from the first chiefly in that it does not attempt to force a quick decision. Underground propaganda and symbolic acts of resistance will play a larger part.

Where there is no quick resolution of the conflict, the initial phase will be followed by one of consolidation and of substantive but generally lower-key resistance. *Selective resistance* is likely to play an important role during this period, that is to say resistance focused on areas or objectives of critical importance in the struggle. It could be focused on preventing the attacker from obtaining major economic or political objectives, or defending institutions and freedoms which are regarded as central to the indigenous culture and to continuing resistance. In Norway the resistance of teachers to the introduction of a Nazi-style curriculum in the schools and to the establishment of a state-controlled union was one example of selective resistance in a critical area; there was also similar resistance by the churches, trade unions, sporting and cultural organizations.[19] One advantage of this selective resistance is that it tends to shift the burden of responsibility from one section of the community to another, rather than involving the whole society all at once in a defiance that would be difficult to sustain. Even in this phase, there will be occasions when all-out resistance by the community would be appropriate—for instance in response to severe brutalities or as a means of supporting particular groups under attack.

Passive and "semi" resistance is also likely to be important during this phase. This can involve go-slows, economic and administrative obstruction, and the kind of general bloody-mindedness that characterised the popular response to occupation in Europe and for that matter is a common feature of trade union and working class resistance to demands which are seen as unreasonable or exploitative. The great advantage of this kind of resistance is that it is difficult to detect and may therefore be carried out with relative impunity even during periods of intense repression. Other forms of indirect resistance may accompany it such as wearing badges, singing resistance songs, observing days of national mourning or celebration and other collective actions which can sustain morale by an open and visible expression of resistance and yet are not so challenging as to bring down on the population the full repressive wrath of the regime.[20]

A campaign which combines this kind of passive and semi-resistance on the one hand, with periodic climaxes involving mass open defiance on the other, could probably be sustained over a long period. It corresponds for instance to the pattern of resistance in Denmark during the German occupation, where low-key resistance in the form of the "civil consciousness" programmes led by Dansk Samling and the Union of Danish Youth, and the *alsangs*—the mass patriotic singsongs—was interspersed with two major "battles"—the rescue of the majority of the Jewish population in October 1943, and the Copenhagen general strike of July 1944.

The last phase of the resistance aims, like Gandhi's Quit India campaign of 1942, to dislodge finally the occupation or client regime. In this phase, open and large-scale resistance will again predominate. It can occur when the balance of forces favours the resistance—when the opponent is weakened and the occupying forces are over-stretched, and when the population has built up the confidence and strength for an all-out effort to achieve liberation.

CIVIL RESISTANCE AS A DETERRENT

The prospect of having to face determined political opposition and mass non-cooperation would not be welcome to any would-be occupier, and the forces that civil resistance bring into play are well understood by governments. Moreover there are instances where the threat of civil resistance has had a dissuasive effect on an opponent. Thus following the successful resistance of the teachers in Norway in 1942, the Quisling regime felt it prudent to drop plans to create a corporate labour system for the country rather than risk a similar confrontation with the unions.[21] And during the Revolt of the Generals in Algiers in 1961, the massive demonstrations against them throughout France, including a token general strike, was certainly a factor in the decision of the generals to abandon any attempt to mount an invasion from Algeria.[22]

But because civil resistance is, generally speaking, a strategy of protracted struggle, an opponent might be tempted in some circumstances to risk facing problems in the longer term for the sake of an immediate advantage. Even so, acts of aggression bring international opprobrium and sometimes immediate and damaging political consequences, and these costs could be much higher where the aggression was against a state resisting solely in a nonviolent way. The prospect of civil resistance by itself may not deter aggression in some situations, especially as no country has yet tried to rely on it as a defence strategy. If it is envisaged as a back-up to military defence, however, it could enhance deterrence by adding to the difficulties of maintaining control after an invasion.

One can distinguish between dissuasion in general and deterrence which is one type of it. Deterrence is generally considered to rely on the threat of destructive reprisals to prevent attack, but it is only one of a number of dissuasive factors. Moreover, "offensive deterrence," epitomized by the nuclear threat to destroy the opponent's society, may actually precipitate preemptive war under some circumstances. Thus a policy which reduced the element of deterrence in a defence policy would not necessarily increase the overall likelihood of war.

There is also a temptation to oversimplify the social psychology of conflict, to reduce it to a matter of the credibility and effectiveness of the threats by one side or the other. However, in the emotional fervour that can accompany a military crisis, the armed forces of the other side may be seen less as a deterrent than as a challenge to be met and overcome, even as an opportunity to vindicate the military prowess of one's own side. A policy of defence by civil resistance might help to defuse this process of psychological escalation, and thus sometimes be more effective in preventing war than a policy of military deterrence. There is not much glory in occupying a country when the only engagements are between the invading forces and unarmed civilians.

The assessment of the risks that Britain or Western Europe would run in adopting a policy of defence by civil resistance depends partly on whether one thinks the Soviet Union is determined to establish control over Western Europe if ever this becomes militarily possible, or whether one expects the Soviet Union to see political and economic advantages overall in developing peaceful relations with Western Europe, and to be daunted by the enormous problems of trying to impose its will by force on complex industrial societies with long traditions of democratic organization. It is certainly debatable whether the Soviet leaders would want to take on the problem of Poland several times over, especially if plans for civil resistance were well prepared and publicized in advance.

CIVIL RESISTANCE AGAINST DICTATORIAL
OR REPRESSIVE REGIMES

Has civil resistance any reasonable prospect of succeeding against a dictatorial regime, or in any circumstances in which the opponent is prepared to resort to extreme repression? The difficulties involved in such circumstances ought not to be underestimated, and the defeat of any particular resistance movement is always possible. Nevertheless, civil resistance has achieved significant successes against dictatorial regimes, and has sometimes persisted in the face of repression.

*   *   *

It is a matter of judgment whether and under what circumstances civil resistance could defeat the attempts of a dictatorial opponent to impose its will on a people through an occupation or the establishment of a client regime. But it is clear that authoritarian regimes are not impervious to the pressures of civil resistance, that significant successes have been achieved in the past, and that divisions can open up within states, however apparently monolithic. Further study is needed of the weaknesses and vulnerabilities of dictatorial regimes so that a more effective civil resistance strategy can be developed in face of threats or attack from them.

Repression

The question of how a resistance can be sustained in the face of severe repression is closely bound up with the above discussion, since dictatorial and totalitarian regimes tend to deal ruthlessly with opposition of any kind. German response to open defiance was usually severe, involving arrest, police trials, deportations, and summary executions. As a result openly defiant actions were generally of short duration. Extreme measures, like the reprisals for the assassination of Heydrich in Czechoslovakia, achieved a period of sullen and resentful compliance, but overall the repression in occupied Europe served to increase the hatred of, and opposition to, the Axis powers. Non-compliance also took forms that were less easy to trace and punish—the go-slows, obstructions, administrative sabotage and so on. Haestrup gives one example from Denmark where a German minesweeper took 26 months to be built instead of the normal 9 months and in the end never did go into service because of successive acts of sabotage.[23]

Occasionally mutiny and disaffection may deprive a regime of the means of carrying out repression, whether the regime is an occupying power or an internal dictatorial regime. In the Iranian agitation of 1978–79, during which some 10,000 people are estimated to have lost their lives, the armed forces were at first loyal to the Shah. However, defections were reported during the latter part of 1978, mainly in the Air Force, and as the unrest continued disaffection spread until in

February 1979 the heads of the armed forces declared their neutrality and recalled their men to barracks.[24]

In the case of foreign invasion and occupation, however, there is usually less contact between the population and the forces involved, and there may be barriers of language, culture, and ideology. Moreover it is more difficult for the individual soldier to melt into the population and avoid detection and punishment.

Units and individual soldiers in an army of occupation have refused orders to fire on unarmed crowds, but this, if it happens at all, is unlikely to be on a scale sufficient to render a policy of repression inoperable. On the other hand mass nonviolent resistance to invasion and occupation would create a dramatic and unusual situation in which many of the normal expectations would be overturned, and in the longer term at least the repression might be blunted. However, while the repression continues it may be necessary to use less overt forms of resistance while efforts are made to divide the opponent and bring international pressure to bear.

In principle extreme repression can always be applied; in practice its extent and ruthlessness can be influenced by the tactics and strategy of the resistance. Civil resistance which avoids the use of violence is less likely to encourage violent reprisals and increases the moral and political cost of using brutality. Its tendency is to inhibit violence by the opponent, though of course there is no guarantee that it will always succeed in doing so.

CIVIL RESISTANCE
AS A SUBSTITUTE FOR MILITARY DEFENCE
AND THE PROCESS OF TRANSITION

Two important reasons for Britain or Western Europe relying substantially on civil resistance for defence are that a major conventional war fought with modern weapons would be immensely destructive and that there would be a serious risk of any such war escalating to the nuclear level. But this in itself does not tell us anything about the viability of alternatives, or about the strengths and limitations of civil resistance as a defence policy.

Civil resistance is, generally speaking, a form of protracted struggle, particularly suited to defending moral, political, and cultural values. But in terms of the other roles that a defence policy is normally expected to play it has limitations. The sanctions that it invokes tend to be cumulative and slow-acting rather than swift and decisive, so that it may not be able to prevent the forcible seizure of territory or attacks upon communities or individuals. In general it is not good at defending territory or recovering it quickly, though it will aim to do so over time through political pressure interspersed with mass direct action. It cannot easily protect interests outside the national territory, for instance to ensure supplies of raw materials. Finally it does not readily lend itself to bilateral or multilateral defence arrangements which, in a military context, may provide collective security.

These limitations do not rule out the notion of a defence based solely on civil resistance. Any defence strategy will be better at doing some things than others, and in choosing a given strategy one is in effect making a statement about defence priorities. Thus by opting for civil resistance, or making this the main feature of defence, one would be giving priority to the maintenance of ideas and values and saying that these are what it is most important to defend.

Two different approaches can be adopted to try to make good the deficiencies of defence by civil resistance. One, obviously, is to think of combining it with forms of military defence—an option that we consider in the next section. The other is to imagine new concepts and structures within a non-military framework.

Possibilities for Extending Civil Resistance

A specially trained and equipped nonviolent force or "peace army," supported by the state or by regional and local bodies, could form a spearhead of resistance in time of attack and carry out peacekeeping work and constructive activities, or be assigned to the UN, under more normal circumstances. Such a body was in fact proposed by Gandhi for India shortly before his death, and a peace army, the "Shanti Sena," was subsequently established under voluntary control. This body intervened successfully in several communal riots and provided a corps of workers for the campaign against government corruption led by Jayaprakash Narayan in the early 1970s.[25] With proper funding and means of transport, such a body might cross national frontiers to support allied countries under attack, send large numbers of resisters to obstruct the occupation of remote but strategically important locations, or send a nonviolent armada to defy a blockade. Here we are moving away from the notion of resistance conducted solely by the civilian population to a broader concept of nonviolent defence in which the resistance by civilians would be spearheaded by specially trained nonviolent forces who could be moved quickly to deal with emergencies. We return to this idea later, to the possible role of a trained corps in UN peacekeeping operations, and to ways in which mutual security arrangements in a nonviolent context might be strengthened.

The Process of Transition

Britain is of course a long way from even considering a defence system based solely on nonviolent resistance; it is not a defence option at the present time in the sense that strengthening territorial forces as a *quid pro quo* for jettisoning nuclear weapons is an option. But the fact that it could not be instituted overnight means that one has to think in terms of a process of transition and acclimatization in which civil resistance would come to be accorded an increasingly important place in defence policy. This process is sometimes referred to as transarmament, to indicate that the intention is not to weaken the defence of the country but to meet at least certain security needs in a different way.[26]

In practice transarmament is bound to be accompanied also by debate and confrontation between advocates of different policies, among them people committed to a totally nonviolent approach. And in fact the process of change requires there to be people with this kind of commitment who can maintain pressure for the adoption of nonviolent methods and who illustrate its possibilities by their activities. In this sense the existence of organizations and groups "demanding the impossible" is essential to the process of broadening the options that are available to society. Transarmament then is likely to be a dialectical process. It could be, for instance, that mass direct action will by example contribute most to the process of acclimatization, and that the capacity for civil resistance by society will develop from below. Official recognition of the notion and interest in its possibilities might not come until a much later stage following a change or several changes of government.

Because change is bound to take time, the question of how far the process should go can be to some extent left open-ended. However, one does then have to consider what changes in the existing defence arrangements ought to be regarded as steps along the way. We return to this in the next section dealing with mixed military and nonviolent strategies.

COMBINING MILITARY
AND NONVIOLENT STRATEGIES

Two sets of questions are central to this discussion. (1) Does the moral basis and social dynamic of civil resistance allow it to be combined with military methods? (2) If there is a mixed strategy, what are the most appropriate military forms to operate in conjunction with civil resistance, and what would be the organizational and other links between the two methods? Chapter 8 discusses questions about the relationship between military and non-military forms of defence if, in the long term, a total changeover to civil resistance is envisaged.

Can Civil Resistance
Be Combined with Military Methods?

Civil resistance may be supported for a variety of reasons and from various moral and political perspectives. Pacifists, who reject any resort to organized lethal violence, might welcome any shift in defence policy which substantially reduced reliance on military means and granted a significant role to civil resistance. For all the contradictions and incompatibilities they may see within such a policy, the move itself would open up debate and could begin a process of more radical change.

Support for civil resistance need not imply commitment to a pacifist ethic. It is possible to believe that in some circumstances the use of military force is justified while acknowledging the value of refraining from violence even in self-defence in the particular social context of an organized campaign of civil resistance. From this perspective there would then be no moral problem about combining nonviolent and military defence in some way—the question would be a strategic and tactical one.

The tactical and strategic calculations are complicated by the fact that civil resistance operates at a variety of levels, and may be adopted for different reasons. If it is chiefly seen as a means of obstruction and harassment, it could fit in very well with a strategy that included conventional or guerrilla warfare, though one would still have to take into account that in a state of warfare, reprisals against civilians would be more likely. If on the other hand the moral and psychological impact of civil resistance is emphasized, and in particular the impact of disciplined nonviolence on the morale of the opponent's armed forces and administrators, then the value of combining civil and military resistance is more questionable. But even where the nonviolent aspect is emphasized, one might not want to rule out altogether the idea of a mixed strategy, though one would need to look carefully at the form that military resistance took and at the relationship between it and the civil resistance.

NOTES

1. Various terms have been proposed for this concept, usually with differing nuances of meaning. "Defence by civil resistance" is adopted here because it is clear and relatively neutral. "Nonviolent defence" might suggest too close an identification with a strictly pacifist approach, and "civilian defence," a term which has been used in the past, has somewhat fallen into disfavour because of the frequent confusion with civil defence. "Social defence" is the term widely used in Germany and France and is intended to convey the notion that this method can be used to defend social gains against internal threats as well as against external aggression; however, its connotation in English is somewhat weak. The American scholar Gene Sharp has proposed "civilian-based defence" and this term is now beginning to be more widely used in the United States; however, we felt that "defence by civil resistance" would probably be more readily understood.

2. Several of these cases are discussed in *The Strategy of Civilian Defence,* A. Roberts, ed. (London: Faber and Faber, 1967). A Penguin edition of this book was published in 1969 under the title *Civilian Resistance as a National Defence: Non-Violent Action Against Aggression,* with a revised introduction by Adam Roberts taking into account the nonviolent resistance in Czechoslovakia to the Soviet and Warsaw Pact invasion of 1968. But as this version is out of print, references are given here to the earlier version. For a discussion of events in Poland during 1980 from the point of view of their significance for civil resistance, see R. Polet, *The Polish Summer* (London: War Resisters International, 1981). See also C. Arbor, *A Study of Civilian Defence,* MA Dissertation 1980, Bradford, University of Bradford, which examines the concept of nonviolent defence with particular reference to the resistance in Hungary in 1956 and

Czechoslovakia in 1968. The Commission is grateful to Christine Arbor for a paper she wrote for us based on part of her dissertation. A research project on civil resistance in Denmark from 1940 to 1945 is being undertaken by Lennart Bergfeldt at the Department of Peace and Conflict Research, Uppsala University, Sweden. Again the Commission would like to thank Lennart Bergfeldt for sending us a copy of a draft chapter covering the period 1940–1943.

3. The idea of nonviolent defence goes back at least to 1852, when it was proposed by Elihu Burritt in the United States. In 1915 Bertrand Russell in his essay "War and Non-Resistance," published in *Atlantic Monthly* in August of that year suggested that "after a generation of instruction in the principles of passive resistance," Britain might disband its armed forces and respond to any invasion with a campaign of non-cooperation. In the period between the two World Wars, writers like Aldous Huxley in Britain, Richard Gregg in the U.S., and Bart de Ligt in Holland, partly influenced by Gandhi's campaigns in India, made similar proposals.

4. Sir Stephen King-Hall, "The Small Countries," *Free Denmark* 1, 5 (August 1942):1. Cited by G. Keyes,"Strategic Non-Violent Defense: The Construct of an Option," *Journal of Strategic Studies* 4, 2 (June 1981):125–151.

5. A key event was the international conference at St Hilda's College, Oxford, in 1964, which led to the publication of Roberts's *The Strategy of Civilian Defence*.[2] From the late 1960s onward, studies appeared in a number of countries, notably G. Sharp's *The Politics of Nonviolent Action* (Boston: Porter Sargent, 1973); A. Roberts's studies for the National Defence Research Institute, Stockholm, *Total Defence and Civilian Resistance* (1972), *The Technique of Civil Resistance* (1976), and *Occupation, Resistance and Law* (1980); A. Boserup and A. Mack's *War Without Weapons: Non-Violence in National Defence* (London: Frances Pinter, 1974), originally published in Danish and commissioned by the Danish government; and various essays and studies, notably by Theodor Ebert (West Germany), Jean-Marie Muller (France), Johan Galtung (Norway) and Gene Sharp (U.S.).

6. In Holland, government interest goes back to 1974 when the defence paper "On the Security of our Existence" included a government policy statement that attention would be given to the problems of social defence (defence by civil resistance). In 1977 the government set up a commission charged with proposing a detailed research programme into nonviolent conflict resolution and defence by civil resistance. Its proposals were published in 1982, but only one of the ten projects it proposed is to be funded by the Dutch government, and the commission itself was dissolved in May 1982. However, some of the other suggested projects may be backed by research institutes or universities.

In Sweden, the studies by Adam Roberts[5] were commissioned by the National Defence Research Institute. In 1972 the Swedish Ministry of Defence financed an International Conference in Uppsala on Non-Military Forms of Struggle. The most significant development, however, was the decision of the Swedish Cabinet in December 1980 (at the request of the Conservative Minister of Defence) to create a working body under a special investigator to present a proposal "for the tasks etc. for a Swedish non-military resistance as a complement to other total defence measures."

Smaller initiatives have been taken by other European governments. In Norway, at the request of the Norwegian Cabinet, the Norwegian Defence Research Establishment prepared a 49-page report, "Non-Military Defence and Norwegian Security," which concluded that nonviolent forms of defence were not an alternative to military defence but that the potential of nonviolent means could not at that time be determined. (However, the Norwegian Defence Commission of 1974 in a brief section on defence by nonviolence concluded that it would lack the desired deterrent and defence capacity and might increase the chances of attack.) In Denmark the study by Boserup, *War Without Weapons*[5] was prepared at the request of the Working Group on Disarmament Questions of the Foreign Ministry. Among the distinguished military men who have become advocates of a system of defence through nonviolent resistance is General de Bollardière in France.

7. C. Von Clausewitz, *On War*, J. J. Graham, trans. (Harmondsworth: Penguin, 1968), p. 119.

8. G. Sharp's *Social Power and Political Freedom* (Boston: Porter Sargent, 1980) has a chapter entitled " 'The Political Equivalent of War'—Civilian-based Defense," pp. 195–261.

9. Numerous articles and books on the resistance in Czechoslovakia have appeared since 1968. See for instance A. Roberts and P. Windsor, *Czechoslovakia 1968: Reform Repression and Resistance* (London: Chatto & Windus for the Institute for Strategic Studies, 1969) or Z. Mlynar, *Night Frost in Prague* (London: Hurst, 1980).

10. The *Le Monde* correspondent in Poland in a report on 1 April 1982 stated that according to reliable sources some 1,700 clandestine broadsheets and bulletins were being published and as many clandestine groups existed to reproduce and distribute them. May 1982 also saw the resurgence of mass demonstrations in favour of Solidarity in Warsaw and several other Polish cities.

11. There is now a vast literature on the Indian Independence struggle which includes accounts and analyses of the Salt March. See for instance G. Sharp, *Gandhi Wields the Weapon of Moral Power: Three Case Histories* (Ahmedabad: Navajivan, 1960) and G. Sharp, *Gandhi as a Political Strategist* (Boston: Porter Sargent, 1979). Other titles are to be found in *Nonviolent Action: A Selected Bibliography*, A. Carter, D. Hoggett, and A. Roberts (London: Housmans, 1970) though of course more has been written since this bibliography was published.

12. J. Haestrup, *Europe Ablaze* (Odense: Odense University Press, 1978), p. 132.

13. Haestrup, *Europe Ablaze:*[12] "The Axis powers had to live with the law that in the eyes of Europe they were ruthless invaders, and had to accept the conditions of invaders. Among these conditions was the dilemma that the captured territories were so vast, and the captured communities so complicated that the Occupying Powers had to seek support to a great extent in the machinery of society in the defeated countries, regardless of how reliable or unreliable they believed them to be. This applied to state as well as regional administration; it applied to the production apparatus; it applied to the transport system and communications network; and it applied to the forces of law and order. In principle, the Occupying Powers had to rely upon the assistance which, in spite of everything, was to be had from these citizens."

14. Haestrup, *Europe Ablaze,*[12] p. 90.

15. Keyes in "Strategic Non-Violent Defense"[4] (p. 139) suggests that the German administrators by 1943 in the face of Danish national integrity had become somewhat half-hearted and allowed themselves to bungle the pogrom of the Jews in Denmark while the Danes carried out the rescue.

16. For further discussion of strategy in civil resistance see A. Roberts, "Civilian Defence Strategy" in *The Strategy of Civilian Defence;*[2] Boserup and

Mack, *War Without Weapons,*[5] who propose a strategic theory derived from Von Clausewitz and argue that unity is the 'centre of gravity' of civil resistance; Keyes, "Strategic Non-Violent Defense,"[4] whose approach is close to that of Boserup, but who argues that morale is the key factor for both the offence and the defence (rather than unity as such), and links this to the proposition that action from principle must be the core of a civil resistance campaign. Keyes sums up his view as follows: "the fast track to failure in nonviolent defense is to use tactics without strategy, strategy without principle, and principle without tenacity."

17. Keyes, "Strategic Non-Violent Defense,"[4] p. 136.

18. Sharp in *Social Power and Political Freedom,*[8] p. 242. The phases of resistance, and the strategy appropriate to them, outlined here are based on Sharp's chapter " 'The Political Equivalent of War'—Civilian-based Defense."

19. See Haestrup, *Europe Ablaze,*[12] pp. 129–131; G. Sharp, "Tyranny Could Not Quell Them" (London: Peace News, 1963); T. Gjelsvik, *Norwegian Resistance, 1940–1945* (London: Hurst, 1979), especially Chapter 3, "The Struggle to Stand Fast." For further titles see Carter et al. *Nonviolent Action,*[11] pp. 44–46.

20. See Keyes, "Strategic Non-Violent Defense,"[4] who discusses the problem of "the weak majority" and the appropriate direction for nonviolent strategy to take in order to take account of it, pp. 139–140.

21. Haestrup, *Europe Ablaze,*[12] pp. 129–131.

22. See A. Roberts, "Civil Resistance to Military Coups," *Journal of Peace Research* 12, 1 (1975):19–36, which examines both the Kapp putsch and the Generals' revolt in Algiers.

23. Haestrup, *Europe Ablaze,*[12] p. 132.

24. See *Keesings Contemporary Archives* 25 (1979):29733.

25. See Narayan Desai, *Towards a Nonviolent Revolution* (Varanasi: Sarva Seva Sangh Prakashan, 1972), where the work of the Shanti Sena during the riots in Baroda is described.

26. On transarmament see for instance A. Roberts, "Transarmament to Civilian Defence" in *The Strategy of Civilian Defence,*[2] pp. 291–301. For a critical assessment of the notion see M. Randle, "Radical Change or Technical Fix?" *War Resisters International Newsletter* 177 (July 1980):5–8.

38. Noncoercive Inducements in International Conflict

Louis Kriesberg

International conflicts are not waged only coercively. Yet most practitioner, popular, and scholarly attention has always been directed at actual or threatened coercion, particularly violent coercion. Recent work has documented the limitations of military coercion and threats of coercion in the pursuit of foreign policy (George and Smoke, 1974). We lack systematic knowledge about the role of noncoercion in international conflicts: about when such means are used, how they are combined with coercion, and under what circumstances they are more or less effective. In this paper, I examine the concepts relating to noncoercion and then review actual instances of the use of positive inducements, as they are mixed with coercion in severe international struggles. I will then analyse the conditions which affect the utilization and effectiveness of noncoercive means in conducting conflicts.

INDUCEMENTS

We must explicate the meaning of coercion and noncoercion as used here. Coercion refers to violent and nonviolent negative sanctions, encompassing their actual employment and their threatened use. This includes the use of military force against an adversary, the threat of bombings, and economic boycotts. Two other modes of conducting a struggle can be distinguished; they are persuasion and reward (Kriesberg, 1973; Gamson, 1968; Deutsch, 1973; Baldwin, 1971). Persuasion refers to one party's efforts to convince an adversary to accede to its requests; the adversary is urged to agree because agreement would be in its own interest or in conformance with its own values. Reward refers to positive sanctions, to offers or grants to the adversary of something it values and made in anticipation of a reciprocating concession. In this discussion, I will call both persuasion and reward positive inducements.

I am distinguishing the existence of conflicts or disputes from the means by which adversaries pursue their goals. A conflict is a situation in which two or more parties, or their representatives, *believe* they have incompatible objectives (Kriesberg, 1973). For example, one party may wish the other to yield a piece of territory it holds and which both wish to possess. In trying to induce the other to yield, a variety of threats, promises, and persuasive arguments will be combined in different ways. The meaning of each inducement is affected by the context provided by the other inducements. The package of inducements varies over time in the course of a struggle, as it escalates and de-escalates. My attention to inducements is focused on the strategy of bargaining more than on the techniques of negotiation.

The distinctions between persuasion, coercion, and reward are conceptually difficult and the problems in conceptualizing the differences underlie issues about how to operationally assess each. At one level, it is clearly recognizable that the properties of punishing actions are quite different from rewarding ones. Those of negative sanctions are employed to deter or to increase the cost to an adversary of doing or being something that is undesired. Positive sanctions are employed to bring about or sustain desired conduct or thoughts. But even this simple distinction has ambiguities when we begin to consider preferences and expectations of the sender and the receiver of such sanctions.

Distinctions between these inducements might be based on the intentions or motives of the sender, on the perceptions of the receiver, on objective standards as set by the observer-analyst, or on the meaning overtly given to the inducement by the sender. Intentions and motives for large collectivities are problematic to say the least; furthermore, they shift as the response of the adversary shifts. Using the perceptions of the receiver as the basis for the distinction draws our attention away from questions about the factors affecting misperception. And to have the observers establish their own criteria may be too irrelevant to the thoughts and actions of the adversaries. The sender's purported meaning, as directed toward the adversary-receiver, is used here to distinguish among the inducements. International actors generally indicate how they want the target of a message to understand it—as a threat, a promise, or a reason to do what they want. This usage allows us to ask about the conditions which affect the choice of inducements and to ask how those inducemens are perceived by the people to whom they are directed.

INTERLOCKING CONFLICTS

I argue in this paper that noncoercive inducements always play some role in international conflict because conflicts are never purely zero sum. There are always some common and complementary interests, even among the greatest of enemies. This is true because the enemies are not unitary entities. Rather, they are complex and overlapping groupings. Consequently, any given conflict is interlocked in many other conflicts and therefore persuasion or reward may be thought useful—perhaps to divide the enemy, to gain additional allies, to solidify support, or for other purposes. I will explicate the ways in which every fight consists of many adversaries.

Each party to any social conflict is made up of many component groups and those groups have somewhat different interests and views about the specific conflict. Each conflict party, in attacking or otherwise trying to get its adversary to change, could pay attention to the several groups making up the other side, differently attempting to threaten or persuade them. Each party to a conflict has allies or potential allies. Each adversary, therefore, has a somewhat different conflict with each member of the opposing coalition. A conflict generally involves several issues and the set of adversaries varies with the issues in dispute. Finally, conflicts generally occur in a series: each dispute may be seen as part of a long-run struggle.

This discussion does not deny that adversaries and observers generally regard one conflict as primary at a given time. But what is regarded as the primary conflict shifts and those shifts are critical for changes in means of conflict. For analytical purposes, here, I consider one conflict as the primary or focal one and examine how it is interrelated with others.

I distinguish six ways in which conflicts are interlocked: (1) serial or nested in time, (2) converging or nested in social space, (3) superimposed or linked, (4) crosscutting, (5) internal, and (6) concurrent. I will briefly discuss each in turn.

First, every conflict may be viewed as one in a series of fights between the same adversaries. Adversaries may choose to bracket a given conflict within a variety of time periods. For example, the American-Soviet conflict may be viewed as occurring as a series of struggles each enduring for several years or as a series of short intermittent crises. In any case, each fight may be viewed as following and preceding others. One implication of this is that every element of a fight may be viewed as setting a precedent for the next one.

Conflicts also converge. Separate groups may coalesce as allies against an adversary or coalition of adversaries. Such coalitions may be based on broadening collective identifications. Thus, the focal conflict may be between two governments and the leaders of each government try to mobilize their domestic constituency, and other people who may share ethnic, religious, or ideological identifications. Adversary parties may also increase in number or scope as they converge on different sides of the issue in contention. Thus, a fight between one government and another may be defined by other governments, peoples, or political movements as a struggle between developed and developing countries and they may choose sides accordingly. The focal conflict may be between large entities and encompass a fight between relatively subordinate entities; in that case, we may speak of proxy wars or a struggle between pawns. Every focal conflict, then, may be imbedded in a broader set of social conflicts or itself may encompass more limited ones.

Superimposition is the third way in which conflicts are interlocked. Few or many contentious issues may be superimposed on each other (Dahrendorf, 19599). Thus, two adversaries may be in a fight over one issue and others are added to the struggle or conversely particular issues may be separated out and put aside. In American-Soviet relations, this has sometimes been referred to as "linkage." At different times, issues about arms control, the war in Vietnam, human rights, and others have been linked or have been de-coupled in adversary negotiations.

Crosscutting conflicts, the fourth type of interlocking conflicts, have been particularly studied by sociologists (Simmel, 1955; Ross, 1920; Coser, 1956; Kriesberg, 1973). Crosscutting conflicts may be based on divisions within and across adversaries or among a set of adversaries allying themselves differently on several issues of contention. In the first case, the protagonists in the focal conflict are each divided on other issues and the adversaries within each protagonist are allied with their counterparts elsewhere. For example, conflicts about petroleum prices and allocations involve governments, managers of multinational oil companies, consumers, and other collectivities which cut across country borders. Crosscutting conflicts are also based on the multiplicity of issues in contention. Thus, if two governments are adversaries on one issue but on the same side against other governments on a different issue, conflicts related to those various issues are crosscutting. For example, we can see some signs of East-West issues crosscutting North-South (developed-developing country) issues.

The fifth kind of interlocking conflicts are the ones which are internal to one of the adversaries. A number of writers have examined the way in which conflicts are linked to internal ones (Simmel, 1955; Tanter, 1966; Wilkenfeld, 1969; Rosenau, 1973; Kriesberg, 1973). Most of this research uses countries as units and concerns the relationship between domestic turmoil and conflict with foreign conflict behavior. However, any major actor in international conflict can be considered to have subgroups within it which themselves may be in contention. Thus, a government consists of many agencies and it competes with opposition groups; or the society may be divided by differences which are the basis for intense struggles. An internal conflict also may be an international one; it may occur within a coalition which is one side in a larger conflict. For example, consider the Cyprus dispute. The Greek and Turkish government fight about Cyprus may be regarded as internal to NATO, which is a protagonist in the focal conflict with the Warsaw Pact Countries. If the struggle between Greek and Turkish ethnic organizations on Cyprus is considered the focal conflict, then each group's alliance with the governments of Greece and Turkey is the basis for a converging conflict.

Finally, the sixth kind of conflict I distinguish is the concurrent conflict. A concurrent conflict is an external one occurring along with the focal one, but it does not involve all the primary adversaries in the focal struggle. Thus, one of the adversaries in the focal conflict has a side fight with another adversary who has no direct relevance to the adversary in the focal conflict. For example, the Egyptian government's involvement in the war in Yemen in the 1960s was concurrent with its conflict with Israel; but insofar as the Israelis were not involved in Yemen, the fight was concurrent with the focal conflict between Egypt and Israel. Furthermore, concurrent conflict may involve *none* of the primary adversaries; it may be happening elsewhere in the world and preoccupying major powers elsewhere; this preoccupation affects the possible involvement of those major powers in the focal conflict.

This discussion has pointed out the many ways in which international conflicts are interrelated. Observers and participants may be paying attention to different focal conflicts. What we call a particular interlocking fight depends on which conflict we regard as salient or primary. Obviously, the participants in a struggle try to define one or another conflict as primary, depending on what they regard as best advancing their interest in the fight. I use the term focal conflict to indicate that we must focus on one conflict at a time, but that other focuses are also, perhaps equally, valid.

CASES AND ACTUAL INDUCEMENTS

This paper is based on analyses of several specific initiatives in the context of enduring international conflicts. More detailed accounts are reported elsewhere (Kriesberg, 1981; Kriesberg and Klein, 1980; Kriesberg, 1980). I have been examining specific escalations and de-escalations in the struggle between Israeli governments and Arab governments and groups and between the U.S. and Soviet governments and allied groups. I have selected some instances in which noncoercive inducements have presumably played a relatively significant role—instances of peace initiatives. These are times when one conflict party, or more than one, has sought to gain an immediate objective by launching a peace effort or de-escalating campaign. These efforts sometimes culminate in one or more negotiated agreements.

Within the Arab-Israeli struggle, I have examined in particular the following cases: (1) the negotiations toward an agreement between the Israeli government and King Abdullah of Jordan in 1949 and 1950, (2) the negotiations in 1953 and 1954 between the Egyptian and Israeli governments, (3) the negotiations about the Johnston plan to establish a Jordan Valley Authority, (4) the cease-fire agreement between Egypt and Israel ending the War of Attrition in 1970, (5) the discussion of a partial withdrawal of Israeli military forces from the Sinai in 1971, and (6) the negotiations between the Egyptian and Israeli governments initiated by President Sadat's visit to Jerusalem in November 1977.

Within the U.S. and Soviet struggle, I have examined two cases in particular. The first pertains to the negotiations related to the Austrian State Treaty, signed in May 1955. This agreement, resulting in the withdrawal of Soviet and Western occupation forces, was associated with the peaceful coexistence campaign which Khrushchev conducted following the death of Stalin. The second case relates to the negotiations leading to the Partial Nuclear Test Ban Agreement in the summer of 1963. This and other agreements were reached after the American University speech John Kennedy gave in June 1963.

All these cases happened within the context of longstanding struggles in which coercive threats and even the use of violence have occurred. The potential for violence on a massive scale was obviously present in the background of all these peace initiatives and moves to relax tension. Nevertheless, within these coercive contexts, mixtures of persuasion, reward, and implicit threats were presented by various groups and directed at adversaries.

Several kinds of rewards and persuasive arguments appeared in the cases examined. Among the positive sanctions offered and promised, the withdrawal of military forces from a territory previously occupied by the military forces occurred in several instances. The Soviet government offered to withdraw its occupation forces from Austria in 1954 and later did so. Some persons within the Israeli government, notably

Dayan, in 1970 raised the idea of a partial Israeli military withdrawal from a part of the Sinai. Another kind of reward is the offer of recognition of legitimacy and assurances of fundamental security. This was offered, in varying degrees, by the Egyptian government toward the Israeli state, most notably at the end of 1977. In both these kinds of rewards, withdrawal of threats implicit in occupation or lack of recognition are offered as rewards. The third kind of positive sanction is a promise not to join an enemy coalition. Thus, Austrian leaders in advancing their interests in having Soviet forces withdrawn from Austria, promised not to ally the Austrian state with the U.S. and its Western allies (Allard, 1970). President Sadat, in the negotiations toward a peace treaty with Israel, variously offered assurances not to join an Arab alliance against Israel.

The fourth kind of positive sanctions used in these cases were offers to forego weapons testing, for example, nuclear weapons testing in the atmosphere. In general, offers to limit certain kinds of weapons development were the essence of bargaining about strategic arms limitations and the associated efforts toward reducing tensions between the U.S. and the Soviet governments. Offers to reduce or limit deployment of military forces were also made in conjunction with peace treaty negotiations between Egyptian and Israeli government representatives.

Fifth, the governments have offered to open their borders to more direct exchange of personal contact. Since the U.S. government and the Israeli government for several reasons have expressed the desire for such openness on the part of the Soviet and Arab governments, Soviet and Egyptian offers to make this possible were presented as positive sanctions.

Finally, a sixth kind of reward was relatively often used: the promise to make particular resources available to the adversary. The resources were quite diverse: they include Egyptian assurances about Israeli use of the Suez Canal and availability of sale of oil from the Sinai. They include the U.S. making available to the Soviet Union the sale of grain and certain kinds of industrial equipment; and the sharing of the waters of the Jordan River among territories bordering upon it.

I have not yet conducted a systematic examination of the variety of persuasive arguments that adversaries have directed at each other. I can nevertheless enumerate several kinds of arguments that were presented. One kind of persuasive effort takes the form of an actor asking the adversary to take its role. The adversary, for example, is assured that what is being sought is necessary for national security and is not intended to be used aggressively or as a threat. For example, during Egyptian and Israeli peace treaty negotiations, Israeli military officers have taken Egyptian officers on tours of the West Bank to demonstrate the Israeli vulnerability to attack if an armed enemy occupied certain positions.

A second kind of argument points out complementary interests which would be enhanced by yielding what is sought. Thus, the Austrian leaders sought to convince Soviet leaders that indeed Austria wanted to be and would remain neutral (Allard, 1970). They argued how neutrality was in their interests and how that would be beneficial to the Soviet Union as well.

A third kind of persuasive argument tries to turn a divisive issue into a problem which is shared and which needs a mutually satisfactory solution. Discussions about arms control often take this form: each side points out that a war would severely damage all parties and hence war constitutes a common problem. Proposals to reduce or limit certain kinds of military developments, then, are presented as reducing a shared problem. In discussions of nuclear weapons testing, particularly testing in the atmosphere, adversaries stressed the common damage that radioactivity released into the atmosphere generated. In addition, Soviet and U.S. leaders could argue that public outcries and protests by other governments constituted a common problem shared by Soviet and U.S. government policymakers.

A fourth kind of argument pertains particularly to the interlocking character of conflicts. One actor may try to convince its adversary that they have a common antagonist against whom they can work together. Thus, in the 1963 discussions in Moscow to negotiate the partial nuclear test ban agreement, some suggestions were made by U.S. officials on the advantages of limiting the nuclear club and the advantage of adding pressure to inhibit China from developing its nuclear weapons capability (Schlesinger, 1965). In conjunction with the Egyptian and Israeli 1977 discussions, suggestions were made that an agreement between the Egyptian and Israeli governments would help exclude Soviet and radical Arab influence in the Middle East and thus serve the common interests of both governments.

Finally, many persuasive arguments are phrased in terms of appeals to common values and norms. For example, appeals are made to fundamental values of freedom, national self-determination, and norms of fairness and equity.

CONDITIONS FOR
USE OF NONCOERCIVE INDUCEMENTS

I now turn to consider the conditions in which noncoercive inducements actually are introduced into a conflict; that is, I offer explanations for international actors resorting to such inducements. I will examine three sets of reasons: those pertaining to one actor's considerations primarily, those pertaining to joint considerations of the adversaries, and those pertaining to considerations of possible intermediaries.

A government or another international actor has several unilateral reasons for applying noncoercive inducements. Naturally, these are variations of the reasons actors use coercion. One set of reasons has to do with placating or seeking to garner domestic support. But instead of seeking to do that by seeming to be tough or hard-line in opposing adversaries, it appears useful to stress moderation and conciliation. This may be the case when there is a new leadership and it wishes to distinguish itself from predecessors who adhered to a relatively hardline in relations with the adversaries. This may also be the case when a leadership group believes that coercive inducements are unavailable and yet some activity is necessary to maintain their leadership. For example, in his memoirs, President Sadat explains that he launched his February 1971 peace initiative because Egypt could not attack Israel and a leader had to maintain a high level of activity (Sadat, 1978).

Noncoercive inducements are also put forward by one actor in order to appeal to, placate, or garner support from groups who are not already fully engaged in the focal conflict. Thus, governments may offer concessions or hold out promises of favors to an adversary in order to appear reasonable in the eyes of other government leaders, for example, as represented in the United Nations. They may also do it in order to gain support or at least acceptance of their demands by the attentive public generally. Sometimes the concessions are made to satisfy or appeal to specific groups outside the primary conflict. Thus the Egyptian government, under president Sadat, has several times taken actions or held out promises to Israel in order to appear reasonable and conciliatory in the eyes of U.S. government policymakers and the U.S. public generally (Khouri, 1976; Heikal, 1975).

An international actor may also propose noncoercive inducements to divide and hopefully split an opposing coalition. Thus, Soviet policymakers may have promoted ideas of peaceful competition and offered to withdraw from Austria in order to inhibit rearmament of West Germany and reduce the solidarity of the U.S. and West European governments against the Soviet government (Khrushchev, 1974). Appeals may also be made to groups within an adversary country to gain support against the adversary government.

Many of the reasons adversaries employ noncoercive inducements pertain to joint considerations. The adversaries recognize, perhaps after some exchange of signals and tentative approaches, that there are common interests which justify a step away from coercion. One such consideration is the apparent convergence of interest among adversaries against other parties. Thus, Soviet and U.S. policymakers in 1963 may have seen some common interests between their countries as against the People's Republic of China (Jacobson and Stein, 1966). In 1977, the Begin and Sadat governments may have seen some common interests in limiting the power of the Soviet Union and of radical Arab groups in the Middle East (Zion and Uri, 1979).

Another consideration is a shared belief that coercive alternatives are not available or are likely to be too costly. The adversaries may believe that coercion is not available; this may arise when all opponents foresee grave risks to escalating coercion. The Cuban missile crisis in October 1962 raised the specter of war vividly to the minds of U.S. and Soviet policymakers; this may have contributed to the readiness of Kennedy and Khrushchev to find alternative ways of pursuing national objectives. Such efforts did follow the missile crisis, eventuating in a series of agreements in the spring and summer of 1963.

Finally, the adversaries may perceive a possible set of complementary interests that can be mutually advanced. Such complementary interests obviously provide the basis for an exchange of rewards. Actualized noncoercive inducements are essential in developing an agreement embodying a comprehensive exchange of positive sanctions.

The third set of considerations pertains to the role of intermediaries. An intermediary may have its own interests in facilitating an agreement between adversaries and encourage one of them to make a positive gesture to the other. Such encouragement may be influential if the support of the intermediary is important. Thus, at various times, the Israeli and the Egyptian governments have attempted to make conciliatory gestures toward the other in order to sustain or gain U.S. policymakers' support. Sometimes the U.S. has promised to make direct contributions that would be beneficial to adversary countries—if they could cooperate with each other. This was the case with the plans for the Jordan Valley Authority, sometimes called the Johnston Plan (Khouri, 1976; Berger, 1965).

In the actual cases examined, the considerations of each adversary, of the adversaries jointly, and of intermediaries all combine to affect the use of noncoercive inducements.

EFFECTIVENESS
OF NONCOERCIVE INDUCEMENTS

Assessing the effectiveness of noncoercive inducements is obviously difficult. What the adversaries want from each other is often obscure; the outcome of a struggle is ambiguous, and the extent to which any given action has contributed to that outcome is difficult to judge. Thus, what Khrushchev wanted to gain in his struggle with Eisenhower and the U.S. policymakers in 1954 and 1955 is obscure. The state of the relationship between the Soviet Union and the U.S. was ambiguous, and the role of Soviet noncoercive inducements in affecting that ambiguous state is certainly difficult to measure.

Acknowledging all this, I will make some observations based on analyses of instances when the use of noncoercive inducements were not effective, when they were to the advantage of one group at the expense of an adversary, and when they contributed to the mutual benefit of two or more adversaries. I will note some of the factors which seem to be associated with the effectiveness of positive sanctions and persuasion.

First, the inducements must be convincing to a wary adversary. This means that the positive sanctions must be able to penetrate suspicions. This requires clarity and often novelty; but a leader may find it risky to offer clear and attractive positive sanctions to an adversary for fear that he will lessen support from his national constituency and his coalition organized in opposition to the adversary. President Sadat's visit to Jerusalem in November 1977 illustrates the power of a striking action in breaking through mistrust in an adversary, but the cost in coalition support is also illustrated.

When agreements between adversaries have been reached, as in the case of the Austrian State Treaty or the Partial Nuclear Test Ban Agreement, noncoercive inducements have played a contributory role. For example, the June 1963 American University speech by John F. Kennedy conveyed effective promises and persuasive arguments, and even small positive sanctions in the form of suggesting that the U.S. may share some responsibility for the Cold War (Gromyko, 1973). But the agreements reached were based upon a convergence of interests among the leaders of the Soviet and U.S. governments for those particular agreements.

Finally, an important element in reaching agreements is the role played by third parties, leaders of countries with strong interests in the issue at stake, but not clearly within the camp of either primary adversary. Thus, in the case of the Austrian State Treaty, the Austrian leaders themselves helped bring about the agreement. In the case of the partial nuclear test ban agreement, the Peoples Republic of China was a significant factor, first in inhibiting Soviet agreement and ultimately making it possible when the alliance with the Soviet Union was ruptured. In the case of several of the peace initiatives taken in the Middle East conflicts, the U.S. and the UN played important encouraging roles (Quandt, 1977).

CONCLUSIONS

In general, coercive, rewarding, and persuasive efforts are limited in bringing about the agreements studied. It must be recognized, in dealing with international affairs, that adversaries can influence each other very little. Coercion, too, has circumscribed effectiveness. If adversaries agree about something, it is because the leaders of each have concluded it suits their purposes and the conclusion is based on domestic circumstances, environmental conditions, and actions of third parties, as well as the actions of opponents. Within each country, public outcries and the judgments of scientists, pressures from the military and defense industry leaders all affect the decisions the country's leaders take. These are difficult for an adversary to affect, but they may be subject to some persuasive efforts over the very long run. Environmental conditions are important in the form of expectations and constraints which other governments, institutions, and past history establish. That is one reason that negotiations once conducted for an extended period of time are difficult to terminate and tend to continue even with little prospect of resolution. The significance of the environmental conditions is such that efforts at manipulation of the environment may be effective.

The analyses also suggest that the inducements which a conflict party uses to gain its objectives are interrelated and they may contradict each other as far as the adversary is concerned. If the various inducements do not support each other, they may nullify each other and make each ineffective. Although carrots and sticks may seem to be usefully combined, unless the blend is skillfully done, each will seem unconvincing.

This analysis suggests one policy implication to me. Thoughtful and reflective consideration of the persuasive and rewarding inducements available to the leaders of each adversary probably would increase their effectiveness. For this to occur, it is necessary to pay attention to the interests and perceptions of the adversaries. At times, this was done by Kennedy and by Khrushchev as well as by others; but having supporting staff who think and develop ideas for such use would increase the range of specific techniques available to each leader and representative, rather than depend on personal intuition and experience. For example, one major issue in making rewards or persuasive communications effective is credibility. How can one party be convincing to an adversary? One way to increase credibility is to demonstrate commitment to a proposed policy by actions which are concordant with it. For example, if the United States government asserts its desire to seek arms control and arms reduction, the development of reconversion plans and legislation would make assertions of sincerity and seriousness of the intentions to reduce arms more persuasive.

In a period when the risks of massive deaths in wars confront us all and matters of great consequence are in dispute, the leaders of all countries should seek ways to pursue their conflicts and yet avert violence. We must all learn much more about how nonviolent coercion can be used in international conflict and we also need to understand how persuasive and rewarding inducements can be effectively used. As we become more familiar with and knowledgeable about nonviolent ways to conduct international conflicts, violence will be less likely to be used.

We need to do more than assess how well, under varying circumstances, noncoercive and nonviolent inducements yield gains for one or more parties in a dispute. We also need to learn about popular and elite conceptions about the effectiveness and intrinsic value of different mixes of coercive and noncoercive inducements. Recourse to coercion and the threats of coercion seems to be natural and patriotic to wide segments of the population in every country. Beliefs in the effectiveness of one means rather than another also affect their actual effectiveness.

REFERENCES

Allard, Sven. *Russia and the Austrian State Treaty.* University Park, Pa.: Pennsylvania State University Press, 1970.

Avishai, Bernard. "Begin vs. Begin." *New York Review of Books,* May 31, 1979.

Avnery, Uri. *Israel Without Zionism.* New York: Collier Books, 1971.

Baldwin, David A. "The Power of Positive Sanctions." *World Politics* 24 (October 1971):19–38.

Berger, Earl. *The Covenant and the Sword: Arab-Israeli Relations, 1948–56.* London: Routledge and Kegan Paul, 1965.

Brecher, Michael. *Decisions in Israel's Foreign Policy.* New Haven: Yale University Press, 1975.

Campbell, John C. *Defense of the Middle East.* Rev. ed. New York: Praeger Publishers, 1961.

Coser, Lewis A. *The Functions of Social Conflict.* New York: Free Press, 1956.

Dahrendorf, Ralf. *Class and Class Conflict in Industrial Society.* Stanford: Stanford University Press, 1959.

Dayan, Moshe. *Story of My Life.* New York: Warner Books, 1977.

Dean, Arthur H. *Test Ban and Disarmament: The Path of Negotiation.* New York: Harper & Row, 1966.

Deutsch, Morton. *The Resolution of Conflict.* New Haven: Yale University Press, 1973.

Eban, Abba. *Abba Eban: An Autobiography.* New York: Random House, 1977.

Gamson, William. *Power and Discontent.* Homewood, Ill.: Dorsey Press, 1968.

George, Alexander L., and Richard Smoke. *Deterrence in American Foreign Policy: Theory and Practice.* New York: Columbia University Press, 1974.

Gromyko, Anatolii Andreievich. *Through Russian Eyes: President Kennedy's 1036 Days.* Washington, D.C.: International Library, 1973.

Heikal, Mohamed. *The Road to Ramadan.* New York: Quadrangle, 1975.

Holsti, Ole R. "External Conflict and Internal Cohesion: The Sino-Soviet Case." In *Communist Party-States,* pp. 337–352. Edited by Jan F. Triska. New York: Bobbs-Merrill, 1969.

Hopmann, P. Terrence, and Charles Walcott. "The Impact of External Stress and Tensions on Negotiations." In *Negotiations: Social Psychological Perspectives,* pp. 301–323. Edited by Daniel Druckman. Beverly Hills: Sage Publications, 1977.

Jacobson, Harold Karan, and Eric Stein. *Diplomats, Scientists, and Politicians: The United States and the Nuclear Test Ban Negotiations.* Ann Arbor: University of Michigan Press, 1966.

Jervis, Robert. *Perception and Misperception in International Relations.* Princeton: Princeton University Press, 1976.

Khouri, Fred J. *The Arab Israeli Dilemma.* 2nd ed. Syracuse: Syracuse University Press, 1976.

Kriesberg, Louis. *The Sociology of Social Conflicts.* Englewood Cliffs, N.J.: Prentice-Hall, 1973.

Kriesberg, Louis. "Interlocking Conflicts in the Middle East." In *Research in Social Movements, Conflicts and Change,* vol. 3, pp. 99–118. Edited by Louis Kriesberg. Greenwich, Conn.: JAI Press, 1980.

Kriesberg, Louis. "Noncoercive Inducements in U.S.-Soviet Conflicts: Ending the Occupation of Austria and Nuclear Weapons Tests." *Journal of Political and Military Sociology* 9 (Spring 1981):1–16.

Kriesberg, Louis, and Ross Klein. "Positive Inducements in Middle East Peace Efforts." Unpublished paper, 1980.

Krushchev, Nikita. *Khrushchev Remembers: The Last Testament.* Translated and edited by Strobe Talbott. New York: Bantam Books, 1974.

Laquer, Walter. *The Struggle for the Middle East.* New York: MacMillan Company, 1969.

McLaurin, R. D., R. D. Maghisuddin, and Abraham R. Wagner. *Foreign Policy Making in the Middle East: Domestic Influence on Policy in Egypt, Iraq, Israel, and Syria.* New York: Praeger Publishers, 1977.

Meir, Golda. *My Life.* New York: G. P. Putnam's Sons, 1975.

Prittle, Terence. *Eshkol: The Man and the Nation.* New York: Pitman Publishing Co., 1969.

Pruitt, Dean G., and Steven A. Lewis. "The Psychology of Integrative Bargaining." In *Negotiations,* pp. 161–192. Edited by Daniel Druckman. Beverly Hills: Sage Publications, 1977.

Quandt, William B. *Decade of Decisions: American Policy Toward the Arab-Israeli Conflict, 1967–1976.* Berkeley: University of California Press, 1977.

Rosenau, James N. "Theorizing Across Systems: Linkage Politics Revisited." In *Conflict Behavior and Linkage Politics,* pp. 25–26. Edited by Jonathan Wilkenfeld. New York: David McKay Co., 1973.

Ross, Edward A. *The Principles of Sociology.* New York: Century Company, 1920.

Sadat, Anwar el. *In Search of Identity: An Autobiography.* New York: Harper & Row, 1978.

Schlesinger, Arthur M., Jr. *A Thousand Days: John F. Kennedy in the White House.* Boston: Houghton Mifflin Co., 1965.

Simmel, George. *Conflict,* translated by K. H. Wolff, and *The Web of Group-Affiliations,* translated by R. Bendix. Glencoe, Ill.: Free Press, 1955. Originally published in 1908.

Sorenson, Theodore C. *Kennedy.* New York: Harper & Row, 1965.

Szulc, Tad. *The Illusion of Peace: Foreign Policy in the Nixon Years.* New York: Viking Press, 1978.

Tanter, Raymond, "Dimensions of Conflict Behavior Within and Between Nations, 1958–1960." *Journal of Conflict Resolution* 10 (March 1966):41–64.

Ulam, Adam B. *Expansion and Coexistence: Soviet Foreign Policy, 1917–73.* 2nd ed. New York: Praeger, 1974.

Wallace, Michael D., and Judy M. Wilson. "Non-Linear Arms Race Models: A Test of Some Alternatives." *Journal of Peace Research* 15, 2 (1978):175–193.

Wilkenfeld, Jonathan. "Some Further Findings Regarding the Domestic and Foreign Conflict Behavior of Nations." *Journal of Peace Research* 2 (1969):147–156.

Wilkenfeld, Jonathan, Virginia Lee Lussier, and Dale Tahtienen. "Conflict Interactions in the Middle East, 1949–1967." *Journal of Conflict Resolution* 16 (June 1972):135–154.

Zion, Sidney, and Uri, Dan. "Untold Story of the Mideast Talks." *New York Times Magazine,* January 21, 1979.

——— **Questions for Reflection and Discussion** ———

1. Should NATO upgrade its conventional forces to reduce its dependence on nuclear weapons? What countries should bear the costs of increased manpower and hardware? Does such a policy represent a long-term solution to the possibility of war involving the superpowers?

2. The readings make a distinction between "offensive" and "defensive" weapons, with a strong theoretical preference for weapons basically "defensive" in character. What standards distinguish between offensive and defensive weapon systems? Do you agree? Do you support the development of ABM systems? Why? Why not?

3. Is the Swiss model of defense applicable globally? Regionally? Would not its worldwide implementation reduce significantly the potential for war? How would you overcome the doctrinal and political barriers to utilization of Swiss-type defense strategies?

4. Is civilian-based defense a supplement to or a substitute for military force? What historical precedents can you cite as examples of civilian-based defense substituting for military force? To what extent might these precedents prove useful in a postnuclear world? What states might successfully implement such strategies at the present time? Do you believe heterogeneous democratic societies possess the discipline necessary to establish and maintain a civilian-based defense system in the absence of immediate threat?

5. What forms might noncoercive inducements take in international conflict? In what current situations might this approach effectively replace the use of force and diplomatic confrontation in achieving U.S. foreign policy objectives? Soviet foreign policy objectives? Is it possible that noncoercive inducements could replace the use of force as global interdependence expands? Isn't this the post–World War II trend? What recent major examples can you cite?

Selected Bibliography

Blechman, Barry M., and Stephen S. Kaplan. *Force Without War: U.S. Armed Forces as a Political Instrument.* Washington, DC: Brookings Institution, 1978.

Boserup, Anders, and Andrew Mack. *War Without Weapons.* New York: Schocken Books, 1975.

Boston Study Group. *Winding Down: The Price of Defense.* San Francisco: W. H. Freeman and Co., 1982.

Carver, Field Lord Marshall. *A Policy for Peace.* London: Faber and Faber, 1982.

Galtung, Johan. "On the Strategy of Nonmilitary Defense: Some Proposals and Problems." In *Essays in Peace Research: Peace, War, and Defense,* by Johan Galtung. Copenhagen: Christian Ejlers, 1976, pp. 378–426, 466–472.

————. "NATO and the States of Western Europe: The Search for an Alternative Strategy." In *Debate on Disarmament,* ed. Michael Clarke and Marjorie Mowlam. London: Routledge and Kegan Paul, 1982.

Gandhi, Mohandas K. *Nonviolence in Peace and War.* New York: Garland, 1971.

Geeraerts, Gustaaf. *Possibilities of Civilian Defense in Western Europe.* New Brunswick, NJ: Transaction Books, 1977.

Morrison, Philip, and Paul F. Walker. "A New Strategy for Military Spending." *Scientific American,* Vol. 239, No. 4 (Oct. 1978), pp. 48–61.

Quester, George H. *Offense and Defense in the International System.* New York: Wiley & Sons, 1977.

Roberts, Adam. *The Strategy of Civilian Defence.* London: Faber and Faber, 1967.

————. *Nations in Arms: Theory and Practice of Territorial Defence.* London: Chatto and Windus, 1976.

Roberts, Adam, ed. *Civilian Resistance as a National Defense.* Harrisburg, PA: Stackpole Books, 1968.

Roling, Bert V. A., "Feasibility of Inoffensive Deterrence." *Bulletin of Peace Proposals,* Vol. 9, No. 4 (1978), pp. 339–347.

Sharp, Gene. *The Politics of Nonviolent Action.* 3 vols. Boston, MA: Porter Sargent Publishers, 1973.

————. *Making the Abolition of War a Realistic Goal.* New York: Institute for World Order, 1980.

Stephenson, Carolyn M., ed. *Alternative Methods for International Security.* Washington, DC: University Press of America, 1982.

Woodward, Beverly. "Institutionalization of Nonviolence." *Alternatives: A Journal of World Policy,* Vol. 3, No. 21 (August 1977), pp. 49–73.

CHAPTER 11

Enhancing World Security Arrangements

The existing international security system has become dangerously obsolete. The war system has made overkill an accepted universal condition, and it is spreading throughout the world at an alarming rate. Remotely controlled missiles and "smart bombs" now can be guided precisely from huge distances, at great speed, and at relatively low cost. Military R&D is fast at work on atomic guns, particle-beam cannons, and other space-age weapons that make existing hardware look almost like toys by comparison. And, accordingly, East-West peace subsists at the mercy of an "exquisite tension" that condemns at least the Northern Hemisphere to the daily threat of extinction. The SALT/START negotiations, if they are not stagnating in the mire of "bargaining chip" diplomacy, produce agreements that "limit" strategic arms at levels beyond what already is possessed. Partly because of 40-odd major and minor conflicts presently ongoing (involving 45 of the world's 164 nations, over 4 million soldier-combatants, and somewhere between 1 million to 5 million deaths to date), world military expenditures now top $650 billion annually, with more than $35 billion going into arms sales, three-fourths to the developing countries where most of these wars are being waged. An estimated 50 to 60 million of the world's peoples are paid through military budgets. Defense ministry employees outnumber all other government employees. Military officers now hold the key power positions in over 40 percent of all developing nations. And, thus, the reasons for pursuing vigorously each and every opportunity to move away from a steadily menacing world order grow every day more and more obvious.

The establishment of the United Nations at the end of World War II represents, of course, the greatest modern effort so far to pursue global security through international cooperation, to minimize resort to large-scale violence, and to build a framework to facilitate the peaceful resolution of international disputes. But member states, especially the Soviet Union and the United States, have not permitted the UN to fulfill its founders' aspirations. Almost from the beginning, the peace-making and peacekeeping missions of the United Nations were disregarded by the major powers—most conspicuously when their vital interests were immediately threatened—and increasingly this pattern of disregard was followed by other countries as well.

Hence, it was not long after the founding of the United Nations that serious proposals for strengthening its peacemaking and peacekeeping functions began to emerge. And as the accelerating nuclearization of traditional power politics became more and more evident, this reformist impulse became increasingly a matter of responsible attention. Together with concern for the creation of durable world financial and economic institutions, the suppression of conventional conflict and the avoidance of nuclear war through *inter*national and *supra*national means soon came to preoccupy scholars and political actors committed to the peaceful evolution of a stable, demilitarized global system.

The most influential and respected proposals among these early recommendations were two alternative plans advanced in 1958 by Grenville Clark and Louis B. Sohn in *World Peace Through World Law*. The Clark-Sohn proposal for achieving world peace through world law called for (a) extensive revision of the United Nations Charter so as to establish the UN as an effective but limited world government, with powers sufficient to prevent or terminate war between states; or (b) the creation of a World Disarmament and World Development Organization, likewise to be endowed with powers necessary to prevent the threat or use of force as an instrument of national policy. The two alternative plans rested upon the premise that eventually governments would recognize the need for conscientious and sustained efforts to achieve total national disarmament, the abolition of war, and a more equitable world order. As the prospects for nuclear and conventional war multiply, in part because of increasing resource scarcities, and as more and more Third World peoples suffer from conditions that are monstrously grim and worsening, the early exhortations of Grenville Clark and Louis Sohn gain new persuasiveness and urgency.

The readings in this chapter reflect a continuing search for multilateral and supranational arrangements capable of handling the problems of militarism and nuclearism. Robert C. Johansen begins by contrasting a range of options relevant to the establishment of a more secure global system, and then offers a comprehensive theory of a security system committed to the fulfillment of basic human needs, including the security of the individual. The excerpts from the Palme Commission Report recommend, in a vein similar to that of the Clark-Sohn proposal, specific modifications in the United Nations Charter to enhance the competence of the Security Council to prevent conflicts or, failing that, to isolate conflicts swiftly, stop the fighting, and restore the peace. In contrast, Silviu Brucan raises the possibility that the United Nations, because it mirrors the power structure that existed at its birth, has outlived its usefulness as a security system, and suggests that a new international authority, reflecting the growing aspiration for a restructured international power system and possessing strengthened conflict resolution capabilities, is now appropriate. Of course, designed to stimulate creative alternative thinking on everyone's part, none of these selections is intended to serve as "the last word" in any way whatsoever. They are intended, rather, as visions to guide the search for solutions to the problem of global peace and security. Accordingly, the reader is invited to consider each in more a tentative than dogmatic spirit.

39. Toward an Alternative Security System

Robert C. Johansen

Three conclusions seem warranted from an analysis of our three- to four-century-old international security system. First, the present militarily competitive international order cannot be expected to prevent large-scale conventional or nuclear war for very long. Despite the appearance of stability in the short run, it is improbable that the international order will avoid major war for as long as a century. A growing number, probably a majority, of scholars now believe this international order possesses a declining capacity to provide security for the world's people.

Second, the international system can change.

Third, the urge to establish a more effective world order has long been present and may either nurture or suffocate fundamental humanitarian values.

These conclusions point toward two others: persons interested in security and humane social change should neither acquiesce in efforts to maintain the present system (because it entails an unacceptably high risk of nuclear holocaust), nor accept a mindless, gradual drift toward a new order (because unplanned change may lead to a global system of hierarchical, unrepresentative institutions hostile to the values of human dignity).

These prospects lead naturally to the following inquiry: Can any policy yield a more secure international order, while at the same time respecting humanitarian values? In answering this question, we will first examine a wide range of policy models and then identify standards for judging the contribution of various policies to a new international order.

CONTRASTING APPROACHES
TO NATIONAL SECURITY POLICY

Seven policy models illustrate the range of options relevant to establishing a more secure global system.

1. Current U.S. national security policy illustrates the first policy model: *a nuclear war-fighting capability.* This posture calls for an enormous, continuously expanding arsenal. More firepower of a more advanced nature is required for a war-fighting strategy than is necessary for simple deterrence of war. Tens of thousands of warheads with precise targeting accuracy imply a strategy to destroy selected military targets, such as opposing missile silos, not a plan simply to threaten general destruction for deterrence purposes.[1] Such a strategy assumes that nuclear war can be controlled, limited, and therefore fought without bringing unacceptable destruction. The purpose, to move toward a capability that could disarm one's opponent in a first strike, makes this an unstable policy. Even though a completely disarming first strike remains impossible, the drive to approach it stimulates the arms race and produces enormous anxiety during crises. Fearing that its adversaries may quickly destroy a large part of its nuclear arsenal, a nation is encouraged to adopt a launch-on-warning policy and thus place its weapons on a hair-trigger. Because weapons must be launched before incoming missiles have arrived, such a policy increases the risk of deliberate or accidental nuclear war.

This posture indicates a willingness to use nuclear weapons first. Military planners designed the MX missile, for example, as an antisilo weapon. But no one wants to destroy a silo after the missile it houses has left, so the MX makes most sense for use in a surprise nuclear attack. The antithesis of a defensive weapon, the MX design increases U.S. invulnerability less than it increases Soviet vulnerability. When the United States increases the other side's vulnerability, the United States also increases its own insecurity.

The desire for a nuclear war-fighting capability represents a quest to find a new functional equivalent to the old nuclear superiority that the United States enjoyed over the Soviet Union during the 1960s. This effort is not a quest for peace. The striving for predominance—a familiar and, for many, an irresistible pursuit in a balance of power system—confirms the need to move toward a more dependable security system.

2. *Mutual assured destruction* was a policy designed more to deter war than to carry out nuclear battles. This policy requires simply that each side be able to destroy its opponent even after suffering a first strike. Former Secretary of Defense Robert S. McNamara and most officials and academic experts during the 1960s and early 1970s strongly endorsed this strategy.[2] No precision guidance systems or additional warheads and missiles would have been required if the United States and Soviet Union had pursued this policy. Indeed, this strategy fell out

of fashion in part because it provided no security rationale for the more sophisticated, more expensive, new generation of weapons that officials, aerospace industries, and the nuclear establishment wanted to build for reasons of vested interests unrelated to security.

For other reasons as well, many advocates of mutual assured destruction during the 1960s became advocates of a war-fighting capability in the 1980s. They abandoned mutual assured destruction as soon as the prospect of destruction became genuinely mutual. Throughout the 1950s and early 1960s the United States was able to inflict massive retaliation upon the Soviet Union for a relatively slight provocation; the Soviet Union, in turn, had no similar capability to devastate the United States.

As this advantage disappeared, "flexible response" gradually came into vogue. Advocates of this doctrine sought to respond to threats or attack with weapons somewhat more proportionate to the threshold of violence that an adversary threatened. This approach emphasized the importance of responses short of all-out nuclear war. On the one hand, a limited conventional attack might be met with a conventional response. Still, the United States always specified that it would not restrict itself from using nuclear weapons just because its adversary did. Tactical nuclear weapons for "limited" nuclear war took on a prominent role in diplomatic bargaining and in preparation for combat. Rather than decrease the reliance on nuclear weapons, flexible response meant that nuclear weapons entered the diplomatic equation at lower thresholds of conflict than ever before. In addition, pinpointing military and industrial targets, rather than exploding large warheads over cities, became a part of U.S. targeting policy for limited nuclear war. Officials developed this posture in part to convince the Soviet Union that an attack on Europe that did not include the United States would be met with tactical nuclear weapons in Europe, since a more massive U.S. nuclear response, which would jeopardize the United States itself, seemed less credible after the Soviet Union developed an intercontinental capacity to destroy the United States. Clearly, this policy opened the way for a nuclear war-fighting strategy.

Once the Soviet Union achieved an intercontinental nuclear force, a U.S. nuclear threat could no longer easily exert leverage over Soviet behavior in areas unrelated to U.S. vital interests, even though the threat to retaliate against a direct Soviet attack on the United States still remained credible. To regain its eroding influence over Soviet behavior—behavior that U.S. officials opposed yet which did not directly compromise U.S. security—Washington developed new strategic doctrine and weapons. In addition, to increase the number of conflicts where the U.S. nuclear arsenal could be brought credibly to bear, the United States broadened its definition of conflicts in which U.S. vital security interests were at stake. Any dispute that threatened U.S. security presumably could be used to justify a resort to nuclear weapons. The alleged right to use force to secure access to Middle Eastern oil illustrates this geographic expansion of interests. The enhanced radiation (neutron) warhead, the land-based cruise missile, the Pershing II, and nuclear artillery all integrated nuclear firepower into U.S. military responses at levels which previously had been reserved for conventional weapons. These new weapons and doctrine enabled the United States to rely even further on nuclear weapons in order to counter the growing Soviet ability to ignore some of the influence that the U.S. had possessed during its period of nuclear superiority. Overall, the evolution of U.S. and Soviet nuclear strategies from massive retaliation through mutual assured destruction and flexible response to a war-fighting capability demonstrates how the present international system generates pressures for a buildup of arms and an erosion of security.

3. A *minimum deterrent* posture differs from mutual assured destruction in that it would deliberately stop the nuclear arms race by resisting political and economic pressures for overkill and by claiming the need for no more than the minimum number of weapons required to destroy one's opponent. According to this doctrine, four hundred survivable warheads would be sufficient to provide a minimum deterrent for the United States, given the size of the Soviet Union and the existence of only 240 Soviet cities of 100,000 or more in population. In contrast, advocates of mutual assured destruction never placed a ceiling on the nuclear arsenal. Thus U.S. deployment of strategic bombs and warheads, which already numbered more than 850 in 1961, rose to 8,500 by 1975, even though the Soviet Union possessed only a few warheads in 1961, 1,000 in 1967, and 2,500 by 1975. In combining figures for tactical as well as strategic weapons, the U.S. Arms Control and Disarmament Agency reported that the United States already possessed 40,000 warheads by 1972.[3]

Contemporary exponents of a minimum deterrent posture favor such policies as a drastic reduction in nuclear warheads and delivery vehicles, a no-first-use pledge, and efforts to avoid increased military threats against the Soviet Union.[4] In this view, increasing U.S. invulnerability makes sense; increasing Soviet vulnerability does not. At the present stage of technological development, several hundred nuclear missiles in submarines offer the most secure deterrent. Submarines provide advantages over the MX, because the size and precision of the MX will increase the threat to the Soviet Union and encourage the Kremlin to expand its arsenal and to adopt a launch-on-warning policy. In any case, further Soviet deployments could make the MX quite vulnerable soon after its deployment.

The Trident II, although sea-based, would not be needed in a minimum deterrent posture because its precision guidance enables it to threaten the Soviet land-based nuclear force. Submarines that can evade a Soviet attack yet remain far enough from Soviet borders to give the Kremlin sufficient warning time provide the most assurance that accidental and preemptive war will not occur. At the same time they still confront the

Soviet leadership with retaliation if they attack the United States. According to these criteria, land-based cruise missiles, which can be easily hidden and moved close to Soviet territory, and Pershing II missiles, which can break Soviet control over their own nuclear forces, would be counterproductive. A minimum deterrent policy would assuage the concern of some Europeans that current plans to modernize NATO nuclear forces reflect a U.S. plan to keep a nuclear war limited to Europe.

As the preceding disussion indicates, mutual assured destruction and a minimum deterrent lead to enormous differences in weaponry. The psychological and political differences are no less significant. Exponents of a minimum deterrent seek to avoid threatening the Soviet Union unless it has made severe, overtly aggressive moves. The goal of this posture is to prevent nuclear war, not to prepare to wage it. Advocates of a no-first-use pledge argue that it would reduce even the risk of a conventional attack by the Soviet Union, because a NATO prepared for a conventional response to a conventional attack poses a more credible deterrent to war than does a nuclear response opposed by many Western Europeans themselves.[5]

Advocates of a minimum deterrent deliberately avoid an arms race by refusing to move beyond minimal levels even though other nations might exceed the minimum. Exponents conclude that the people of the world and even the people of one superpower are safer with only one nuclear war-fighting capability in existence than they are with two—even though the preferred outcome, of course, would be to have none. If one nuclear war-fighting capability is not countered by a second, the odds for escalating tensions and for war by accident or miscalculation diminish considerably.

4. A *defensive weapons system,* based on conventional arms, has received surprisingly little attention, especially given its special relevance to Europe. This approach assumes that genuine security and arms restraint can best be achieved through military power which is ample for defense but which cannot be used for offensive purposes.[6] Those weapons that threaten one's opponent should be eliminated, without negotiations, while other weapons should be designed and deployed to mount a strong defense.

According to this view, the idea that offense provides the best defense "should be a rule of tactics and not of strategy."[7] Advocates argue that a sharp distinction should be made between offensive and defensive uses of all weapons. Although the distinction is always subject to argument, Freeman Dyson states that its main implications are clear: "Bombers are bad. Fighter airplanes and antiaircraft missiles are good. Tanks are bad. Antitank missiles are good. Submarines are bad. Antisubmarine technology is good. Nuclear weapons are bad. Antiballistic missile systems are good." Dyson acknowledges, "This list of moral preferences goes flatly against the strategic thinking which has dominated our policies for the last forty years." Because it goes against "accepted dogmas," it may offer hope for escaping the policy agenda which entraps us.[8]

Unlike the first three models, a defensive posture can succeed in the presence of an inequality of military power as long as it is an excess of defensive capability over offensive capability. Each country can enjoy its own superiority of defensive power without making other states insecure. No government should be unhappy with defensive inequalities because they threaten no one.

For this reason, a defensive system, unlike nuclear deterrence, encourages stability. As discussed earlier, deterrence bears the fatal destabilizing flaw of threatening an opponent, even to the point of committing national suicide. Nuclear deterrence relies on vindictiveness. It has no credibility without willingness to retaliate after being destroyed oneself, even though retaliation can no longer save one's society or do more than further crush civilization and the environment. A continuously credible deterrent functions with confrontation, brinksmanship, and arms buildups.

Deterrence, if strictly defined, refers to the coercive influence that results from threats to destroy a potential attacker's assets. The threatened destruction deliberately and vastly outweighs any possible benefits to be derived from attack.[9] Deterrence is not posed directly against the attacking forces. In contrast, defense mounts force to repel an attack and to make the attack fail. Discussion on European security today obscures the line between these two concepts. Nuclear weapons, which have been used mainly as instruments of deterrence, are now being increasingly discussed as if they could be employed in a defensive role. This not only intensifies the arms competition but also causes greater public anxiety over the prospect of nuclear confrontation.

It can be argued that a defensive weapons system cannot provide defense against nuclear attack without dismantling nuclear arsenals worldwide. This in a fundamental sense is true, but it should be noted that *all* approaches share the inability to avert a determined nuclear attack, including the most forbidding variety of a nuclear war-fighting capability. Furthermore, those nations possessing no nuclear weapons are usually not targeted for nuclear attack by countries with nuclear weapons. If, in addition, defensive emphasis reduces arsenals more successfully than do other policies, then it produces a superior security yield. Potentially offensive arms carry the disadvantage of stimulating arms races, threatening opponents, and ultimately leading to greater insecurity for all.[10]

5. A policy to establish a *peacekeeping federation* seeks to strengthen regional and global international organizations so they can verify and eventually enforce multilateral arms reductions. Advocates of this approach believe that a decentralized balance of power system can never provide lasting peace and, therefore, should be replaced. No mystery surrounds the type of system that can keep peace. After all, most disputes

inside national societies are resolved without violence. Domestic conflicts often involve millions of people with different languages, religious traditions, races, and lifestyles. If such numbers can coexist peacefully, then the appropriate conditions and political institutions, if established, could also provide peace for all of the planet's citizens.

According to this view, peace requires a worldwide political organization which includes all societies. In *World Peace Through World Law,* Grenville Clark and Louis Sohn provide the classic expression of this approach. They describe in detail a reformed United Nations system with the purpose of creating "an effective system of enforceable world law in the limited field of war prevention."[11] Strengthening the rule of law and achieving comprehensive disarmament are two central goals. To help accomplish the first, a central authority would replace the existing system of relative international anarchy. The second, once accomplished, would eliminate the capacity of states to overrule that authority's enforcement of peace. The armed forces of all nations would be gradually, simultaneously reduced as international institutions matured. A global agency would retain a limited policy capability to patrol contested borders and prevent efforts by any nation to rearm. Each state would diminish its sovereign authority to make war, in return for the consent of other states to assign new legal authority to organs acting on behalf of the community's common interest in peace. The emphasis on federalism signals that the new global governance should be limited, although critics question whether a central organ could possess sufficient power and authority to keep peace without having so much power that it would drastically transform national sovereignty in other areas.

The importance of this policy approach lies more in its theoretical insight than its immediate political appeal. A surprisingly large number of scholars accept the contention that peace requires some system of effective global governance.[12] Yet because they consider it unattainable few work toward creating the conditions to bring a world federation into being. Since the most serious political liability of this approach remains widespread disbelief in its attainability, advocates might at first encourage the economic, political, and attitudinal conditions needed for the adoption of more modest forms of policy coordination at the global level.

Feasibility aside, no one should consider the achievement of world federation equivalent to the maintenance of peace. Wars *do* sometimes occur within a single governmental entity. And peace sometimes reigns between countries that are politically separate. Nonetheless, a dependable peace without more global governance seems a more remote possibility than the growth of global governance itself.

6. A security policy based on *civilian resistance* for national defense is rooted in an understanding, common to all five preceding policies, that the use of power is necessary to defend one's country against external attack. But, unlike the advocates of other approaches, advocates

of civilian resistance limit the instruments of power or coercion to nonviolent means. This strategy is rooted in a careful—even if controversial—appraisal of political and military power. The accumulated evidence shows that the power of nonviolent action is usually underestimated, that the utility and applicability of modern military power is often overestimated, and that the costs to one's own society of waging violent conflict are seldom weighed accurately before sending armed forces into action. The leading U.S. exponent of this approach, Gene Sharp, contends that the power of nonviolent action, including strikes, boycotts, obstruction, and total noncooperation, often can resist an aggressor and eventually defeat an occupation force more effectively than can violent resistance.[13]

In addition, advocates stress that protecting a society's democratic values and institutions is more important, strictly speaking, than maintaining control over territory at extreme cost to basic values. Civilian resistance, according to this view, can protect preferred values and institutions more effectively than a military posture that risks the complete unraveling of the social fabric if deterrence fails or the subordination of democratic values to the demands of a garrison state if deterrence "succeeds."

A carefully planned civilian resistance campaign against an external invader has never really been tested. Yet even without advance training or well-defined leadership utilizing a comprehensive strategy, nonviolent action has succeeded in a surprising number of historical cases.[14] The effectiveness of the Norwegian resistance in neutralizing many policies of the German occupation forces in World War II is instructive.

This policy approach is unlikely to receive widespread support until it has been adopted as a security policy in one or two national contexts. The governments of Sweden and the Netherlands have conducted preliminary studies of this strategy but without impact on their security policies. The indifference to civilian resistance, even by small states, reveals the psychological and intellectual inertia of contemporary leadership, as well as the familiar tendency of generals and civilian experts to prepare for the last war. Danish, Norwegian, and Belgian societies, for example, presumably are aware that they cannot defend themselves militarily against outside attacks by any major power. They also know that if they totally renounced the use of force they would be less likely to be targets for nuclear or conventional attack. Furthermore, with advance planning and training, their populations, firmly committed to national independence, could conduct a civilian resistance campaign of indefinite duration with sufficient courage and determination to make it at least as effective as military defense and probably less costly. If countries such as these would adopt civilian resistance or nonmilitary defense policies, they could, by experience and example, probably contribute far more to their own and to human security than they now do by membership in NATO.

7. We can imagine yet another policy, one that aims at achieving *global security*.[15] For reasons of prudence and ethics, its purpose is to provide security equally for all people. In practice, security for one is connected with security for all. In ethics, it is not right that security for one nation should be purchased at the price of insecurity for another. This world view is informed by an appreciation of diplomatic history and scientific studies of war. It is realism without dogma. Given humanity's unlosable knowledge of the technology of destruction and willingness to use it, this approach finds lasting security possible only with effective efforts to abolish war itself. According to this view, the current international system is, at its base, a war system. Although this system persists with such resilience that it *seems* to be a part of nature, in fact human beings created it. Human beings can transform it.

Such thinking is not new. Yet previous generations have dismissed it as utopian, or at best before its time. But no longer. Eminent realists, if they have avoided dogmatism, now ask how, not whether, to transform the international system. George Kennan, for example, concludes that even "the earliest possible elimination of nuclear weaponry . . . would not be enough, in itself, to give Western civilization . . . an adequate chance of survival. War itself, as a means of settling differences . . . will have to be in some way ruled out."[16]

Toward that end, a global security policy includes five distinguishing features. First, it tries to prevent the desire for short-range advantages from dominating decisions at the expense of long-run interests. Simply taking a longer view often would yield far-reaching security dividends. Consider, for example, the Soviet and U.S. proposals in 1982 for curtailing the arms race in Europe. On the one hand, the Soviet Union has offered to halt further deployment of SS-20 missiles and has promised to dismantle "hundreds" of intermediate range missiles (SS-4s, SS-5s, and SS-20s) targeted on Europe if in return the United States would not deploy its Pershing II and cruise missiles as planned. On the other hand, President Reagan has offered to forego deploying those same missiles if in return the Soviet Union would dismantle all of its intermediate range missiles targeted on Europe. Both sides categorically rejected the other's proposals as one-sided and totally unrealistic.

Yet any reasonably detached analyst would conclude that either side would be better off in the long run if it simply accepted the other's proposal outright. If by dismantling SS-20s the Soviet leaders could halt the arms buildup before NATO deploys the extremely destabilizing, next generation of nuclear weapons in Europe, they would increase the security of the Soviet people. Similarly, if by cancelling the deployment of the Pershing II and cruise missiles NATO countries could halt the further buildup of Soviet and nuclear arms targeted on Europe, they would benefit enormously. U.S. and Soviet rejection of one another's proposals suggests that the two governments do not want to end the arms race so much as to shape its continuation.

Second, the global security approach emphasizes the importance of providing greatly expanded positive incentives rather than relying largely on negative military threats as the means to influence other nations' security policies and to establish a dependable security order. To initiate arms reductions, for example, a state might independently announce that it was halting the testing and deployment of all new nuclear weapons for six months, and that it would extend that period indefinitely if the other side would reciprocate. Contrast this approach with the more common U.S. strategy of building new weapons for bargaining chips in order to threaten the Soviet Union into negotiating seriously for arms reductions. Positive incentives—whether an easing of the arms race, an increase of equitable political representation in international organizations, an extension of favorable trading status, or an offer of other economic benefits—are essential to building a norm against the use of force. On the other hand, military incentives, such as a threat to use national military force to resolve an issue, reinforces the idea that force may be used as a legitimate instrument of foreign policy. This reinforcement occurs even if the use of force is for defensive purposes, because defense is typically self-defined, rather than specified by central institutions representing the world community.

We can prevent any potentially aggressive government from precipitating a war if we can insure that, in the eyes of its governing officials, the benefits of peace outweigh the anticipated benefits of war. Thus policymakers face two broad alternatives in designing policies to deter aggression: they may decrease the benefits of war or increase the benefits of peace. The benefits of war to the Soviet Union or the United States can hardly be decreased further since each has the ability to destroy the other completely. Therefore, the only remaining rational strategy is to increase the benefits of peace.[17]

The emphasis on nonmilitary incentives to channel governments' behavior naturally suggests an expanded role for international organizations or regimes to facilitate cooperation and to regulate intergroup conflict. Transnational public organizations, such as a permanent, individually recruited international police force and an international satellite monitoring agency, might be established. These organizations could lay the basis for later establishing a global authority to enforce arms reduction and prohibit the use of force. In these areas a global security policy draws upon insights from the preceding policy models. Like a peacekeeping federation, regional and global institutions would be established to help resolve conflict peacefully. However, in this instance representation in such institutions would be more complex and would include functional and private organizations as well as national governments. Learning from the advocates of civilian resistance, governments and private organizations might initiate efforts to organize nonviolent measures to help pacify the international system or to restrain dictators.

Third, a global security policy emphasizes a positive image of peace which includes much more than war prevention. At the most general level, the values preferred in a global security policy may be expressed as human rights: (1) the right to peace and to freedom from the threat of genocide and ecocide; (2) the right to security of person against arbitrary arrest, torture, or execution; (3) the right to traditional civil and political liberties; and (4) the right to fulfill all basic needs essential to life.[18] More concretely, to secure the rights and basic needs of all people becomes as important a guideline in decisionmaking as to secure the institutions of the state. Eliminating the causes of violence, such as poverty and economic inequity, and building the institutions of enforceable peace, such as an effective global monitoring agency for *all* nuclear reactors and fuel processing centers in the world, receive high priority. These more fundamental security goals have in the past been subordinated to a maneuvering for short-term geopolitical advantage.

As indicated at the outset and of most immediate relevance to the field of military affairs, this approach seeks not only to prevent war but eventually also to abolish it as a legitimate institution. Toward that goal, policies aim to reduce arms and to curtail the influence of the military outlook on decisionmaking. Progress toward the demilitarization of all societies is an important goal of global policy because nothing less can fulfill the human need for security. Moreover, demilitarization facilitates the realization of other preferred values, such as a fair distribution of world resources, a lifting of military repression, and a respect for the environment.

This approach does not assume that a quick abolition of national military forces is possible. But, unlike existing military and arms control policies which tolerate unending reliance on arms, this policy seeks to diminish the importance of arms as points of political leverage, wherever possible, without inviting other actors to engage in aggression. The goal is gradually to increase reliance on nonmilitary defenses, both national and global, while decreasing reliance on military power. This policy moves toward nonnuclear weapons that are specifically designed for defense; places the monitoring of world military deployments and the patrolling of some borders under international auspices; and insures that representation in regional and global institutions becomes more equitable.

Fourth, this approach moves beyond the familiar, singular focus on security for one nation-state. All people of the human race, not one national segment of it, consciously become the beneficiaries of security policies. A sense of species solidarity and global citizenship begins to coexist with more traditional national identity. Similarly, within a society, security should be for all classes of people, not just primarily for the ruling elite.[19]

With a concern for the security of the whole nation and the whole human race, rather than merely for parts of either, a new attitude toward "foreign" societies develops. The distinction between "our" government and "their" government begins to fade. Once the nuclear and environmental policies of "foreign" governments directly affect each of us, the actions of other governments become almost as important to us as the actions of our own. In this sense, those governments become "my" governments as well, not because I have elected their officials or sanctioned their politics, but because their decisions affect my life. Similarly, the U.S. government remains "my" government even when it does what I deplore and when I have voted against its elected officials. Whether we like it or not, in the nuclear-ecologically fragile age, all governments become "my" government.[20]

This new way of viewing governments spawns a new way of viewing their interactions. Diplomatic confrontation between two societies, especially when filled with hostility and hatred, loses the virtue it had in the past. For one's government nearby to be militarily number one in the world does not radiate the same glory. One's more distant governments must bear the burdens of military inferiority. Even worse, in the struggle for a military edge, the social and human costs are insufferable: because my various governments compete militarily, they unconscionably squander scarce resources, render many industrious people jobless, and deprive even the employed of means to secure a decent life for their families.

Fifth, in this worldview normative boundaries are at least as important as territorial boundaries. This diplomatic emphasis stems from a grasp of the profound significance of nuclear technology. As Michael Mandelbaum concludes after lengthy study of the consequences produced by the invention of nuclear weapons, "so drastic are these changes that they call into question the very purpose for which all weapons have been used in the past—the conduct of war."[21] In this era the prevention of major war can be no less important than the prevention of territorial conquest. Of course, the diplomatic alternatives are not often so starkly set before us; usually more than two alternatives exist, and the historical outcomes of the threat to conquer or the threat to respond with nuclear weapons are seldom clear.

Mandelbaum's point bears a special urgency for Europeans. Horrifying as war may have been in the prenuclear age, most people preferred to risk its consequences rather than allow one European power to dominate the rest. But a growing number of Europeans now believe that the consequences of nuclear war in Europe would be more catastrophic than one nation's domination of the continent, deplorable though this would be. Because such an idea shatters traditional security calculations, a new diplomatic direction, such as suggested in a global security policy, is called for. A global security system provides a rational way to avoid the unacceptable military risks of escalating nuclear arms, on the one hand, and the unacceptable political costs of acquiescing in nuclear blackmail, on the other.

Even from the perspective of a continental power like the United States, security is probably advanced more by promoting a standard against *all* uses of nuclear weapons than by engaging in nuclear threats over any issue. Every threat to use nuclear weapons undercuts the obligation against use. Given this reality, the most vital front line of defense becomes not a new generation of nuclear weapons but a new code of international conduct to restrict the use of military power. This requires moving in a non-nuclear direction—toward conventional defense, world federation, civilian resistance, or global security.

The central means for establishing the new code of conduct is not a politically ineffective outlawry of war in a new Kellogg-Briand Pact, but an amassing of the nonmilitary incentives, mentioned above, to influence even reluctant nations to rely more on transnational processes for their security and less on national military power and self-help. In addition to the informal influences created by a new diplomacy, there also should be formal intergovernmental agreements and monitoring agencies as well. Together, these could eventually constrain the war-making function of national sovereignty. But the purpose is not to abolish the nation-state, it is to enable the nation-state to exercise its sovereignty more safely in other areas.[22]

A global security policy acknowledges that in the nuclear age nations cannot be secure and still be fully sovereign. This is a dramatic reversal of the time-honored truth, now an untruth, that to be secure a nation must be sovereign. For U.S. citizens to be secure requires some limits on the sovereignty of other nations and some control over what other nations can do to the United States. For the United States to reject a degree of control by other nations over U.S. actions means in turn that the United States cannot obtain control over the behavior of others—except through imperial domination, which is no longer a reasonable possibility. In short, to gain limits on the military behavior of others requires willingness to accept limits on oneself. To achieve fair and dependable restraints on the use of force should be the overriding purpose of diplomacy. To achieve such limits is worth paying a price at least as high as now is paid to continue the arms buildup, which decreases our security over time and speeds the decay of human civilization.

The normative boundaries that are to be progressively adjusted and firmly maintained against erosion should differentiate between policies that lead toward justice and injustice, as well as toward peace and war. In practice, the defense of fundamental humanitarian values should begin to assume an influential role in policymaking, a role formerly reserved almost exclusively for the defense of national territory and the assertion of geopolitical advantage. Before U.S. cruise missiles were placed in Europe, for example, people would ask: how does the pending deployment realize the values of peace and security for all people? The old diplomatic approach would have asked: how do the new missiles add to the military strength of the U.S. government?

Because the significance of territorial boundaries recedes in this worldview, the global security approach attenuates the traditional prohibition against intervention in the internal affairs of another state. This change, however, would be limited to authorized intervention aimed at implementing norms established by the world community. Unilateral intervention, which sometimes now occurs in violation of traditional international law, would continue to be prohibited. Humanitarian intervention by an authorized international organization might be used to feed starving Kampucheans, to establish a demilitarized corridor for refugees during war in Lebanon, and at some point even to provide a trusteeship government to dismantle *apartheid* and elect a majority government.

Of course, national boundaries and the importance of territory do not disappear. By its nature, human security always occurs in a particular place. But, according to this view, if the security of all people is to increase, then the importance of territorial boundaries must diminish and that of political, legal, and ethical boundaries for human behavior must increase. This rationale deems it better to strengthen a norm against all use of nuclear weapons than to bolster through nuclear deterrence one's defense of disputed territory. Which side of a national boundary one lives on, important though this may be, can hardly be more important than averting nuclear war which will create enormous loss of life on both sides of the border. Although this thought is unpleasant, denying its truth makes no one more secure.

The motivating force for emphasizing the "human interest" more and a narrow national interest less stems not from sentimental globalism, but from prudent calculations of security needs.[23] As Herz explains, "the new realism of universalism puts . . . the common interest in survival before the traditional interest in seeing one's opponent commit mistakes."[24] The security of one society cannot be achieved without at the same time securing other societies. For example, if either superpower develops new weapons, such as SS-20s or Pershing IIs, in pursuit of increased security for itself, the other will attempt to acquire similar or superior weapons, thus leaving both sides less secure as a result. The most effective way to increase the willingness of all societies to move toward a less militarized global security system is to increase their stake in such a system. Happily, these pragmatic security considerations dovetail with the humanitarian values esteemed by morally sensitive persons in every corner of the globe.

This discussion of global security policy completes our examination of alternative policy models. The next step is to identify criteria for selecting the most useful concrete policies.

EVALUATING POLICIES

Whenever policymakers choose one policy over another, they employ criteria for judging which will best serve their preferred values. Because these criteria are usually implicit rather than explicit, they often amount to little more than assumptions inherited from a bygone age. The result, then, is the unquestioned application of nineteenth-century balance-of-power dictates to the technological conditions of the twentieth century.

Just as generals prepare new strategies for fighting the most recent war rather than the next one,[25] so diplomats also prepare to resolve conflict using policies and institutions appropriate for an age that has disappeared. That is why conservatives and liberals alike have been unable to shape an effective U.S. diplomacy in recent years. To illustrate, the use of implicit, unexamined criteria encourages policymakers to select new weapons based on the assumption—which was perhaps correct in an earlier age—that more arms equals more security. Today new arms usually stimulate counter armaments that pose new threats to oneself. Therefore, unless the criteria are changed for selecting policies, misguided choices will result.

By making criteria explicit, policymakers can more easily detect which criteria are outmoded and which policies advance preferred values like peace and security. Explicit criteria for assessing alternative directions—for example, to produce the MX missile or to freeze the nuclear arms buildup—also help ferret out the policymaker who in fact seeks national power under the guise of seeking world peace. Until there is a clear, well-known basis for judging whether a given policy leads to war or peace, to global equity or to national hegemony, the public cannot easily identify those people who pursue hidden goals which violate the public interest. Only when the criteria for evaluating policies have been made explicit will policymakers be able to select appropriate means to achieve preferred ends, or the public be able to identify the officials who genuinely seek professed ends.

What criteria can we use? Diverse studies of the causes of war and the conditions of peace suggest at least four tests to determine whether policies increase the prospects for peace. Although these guidelines may be insufficiently precise to reflect short-term shifts in the likelihood of war, they do indicate the policy direction that will make the international system less conducive to war.

A synthesis of earlier research suggests that the prospects for peace and security increase as societies demilitarize, depolarize, denationalize, and transnationalize the global political system. These four qualities may be stated as *goals* for nation-states or as *processes* for domesticating the international system. Table 1 provides a summary of the trends which make the global system more peaceful or more war prone. Columns 1 and 3 describe national security policies that characterize the ends of the four continua. The central column contains illustrative questions for evaluating the degree to which policies encourage system change on the four continua.

The militarization-demilitarization continuum reflects the following components: (1) the ratios of national military expenditures to the quality of life within the society, to gross national product, and to world military

TABLE 1. The Evaluation of Policies to Improve the Capacity of the Global System to Maintain Peace

HIGH LIKELIHOOD OF WAR 1	Illustrative Questions for Policy Evaluation 2	HIGH LIKELIHOOD OF PEACE 3
MILITARIZATION ↕	(military factors)	DEMILITARIZATION ↑
Security policy pursues traditional diplomacy backed by increasing military power.	To what extent does a policy reduce preparation for war, reduce the costliness of war if it occurs, increase the prospects for arms reductions, reduce militarily coercive relations between and within nation-states, and increase the capacity of the global system for war prevention?	Security policy expands the use of non-military power while constricting the use of military power.
POLARIZATION ↕	(political, economic, and ecological factors)	DEPOLARIZATION ↑
Despite rhetoric to the contrary, policy in practice aims to maintain or accumulate more national power and wealth in the short run.	To what extent does policy serve broad global constituencies, rather than a limited national, regional or bloc constituency?	Policy aims to fulfill all human needs in the short- and long-range future.
NATIONALIZATION ↕	(social and psychological factors)	DENATIONALIZATION ↑

To what extent does policy build human solidarity (identification across national boundaries)? Does policy encourage people to acknowledge their commonalities?

Security policy educates the public to feel a sense of species solidarity.

Policy emphasizes the need for multilateral cooperation with all nations to achieve mutual benefit.

Security policy deliberately attempts to establish the individual as an important subject in international law; human rights covenants are ratified and enforced within a government's own society and elsewhere insofar as possible.

TRANSNATIONALIZATION

(institutional factors)

To what extent does policy develop more effective (representative, equitable, functionally useful, non-territorial) world organizations?

STATE CENTRICITY

Security policy educates the public to be nationally exclusive in identity.

Policy emphasizes the need for alliance tightness or for unilateral acts of military self-help.

Security policy assumes that the national government is all that matters in international relations. Individuals are treated as means to the ends of state power and wealth.

Intergovernmental organizations without national veto power and transnational institutions are feared, shunned, or nominally accepted, but without enthusiasm for institutional innovation to encourage the four processes associated here with peace.

Private organizations and religious groups are encouraged to leave security policy to the government.

Participation in intergovernmental and transnational organizations aims to increase their capacity to help demilitarize, depolarize, denationalize, and and transnationalize world society.

Private organizations, religious groups, and individuals participate in efforts to make peace through transnational linkages. Individuals relate directly to people of other countries without channeling contacts always through their national capital.

expenditures; (2) the extent to which weapons are restricted to defensive purposes or instead threaten other countries; (3) the nature and scale of arms sales; (4) the number of overseas military installations; (5) the military assistance given to other governments; (6) the prominence of military influence in policymaking; and (7) overall reliance on military instruments in diplomacy. Data for one country should be compared over time and viewed, of course, in comparison both to the parallel activity of rival states and to worldwide totals.

The other criteria are perhaps more difficult to specify. Whereas demilitarization pertains to military affairs, depolarization applies to political and economic conditions, denationalization to social, cultural, and psychological factors, and transnationalization to institutions. More specifically, depolarization reflects political and economic efforts to soften rigid bloc and alliance boundaries, to diminish East-West and North-South conflicts, and to reduce antagonism between adversaries wherever possible. Hegemonic states, for example, should tailor their political and economic policies to achieve greater equity for all societies. Reciprocity in economic and political relations, regardless of a state's ideology, is the touchstone of depolarization.

To illustrate, an industrialized country like the United States would be advancing depolarization if it met the UN's goal of contributing 0.7 percent of its GNP annually to the economic development of poor nations, if it ratified the Law of the Sea Treaty obligating the world community to reserve some benefits of the common heritage for the world's poor, if it agreed with the Soviet Union to prohibit all nuclear weapons tests as most nonnuclear states have requested, and if it withdrew all its nuclear weapons to points at least 500 kilometers from the line separating NATO and Warsaw Pact nations in Central Europe.

Denationalization extends the lines of personal and group identity beyond the nation. It seeks to nurture universal respect for human dignity and to promote a political culture of human solidarity. It actively develops political and moral support for the measures required to make progress in demilitarization, depolarization, and transnationalization. A society contributes to denationalization if it actively educates its population about the need for reducing the role of military influence in domestic and international life and for building representative institutions for management of international conflicts. This education should occur through its public schools, in statements by public officials, in its legislative programs and use of public revenues, and in its diplomacy.

Because nationalism contributes to unfair discrimination against other groups, similar to that which accompanies racism, denationalization is analogous to antiracist education and action. It cleanses nationalism of its most harmful qualities. One test of denationalization is the extent to which a government avoids stirring up chauvinism through frequent military threats or shows of force and resists the temptation to mislead the public through slanted use of classified information and propaganda based on national stereotyping. Applying universal human rights standards as opposed to national security considerations to determine the eligibility of other governments for development aid is another example of denationalization, as is the building of public support for the submission of international disputes to impartial international judicial settlement.

Transnationalization describes the process by which individuals, private organizations, and governments institutionalize the means for peaceful resolution of conflict and a dependable protection of security. The growth of equitable organizations that transcend national boundaries can both shape the content and strengthen the obligatory quality of a new code of international conduct. Without the growth of private and public transnational organizations to help bridle national excesses, state behavior would too easily relapse into the pursuit of national vested interests at excessive cost to the global commonweal.

Measures might include efforts to strengthen multilateral regimes, rather than to rely on bilateral diplomacy, for peacekeeping, for monitoring arms control agreements, for curtailing intervention in nonaligned states, for promoting economic development, and for settling disputes. A country contributes to transnationalization if it actively seeks to create formal organizations or informal arrangements for the preceding activities, if it accepts without reservation the compulsory jurisdiction of world and regional courts, and if it generally fulfills its duties as a good global citizen in existing international organizations like the United Nations.

Each of these four interrelated processes of moving toward global security suggests three foci for examining any country's foreign policy options: (1) a national government's relationship to its major rival(s); (2) a national government's relationships to other states of substantially different power and position in the global hierarchy; and (3) a national government's relationship with its own people. For example, steps toward demilitarization include these dimensions: reducing the likelihood of war between rivals, reducing the residue of imperialism, and reducing military influence or repression within societies. For NATO and Warsaw Pact countries, these three areas correspond respectively to the tensions between East and West, between North and South, and between rulers and ruled. For states not part of the conflicts between NATO and Warsaw Pact nations, the first area of conflict might be with a regional rival (e.g., Iran and Iraq). These foci also suggest three points of entry into the process of change.

The prospects for peace improve to the extent that governments pursue the policies described in column 3. On the other hand, some or all of the following conditions, reflecting column 1 of the four continua, usually precede war: (1) arms buildups and heavy military influence in decisionmaking; (2) intense international polarization, inflexible alliance structures, and economic exploitation; (3) exclusive national identification (often buttressed with ideological rigidity and laced with racial overtones) achieved at the expense of external scapegoats; and (4) uninfluential or unfair transnational interactions.

During periods of war, policies most fully incorporate the attributes of column 1. How can the conditions of war in column 1 sometimes produce a period of peace which often reigns after a war ends? As illustrated in World War II, the chain of social forces suddenly snaps at the conclusion of wars, with one side forced to capitulate to the other. Surrender, in which one side's military forces are immobilized and totally exposed to the demands of the other, is a radical act of demilitarization. So profoundly does demilitarization contribute to peace that even coerced demilitarization produces peace if it is accompanied by depolarization between former belligerents.

In such instances, after surrender the previous degree of polarization falls sharply, alliance patterns once again become flexible, prejudicial national stereotyping tapers off, and more positive forms of transnational collaboration flourish. Military capitulation opens the way for the victorious power to act magnanimously, as the United States did in helping to reconstruct Germany and Japan after 1945. The immediate postwar years are usually the most fertile period of each long cycle in international politics. The demilitarization of the capitulating government does more to bring future peace than does the military prowess of any victor, although the victor's nonmilitary diplomacy following the war plays a decisive role. In sum, demilitarization and the attendant qualities noted in column 3 produce peace; peace does not grow out of the conditions of war itself.

Lasting peace did not follow World War I because the conditions of column 3 were never very fully developed. There was no period of magnanimity. Depolarization never occurred. In a sense, World War II was a continuation of World War I. The period following the Second World War held more promise, especially because of transformed roles for Germany and Japan, but opportunities for institutionalizing a less militarized system of international relations were not imaginatively seized. Instead, a nineteenth-century diplomatic orientation stimulated the Cold War between the United States and the Soviet Union.

We can now apply the four criteria to the policies previously discussed and listed here in Table 2. These criteria call sharply into question the utility of present U.S. and Soviet policies, for they are the antithesis of *demilitarization*. The development of more advanced intercontinental and intermediate-range ballistic missiles, more accurate guidance systems, new cruise missiles, larger nuclear submarines, new strategic bombers, satellite targeting systems and antisatellite warfare capability, thousands of additional warheads, more battleships and aircraft carriers—all stimulate reciprocal action by a rival nation. New deployments also whet the military appetites of less militarized, smaller states and encourage them to conclude that a key to being taken more seriously in the diplomatic world is to possess additional weapons, perhaps including

TABLE 2. Approaches to Security Policy

System of World Order	Policy Model	Illustrative Exponent	Major Security Beneficiary
Interstate (im)balance of military power	1. nuclear war-fighting capability	Brown Brzezinski Gray Weinberger	national elite
	2. mutual assured destruction	McNamara	national elite
	3. minimal nuclear deterrent	Boston Study Group	national elite
	4. defensive weapons system	Fischer Boserup Dyson	national society
	5. world peacekeeping federation	Clark & Sohn	national society
	6. civilian resistance as a national defense	Sharp Roberts	national society
Transnational balance of nonmilitary power	7. global security	*	all people

*Although this policy model is my own formulation, it benefits from the path-breaking work of Johan Galtung, *The True Worlds* (New York: Free Press, 1980); Richard Falk, *A Study of Future Worlds* (New York: Free Press, 1975); Charles Beitz, *Theory and International Relations* (Princeton: Princeton University Press, 1979); Myres S. McDougal, Harold Lasswell, and Lung-chu Chen, *Human Rights and World Public Order* (New Haven: Yale University Press, 1980); Richard Falk and Yoshikazu Sakamoto, "A World Demilitarized: A Basic Human Need," *Alternatives: A Journal of World Policy*, Vol. 6, No. 1 (1980), pp. 1–16; and Jan Oberg, "Disarmament, Conversion and Transformation: Some Elements of a Strategy Towards Constructive Defence and Peaceful Development," *Bulletin of Peace Proposals*, Vol. 10, No. 3 (1979), pp. 308–314.

nuclear arms. Stimulated by the example of the world's leading military powers, a majority of the world's societies now face increasing military influence in their political processes.

Policies at the top of Table 2, especially those relying on nuclear weapons, *polarize* world affairs to an unprecedented extreme. They violate the common interests of a global constituency. The priorities of military competition exacerbate poverty and economic uncertainty. They lead one society openly to prepare to destroy the people of another for the misdeeds of their government over which they frequently have little direct control. As the possibility of war perseveres and resources become more scarce, the militarily strong will increasingly compete for allies and for political influence in the governments of nonaligned countries, intending to gain access to bases and resources and to deny them to their military rivals. No land stands outside superpower rivalry. Global polarization inflames regional subpolarizations. Together, they make nonviolent resolution of conflict far more difficult.

The policies at the top of Table 2 also inhibit the *denationalization* of human affairs and discourage the growth of human solidarity across national boundaries. Indeed national jingoism, not a sense of world-mindedness, helps raise the massive taxes required to pay the enormous costs of a nuclear warfighting capability. Democratic societies bent on high military expenditures and the projection of power globally *need* a national enemy to help divert money from social programs to military production. Wasting scarce resources hurts almost everyone globally, but the burden falls most heavily on the poor. To justify inequity, a rich nation will frequently discriminate unfairly against other nationalities through its trade, aid, and immigration policies. In addition, expensive preparation for war usually deepens potential class conflicts. It benefits the governing elite, their supporters, and those connected with military production, while the rest of the society pays war taxes and reluctantly raises conscripts. Leaders often stimulate nationalistic fervor to turn attention away from a government's failures. In general, advocates of nuclear deterrence implicitly deny respect for human life, especially for people of other nationalities, and for nature. The threat to use nuclear weapons, which is essential to maintaining the deterrent's credibility, is in fact a threat to commit genocide and crimes against other nations.

Finally, policies 1 and 2 impede the effort to develop more effective *transnational* institutions. Superpower nuclear rivalry and the subordination of pressing human needs to the pursuit of geopolitical advantage stifle the growth of equitable and humane world organizations. Even the arms control efforts of the superpowers seldom encourage the development of international organizations for peacekeeping. Rather than working seriously in a multilateral framework, Moscow and Washington prefer bilateral negotiations in order to minimize the influence of views from less militarized societies; the superpowers oppose international monitoring and verification of existing bilateral arms agreements; and they prefer accords, if at all, that slow development in a weapons area they no longer value, while allowing the development of new weapons in other, uncontrolled areas.[26] This maintains their military superiority over weaker countries.

The policies in Table 2 are ranked according to how much they demilitarize, depolarize, denationalize, and transnationalize the global political system. Table 3 contains the basis for the rankings. Although crude, such explicit approximations are preferable to hidden assumptions without any clear calculus at all. Future research certainly can improve the quality of the estimates. At the least, these rankings can help to focus debate on whether a nuclear war-fighting capability, for example, in any way helps to demilitarize or depolarize international relations.

Applying the criteria of demilitarization, depolarization, denationalization, and transnationalization to the policies that dominate the agendas in Washington and Moscow forces one to reach a painful conclusion: current U.S. policy leads toward war. By pursuing its present course the United States marches toward national suicide, and perhaps toward the death of civilization. U.S. policy undermines, rather than increases, the capacity of the global system to prevent violence. Similar criticisms could be made of the Soviet Union, but neither side's current failures justify the other's reckless military deployments.[27]

Existing policies at the top of Tables 2 and 3 may seem sensible for those operating under the assumed conditions of the nineteenth-century balance of military power. But those conditions no longer exist. And the policies which have been derived from them now contribute more to the causes of war than they do to the conditions of peace. Nuclear weapons may make political leaders somewhat more cautious, but they do not increase the capacity of an antiquated international system to provide security or abolish war. Indeed, they further strain an international structure already extended far beyond the limits of reliability.

Certainly it would be simplistic to think that the United States might quickly jump from a nuclear war-fighting strategy to the abolition of war or even to a strictly defensive posture based on conventional weapons. Yet it is not unreasonable to think that the United States should now commit itself to steps in that direction.[28] Policy changes obviously need to be planned carefully, with ample safeguards to avoid diminution of security at any point along the way. Yet the most frightening prospect is not the risks involved with change. It is the absence of any effort to devise policies that at the very least would move us away from a war-fighting capability and toward a minimum deterrent, to say nothing of efforts to establish a warless world.

Our remaining task is to identify several achievable steps in that direction.

TABLE 3. The Contribution of Various Policies to Peace and Security: A Tentative Estimate

Policy Model	Demilitarization	Depolarization	Denationalization	Transnationalization	Total
		(5 point scale of approximation)			
1. war-fighting capability	0	0	0	0	0
2. mutual assured destruction	1	1	0	0	2
3. minimal deterrent	2	2	0	1	5
4. defensive-weapons system	3	4	2	2	11
5. peacekeeping federation	4	4	4	4	16
6. civilian resistance	5	4	3	4	16
7. global security	5	5	5	5	20

WIDENING THE LIMITS OF THE POSSIBLE

The policy models outlined above define a range of policy choice that begins with a high degree of militarism and ends with global security. The policies toward the bottom of Tables 2 and 3 are most likely to promote security and other preferred values. But these are not considered seriously in policy debates. They are presumed to be infeasible, given the harsh realities of international politics. Yet the presumption that steps cannot be taken toward global security is rooted as much in dogmatic beliefs and misperception as in the harsh realities themselves, of which there are admittedly many. In addition, the policy agenda is kept limited in part by those who fear that a loss of vested interests might accompany movement toward a more equitable and less militarized social order.

The repressed agenda of policy alternatives can be opened wide. We have grown accustomed in the past twenty years to a narrower, less hopeful, more barren diplomacy than characterized even earlier times when the handwriting of interdependence was not yet clearly on the wall. In contrast to the worldview that prevails today, as described at the outset of this essay, a more open attitude existed during the 1950s and 1960s, when at least a few people in the U.S. government worked for general and complete disarmament under effective international control. Indeed, the United States and Soviet Union formally agreed to principles to guide a disarming process and accompanying verification.[29] During those years the U.S. Ambassador to the United Nations, Adlai E. Stevenson, delivered an address to the UN entitled "Working Toward a World Without War," in which he proclaimed openly that to achieve such a world "inevitably requires an alternative [international] system for coping with conflict."[30]

Even then astute historians understood that nuclear weapons were forcing a departure from past understandings of self-defense and legitimate security needs. They could already sense the warping of the policy agenda. In 1959 George Kennan wrote that "this commitment to the weapons of indiscriminate mass destruction which has dominated our strategic thinking, and increasingly our political thinking, in recent years, represents a morbid fixation of the most fateful and hopeless sort. No positive solution to any genuine human problem is ever going to be found this way."[31]

Because we have mistakenly assumed that an improved security order is not possible, we have been unimaginative in constructing policies that are modest enough to be implemented now without jeopardizing national security, yet that are substantial enough to promise fundamental improvements in the existing order. As a result, we have made the long-range goal of system transformation seem needlessly farfetched. Our search should be for policies to initiate a *process* leading toward a new international security order—one which matures as it is gradually demilitarized—rather than for an immediately workable, detailed, alternative system itself. As world conditions change, one can draw and redraw more sharply the sketch of what can and should be developed. Even with the present context of U.S.-Soviet hostility and increasingly unstable deterrence (policy 1), it is possible to look toward the eventual abolition of war in a system of global security (policy 7). Several examples illustrate a sensible, modest response to the four guidelines for increasing security mentioned above. One particular example may especially help to demilitarize the international system, while another may help to depolarize or denationalize it. Yet often the most effective policies will produce results in several or all four interrelated areas at once. The purpose here is not to present an exhaustive list of proposals, but to illustrate how to begin making progress in all areas.

First, the establishment of an international satellite observation agency could be a step toward transnational monitoring of world military capabilities. Such an agency could inspect arms control agreements that have already been ratified, and new ones that might come into force. Its mere presence might discourage provocative military buildups or maneuvers and attempts at infiltration of armed forces or equipment across borders.[32] A monitoring agency could, furthermore, help resolve U.S. claims about arms flows into El Salvador. It could also provide an impartial means of detecting and thereby possibly of discouraging missile tests or secret nuclear explosions by countries on the threshold of developing nuclear weapons. Direct observation would give states that do not possess nuclear weapons a higher stake and more equity in a stable nonnuclear security system. They understandably have little sympathy for the current security system, in which the nuclear superpowers have a monopoly on both the most destructive weapons and the capacity to observe their testing, location, and use. If the least militarized states had access to a global monitoring agency, then those states without a vested interest in high levels of military preparedness might be able to exert greater leverage to halt the proliferation of nuclear arms by present and potential nuclear powers. Perhaps most importantly, the creation and early use of such an agency would enable it to acquire the vital experience and reliability that will be essential if reductions of armaments are ever to proceed very far.

The establishment of a global monitoring agency need not wait for any other event. The technological capacity already exists, and it is well within the financial reach of the UN community. Governments like the United States and Soviet Union could retain their own national means of verification, operating independently of the proposed transnational public agency.

The reluctance of the superpowers to subordinate the slightest short-range national advantage to long-range human interests and their resistance to facilitating even modest system change is indicated in their reception of a French proposal calling on the United Nations to study the establishment of an international satellite monitoring agency. Over 120 nations voted for the proposal, but not the Soviet Union, its allies, and the United States. U.S. Ambassador Adrian Fisher declared that the project is "not feasible, necessary or desirable."[33] Soviet Ambassador Viktor Issraelyan expressed a similar view, saying the proposed verification agency would simply create the appearance—"a wholly superficial appearance"—of making progress in the control of arms.[34]

Second, the creation of a permanent global police force would also help set the institutional stage for gradual system change. What is proposed would differ from past UN peacekeeping experience in two ways: This police force would be permanent, and it would consist of individually recruited persons instead of contingents from various national military forces. Such a force, loyal to authorities acting on behalf of the world community, could not be suddenly dissipated by the unanticipated withdrawal of national contingents from *ad hoc* UN forces, as occurred along the Egyptian-Israeli border in 1967. Because it would be more efficiently integrated, more readily available, less subject to charges of unreliability due to allegedly divided loyalties, and better able to build useful precedents over time, a permanent global police force would be a further small step in the process of domesticating the international system.[35]

To help denationalize narrow group identities within the international system, it is useful to rethink ways that legal settlement might be more creatively used. Many international commercial transactions occur every day, of course, and are subject to international legal regulation and control. Yet there is resistance to expanding this experience into more highly political areas. Partly because the use of international courts and arbitration was oversold in a previous era, its marginal utility in political areas can hardly be taken seriously now. Nonetheless, the sooner judicial settlement becomes a more routine means of settling modest political disputes, the sooner the world community will begin to turn toward nonmilitary resolution of more sensitive political questions.

Highlighting successful uses of international legal processes, even if modest, can help dampen existing prejudices against transnational or supranational institutions. Psychological openness to and social acceptance of a legitimate role for transnational institutions can in themselves go far toward transforming international relations—even without any immediate institutional changes. Whenever a conflict arises, it is not inherently either a military issue or a legal one. People may choose whether to resolve it through military, political, or legal means. Issues can be moved from one category to another. If parties to a dispute choose to view an issue as a legal question, a judicial process can handle it. The International Court of Justice exists, but awaits more serious use. To remedy this, the United States should encourage the use of the world court and regional courts, and finally accept without reservation the compulsory jurisdiction of the International Court in all disputes with other states similarly accepting this provision.[36] To be sure, this would be a largely symbolic act in the short run, but it would also be a virtually costless one that could play an important role during a time of transition to new beliefs and a system of global security.

The only means that can be effective in establishing the preferred rules and institutions of a less militarized security system are to be found in nonmilitary conduct. Because behavior so heavily influences the code of conduct in international affairs, the existing security system is reinforced and the growth of a new, more appropriate security system is stunted by every use of military power, no matter how wisely exercised or justified in terms of maintaining stability. The key to progress is more imaginative development and use of nonmilitary incentives to encourage others, even one's rivals, to help establish preferred global norms.

Third, a ban on all nuclear tests would directly help to depolarize and demilitarize the international system.[37] It would begin, in a small way, to recognize the importance of serving a broader global constituency. This is the one step that nonnuclear weapons states have asked as the price of their foregoing nuclear weapons themselves. Until the United States and the Soviet Union take this small step toward making the nonproliferation regime less inequitable, their nonproliferation policies lack political credibility. The Reagan administration's termination of negotiations on a treaty for a comprehensive test ban after it was nearly completed demonstrates the reluctance of the most heavily armed states to demilitarize. Because the development of new kinds of warheads depends on tests, a comprehensive test ban would at least help to halt the current militarization process.

Offering more generous, equitable terms for economic cooperation and decisionmaking with Third World states would also help depolarize efforts to create norms for the stabilization of trade in important commodities like food and oil—to everyone's long-term benefit. Such depolarization would also relieve some of the pressure the economically dispossessed must now feel to acquire more weapons in order to gain a fair share of the world's economic benefits.

Fourth, the establishment by Moscow and Washington of a nonintervention regime would yield progress in both depolarization and demilitarization. Either the Soviet Union or the United States could offer, without prior negotiations, to refrain in the future from sending any of its armed forces into any nonaligned country, *even if invited,* in return for a promise from the other superpower to show the same self-restraint. Such an agreement might have kept the United States out of Vietnam and the Soviet Union out of Afghanistan. If successful, it also would stabilize the volatile Persian Gulf region and should make rapid deployment forces unnecessary. A nonintervention regime would reflect converging interests among the East, West, and South. The United States and Soviet Union each have an interest in keeping the other out of nonaligned countries, and the Third World supports the exclusion of both superpowers.

Dogmatic realists and a compliant public put an almost singular emphasis on bilateral negotiations as the best means to halt the U.S.-Soviet arms buildup. This narrow approach is largely responsible for the failure to reduce arms over the past 35 years, despite several thousand diplomatic meetings on the subject. Arms control negotiations, which sometimes serve to increase armaments rather than to decrease them, raise these problems: (1) they often take years to complete, thus legitimizing a continuing buildup while officials and the public wait for a negotiated halt; (2) they give exaggerated attention to tallying the number of weapons one side may need to acquire in order to equal the other; (3) they stimulate the development of new weapons for use as bargaining chips; and (4) they seldom focus on the next generation of weapons, which both sides plan to deploy even if negotiations "succeed."[38] Serious efforts at demilitarization, therefore, should begin by emphasizing independent initiatives coupled with an invitation to other countries to reciprocate. Negotiations formalizing tacit agreements can come later.

Perhaps the most promising initiative that the United States or Soviet Union could take independently would be to freeze the testing, deployment, and production of all its new nuclear weapons and delivery systems for six months or a year, and invite the other to reciprocate. This could begin the process of moving away from policies at the top of Tables 2 and 3. No unacceptable security risks would be involved, since relatively high verification reliability is possible for a comprehensive, across-the-board nuclear freeze.[39] Certainly no violations modest enough to be undetected would be large enough to offset the enormous excess military capacity each side now possesses. Even if reciprocation did not occur, no serious security losses would result in the six- to twelve-month period, given the more than adequate deterrent capability already available.

Sixth, another desirable step, which the Soviet Union has already taken as an independent initiative, would be for the United States to pledge that it would never again be the first to use nuclear weapons in combat. Although the benefits of such a commitment are somewhat limited, given the possibility that the promise may not be honored in war, it nonetheless would produce these positive effects: (1) it would reduce the likelihood that a conventional war would escalate to a nuclear war; (2) it would dampen the nuclear arms race between the superpowers, because the pressure for new weapons today comes from the desire to acquire weapons that would have to be used first to be effective; (3) it would reduce the prospects for the spread of nuclear weapons to additional countries; and (4) it would facilitate a wider recognition of the human qualities of people living in a rival country.

Seventh, initiatives for demilitarization, depolarization, and the other areas can, of course, also be taken by small powers. To avoid becoming targets for clandestine intervention or strategic bombing, small states may increasingly find it in their interest to stay out of military alliances, to reduce their dependency on and involvement with military powers, and to establish nuclear-free or demilitarized zones wherever possible. Even if these are begun in seldom-used areas, such as the high seas, these zones could be established and then gradually expanded. A very carefully constructed proposal for a Nordic nuclear-weapons-free zone, which would include Finland, Sweden, Norway, and Denmark, seems eminently reasonable and should be implemented as soon as is politically possible.[40] It is particularly attractive because it includes one state which has signed a treaty of friendship with the Soviet Union, one neutral state, and two members of NATO. Such a Nordic zone would advance the nuclear demilitarization of NATO in the North, as well as open a door for depolarization between NATO and Warsaw Pact nations. Eventually one or more countries in the Warsaw Pact, perhaps beginning with Romania, could reciprocate. If the Nordic zone established verification procedures open to the global community, as suggested, this measure would also help transnationalize and denationalize the international system. It could be the first step toward the denuclearization of a zone through all of Central Europe.

This is a modest set of proposals. None of these steps separately nor all of them together are a sufficient response to the security crisis in which we live today. They simply illustrate that it is possible to transcend today's narrow policy agenda, which is limited by an unwarranted faith in the balance of military power. Too often this agenda is accepted as normal or sacrosanct. Additional, more far-reaching suggestions could be developed from the arguments for a defensive weapons approach, for civilian resistance, for world federation, and, of course, for global security.

But critics resist even the modest steps proposed here. If countries move toward demilitarization at varying paces, critics point out, then national and world security will be in jeopardy. This reservation no doubt has some validity. But if used to reject all suggestions for change, it becomes a facile excuse for doing nothing. Many of these proposals can be implemented with no security losses, even if not reciprocated. Publics and leaders share an obligation to take clear initiatives, to tie these steps publicly to an overall change in diplomatic direction, and to provide as many economic and political incentives as possible to induce reluctant nations to come along. This approach has not been tried since World War II.[41] Until it has been, to claim that the United States cannot move forward until the Soviet Union does is cowardly and irresponsible—cowardly because that claim indulges our unwillingness to take as many risks for lasting peace as we take for deepening militarism, and irresponsible because we sacrifice far more human interests and resources in the pursuit of an illusory military security than we devote to prudent steps toward a more dependable security system. U.S. diplomacy falls far short of taking steps so far-reaching that anyone can honestly say this nation has reached the outermost limit it can travel toward global security before pausing until the Soviet Union comes along.[42] An identical argument for Soviet initiatives can and should be put to the Soviet Union, of course, as well as to militarily less strong countries which also have shown little imagination and boldness in exerting pressures for reversing the arms race.

NEW IDEAS AMID OLD PRACTICES

In conclusion, it is unnecessary to accept the permanency of an international order in which nuclear war may be as inescapable as death itself. A new international security order is a serious possibility, and carefully constructed policies leading toward it seem reasonably capable of maintaining security in the short run while leading toward a more effective security system in the long run. Yet, the analysis of seven policy orientations demonstrates that the United States and Soviet Union now are moving in precisely the *wrong* policy direction. The new weapons on the drawing boards promise policies in the 1990s that will more severely threaten the security of the nation and the survival of the species than does the nuclear war-fighting posture currently in vogue. Recent history suggests that military powers—regardless of ideology—will take constructive steps toward global security only if an energetic public, in many parts of the world, insists that together we subordinate the pursuit of national power and wealth to the call for human survival and dignity.

NOTES

1. For example, see Colin S. Gray and Keith Payne, "Victory Is Possible," *Foreign Policy,* No. 39 (Summer 1980), pp. 14–27; Harold Brown, *Department of Defense Annual Report Fiscal Year 1981* (Washington, D.C.: Government Printing Office, 1980), especially Chapters 1 and 5; and Department of Defense, *Annual Report Fiscal Year 1982* (Washington, D.C.: Government Printing Office, 1981), pp. 37–62.

2. See, for example, Herman Kahn, *On Thermonuclear War* (New York: Free Press, 1969); Bernard Brodie, *Strategy in the Missile Age* (Princeton: Princeton University Press, 1960); and Henry Kissinger, *Nuclear Weapons and Foreign Policy* (New York: Harper Row, 1957).

3. Neville Brown, *Nuclear War: The Impending Strategic Deadlock* (London: Pall Mall Press, 1964), p. 128; Stockholm International Peace Research Institute, *SIPRI Yearbook of World Armaments and Disarmament 1969–70* (Stockholm: Olmqvist and Wiksell, 1970), p. 380.

4. See Robert Jay Lifton and Richard Falk, *Indefensible Weapons: The Political and Psychological Case Against Nuclearism* (New York: Basic Books, 1982), especially Chapter 14. George Kennan describes the need for major cuts in strategic weapons and for a more practical stance toward the Soviet Union in *The Nuclear Delusion: Soviet-American Relations in the Atomic Age* (New

York: Pantheon, 1982), and Solly Zuckerman argues that the superpowers' nuclear arsenals are far in excess of what is needed for minimal deterrence in *Nuclear Illusion and Reality* (New York: Viking Press, 1982). In *The Price of Defense* (New York: New York Times Books, 1979), the Boston Study Group recommends, at least for the immediate future, the maintenance of a larger number of warheads than a minimum deterrent requires in the long run. Nonetheless, their purposes are similar to that of a minimum deterrent posture: to achieve a self-imposed, strict numerical limit on U.S. nuclear deployments, and to establish a clear political limit on the employment of a deterrent force so its only function is to deter the use of nuclear weapons.

5. McGeorge Bundy, George F. Kennan, Robert S. McNamara, and Gerard Smith (note 3), p. 765.

6. See Johan Galtung, *The True Worlds* (New York: Free Press, 1980), pp. 179–254, 363–376; Dietrich Fischer, "Invulnerability Without Threat: The Swiss Concept of General Defense," *Journal of Peace Research,* Vol. 19, No. 3 (1982); Freeman Dyson, *Disturbing the Universe* (New York: Random House, 1979), Chapter 13; Harry B. Hollins, "A Defensive Weapons System," *Bulletin of the Atomic Scientists,* Vol. 38 (June/July 1982), pp. 63–65; Randall Forsberg, "Confining the Military to Defense as a Route to Disarmament," mimeographed, 1981; Anders Boserup, "Deterrence and Defense," *Bulletin of the Atomic Scientists,* Vol. 37 (December 1981), pp. 11–13; Anders Boserup, "Nuclear Disarmament: Non-Nuclear Defense," in Mary Kaldor and Dan Smith, eds., *Disarming Europe* (London: Merlin Press, 1982), pp. 185–192.

7. Dyson (note 6), p. 144.

8. Ibid., p. 143.

9. Dyson (note 6) finds intercontinental nuclear missiles and missile-carrying submarines to be "purely strategic offensive weapons . . . for which no genuinely defensive mission is conceivable" (p. 144).

10. Dietrich Fischer (note 6), p. 7.

11. Grenville Clark and Louis Sohn, *World Peace Through World Law,* 3rd ed., rev. (Cambridge: Harvard University Press, 1970). See also Norman Cousins, *In Place of Folly* (New York: Harper, 1961); Emery Reves, *The Anatomy of Peace* (New York: Harper, 1945).

12. Hans Morgenthau, for example, in his classic book on the balance of power, wrote that "the argument of the advocates of the world state is unanswerable: There can be no permanent international peace without a state coextensive with the confines of the political world." *Politics Among Nations,* 5th ed. (New York: Knopf, 1973), p. 489. Although not advocating world federation, Michael Mandelbaum explains that "the persistence of the 'anarchic' structure of international politics . . . prevented the erection of an insurmountable barrier to all wars." *The Nuclear Question: The United States and Nuclear Weapons, 1946–1976* (Cambridge: Cambridge University Press, 1979), pp. 189, 223. Inis Claude, *Power and International Relations* (New York: Random House, 1962), reports that the concept of world government enjoys "widespread acceptance as the theoretically correct solution to the problem of the management of power" (p. 209).

13. Gene Sharp, *The Politics of Nonviolent Action* (Boston: Porter Sargent Publisher, 1973); Sharp, "Making the Abolition of War a Realistic Goal " (New York: Institute for World Order, 1980); and Sharp, *Making Europe Unconquerable: Civilian Based Defense and Deterrence* (New York: Institute for World Order, forthcoming 1983).

14. See the sources in note 13 and also Adam Roberts, ed., *Civilian Resistance as a National Defense* (Baltimore: Penguin, 1967).

15. Although this policy model is my own formulation, it benefits from the path-breaking work of Johan Galtung, *The True Worlds* (New York: Free Press, 1980); Richard Falk, *A Study of Future Worlds* (New York: Free Press, 1975); Charles Beitz, *Theory and International Relations* (Princeton: Princeton University Press, 1979); Myres S. McDougal, Harold Lasswell, and Lungchu Chen, *Human Rights and World Public Order* (New Haven: Yale University Press, 1980); Richard Falk and Yoshikazu Sakamoto, "A World Demilitarized: A Basic Human Need," *Alternatives: A Journal of World Policy,* Vol. 6, No. 1 (1980), pp. 1–16; and Jan Oberg, "Disarmament, Conversion and Transformation: Some Elements of a Strategy Towards Constructive Defence and Peaceful Development," *Bulletin of Peace Proposals,* Vol. 10, No. 3 (1979), pp. 308–314.

16. Kennan (note 4), p. xxvi.

17. For discussion of this point see Robert C. Johansen, *Jimmy Carter's National Security Policy: A World Order Critique* (New York: Institute for World Order, 1980), pp. 29–34.

18. On the need to modify the present international system to advance these rights, see Robert C. Johansen, "Human Rights in the 1980's: Revolutionary Growth or Unanticipated Erosion?" *World Politics,* Vol. 35, No. 2 (January 1983).

19. On this point, see Richard Falk, *Toward Security for People* (New York: Institute for World Order, forthcoming 1983).

20. For elaboration, see Robert C. Johansen, "A Philosophy of Peace Appropriate for the Nuclear Age," UNESCO, forthcoming.

21. Mandelbaum (note 12), p. 3.

22. Mandelbaum states that "For nuclear weapons to be abolished, sovereignty would have to be abolished." Ibid., pp. 5–6. While strictly speaking this may be correct, it seems to me politically more useful and certainly no less accurate to stress that sovereignty in practice is not absolute. It is possible to curtail the capacity to make and use nuclear arms without destroying the authority of national governments to continue exercising sovereignty in many nonmilitary areas.

23. An elaboration of the concept of the human interest is in Robert C. Johansen, *The National Interest and the Human Interest: An Analysis of U.S. Foreign Policy* (Princeton: Princeton University Press, 1980), pp. 20–27, 364–408.

24. John Herz, *International Politics in the Atomic Age* (New York: Columbia University Press, 1959), p. 304.

25. Plans for fighting a limited and/or protracted nuclear war, utilizing nuclear explosives almost as conventional battlefield weapons, may illustrate this point for our generation.

26. For example, the United States and Soviet Union agreed to a ban on the atmospheric testing of nuclear weapons by allowing themselves to continue testing underground. They have conducted more tests underground since the 1963 treaty than they did above ground before the treaty. The treaty helped limit fallout, but did not dampen the arms race. For further elaboration of the ineffectiveness of arms control, see Johansen (note 23), pp. 44–104; and "SALT II: Illusion and Reality," *Alternatives: A Journal of World Policy,* Vol. 5, No. 1 (1979), pp. 43–58.

27. It is necessary to acknowledge that the United States has generally led the arms race for more than three decades, with the Soviet Union attempting to catch up.

28. Of course the Soviet Union or other countries should also be pressed to play a leadership role in global demilitarization.

29. United States Arms Control and Disarmament Agency, *Toward a World Without War: A Summary of United States Disarmament Efforts—Past and Present* (Washington, D.C.: Government Printing Office, 1962), pp. 10–28. The point is not that the U.S. made extensive efforts to implement such ideas, but that they were not excluded from public debate and policymakers' discussions. Although the United Nations also expressed unanimous support for the U.S.-USSR Joint Statement of Agreed Principles (sometimes called the McCloy-Zorin principles), U.S. officials never worked to implement them because the Pentagon refused to support efforts to follow through.

30. Stevenson delivered this speech to Committee I of the United Nations, November 15, 1961. The text is reprinted in United States Arms Control and Disarmament Agency, *Disarmament: The New U.S. Initiative* (Washington, D.C.: Government Printing Office, 1962), p. 18.

31. Kennan is quoted by Dyson (note 6), p. 147.

32. An international satellite monitoring agency might even occasionally increase rational deliberation in U.S. foreign policymaking, insofar as it might prevent ill-conceived interventions that depend on secrecy for success, such as the secret bombing of Cambodia during the war in Vietnam, the abortive U.S. effort to rescue U.S. diplomats in Iran in 1980, and the support given to Cuban exiles who invaded Cuba at the Bay of Pigs in 1960.

33. UN General Assembly, First Committee, A/C.1/33/PV.53 (November 29, 1978), pp. 37–38. Also quoted in Homer Jack, "Disarmament at the 33rd UN General Assembly," *WCRP Report* (New York: World Conference on Religion and Peace, 1979), pp. 22–23.

34. UN General Assembly, First Committee, A/C.1/33/PV.53 (November 29, 1978), pp. 36–37.

35. For a more comprehensive treatment of these issues, see Robert C. Johansen and Saul H. Mendlovitz, "The Role of Law in the Establishment of a New International Order: A Proposal for a Transnational Police Force," *Alternatives: A Journal of World Policy,* Vol. 6, No. 2 (1980); Derek Bowett, *United Nations Forces* (New York: Praeger, 1964); Lincoln P. Bloomfield, *International Military Forces* (New York: Little Brown, 1964); and Richard Falk and Saul Mendlovitz, *The Strategy of World Order,* Vol. 3, *The United Nations* (New York: World Law Fund, 1966), Chapter 9.

36. This step would require nullification of the Connally reservation, which enables the United States to decide whether the court should have jurisdiction in a dispute.

37. A treaty for a comprehensive test ban has been virtually completed for several years. The obstacle to consummation has been the desire of military officials to continue testing.

38. For documentation of these points, see Johansen (note 23), Chapter 2.

39. See Randall Forsberg, "A Bilateral Nuclear-Weapon Freeze," *Scientific American,* Vol. 247 (November 1982), pp. 52–61.

40. Erik Alfsen et al., "A Nuclear Weapon-Free Zone in the Nordic Countries: A Preliminary Study," *Bulletin of Peace Proposals,* Vol. 13, No. 3 (1982), pp. 189–200.

41. No nation that has refused to accept the unqualified compulsory juris-diction of the world court, to take an almost ludicrous example, can make a credible claim to wanting the rule of law to replace the rule of force. What

shape would U.S. diplomacy and international institutions take if officials and the public sought to improve the credibility of that claim with as much energy, money, and brainpower as we devote to maintaining the credibility of our threat to use nuclear weapons?

42. During the past four decades perhaps the Baruch Plan, based on the Acheson-Lilienthal Report, came the closest to being such a positive diplomatic initiative. But even this contained a one-sided advantage for the United States in its possession of knowledge about making the atomic bomb. (Nonetheless, the world would doubtless have benefitted enormously if the Soviet Union would have been willing to negotiate an agreement based on the Baruch Plan.) Failure to reach agreement could have intensified efforts to suggest a more equitable comprehensive proposal, rather than to move toward more technical study and advocacy of arms control.

40. Elements of a Programme for Arms Control and Disarmament: Strengthening the United Nations Security System, Regional Approaches to Security, and Economic Security

Independent Commission on Disarmament and Security Issues

[W]e focus [now] on the need to promote international security in a global context with emphasis on the developing world.

STRENGTHENING THE UNITED NATIONS SECURITY SYSTEM

[In order to achieve disarmament, we] are convinced of the need to strengthen the security role of the United Nations. A new conceptual approach must be developed in order to promote common security in the world at large.

More Effective Use of the Security Council and the Secretary General

Within the UN, primary responsibility for maintaining international peace and security rests with the Security Council. Regrettably, states have tended only to turn to the Council as a last resort when conflict has already, or is on the verge of breaking out. If they are to be persuaded to shed this attitude, *the Security Council itself must enhance its capacity to preempt conflicts. The permanent members, in particular, should seek to foster a close understanding and collaboration among themselves and encourage a mutually supportive partnership with the Secretary General to facilitate initiatives under Article 99 of the Charter.*

Article 99 specifically authorizes the Secretary General "to bring to the attention of the Security Council any matter which in his opinion may threaten the maintenance of international peace and security." *The Security Council should adopt an initiating resolution explicitly calling upon the Secretary General to bring to its immediate attention potential threats to the peace. In addition, we recommend that the Secretary General should report to the Council on a regular basis throughout the year. There should be a special annual "state of the international community" message to be delivered in person by the Secretary General to a meeting of the Security Council with the Foreign Ministers in attendance.* This message should be delivered at a public session so that all states become aware of the Secretary General's assessment. It should be followed by a private discussion of its implications by the Foreign Ministers of Security Council members. They should attempt to identify specific measures which the Council might take to head off possible conflicts.

To help assert the UN's primacy in international peace and security and to enhance the role of the Security Council we believe that it would be useful for the Council to hold occasional meetings outside UN headquarters. This would provide the opportunity for a more focused discussion and consultation on the problems of a particular region.

Collective Security—A First Step

A key proposal in our recommendations is the implementation of a modified version of the UN Charter's concept of collective security. Its basis would be political agreement and partnership between the permanent members of the Security Council and Third World countries. Its scope would be limited to Third World conflicts arising out of border disputes or threats to territorial integrity caused by other factors. Its purpose would be to prevent the conflicts from being settled by armed force, and not to pronounce on the substantive issues in dispute. It would be underpinned by an understanding—"concordat"—among the permanent members of the Security Council to support collective security action, at least, to the extent possible, of not voting against it. The cooperation of the permanent members of the Security Council is particularly important. Their consent is a prerequisite for the effective functioning of the United Nations in maintaining international peace and security.

As distinct from peacekeeping operations, collective security procedures would have anticipatory, preventive, and enforcement elements. They would all be integrally linked, each reinforcing the other.

At the anticipatory and preventive levels three phases of UN action would be necessary:

(i)   On being alerted by at least one of the disputing parties to the danger of a possible conflict, the Secretary General would constitute a *fact-finding mission* to advise him on the situation.

(ii)   If circumstances warrant, and with the consent of at least one of the disputing parties, the Secretary General would seek the authorization of the Security Council to send a *military observer team* to the requesting state to assess the situation in military terms and to demonstrate the Council's serious concern.

(iii)   In the light of circumstances and the report of the military observers, the Security Council would authorize the induction of an appropriate *UN military force* at the request of one of the disputing states with a view to preventing conflict. This force would be deployed within the likely zone of hostilities, in the territory of the requesting state, thereby providing a visible deterrent to a potential aggressor.

All three phases would be covered by the political concordat among the permanent members of the Security Council whereby they would commit themselves to support particular types of collective security action, and thereby placed on an assured basis.

The introduction of substantial UN forces before the outbreak of hostilities would, in most cases, prevent violations of territory from occurring at all. Nevertheless, there could be situations where violation of territory might still take place with an attack so sudden as to preempt the possibility of effective preventive measures. In such circumstances limited enforcement measures would become necessary. The first objective would be to establish a negotiated cease-fire. The Council would call on the warring parties to cease hostilities and notify them of the dispatch of collective security forces to establish and maintain an effective cease-fire. The parties would be asked to cooperate fully in the achievement of this objective, it being clearly understood that UN forces would have the right of self-defence if attacked by either of the two warring parties.

Full-scale collective security enforcement action would, of course, imply restoration of the *status quo ante* through military means. This is the ultimate deterrent enshrined in Chapter VII of the Charter. Although not realizable in the immediate future, it must remain a goal towards which the international community works.

For the present, other means could be used to ensure that aggression does not prevail. The introduction of a cease-fire should be accompanied by an appeal by the Security Council to the aggressor state to withdraw its troops to its original borders. In the event of a refusal to comply, the Council would immediately consider ways of enforcing its will through the other provisions of Chapter VII, including the imposition of mandatory economic sanctions.

Process of Implementation

We identify the following key components for implementing our approach to collective security:

(i)   *Third World support.* The Non-Aligned Movement has long been an advocate of a strengthened UN role in international security. Its support would be critical in facilitating the proposed concordat among the permanent members of the Security Council.

(ii)   *A political concordat among the veto powers.* The scope of this concordat would be limited, in both procedural and operational terms. The permanent members of the Security Council would be committed to supporting collective security action in the manner described, and, at least to the extent possible, to not vote against it.

(iii)   *An operational structure for UN standby forces.* Article 43 envisages agreements between the UN and member governments on the provision of military standby forces. The Military Staff Committee should be reactivated and strengthened for this purpose. Furthermore, the respective roles of the Secretary General and the Military Staff Committee would need to be carefully considered so as to ensure that enforcement action by the UN is not allowed to become, or perceived by Third World countries to be, a vehicle for great power interference. Standby forces should not be recruited exclusively or overwhelmingly from the forces of the permanent members of the Security Council. We consider it particularly important that a greater number of Third World countries should become potential contributors of standby forces. This objective could be accomplished most readily on a regional basis. Where states of the region deem it suitable, regional or subregional cooperation for the establishment, equipping, and training of standby forces along the lines that have already been successfully developed by the Nordic states should be actively encouraged.

The presence of standby forces in a particular region where it was thought that enforcement action might be required would mean that they could be rapidly deployed to the scene of the conflict, either to be stationed on the border as a deterrent to aggression or to establish a cease-fire as soon as possible after a violation of territory has taken place. In the case of Africa, arrangements establishing standby forces within the region, moreover, would provide the necessary military infrastructure to enable the Organization of African Unity to effectively contribute to peacekeeping operations which it may have itself initiated, even though the necessary funding and specialized technical support might still have to be provided under UN auspices.

Specifically, in connection with the proposal for establishing a

UN collective security system, we envisage that regional organizations could play a vital role in alerting the Security Council and the UN Secretary General to the danger of an imminent threat to the peace and in supplementing UN efforts to maintain peace.

Improved Capability for Peacekeeping

Since our proposal on collective security will not apply to all conflict situations, there will be continuing need for UN peacekeeping operations. We recommend that a small complement of professional military personnel be included in the staff of the Under-Secretary General for Special Political Affairs who is responsible to the Secretary General for the coordination and management of all peacekeeping operations.

Participation in peacekeeping operations is not compulsory but voluntary and only a small number of countries have responded to the UN's call in the past. *We believe steps should be taken to encourage wider participation in peacekeeping through:*

(a) *A General Assembly resolution requesting states to incorporate training for peacekeeping as part of their armies' basic training course, assisted by a standard training manual issued by the UN Secretariat.*

(b) *A joint undertaking between states with experience in peacekeeping and an appropriate UN agency to assist in the training and equipping of troops from Third World countries.*

(c) *Regional arrangements to promote units for peacekeeping duties on a standby basis.*

(d) *The stockpiling of certain types of equipment and supplies which are always necessary. This would improve the capacity of the UN to undertake peacekeeping operations at short notice. The major powers should be asked to contribute transportation aircraft and special units for logistic and signals support; other states should be asked to earmark units for medical services, including field hospitals. Contribution of special units would also improve capabilities for disaster relief operations.*

The UN also must be prepared to respond to new kinds of challenges to international peace and security. For example, the emergence of extensive piracy in the areas off Southeast Asia might suggest the creation of a small UN naval patrol force based on the voluntary assignment of naval vessels and crews to UN duty by member states, and the consent of the littoral states.

AN APPROPRIATE FUNDING MECHANISM
WITH BUILT-IN AUTOMATICITY

The UN has experienced great difficulty in eliciting the financial contributions necessary to pay for peacekeeping operations from some member states, including one or two members of the Security Council. We believe that collective security operations and, for other purposes, peacekeeping ones as well, need to be financed through an independent source of revenue.

We underline the importance of adopting a means of automatic financing that spreads the burden widely and fairly throughout the international community. All will benefit, all should contribute.

Pending agreement on automatic funding from an independent source of revenue, we recommend that the General Assembly should agree on a specified percentage surcharge to be added to the assessed contributions of all member countries to the regular budget. These moneys would be placed in a special reserve fund earmarked for implementing all aspects of collective security operations. Current peacekeeping operations, too, would benefit from a similar approach.

REGIONAL APPROACHES TO SECURITY

The Commission's recommendations for strengthening the UN's security system stem from the conviction that there is no alternative to preserving and enhancing the primacy of its role in maintaining international peace. Although Third World countries in recent years have increasingly sought to handle their own conflicts outside the UN, in many of the conflicts neighbouring countries take opposing sides. This demonstrates that a regional approach can often prove inadequate or counterproductive. There are some situations in which a regional forum could provide a more appropriate framework than the UN for arriving at a political settlement, but even in such cases financial and operational limitations at the regional level sometimes work against effective security solutions.

Regional approaches should, therefore, be viewed not as substitutes for UN action, but as a means of complementing and strengthening it. There is a need to develop an operational connection between regional security initiatives and the UN security system. This kind of link, moreover, would be fully in accord with Chapter VIII of the Charter which explicitly anticipates that regions might wish to establish their own arrangements for dealing with matters relating to international peace and security. It makes only two provisos: that these arrangements and bodies must be "consistent with the purposes and principles of the United Nations," and that "the Security Council shall at all times be kept fully informed of activities undertaken or in contemplation under regional arrangements or by regional agencies for the maintenance of international peace and security."

There is a great unexplored potential at the regional level not only to meet and resolve actual conflict situations as they arise, but also to promote a general sense of security through cooperative measures with the aim of facilitating disarmament, encouraging policies of mutual restraint, and improving the economic welfare of member states. In making the recommendations set out below, however, the Commission has been conscious that the various regions and subregions differ widely in respect both of indigenous rivalries and the degree of involvement by the major powers. We fully appreciate that any initiative for regional cooperation will require regional consensus, but we are convinced that consensus can in turn be consolidated and expanded through cooperation.

Regional Conferences on Security and Cooperation

The Commission recommends that the countries making up the various regions, and in some instances subregions, of the Third World consider the convocation of periodic or ad hoc Regional Conferences on Security and Cooperation similar to the one launched in Helsinki for Europe in 1975. Regional Conferences on Security and Cooperation could add new substance to the concept of common security. The priorities must be developed by the countries concerned and reflect the circumstances in the individual regions both with respect to agenda and participation. The Secretary General of the United Nations should be invited to participate.

It is envisaged that the Regional Conferences could provide an overall framework for cooperation not only on matters directly relating to security, but in the economic, social, and cultural spheres as well.

In the area of security, the Conferences could consider such matters as adoption of codes of conduct and confidence-building measures, establishment of zones of peace and nuclear-weapon-free zones, and agreements on arms limitations and reductions. Subsidiary bodies could be set up to deal with aspects of implementing the Conferences' decisions or to carry out any further studies that might be required. Depending on the character of their membership, Regional Conferences might consider it useful, for instance, to establish a Boundaries Commission to investigate and make recommendations on solutions for border disputes or a similar body to look into difficulties arising from the demarcation of territorial waters and exclusive economic zones. Regional study institutes could be created to analyse security issues of direct relevance to the particular region and to formulate recommendations for the consideration of the Conference; such institutes should be funded by governments and possibly receive a financial input from the UN as well, but should be allowed to operate independently of government direction.

The Regional Conferences would also be the appropriate bodies for launching any regional peacekeeping or peacemaking initiative to meet a given crisis situation. It would, however, be essential for them to keep the Security Council fully informed about any specific security arrangements contemplated. We further recommend that general working procedures for tying regional security arrangements into the UN security system should be formulated. These should preferably be established soon after the Regional Conference is constituted so as to create a standby operational framework for activating cooperation with the UN to cope with conflict situations when it is needed.

In our opinion, the concept of regional security will be unlikely to take root unless it is sustained by programmes for economic cooperation to encourage countries to see themselves as having a national stake in actively working to achieve regional harmony. An important focus of the Regional Conferences must therefore be the establishment of joint projects that are designed to benefit all participating states. The UN's regional economic commissions could have an important part to play in this connection—the Economic Commission for Europe, for example, has performed a valuable function in assisting the development of the Conference on Security and Cooperation in Europe. Involvement of these Commissions would moreover ensure a UN contribution of funds and technical assistance for security building through economic cooperation. This would provide an effective infrastructure for the link between regional security initiatives and the UN security system.

The Regional Conferences could also consider schemes for regional cooperation on the peaceful exploitation of nuclear energy in a manner which would strengthen an equitable non-proliferation regime. Regional cooperation could comprise regional fuel banks, plutonium storage schemes and arrangements for spent fuel management. It could provide structure and substance to general international projects which should be drawn together by the International Atomic Energy Agency.

Zones of Peace

The creation of zones of peace has been proposed most notably for the Indian Ocean and Southeast Asian areas.[1] Within the zone, peace should be maintained by the countries themselves through the peaceful resolution of disputes in a context of political and economic cooperation, as well as mutual military restraint. An essential factor in ensuring its viability, however, is agreement by outside powers to respect its purposes and specific provisions.

Zones of peace would be a flexible mechanism for developing cooperation at the subregional level, while the proposed Regional Conferences on Security and Cooperation could provide a general framework for considering objectives and experiences of the different zones within their region and for establishing links between them. States within the zones could cooperate on developing a code of conduct and confidence-building measures as well as on an agreement to limit arms competition. Some important suggestions along these lines were put forward by the President of Mexico in February 1982 as part of a proposal to further a relaxation of tensions in Central America. The main elements encompass renunciation of all threats or use of force, balanced reduction of military troops in the area, and a system of nonaggression pacts.

It is important to note that the Kuala Lumpur Declaration of 1971 on the establishment of Southeast Asia as a Zone of Peace, Freedom and Neutrality was issued by a grouping of countries which had already put significant emphasis on economic, social, and cultural cooperation and had formed themselves into the Association of South East Asian Nations to further this objective. Similarly, the Economic Community of West African States started its existence in 1975 as a purely economic grouping and in 1981 its sixteen West African member states adopted a Protocol on Mutual Assistance in Defence Matters. The Gulf Cooperation Council, established in 1981 with the ultimate aim of achieving unity of their six member countries, has likewise stressed the need to build "coordination, integration and cooperation in all fields."

The Commission considers that the concept of zones of peace could be an important contribution to the maintenance of international peace and security. Political difficulties that might seem to militate against its realization in the immediate future should not, in our view, inhibit groups of countries from continuing their work towards the establishment of such zones as a long-term objective.

Nuclear-Weapon-Free Zones

The Commission believes that the establishment of nuclear-weapon-free zones on the basis of arrangements freely arrived at among the states of the region or subregion concerned, constitutes an important step towards non-proliferation, common security, and disarmament. They could provide mutual reassurance to states preferring not to acquire or allow deployment of nuclear weapons as long as neighbouring states exercise similar restraint. This would improve the chances for the region not to become enveloped in the competition of the nuclear-weapon states. The nuclear-weapon states would have to undertake a binding commitment to respect the status of the zone, and not to use or threaten to use nuclear weapons against the states of the zone.

The Treaty of Tlatelolco, prohibiting nuclear weapons in Latin America, is a path-breaking regional arrangement in this field. A party to it is not bound, though, until all the signatories have completed ratification, unless it waives this condition. Brazil and Chile have not done so. At present the treaty is in force for twenty-two Latin American states. Argentina has signed but not ratified the treaty. Cuba has neither signed nor ratified. The Commission strongly urges all states concerned to adopt all relevant measures to ensure the full application of the treaty.

Proposals for creating nuclear-weapon-free zones in Africa, the South Pacific, South Asia and the Middle East have been put forward in the United Nations and have received support in the General Assembly. The process of establishing nuclear-weapon-free zones in different parts of the world should be encouraged with the ultimate objective of achieving a world entirely free of nuclear weapons.

Should it prove impossible to agree on legally defined nuclear-weapon-free zones, states could, as an interim measure, pledge themselves not to become the first to introduce nuclear weapons in the region. The nuclear-weapon states would have to guarantee the countries concerned that they would not be threatened or attacked with such weapons.

ECONOMIC SECURITY

The present condition of the world economy threatens the security of every country. *The Commission believes that just as countries cannot achieve security at each other's expense, so too they cannot achieve security through military strength alone.* Common security requires that people live in dignity and peace, that they have enough to eat and are able to find work and live in a world without poverty and destitution.

The Costs of Military Spending

Military competition reduces both military and economic security. Military spending is part of the problem, not part of the solution. The human cost of military effort has long been apparent in a world where more than 1,000 million men, women, and children have no chance to learn to read and write, and more than 600 million are hungry or starving.

But the economic problems of the 1970s and early 1980s make the waste of human effort even more intolerable. The presumed economic benefits of military spending are a dangerous illusion. Increased military spending would make our economic problems worse, not better. Military expenditure is likely to create less employment than other forms of public expenditure, with greater risks for inflation and for future economic growth. These dangers are exacerbated by the peculiar character of the modern military effort, with its increasing emphasis in both developed and developing countries alike on expensive, technologically sophisticated armaments. All but a very few countries now face the most troubling choices in deciding how to spend their limited government revenues— on health programmes or on improving the lives of old people, on unemployment benefits or on investment in economic growth and development, on education or on foreign aid. The costs of military spending must be counted in terms of these other opportunities forgone.

Disarmament and Development

The link between disarmament and development, in the new economic context of the 1980s, is close and compelling. The "crisis" in the world economy described by the Brandt Commission in 1980 has become even more serious. The military tensions analysed in the present report have been a major contributory factor in making this crisis worse. But the process of building common security could help to resolve it. In the first place, for several developing countries, military expenditure, particularly on sophisticated imported weapons, threatens the economic development which is the only basis for lasting security. In the second place, revenues now used on the military could constitute a major source for increasing development assistance by developed and capital-surplus countries. Some governments argue that they cannot increase or even maintain their foreign aid because of competing domestic claims on government resources. These claims are real and urgent. But even a tiny share of the expenditure currently going to military purposes—about $650 billion a year—would go a long way towards resolving the Third World's pressing needs. Third, reductions in military spending would increase the prospects for resumed growth in the world economy, and thus for worldwide economic security. Developing countries need to import the goods and services that developed countries need to export. Resources saved from the military could finance this expansion. We share the view that such economic recovery is an essential investment in future security.

Limiting military competition would have immense benefits for the security of all countries; it would have economic benefits as well. Reductions in military spending will provide resources to reduce poverty and increase social well-being even in the richest military powers. They should also provide resources for development.

Schemes for linking disarmament and development will be different in different countries and regions. In countries with large military expenditures, they should take the form of releasing resources from defence budgets for foreign development assistance. The main military powers spend from four to over one hundred times as much on defence as on foreign economic aid. A ten percent cut in procurement by the nuclear powers alone would be more than enough to double total foreign aid and other financial flows to the thirty-one least-developed countries. Such rather mechanical calculations would probably not lead to appropriate targets, although there is certainly need for international cooperation in discussing the various possibilities for verifying the switching of resources from the military to development. It might be possible, instead, to devise targets described in physical terms; countries might announce that they would use funds from their defence budget to build a fertilizer factory, for example, or to contribute the services of a hundred paramedical workers. It is up to the imagination of people in each country to find ways to participate in such "peace competition."

Regional Conferences
on Disarmament and Economic Security

It is essential that people and governments in all regions should participate in finding new resources for development. The Commission urges that one of the first topics for the Regional Conferences described above, including the Conference on Security and Cooperation in Europe, should be disarmament and economic security. *Countries should consider convening a high-level conference to discuss common problems of economic security, and their common interest in reducing the regional costs of military spending.* Such a conference could provide an opportunity to inform people and governments about the economic costs of military competition; to initiate cooperation in providing information and analysis about military spending; to initiate common efforts to achieve more security at less cost.

The Commission urges that the Regional Conferences launch major campaigns to increase public awareness of the dangers of military competition, including the dangers for economic security. Such campaigns should be an initial step in a continuing long-term public-education effort. Their cost could be met with a small fraction of one percent of regional military expenditure. The United Nations should coordinate the efforts of regional conferences and participate actively in the information campaigns.

The Commission finds it unacceptable that a substantial share of the world's scientific potential be devoted to ever more refined forms of destruction, while our countries urgently need research into preventing and curing disease, into new methods of food production, into alleviating the problems of old people, and into preserving the physical environment. The Regional Conferences should consider ways of converting to civilian uses the scientific and technical resources now consumed for military purposes: from research and development workers and facilities in developed and certain developing countries to technicians with scarce industrial skills throughout the world. The real social costs of devoting resources to military spending vary greatly in different regions, and should accordingly be discussed at a regional level. *The Regional Conferences should propose detailed programmes to use military skills for urgent civilian needs in the particular region. Such schemes should include national plans to convert specific military facilities—research establishments or other military installations—to civilian purposes.*

Common Security and Common Prosperity

We share the conviction of the Brandt Commission that the South and the North, the East and the West have "mutual interests" in economic progress. No country can resolve its problems alone. A reduction in the present high levels of military spending would therefore be in the economic interests of all countries, even those who spend relatively little on their own military efforts.

The principle of common security asserts that countries can only find security in cooperation with their competitors, not against them.

No country can hope to win military advantage by out-running its competitor in an economically costly arms race. All countries are hurt by the economic difficulties of the major economies. Common security is not only a matter of freedom from military fear. Its objective is not only to avoid being killed in a nuclear apocalypse, or in a border dispute, or by a machine gun in one's own village. Its objective, in the end, is to live a better life: in common security and common prosperity.

NOTES

1. See *Final Document of the Tenth Special Session of the General Assembly,* New York, United Nations, 1972, A/RES/S-1012 pp. 14–15; and *Study on All the Aspects of Regional Disarmament,* New York, United Nations, 1981, A/35/416 pp. 15–19.

41. The Establishment of a World Authority: Working Hypotheses

Silviu Brucan

INTRODUCTION

As we approach the end of the twentieth century, the world is entering a stage in which every major development—whether an essential resource becoming scarce, a social or political upheaval—seems to acquire such magnitude and involve consequences so ominous that new international arrangements are required to contain, control, and direct them. The globalization of the phenomena, processes, and problems besetting our world has turned the establishment of an international institution capable of controlling and managing them into the central question of world order.

In the 1960s, a world institution was proposed with the exclusive purpose of preventing a catastrophic nuclear war. Very soon, however, it became clear that such a partial approach is thoroughly inadequate. To build a new international institution one must deal with the *whole,* not with its parts; even the elimination of war is preconditioned on the solution to global economic and social problems that have proved unmanageable under present international organizations.

In fact, the general disorder prevailing now in various international activities informs us that we are on the threshold of a new era in the history of international relations. As I view this, we are going through a period of transition—from the *international state system* to the emerging *world system.* Whereas in the former, the nation-state is the prime mover and its inputs are predominant in shaping the system and determining its behavior, in the latter, it is the reverse effect of the world system that is beginning to prevail over its subsystems, adjusting them all to its own motion. No longer is the nation-state functioning as a self-contained social system whose decisions are determined inside; outside factors now increasingly participate in national decisions and governments are totally inept in coping with them.

Apparently, international relations and transnational activities are growing so interdependent, so systemic, that the world system acquires a drive of its own. And since such a drive has no conscious direction and rationality, it is imperative that a world authority control and direct its motion. It is in that historical perspective that I intend to deal with the issue of the new world institution.

THE HISTORICAL CASE

Throughout history, international organizations or institutions have always mirrored the contemporary world power structure and the respective stage in the evolution of international relations. The issue now involves chiefly the management of power in international society and the ways and means of securing the smooth functioning of relations among its political units. Here, one must proceed from the fact that in the international arena there is no center of authority and power like the state in national society. Over the ages, this vacuum has been filled by various schemes substituting for a central power and endeavoring to perform in the international sphere order-keeping and integrative functions—if possible, through international organizations.

Such a necessity became particularly critical with the formation of the modern international system in the historical period in which the expansion of capitalism coincided with the making of nation-states in Europe—a symbiosis that left its mark on the whole system and its behavior. The capitalist mode of production gave an impetus to the extension of trade and to the creation of the world market, overcoming the isolation of countries and continents typical of the Middle Ages and feudalism. Nation-states provided the basic political units that would constitute the structure of the system.

Although not an international organization, the Concert of Europe (1812–1914) was the first comprehensive scheme for coordinated management of world order. It was based on the premise that each of the four or five participating European powers could enforce common decisions in its own sphere of influence. A classical balance-of-power scheme, the Concert of Europe was hailed as the "golden age of diplomacy" stretching over a century of "international order and stability." Yet, if one looks deeper into the matter, one finds that this Golden Age witnessed the imperialist conquest of Africa, Asia, and Latin America that kept the colonial powers so busy overseas that Europe remained necessarily peaceful for a while.

The League of Nations, endowed with a Covenant, an Assembly, a Council, and a Permanent Secretariat, constituted a radical departure from previous arrangements. It was a real organization with a legal personality, a structure, and agencies of its own. The League was a step forward in international society, responding to the growth of international activities after World War I. Its membership reached more than 30 nations, for the first time providing small nations with an opportunity to participate and be heard in an international forum. Yet, the League reflected the predominant position of Britain and France, allowing them to control the organization and to use it for their imperialist ends. Hence the Covenant did not specifically outlaw war—an expression of an epoch in which force was still considered the final arbiter of international conflict.

The United Nations is an organization much more democratic and universal in membership and more advanced in its principles. However, while most of the principles and purposes of the UN Charter reflect the new openings in world affairs after World War II, the mechanism of the governing structure of the UN bears the imprint of the power realities of 1945. The Big Five of the victorious coalition were given a privileged position as permanent members of the Security Council with a right to veto any resolution that did not suit their particular interests. The practical consequence has been that the UN is unable to take effective action whenever one of the great powers is directly or indirectly involved in a conflict. Thus, very few military outbreaks can be resolved by the UN, for we live in a world in which power is ubiquitous. What is more, as one author puts it: "In relations among the Great Powers, decisive for the maintenance of world peace, international organizations stand exposed to perpetual defeat."[1] The total impotence of the UN in halting the insane nuclear race is a case in point.

Since power relations are never static, the evolution of the UN has followed postwar shifts in the worldwide distribution of power. For the first 15 years, the United States, as the leader of both the Western world and of the Latin American nations, controlled more than two-thirds of the votes and could easily prevail over the group of socialist states in the General Assembly. By the end of the 1950s, a new political factor began to assert itself in the UN: as Latin American nations joined the Third World, the voting pattern within the UN shifted dramatically. In this respect, then, the UN has come a long way—from the "blunt truth that far more clearly than the League, the UN was essentially conceived as a club of great powers"[2] to the present state of affairs in which the great powers complain about the "tyranny of the majority."

From a strictly juridical angle, power simply does not exist in the UN. Article 2, paragraph 1 of the Charter solemnly proclaims: "The Organization is based on the principle of the sovereign equality of its members." The same principle is implicit in Article 18 which gives each member of the General Assembly one vote. To be sure, there are political analysts who take these provisions at face value as though world politics were guided by legal criteria and rules. Actually, international power relations are marked by great discrepancies, and the distribution of power in the real world merely points up the gap between juridical principles and power realities. Hence the theory of the "weighted vote" is essentially an attempt to eliminate this gap and to duplicate in the UN the power relations prevailing on the international scene.

The contrast between world law and world reality may well be the underlying reason why in recent years issues involving the great powers have been gradually removed from the UN. The major protagonists feel they are in a better position to promote their interests outside a setting that has become too egalitarian and democratic for power politics. Apparently, the nuclear stalemate outside the UN has been compounded by a political stalemate within the organization. On the one hand, to be effective, key UN decisions require the agreement of the great powers; on the other, neither the United States or the Soviet Union nor any combination of the major powers can any longer move the UN to act against the interests of the Third World.

This is a structural crisis that must be carefully examined. To begin with, while the drafters of the UN Charter recognized the state of international relations after World War II and decided to codify it as an international state system functioning according to the principle of national sovereignty, their underlying assumption was that such a system could be run by an organization in which the great powers could act as coordinate managers of world order on the premise that each one would enforce UN decisions in its own sphere of influence. This basic constitutional assumption reflected the ideology of an epoch in which power realities were skillfully disguised in the liberal rhetoric of international law.

At the time of the Concert of Europe, four or five powers were able to apply such a scheme because there were actually very few sovereign states in the other continents: the colonial empires of the European powers practically covered the whole planet. Such a scheme, though gradually altered, continued to function in the years of the League and seemed still workable at the time when the UN was set up. It was not until the 1960s, when the political configuration of the world radically changed, that it became obvious that such a scheme could no longer work. Social revolutions in Eastern Europe, China, and elsewhere had considerably enlarged the number of countries dropping from the capitalist system. The national liberation movement expanded rapidly: almost 20 Arab states appeared, while in Africa and Asia dozens of new states arose over the ruins of the French, British, Dutch, and, lastly, Portuguese empires. Indeed, the number of sovereign political units around the world has multiplied to well above 150, and so has the membership of the United Nations.

And it is not only the map that looks different. Though the new states started with a backward economy and therefore have had to retain economic links with their former metropoles, the political activation of the mass population stimulated by independence, increasing education, and touches of modernization and industrialization, has resulted in a powerful thrust of national resurgence that has swept world politics. While it is true that this resurgent movement does not involve power in the traditional sense of the term, it has nevertheless produced a new international setting in which it is no longer possible for the major powers to run the world, or even to exercise effective control over their allies, partners, or clients. Actually, we are witnessing the most decentralized international system in modern history.

Perhaps the greatest merit of the UN lies in its capacity of accommodating the decolonization struggle and the support it gave the new nations in achieving statehood. In fact, the UN has helped extend the state system to all continents, making the system truly international. The UN Charter proved well drafted for this historical task while the organization displayed flexibility in adapting to its requirements.

Having accomplished this mission, the UN seems to have reached its historical limits. Apparently, the UN was neither conceived nor equipped to deal with the global problems that have come to the fore in recent years (the nuclear arms race and proliferation, development, world resources and the energy crisis, ecological deterioration, etc.), or with the economic and financial disorders that trouble the world today. These problems and tasks actually belong to new historical conditions so different from those which produced the UN. The very principle of sovereignty that made the UN system work and enabled it to successfully carry out the internationalization of the state system is now the single greatest barrier in coping with the problems now confronting the international community.

To sum up the historical case with the extension of the state system all over the world, international organizations can no longer work as instruments of great powers, nor can international organizations substitute for a center of authority whilst their activity depends on the political will of 150 member-states with conflicting interests, objectives, and views. A new type of international institution must now be established having the authority to plan, to make decisions, and to enforce these decisions.

WHY A WORLD AUTHORITY?

Ours is a world in which changes on the international scene are so rapid that decisions made today must be necessarily conceived in terms of tomorrow. This is even more so when the issue is a world institution designed to accommodate world developments in the decades to come.

The world of the next decades will be a "small world" in which the per capita GNP of the developed nations will still be 12 times that of the developing nations, even if the growth rates set by the UN for the year 2000 were achieved. The population of the developing nations, however, will be five times that of the developed world. Anyone who puts these two sets of figures together must realize that the explosion will not be limited to population. We will live in a world in which it will take about two or three hours to fly from Caracas to New York or from Lagos to London, a world in which the Bolivian or the Pakistani will see on television every night how people live in the affluent societies, a world in which there will be no suburbia for the rich to insulate themselves from the poor.

While the insane nuclear arms race will continue generating its own perilous moments in the drive for first-strike capability and military superiority (whatever that means in overkill terms), the world of the next decades will live and sleep with a balance of terror in the hands of 20 or so ambitious nations armed with atomic weapons, not to mention terrorist groups using atomic bombs for blackmail or ransom. With the shift of the superpower confrontation to the battlefields of the Third World, the arms race will continue to be exported to Africa, Asia, and Latin America, infecting a growing number of developing nations with militarism, dominance appetites, and regional policeman roles. As the pillars of the old order crumble one after the other, the world of the coming decades will look like New York, Tokyo, or Paris, without traffic regulations and policemen.

The present dislocations in the world market and the recurring disruptions in the monetary system, compounded by the chaos of oil prices, are but signals of a long period of instability ahead for the world economy. We can thus expect an equally long period in world affairs that will involve great dangers of military adventurism and neofascism caused by the desperate attempts of finance and corporate capital to hold on to its challenged positions. It is the belief of this writer that the remaining two decades of this century may go down in history as its most critical and explosive period. For never before have so many social and poiltical contradictions requiring structural changes converged in a world so small and so capable of destroying itself.

Surely, the United Nations is not equipped to deal with problems of such nature and magnitude. A decision-making system with 150 independent participants is in itself a prescription for ineffectiveness in dealing with global problems. A strong and effective world institution is *the only rational solution* to the kind of global problems confronting us today. What else could break the war system by halting the arms race and reversing its trends while planning and managing the conversion to a peace economy without serious disruptions? Twenty years of disarmament negotiations have resulted in a complete failure. Military expenditures have reached monstrous proportions while nations, starting with the great ones, feel less secure than ever.

Within present international arrangements, nothing can stop the escalation of the nuclear arms race, the most aberrant product of power politics. The nuclear arms race seems very little affected either by rational economic arguments or by moral standards; it remains untouched by the most terrifying prospects and is stronger even than man's instinct for self-preservation. To keep the war system going, even "peace agreements" like that of Camp David are supposedly buttressed by arming to the teeth the two partners—Egypt and Israel; so-called arms controls treaties, like SALT II, are actually used as a springboard for a new escalation in armament expenditures.

Equally inefficient are the efforts by present international organizations to deal with development. Two "Development Decades" have elapsed under the UN's aegis, and the abysmal gap between the haves and the have-nots is growing wider. In the years since 1974, when the UN adopted the historic resolution on the establishment of a New International Economic Order, it has become all too clear that no significant headway will ever be possible without some sort of global planning and management designed to ensure that the transition toward a new order is not marred by disruptive competition and chaos for industrial nations and developing ones alike. Such global planning is inconceivable without a world authority.

Furthermore, even a partial agreement in North-South negotiations will come up against the issue of enforcement. *Who* will make sure that all the parties involved will observe the terms of the agreement? The real choice is between a world authority and the laws of the market, which systematically work in favor of the rich. As for the latter, global planning is also imperative if the industrial nations are ever to come out of their present economic and financial crises. Thus a world authority is a *must* for both.

In recent years, international UN conferences have brought to the fore the enormity of such world problems as the human habitat, population growth, transfer of science and technology, ecological deterioration and pollution, food, etc. They all point in the same direction: the need for global planning and management. To cite but one such problem, merely to build the physical infrastructure of the human habitat—houses, schools, hospitals, factories, new cities, etc.—required before the end of the century entails a construction job similar in scope to that accomplished since the Middle Ages. And what about the task of providing work for the 350 million able-bodied men and women currently underemployed or unemployed, the one billion or more new jobs that will be needed for children now being born?

Finally, while people are worried about the depletion of nonrenewable resources, the so-called renewable ones face more imminent dangers: the rapid degradation of the tropical rain forests, the advance of desertification, and an accelerating extinction of animal and plant wildlife. If these processes are not halted, we are bound to lose drastically in terms of health, habitat, and quality of life.

THE WORLD SYSTEM

I submit that neither the convergence in time of global problems, nor the commonality of their nature and scope are accidental. Although they seem to be products of a chaotic amalgamation of factors, processes and phenomena, there is a certain logic in their appearance, manifestations, and magnitude. I think they actually inform us about something fundamental taking place in the very system of international relations: the emergence of the world system.

Here I must point out that there are various approaches to studying the world system and the timing of its appearance. Immanuel Wallerstein, in a monumental work, relates it to the expansion of capitalism, starting with the fifteenth century, when the origins and early conditions of the world system, then exclusively European, appeared.[3] Other authors stress the role of great powers (starting with Portugal) in the formation of the world system since 1500. Although I agree with Wallerstein's focus on the role of capitalism in the formation of the world economy, I consider that political developments did not necessarily parallel the economic ones, as illustrated by the Absolutist State—the maker of modern nation-states in Europe. What followed was essentially a state system, then exclusively European, extending only lately to all continents.

I suggest that the watershed in the creation of a global system encompassing the whole world and functioning with sufficient regularity to impose certain recognizable patterns of behavior on all its subsystems is primarily related to the scientific-technological revolution. It is this revolution that has made communication universal, information instantaneous, transportation supersonic, and modern weaponry planetary, and that has allowed for a global sphere of multilevel interdependencies to emerge and function with a unifying and integrating force. Therefore, I place the appearance of the world system at the middle of the twentieth century, when major breakthroughs in science started to be applied on a large enough scale to become consequential in world politics. Previously, large sections of the world had remained isolated and practically unaffected by central events—even by the two world wars.

The important point is that 'world system' is the conceptualization best suited to explain the new global problems that have arisen in recent decades. Certainly, development, ecological equilibrium, nuclear proliferation, or the energy crisis cannot be dealt with adequately in the context of the "world system of the 1500s" or, for that matter, of the 1800s, for the very simple reason that they were not world problems then. And they were not problems then because there was no world system to account for their global scope.

As I mentioned earlier, what distinguishes the world system from the present international state system is to be found in the relationship between the two levels of systemic motion—the national and the world level. The first level covers the nation-state as the basic political unit of the international system; the second takes the world system and global dynamics as its starting point. To be sure, there is constant interaction between the two. But, whereas in the present international system, the nation-state is still the prime mover whose decisions and performances eventually produce the functioning principles and prevailing patterns of behavior, in the world system, it is the reverse.

A typical effect of the world system upon nation-states is being felt in military policy. Since nuclear missile weapons are planetary both in destruction and delivery capability, nuclear policy acquires a global scope that transcends alliances and overrides all other considerations, including ideological ones. Globalism has led the U.S. and the USSR to stubbornly preserve their monopoly of basic decisions on war and on nuclear strategic weapons. The two nuclear treaties (test-ban and nonproliferation) jointly drafted by American and Soviet experts, as well as SALT I and II, reflect this basic policy. China's advocacy of a strong Western European defense is also inspired by the nuclear logic and the power game it regulates.

The global power rivalry, continuously fed by the arms race, makes for a war system with a drive of its own. This may well explain why the nuclear arms race goes on and on in spite of the fact that already, in the late 1960s, the arsenals of the superpowers were sufficient to destroy the world and kill everybody many times over. The overall effect of the world system is apparent in the active participation in the nuclear arms race of all great powers, irrespective of their domestic system, and in the tendency it generates in other ambitious nations—some of which are still in a preindustrial stage—to go nuclear.

It is in international economic relations and activities that the world system is at its best in influencing nation-states. International trade has been converted from an exclusive club of the big exporting nations into a real world activity. The rate of growth of world exports is rising faster than the growth rate of either production or average GNP. Thus, national economies are increasingly dependent on foreign sources of raw materials and modern technology, and on foreign outlets for their products. The energy crisis highlighted the dependence of most powerful states on oil imports; indeed, interdependence is the law of the world.

The globalization process powered by modern technology is a basic feature of international economic relations. It is a factor so strong that it overpowers even ideological prejudices: joint ventures between socialist states and multinational corporations are cropping up every day. The current economic and financial disorder is truly global with all nations, including socialist ones, feeling its effect.

The attempt of the industrial states to plan their economic development (OECD Scenario for 1980) as well as the strategy set by the regular summit meetings of the seven rich have both ended in complete failure, proving once more that the industrial nations cannot overcome . . . crises by planning in a closed circuit. Equally self-defeating are the barriers raised by these countries against industrial goods of developing nations; thus, the very purchasing power of the latter for buying industrial equipment from the West is reduced. Only by global planning could the present crises be overcome. Gone are the days when economic policies of nations were decided inside; now even major industrial nations, such as Great Britain and Italy, have to develop their annual budget in accordance with the instructions of the International Monetary Fund. Outside factors are now integral to the major economic policies of all governments.

Briefly, in both the military and economic domains, *the world system causes nation-states to make adaptive decisions that they would not make in response only to domestic wants.* The impact of the world system upon its basic units, the nation-states, is thus felt in all major areas of foreign policy, and, as far as we can tell, the tendency of these external stimuli in determining the behavior of nations is going to grow.

A NEW SYSTEM—A NEW INSTITUTION

Historically, the case for a world authority rests on the emergence of the world system eroding the present international state system. It logically follows that a new system of international relations requires an adequate institution to establish its corresponding world order and secure its smooth functioning during the long transition period from the old system to the new one. To be explicit in what we are talking about, by world order I mean a pattern of power relations among states capable of ensuring the functioning of various international activities according to a set of rules—written and unwritten.

Thus far, the discussion of a new international or world order has been dominated by moral, religious, ideological, and, lately, juridical and economic principles and values. Surely, none of these criteria should be overlooked since each provides some of the motivations underlying large-scale human actions so essential to such an undertaking. What is still lacking is conceptual clarity and scientific groundwork, particularly in bringing into focus the fulcrum of politics which is and remains decisive in settling the issue of world order.

A serious intellectual effort is required to fill this gap. Here are my suggestions regarding the directions of such research work and how to go about it.

1. Since the issue involved is chiefly the management of power in international society, I submit that the first thing that must be worked out is the ways and means for the establishment of an international institution wielding power of its own. In practical terms, this means that a transfer of power—a partial and gradual one, to be sure—would have to take place from nation-states to the new institution. The transfer of power to the World Authority being assumed to be gradual, it follows

that during the transition period world order will be maintained by a *duality of power:* the nation-state retaining most of its sovereign prerogatives and the World Authority exercising power in international affairs to the extent of its delegated authority and competence.

2. The concept of World Authority is different from that of world government. The latter presupposes the dissolution of nation-states and the creation, instead, of a single governing body designed to run the whole world, whereas the World Authority requires the nation-state to be maintained with only a partial transfer of power to the new institution so as to enable it to operate effectively within its limited area of competence.

3. It is assumed that the World Authority will be initially entrusted with two major tasks: *peace maintenance* with a view to enforcing general disarmament and eventually abolishing war, and the *restructuring of international economic relations* with a view to overcoming the present economic crisis and eliminating the glaring inequality between the developed and developing nations. Securing peace actually means breaking the war system by halting the arms race—its specific form of movement—and reversing its momentum. This also involves the gradual dismantling of military forces and organizations parallel with the establishment of a *world police force* and a *world tribunal,* which are needed to make sure that the decisions of the World Authority are enforced, to intervene whenever the law is violated, and for the peaceful settlement of disputes.

4. The choice of government, of its economic, social, and political system will remain the inalienable right of each nation. The World Authority will see to it that no foreign power interferes with such internal affairs of member-states. As the existence of a national police force does not prevent citizens from exercising their constitutional rights, so will the World Authority and police force not prevent nation-states from exercising their sovereignty in all spheres of domestic activity, nor will they be able to interfere with the struggle of exploited classes or oppressed minorities for a better society. Briefly, it is only the *use of force* in interstate relations that will fall within the competence of the World Authority.

5. While we live at a time when nationalism is stronger than ever and nations are extremely sensitive about their sovereign rights, experience shows that nations are nevertheless prepared to transfer some of their prerogatives, provided they are impressed by the advantages deriving therefrom. Recognizing that it is in their best interests that foreign airplanes should fly over their territory and across their frontiers, national governments have accepted the establishment of the International Civil Aviation Organization, and have abided strictly by its rules. Also, such activities as weather control, shipping, control of contagious diseases, have been entrusted to international organizations wielding some power of their own. Therefore, a thorough study should be undertaken to

examine the kind of requirements to be met before governments would be willing to hand over national prerogatives to the World Authority in such activities as peace maintenance and economic relations. Since we are dealing with nations having conflicting views, both as to objectives and as to methods, such a study must find compromise solutions to accommodate everyone.

6. Confidence-building measures are essential in the case of a supranational institution, particularly on matters of national security, disarmament, and a world police force—where fears and suspicions reach their highest intensity.

7. *Economics of a warless world:* The question of conversion to a peace economy must be reexamined in the context of the present economic crisis and strategy of development.

8. *Politics of a warless world:* What kind of restrictions and pressures are necessary to apply to the nation-states, particularly great powers, in order to prevent them from using force, and eventually to abolish war? Given the dynamics of power politics, how can the World Authority contain and control it?

9. *The law of a warless world:* A totally new legal framework must be formulated, keeping in mind the conceptual novelty of a supranational institution and allowing for a gradual process toward that goal. The new constitution must spell out clearly what kind of authority and power and over what substantive areas, will be entrusted to the World Authority; also what kind of safeguards will be necessary to prevent organs of the new institution from encroaching upon areas remaining under the authority of nation-states. Finally, the jurists will also have to examine the creation of a world tribunal to establish ways and means for settling disputes.

10. *The new institutions:* The World Authority with its enforcement agencies must be conceived and spelled out functionally in terms of membership, structure, organizations, distribution of power and representation, deliberative and executive bodies, secretariat, rules of procedure, etc. Here the authors will have to devise the new institutions in such a way as to allay the fears that the World Authority once constituted may abuse its powers and become a Frankenstein monster that will terrorize us while we are unable to control it. This issue is paramount in terms of political feasibility; for, unless we assure people that they need not fear abuses from the World Authority, the political will for establishing the new institution is not likely to be forthcoming.

Equally important in this respect is to convey the feeling that in the organization of the World Authority there will be fair and equal opportunities for all nations, irrespective of size, power, and wealth. Experience has implanted in the small and poor nations fear and suspicions against misuse and manipulation of international organizations by the powerful and rich nations. A fair system of representation and distribution of power should allay such fears.

In practical terms, the UN could be instrumental in the initiation phase of the new institution, providing the proper forum for discussion of its principles, organization, and structure. What is more, the new institution will probably have to make use of the experienced staff and vast facilities of the UN, once the latter would cease to exist.

CONCLUSION

Let me frankly admit that a world authority, however rational its establishment, and however persuasive its historical case, is far ahead of present political and ideological realities and, therefore, its very idea is bound to encounter formidable resistance. Paradoxically, those who need it most, fear it most.

In fact, the changes that require the setting up of such an institution have come so rapidly in international life—quicker than a generation's span of time—that political thought and practice have been left well behind. In no other domain is there a contrast so great between the speed of change and the nature of problems, on the one hand, and the political institutions supposed to deal with them, on the other hand. And yet, horrendous problems are piling up, threatening our jobs, the peace we cherish, the air we breathe, the cities we live in, the planes we fly in, and, in the last analysis, our very existence as human beings.

In a world divided by power, wealth, and ideology, probably the most difficult assignment will be the building of a model for the World Authority equally attractive and reassuring for all nations. While the citizens of great and developed nations should look at the World Authority as the safest way of avoiding a nuclear catastrophe, the citizens of the Third World should look at it as the best way of building a more democratic and equitable world order. As for the socialist nations, who are interested in both the maintenance of peace and the establishment of a more equitable economic order, surely "peaceful coexistence," however noble a principle, is still an "armed peace," and as such is no guarantee whatever against the outbreak of wars—not even among socialist nations themselves. It is only a world authority that can provide such a guarantee. For a Marxist, it should be clear enough that imperialism will never give up its privileged positions without resorting to the "biggest bang" at its disposal, nor will the advanced capitalist states willingly renounce their commanding positions on the world market. What could socialism mean on a radiated planet?

Apparently, with the emergence of the world system, everybody must think anew and act anew.

NOTES

1. Stanley Hoffmann, *Organisations Internationales et Pouvoir Politique des États* (Paris: Armand Colin, 1954), p. 412.
2. George Ball, "Slogans and Realities," *Foreign Affairs* 47, 4 (July 1969):625.

3. Immanuel Wallerstein, *The Modern World-System* (New York: Academic Press, 1974), Vol. 1, Introduction.

———— **Questions for Reflection and Discussion** ————

1. What does Johansen identify as the basic problems with the present international security system? Are you confident that current approaches to the prevention of major war will last indefinitely? What alternatives are there to a balance-of-power approach to international peace and security? Is the world security system suggested by Johansen a desirable alternative? Realistic? How can policymakers overcome the temptation to achieve short-term geopolitical gains in order to build a more secure global order?

2. Why have governments failed to make effective use of the United Nations? What flaws in the United Nations Charter require remedy? What are the potential political and military ramifications of the changes recommended by the Palme Commission? Would the UN be willing to take action against an errant superpower? Would you be willing to serve with UN peacekeeping forces or to have your society bear a proportion of the manpower and hardware costs in policing conflicts that might have no direct bearing upon your country? Would you commit yourself to service in a transnational police force? Do you favor its establishment?

3. Should a new international organization be created to deal with global security? What configuration might it take? How would different national societies be represented? Would a new global institution, with a fresh mandate reflecting current political and economic interdependencies, be more likely than present-day institutions to gain compliance in the realm of arms control and disarmament? What should be the role of the United States in facilitating this new organization? Should the United States transfer ultimate control of its nuclear arsenal to a multilateral or supranational agency?

Selected Bibliography

Angell, Robert Cooley, *The Quest for World Order.* Ann Arbor, MI: University of Michigan Press, 1979.

Boulding, Kenneth. *Stable Peace.* Austin, TX: University of Texas Press, 1978.

Clark, Grenville, and Louis B. Sohn. *World Peace Through World Law.* 3rd ed., enlarged. Cambridge, MA: Harvard University Press, 1966.

Falk, Richard A. *A Study of Future Worlds.* New York: Free Press, 1975.

Galtung, Johan. *The True Worlds.* New York: Free Press, 1980.

Johansen, Robert C. *Toward a Dependable Peace: A Proposal for an Appropriate Security System.* New York: Institute for World Order, 1978.

Johansen, Robert C., and Saul H. Mendlovitz. "The Role of Law in the Establishment of a New International Order: A Proposal for a Transnational Police Force." *Alternatives: A Journal of World Policy,* Vol. 6, No. 2 (July 1980), pp. 307–337.

Manley, Robert H., ed. *Building Positive Peace: Actors and Factors.* Washington, DC: University Press of America, 1980.

Mische, Gerald, and Patricia Mische. *Toward a Human World Order: Beyond the National Security Straightjacket.* New York: Paulist Press, 1977.

Mische, Patricia. "Re-Visioning National Security: Toward a Viable World Security System." In *Alternative Methods for International Security,* ed. Carolyn M. Stephenson. Washington, DC: University Press of America, 1982, pp. 71–86.

Randle, Robert F. *The Origins of Peace.* New York: Free Press, 1973.

Stanley, C. Maxwell. *Waging Peace.* New York: MacMillan Co., 1959.

Stephenson, Carolyn M., ed. *Alternative Methods for International Security.* Washington, DC: University Press of America, 1982.

Wynner, Edith, and Georgia Lloyd, eds. *Searchlight on Peace Plans.* New York: E. P. Dutton and Co., 1944.

CHAPTER 12

Promoting
Systemic Transformation

In the introduction to his recent book *The Nuclear Delusion: Soviet-American Relations in the Atomic Age,* former U.S. Ambassador to the Soviet Union George F. Kennan makes the following "confession":

> I am now bound to say that while the earliest possible elimination of Soviet weaponry is of no less vital importance in my eyes than it ever was, this would not be enough, in itself, to give Western civilization even an adequate chance of survival. War itself, as a means of settling differences at least between the great industrial powers, will have to be in some way ruled out; and with it there will have to be dismantled (for without this the whole outlawing of war would be futile) the greater part of the vast military establishments now maintained with a view to the possibility that war might take place. The reasons for this conclusion are multiple; but among them are, first, the recognition that the weapons of this age—even the so-called conventional ones—are of such destructiveness that there can be no clear line between the discriminate ones and the weapons of mass destruction; and second, the similar recognition that so extensively has public understanding and official habit been debauched by the constant encouragement given it to perceive the military balance primarily in nuclear terms that it would probably be incapable of making these fine distinctions between one kind of weapon and the other in time of war, and the use of the immensely destructive "conventional" weapons would in all probability slip over into the use of those to which the term "conventional" could not properly be applied.

In effect, Ambassador Kennan is saying that the achievement of nuclear disarmament and, indeed, the survival of Western civilization itself depends ultimately and ineluctably upon basic social change. As he continues: "[T]he course of international life is not, and cannot be, determined over the long term by specific treaties or charters agreed upon at a single moment in history and reflecting only the outlooks and circumstances of that particular moment. It is the ingrained habits and assumptions of men, and above all men in government, which alone can guarantee any enduring state of peaceful relations among nations."

To be sure, disentanglement from a tradition of militaristic power politics toward a world in which individual freedom, dignity, and security are ascendant presents a formidable task that clearly must span generations—assuming, that is, that we have the wits to avert nuclear omnicide. Though the present world order already is embarked upon an accelerating course of fundamental transformation, basic institutions are durable, including the institution of nuclear deterrence, and not easily given even to modest change. But fundamental normative, procedural, and institutional change there must be; for on final analysis the problem of nuclear disarmament, and still more so the problem of general and complete disarmament, is a problem of system transformation. It is doubtful whether we can rid ourselves of the nuclear habit without getting rid of the war habit, and it is certain we cannot get rid of the war habit without committing ourselves to ways of thinking and acting—now dreadfully lacking—that reflect, in our norms, our procedures, and our institutions, a sensitivity to the preciousness of life and to the possibilities for upgrading human existence.

There is, of course, a very real danger in casting the problem of nuclear disarmament in this way. It has the potential for making this already difficult problem seem all but insurmountable, for regenerating a sense of futility and fatalism about the future, despite the embryonic peace movement that has taken hold in Western Europe and begun now to spread elsewhere. At the same time there lies within this broad view of the problem the seed for reducing immobilizing despair, for instilling a posture of hope in relation to the future. Fundamental to the process of system transformation is the reorientation of individual values, political life-styles, and community goals, and when this connection is truly understood there emerges among us, refortified by our innate urge for survival, a sense of personal empowerment regarding our ability to effect significant social change. A genuine reorientation of individual values, political life-styles, and community goals toward a more peaceful vision of the future than has prevailed in the past is, in other words, one of the most significant ways we have to reorient our national and world societies toward global peace and security.

The readings in this chapter take these observations as their starting point and offer to us a wide range of thinking on how to shape an environment that is responsive to denuclearization and disarmament. In the opening selection, Rajni Kothari contends that a new consensus concerning the inevitability—not merely the necessity—of basic system change must be developed, a consensus that is cognizant of the need to adjust social institutions to the growing interdependencies of national societies. Mary Kaldor, accepting the need for such system transformation, offers important insights into the task of converting military economies into peaceful ones. Chadwick Alger, also accepting the need for basic structural change, looks to the reconstruction of national polities to decrease individual political marginalization and promote a more global human outlook. Finally, Robert Lifton and Richard Falk, seeking to nurture the consensus of which Kothari speaks, close the chapter (and our text) with a *cri de coeur,* a call to each of us to accept personal responsibility in pressing for a world that is free from geopolitical machinations and the constant threat of a devastating cataclysm nobody wants.

42. Survival in an Age of Transformation

Rajni Kothari

A mood of pessimism seems to have pervaded the campaign for disarmament over the last twenty-five years. Writing and pleading about it seems to be a futile exercise, for the world of action moves on a different plane and is found to be totally insensitive to the very large body of opinion—and popular movements—in favour of disarmament. If there is one area where there is a total alienation between the world of thought and the world of action, it is indeed the field of disarmament.

APPROACH TO DISARMAMENT

Could it be that the whole effort at promoting disarmament has gone on in an unrealistic manner, in a manner that is historically naive and conceptually empty? Could it be that, because of their fragmented nature, both scientific efforts and practical proposals dealing with disarmament, as with development and the forging of a new economic order and other facets of global endeavour, are pursuing their task in a rather abstracted and specialized manner instead of locating it in a comprehensive and holistic perspective and strategy? To me, at any rate, this seems to be the case.

There is something highly utopian in the manner in which we have approached the problem of disarmament—as if it could be achieved herein and by itself. We should no doubt be greatly concerned about the terrifying magnitudes that the stockpiling and continuing refinement of ever more deadly armaments are assuming as also about the undeniable fact that the arms race is really getting out of hand. But it is also true that if one expects to make any dent on this rather complex problem, one must take cognizance of the larger historical context in which it is located. It is the context of a major transformation taking place in several spheres of world reality simultaneously. It is a transformation that could lead either to a world more peaceful and secure as well as more just and humane, or to a world racked by increasing turbulence, by a greater sense of insecurity among the major centres of power and hence to a further tightening of the structures of domination and exploitation, producing in its wake an intensification of the arms race on the one hand and domestic repression on the other, preemptive countermoves against forces of change, growing domestic turmoil and regional conflagrations, and as these get out of hand, an eventual catastrophe which no one could control once it starts taking place.

That we live in a period of rapid transformation is now widely recognized and has of late become almost a cliché. However, the necessary scientific effort geared to both *understanding* the nature of the transition that this implies and *enabling* people to deal with it seems to be lagging behind. The most fundamental problem posed by such transition, as in earlier periods of major transformation, pertains to the elementary question of human survival and the survival of civilization. We seem to be back again to the basic predicament of man: will he survive? Will he be able to contain the forces of change and conflict that he has himself engendered in the pursuit of civilization and turn them into instruments of change and reconstruction towards a new order? Or will he, refusing to work for the latter, confine himself to ad hoc tinkering of reality through instrumentalities fashioned for a different age in the mere hope that ultimate catastrophe will somehow be avoided, in the meanwhile permitting the cleavages to sharpen and fragmentation to deepen?

However, while the basic predicament that we in our age face is in its most elementary sense the same as in the earlier periods of trans-formation, it is fundamentally difficult in both scale and depth. Scale-wise, it encompasses the whole human race with the danger of its total eclipse. Depth-wise, it is no longer limited to contending regimes and ruling classes but extends to entire populations all the way down to the poor and the dispossessed. It is a new and dramatic phase in the struggle for human survival—the stakes are high, the arena is the whole globe and the actors are the peoples of the world as well as the numerous States and nationalities in which they are encapsuled.

It is this all-encompassing canvas of new and unprecedented forces of change that should engage the minds of those who seek to achieve peace through disarmament. For one thing is clear. Peace, unless it emanates from and is rooted in a structure widely seen to be just and fair, can be highly stultifying to the forces of change and reconstruction. There are different reasons for which different groups desire peace. Those not so entrenched want peace on the basis of justice and a share in power and decision-making. In their view, a structure of inequity and exploitation is the primary source of conflict and violence.

These observations apply as much to the international order as to the national and regional ones. It is a characteristic of our contemporary world that this structure of inequity extends to both socio-economic and politico-strategic dimensions. It is a situation of cumulative inequity in which a fantastic command over instruments of violence and military power reinforces and supports a system of economic and political domination. Hence the interest of those outside the dominant structure of power in peace and disarmament. But the essential nature of this interest and striving should be understood. It perceives disarmament as a component, indeed an essential component, of a global effort towards transforming the world polity with a view to building a more just and equitable order. It is only on the basis of such an order that a lasting structure of peace can be achieved according to this view.

It is to this basic dialectic at the present juncture of world history—the dialectic of peace and equity and of survival and transformation—that this paper will address itself.

THE CONTEXT OF WORLD HISTORY

The unfolding dialectic of world history is entering its most comprehensive and perhaps the most problematic phase—at once unnerving and creative. It heralds a process of fundamental mutation in the history of the human species, giving rise to far-reaching changes in the arrangement of human affairs: in the structuring of global power relations, in the encounter of civilizations, and in the arenas of class, region, ethnicity, and religion. And yet few, if any, seem to have a clue to the real nature of this transformation.

It is a phase in which the so-called peripheries of the world political structure are responding to the very concepts of self-determination and sovereignty that the leaders of Great Powers had proclaimed and in which it is the latter that are found to defend the status quo and stall the forces of change with all the resources and skills at their command—negotiations meant to tire the opponent out and coopt him, barriers to freedom of trade, communication and movements of people, lethal weaponry, and war.

It is a phase in which domestic social structures are getting deeply destabilized, with the poor and the oppressed both rising in revolt and being put down by populist rhetoric on the one hand and by a repressive State apparatus on the other.

It is a phase in which the struggle for human rights is also drawing upon deeper springs of identity and authenticity, against domination and alienation, and for human and cultural dignity.

It is a phase in which the conflict between tradition and modernity is turning upside down, with modernity becoming the creed of the Establishment and orthodoxy and traditional civilizations struggling to provide radical critiques and alternatives to it. The outcome of such movements, dramatically posed by the Iranian revolution, is by no means certain, however, and could well lead to a revival of old animosities and produce a new spate of uncontrolled violence and atrocities while the defence of modernity—and its main bearers within the State system—

may also get more adamant and fierce in a last-ditch battle for survival. The encounter of civilizations, under such conditions, instead of pluralizing the human condition and rooting it into authentic indigenous streams, each as valid as the other, may lead to an erosion of human civilization as such.

Struggle for Survival

The struggle for survival is thus endemic to and an inherent part of the struggle for transformation of the world. The issue of peace in our age is deeply embedded in this phenomenon. There will be no peace until the process of transformation makes significant strides. And this is not going to be easy. For the age of transformation that we are living in is also an age of mind-boggling paradoxes. It is a paradox in which the erstwhile dynamic agents of change (both the Pax Americana with its theory of economic development and the Soviet Vanguard with its theory of world revolution) have turned to defending the status quo; in which modernizing elites are found askance at the sight of the masses asking for their share in modernity; in which both modernity and revolution have turned sour; in which the battle over alternative universals is turning into a series of particulars; and in which the search for peace and security is turning into ever expanding arenas of strategic checkmates and military escalations. If it is an age of transformation, let us also recognize that it is an age in which the most powerful actors (globally, nationally, locally) are pitched against allowing the transformation from fulfilling itself, if need be by resort to violence—externally and internally.

The Paradox of Transformation

This paradox of transformation reveals itself in a series of dramatic contrasts and contradictions. It is found in the mounting piles of ever more deadly armaments on the one hand and the growing hordes of the very poor and undernourished people living in conditions of extreme deprivation including starvation on the other. We are witness to a great schism in the human community, dividing the world into extremes of affluence and deprivation, with concentrations of poverty and scarcity and unemployment and deprivation in one vast section of mankind and of overabundance and overproduction and overconsumption in another section of the same species. A century of unprecedented material progress has also been one of sprawling misery and increasing deprivation. An age that has witnessed the end of empires and has seen the dawn of independence for so many nations has also turned out to be an age of increasing domination of the world by just a few powerful nations. Despite world agricultural production having been ahead of population growth, food availability has become a serious problem for millions of people. On balance there is a net flow of nutritional resources from the poorer and more populous to the richer and less populous regions of the world. What appear to be slightly more generous immigration policies of rich countries with low densities have in effect become policies of sucking the most skilled technical manpower from the poorer regions. Policies of "aid" as transfer of technology and resources from the industrialized regions have in effect turned out to be a net drainage of surpluses from the latter.

Industrialization was supposed to put an end to the condition of scarcity for mankind as a whole. In fact, it has made even the basic necessities of existence more scarce and inaccessible for an increasing number of human beings. Modern education was supposed to lead to continuous progress and enlightenment for all and to greater equality among men and women. On the contrary, it has produced a world dominated by experts and bureaucrats and technocrats and one in which the ordinary human being feels increasingly powerless and is manipulated by forces beyond his control. Similarly, communication and transportation were supposed to have produced a small world in which the fruits of knowledge and development in any part of the world could become available to all the others. But modern communication and fast-moving transportation have in fact produced a world in which a few metropolitan centres are sucking a large part of world resources and depriving the other regions of whatever comforts and skills and local resources they once used to enjoy. Surely, then, there is something more deeply wrong with the structure of this world than the mere production of nuclear weapons or the economic handicap of the poorer countries. The world we live in is indeed very badly divided, but the divisions are more fundamental than merely ideological, military, or economic.

A Deeply Divided World

The most critical of these divisions is no doubt political, between States and between sets of States—East and West, South and North, Orient and Occident. Underlying these divisions is a crisis of the modern State in both its internal and its external manifestations. This is so everywhere but especially in the more vulnerable States of the Third World which were meant to be instruments of liberation from inequitable social structures and to provide new foci of identity and dignity but which are turning out to be willing or unwilling allies of the status quo. These States find themselves increasingly incapable of coping with the unprecedented demands on their resources and leadership, and their stability and security are being threatened from mass turmoil on the one hand and global pressures of energy, the arms race, and economic recession on the other. A world based on such unstable and insecure States cannot provide a framework of peace and security. It can only produce growing conflicts and divisions.

There are other divisions, potentially no less troublesome, to which thinkers are only now beginning to pay attention, and as yet rather dimly. The most important among them is the division between generations. By this I do not only mean what is usually known as the generational conflict between old and young. This is of course important and quite serious and has not received systematic attention despite a great deal of talk about it. But what I have in mind is something more comprehensive, namely the division between the present and the future, the future including both the very young amongst us and the yet unborn generations. Never before has this concern with the future been of such immediate relevance and urgency as it is today.

Nor is the issue of human survival limited to the human species—the present and the future. For with the survival of this species is inextricably bound the survival of other species and forms of life and of inanimate nature, with all of which it is in fact united through a common organic bond and without whose health and abundance its own survival is at stake. Increasingly man is destroying, almost without bounds, various other species, vegetation, gaseous and chemical sources of life and the seabeds and rocky land whose bounty has been the cause of so much imagination and sense of unity and joy and creativity among humans. Springing from the unending acquisitiveness of technological man and the decline in his sensitivity to his own kind in other regions and generations and to other forms of life, he has been on a rampage that threatens the survival of other species and forms of creation.

The Problematique

What then is the most comprehensive problematique of the human condition at the present juncture of world history? It is, in one word, survival—survival of the species, survival of civilization, survival of the whole creation, and survival of the State as an instrument of change and liberation, identity, and dignity. The problematique is affecting institutional structures, the behaviour of people, and their psychic responses. It is found in the currently widespread feeling of uncertainty and insecurity at all levels which seems to overshadow the earlier sense of confidence and certitude—about the theory of development, about the prospects for peace, about continuity of human progress, and about civilization and its underlying unity.

CRISIS OF THE SYSTEM

In large parts of the world there is increasing evidence of growing incapacity to cope with emerging problems and crises, both domestically and internationally. The old confidence has given way to a mood of concern, perplexity, and confusion. This is understandable, for we live in a period of fundamental transition. The postwar world, which was characterized by recovery from the ravages of economic depression, war, fascism, and colonialism on the one hand and renewed competition for global power on the other, had achieved a measure of stability through an essentially managerial response to a new situation. The chief architects of this managerial response were the two superpowers with their rival systems of alliances and a doctrine of deterrence which, as the dangers of such a doctrine eventually became clear, was fortunately restrained by a period of détente and a complicated balancing of world power. Other expressions of this managerial response included a modicum of development assistance for the countries most affected by centuries of colonialism and a modest effort at creating an institutional framework of conciliation, debate, relief, and welfare under the United Nations system. This managerial response was by no means satisfactory, as it ignored basic issues of structural change and cultural diversity. But it did work for a time in preventing sources of conflict and tension from leading to a major catastrophe.

This system is no longer working. We are already in the throes of a growing breakdown of this system. It is breaking down not simply in respect of larger structural and cultural issues that are engaging sensitive minds everywhere but even in respect of managerial efficiency, sustenance of growth rates and provision of certain minima for human survival, and maintenance of a framework of peace and security. The world economy has already entered a period of stagnation and paralysis, the old engines of growth in the industrialized world seem to have reached their limit, the energy crisis is taking a heavy toll everywhere and the simultaneous onslaught of unemployment and inflation is fast eroding the framework of economic stability that had been constructed following Bretton Woods, the philosophy of economic aid and the role of the dollar and other global reserves in preserving the old international economic order.

Major countries like the United States are fast losing their influence partly due to a decline in their economic influence in the world, partly due to their incapacity to adjust to new political realities, and partly, independently of both these factors, due to major strains in the erstwhile Western alliance under the growing pressure of larger world forces. There develops an obvious danger when major centres of technological and military might find themselves unable to cope with a new situation as they are likely to fall prey to irrational responses unless new and saner forces can inject a large measure of restraint and statesmanship.

Meanwhile, the socialist world is also in a state of flux partly as a result of the fast-changing world economic and political situation, which has cast a shadow on the framework of détente and has led to a new resumption of superpower rivalry, but partly also as a result in their case too of older assumptions not working (such as the prognosis of imperialism and its nemesis, the theory of a world proletariat and the tactical line of coexistence). Alongside, new forms of nationalism are intervening at various points in the old edifice and new and untidy alignments in regional contexts are undermining the cohesion of the socialist world and its special relationship with ex-colonial countries.

In the Third World itself there is a whole set of disturbing signs. While there has taken place a considerable rise in both consciousness of political and economic power and actual assertion thereof and while there is little doubt that the new engines of growth and dynamism must come from the newly industrializing parts of the Third World and from the enormous resources that the poor of the world must provide (both as productive forces and as new markets), the countries of the Third World are also caught up in deep conflicts both at home and abroad. They are no longer able to work unitedly (except in verbal confrontations in the United Nations) and, bewitched as they are by outworn assumptions about economic planning, technological transfers, and the model of a modern technocratic State which they seem unable to control and which tends to either perpetuate older forms of neocolonialism or foster new ones, the elites of the Third World are fast losing their leverage in world affairs. As latecomers in both the game of the world politics and in the processes of modernization and industrialization, these elites seem to view these matters in old power terms, whereas the real issues are increasingly of a different order. There is a need to think of both development and power anew but this is not forthcoming.

The non-aligned world, the Group of 77, the concept of collective self-reliance, and the call of a new international economic order all seem to be in a jam. They may perhaps be useful in putting up the necessary resistance to Western domination but they hardly provide sufficient bases for preparing the countries of the Third World to deal with their own problems either jointly or severally. They do not seem to agree on even setting up a powerful Secretariat or on sponsoring a major research and information system which can match with the efforts of the OECD group of countries. As a prisoner of its own rhetoric which more often than not reflects more its powerlessness than its power and being still immersed in archaic and often reactionary structures at home, the Third World presents a picture of growing fragmentation and chaos. This is hardly a condition in which to join the North-South dialogue based on any confidence of one's own position or strength. No wonder that the dialogue too has become an empty ritual and has in effect all but collapsed. Nor does it seem likely that the much-talked-of South-South process will take off, given the short-sighted view of "national interest" in most of the South, the simmering regional conflicts leading to arms buildup in most regions, and the drive of the larger and more capable of the Third World nations towards playing hegemonical roles in the various regions. This posture of the Third World suits the global corporate structures of both world capitalism and world militarism.

A Process of Fragmentation

Such a picture of all-round fragmentation in which the superpowers have lost their capacity to provide any framework of stability and security, and in which the old alliances are disintegrating and new movements for structural change in the world have failed to make any headway, is further compounded by an increase in the spate of violence both domestically and internationally, and a fast-spreading virus of militarization in all regions of the world for which some powerful countries of the North are providing the fuel and the fodder. There is also a much heightened competition for scarce resources, a growing depletion of the natural environment and the protective cover of the biosphere in the craze for technological power often wholly unrelated to real needs of the people, and, consequent upon all this, a desperate struggle for human survival and sanctity of life and its values at all levels of the globe. Unless major infusions of both knowledge and statesmanship intervene in the process, we are likely to witness a series of localized and not-so-localized wars and unexpected mutations in power relations among major States for which we may be wholly unprepared. Large and uncontrolled movements of millions of people across State boundaries—a process that has already begun—are likely to further sharpen domestic strife and economic collapse, challenging the stability of regimes and producing a breakdown of civil society. Failure to manage these accumulating sources of tension and intervene through necessary structural and institutional changes may well lead us without much forewarning to a psychic condition which may produce the ultimate nemesis of a nuclear war.

Now such a prognosis of possibilities of fragmentation, chaos, and probable catastrophe is not a result of evil forces working themselves out along some inexorable logic of unfoldment or of the doings of some mad and stupid men in power. On the contrary, the reasons for such a state of affairs are to be found in some very positive and historically inevitable forces of change—the stirring of consciousness among millions of hitherto suppressed people everywhere, the rise of Third World societies in the global framework of power and position, the radical shifts in the global structure of economic and political power, and in the demand for world resources, the resurgence and revitalization of ancient civilizations and world religions and their assertion of alternative perspectives on fundamental issues facing humanity. Critical rethinking on values, perceptions, and cosmologies are in the offing in the wake of new forms of consciousness, new explorations of the human mind, and new awareness that the old ways will not do and that there is need to find new answers, produce new skills, and generate new forms of knowledge to deal with a new human problematique—in a way to restore vision and perspective but to do so by taking cognizance of new secular and spiritual forces at work. The long period of decline of institutions and of capabilities has also been one of new expressions of the human spirit.

Growing Alienation

It is the huge and widening gap between these new mutations and the old and obsolete institutional mechanisms of deliberation and decision-making persisting at both national and international levels that accounts for the present crisis. It is this birth of the new in the confines of the old that lies behind the conflicts and confrontations we are witnessing. Many of them, though not all, are inherent in a process of rebirth and rejuvenation. The prevailing systems of management are inevitably unable to fathom the forces that are at work and provide the necessary restructuring of institutional, technological, and power relationships. Governments and political party machines are no longer able to aggregate interests, hold allegiances, and mediate between contending forces. The incipient intrusion of the mass media and the virtual transfer of major political functions to bureaucracies and "experts" everywhere have transformed the nature of the State, in both liberal and socialist countries as well as in the as yet nascent politics of the Third World.

There is then a growing alienation between the awakened masses at the bottom and the modes of conflict resolution that are still highly centralized and technocratic. Similarly, the relationship between choices of technology and processes of social and political transformation are increasingly at odds, producing further alienation. But, above all, the universities, scientific bodies, and expert meetings (which have multiplied at a phenomenal rate in recent decades) are all lagging far behind in coming to grips with the new realities. Their place seems to be taken by the purveyors of capsuled knowledge—the media, the smart salesmen of corporate interests, the experts and "advisers" from foreign aid agencies, as well as phoney spiritualists and the gurus—who are of course unable to provide new answers but who have a mesmeric effect in a world of rapid changes and increasing insecurities. The same is the case with planning bodies and financial institutions, the economic pundits, the management specialists, and the disseminators of so-called innovations and inventions. This pervasive process of alienation that has produced a non-functioning structure of governance and decision-making everywhere is above all to be traced to this deep schism between the world of knowledge and the world of reality. Continuous and even exponential expansion of knowledge does not seem to increase the capability to deal with real problems. This is the biggest and sharpest alienation of all and one that lies behind the heightened sense of insecurity all around.

Role of Knowledge

This is because reflecting and reinforcing the fragmentation of the world discussed above is the fragmentation of the knowledge system produced by the modern conception of science. So much so that even the elementary and integral issue of survival in an era of strife is broken up into so many fragments. Thus the social anthropologist's concern with processes of strife within and between communities, the economists's concern with the material basis of world crisis, and the psychologist's explorations with the deeper springs of human destructiveness, on the one hand, and the study of peace and security by experts in international relations and strategic studies, on the other, are hardly ever informed by a common conceptual paradigm or vision, and even less by a coherent framework of praxis and intervention in the historical process. The result is that reality is broken up into bits and pieces according to the logic of academia and technocrats rather than according to the logic of the reality itself, and the bits and pieces are then pursued in separate and watertight compartments.

Such an approach to human knowledge is not unproductive. On the contrary, we are witnessing one of the biggest explosions in human knowledge of all times. In fact, it is because of its fragmented character that it is becoming increasingly divorced from the reality it seeks to comprehend. The explosion has not increased our capacity to deal with the vital problems and crises that confront us. Thus, just at a time when the frontiers of research in psychology and social anthropology have revealed the fragility of human collectivities, there have been other frontiers of research that have produced the most devastating structure of destruction, not only in terms of stockpiles of weaponry and other hazardous technologies but also in terms of doctrines of waging and winning catastrophic wars. Just at a time when large strides in consciousness have generated deep ferment and awakening at the bottom of the world pyramid, paving the way for fundamental democratization of societies, there has also taken place increasing sophistication in the means of phsysical repression and genetic control of entire societies, giving rise to an equally fundamental assault on human freedom.

Crisis of Values

Closely related to this crisis in the world of knowledge and its incapacity to deal with the problematique of survival is the crisis in values. This crisis has arisen out of the obsolescence of earlier assumptions about the human condition—the assumption of a linear and continuous march of progress benefiting the whole of humanity; the assumption about the benign nature of government and the bureaucracy in mediating societal affairs (which was further fortified after the collapse of empires and the rise of colonies into independent nationhood); the infrastructural assumption about the aggregative role of political parties and the federal process in liberal democratic systems and of the Welfare State in both liberal and socialist systems; the broader and culturally crucial assumption about the territorial structuring of human loyalties and identities; and, above all, the assumption of peaceful relations between man and man and the close linkage between "development" and peace.

All these assumptions and beliefs which underlie the modernist world view are today in a state of flux, if not in disarray. This has produced a state of normative and moral vacuum. The various paradoxes of transformation laid out earlier arise out of this characteristic of the contemporary human condition. There is also a political reason for this disarray of a paradigm of thought which held sway for so long. It was essentially an apolitical paradigm and it left out the crucial problem of power and the issue of distributive justice. This was possible to do until the imperial cushion enabled management of demands from the lower classes in the metropolitan centres and kept out of view the emerging chasm between those centres and their colonial outreach. Even after the emergence of newly independent countries, it was obfuscated by the dominant theories of development and modernization—no less apolitical than the theory of progress—according to which problems of poverty and inequity could be handled through a managerial model of economic transformation. This was further buttressed by a conception of State and nation building according to which erecting cohesive centres of power in each country would also provide the basis of genuine independence and autonomy.

Today, following the collapse of these theories and the startling evidence of increasing inequity and exploitation between and within societies, the problem of power relationships has emerged as the central issue in defining the human condition and is affecting the consciousness of people as well as of States. It is a condition of sharpening dualism (a) between the imperial centres and peripheral societies and (b) between the rich and poor of the world, the two dimensions converging in an intricate and all-encompassing battle for survival at a variety of levels.

THE SPECTRE OF INSECURITY
AND THE STRUGGLE FOR SURVIVAL

The issues of peace and security need to be viewed in this context of a struggle for survival at various levels—all the way up and all the way down—and the accompanying sense of insecurity that propels it.

Survival of Life

For millions of people (around the world but mainly in the South), it is a struggle for simple physical survival, though for them it is also a struggle for social and cultural values and their defence against external encroachments. One-third of the world has no access to potable water, no purchasing power to buy adequate food even though it may be available, no shelter worth the name, and no defence against erosion and plunder of community resources in the form of land, forests, and rivers. Natural calamities are on the increase in these regions, each subsequent flood or famine proving more disastrous than the earlier one, their primitive life support systems collapsing against the onslaught of a mindless technology. There is the prospect of millions of people starving long before the turn of the century. The peasant rebellions and lower class struggles prompted by these conditions are meanwhile being ruthlessly suppressed by an increasingly repressive State apparatus the technology for which keeps being supplied from imperialist powers keen on maintaining "peace" and the authority of ruling juntas.

Survival of Life-style

For millions of others, however, the struggle for survival takes a different form, namely the defence of living standards and life-styles already achieved, and of control over and cornering of resources needed for this purpose. There is evidence of anxiety and insecurity in this respect in the North, the "challenge from the Third World" being perceived essentially along these lines, as a threat to the maintenance of and indeed continuous rise in the living standards of the North. This is the new and most dangerous conception of "national interest" that lies behind the strident resource diplomacy of Western nations, especially the United States, as well as new strategic doctrines developed for the maintenance of global supremacy. This is likely to be the most important reason for the insecurity of the powerful in the face of challenge, reflected also in similar insecurity of the privileged within individual societies against the challenge from the bottom. Perhaps more wars will be fought on this single issue than any other. And more repression and atrocities will be committed on the poor and the oppressed on the same issue, notwithstanding all the rhetoric of a new economic order at the international level.

It is the issue of contending life-styles—and their politics. The prevailing conception of life-style has given rise to a global structure of political and economic power that has become increasingly inequitable and ridden with conflicts. It has led to a blotting up of world resources in a few centres and provides one of the major sources of stratification of the species—both internationally and domestically.

There are three vital aspects of the scenario of this growing conflict. The first is the global structuring of relationship between resources and human beings in which a minority of nations has, in pursuit of a parasitic and wasteful style of life, shored up a large part of world resources. The second aspect is the spread of the same style of life among the dominant strata of the Third World which has produced deep divisions in these societies, both within each of them and between them severally. The third aspect emanates from the first two and consists in the growing conflict over the access, distribution, and control over world resources for maintaining and raising standards of consumption and life-style that have been achieved by the industrialized world and, through emulation and prompting, by the privileged strata of the developing countries.

Survival of the State

Based largely on this schism over control of material resources and productive forces but also somewhat independent of it are sources of insecurity and threat to survival of social and political structures in various regions of the world, both in respect of local hierarchical orders and in respect of the integrity and survival of national economies and nation-states themselves. In Zaire and Chad, in Pakistan and Afghanistan, in the Gulf area generally, in parts of Central America, in Zimbabwe and Uganda, and as years go by and with the growing movement of peoples across legal boundaries, in India, the Vietnam peninsula, and Southeast Asia as a whole, the issue of survival and security of existing national boundaries may prove crucial to their stability and security as States. Nor is this phenomenon of internal convulsions of new nationalities affecting the security of existing States limited to the Third World. It is also likely to affect the North, in the United Kingdom, in Belgium, in Canada and before long in Eastern Europe. The crises of an economic kind and the struggle of social and regional components of existing States over scarce resources will reinforce these political cleavages, sharpen hostilities, and produce repression and violence of established State structures (consider the trauma of Irish nationalism). And all this would look even more serious if seen with reference to the tumultuous changes in regional power equations that will be occasioned by the highly convulsive and destabilizing politics of countries like Israel and South Africa.

Survival of Power Structures

Quite apart from these sources of tension and disaffection from within the social and territorial structure of nation-states, there are international forces at work which are producing a sense of uncertainty and insecurity about the political future of major world regions. Partly caused by the intricate and intransigent politics of energy and the consequent viability of major economies, and partly fuelled by the continuing military perception of dealing with essentially political issues, these countries are caught in an embattled struggle for survival on strictly political grounds. Egypt, India, Saudi Arabia, Indonesia, the European "great powers," Iran, even Japan, and the until now unruffled socialist bloc face a convergence of fast-changing geopolitical, demographic, techno-economic, and domestic political situations. Each of them will be confronted by new mass awakening and new challenges in respect of intellectual grasp and ideological orientations and by new expressions of dissent and revolt against established ways of thinking about national interest and national security. In the years and decades to come, the global economic crisis, caused by the twin pincers of energy cost and military budgets, is likely to shake the complacency of earlier alignments—and also the non-alignment of those who have so far refused to fall in line—and push them along hitherto uncharted paths. All this will add to the sense of uncertainty and insecurity.

Survival of the State System

Finally, the superpowers themselves exhibit the same sense of insecurity in the face of global realignment of forces, the decline in credibility of erstwhile posture, the failure of long-held doctrinal and ideological positions, and above all the almost total unworkability of long-developed strategies and trajectories of national and international security which however will continue to be even more strongly clung to in the absence of the will and willingness to undertake major restructuring of the international system. All of this is likely to give rise to a sense of desperation and frustration in the various arenas of international politics, transforming a steady competition for power and scarce resources into erratic and adventurist acts of preemption and checkmate on a world chess board whose basic rules continue to be violated under conditions where both the number of players and their moves become unpredictable.

In sum, lacking determined intervention for restructuring the whole global enterprise, the various levels of insecurity and various drives for hegemony on the one hand and holding operations and sheer politics of survival on the other will only accentuate the arms race, repressive State structures, and growing anomie and turmoil in the State system (not just the domestic socio-economic bases thereof).

THE PROBLEM OF PEACE
IN AN ERA OF TRANSFORMATION

Such an overview of specificities of the emerging global problematique can be restated in a somewhat simplified manner which also happens to be the crux of the matter. It is that the two basic dimensions on which the human prospect is based are survival and transformation— or, to put it in more conventional language, on peace and development— and that the two dimensions are inextricably intertwined. The contemporary human condition is one in which there is recession on both these dimensions and in which the vision of an integral and unified human future based on bonds of solidarity and shared destiny is more remote than ever.

Interrelationship

Let us look more closely at this interrelationship. As we move into an age when the superpowers will be unable to stem or control international conflicts and wars and the United Nations itself may be paralysed by the growing conflict between the North and the South, the East and the West, and within each of these world segments, the State system as it is presently constructed will be unable to provide peace and security and all progress on disarmament and human rights will come to a standstill if not reversed. Similarly, as the international system becomes even more precarious and as it further strains national and local resources and institutions, and as old engines of growth and dynamism begin to give way, there will be a need to pay special attention to restructuring the world economy, generate new engines of growth in the newly industrializing countries by drawing upon the numerous resources of their vast populations and their rich and ancient civilizations and scientific traditions. The problems are fundamentally international and global in both respects.

I do not subscribe to any universal theory of human behavior or to globalism based on such a universalist view. It is rather the structure of interrelationships and linkages that has permeated the individual and social condition that interests me and needs to be taken cognizance of in our thinking about the human predicament and ways of dealing with it. It is from such a perspective that the close intertwining of the prospects for peace and the challenge of transformation emerges.

Global Structuring

Let us elaborate on this particular perspective on the global structuring of the human predicament. It will not do any more to think in local, regional, or even North-South terms. Though I strongly believe in the primacy of the Third World in any strategy of world transformation— both in respect of historical analysis and in respect of a paradigm of action, I am convinced that it is not any longer possible to think of either development or peace in a narrow Third World sense, and also that the developed world itself faces serious problems of maldevelopment, exploitative structures, militarization of science and technology, and cultural erosion. Equally, it is no use thinking on single dimensions. Thus while it is important to deal with hunger, it is idle to do so without at the same time ensuring survival to the poor and the hungry. Moreover, unless one deals with and eliminates the sources of war, the resources and political will needed to deal with hunger and poverty will just not be available. The contrary is also true: unless we develop the necessary human capacity to mount a frontal attack on the worst forms of misery and despair and the conflicts and tensions inherent in such a human condition, we will never succeed in removing the sources of violence and war. The way to this dual challenge facing us—of war and poverty—lies not in some blind faith in technology and its continuous expansion but rather in bringing the human being back at the centre of the development process as well as at the centre of creating a peaceful and harmonious world.

At this point it is necessary to add a third dimension to those of peace and development, one that follows from the perspective on those two spelt out above but which needs to be handled conceptually as a third lever in dealing with the global human condition. This has to do with the whole question of science and technology. In the uncritical preoccupation with technological advances, the older vision of science as a liberator of the human spirit has receded in the background and its vital link with the civilizational process has been snapped. It is necessary to restore this link by involving leading scientists and humanists in a common dialogue on the prospects and crises facing humanity.

TOWARDS A NEW PARADIGM OF PEACE AND TRANSFORMATION

It follows that the problem of peace and security is related to the profound and turbulent changes of our time and hence requires an agenda of structural transformation and cultural change necessitated by this turbulence. We will have to include in the paradigm of peace the need to build human and institutional capabilities for carrying through major restructuring of the human polity, with minimum recourse to violence and human destruction and by arresting the suicidal and self-destructive proclivities in human culture and psyche.

Let me restate my position in a summary form by listing the major parameters of the unfolding human condition in this last leg of the twentieth century and the transition to the twenty-first which calls for consideration and creative response:

(i)   the fact that the superpowers and the State system presided over by them are unable to manage the sources of tension and instability in the international order, respond in a responsible manner to the radical shifts in the global distribution of power that have taken place, and provide a new basis of peace and security in the world;

(ii)   the fact that domestic political systems (across ideological differences and regime types) are increasingly unable to cope with the demands generated on them as a result of mass awakening and the breakdown of the old "consensus";

(iii)   the fact that the basic social and human thrust of our time is towards equity of an all-encompassing type, all the way from the power structure of the international order to the availability and distribution of world resources, to social structures and moral bases of diverse societies, all of it giving rise to a totally new scale and types of expectations and demands on the world political process;

(iv)   the fact that the political, managerial, and technocratic elites of the world, faced by new challenges and threats to their hegemony, are feeling insecure and caving in, and are resorting to archaic methods of dealing with revolutionary forces through repression, terror, and coercion, all in the name of "stability" and "law and order" and "peace" on the one hand and "development" on the other;

(v)   the fact that increasingly this fighting back by entrenched interests is by resort to armaments and militarism and the transformation of civil societies into national security States and the transformation of the international order by a balance of ever escalating instruments of destruction and terror (including military interventions and virtual occupation of alien territories);

(vi)   the fact that increasingly this backlash is destabilizing and undermining the cohesion and security of the State in large regions of the world, especially in the fragile and vulnerable regions of the Third World. No formula of international security is possible without the security of the State, still the basic unit of human organization (even if in a long-term process of transition towards a different configuration of human structures);

(vii)   the fact that other components of the international order that were devised after the Second World War are giving way too, most strikingly the international monetary system plunging the world into a global economic crisis, but also other international conventions and protocols, notably in the fields of energy, ecology, oceans, and space, giving rise to a world energy crisis and an environmental crisis of major proportions;

(viii)   the fact that ethnicity and large movements of peoples are taking deep and potentially dangerous forms in various parts of the world, consequent upon both the new assertion of parochial identities within national politics and intrusion of new parochialisms through mammoth migrations of people across national frontiers;

(ix)   the fact that traditional restraints on violence and anomic behaviour are giving way in large parts of the world and at so many levels;

(x)   the fact that in the meanwhile the countervailing forces and alternative systems that showed promise at one stage are equally in disarray, with the breakdown of cohesion and solidarity of the Third World, the erosion of youth and counterculture movements and the frustration of traditional disarmament and peace movements in the North;

(xi)   the fact of a likely collision of civilizations (and not just of secular ideologies and the power structures that sustain them) as a result of all these forces at work, posing the most basic of all challenges to human survival—the survival of human civilization;

(xii)   but also the fact that on the other hand new and pervasive forms of awakening and renewal are underway in large parts of the world through the reassertion and regeneration of old religions and cultures, posing a major challenge to the prevailing international order and, by forcing a reformulation of the earlier conflict between the sacred and the secular in a totally new historical context, also posing fundamental challenge to world religions and their capacity to contain the forces of chauvinism, hatred, and violence and provide a new basis for global consciousness and human solidarity; and finally

(xiii)   alongside these deeper stirrings, the rise of new movements within the secular framework of societies and the international order— all the way from the assertion of legitimate rights by oppressed people and communities within individual States to transnational movements for a just world to new and radical popular movements for disarmament and "people's security."

It is this multidimensional field of concern and perspective that we need to deal with. The problems of human survival, peace, and security would, in this way of approaching them, get focused on the most basic of all tasks facing the world community: evolving a strategy of peaceful and by and large a nonviolent restructuring of the prevailing international system as well as its various component structures within States, an essentially global task but a global task that is simultaneously pursued in international, regional, and national settings. The threats to human survival and peace are as ominous and brutalizing in the latter two settings as in the former. Indeed it may well be that the unfinished task of structural transformation in national and regional settings, producing in its wake immense power vacuums, crises of legitimacy, and confrontation between revolutionary movements and regimes of repression, would provide triggering points of destabilizing global strategic and military balances and in course of time pushing them to the precipice.

This, then, is the comprehensive problematique of peace and security in a world that is already in the throes of fundamental transformation, and is crying for a comprehensive strategy of peaceful reconstruction towards a new and alternative social and international order, with appropriate economic, technological, cultural, and institutional underpinnings.

In the words of Soedjatmoko, the Rector of the United Nations University, we need to:

start from the premise of the inevitability of a large and profound social and structural change at both the global and the national level. If one accepts that premise, then the problem of peace can be dealt with as the problem of how to reduce human and social cost in the process of social transformation and how to enhance the capacity of humankind to articulate and resolve conflicts and violence among nations as well as inside nations or within a society.

RECONCEPTUALIZING DISARMAMENT

It is against this larger socio-historical context of peace and development or, as I prefer to call it, survival and transformation, that the issue of disarmament needs to be conceived. For, here too, there is need for reconceptualization and for basic rethinking on the framework of assumptions that informs the field. We have to challenge the assumptions and break out of them—the assumption, for instance, of the reality of a bipolar world that used to inform our perception of world politics and to a large extent still does, consciously or unconsciously; the assumption that issues of peace and security are determined by existing technology, nuclear and otherwise, and prevailing military R&D; and the assumption of balance of power and the management of world affairs through such a balance.

Similarly, the conception of disarmament with an incremental perspective of moving step by step, through arms control and peace negotiations, to ultimate general disarmament will have to be given up. We have to make a quantum leap in our intellectual perspectives. We have to explode the myth that has been steadily cultivated round the world, including the strategic research community, that there can be a realistic nuclear deterrent (which rests on the assumption of preparing for a nuclear war in order that it does not take place). Once this is done, all the effort at building parities in nuclear capacities at an ever escalating rate, or of building nuclear counterforce as a doctrine of defence, will become meaningless and the undoing of the nuclear arms race will come to be placed as a first priority on the agenda of world security. With this it will become clear that without this first and paramount prerequisite of achieving peace and security, no progress in disarmament is possible. And the problem of disarmament will be liberated from all the cobweb of strategic thinking that has held the field for so long. For instance, the whole question of nuclear peace zones will have to be seen in a proper perspective. Until the nuclear arms race between the superpowers is tackled and tackled frontally, the prospect for disarmament remains dim. Let us also not forget that there is taking place, as part of this superpower conception of their security, clandestine transfers of various levels of nuclear armaments to the most sensitive regions of the world—South Africa, the Middle East, and the Indian Ocean, as well as Western Europe. The issue of regional security cannot be seen in isolation from this global context.

Once this is recognized, many other issues will be highlighted, issues that are as clear as daylight but are somehow not grasped. For instance, it is clear by now that if the resources of the world are spent at the present rate on military technology and the arms race and on arms industries that keep producing and transferring ever more sophisticated armaments to the Third World, the cost to the people of the industrialized countries will be disastrous, with both inflation and unemployment knowing no bounds and with wars becoming the only answer to economic recessions.

We have to think of peace and disarmament as critical to human survival and to the survival of civilization. At the present moment the world is gripped at all levels by a rising sense of insecurity, all the way down and all the way up, as we have shown, from the behaviour of the superpowers themselves to the very bottom of societies among the world's poor who are being continuously denied their due—thanks to the rapacious character of modern technology which is being made more and more rapacious and menacing due to the demands of militarism and military technology. We have to think of security in terms of people's security and of peace as an aspect of people's participation in the building of a new human civilization. What we have today, instead, is people's insecurity and vulnerability in the face of mounting threats to their minimum sustenance, their lives, and their ecology. Such people cannot participate meaningfully in the civilization process.

We have to think of the nature of the State in our times under the shadow of rising insecurity and in the global context of regional wars and war-preparedness everywhere. There is taking place an increasing pressure on national economies consequent upon the withdrawal of vital resources for sustaining the arms race and high technology. Thus withdrawal is hurting the poor and the weak the most and giving rise to unrest and turmoil that nascent States are unable to deal with, except through becoming more and more repressive—hardly a condition for security and survival. In large parts of the world, the State is weakening and collapsing as a framework of conducting human affairs, especially from the point of view of the people, their survival, their development, and their future. The issue of disarmament cannot be divorced from the need for security of the State, of all States and of all peoples. In the absence of such security, disarmament has no future.

In the field of peace and security, the scenario is one of growing danger. The nuclear arms spread is already on and cannot be prevented—except by the superpowers themselves changing their course. Militarization is getting globalized and is engulfing the whole world. Worst of all, the most responsible countries in the world seem to be set on a hazardous and dangerous course. This peculiar brand of militarization based on more and more sophisticated weaponry is becoming the largest drag on world resources and is undermining all efforts at growth and development. Indeed it is offering the prospect of a continuous decline in human standards.

It is important to understand how this is happening. There is a whole system of military R&D which is in fact quite unlike all other R&D and is becoming the propelling mechanism of a grotesque arms race which is becoming perpetual and *ad infinitum*. Important and leading sectors of the national economies of leading countries have become oriented to this phenomenon. Meanwhile a whole lot of conceptual defences have been built around it and the human mind is getting immunized to it.

It is necessary that the thinking on disarmament rises to the challenge posed by this empirical reality of growing apathy and insensitivity in the face of imminent danger. Underlying all the major crises facing the world is a crisis of the intellect. This is so in development theory and the same is the case in the field of peace and security. Thinking will have to go beyond arms control and strategic studies, beyond the "disarmament and development" school, even beyond demilitarization and the nonviolence schools of thought, though undoubtedly drawing on the strengths of some of these. It will have to be along a more comprehensive and holistic approach to the whole problem of survival. It will have to deal with the nature of the contemporary State, with the sources of violence, with the conflict over resources, with the sweep and consequences of military R&D, and, above all, with the role of the United Nations system and how to restore to it its true categorical imperative from which it seems to have somehow strayed away. Let it be reminded that its principal task is to provide a framework of survival and security as a basis for a more humane and just world order. As set out in its Preamble, the primary purpose and *raison d'être* of the

United Nations is "to save succeeding generations from the scourge of war."

The new thinking on disarmament will have to deal with specific regional contexts and with the interrelationship of conflict and violence and insecurities in domestic settings with the same phenomena in regional and global settings. This calls for nothing short of a comprehensive doctrine on an *ecology of disarmament.*

It is of course not enough to leave all this to the realm of thought and discussion. There is a need for a sustained analysis and exposure of all this in a manner that goes beyond expert debates and disarmament committees and commissions. There is a need for a direct and persuasive programme of public debate on all this, focusing especially on the increasingly hazardous weapons technology as a whole which too is emanating and spreading from the same metropolitan centres of the power structure of world militarism.

There is also a need to connect such public debates with action movements wherever these focus on the same issues. Indeed, it is necessary to view thinking and debates themselves as part of a paradigm of action. There are taking place around the whole world a wide variety of popular movements against sources of deprivation, terror, militarism, and authoritarianism. There is a need to relate these grassroot efforts, as well as more macro movements around antinuclear, ecology, feminine, and national self-determination efforts of sensitive statesmen and intellectuals throughout the world. The role played by the citizenry of the world, and of popular movements, in influencing the world political process has not been adequately stressed so far. It is high time it is.

In sum, there is (a) the role of sustained debate and building of public opinion, (b) the role of popular movements, (c) the role of the United Nations, and (d) the role of individual governments and their regional and interregional organizations in a common effort towards a global movement for peace and transformation.

43. Disarmament:
The Armament Process in Reverse

Mary Kaldor

Stopping cruise missiles is not just a matter of convincing the politicians. Time and time again, the statesmen of the world have met together in international fora and expressed lofty and commendable ambitions for peace and disarmament. Yet hardly anything of practical value has ever been achieved. New and more deadly kinds of weapons continue to be acquired: war and militarism continue to characterize international relations. It appears as though disarmament, which is viewed as an international act of will, is quite unrelated to armament, which is a national process involving people, money, and institutions deeply embedded in the fabric of our society.

If the campaign for European nuclear disarmament is to succeed, we need to see it, not just as a campaign to change the political will of Europeans—important as that is—but, more profoundly, as the first step in a process which reverses the process of armament. The aim would be to undermine the ideas and institutions which foster the arms race, to rechannel the energies which are currently devoted to militarization into other new directions, and create, so to speak, a vested interest in socially productive as opposed to destructive ends. The act of will that is currently thought of as disarmament would present the final blow to a crumbling military-industrial edifice, the last and perhaps least act in a series of events which totally transforms the current political, social, and economic environment of armaments.

Every armament process has its time and place. The culture which invented the stirrup was quite different from the one which developed the gun. The capitalist armament process and what is more or less its mirror image in the centrally planned economies has its own unique properties. This essay is an attempt to sketch out these properties and to see what they imply for disarmament.

THE ARMAMENT PROCESS

Modern armed forces both East and West are dominated by armaments: what one might call the fixed capital of warfare. In countries like the United States, Britain, or France which are major arms producers, the procurement of arms accounts for about half the military budget and the same is probably true of the Soviet Union. Moreover, the procurement budget is dominated by a few major weapon systems, i.e., warships, aircraft, or armored fighting vehicles, that combine a weapons platform, a weapon (gun, missile, torpedo), and the means of command and communication. In the U.S., for example, the Trident submarine, the new nuclear-powered aircraft carrier, and a handful of guided missile destroyers and frigates, account for about two-thirds of the naval procurement budget. The MX missile, together with the latest Air Force fighters F-15 and F-16, is equally important to the Air Force, while the new XM-1 battle tank accounts for a major share of the Army budget. The same is true in Britain and France. In Britain, the Multi-Role Combat Aircraft (MRCA) Tornado accounts for around 40 percent of the Royal Air Force (RAF) budget: the three antisubmarine warfare cruisers, which are actually small aircraft carriers with their associated escort and support ships, probably account for a fifth to a quarter of the British naval procurement budget.

The concept of the weapon system can be said to have originated in the first prolonged period of high peacetime military spending, namely the Anglo-German naval arms race before World War I. Socially, the rise of the concept may be likened to the replacement of tools by machines. Whereas formerly the weapon was the instrument of man, now it appears that man is the instrument of the weapon system. A weapon system demands a rigid technical division of labor that admits little variation in the social organization of the men who operate it. Equally, the weapon system, like the machine, guarantees the existence of certain types of industry for its manufacture.

Although in almost all industrialized countries armed forces have been pruned and centralized since the war, they remain functionally organized around the weapon system. Hence, navies are organized by ship, with groups of ships organized hierarchically into task forces. At the apex of the American surface Navy is the aircraft carrier, requiring destroyers and a submarine or two for protection, aircraft to fly from its deck, and supply ships of various kinds for replenishment. The bomber and the battle tank have a similar role in the Air Force and Army. The Air Force is divided into bomber, fighter, and transport commands. The Army is made up of armor, artillery, parachute, or infantry units, but the armored units are the core of the combined arms team. The functional autonomy of individual services or military units is achieved through independent strategies associated with particular weapon systems. This would explain why strategic bombing is so central to the U.S. Air Force or why the British Navy remains committed to the oceangoing role associated with carriers long after the abandonment of overseas commitments. In the Soviet Union, for example, land-based medium- and long-range ballistic missiles constitute the basis for a separate service, the Strategic Rocket Forces.

The strategic doctrine of any particular military unit can thus be expressed in the military specifications for a particular weapon system; that is to say, in a set of specified performance characteristics. These, in turn, are the product of the manufacturing capabilities of a particular enterprise. Hence, the weapon system is the link between the enterprise and military unit, the embodiment of a persistent military-industrial alliance.

WESTERN COUNTRIES

In the West, the design, development, and production of weapon systems is, by and large, undertaken by a few large companies known as prime contractors. In general, the prime contractors are the manufacturers of weapon platforms—aircraft, shipbuilding, automobile, or engineering companies; they assemble the complete weapon system, subcontracting subsystems like the weapons, the engine, the electronics, and components in such a way as to create an independent network of big and small companies. The prime contractors tend to specialize in particular types of weapon systems: Boeing and Rockwell are bomber enterprises;

Dassault in France and British Aerospace make combat aircraft, Westland Aircraft makes helicopters; Electric Boat (now part of General Dynamics) and Vickers Barrow (now part of British Shipbuilders) make submarines.

The prime contractors are among the world's largest companies. Since World War II, between forty and fifty U.S. companies have regularly appeared on *Fortune's* list of the top 100 companies and on the Pentagon's list of the 100 companies receiving the highest prime contract awards. Their stability, in both America and Europe, has been widely noted. Firms have been amalgamated or nationalized, especially in Europe, but basically there has been very little nationalization. The plants which receive prime contracts from major weapon systems have remained much the same, under different names, for thirty years. There has been more specialization and an increased amount of subcontract work both among the prime contractors and the outside firms, especially in the electronics industry. Also, the composition of subcontractors has varied enormously along with changes in technology and the business cycle—thousands of subcontractors regularly go bankrupt during recession. But among the prime contractors, there have been few, if any, actual closures in the postwar period. Equally, there have been no new entries into the major weapons markets. The consequence is that a specific mix of skills and physical equipment, and a specific set of relationships with customers (the military units) and suppliers (the subcontractors), has been preserved—in effect, a specific manufacturing experience which corresponds to a specific military experience.

Although several of the big arms manufacturers in Europe have been nationalized, the prime contractors operate according to the principles of private enterprise. They need to maintain their independent viability and this, in practice, means the constant search to find new markets, and to maintain or increase profit margins. Frequently, U.S. defense contractors testify to the intensity of competition—"a continuous life and death struggle to obtain defense contracts."[1] The fact that this competition takes a technological rather than price form has to do with the peculiarity of the arms market—the government as sole customer. Firms put more emphasis on the ability to offer improvements to the product than on the ability to reduce the cost of production—in the end, the government pays.

In essence, then, the Western armament process is characterized by a contradictory combination of stability and competition. The armament sector could be described as a semiplanned sector. On the supply side, it is monopolistic, i.e., has one customer, and on the demand side, it is oligopolistic, i.e., has a few competitive suppliers. On the demand side can be found all the complex mathematical techniques that are typical of a centrally planned system and, on the supply side, can be found the preoccupation with profit margins, contracts, markets, etc., that are the hallmark of private enterprise. Inevitably, these two aspects are reflected in the final product, the weapon system.

In a planned system, unless there is some overriding objective like victory in war, a plan tends to reflect the objectives of the institutions that participate in the plan, to express the various interests of the plan's constituencies. In other words, consumer sovereignty in a planned system is rare because the people who draw up the plan are strongly influenced by the people who carry it out. In peacetime, without external stimulus of war, decisions about what is "needed" for defense tend to be taken by the "experts," generally those who have gained their formative experience in the armament sector. Such decisions tend to be "autistic"— the outcome of the institutional interests of the user and producers. Because the Soviet Union has always lagged behind the United States technologically, the need for any particular weapon system has been assessed against an idea of what the Soviet Union might possess when the weapon system eventually, five or ten years later, enters operational service. This idea owes more to the subjective imagination of the designers than to any hard knowlege about what is happening in the Soviet Union.

The designers are the products of their military-industrial environment. The *competition* between prime contractors propels technology forward as each corporation attempts to offer something better than its competitor and something the military, at least in the U.S., can justify to Congress. And yet this technology dynamism is confined within certain limits— limits that are defined by the *stability* of military and industrial institutions, a stability which is guaranteed by the planning system. The result is an entirely introverted form of technological change, something which has been described as "trend" or "routinized" innovation.[2]

Trend innovation has found its characteristic form in the follow-on imperative.[3] The form and function of the weapon system have not changed much since 1945. Technical change has largely consisted of improvements to a given set of performance characteristics. Submarines are faster, quieter, bigger, and have longer ranges. Aircraft have greater speed, more powerful thrust, and bigger payloads. All weapon systems have more destructive weapons, particularly missiles, and greatly improved capabilities for communication, navigation, detection, identification, and weapon guidance. Each contractor has designed, developed, and produced one weapon system after another, each representing an incremental improvement on the last. For Boeing, the Minuteman Intercontinental Ballistic Missile followed the B-52 strategic bomber, which followed the B-47. Between 1952 and 1979, Newport News's yards have produced no fewer than nine aircraft carriers, each bigger, and better than the last, bow to stern in the best follow-on tradition. And in Europe, Dassault has produced the famous series of Mirage fighters; Westland has manufactured one helicopter after another; and the submarine which the British propose to construct in order to launch the American Trident missile is likely to continue a tradition at Vickers Barrow that goes back, with interruptions, as far as the 1890s.

The idea that each weapon system must have a follow-on has become self-perpetuating. Each corporation has a planning group whose sole function is to choose suitable successors for weapons currently being produced and which maintain close contact with consorts in the military. The planning procedure is supposed to be an exercise in prediction. In actual fact, because of the intimate relationship with the armed services it becomes a self-fulfilling prophecy. Even so the system has not worked smoothly, and it has taken periodic industrial crisis to initiate the full range of new projects. Such was the crisis which followed the winding down of the Vietnam war in the early 1970s. The pressure on the defense budget which we are now witnessing is partly the result of projects initiated during that period.

Each follow-on is bigger and "better" than its predecessor. As weapon systems approach the limits of technology, they become increasingly complex and costly. It becomes harder and harder to achieve incremental improvements to a given set of performance characteristics. Although the basic technology of the weapon platform may not have changed much, such improvements have often entailed the incorporation of very advanced technology, e.g., radical electronic innovations such as microprocessors, or nuclear power for submarines, and this has greatly increased the complexity of the weapon system as a whole. And as the weapon system becomes more complex, more labor and materials are required for development and production, greatly increasing the total cost.

The weapon systems of the 1970s represent what one might describe as a quantum leap in expense and grotesque elaboration. The monstrous MX missile with its luidicrous racetrack system will cost somewhere from $33 billion (the official figure) to over $100 billion (an estimate made in April 1980).[4] It will involve the biggest construction program in the history of the United States. The obese Trident submarine, which is too big to get out of the channel where it was built, will cost much the same. The real cost of producing the British-German-Italian Multi-Role Combat Aircraft will be slightly greater than the *entire* production costs of the Spitfire before and during World War II. A recent U.S. General Accounting Office report concluded:

The cost problem facing the US military is growing worse and no relief is in sight. The so-called "bow wave" of future procurement costs is growing beyond the point of reasonableness. Current procurement programs are estimated to total about $725 billion. If these costs are spread over the next ten years (a conservative projection) the annual average of $72.5 billion will be more than twice the current funding levels.[5]

Yet many people, and not just those who question the whole basis of modern strategy, are beginning to wonder whether the extra money will buy any real increase in military utility. A number of strategic writers have come to criticize the criteria for technical improvements to weapon systems.[6] Many of the indicators of military effectiveness are thought to be no longer relevant to modern warfare. For example, the development of naval aircraft and submarines has meant that speed is no longer important for surface ships. Likewise, aircraft speed is only of advantage in fighter roles. The cost, complexity, and size of modern weapon systems consequent upon the so-called improvements in performance characteristics may turn out to be a positive liability. In the hostile environment of the modern battlefield, where the accuracy and lethality of all munitions have greatly increased, size and vulnerability go hand in hand. Complexity greatly increases unreliability, reduces maneuverability and flexibility, and creates enormous logistic problems. The U.S. Air Force's First Tactical Air Wing, whose motto is "Readiness is our Profession," recently failed a test given by the Air Force's Tactical Command to see if it was ready to mobilize for a war in the Middle East. Only twenty-three of the sixty-six F-15 aircraft were "mission capable" because of engine and parts failure, lack of spares, shortages of skilled technicians, etc.—and these problems are not untypical of Western weapon systems in general. Likewise, cost is a disadvantage because of the high attrition rates of modern warfare and because budgetary limitations lead to savings on such essentials as ammunition, fuel, spares, military pay, training, etc. The huge support systems and the overburdened centralized command systems associated with the modern weapon system are very vulnerable and could be easily disrupted in a war. Indeed, the experience of war in Vietnam and the Middle East—the problems of vulnerability, logistics, communications, etc.— has called into question the whole future of the weapon system. Destructiveness and effectiveness are no longer synonymous—if they ever were.

The degeneracy of the weapon system is not without its effects on Western economy and society as a whole. As an object of use, the weapon system is the basis of military organization both within individual nations and within the alliance as a whole. It is, at once, a symbol of legitimacy and Western unity. The dominance of American weapon systems reflects the dominance of American strategic thinking and the American defense industry. The proposals for ground-launched cruise missiles could be interpreted as an attempt to reassert that domination. As the military rationale for such systems becomes more and more remote and rarified, so their usefulness in holding together, as it were, the Western alliance becomes more open to question.

As an object of production, the weapon system is part of modern industry and its development has to be understood as consequence and cause of broader industrial tendencies. In a capitalist system, the market mechanism ensures rapid technical change. As production processes are adapted to meet changing demands, the whole economic structure undergoes radical alterations. Companies, industries, sectors, and regions rise and fall according to the dictates of the market. As the product of a semiplanned sector, armaments can interrupt this process. In so far as they guarantee the stability of military-industrial institutions, of the major corporations, armaments can help to alleviate crises. But capitalist crises produce change. That same stability has the effect of freezing industrial structure and postponing change. In so far as armaments are themselves subject to the capitalist dynamic they can also drag the economy along their own technological cul de sac, passing on the degeneracy of overgrown trend innovation. In effect they can preserve and even extend industries that would otherwise have declined and at the same time fetter the emergence of new dynamic industries. This is one reason for the persistance of mechanical engineering and shipbuilding in Britain or the automobile and aircraft industries in the United States. The absorption of resources by these declining sectors, the distorting effects of armament-induced ways of thinking about technology on new as well as older industries, are among the factors which help to explain the backwardness of arms-intensive economies like Britain and the United States compared with, say, West Germany and Japan.

THE SOVIET UNION

There is a remarkable parallel to be drawn with what happens in the Soviet Union. The armament sector in the Soviet Union could be described as the inverse of the Western armament sector. On the supply side, arms are produced by the same kinds of enterprises that characterize the centrally planned economy as a whole. Unlike those in the West, research institutes, design bureaus and production plants are organized as separate entities under the control of nine different defense ministries. The stability of these institutions, together with their suppliers, is guaranteed by the system of planning and budgeting. Unlike the West, where competition, the pressure for technical advance, the winning or losing of contracts may lead to the amalgamation of design teams and prime contractors and to massive shifts in the composition of subcontractors, the various industrial organizations are assured of a steady flow of work. If the stability of the prime contractors slows down the process of industrial change in the West, then this same tendency for conservatism and continuity is typical of the Soviet economy as a whole.[7]

On the demand side, however, armaments are characterized by competitiveness (with the West). Armaments in the Soviet Union are privileged products; it is often said that the armament sector is the only sector in the Soviet system which enjoys consumer sovereignty, and this is evident in the priority system. The armament sector receives the best machinery and parts; it can commandeer scarce materials; defense employees earn higher incomes and obtain better nonmonetary benefits; requests and orders from the administration tend to be dealt with more quickly. Many commentators have remarked on the unusual degree to which the consumer can ensure that specifications are met and can overcome resistance to demand-induced changes. From time to time, the leadership has imposed new solutions for forcing technology in order to initiate such programs as nuclear weapons, jet engines, missiles, etc. In general, these programs were a response to developments in the West, which was always one technological step ahead of the Soviet Union.

Hence, because of the degree of consumer sovereignty, the armament sector can represent a mechanism for change in the Soviet system. This was certainly the case in the 1930s, when military competition with Germany could be said to have been the overriding objective of the Soviet planning system. It can be argued that it was through the armament sector that the economy was mobilized.[8] The armament sector continues to transmit new technology into the Soviet system: however, precisely because of the nature of the Western armaments, technologically induced change of this kind may prove distorting and not progressive.

DISARMAMENT

The weapon system is the basis of modern military organization. It holds together the two great military alliances and divides East from West. And yet, paradoxically, the sector which produces the weapon system is also the conceptual *link* between the two societies. For it introduces an element of planning into the capitalist system; it thus helps to stave off crisis but, at the same time, slows down change. And it introduces an element of competition into the Soviet Union, inserting a mechanism for change.

In the past, the armament sector may have worked quite well in blunting some of the contradictions of each society. This is no longer true. The declining military effectiveness and growing cost of armament are gradually undermining the political weight of the superpowers and sapping their economic strength. The crisis of the armament sector has thrown up new forms of conflict and protest. New political and economic rivalries in the West, and consumer dissatisfaction, dissidence, and increased repression in the Soviet Union are all elements of a wider breakdown in the postwar international system of which the armament sector is a central part. The crisis has drawn a response from within the armament sector, as well as elsewhere, from soldiers ill-prepared for new forms of conflict (as in Vietnam), and from workers in the defense industry, concerned about employment. The new situation represents an opportunity for change. It entails the risk of war and of rearmament. But it could alternatively initiate a process of disarmament by channeling the new protests into positive directions.

Most disarmament efforts are aimed at the role of armaments as objects of use. To reverse effectively the armament process, we also need to undermine their role as objects of production. We need to campaign against cruise missiles. But we also need to change the military-industrial culture which created them.

Industrial conversion is one way of achieving this. In a sense, any form of economic development represents a continual process of conversion—of finding new products and phasing out old ones. The conversion from arms to peaceful production would be merely one aspect of this process. Different societies have different mechanisms for conversion. The capitalist economy depends on the market as a method of allocating resources. It involves anarchy, dislocation, structural unemployment, and periodic crisis. The alternative is the central planning mechanism of the socialist countries which leads to rigidity because biases in government reflect vested bureaucratic interests. It thus avoids crises but, at the same time, is much more resistant to change than is the capitalist system.

The conversion from war to peace needs to be seen *not* as the *technical* process of converting swords to ploughshares, but as a *social* process of finding a new mechanism for the allocation of resources. Mere technical conversion from war to peace could never be sufficient. In a sense, we have already experienced this in the nonmilitary products of the arms companies—the U.S. and Soviet space programs, Concorde and the TU-144, nuclear energy, various American rapid urban transit systems, and environmental products. These have become what one might call quasi-weapon systems—similarly elaborate and expensive, with, in the end, similar economic consequences. Further, these products could never provide perfect substitutes for armaments since they do not command the same urgency. It would be difficult to justify increased expenditure on space or artificial hearts in times of economic recession.

Conversion needs to be seen as a way of creating a new economic system which would minimize those problems that create opportunities for conflict and the pressure for armaments. Such a system would combine the positive elements of planning with positive elements of free enterprise, instead of, as in the armament sector, the negative elements of both. The Western armament system, as we have seen, is characterized by planning on the demand side and competition on the supply side. The Western form of military technical change, the outcome of this system, is transferred to the Soviet Union through the consumer sovereignty that is the unique characteristic of the armament sector in the Soviet Union. What is needed is a system of consumer sovereignty in which the consumer is not a military establishment engaged in a competitive arms race but an ordinary person—in other words, planning, under democratic control. How is this to be achieved in practice?

A sturdy democracy originates in popular movement, even though such movements must eventually find an institutional expression. Already, trade unions in the defense industry in Britain, West Germany, the United States, Italy, and Sweden have begun to express interest in the idea of conversion. This interest has proceeded farthest in Britain, where the workers of Lucas Aerospace and Vickers have earned a worldwide reputation for their proposals and campaigns to achieve socially useful production.

The principle that underlies the Lucas Aerospace Corporate Plan,[9] the Vickers pamphlets,[10] and various proposals from workers in other companies, including Rolls-Royce ("Buns Before the Gutter"), BAC, and Parsons, is the simple but revolutionary idea that in a society where there are substantial unfilled needs it makes no sense to put people, who could be making products to fill those needs, on the dole or into arms manufacturing. Neither the market mechanism nor central planning has proved very efficient at marrying social need to available resources. The alternative is to propose products which emanate from direct contacts between producers and consumers. This is the basis of the various worker plans.

In developing their ideas, the unions found it necessary to develop links with unions in supplier industries and with consumer organizations. Partly, this was in order to establish technical and social feasibility. For example, proposals by Rolls-Royce workers for gas turbine propulsion for merchant ships turned out to be an oversophisticated, marginally useful suggestion. More importantly, it provides a more effective method of putting political pressure on management and the government. Many of the ideas clash with priorities currently established by the government, which tend to reflect existing vested interests. Hence the shop stewards proposed energy conservation equipment and alternative forms of energy based on wind and waves; yet official energy priorities stress North Sea oil, coal, and nuclear energy. They also proposed new kinds of rail vehicles or ways of revitalizing Britain's canal system; yet transport policy places the emphasis on roads rather than railways or canals. The workers have consequently joined forces with organizations like the antinuclear energy movement or Transport 2000, which lobbies against the unplanned growth of the automobile infrastructure. On more mundane levels, unions in British Leyland pressed their management to purchase a scrap metal baler, one of the ideas put forward by the Vickers Shop Stewards. Lucas Aerospace Shop Stewards at Burnley worked closely with the local council with the idea of meeting local needs. These informal alliances between producers and consumers could provide the basis for future planning agencies which would reflect a different sort of social priorities from those that currently hold sway.

Ideally, these links should be international, for there is always the risk that social criteria for resource allocation could turn out to be national, and hence divisive on a global scale. At both Vickers and Lucas Aerospace, some international links have been forged. Vickers workers have visited India (where they helped to establish a tank factory) and Iran (where they were shocked to hear of the way Chieftain tanks had been used). They have proposed various kinds of equipment for irrigation and for water purification. Lucas Aerospace workers have discussed the possibility of adapting a road/rail vehicle they have invented for use in Tanzania and Zambia with the governments of those countries.

The Lucas Aerospace workers have actually achieved some success in pressing their management to undertake the manufacture of socially useful products. For the first time, workers are inserting their own criteria, as both producers and consumers, into the choice of products. They are, in a sense, developing a new mechanism for conversion, which, if it spreads, could change the composition of power in existing institutions—local councils, regional development councils, the Industrial Manpower Commission, the Atomic Energy Commission, for example—and which could eventually be embodied in a new set of planning institutions which set priorities according to the social needs of consumers and which guarantee stable, although mobile, employment.

Any campaign for disarmament must join forces with workers in the defense industry in demanding conversion. Conversion—along with other more traditional disarmament issues—could build upon the growing fissures within the armament system and direct current frustrations toward disarmament rather than war. It could help to initiate a process of conversion which would *precede* disarmament. Conversion would thus be seen as a way of achieving disarmament rather than a thorny problem to be solved after the politicians had finally willed the reduction of armaments. Conversion would not just be a matter of turning swords into ploughshares. It would be a matter of creating a new mechanism for the wider process of economic conversion, matching the desperate needs of the modern world with resources that are either misused or not used at all. It could thus undermine the political and economic basis for armaments in advanced industrial countries and it would help to overcome the structural problems, weaknesses, and divisions of different economic systems. Hence it could help to remove the causes of war.

NOTES

1. National Security Industrial Association, quoted in J. E. Fox, *Arming America: How the US Buys Weapons* (Cambridge, Mass: Harvard University Press, 1974), p. 101.

2. See Morris Janowitz, *The Professional Soldier* (New York: Free Press, 1960).

3. See James Kurth, "Why We Buy the Weapons We Do," *Foreign Policy* 11 (1973).

4. Science Supplement, *New York Times*, April 15, 1980.

5. *Impediments to Reducing the Costs of Weapons Systems*, Report to the Congress of the United States by the Comptroller General, PSAD-80-6, November 1979, p. 3.

6. See, for example, Stephen Canby, "The Alliance and Europe, Part IV, Military Doctrine and Technology," Adelphi Paper No. 109 (London: IISS, Winter 1974-75).

7. See Alec Nove, *The Soviet Economic System* (London: Allen & Unwin, 1977).

8. See Julian Cooper, "Defence Production and the Soviet Economy, 1929–41," CREES Discussion Paper, Soviet Industrialization Project Series SIPS, No. 3, 1976.

9. Lucas Aerospace Combine Committee, *Corporate Plan* (1976).

10. Vickers National Combine Committee of Shop Stewards, *Building a Chieftain Tank and the Alternative Use of Resources* and *The ASW Cruiser: Alternative Work for Naval Shipbuilding Workers* (1978).

44. Reconstructing Human Polities: Collective Security in the Nuclear Age

Chadwick F. Alger

As I write there is a great surge of public concern about the arms race. The nuclear freeze movement has galvanized an unusually broad coalition that has carried the campaign not only to the U.S. Congress, but also to state legislatures and referenda, and to town and city councils and referenda. In a relatively short period of time, thousands of people in local communities throughout the United States have learned a great deal about nuclear weapons and military strategy, as revealed in symposia and debates in hundreds of communities and testimony before many city councils and state legislatures. Serious challenge is being offered to the long-held assumption that only a small politico-military elite is competent to participate in military policymaking. These are encouraging developments to those who believe that domination of foreign policy-making by this small elite has produced excessive dependence on arms as an instrument in foreign policy.

On the other hand, if one takes the long view, optimism evaporates. There have been surges of public concern for arms races in the past. Are we experiencing another temporary peak of public concern that will again be followed by a return to widespread apathy?

This chapter attempts to shed light on why apathy is more normal than active concern and suggests strategies for overcoming apathy. The analysis proceeds out of three key assumptions. First, arms have become the centerpiece of U.S. foreign policy because of inability to mobilize support behind other approaches for dealing with world social and economic problems. Second, creative U.S. involvement in efforts to solve world social and economic problems will not become possible unless this involvement is supported by movements with widespread participation and staying power. Third, the development of such movements requires the creation of new opportunities for sustained grassroots participation in world affairs.

The inability of the United States to sustain creative involvement in efforts to solve world social and economic problems is reflected in the dramatic contrasts between some values and beliefs widely espoused within the United States and those values and beliefs reflected in the external relations of the national government. Here are four examples.

First, we pride ourselves on being a nation of law and widely advocate the rule of law in international relations. Yet in 1982 the United States Government, along with only four other countries, voted against the new Law of the Sea Treaty. This historic treaty, consummating a decade of drafting and negotiation, provides a rule of law for seventy percent of the surface of the earth. With minor exceptions, the U.S. rejection of the treaty is largely ignored by the media, little known by the public, and little debated. Why?

Second, most people in the United States are proud of the degree to which their society protects human rights. There were widespread positive responses to President Carter's emphasis on worldwide human rights during his presidential term. But the United States has not ratified the two covenants that move toward implementation of the United Nations Universal Declaration of Human Rights—the Covenant on Civil and Political Rights and the Covenant on Economic, Social and Cultural Rights. These treaties were negotiated and signed by the United States Government in 1966, but not even submitted to the Senate by the President until more than a decade and a half later. Despite widespread media attention to human rights, there is virtually no public debate or even concern about the failure of the United States to ratify these agreements. Why?

Third, the gap between the rich and poor of the world is growing, accompanied by widespread suffering. There is growing animosity between industrialized and Third World countries that threatens future access by the United States to important resources and markets and increases the likelihood of revolution, terrorism, and repressive regimes in the Third World. Many people in the United States are concerned about Third World poverty. Hundreds of voluntary groups are expending substantial resources to help Third World people in need. But in contrast, their national government leads a very small minority of industrialized countries in the United Nations which refuses to negotiate seriously on Third World demands for a New International Economic Order. The prime issue is not aid, but desire for change in patterns of trade, investment, and technology transfer that keep the Third World on the bottom of the global division of labor. Nevertheless, most citizens, and most of the media as well, still treat North-South issues as fundamentally a demand by the South for more aid. They seem unaware that there is an historic struggle now in progress in which the South, now that it has acquired "political" self-determination, is struggling to get economic self-determination, without which their newly won political independence is a hollow shell. Very significantly, they are trying to use peaceful procedures largely designed by the West for this purpose—the United Nations. Why do the people and the media in the United States neglect and not understand these North-South issues?

Fourth, the United States Government now frequently withholds or threatens to withhold legally binding financial support for United Nations agencies, and threatens withdrawal from these agencies when decisions are taken with which the U.S. Government disapproves. This bizarre behavior is widely applauded in the United States, by media and citizens, and rarely is challenged. Yet it undermines the legal foundations of the United Nations. No other member has employed this tactic so frequently or blatantly. In contrast, if an exceedingly wealthy member of a city council in the United States were to threaten nonpayment of taxes or secession of his estate from the town, the population would most certainly rise up in scathing disapproval. Why do these same citizens not object to the behavior of their national government in the ILO, UNESCO, the IAEA, and the United Nations proper?

Related to this puzzling behavior is the widespread belief in the United States that the U.S. Government makes excessive financial contributions to the United Nations. This is likely a result of the fact that the United States is the wealthiest country in the world and pays the largest percentage of the budget—twenty-five percent. But few know, including the media, that the U.S. ranks about fiftieth in contributions as a percentage of GNP. Likewise, few know that over half of U.S. contributions are voluntary, for programs which the U.S. Government chooses because it deems them to be in its interest. This produces an astounding anamoly: people who say they believe in an international society based on law and peace very grudgingly spend four dollars per capita on the United Nations system and much more readily spend $500 per capita on weapons. How can they be so miserly in financial support for a global organization largely based on Western political values and at the same time so thoughtlessly acquiesce in the construction of nuclear bombs having 700 times the destructive power of the bomb dropped in Hiroshima?

The point is not that all people believing in world peace through law and justice would automatically be expected to support the new Law of the Sea Treaty, the human rights covenants, global negotiations on a New International Economic Order, and increased financial support of the United Nations. These are frontier issues in a period of extensive and complicated changes in the world systems. Devising policies on these issues in a manner that would support peace and justice is no simple matter. But it is difficult to understand why these issues are not the subject of widespread public attention and debate, and why most people do not even perceive them as present. All have a direct bearing on the possibilities for peace and justice in the world and, indeed, on the likelihood of the survival of our civilization itself. They are, in fact, strategies for acquiring *collective security* in the broadest sense, for humanity. Why, then, such ignorance and disinterest? Why are a few governmental officials making and carrying out policies on these issues without public cognizance or concern? Why such great public and media silence?

As a professor of international relations I have for many years tried to understand the reasons for the puzzling ignorance of the American public about world affairs and have long been distressed at how few college and university students received adequate education about the world. In the late 1960s, after more than a decade of research and teaching in the United Nations, I became astounded at the widespread lack of knowledge about the UN system, even among people with a college education, including most of my academic colleagues. Is it because, as a continental nation, most of our citizens are distant from borders and from centers of international activity? Perhaps. But why do traditions of citizen disinterest and ignorance about world affairs persist in an age of obvious interdependence, in an age of potential nuclear annihilation? What kind of programs can help people in the United States overcome illusions of detachment, only temporarily interrupted when dramatic events demand supreme sacrifice, as in 1915, 1941, 1950, and the late 1960s?

I began to ponder this question seriously in May 1971 as I stood arm in arm with faculty confronted by a crowd threatening to burn down a university building with torches. As the crowd charged, I wondered: Why have people waited so long to find out what has been going on in Vietnam? Why have they waited so long to act? Why do they lash out here when those responsible for the policies are elsewhere?

In the decade since that night of the torches, I have spent much of my life trying to answer these and related questions by moving the focus of my research from the United Nations to local communities (particularly Columbus, Ohio).[1] The reorientation has proved instructive. It has led me to conclude that the weakest element in the emerging global polity—which today includes, of course, the growing numbers of individuals and groups who fear the nuclear arms race to be out of control—is not in global institutions, as inadequate as they may be, but in organization for participation in world affairs at the local level. This is reflected, ironically, in the practices and outlooks of international education, globally connected voluntary associations, internationally oriented nongovermental organizations, and "cosmopolitans" in local communities. Each of these elements contribute to the lack of grassroots competence to participate effectively in world affairs. Each thus hamper efforts to overcome public apathy in relation to such major human struggles as the nuclear freeze and related movements. And each therefore must be reconceptualized and transformed if the emerging global polity is going to ensure the public interest and participation in world affairs upon which true collective security in the nuclear age absolutely depends.

RESTRAINTS ON INTERNATIONAL PARTICIPATION

International Education

A problem with international affairs education and research is that it has tended to wall people off from the world in three ways. First, it has focused almost exclusively on the activities and policies of distant decisionmakers who operate out of those places where there are stars on world maps—national capitals. Second, primarily concerned with the conflicts of the big powers, it has ignored the extensive international involvements of consumers, workers, farmers, members of ethnic and religious groups, and other ordinary people in cities, towns, and countryside, and also the extensive international relations of local institutions, such as banks, corporations, universities, churches, and military bases. Finally, it teaches about other parts of the world as distant and strange cultures, far from local cities, towns, and countryside, even while local linkages to these faraway places are extensive, through banks, corporations, universities, religious groups, military bases, and ethnic communities. This style of education creates illusions of detachment from the world; it creates a *perceptual gap*. Most people believe that activities that are called world affairs or international relations or foreign policy happen "out there" somewhere—beyond their city or town, beyond their state or province. They know that "it is an interdependent world" because everyone says it is. And they sense that world systems affect prices and employment, and that nuclear bombs may come out of the sky someday. But they don't have knowledge of how these world processes affect them because things that really count happen "out there"—in Washington, Moscow, Brussels, Peking, and so forth.

As a result of this perceptual gap, people develop a *peripheral mentality*. Despite the fact that their lives are intertwined with world processes—as workers, as consumers, as members of world religions and ethnic groups, as potential draftees, as potential victims of nuclear weapons—they feel distant from the world. This was dramatically documented when we asked a man on a streetcorner in Columbus, Ohio: "In what ways is Columbus connected with the world?" He replied: "I don't think it is connected anywhere." Yet he was in the shadow of a bank with satellite linkages around the world, near a state office building that housed the state office of international trade with branches in Brussels, Dusseldorf, and Tokyo. He also was near the world headquarters of a multinational corporation with plants in some thirty countries and branches in more than a hundred. He was within a few miles of a Defense Department supply base that ships military supplies around the world. And he was within a few miles of an Air Force base that was then rotating bomber crews to Vietnam.

Intimately associated with the perceptual gap is a *participatory gap*. Whereas the perceptual gap proceeds from traditions in teaching and research, and from images of the world presented by the media, the participatory gap is a consequence of traditions of the nation-state system that dictate that a small elite in each national capital will take care of "foreign affairs." This is true worldwide, whether the country is large or small, authoritarian or democratic. Foreign policy, it is said, is difficult and complex and requires knowledge and information that only a few can possess. A small elite are believed to be uniquely—and exclusively—competent to divine the "national interest," and as a result "public education" on foreign policy has consisted largely of programs for passing "down" to the people definitions of the "national interest" and policies that it is said will fulfill these interests.

Finally, the participatory gap produces a *myth of incompetence*, which asserts not only that people don't know enough about world affairs to participate in foreign policymaking, but also that they cannot learn. This contributes to their disinterest in learning about world affairs. Why learn if it is impossible to participate? And, of course, people also are deprived of the continual learning that comes from participation. Meanwhile, a small elite does participate and does learn how to fulfill *their* interests—which they label the "national interest."

In sum, international affairs education fosters a perceptual gap which in turn produces a peripheral mentality, hence a participatory gap, and almost inevitably, therefore, a myth of incompetence. Accepting myths about their own incompetence and feeling that they live in the periphery "far away from where things really happen," most people see it as unthinkable that they can or should play a part in the foreign policymaking of their national government. This disempowerment, which we may call *marginalization*, becomes a self-fulfilling prophecy that also is accepted by the media and by educators in our schools, colleges, and universities. It is a phenomenon that seriously—negatively—affects the peace movement as well as other globally oriented initiatives.

Globally Connected Voluntary Associations

But this is only the tip of the iceberg because people are marginalized not only by educators and the media but also by the very organizations whose purpose it is to offer avenues for public participation in issues of public policy—voluntary associations. These associations, e.g., church denominations, labor unions, fraternal groups, and professional associations, tend to be organized in the image of the nation-state, and are as distant from their rank and file as the U.S. Secretary of State. As with national governments, their "foreign affairs" generally are run in a national headquarters by a small elite who tend to believe that their memberships are and always will remain incompetent relative to international issues. Generally this elite takes part in the international nongovernmental organization (INGO) through which most national associations extend their interests and values worldwide—as in international labor unions, worldwide religious organizations, etc; but members of local groups rarely hear of these activities and generally don't even know of the existence of the international counterparts to their local organizations. The international union and the world church body are as distant from the rank and file as is that array of UN agencies such as ECOSOC, UNESCO, and UNICEF whose initials confuse the average citizen.

Because international concerns tend to be more exclusively handled by the national office than are other concerns, the international expertise of national voluntary associations tends to be concentrated there too. It is unusual to find a sub-unit specializing in international affairs in the state or regional offices of these associations, and because there is a tendency for their national offices to be congregated in a few cities the nongovernmental professional specialists in international affairs are concentrated in these cities as well—particularly Washington and New York. Aided and abetted by the government and the media, this produces a brain drain of international specialists—who are trained in colleges and universities throughout the country—to a few centers of international activity, thereby depriving local associations, and communities, of easy access to them. Also, because international specialists in the voluntary associations, the government, and the media are congregated in a few cities, these cities become the places where things international *appear* to happen. Here is where the foreign policy agendas are created, and these are the activities on which the media fix their attention.

This social structure, through which U.S. society relates to and knows about the world, places great limits on the degree to which education alone can overcome the marginalization of the public from world affairs. Even that small minority in local communities who receive formal education in world affairs find few opportunities for direct local involvement in international issues in ways that can motivate continued learning and long-term participation. That even smaller minority that aspires to professional careers in world affairs must leave their local community in order to find employment—whether it be in voluntary associations, the government, or the media. The social structure this creates—the centralization of professional competence in world affairs— marginalizes the rest of the society from world affairs decisionmaking.

Furthermore, this social structure produces barriers between people working on social issues locally and people working on the same issues internationally. For example, people working for human rights locally tend to know very little about efforts to guarantee human rights worldwide, through multilateral institutions and conventions. People involved in local environmental issues, including air and water pollutants that enter world ecological systems, also are uninformed about efforts to develop worldwide programs and institutions. And the same is true of people challenging multinational corporations; they are not aware that their concerns are identical to certain key issues in the Third World demand for a New International Economic Order.

In sum, there is a tendency for local activists on social issues to be cognizant of state (province) and national organizations and networks relevant to their concerns, but unaware of organizations and networks that transcend the borders of their nation. Instead, there is a division of labor by which people in national offices, located in centers through which external relations are controlled, tend exclusively to handle these so-called "foreign policy issues," and this prevents or tends to prevent the mobilization of grassroots movements for social change on the international dimensions of issues on which local attention is focused. This is a large reason why local human rights and civil rights groups are silent on ratification of the human rights covenants, and why local groups working for economic justice seem to be wholly oblivious to the unwillingness of their national government to negotiate with the Third World on New International Economic Order issues. The same is true in the field of arms control and disarmament.

Internationally Oriented Local Voluntary Associations

There are, of course, people in all communities who are deeply interested and active in local voluntary associations having an international emphasis. Important are educational activities (such as world affairs councils and UN Associations), high school and adult exchange programs, organizations directly and indirectly helping people in need in other countries, and organizations assisting with local resettlement of refugees. But the agendas of these associations are strongly influenced by the centralized social structure for involvement of the society in the world, and again local leaders defer to leaders in national offices. Also, local people who are actively involved in world affairs generally tend to defer to Washington and New York foreign policy establishments on foreign policy issues deemed important by these establishments. Accordingly, local people fulfill their international interests by involvement in an array of international activities that are deemed appropriate for citizens with international concerns: education, exchange, foreign assistance, refugee relief and settlement, and the like. Indeed, the U.S. Department of State, the Agency for International Development, and the U.S. Information Agency have for years had modest programs devoted to stimulating and channeling these kinds of activities in ways that are supportive of governmental foreign policy.

Thus, because they tend to deal with the consequences of national government foreign policies rather than to engage in activities that might change these policies, even those local people highly active in international activities are substantially marginalized from participation in the foreign policy decisionmaking of their national government. For example, in response to the fact that national government policies often generate conflict that threatens violence, voluntary associations respond by participation in exchange programs so as to diminish hostility and decrease the likelihood of violence. To offer another example, one might expect that many people active in nongovernmental organizations that are engaged in Third World assistance might also be actively engaged in efforts to overcome U.S. Government unwillingness to participate in global negotiations on New International Economic Order issues. But most of these people are only engaged in aid and relief activity that deals with the consequence of the existing international economic order, and not at all involved in efforts to change this order. And to offer still another example, those involved in refugee relief and settlement are rarely involved in efforts to change the policies that create the need for people to flee their countries—policies that arm authoritarian regimes and that support military responses (rather than change and negotiation) to demands by Third World people for economic and social justice.

The point here is *not* that the traditional tasks of local people active in international activity are unworthy or unimportant. Rather, we are emphasizing that the tasks traditionally allotted to local people tend to deal with the consequences of national foreign policies rather than with formulation of the policies themselves. In dealing with consequences (i.e., suspicion and mistrust among peoples, poverty and malnutrition, homelessness, etc.), local people tend not to be involved in that kind of participatory learning that would deepen their understanding of the world structures and systems that create these conditions. Consistent with this division of labor between national officials and local citizens is a widespread tendency of involved local people to defer to national government officials on major foreign policy decisions. Although most of these local people have advanced education and while many have had significant international experiences through travel, they tend to believe that they are incompetent to deal with what they discern to be really "important" foreign policy issues. A classic example is military policy, including arms control and disarmament policy.

Cosmopolitans in Local Communities

We turn now to the "cosmopolitans," those people who reside in numerous local communities but who have considerable influence in world systems through their positions in transnational corporations (TNCs) or knowledge production and dissemination. They are to be found in the headquarters and branches of corporations and in universities and research institutes throughout the country; and they deserve the label "cosmopolitan" because they are more a part of world systems than of their local communities. Corporation officials control world systems of mining, production, communication, shipping, finance, and accounting. They circle the globe frequently and have penetrating understanding of world systems that affect or might attempt to exercise control over their activities. Those involved in world knowledge systems receive information from, and disseminate information to, colleagues in several continents and meet with them in small groups and world conferences around the world. They often travel to such world system megacenters as New York, Washington, London, and Brussels to share their knowledge with the powerful and to appeal for funds for continued support of their work. Because of jet engines and satellite communication it is increasingly possible for individuals to play influential roles in world systems from many places.

These cosmopolitans are in some respects dramatic exceptions to the marginalization of local people from effective participation in world affairs. After all, they do participate significantly from many places throughout the country. Yet, in another sense, they offer dramatic insight into the process of marginalization. For the most part, local people have little knowledge about the global ventures of cosmopolitans in their midst, and, since these activities are largely unperceived locally, local people miss opportunities to learn, through vivid firsthand experience, how world systems work, how their community is affected by them, and how they in turn affect local people elsewhere in distant places. Also, they miss opportunities to learn about possible ways in which they, in cooperation with local citizens, might affect world systems by exercising local control over these activities. While these international specialists, unlike those lost to the brain drain, do not physically move their residences to centers where foreign affairs for the society are controlled, they tend not to apply and share their knowledge in ways that shed local enlightenment beyond their own institutions. Rather, their identity is with colleagues in the world systems in which they operate and with the needs of powerful figures in centers from which the external relations of their society are controlled. Thus, they too play a part in marginalizing most local people from world affairs decision-making.

In the aggregate, cosmopolitans are very influential in shaping the influence of United States society on the world, through world systems in agribusiness, food processing, mineral exploitation, manufacturing of consumer goods, computers, banking, print media, films, TV programs, textbooks, recordings, manufacturing technology, and the like. The policies of these cosmopolitans are naturally dictated by their desire for profits, for overpowering their competitors, for creating and maintaining jobs for themselves and their colleagues and employees, and for seeking out and overcoming challenges in ever new parts of the world. However, although in the aggregate they have tremendous influence on the role United States society plays in the world, and on the condition of humankind, their decisions are not for the most part made with these consequences in mind. This does not mean that they are not responsive to the foreign policy needs of their country, to the needs of other countries, or to needs expressed in global problems. They do respond to demands for food, for housing, for clothing, for medicine, for educational materials, for pollution control devices, and for arms. They may even advertise that they are helping Third World development, feeding the hungry of the world, cleaning up the atmosphere and water, curing disease, and ensuring national security. But it is very important to understand that these policies are not necessarily the most effective ways in achieving these ends, or even effective at all. This is because their basic end is to market a product or service as widely as possible rather than to find the most effective means for achieving the advertised goal. For example, food may be exported to areas with food shortages, thereby undermining local markets and creating greater food shortages over the long run. Or, consumer goods for an urban Third World elite may be produced by using scarce foreign exchange, local capital, and trained people that are more desperately needed in rural areas.

The net effect, thus, is that powerful institutions in the United States have tremendous impact on world systems, and thereby on many individuals, communities, and institutions around the world, but that the intellectual skills of these cosmopolitans are trained on the employment of means rather than on a searching concern for long-term solutions to problems. The means may be new missiles that contribute to arms races, tanks that strengthen authoritarian rulers, wheat or processed foods that make local people dependent on imported food, textbooks, films, or TV programs that undermine local culture. The result is that a substantial portion of the influence of U.S. society on the world is produced without serious concern for the kind of world it is creating over the long term.

The consequences of this projection of means is perhaps most dramatically portrayed in arms production and sales. Between one-third and one-half the research and development activity in the United States is devoted to research and development for military purposes. For most of the scientists and technicians involved, this activity is basically a means for applying their talents, maintaining and expanding their research institutions and departments, and acquiring a livelihood. In the same way, local workers, local government officials, and local businesses support such projects as the B-1 Bomber because they bring contracts to local factories. For those involved in the manufacturing of weapons, as well as those involved in R&D, rarely is the policy behind weapons development a matter of prime concern. Yoshikazu Sakomoto insightfully comments on how weapons production in the United States has extended beyond the personal rewards of scientists, management, and workers directly involved to a means for maintaining the U.S. position in the world economy:

Increasingly it is argued that the United States must continue to be the leader in the development and manufacture of ultra-modern weapons in order that she may maintain her competitiveness in the export market and improve her balance of payments. It is pointed out, in particularly that since the main export market for arms is the Middle East, they constitute ideal collateral export goods for securing the supply of oil as a source of energy. This shift is occurring parallel to a decline of the dominant position of the United States in the international economy. Under these circumstances, since it can be argued that the securing of the supply of oil would benefit the *entire* nation, military-industrial complex is no longer viewed, as in Eisenhower's case, as an exclusive group which is posing a threat to the people, but is instead pictured to be bringing *benefits* to the people.[2]

Thus, in the name of improving the balance of payments, the United States stimulates arms races and militarization around the world.

In sum, while local cosmopolitans do control global systems, for the most part their primary ends are the selling of their products and services; and with the masses essentially marginalized from participation in foreign policymaking, even local people who are internationally active in educational, exchange, and aid activities, there is little grassroots influence brought to bear upon issues of high State policy. Nowhere is this more evident than in relation to the nuclear arms race over the last thirty to forty years.

CURRENT EFFORTS TO OVERCOME MARGINALIZATION

Of course, there are groups attempting to break through the restraints posed by the prevailing social structure for external relations and to mobilize grassroots participation in world affairs. One example is Amnesty International, in which local chapters work for the release of prisoners of conscience in other countries.

There also are numerous examples of efforts to influence the worldwide activities of multinational corporations. INFACT, built upon a grassroots boycott of Nestle products, has waged an heroic campaign to get the corporation to subscribe to a code for marketing infant formula, particularly in the Third World; and they deserve substantial credit, along with numerous allied organizations, for the code for marketing infant formula passed by the World Health Organization—with only one dissenting vote (the United States). Similarly, a campaign against apartheid has targeted meetings of stockholders of multinational corporations doing business in South Africa, and also local banks, churches, and universities with South African investments. Perhaps influenced by local government resolutions against the Vietnam war, the movement has stimulated the introduction of anti-apartheid legislation in fifteen state legislatures and seventeen cities and counties. Generally this legislation is directed toward requiring government funds (usually pension funds) investing in corporations doing business in South Africa to divest of these investments.[3]

Presently there is a remarkable expansion of organizations, with substantial grassroots strength, working on arms control and disarmament issues. Older organizations such as the Women's International League for Peace and Freedom and SANE have been joined by a great number of new organizations, such as the Nuclear Weapons Freeze Campaign, Peace-Pac for the Prevention of Nuclear War, the National Mobilization for Survival, and many others. There also is an exciting outreach to occupational and professional groups through organizations such as the Physicians for Social Responsibility, the Union of Concerned Scientists, The Lawyers Committee on Nuclear Policy, Musicians Against Nuclear War, Student Teachers to Prevent Nuclear War, and even Ranchers for Peace. Also significant is the fact that organizations traditionally focused on domestic issues have joined the movement to control nuclear weapons, such as Common Cause's Campaign to End the Nuclear Arms Race. Betty Bumpers, after initial success in Arkansas, has organized Peace

Links (Women Against Nuclear War) on a national basis, working largely through mainstream local groups such as garden clubs.

This flurry of activity, apparently largely stimulated by fear created by President Reagan's arms buildup and bellicose statements to the Soviets, has been encouraging to those concerned about the dangers of nuclear war. But a question on the lips of many is: "Can the movement be expanded and sustained long enough to bring about fundamental changes in government policy and in the economic and political processes that support arms buildups and produce arms races?"

Any answer to this question must be very speculative. A useful answer requires an assessment not only of factors limiting progress of the movement and factors facilitating it; it also requires creative suggestions that can enhance possibilities for growth and eventual success.

On the positive side is evidence of considerable grassroots concern for arms issues, as revealed by the November 1982 referenda in the United States on a proposed bilateral freeze on the testing, production, and deployment of nuclear weapons by the United States and the Soviet Union. Also positive has been the ability of the free campaign to create an agenda on which organizations with a diversity of views can agree. And very significant, too, has been the mobilization of concern beyond the small group of peace organizations that often have talked only to themselves. Involvement of organizations such as Common Cause and participation of numerous professional and occupational associations is highly significant. Whether or not these organizations are able to keep arms issues on their agenda will be a significant indicator of whether a sustained movement is taking place.

On the negative side are indications that support for the freeze movement and the flurry of new organizational efforts on arms issues are responding primarily to fear generated by President Reagan. This fear may dissipate as he responds by engaging in arms negotiations and clothes his policies in peace symbols, such as labeling the MX missile the "Peacekeeper." As fear subsides, things will return to "normal" wherein foreign and military policy is left in the hands of the President and the marginalization of most of the people from policymaking will continue. This negative judgment is based on the assumption that two requirements must be met to achieve the sustained public participation that would alter excessive dependence on arms as means for achieving foreign policy goals. First, there must be widespread possibilities for citizens to learn about and express their concerns about arms issues, such that it comes to be widely accepted that "the people" are competent to make judgments on these issues. This must include substantial participation in many local communities. Second, these possibilities for participatory learning must include significant foreign policy issues other than arms issues, such as the new international economic order, the law of the sea, human rights, and so forth. This is based on the belief that concern for arms policy is largely based on fear and that a foreign policy not based on fear will require widespread citizen competence to understand and support positive efforts to build a world of peace and justice. It is ironic that fear should play such a prominent part in the foreign policy of the most powerful country in the world. Fear on the part of the national government has produced excessive reliance on weapons as an instrument of foreign policy. This emphasis has in turn produced fear on the part of the people that government policy may lead to their incineration. But the public is not widely involved in issues which offer positive possibilities for shaping a world responsive to human needs.

BUILDING LOCAL STRUCTURES
FOR SUSTAINED GRASSROOTS PARTICIPATION

Our analysis suggests that sustained grassroots participation requires diminution of the control of a few centers over external relations through the development of organized competence for participation in world affairs in hundreds, even thousands, of local communities. This demands strong local organizations and traditions that support lifelong participatory learning about world affairs for substantial numbers of people in many local communities. Without this kind of strong local base, efforts to mobilize public concern for world affairs issues, including arms control and disarmament issues, will continue to be episodic. They will not have the staying power required to challenge the military-industrial-technological-labor-academic-managerial-political complex that presently dominates the external relations of the United States. And they will not have an indispensible resource for challenging this powerful complex, namely, multitudes of people with widening knowledge about their involvement in the networks of humanity and growing capacity to activate their values and interests in these networks.

It is obvious that overcoming centuries-old traditions for dealing with world affairs will be no easy task. In fact, we are suggesting nothing less than a reconstruction of those social structures that link together the diverse polities that make up humanity. Building on our earlier analysis, we conclude that sustained participation in world affairs issues in any local community would be strengthened by five kinds of activity: (1) international education that informs citizens on the international involvements of their daily lives and on the international involvements of their own community; (2) putting international issues on the agendas of state and local units of voluntary associations, such as labor and churches; (3) participation in policymaking on major international issues by local people active in nongovernmental organizations with an international emphasis; (4) involving local issue groups, such as environmental, civil rights, consumer, senior citizens, and women's groups in the international dimension of these issues; and (5) making local cosmopolitans more visible to local communities and extending local influence over their activities. Let us consider each in sequence.

1. International education that informs citizens of their personal international involvements, and those of organizations in their community, is the first step in eroding the false perceptual gap between individuals and the world systems that have so much influence on their lives. In this approach, elementary school instruction in world affairs would begin with the world relations of local individuals and institutions. When sustained through middle school, high school, college, and in nonschool settings, this kind of education converts a local community and region into a laboratory for learning about world systems in banking, trade, health, military, agriculture, manufacturing, communications, and a host of voluntary activities such as scouting, service groups, churches, sports, and the like. Concrete examples drawn from the local community make things concrete and immediate that otherwise seem abstract and apparently irrelevant.[4]

2. Putting international issues on the agendas of state and local units of voluntary associations, such as churches and labor unions, does not mean, of course, only those issues that have been identified as "important" by the national office. As local communities grow in their competence to perceive and understand their specific links to the world, issues that are locally important will be identified. There are obvious examples that already are highly visible, such as the impact of imported cars and steel on local unemployment, as well as the impact of grain exports on local farm income. Presently these tend not to become issues until local unemployment or prices have dramatic negative impact on local people, and this means, then, that it usually is too late for those most directly involved to deal with the issues. Another example would be numerous efforts to convert local manufacturing plants building weapons to plants that would build goods more responsive to human needs and that would thereby employ even more workers. But up to now, conversion proposals have not engendered much local support and defense spending still draws widespread support of labor, despite the fact that it tends not to create as many jobs as alternative kinds of employment.

3. Involving people active in internationally oriented local voluntary associations in international issues would seem to flow naturally out of their involvement in international educational, refugee, aid, and exchange activity. They would be encouraged to deepen their understanding of the world systems in which these activities are enmeshed, as with the link between hunger and poverty, and the connection between poverty and world economic processes. The need for this kind of education has already been identified by some organizations, as revealed in the new development education projects of economic aid programs such as CARE and CROP/Church World Service. But no effort has been made to break down the division of labor whereby the local "internationals" engage in activities that deal with the symptoms of problems created by States and world systems while it is left to the national governments and a relatively small group of foreign policy elites to set policies that deal with the underlying causes.

4. Involving local issue groups, such as environmental, civil rights, consumer, senior citizens, and women's groups in the international dimension of these issues would require breaking down the territorial boundaries that limit the perspective of most local activists. Some of these groups are local units of national associations that would be included in Activity 2 above, but many groups that have sprung up in local communities are locally based responses to local problems. Most seem to recognize the necessity of networking on a local community, regional, or even a national basis. And some recognize that the problems they are addressing flow across national borders. But very few know about transnational organizations dealing with similar problems or have contact with similar movements in other countries. Yet most are attempting to deal with problems that are importantly affected by world systems. Most are attempting to affect the policies of powerful financial, manufacturing, and communications organizations that are international in scope. They would be more effective if they developed strategies, in concert with other groups, that extend to this scope. In so doing, they would help fill a void in public activism on international issues concerned with human rights, political economy, the environment, and, not least, the arms race.

5. Locally resident cosmopolitans are living examples to local people that their communities are not as distant from the world "out there" as they had believed. As local people become more cognizant of their links to the world, the activities of these cosmopolitans will become more visible. As local people grow in understanding of how world systems work, they will aspire to exert influence over them. Locally resident cosmopolitans offer possible channels through which local people can have impact on world systems. Local workers can have influence on employers, stockholders on owners, bank depositors on bank investments, students and citizens on the overseas activities of universities, and so on. As local people attempt to influence local cosmopolitans, the isolation of cosmopolitans from the influence of local interests and values will diminish.

LOCAL COMMUNITIES AS DYNAMIC NODES IN WORLD SYSTEMS

How might these activities be spurred in a specific local community? Indispensible would be local leadership that believes that it is the responsibility of the local community to offer lifelong opportunity for citizen education and participation in world affairs. This belief must be shared by some educational leaders at all levels, from kindergarten to senior citizens. Furthermore, education at all levels must be inclusive of the world dimension of local life. This belief must be shared by some leaders in local international associations. They must view their activities not only as service activities but also as important avenues for participatory learning about world affairs. Some leaders in other local voluntary organizations must believe it important that local people learn to cope with the international dimension of labor problems, ecology, human rights, etc. Also sharing this belief must be some cosmopolitans, particularly those in universities and research institutes. They must serve the knowledge needs not only of institutions and leaders in distant centers but also of people and organizations in their own community.

Collaboration among leaders across these vital sectors, perhaps only a few individuals at first, can commence the process of making their community a dynamic node of world systems. We have a vision of how the process might develop. Gradually, concern about world linkages and issues would be found at all educational levels and in many disciplines. Organizations with a great diversity of policy and activity concerns would be involved in world affairs. Local and regional offices of national organizations would have specialized staffs for world affairs. Whatever the policy domain—energy, population, unemployment, civil rights, pollution, consumer affairs, militarism—local people would be cognizant of the impact of world systems on these issues and of the possibilities for working with people in other countries on these issues through both international governmental and nongovernmental organizations. Local media would be much more concerned about world affairs because of increased local interest and increased local activity.

There would be much local debate and controversy over world affairs issues. Foreign policy issues would be very significant in congressional and senatorial campaigns. Schoolboard candidates would debate the adequacy of world affairs education in local schools. Some local consumers, importers, and retailers would argue for trade preferences for Third World products. Workers and management from local firms producing competitive products would argue against them. Most local workers and owners of small business enterprises would argue for more stringent local and UN regulation of transnational corporations, while local owners and managers of bit corporations would likely be against them. Local workers and peace groups would join forces in demanding that military production in local plants be replaced with the production of more labor-intensive products. The city council would debate whether the city office of development should work toward the elimination of all military-related production and bases and declare the city to be an open city immune from bombardment under international law.

Local human rights groups, frustrated with slow Senate progress in ratifying the Covenant on Civil and Political Rights and the Covenant on Economic, Social and Cultural Rights would appeal to local individuals to implement the covenants in accordance with the plea in the preambles of each:

Realizing that the individual, having duties to other individuals and to the community to which he belongs, is under responsibility to strive for the promotion and observance of the rights recognized in the Covenant.

This would lead to cooperation among local civil rights organizations, churches, and unions in a yearly survey of how well the local community is doing in implementing these conventions.

This local approach to human rights eventually would spread to many cities and towns through organizations such as the League of Cities in the United States, and to other countries through "sister city" relations and organizations such as the International Union of Local Authorities. Local frustration with the slow pace of ratification and implementation of the UN human rights covenants eventually would stimulate the drafting of a Declaration of Equitable Relations Among Human Settlements. The convention would emphasize the importance of a "balance of payments" in the world exchanges of human settlements, i.e., a balance for each settlement between values received from, and values exported to, the world. For example, this might influence a settlement to calculate whether its voluntary health assistance to the Third World is adequate "payment" for local doctors trained in the Third World. An optional protocol would declare:

> Whereas it is the fundamental purpose of human settlements to protect and nourish human life, to preserve the cultural achievements of past generations and to support future human growth and achievement, and the hope for the future this requires, we hereby declare: this human settlement will not permit within its boundaries the manufacturing or stationing of weapons of mass destruction or training in their use. This settlement is declared to be an open city immune from bombardment under international law.

National and international unions of cities and local authorities would develop procedures for monitoring the degree to which local settlements were living up to the Declaration on Equitable Relations Among Human Settlements. Particularly relevant in the development of standards, and in the monitoring of their fulfillment, would be UN information systems, conventions, and declarations. Valuable information would come from activities such as Earthwatch (coordinated by the UN Environment Program), WHO health statistics, and UNESCO educational data. Relevant standards would come from sources such as ILO conventions and labor standards and the UN conventions on racism and on women's and children's rights. Examples of relevant normative declarations would be the Charter on the Economic Rights and Duties of States and the Cocoyoc Declaration, particularly its appeal to individual responsibility. The declaration is fearful that individuals involved in "the international power structure" will perpetuate "economic dependence" with centers "exploiting a vast periphery and also our common heritage, the biosphere":

> To those who are the—sometimes unwilling—tools of such designs—scholars, businessmen, police, soldiers and many others—we would say: "refuse to be used for purposes of denying another nation the right to develop itself." To the natural and social scientists, who help design the instruments of oppression we

would say: "The world needs your talents for constructive purposes, to develop new technologies that benefit man and do not harm the environment."[5]

These local applications would not only make UN information sources, standard setting, and normative declarations relevant to local people; they would begin to involve the people of the world in activities that are creating minimum standards for human life on the planet.

Great national, regional, and global congresses of cities and local authorities would be held in which evolving standards for equitable relations among human settlements would be debated. These would sometimes pit giant cities against smaller settlements, industrial cities against nonindustrial settlements, landlocked against coastal, prosperous against poor, etc. Nevertheless, there would be general agreement that important new means were being created to enable humankind to cooperatively address problems encountered by people everywhere—inadequate housing, pollution, crime, unemployment, unrewarding labor, and lack of opportunity for local people to participate in decisionmaking for world systems that shape conditions in local communities. These activities would open up an array of new approaches to security, and as a result collective security would acquire a totally new meaning.

As local communities became dynamic nodes in world systems, the centrality in world systems of national capitals and their institutions would diminish. Their military establishments would decline in importance and would find it increasingly difficult to acquire resources because people would have found alternative means for acquiring security. The ability of national capital institutions to control external relations of each society would diminish because they would no longer monopolize relevant information and local people would no longer defer to their judgment. Where useful functions are performed, their importance would continue, but where not useful they would lose their legitimacy.[6] Local competence and initiative would erode legitimacy based strictly on the dying mythology of the nation-state system. People would tend to find the national capital institutions in the big States least useful—as in Moscow and Washington. Particularly in big countries, local communities able to develop their own approach to the world would find that regional cooperation is more responsive to their needs. Sometimes these regional arrangements would follow old provincial lines. Often they would transcend international borders, as in the U.S.-Mexican border region, several U.S.-Canadian regions, and in the Caribbean basin. These regional arrangements, involving only regions of the United States, would make U.S. participants seem less threatening—to Caribbean countries, to regions in Mexico and to regions in Canada—than are relations with Washington.

Old centers that now exercise substantial control over activities of international nongovernmental organizations (from New York, Washington, London, Paris, Brussels, etc.) also would decline in importance as people from local communities would participate more actively in these organizations. Most likely, completely new criteria for participation and representation would be developed. Rather than the national chapter as the unit of representation, it might become the region or perhaps a certain number of local chapters. These nongovernmental activities would grow in influence as they are able to mobilize grassroots support more successfully.

Appropriate relationships between a multitude of new centers of world concern and participation and the United Nations system would become a much disputed issue. Initially these new centers would bring pressure on their national governments to change their policies in the United Nations to be more reflective of local needs and interests and less responsive to power politics and the preferences of national capital elites. Frustrated at the slow response to their demands, world conferences of local authorities would demand that a second house of the General Assembly be created that would offer opportunity for direct representation of local communities, probably selected by regional conventions. This proposal would be challenged by increasingly influential international nongovernmental organization (INGO) leaders who would criticize the "localist" tendencies of such representation and urge that the proposed second house of the General Assembly be made up instead of representatives of INGOs. More radical critics of the nation-state system would argue that the State basis of UN membership is a fatal flaw that cannot be cured by tinkering. Instead, they would advocate a new world organization in which people are directly represented. INGOs and local communities would be the most mentioned bases of representation in these plans. Some would argue for one or the other, and some would argue for a completely new world assembly that is a combination of the two.

Thus grassroots participation would launch a revolution, in thinking and practice, about relations among the diverse polities of the world and about their participation in a variety of transcending polities for humanity. For the first time: (1) local polities would have a place in visions of polities for humanity; (2) this would make grassroots contributions to these visions possible; and (3) it would also make these visions locally actionable. Initially this burst of creativity and diversity would be confusing and even threatening to that small cosmopolitan elite that has so far monopolized the task of producing "future world orders." But gradually they would come to understand that their monopoly was the main reason why their visions were universally ignored.

CONCLUSION

In conclusion, there may be readers who feel that we have strayed a long way from the essential concerns of this volume: the nuclear arms race, specifically, and the arms race, in general. Accordingly, the three assumptions set forth in the introduction to this essay may bear repeating:

(1) arms have become the centerpiece of U.S. foreign policy because of inability to mobilize support behind other approaches for dealing with world social and economic problems; (2) creative U.S. involvement in efforts to solve world social and economic problems will not become possible unless this involvement is supported by movements with widespread participation and staying power; and (3) the development of such movements requires the creation of new opportunities for sustained grassroots participation in world affairs. We have spelled out in some detail the action implications which attend each of these assumptions. As parting words they might be stated more bluntly: (1) arms races will continue until our actions motivated by fear of incineration are matched by our actions motivated by the desire to overcome widespread social and economic injustice in the world; (2) arms races will continue until our actions toward both justice and peace are pursued on a permanent basis—as a way of life, for decades rather than for a few months or years; and (3) arms races will continue until our actions are directed toward the fulfillment of ever more creative visions of a world of peace and justice—visions that are the collective product of widespread participatory learning.

NOTES

1. This work is reported in Chadwick F. Alger, "'Foreign' Policies of U.S. Publics," *International Studies Quarterly*, Vol. 21, No. 2 (June 1977), 277–318; "People in the Future Global Order," *Alternatives*, Vol. 4 (1978-79), 233–262; "The Impact of Cities on International Systems," in Krishna Kumar, *Bonds Without Bondage: Explorations in Transcultural Interactions* (Hawaii: University of Hawaii Press, 1979); "Creating Participatory Global Cultures," *Alternatives*, Vol. 6 (1981), 575–590; "Participation of Local Communities in Building Future Worlds," in R. Strassoldo and G. Delli Zotti, eds., *Cooperation and Conflict in Border Area* (Milano, Italy: Franco Angeli Editore, 1982).

2. Yoshikazu Sakomoto, "Global Armament Dynamics: A Critical Review," p. 6, no date.

3. Jan Love, "Foreign Policies of State and Local Governments: Anti-Apartheid Divestment Campaigns," International Studies Association 23rd Annual Convention, March 1982, pp. 8, 9.

4. Some examples of the approach suggested that have been developed out of the Columbus in the World project: for elementary school, David C. King and Charlotte C. Anderson, "The United States in the Global Community," in *Windows on the World: The United States* (Boston: Houghton Mifflin, 1976), Unit 4, 143–177; for grades 8–12, Robert W. Woyach, *Making Decisions: Our Global Connection* (Columbus, Ohio: Columbus Council on World Affairs, 1980); for college students, Chadwick F. Alger and David G. Hoovler, *You and Your Community in the World* (Columbus, Ohio: Consortium on International Studies Education, 1978); and for adult discussion groups, *Columbus Great Decisions 1982* (Columbus, Ohio: Mershon Center, Ohio State University, 1982). The last was prepared for Great Decisions groups in Columbus as an addendum to materials produced by the Foreign Policy Association of New York City. This material focuses on local decisions with respect to local manufacture of infant

formula marketed in the Third World and Ohio General Assembly resolutions on a nuclear freeze and South African apartheid.

5. The full Cocoyoc Declaration can be found in *International Organization*, Summer 1975, 893–901.

6. The changing role of national capital institutions that is envisaged also implies simultaneous strengthening of grassroots participation in all public policy issues, not just those most significant for world affairs. For more extended discussion see Chadwick F. Alger, "Reconstruction of Global Polity," in Shri Brahmandji, *Jayaprakash: Man and Thoughts* (New Delhi: Jayaprakash Academy, in press).

45. Obtain the Possible: Demand the Impossible

Robert Jay Lifton and Richard A. Falk

Participation in the surging popular movement of opposition to nuclearism is making many people more hopeful about the future. Yet this new hopefulness is often closely connected to an arousal of fear and anxiety, and is certainly fragile, being vulnerable to disillusionment. The present spirit of the antinuclear movement is captured by W. H. Auden's words:

"We who are about to die demand a miracle." Demanding a miracle is itself an affirmation of life, exhibiting, at the same time, an uplifting clarity about the gravity of the danger.

The miraculous applies to freeing the planet of nuclearism altogether. Such a prospect seems beyond the horizon of what is possible. Complete nuclear disarmament is not really plausible so long as leaders hold a Machiavellian world picture, and perhaps, so long as the organization of political life is based upon grossly unequal sovereign states competing militarily for scarce resources. Common sense illustrates the difficulty of achieving total nuclear disarmament in the world as we know it, even assuming good will on the part of the main governments, which it is misleading to assume either for ourselves or our adversaries. Suppose we imagine a situation in which nuclear disarmament had been agreed upon and implemented, but national sovereignty and the war system remained. It seems inconceivable that a government faced with the prospect of defeat in a major war, yet retaining the knowledge and technology to reconstruct nuclear weaponry would refrain under such conditions. Realizing this prospect, a government would assume that its adversary might try to evade the disarmament agreement at least to the extent of retaining a small hidden stockpile as a hedge against a rearmament race or nuclear blackmail. To prevent this evasion of a disarmament treaty, given the grave consequences at stake, would require a highly reliable system of verification, itself a nonnegotiable barrier to agreement, given the apprehensions associated with sovereignty. But more than this, since the bomb cannot be disinvented and since the technology will become more and more accessible, it must be supposed that any political actor faced with the prospect of defeat would revive at the onset of crisis its nuclear weapons option. When these considerations are understood, it becomes clear that war, in general, not nuclear weapons in isolation, must become the inevitable focus for any serious effort to overcome *nuclearism*. Like the Zen archer, the dedicated antinuclearist must aim above the target to strike the bull's-eye.

To get rid of war, however, requires a new type of world order, including a far stronger sense of human identity to complement and complete the various partial identities of nationalism, religion, race, and ideology. The end of war implies, in effect, the displacement of Machiavellianism by a holistic world picture.

For all these reasons, then, it seems impossible, as matters now stand, to achieve nuclear disarmament, despite its necessity. As long as nuclear weapons remain a central basis of national security, the danger of their use will condition our experience—at times mitigated, at other times, such as the present, magnified. Additionally, reliance on nuclear weapons inevitably concentrates antidemocratic authority in governmental institutions and builds such a strong permanent disposition to engage in ultimate war as to negate the atmosphere and structure of genuine peace. We can never taste real peace again until we find the means to eliminate nuclear weapons altogether.

Yet we need not wait. There are many things we can do to make the world safer and saner, thereby also creating opportunities for more fundamental changes to occur. We can greatly reduce the risks of nuclear war, as well as dramatically reduce the drain upon the world's precious resources. It is possible to foster a political climate in which leaders are induced to take steps, gradual and partial in character, but highly significant in their cumulative effect. The antinuclear movement, while finally demanding the impossible, is tactically focused on attainable goals: freezing the arms race, renouncing first-use options and limited war doctrine, opposing the deployment of specific weapons systems (for example, neutron bomb, Pershing II, cruise missile), establishing nuclear-weapons-free zones (such as the Indian Ocean, the Korean peninsula, Europe), prohibiting all further flight testing of missiles, and underground testing of warheads.

These tactical goals will themselves not be easy to attain. There are powerful, vicious, mystifying, and self-mystifying social forces tied up with the reign of nuclearism. Politicians are surrounded by advisors who contend that whatever danger of nuclear war exists is attributable to their enemy, and preserving "peace" depends on achieving nuclear superiority for oneself. There are, in other words, . . . powerful nuclear illusions that keep the arms race going and oppose by all available means popular demands for minimizing the dangers of nuclear war. Some nuclearists in and close to power centers will surely resort to a mixture of deceit, nominal accommodation, infiltration and provocation, and outright repression before giving way to democratic peace pressures. The antinuclear movement, without losing its enthusiasm, will have to develop a politics of struggle and resistance if it hopes to achieve major results. There is no assured way to get from here to there, even if there is defined in the relatively limited terms of stabilizing the role of nuclear weaponry.

Also, bureaucracies are unfortunately more durable than either politicians or popular movements. Politicians can respond to shifts in mood and might even be persuaded to implement serious antinuclear goals. We see that beginning to happen here and in Western Europe and Japan. It is an impressive tribute to the extraordinary vitality and strength of the antinuclear movement. Yet the roots of militarism are deeply embedded in the huge, implacable structures of governmental bureaucracy and reach out to encompass powerful, privileged sectors of the economy, including parts of the media. If past behavior is any guide, this faceless, durable bastion of nuclearism is certain to organize a variety of responses to the popular movement, perhaps even largely behind the backs of the main politicians, hoping to disillusion, or at least outlast, protest activity. Consider the following: Stalin was repudiated, but Stalinism remained, not exactly as before but essentially a regrouping of the same forces to maintain a basically repressive relationship between the Soviet state and the Soviet people. Bureaucracies are notoriously hard to reform so long as they remain intact.

Since popular movements are difficult to sustain (Americans being particularly prone to quick disillusionment), it is essential that its guiding spirits possess and impart a vision of what needs to be done, and how to do it. There is a special requirement present here, as well. To oppose nuclearism effectively does impose a difficult and special requirement that we connect tactical demands with a commitment to perseverance in pursuit of essential long-range objectives. Either without the other will collapse: the moral passion that gives grassroots politics its edge depends largely on an overall repudiation of nuclearism in any form, while the emphasis on attainable goals builds needed popular confidence that victories over nuclear forces are possible, that ordinary people can mobilize and wield decisive power, and that a path can be eventually found to overcome, once and for all, the nuclear menace.

Most current action within the peace movement is dedicated, whether deliberately or not, to *stabilizing* rather than *eliminating* nulcearism. The goal is to force a shift from certain *adventurist* forms of nuclearism (arms race, counterforce strategy, first-strike options, limited war and war-fighting scenarios) toward some variant of a *defensive* nuclear posture (nuclear weapons are retained, but their role is strictly limited to providing protection against nuclear blackmail and surprise attack by an enemy state).

Recalling the discussion of world pictures, it seems evident that the shift toward a more defensive nuclear posture can be achieved by stages and can partly rely on the methods of politics-as-usual, including the logic and dynamics of the Machiavellian world picture. It is not surprising, then, given the self-destructive dangers of adventurist nuclearism, that many prominent Machiavellian "realists" are beginning to lend their support to popular demands for greater moderation when it comes to nuclear weapons policy. These welcome defections from the upper ranks of policymakers greatly enhance prospects for influencing formal institutional policies. A stifling consensus is replaced by a political process consisting of pressures and counterpressures that reflect the interplay of special interest groups, social forces, and competing images of realism. At the center of dispute is the proper content of national self-interest and security requirements in relation to the various facets of nuclear weapons policy.

Only within the altered climate created by the popular movement do we find elite figures advancing their own proposals for moderation. In the late 1970s militarist forces within and without the governing structure had succeeded in dominating policy with a predictible heightening of East-West tensions and quickening of the arms race. Only the unexpected reactions of public opinion, alarmed about rising nuclear war risks, created a serious possibility of challenging nuclear adventurism at the level of national debate. The tricontinental peace movement now enables even mainstream politicians and journalists to consider openly, and even support, policies designed to move toward more moderate roles for nuclear weapons. At this point it is astonishing to observe even an avowedly militarist president clamoring aboard the arms control bandwagon. It may well turn out to be an optical illusion. Strong grounds for skepticism remain. The Reagan forces could merely be riding out the antinuclear storm, hoping to calm things down enough to go forward with their basic thrust toward nuclear superiority and an interventionary foreign policy. It seems realistic, rather than cynical, to suppose that the current American leadership would like to place the onus of their arms race on Soviet shoulders so as to convey the sense that the United States has tried and failed, and now has no choice but to proceed with a further military buildup. However it may also be possible that the drive to remain in the White House will convince even confirmed cold warriors and superhawks that dramatic progress toward stabilizing nuclearism can alone bring them victory on the domestic scene. Everyone recalls that it was that impeccable anti-Communist, Richard Nixon, who in 1972 turned a conciliatory visit to Red China into a great electoral triumph. Ironies never cease. Now it may be the turn for an ardent militarist like Reagan to deliver the goods on arms control and world peace.

While it is important not to be duped by powerfully entrenched militarist interests, it is also desirable to be receptive to changes by leaders, however opportunistic their motivation. In one sense, the popular movement against nuclearism has achieved substantial success when it rewards peace-minded leadership at the ballot box. In fact, shifting the calculations of politicians is the most hallowed democratic method of reorienting policy and should be respected. Beyond even this kind of healthy pragmatism, however, lies a more genuine possibility of shifting the inner balance of feelings operative among our war-makers. Even the most ardent militarist admits that a nuclear war would be a disaster, and some part of his being must be touched by efforts to minimize these risks.[1] The distinctiveness of the nuclearist menace is that all of us, including even nuclearists and their families, are potential victims in the fullest sense. The kind of benefit that some derive from positions, power, wealth, and influence associated with present patterns of nuclearism would be forever destroyed by the personal tragedy brought about by nuclear war. Conversions among the elite have already taken place, and there must always be a readiness to welcome with open arms those who genuinely renounce nuclearism. In this central sense, the antinuclear movement, despite its destiny of struggle, has no permanent or inevitable enemies.

What blocks many from recognizing their own deeper affinities with the peace forces, aside from their preoccupation with defending special interests, are certain insulating thought-forms that have grown up over the centuries to bolster the militarism of the Machiavellian world picture, despite its growing absurdity as a rational ground for security. I have in mind here particularly the paradoxical idea, enchanting to foreign policy specialists and former national security advisors, that peace is most effectively pursued through preparation for war. This posture toward war and peace enables one to reconcile ethical and survival concerns with the most adventurist forms of nuclearism. As such, it inhibits a recognition of the dangers of the nuclear arms race, allowing at most tactical adjustments in response to political pressure. The contrary position taken by the antinuclear movement is that preparations for war are themselves a cause of war, that arms races have through international history displayed an overall tendency to heighten tensions, produce crises, and lead to wars.

I think it is particularly important to challenge the mental armor of nuclearism at this stage. For this reason, it seems useful to highlight the immorality, illegality, and illegitimacy of nuclear weapons and tactics.[2] Such an emphasis is also consistent with a series of United Nations General Assembly resolutions declaring that "the use or threat of use of nuclear weapons should . . . be prohibited, pending nuclear disarmament."[3] The most effective way to push ahead on this front is through a global insistence on a no-first-use policy pertaining to nuclear weapons, an insistence that earlier might have prevented a nuclear arms race altogether . . . , but even now could contribute greatly to a more stable world.[4] Such a step would make the crucial acknowledgment that these weapons can never be legitimately threatened or used for the ends of state power, however helpful it may seem in a particular set of circumstances. It would be beneficial to have such a declaration of no-first-use solemnized in a formal statement subscribed to by all governments. Part of the appeal of such a no-first-use arrangement is its simplicity: it is equal, easy to negotiate or can consist of unilateral declarations, requires no monitoring or verification, and contributes to overall security. The importance of this step is not only as an official statement of policy but also to persuade governments to abandon the forward or battlefield deployment of nuclear weapons, especially in Western Europe. A government of a superpower is unlikely to make a declaration of this sort in solemn form without adapting its war plans and deployment patterns.

Some Western specialists say that Europe, South Korea, or the Persian Gulf cannot be defended without threatening to respond to conventional attacks with nuclear weapons. There are many reasons to believe that the new conventional weaponry that is becoming available, including the latest in precision guided munitions and antitank technology, can meet defense requirements at current levels, or less, of expenditure. Contrary to the protestations of nuclearists, it is not necessary to militarize further other dimensions of domestic and world politics to compensate for taking this large step toward the stabilization of nuclearism. Note, also, that a no-first-use posture is fully compatible with a wide range of other arms control proposals, including the nuclear weapons freeze, prohibitions on new weapons system and further testing, creation of nuclear-free zones, restraints on conventional weaponry, and a diplomacy of nonalignment for countries formerly allies of one or the other superpower.

Some critics complain that a no-first-use pledge is worthless, consisting of mere words, lacking any provision for sanctions, enforcement, or verification. Its verbal character, they argue, creates a one-sided trap for the more peace-minded states in the world, while placing no obstacle whatsoever in the path of an aggressor government. Here again the reasoning of defenders of the nuclear status quo seems poor. Except for possibly the United States, no other country has the slightest incentive other than in a situation *in extremis* to threaten or use nuclear weapons. If the United States were to adopt a no-first-use posture, it would certainly at the same time alter accordingly its contingency plans and capabilities, while the fear of what a beleaguered country might do if at the edge of survival and in possession of nuclear weapons seems almost irrelevant. Of course, no regime of restraint can promise perfect compliance. All rules of inhibition are susceptible to violation in any situation where political survival is deeply threatened, and yet even here, the situation would be no worse than what exists without the declaration. The importance of no-first-use thinking and practice is to discourage resolving crises by the temptation of recourse to nuclear threats. Even with a no-first-use orientation firmly in place, it will remain dangerous to press hard for military victory in conflicts touching on the vital interests of states that retain nuclear weapons or are closely aligned to such states. The Falklands/Malvinas War of 1982 vividly shows the helplessness of international society as a whole when the "honor" of sovereign states is drawn into question, especially if a military confrontation is popular at home and officials of the adversary governments are eager to distract criticism with an overseas sideshow. This helplessness has resulted in a stream of costly, senseless wars over the course of history, perhaps World War I being the clearest major instance in our century. No rule of conduct can hope to do more in a world of sovereign states than build a framework of inhibition that over time reshapes attitudes and expectations about the role of nuclear weapons, and by such alteration builds new possibilities for further denuclearization.

If moderate postures (that is, as a weaponry of ultimate recourse when total defeat is in prospect) evolve into purely defensive nuclear postures (that is, a weaponry retained only as protection against the nuclearism of others), then a fundamentally different situation would exist. True, even a defensive conception of nuclear weaponry might produce various forms of anxiety about whether the capabilities and intentions of the other side could not mount a successful disarming first strike (thereby destroying the hedge), and such speculation, possibly induced by maliciously false intelligence reports, could, if believed, create renewed pressures to resume the nuclear arms race despite the adoption of declarations of prohibition, freeze arrangements, and a host of other arms control measures. As long as the weaponry continues as an existing part of the security package then the structure of nuclearism, however contained, will cast its long shadow across our lives, posing in some form risks to human survival, impairing democratic relations between state and society, and, very likely, inducing a tensed reliance on non-nuclear militarism to offset the diminishing role of nuclear weaponry in an unchanged global political context. A central source of persisting anxiety will be the forward march of technology, making the weaponry of mass destruction more and more accessible to virtually all governments and discontented groups; the problems of proliferations will remain and jeopardize any international framework based on purely defensive conceptions. Furthermore, so long as the war system persists, a purely defensive posture for nuclear weapons would always be drawn into question whenever a government possessing nuclear weapons was facing the prospect of a major military defeat. Worthy and ambitious as is the shift to a purely defensive posture, it cannot hope to be entirely stable, and yet, as Jonathan Schell tirelessly underscores, the weaponry cannot be disinvented. We again confront here the apparent unresolvable tension between our need to get totally rid of this weaponry and the apparent impossibility of doing so. This tension expresses in clearest form the specific nature of the nuclear trap. History must be reversed, but history, by its nature, is irreversible.

Yet the finality of this formulation may itself be a trap set by ourselves, by our way of thinking. Nuclear weapons may "disappear" when other arrangements render them "irrelevant," when, for instance, the defense of our national boundaries relies no more on military capabilities than does the security of Pennsylvania in its relationship to New Jersey or Ohio. We get a glimpse of this possibility in the mutual relations of Western Europe countries since 1945 or of Canada and the United States in this century.

To overcome nuclearism, as such, requires quite a different sort of action than increasing the rationality and prudence of existing political leaders or of moderating institutional arrangements. It rests on the live possibility of establishing an orientation toward security that is not wedded to militarist strategies of geographical defense. It presupposes, in other words, supplanting the Machiavellian world picture with some version of a holistic world picture. Such a process would automatically transform the role and character of political institutions, eliminating a society's dependence on the existence of an enemy to achieve identity and coherence. A holistic world picture defines group coherence positively by a capacity to satisfy basic human needs of all people without damaging the biosphere or weakening reverence for nature. This holistic alternative is struggling in various ways to emerge in our thought and action, although as yet its influence seems weak and marginal, often expressing itself more in relation to ideas about diet and health than reshaping our sense of the political. It is important for the movement against nuclearism to grasp that realizing its goals is inseperable from the triumph over time of this holistic orientation. At this stage, this understanding may require nothing more substantive than a receptivity to such a possibility and a clarity about the desirability, yet limited horizons, of actions designed to diminish the dangers of nuclearism in its current forms.

There are a few additional orienting comments about action that flow from an acceptance of the long-range necessity for holistic politics.

CONTRA UTOPIANISM

A holistic vision does not imply a blueprint for the future, much less does it imply covert support for the project of world government or for the formation of a superstate; only in the process of gaining ascendency can the holistic world picture evolve appropriate institutional forms, but we can anticipate that they will not be reproductions on a global scale of the sort of governmental arrangements now associated with the sovereign state. Decentralization of power and authority will be paramount, as will efforts to coordinate economic, social, and cultural relations without reliance on bureaucratic oversight. New technologies for dispersed participation in shaping and sharing information may be one of the keys helpful for unlocking the future. Finally, the holistic prospect is not cut off from historical processes of evolution, as is the case with utopias that are posited as fully wrought solutions. We require a politics, as well as an imagery, of transformation.

CONTRA MILITARISM

Militarism is difficult to define clearly. It involves both a state of mind and a set of supportive societal arrangements. The essence of modern militarism is a comprehensive reliance on instruments of violence in the pursuit of national security. Militarism is also tied to technology. A militarist state of mind does far less damage, as a rule, under conditions of primitive technology, although even this direct assertion needs to be qualified. If, as is the case in the nuclear age, the consequences of militarism are catastrophic, then even the unabashed militarist is inhibited to a certain extent. Militarist guidance of foreign policy without any nuclear weaponry on the scene would undoubtedly have already produced World War III by now.

The rejection of militarism is wider than the rejection of nuclearism, but it is integral to it. And, in fact, the rejection of nuclearism without the substantial modification, if not outright rejection, of militarism is, finally, a futile project. Although nuclearism represents something that reaches far beyond the mere application of military technology according to the dictates of the Machiavellian world picture, its incorporation of specific weapons of war proceeded within this traditional framework. It may not be necessary, at least at the outset, to confront militarism with pacifism, but overcoming militarism will eventually depend on the existence of nonviolent alternatives to achieve security for peoples and nations.[5] One important way to dilute militarism is to confine military capabilities and foreign policy to the strict circumstances of *defensive necessity*, as well as to draw distinctions between the defense of governments and of people. Of course, defense is an elastic concept, but my intention is to emphasize a real change of heart that seeks to restrict sharply the role of military weapons of all kinds.

The arrival of a sheriff in a western town during the early part of the last century brought a different kind of order *only* if the expectations about violence changed for most of the inhabitants. Without such a shift the new *forms*, and even *capabilities*, could not enhance security in the community and might indeed have produced a reliance on higher levels of violence on all sides.

Unless antinuclearism evolves in the wider setting of antimilitarism there is conjured up the prospect of a renunciation of the nuclear option combined with a vast buildup of conventional weaponry, a revival of the draft, an enormous peacetime army deployed around the world, thus creating an overall darkening prospect of major wars fought with weaponry of far greater savagery than used in World War II, as well as the persisting prospect of nuclear rearmament. The kind of popular momentum created by antinuclearism would, if it succeeded, also move naturally in an antimilitarist direction, questioning the ethics and viability of interventionary diplomacy and realizing the need to diminish those nonmilitary causes of war related to food and energy supplies, world poverty, and environmental decay.

CONTRA A NARROW AGENDA

There is a view frequently found among antinuclear activists that their concerns can be treated apart from others, arguing that the removal of the danger of nuclear war constitutes the necessary ground that must be achieved first if other social and political challenges are ever to be faced. This insistence on priority, however well conceived, tends to misunderstand the political conditions that must come to exist if an antinuclear movement is to achieve even limited success in both East and West. We need to consider what quality and quantity of social forces must be mobilized to challenge effectively the nuclear national security state in both superpowers. When we do this it becomes obvious, I think, that labor and minority discontent, peace activism by leading church groups, popular demands for liberty and social justice, and attacks on the corruptions and repressiveness of the bloated state create bonds of transnational dimension that can also easily become bearers of anti-militarist and antinuclearist sentiments. The success of Polish Solidarity, as most leaders in the European Nuclear Disarmament movement understood, would strengthen their prospects; its defeat would be de-moralizing and debilitating, in part constituting a reassertion of the primacy of Soviet militarism and an uncertainty about whether a Western-centered movement for peace is not, in the end, self-defeating.

If antinuclearism succeeds in influencing policies of nuclear govern-ments it will be because it prevails through struggle, a struggle that includes the persuasiveness in debate of antinuclear forces. Persuasiveness is an important instrument to mobilize portions of the citizenry and to sow doubts in the nuclearist consensus, but it is by itself not nearly enough. Coalitions must be struck with social forces animated by discontent about the *status quo*. The nuclear national security state has grown into a powerful apparatus of coercion that can be and would be trained upon any opposition movement that threatened its dominion. The more broadly conceived the movement, the harder to break its will and morale.

It is pure illusion to suppose that there exists an apolitical and nonmilitant path to a nuclear-free United States or world. It is a further illusion to suppose that a political path can be discovered that is not beset by obstacles and struggle. Prospects for a nonviolent struggle toward these ends is likely to depend, in large part, on how broadly based and strongly motivated such an oppositional movement can become. In this regard, the particular characteristics of the movement need to be understood by its various segments. On the one side are the present fragments of the American political elite and generally conservative professionals, including doctors, lawyers, and engineers that have formed their own antinuclear pressure groups. On the other side are present more militant groups that oppose nuclearism as part of a wider struggle against the modern state and its injustices. In between are an array of other orientations, including a wide variety of positions emanating from church activism on the nuclear issue. The capacity of the overall movement to grow more powerful and successful will depend greatly on the wisdom of its leaders, especially their ability to regard the diversity and multileveled character of the antinuclear movement as an expression of democratic vitality rather than as an indication of disunity and weakness.

CONTRA SECULAR ABSOLUTISM

Over time the modern state, even in societies proudest of their democratic identity, has adopted absolutist prerogatives and moved steadily in authoritarian directions. Nowhere is this tension between democratic creed and antidemocratic practice more evident than in relation to nuclear weapons diplomacy. The same leaders who insist that the major stake in international conflict is the fate of democratic governance have steadily eroded democratic content in the name of national security.

It is well to recall the early American antipathy to peacetime military establishments of any kind, phrased as opposition to so-called "standing armies." Even Alexander Hamilton, in so many ways an architect of governmental centralism, joined in the then prevalent belief that, as set forth in Federalist Paper No. 8, the standing armies of Europe and their perpetual readiness to engage in war "bear a malignant aspect to liberty and economy" for the country involved.[6] The founders of the American republic believed that advantages of geography and of political ideology would provide the United States with a general circumstance of security without militarism.

A similar disposition underlay, of course, the preoccupation with creating checks on possible abuse of presidential powers. The entire Constitution was drafted in light of the central doctrine of "the separation of powers" and the closely aligned notion of "checks and balance." The founders of our republic sought to avoid, above all else, a re-creation in some new format of royalism and of leaders, who like the kings of old, could claim to rule by divine right. The American idea was to limit presidential authority by combining rules of substance with restraining procedures. Indeed, given the stern religious teachings of early America, including a preoccupation with original sin, the constitutional framework was conceived as a buffer against weakness and evil inherent in the human condition. The requirement that Congress participate in a declaration of war was specifically intended to prevent the president from having the power to commit the country unilaterally to war.

Over time there have been many encroachments on this conception of peacetime governance, a variety of accommodations to practical necessity without any formal adjustments by way of constitutional revisions. The avoidance of standing armies gave way to an expanding permanent military establishment. The Executive Branch claimed various privileges to keep national security information secret. The Congress and the public tolerated, even encouraged, a variety of recourses to armed force without prior declarations of war, American involvement in the Korean and Vietnam wars being the most spectacular instances.

All these tendencies helped to set the stage for the advent of nuclear weaponry that has put a permanent seal of inevitability on the imperial presidency. The nuclear national security state is a new, as yet largely unanalyzed, phenomenon in the long history of political forms. Being constantly ready to commit the nation (and the planet!) to a devastating war of annihilation in a matter of minutes on the basis of possibly incorrect computer-processed information or pathological traits among leaders creates a variety of structural necessities that contradict the spirit and substance of democratic governance: secrecy, lack of accountability, permanent emergency, concentration of authority, peacetime militarism, extensive apparatus of state intelligence and police. No king ever concentrated in his being such absolute authority over human destiny, not just in relation to his own people but for humanity as a whole. War as the sport of presidents has become the ironic, dreadful descriptive circumstance, an outcome brought about by the combined impact of the growth of statism and of the characteristics of the technology of war now available to leaders of the superpowers.

Indeed, nuclearism has caused a cultural, as well as a political and constitutional, breakdown. The unconditional claim by finite, fallible human beings to inflict holocaustal devastation on an unlimited scale for the sake of national interests and on behalf of any particular state is an acute variety of idolatry—treating the limited and conditional as if it were unlimited and unconditional. Our religious leaders have been slow to respond, complacent in their own secularism, and have tended to acquiesce in whatever powers the state claims for itself beneath the banner of national security. An encouraging recent sign is a dramatic weakening of deference to secular absolutism within the religious community when it comes to nuclear weapons policy. An increasing number of spiritual leaders with an array of denominational backgrounds are speaking out, to date mainly on the pernicious nature of nuclear weapons but also in strong support of individuals who stand apart from the state in a posture of resistance.

The erosion of democracy, while serious, is by no means final. In fact, if popular forces succeed in altering nuclear weapons policy it will have an overall revitalizing effect on our entire political process. Thomas

Jefferson, always dubious about the capacity of constitutional arrangements ("a mere thing of wax"), put his trust for the maintenance of democratic vitality in "an energetic citizenry." One of the features of the nuclear national security state is to demobilize the citizenry as totally as possible on the most crucial questions facing the society. Only an energetic citizenry can hope to modify the political climate sufficiently to create space for new leadership and different directions of official policy. To combat nuclear militarism in the United States certainly requires an even more energetic citizenry reinforced by a cultural and religiously active appreciation that the authority of the state has degenerated into a new and acute species of idolatry.

At this time political analysts are in a position comparable to that of seismic specialists called upon to predict the intensity and date of an expected earthquake. There are many warning tremors. The political fault lines are so wide and deep that when it comes, the eruption could shake the strongest institutional foundations, but we cannot be sure whether this shattering of our order will come sooner or later, or what precise form it will take.

On a more concrete level, a distinction can be drawn between proximate goals that can be stated quite concretely and more distant goals that will have to be specified as they are approached. The essence of an antinuclearist orientation, given the realities of the world as we know it, involves a renunciation of the nuclear option combined with the retention of a limited number of nuclear weapons as an instrument of ultimate resort, confined in its potential role to a nuclear retaliation to a nuclear attack. The ethics and politics of this renunciation should help center a popular movement in the United States and would, I feel confident, find a resonant response elsewhere, including the Soviet Union. Such an expectation is not based on any perception of untapped altruistic energies being set loose. Quite the contrary. Selfishness would lead other countries to join with us in this process of nuclear renunciation, partly because it is the United States alone that has made such a strong investment over the years in maintaining the nuclear option against all challengers. I would not want to pretend that this dynamic of partial renunciation will come about easily. Its realization would represent a profound reversal of field with respect to the lineaments of security in the nuclear age.

If antinuclear sentiments take command, even more ambitious goals would then seem attainable: namely a determined assault on "the war system" in its totality, including national and transnational subsystems of special privilege, exploitation, and repression. In effect, the pursuit of humane governance is a goal on all levels of social organization from the family to the world. Such an animating vision may never be fully attainable, but its pursuit seems implicit in any serious engagement to work toward liberating our planet and our species from the nuclear curse that has been laid so heavily upon it.

This great struggle for global transformation encompasses normal politics, but it is also far broader than any strictly political experience, resembling more the emergence of a new religion or civilization on a global scale than a change, however radical, in the personnel or orientation of political leaders. In essence, as the transformation proceeds, the ground of politics will shift, and by shifting, will cause turmoil and confusion as new tendencies grow stronger, while the old structures, despite being undermined, remain in place and may through the desperate efforts of their stalwarts, embark on even more aggressive and adventurist paths. The avoidance of a crash landing of the old order is obviously a high priority under these circumstances. One form of constructive politics in such a setting are forms of thought and action that incorporate positive aspects of the past rather than insisting on its utter repudiation or a complete break. The pain of transition could be considerably eased by regarding attitudes of reconciliation as a cardinal virtue alongside those of perseverance and commitment.

Some words by James Douglass, theologian and antinuclear activist, provide a concluding vector: "a way of stopping the world in an end-time of global violence is, above all, a way not of speculation but of practice—a way of living and acting out a day-to-day personal and communal struggle for a liberating, transforming truth for humanity."[7] There are many paths that ascend the mountain, but we dare not any longer evade the challenge of the long, difficult climb. The vision from the peak will surely be a holistic panorama. And yet, there is no real suspense. In the most profound sense the holistic world picture is available to all of us now; we can simply cease to be Machiavellians whenever we choose. Each individual withdrawal of energy and consent strengthens collective capacities to fashion life-sustaining alternatives for the society as a whole. If only we are alert, all of us have this extraordinary vitalizing opportunity to create together a postnuclear history.

NOTES

1. There is a deep self-mystification that interferes with such awareness. Militarists continue to believe that the path to peace is to deter the other side by being even stronger and that the path to war is to tempt enemies to commit aggression. This obsolete mind-set, which has elements of insight, needs to be understood, analyzed, and discredited as effectively as possible. As long as it dominates the thinking and feeling of policymakers and opinion-shapers, it will allow those in power to oppose peace forces in good faith. For an important attempt along these lines see Richard J. Barnet, *Real Security: Restoring American Power in a Dangerous Decade* (New York: Simon and Schuster, 1981).

2. For an extended discussion see Richard Falk, Lee Meyrowitz, and Jack Sanderson, "Nuclear Weapons and International Law," World Order Studies Program, Princeton University Center for International Studies Occasional Paper No. 10, 1981, pp. 1–80.

3. The most recent formulation is contained in G. A. Resolution 36/911, in Report A/36/751 (1981). It was adopted by a vote of 121 to 19, with 6 countries

abstaining. The opposition included the United States and most of NATO, while both China and the Soviet Union voted in favor of the resolution.

4. For analysis to this effect see McGeorge Bundy, George F. Kennan, Robert S. McNamara, and Gerald Smith, "Nuclear Weapons and the Atlantic Alliance," *Foreign Affairs* 60 (1982):753–768.

5. For an important effort to rethink security and foreign policy see Robert C. Johansen, *The National Interest and the Human Interest* (Princeton, N.J.: Princeton University Press, 1980); Johansen, "Toward a Dependable Peace: A Proposal for an Appropriate Security System," World Order Models Project Working Paper No. 8 (New York: Institute for World Order, 1978).

6. Jacob E. Cooke, ed., *The Federalist* (Cleveland, Ohio: World Publishing Co., 1961), p. 44.

7. James Douglass, *Lightning East to West* (Portland Oregon: Sunburst, 1981), p. 65.

—————— Questions for Reflection and Discussion ——————

1. Do you agree that the global political order is in the process of profound change? Is it possible that undesirable forms of governance might emerge? If so, what steps should be taken to offset the possibility? Are you prepared to accept responsibility in developing an international structure that enforces human rights and meets human needs?

2. How would you encourage national policymakers to diminish sovereign control of military forces and to rely on supranational approaches to world peace? What tools are available for eliminating the adverse, militaristic consequences of nationalism? How would you attempt to redirect national energies to meet global problems?

3. According to Mary Kaldor, what are the "properties" of the capitalist armaments process? The central planning armaments process? Are they coextensive? What basic task for proponents of disarmament does Kaldor set? Why is a focus on simply the elimination of weapons insufficient? Why must economic conversion occur? Phenomenologically, what does it represent? What examples of conversion does Kaldor cite? What is the potential for expanded efforts at conversion?

4. Does marginalization of the public's role in formulating foreign policy represent a failure of democratic principles? What methods does Alger suggest for overcoming elitist control of national conduct at the global level? What are the probable effects of infusing public perceptions and values into the foreign policy process? Would you expect less frequent use of force due to an increasing public sense of globalism? What is the hierarchy of your personal loyalties? Do you have a sense of obligation to contribute to worldwide human progress, a sense of humanistic globalism?

5. What forces are currently at work for nuclear arms control and disarmament? What role do Lifton and Falk assign to the individual reformist? How would they institutionalize a disarmament dynamic in international relations? What socioeconomic and psychological changes are necessary, if any, to develop and maintain mass, effective political commitment to demilitarization? On final analysis, would not such a global order be imminently superior to the current system? What barriers are there to the evolution of a new order, other than human perceptions and want of confidence in change?

Selected Bibliography

Alger, Chadwick F. "Creating Participatory Global Cultures." *Alternatives: A Journal of World Policy*, Vol. 6, No. 4 (Spring 1981), pp. 575–590.

Bahro, Rudolf. "A New Approach for the Peace Movement in Germany." In *Exterminism and Cold War*, ed. New Left Review. London: Verso Editions and NLB, 1982, pp. 87–116.

Barnet, Richard J. *Roots of War*. New York: Atheneum, 1972.

Bayer, William H. *Education for Annihilation*. Honolulu: Hogarth Press–Hawaii, 1972.

Beitz, Charles, and Michael Washburn. *Creating the Future: A Guide to Living and Working for Social Change*. New York: Bantam Books, 1974.

Beres, Louis René. *People, States, and World Order*. Itasca, IL: F. E. Peacock Publishers, 1981.

_____. "Steps Toward a New Planetary Identity." *Bulletin of the Atomic Scientists*, Vol. 37, No. 2 (Feb. 1981), pp. 43–47.

Beres, Louis René, and Harry L. Targ. *Reordering the Planet: Constructing Alternative World Futures*. Boston: Allyn and Bacon, 1974.

Beres, Louis René, and Harry R. Targ, eds. *Planning Alternative World Futures*. New York: Praeger Publishers, 1975.

Chatfield, Charles, ed. *Peace Movements in America*. New York: Schocken Books, 1973.

Dumas, Lloyd J., ed. *The Political Economy of Arms Reduction: Reversing Economic Decay*. Boulder, CO: Westview Press, 1982.

Falk, Richard A. *A Study of Future Worlds*. New York: Free Press, 1975.

_____. "Normative Initiatives and Demilitarization: A Third System Approach." *Alternatives: A Journal of World Policy*, Vol. 6, No. 2 (July 1980), pp. 339–356.

Galtung, Johan. *The True Worlds*. New York: Free Press, 1980.

Haavelsrud, Magnus. *Approaching Disarmament Education*. Woburn, MA: Butterworth Publishers, 1981.

International Workshop on Disarmament. "Disarmament for a Just World: Declaration of Principles, Proposal for a Treaty, and Call for Action." *Alternatives: A Journal of World Policy*, Vol. 4, No. 1 (1978), pp. 155–160.

Keys, Donald. *Earth at Omega: Passage to Planetization*. Boston: Branden Press, 1982.

Kothari, Rajni. *Footsteps Into the Future*. New York: Free Press, 1974.

Lakey, George. *Strategy for a Living Revolution*. New York: Grossman Publishers, 1973.

————. *A Manifesto for Nonviolent Revolution.* Philadelphia, PA: Movement for a New Society, 1976.

Magri, Lucio. "The Peace Movement and Europe." In *Exterminism and Cold War,* ed. New Left Review. London: Verso Editions and NLB, 1982, pp. 117–134.

Melman, Seymour. "Conversion from Military to Civilian Economy." *Annals of the New York Academy of Sciences,* Vol. 368 (1981), pp. 93–102.

Mendlovitz, Saul H., ed. *On the Creation of a Just World Order.* New York: Free Press, 1975.

Paige, Glenn D. "Nonviolent Politics for Disarmament." *Alternatives: A Journal of World Policy,* Vol. 6, No. 2 (July 1980), pp. 287–305.

————. "Political Leadership, Followership, and Education for Disarmament." *Gandhi Marg,* Vol. 4, Nos. 2–3 (May–June 1982), pp. 356–405.

Preiswerk, Roy. "Could We Study International Relations as if People Mattered?" In *Peace and World Order Studies: A Curriculum Guide.* 3rd ed. New York: Institute for World Order, 1981, pp. 2–23.

Rockman, Jane. *Peace in Search of Makers.* New York: Judson Press, 1979.

Sharp, Gene. *Social Power and Political Freedom.* Boston: Porter Sargent Publishers, 1980.

Somerville, John. *The Peace Revolution: Ethos and Social Process.* Westport, CT: Greenwood Press, 1974.

Thompson, E. P., and Dan Smith, eds. *Protest and Survive.* New York and London: Monthly Review Press, 1981.

Wagar, Warren W. *Building the City of Man.* San Francisco: W. H. Freeman and Co., 1971.

Wallensteen, P., ed. *Experiences in Disarmament: On Conversion of Military Industry and Closing of Military Bases.* Uppsala, Sweden: Uppsala University, 1978.

Wallis, Jim, ed. *Waging Peace: A Handbook for the Struggle to Abolish War.* New York: Harper & Row, 1982.

Weston, Burns H. "Contending with a Planet in Peril and Change: An Optimal Educational Response." *Alternatives: A Journal of World Policy,* Vol. 5, No. 1 (June 1979), pp. 59–95.

Appendix A: Glossary of Terms

AAM. See *Air-to-air missile.*

ABM. See *Antiballistic missile.*

ABM Treaty. See under *Antiballistic missiles.*

Accidental nuclear war. A hostile exchange of nuclear weapons initiated by human error or technical malfunction.

Active penetration aid. A weapon that helps a nuclear delivery system breach enemy defenses. Air-to-air and air-to-surface missiles are examples. See also *Passive penetration aid; Penetration aids.*

ADM. See *Atomic demolition munition.*

Advanced Technology Bomber (ATB). A manned bomber capable of eluding enemy radar detection because of design and materials. Also known as the "Stealth bomber."

Aerospace defense. An inclusive term encompassing all measures to intercept and destroy hostile aircraft, missiles, and space vehicles or otherwise neutralize them. See also *Air defense; Antiballistic missile.*

This glossary has been prepared primarily from the following sources: Ground Zero, "Glossary of Nuclear War Terms," in *Nuclear War: What's In It for You?* (New York: Pocket Books, 1982), pp. 250–263; Marek Thee, ed., "Glossary of Terms, Acronyms and Abbreviations Frequently Used in Writings Dealing with Military Policy and in Arms Control and Disarmament Negotiations," in *Armaments, Arms Control and Disarmament* (Paris: UNESCO Press, 1981), pp. 407–420; Stockholm International Peace Research Institute, ed., "Glossary," in *The Arms Race and Arms Control* (London: Taylor & Francis, 1982), pp. IX–XXI; and U.S. Arms Control and Disarmament Agency, *SALT Lexicon*, revised ed. (Washington, DC: U.S. Government Printing Office, 1975). The selection of terms has been made to facilitate lay understanding of the technical literature associated with nuclear weapons and warfare, and is not restricted to the terms used in the readings.

Airborne alert. A state of readiness designed to reduce reaction time and increase survivability by maintaining combat-equipped aircraft aloft on a continuing basis or during times of tension. See also *Ground alert.*

Airborne Warning and Control System (AWACS). An air-based defense system carrying radar and navigation and communications equipment designed to detect, track, and intercept attacking aircraft.

Airbreathing system. Any delivery system that operates entirely within the earth's atmosphere. Manned aircraft and cruise missiles are examples.

Air defense. All measures to intercept and destroy hostile aircraft and cruise missiles or otherwise neutralize them. Equipment includes interceptor aircraft, surface-to-air missiles, surveillance devices, and ancillary installations.

Air-launched ballistic missile (ALBM). A ballistic missile transported by and launched from land- or sea-based aircraft and/or lighter-than-air conveyances such as blimps, balloons, and dirigibles.

Air-launched cruise missile (ALCM). A cruise missile designed to be launched from an aircraft. See also *Cruise missile.*

Air-launched miniature vehicle (ALMV). A self-propelled explosive device launched from an airborne interceptor against an enemy's satellites.

Air-to-air missile (AAM). A missile used in aerial combat against enemy aircraft and cruise missiles.

Air-to-surface ballistic missile (ASBM). A ballistic missile launched from an aircraft against a target on the earth's surface.

Air-to-surface ballistic missile carrier. An airborne carrier for launching a ballistic missile capable of a range in excess of 600 km against a target on the earth's surface.

ALBM. See *Air-launched ballistic missile.*

ALCM. See *Air-launched cruise missile.*

Alliance or regionally oriented (related) systems. Nonstrategic nuclear systems deployed by the U.S. and the USSR to carry out responsibilities owed to their respective allies and to help maintain regional power balances. Such systems vary from long-range theater nuclear forces to battlefield nuclear weapons.

ALMV. See *Air-launched miniature vehicle.*

Antiaircraft defense. See *Air defense.*

Antiballistic missile (ABM). Any missile used to intercept and destroy hostile ballistic missiles or otherwise neutralize them. Antiballistic-missile defense equipment includes weapons, target acquisitions, tracking and guidance radar, plus ancillary installations having the same purpose.

ABM Treaty. One of four agreements known collectively as the SALT I agreements. Signed in Moscow on May 26, 1972, the treaty entered into force on October 3, 1972, and is of unlimited duration. The original terms limited each side to two ABM deployment areas (one national capital area and one ICBM silo launch area) with restrictions on the deployment of ABM launchers and interceptor missiles (100 per area) and ABM radars at these areas. A protocol to the treaty, signed in 1974, further restricted each side to only one ABM deployment area.

Antisatellite system (ASAT). A weapon system designed to destroy enemy surveillance and hunter-killer satellites.

Antisubmarine warfare (ASW). All measures to reduce or nullify the effectiveness of hostile submarines.

Arms control. Any measure limiting or reducing forces, regulating armaments, and/or restricting the deployment of troops or weapons that is intended to induce responsive behavior or is taken pursuant to an understanding with another state or states. See also *Arms limitation; Disarmament.*

Arms limitation. An agreement to restrict quantitative holdings of, or qualitative improvements in, specific armaments or weapon systems. See also *Arms control; Disarmament.*

Arms stability. A strategic relationship in which neither side perceives the necessity of undertaking major new weapon programs in order to avoid being placed at a disadvantage.

ASAT. See *Antisatellite system.*

ASBM. See *Air-to-surface ballistic missile.*

Assured destruction. A highly reliable ability to inflict unacceptable damage on any aggressor or combination of aggressors at any time during the course of a nuclear exchange, even after absorbing a surprise first strike.

ASW. See *Antisubmarine warfare.*

ATB. See *Advanced Technology Bomber.*

Atomic bomb. A weapon based on the rapid fissioning of combinations of selected materials, thereby inducing an explosion (along with the emission of radiation).

Atomic demolition munition (ADM). Stationary nuclear explosives designed for military application, also known as nuclear land mines.

Attack aircraft. See *Strike aircraft.*

Attack submarine. A submarine designed to destroy enemy naval vessels (including submarines) and merchant shipping.

AWACS. See *Airborne Warning and Control System.*

B-1. A new U.S. strategic bomber with a 34,000-km payload capable of flying intercontinental missions without refueling.

B-52. An all-jet heavy bomber used in the U.S. Strategic Air Command (SAC) since 1955.

Backfire. The NATO designation of a modern Soviet two-engine swing-wing bomber.

Ballistic missile. A pilotless projectile propelled into space by one or more rocket boosters. Thrust is terminated at some early stage, after which reentry vehicles follow trajectories that are governed mainly by gravity and aerodynamic drag. Mid-course corrections and terminal guidance permit only minor modifications of the flight path.

Ballistic missile defense (BMD) system. A weapon system designed to destroy offensive strategic ballistic missiles or their warheads before they reach their targets. See also *Antiballistic missile; Charged-particle beam; Laser.*

Battlefield nuclear weapons. A term generally meant to refer to nuclear weapons used against enemy conventional and nuclear forces at close quarters (within 200 km).

BMD. See *Ballistic missile defense system.*

Bomb. A weapon dropped from a manned aircraft of any sort. Gravity is the primary force, but "smart" bombs can be guided electronically.

Breeder reactors. Reactors in which the process of fission enhances the concentrations of fissionable materials in the fuel or in a "jacket" covering the reactor, thereby producing more fuel than is used.

Bus. See *Postboost vehicle (PBV).*

Carrier. Any vehicle designed to deliver weapons to a target or to stand-off release points. Aircraft, aircraft carriers, and submarines are examples. See also *Stand-off.*

CBM. See *Confidence-building measures.*

CD. See *Committee on Disarmament.*

CEP. See *Circular error probable.*

Charged-particle beam. An intense beam of subatomic particles, usually electrons, capable of destroying animate objects. Of potential BMD application.

Circular error probable (CEP). A measure of the delivery accuracy of a weapon system. CEP is the radius of a circle around a target into which a weapon aimed at the target has a 50 percent probability of falling.

Civil defense. Passive measures designed to minimize the effects of enemy action on all aspects of civilian life, particularly to protect the population and production base. Includes emergency steps to repair or restore vital utilities and facilities.

CM. See *Cruise missile.*

CMC. See *Cruise-missile carrier.*

Cold launch. A "pop-up" technique that ejects ballistic missiles from silos or submarines using power plants that are separate from the delivery vehicles. Primary ignition is delayed until projectiles are safely removed from the missile container/carriers.

Collateral damage. The damage to surrounding human and nonhuman resources, either military or nonmilitary, as a result of action or strikes directed against enemy forces or military facilities.

Combat radius. The distance an aircraft loaded as required can fly from base to target and return employing axes, speeds, and altitudes most likely to guarantee success against armed opposition.

Command/control. An arrangement of facilities, equipment, personnel, and procedures used to acquire, process, and disseminate information needed by decisionmakers in planning, directing, and controlling operations.

Committee on Disarmament (CD). A multilateral arms control negotiating body based in Geneva which is composed of forty states (including all the nuclear-weapon states). The CD is the successor of the Eighteen-Nation Disarmament Committee (ENDC, 1962–1969) and the Conference of the Committee on Disarmament (CCD 1969–1978).

Confidence-building measures (CBM). Political and/or military arrangements allowing potential adversaries to reduce the possibility of conflict caused by incorrect assessments of the other's military movements. Standard examples include notification of military exercises and movements above a defined level, limitation of military maneuvers to low tactical levels close to national frontiers, prohibitions on live ammunition during military exercises and movements, and exchanges of observer personnel and liaison.

Conventional (forces, war, weapons). Military organizations, hostilities, and hardware that exclude nuclear, chemical, and biological capabilities.

Counterforce capability. The ability to destroy enemy military forces. Generally used with reference to the destruction of an adversary's strategic nuclear weapon systems.

Counterforce strategy. A strategy of using nuclear weapons to destroy the opponent's nuclear and general military forces. The main consequence of adopting such a strategy is the need for large numbers of extremely accurate nuclear weapons.

Counterforce strike. An attack aimed at an adversary's military capability, especially its strategic nuclear capability.

Countervalue attack. An attack aimed at urban-industrial targets, sometimes referred to as a "city-killing" attack.

Countervalue strategy. A strategy of targeting nuclear weapons on the opponent's cities and industrial areas. Compared to counterforce strategy, this strategy requires fewer and less accurate nuclear weapons.

Coupling (strategic). The linking of a lower level of conflict to the use of strategic deterrent forces.

Crisis stability. A strategic force relationship in which neither side has any incentive to initiate the use of strategic nuclear forces in a crisis situation.

Cruise missile (CM). A guided missile that uses aerodynamic lift to offset gravity and propulsion to counteract drag. A cruise missile's flight path remains within the earth's atmosphere. Cruise missiles fall into three categories: LRCMs, or long-range cruise missiles (over 3,000–3,500 km); MRCMs, or medium-range cruise missiles (1,000–3,000 km); and SRCMs, or short-range cruise missiles (under 1,000 km).

Cruise missile carrier (CMC). Any vehicle equipped for launching a cruise missile.

Damage limitation. A term used in nuclear-strategy debates to indicate a situation in which one side, believing an attack to be imminent, launches a preemptive strike with the objective of reducing the opponent's nuclear forces and therefore the severity of the expected attack.

Defense in depth. Protective measures in successive positions along axes of enemy advance, as opposed to a single line of resistance. Designed to absorb and progressively weaken enemy penetrations.

Delivery system. See *Nuclear delivery system.*

Delta-class submarine. U.S. designation for the mainstay of the Soviet nuclear-powered SSBN fleet. Armed with 12–16 SLBMs, Delta submarines carry either single- or multiple-warhead missiles.

Depth bomb. A nuclear device exploded underwater to destroy a nearby enemy submarine.

Deterrence. Any strategy whose goal is to dissuade an enemy from attacking. See *Nuclear deterrence.*

Disarmament. The reduction of a military establishment to some level set by international agreement. See also *General and complete disarmament.*

Dual-capable system. A system capable of delivering either conventional or nuclear warheads.

ECM. See *Electronic countermeasures.*

Electronic countermeasures (ECM). A form of electronic warfare that prevents or degrades effective enemy uses of the electromagnetic spectrum. Jamming is a typical tactic.

Enhanced-radiation weapon (ERW). A nuclear weapon designed to limit collateral damage by relying on radiation rather than blast to attack enemy ground forces. Also known as the neutron bomb.

Essential equivalence. The term as currently used refers to approximate equality in the overall capabilities of opposing strategic offensive forces.

Euro-strategic weapons. Long-range theater nuclear forces currently assigned combat missions in the European theater of operations.

Fallout. Radioactive particles carried into the upper atmosphere by a nuclear explosion that fall to earth downwind from the explosion, usually via rain.

Fighter aircraft. Tactical aircraft used primarily to gain and maintain air superiority.

Fighter-bomber. See *Strike aircraft.*

First-strike capability. The ability to destroy all or very nearly all of an enemy's strategic nuclear forces in a preemptive nuclear attack. See also *Preemptive strike; Second-strike capability.*

First-strike strategy. A strategy adopted by a nuclear-weapon state whose nuclear weapons, being vulnerable to an attack, must be used before an attack is launched.

Fissile (or fissionable) material. Isotopes (variants) of certain elements—such as plutonium, thorium, and uranium—that emit neutrons in such large numbers that a sufficient concentration will be self-sustaining, continuing to produce increasing numbers of neutrons until it is damped down, explodes, or the material is exhausted.

Flexible response. A strategy for controlling escalation whereby an enemy's escalatory step is met with a measured response designed to limit the intensity of the conflict to its lowest possible level while denying the enemy its political-military objectives.

FOBS. See *Fractional Orbital Bombardment System.*

Fractional Orbital Bombardment System (FOBS). A missile that achieves an orbital trajectory but fires a set of retrorockets before the completion of one revolution in order to slow down, reenter the atmosphere, and release the warhead it carries into a ballistic trajectory toward its target.

Fratricide. The destruction or neutralization of one nuclear weapon by another belonging to the same country or coalition. Blast, heat, and radiation all may contribute.

FROG (free rocket over ground). NATO designation for an unguided Soviet surface-to-surface missile designed for battlefield use.

Functionally related observable differences (FRODs). The means by which SALT II provides for distinguishing between those aircraft capable of performing certain SALT-limited functions and those that are not. FRODs are differences in the observable features of aircraft that specifically determine whether or not they can perform the mission of a heavy bomber, whether or not they can perform the mission of a bomber equipped for cruise missiles capable of a range in excess of 600 km, or whether or not they can perform the mission of a bomber equipped for ASBMs.

General and complete disarmament. The goal established by the United Nations General Assembly in the field of disarmament. It involves disbanding armed forces, dismantling military establishments, eliminating stockpiles of nuclear, chemical, bacteriological and other weapons of mass destruction, and discontinuance of military expenditure according to an agreed sequence of balanced measures under strict and effective international control. The ultimate outcome would be that States would have at their disposal only those nonnuclear armaments, forces, facilities, and establishments as are agreed to be necessary to maintain internal order and to protect the personal security of citizens.

General-purpose forces. All combat forces not designed primarily to accomplish strategic offensive or defensive missions. Tactical aircraft are an example. See also *Strategic nuclear weapon systems.*

GLCM. See *Ground-launched cruise missile.*

Gravity bomb. See *Bomb.*

Ground alert. A state of readiness designed to reduce reaction time and increase survivability by maintaining combat-equipped aircraft and crews ready to take off quickly. It may be routine procedure or be practiced only during times of tension. See also *Airborne alert.*

Ground-launched cruise missile (GLCM). A cruise missile launched from ground installations of vehicles. See also *Cruise missile.*

Ground zero. The point on the earth's surface (i.e., the geographical coordinates) at which a nuclear weapon is detonated. For an airburst, it is the point on the earth's surface directly below the point of detonation.

Hard target. A target protected against the blast, heat, and radiation produced by nuclear explosions. There are many degrees of hardening.

Hard-target kill probability. The likelihood of a specific strike destroying a target designed to withstand blast, heat, or radiation from a nuclear attack.

Heavy ballistic missile. For the purposes of SALT II, ballistic missiles are divided into two categories according to their throw-weight and launch-weight: light and heavy. Heavy missiles (ICBMs, SLBMs, and ASBMS) are those missiles that have a launch-weight or throw-weight greater than the launch-weight or throw-weight of the Soviet SS-19 ICBM.

Heavy bomber. The term used in SALT II to describe those aircraft included in the aggregate limitations of the agreement. See also *Strategic bomber.*

Horizontal proliferation. The spread of nuclear capabilities across states and/ or nongovernmental entities.

Hot-launch system. A system in which full ignition of the main engine of a ballistic missile occurs in its silo.

Hunter-killer submarine. See *Attack submarine.*

Hydrogen bomb. See *Thermonuclear weapon.*

IAEA. See *International Atomic Energy Agency.*

ICBM. See *Intercontinental ballistic missile.*

Independent nuclear forces. Nuclear forces not controlled by the U.S. or the USSR.

Inertial guidance. A system that measures acceleration and relates it to distances traveled in certain directions. Designed to steer ballistic missiles over predetermined courses, using data generated solely by devices in the missiles.

Interceptor. An air-defense aircraft designed to identify and/or destroy hostile airbreathing weapons systems such as bombers and cruise missiles.

Intercontinental ballistic missile (ICBM). A land-based fixed or mobile rocket-propelled vehicle capable of delivering a warhead across intercontinental ranges. Once outside the atmosphere, ICBMs fly to a target on an elliptical trajectory. An ICBM consists of a booster, one or more reentry vehicles, possibly penetration aids, and, in the case of a MIRVed missile, a postboost vehicle (PBV). For the purposes of SALT II, an ICBM is considered to be a land-based ballistic missile capable of a range in excess of 5,500 km (about 3,000 nautical miles).

Intercontinental ballistic missile (ICBM) silo launcher. An ICBM silo launcher, a "hard" fixed ICBM launcher, is an underground installation, usually of steel and concrete, housing an intercontinental ballistic missile and the equipment for launching it.

Intermediate-range ballistic missile (IRBM). A ballistic missile with a range of 1,500 to 3,000 nautical miles (2,800-5,500 km). See also *Ballistic missile.*

International Atomic Energy Agency (IAEA). The international organization belonging to the United Nations system charged, among other things, with monitoring the production and use of special fissionable materials.

IRBM. See *Intermediate-range ballistic missile.*

Kiloton. One thousand tons (of TNT equivalent).

Laser. A device which produces an intense beam of light entirely of the same wavelength. Potential military applications include BMD and ASAT missions.

Launcher. The equipment that launches a missile. ICBM launchers are land-based launchers, which can be either fixed or mobile. SLBM launchers are the missiles tubes on a ballistic missile submarine. An ASBM launcher is the carrier aircraft with associated equipment. Launchers for cruise missiles can be installed on aircraft, ships, or land-based vehicles or installations.

Launch-on-warning. Retaliatory strikes triggered upon notification that an enemy attack is in progress, but before hostile forces or ordnance reach friendly soil.

Launch-weight. The weight of the fully loaded missile itself at the time of launch. This would include the aggregate weight of all booster stages, and postboost vehicle (PBV), and the payload.

Liquid-fuel systems. Ballistic missile propulsion systems that rely on liquid fuel. Military ramifications include comparatively high maintenance costs and risk of accidents when compared with solid-fuel systems. See also *Solid-fuel systems.*

Loiter time. The length of time an aircraft can remain aloft in any given location, pending receipt of further orders. Depends primarily on fuel capacity, consumption rates, refueling capabilities, and pilot fatigue. Loiter capabilities for missiles are a future possibility.

Long Range Aviation. Soviet military bureaucracy in control of intercontinental and medium-range land attack bombers assigned strategic- and theatre-level missions.

Long-range theater nuclear forces. Comprises nuclear delivery systems with ranges exceeding 1,000 km but less than 5,500 km. Weapons typically included in this category are IRBMs, MRBMs, some types of SLBMs, and medium-range bombers and strike aircraft.

LRCM. See *Cruise missile.*

LRTNF. See *Long-range theater nuclear forces.*

MAD. See *Mutual assured destruction.*

Maneuverable reentry vehicle (MaRV). A ballistic missile warhead or decoy whose accuracy can be improved by terminal guidance mechanisms. See also *Mid-course correction.*

Manned penetrator. Strategic bombers and tactical aircraft whose performance depends on pilots and/or crews.

MaRV. See *Maneuverable reentry vehicle.*

MBFR. Mutual and balanced force reductions or mutual balanced force reduction. See *Mutual force reduction.*

Medium bomber. A multi-engine aircraft that lacks intercontinental range without in-flight refueling, but is suitable for strategic bombing under special circumstances. See also *Strategic bomber.*

Medium-range ballistic missile (MRBM). A ballistic missile with a range of 600 to 1,500 nautical miles (1,100-2,800 km). See also *Ballistic missile.*

Megaton. One million tons (of TNT equivalent).

MFR. See *Mutual force reduction.*

Mid-course correction. An in-flight amendment to the trajectory of a ballistic or cruise missile, by any means whatsoever, for the purpose of improving accuracy. See also *Terminal guidance.*

Militarily significant. A phrase used in reference to the acquisition of superior counterforce or war-fighting capabilities.

Military-industrial complex. A term coined by President Eisenhower to describe the combined interests of the armed forces and the defense industry in obtaining new weapon systems.

MIRV. See *Multiple independently targetable reentry vehicle.*

Mobile launchers. A surface vehicle by which land-mobile ballistic missiles can be moved into position, prepared for launch, and fired.

Mobile missile. Any ballistic or cruise missile that depends partly or entirely on mobility to ensure prelaunch survivability. Carriers may be aircraft, ships, or motor vehicles.

Mobile target. Any target in motion at the time it is attacked.

MRBM. See *Medium-range ballistic missile.*

MRCM. See *Cruise missile.*

MRV. See *Multiple reentry vehicle.*

Multiple independently targeted reentry vehicle (MIRV). A missile payload comprising two or more warheads that can engage separate targets. See also *Multiple reentry vehicle; Reentry vehicle.*

Multiple reentry vehicle (MRV). A missile payload comprising two or more warheads that engage the same target. See also *Multiple independently targeted reentry vehicle; Reentry vehicle.*

Mutual and balanced force reductions (MBFR). See *Mutual force reduction.*

Mutual Assured Destruction (MAD). The mutual capacity to inflict massive countervalue damage after absorbing a full-scale counterforce strike.

Mutual force reduction (MFR). Negotiations between nineteen NATO and Warsaw Pact countries begun in Vienna in 1973 to discuss the mutual reduction of forces and armaments in Central Europe.

Mya-4 Bison. NATO designation for a Soviet four-jet long-range strategic bomber. First deployed in 1956, it has an estimated payload of 10,000 kg, a maximum speed of 900 km per hour, and a typical range of 6,000 nautical miles (11,200 km).

National Aviation. The Soviet military bureau responsible for Soviet aircraft intended for use against an enemy's maritime forces.

National command authority (NCA). The top national security decisionmakers of a country.

National technical means of verification (NTM). Assets that are under national control for monitoring compliance with the provisions of an agreement. NTM include photographic reconnaissance satellites and aircraft-based systems (such as radar and optical systems), as well as sea- and ground-based systems (such as radar and antennae for collecting telemetry).

Neutron bomb. See *Enhanced-radiation weapon.*

North American Aerospace Command (NORAD). U.S. military bureau responsible for the defense of U.S. airspace. See also *Air defense.*

NPT. See *Nuclear Non-proliferation Treaty.*

NTM. See *National technical means of verification.*

Nuclear-capable. See *Dual-capable system.*

Nuclear delivery system. A nuclear weapon, together with its means of propulsion and associated installations. Includes carriers such as aircraft, ships, and motor vehicles. See also *Nuclear weapon.*

Nuclear deterrence. A strategic doctrine based on the assumption that a potential aggressor can be dissuaded from provocative action or war by (a) the possession of nuclear forces sufficient to deny the enemy its political-military objectives at any level of conflict (counterforce deterrence), or (b) the possession of nuclear forces sufficient to launch a massive urban-industrial retaliatory strike (countervalue deterrence). See also *Counterforce strategy; Deterrence; Mutual Assured Destruction.*

Nuclear device. Sometimes used to refer to a nuclear explosive that may (a) be intended for nonmilitary uses such as construction, hence a peaceful nuclear explosive, or (b) be too heavy and/or too cumbersome for delivery on military targets and hence is useful only for test purposes.

Nuclear material. See *Fissile material.*

Nuclear Non-proliferation Treaty (NPT). The multilateral agreement officially known as the Treaty on the Non-proliferation of Nuclear Weapons, signed in London, Moscow, and Washington on July 1, 1968, and entered into force on March 5, 1970. The treaty prohibits: (a) the transfer by nuclear-weapon states to any recipient whatsoever of nuclear weapons or other nuclear explosive devices or control over them; (b) the assistance, encouragement, or inducement of any non–nuclear weapon state to manufacture or otherwise acquire such weapons or devices; and (c) the receipt, manufacture, or other acquisition by non–nuclear weapon states of nuclear weapons or other nuclear explosive devices.

Nuclear parity. Rough equivalence between the nuclear forces of opposing countries. Equivalence can be defined in a number of ways: number of launchers; number of individually deliverable warheads; total deliverable explosive power; or throw-weight.

Nuclear proliferation. The process by which one state after another comes into possession of some form of nuclear weaponry, and with it the potential to launch a nuclear attack on other states.

Nuclear reactor. A mechanism fueled by fissionable materials that give off neutrons, thereby inducing heat. Reactors are of three general types: (a) power reactors, in which the heat generated is transformed into power in the form of electricity; (b) production reactors, which are designed primarily to increase concentration of certain fissionable materials, such as plutonium 239; and (c) research reactors, designed primarily to produce isotopes (variants) for some materials and/or to induce radioactivity in others, for applications in genetics, medicine, and so forth.

Nuclear reprocessing. The separation of radioactive waste (spent fuel) from a nuclear-powered plant into its fissile constituent materials. One such material is plutonium, which can then be used in the production of atomic bombs.

Nuclear safeguards. Any number of ways to protect nuclear power or production reactors from accidental spillage of nuclear waste, from theft of nuclear materials, or from the diversion of these to unauthorized purposes, such as weapons production.

Nuclear terrorism. Terrorism is the systematic use of terror as a means of coercion. Nuclear terrorism involves the use or threatened use of nuclear weapons or radioactive materials by an actor, either state or nongovernment.

Nuclear Test Ban Treaty. See *Partial Test Ban Treaty.*

Nuclear weapon. A bomb, missile, warhead, or other deliverable ordnance item (as opposed to an experimental device) that explodes as a result of energy released by atomic nuclei by fission, fusion, or both. See also *Thermonuclear weapon.*

Nuclear-weapon-free zone (NWFZ). A region or group of states from which all nuclear weapons are banned.

Nuclear-weapon state. A nation-state possessing nuclear weapons, whether fission, fusion, or both.

NWFZ. See *Nuclear-weapon-free zone.*

Overkill. A destructive capacity in excess of that required to achieve stated objectives.

Partial Test Ban Treaty (PTB). The multilateral agreement officially known as the Treaty Banning Nuclear Weapon Tests in the Atmosphere, in Outer Space and Under Water, signed in Moscow on August 5, 1963, and entered into force on October 10, 1963. The treaty prohibits "any nuclear weapon test explosion, or any other nuclear explosion" in the atmosphere, in outer space, or under water (as its official title proclaims).

Passive penetration aid. A harmless device that helps a nuclear delivery system breach enemy defenses. Chaff and electronic countermeasures are examples. See also *Active penetration aid; Penetration aids.*

Payload. The ordnance delivered by any system, expressed in numbers of bombs, stand-off weapons, and missile warheads, and/or in terms of yield (kilotons, megatons).

PBV. See *Postboost vehicle.*

Peaceful nuclear explosion (PNE). A nonmilitary use of a nuclear demolition, e.g., for the purpose of digging canals or harbors, creating underground cavities, etc.

Penetration aids (Penaids). Devices employed by offensive weapon systems, such as ballistic missiles and bombers, to increase the probability of penetrating enemy defenses. They are frequently designed to simulate or to mask an aircraft or ballistic missile warhead in order to mislead enemy radar and/

or divert defensive antiaircraft or antimissile fire. See also *Active penetration aid; Passive penetration aid.*

Penetration capability. The ability of offensive (nuclear) forces to penetrate defenses.

Permissive action links (PAL). Electronic systems for the control of nuclear warheads whereby these can be armed only if positive action to this end is taken by a duly constituted authority, such as the President of the United States or the Supreme Allied Commander, Europe.

Plutonium recycling. A process whereby plutonium in the spent fuel of reactors is separated from other fissile materials and reused either as reactor fuel (see *Breeder reactors*) or for atomic weapons.

PNE. See *Peaceful nuclear explosion.*

Point target. A target located by a single set of geographic coordinates on operational maps. Missile silos are representative.

Polaris submarine. U.S. nuclear-powered ballistic missile submarine operational during the 1960s and 1970s. All U.S. Polaris submarines have been replaced by Poseidon SSBNs. See also *Poseidon submarine; Trident submarine.*

Poseidon submarine. U.S. nuclear-powered ballistic missile submarine (SSBN) armed with 16 Poseidon C-3 or 16 Trident C-4 MIRVed SLBMs. The Poseidon submarine force currently forms the backbone of the sea-based component of the U.S. strategic triad. See also *Submarine; Trident submarine; Triad.*

Positive control. Standard procedures that prohibit the accidental launch of ballistic missiles. Aircraft launched on warning return to base unless they receive coded voice instructions that can be authenticated.

Postboost vehicle (PBV). Often referred to as a "bus," the PBV is that part of a missile's payload carrying the reentry vehicles, a guidance package, fuel, and thrust devices for altering the ballistic flight path so that the reentry vehicles can be dispensed sequentially toward different targets. Ballistic missiles with single RVs also might use a PBV to increase the accuracy of the RV by placing it more precisely into the desired trajectory.

Postlaunch survivability. The ability of any given delivery system to breach enemy defenses and attack designated targets. See also *Prelaunch survivability.*

Preemptive strike. An attack launched in the expectation that an attack by an adversary is imminent and designed to forestall that attack or to lessen its impact. Usually refers to a strike on an adversary's delivery vehicles, weapon stocks, and other components of nuclear forces.

Prelaunch survivability. The ability of any given delivery system to weather a surprise first strike successfully and to retaliate. See also *Postlaunch survivability.*

Protracted nuclear war. An ambiguous term referring to a continuing exchange of nuclear attacks, presumably short of massive countervalue exchanges.

PTB. See *Partial Test Ban Treaty.*

Quick-reaction alert. Readiness procedures designed to reduce reaction times and increase the survivability of tactical aircraft, mainly in the NATO area. See also *Ground alert.*

Radioactive materials. Those giving off Beta rays, Gamma rays or other forms of radiation. Radioactive materials may or may not be fissionable.

Radiological weapon. A device, including any weapon or equipment, other than an explosive nuclear device, specifically designed to disseminate radioactive material so as to cause radiological damage to human and nonhuman resources.

Rapid reload/refire capability. The ability of a delivery system to conduct multiple strikes. This characteristic is at present confined to aircraft, but land-mobile missiles and hard-site ICBMs have the potential. Submarines conceivably could be replenished at sea, but a significantly greater time lag would occur.

Recall capability. The ability to retrieve weapons and/or carriers after launch-on-warning. Recall may be directed by communications or occur spontaneously in the absence of authenticated orders to attack targets.

Reentry vehicle (RV). That portion of a ballistic missile which carries the nuclear warhead. It is called a reentry vehicle because it reenters the earth's atmosphere in the terminal portion of the missile trajectory.

Rem. An acronym for "Roentgen Equivalent Man," a measure of radiation exposure which indicates the potential adverse impact on human cells.

Retrofit. To upgrade existing weapons systems by installing state-of-the-art modifications.

RV. See *Reentry vehicle.*

SAC. See *Strategic Air Command.*

SALT. See *Strategic arms limitation talks.*

SAM. See *Surface-to-air missile.*

Saturation attack. The use of weapons en masse to overload enemy defenses and/or blanket areas that contain known or suspected targets.

Second-strike capability. The ability to mount a nuclear attack after a first strike by the opponent. For a strategy of deterrence, the object is to convince the enemy that, no matter what it does (in a first strike), you will retain the forces necessary to deny it its political-military objectives or its capability to deliver an unacceptably severe second strike. See also *First-strike capability; First-strike strategy.*

Shelter. A revetment or other protective construction above ground, designed as a prelaunch shield for a nuclear delivery system and/or crew. Effective in varying degrees against atomic effects, depending on weapon yields and distances from ground zero. See also *Silo.*

Short-range attack missile (SRAM). An air-to-ground missile with a nuclear warhead deployed on U.S. strategic bombers (FB-111 and B-52) since 1972. Its main purpose is to attack enemy aircraft defenses (for example, antiaircraft missile sites) to enable the bombers to penetrate to their primary targets. Its maximum range is 160 km. See also *Cruise missile.*

Short-range ballistic missile (SRBM). A ballistic missile with a range of less than 1,000 km. See also *Ballistic missile.*

Silo. Underground facilities for a hard-site ballistic missile and/or crew, designed to provide prelaunch protection against atomic effects. High-yield precision weapons are needed to destroy the most durable construction. See also *Shelter.*

Single integrated operational plan (SIOP). The U.S. plan for nuclear retaliation. If deterrence fails, it affords the President many options, regardless of circumstances.

SLBM. See *Submarine-launched ballistic missile.*

SLCM. See *Submarine-launched cruise missile.*

Soft target. A target not protected against the blast, heat, and radiation produced by nuclear explosions. There are many degrees of softness. Some missiles and aircraft, for example, are built in ways that ward off certain effects, but they are "soft" in comparison with shelters and silos. See also *Hard target.*

Solid-fuel system. A propulsion system that permits the launching of a ballistic missile with comparative swiftness. See also *Liquid-fuel system.*

Spent fuel. Fuel that has been in use in a reactor for some time and thus has a changed composition and a diminished ability to give off neutrons.

SRAM. See *Short-range attack missile.*

SRBM. See *Short-range ballistic missile.*

SRCM. See *Cruise missile.*

SS. U.S. designation for a diesel-powered attack submarine (or "submergible ship"). See also *Submarine.*

SSB. U.S. designation for a diesel-powered ballistic missile submarine. See also *Submarine.*

SSBN. U.S. designation for a nuclear-powered ballistic missile submarine. See also *Submarine.*

SSG. U.S. designation for a diesel-powered cruise missile submarine. See also *Submarine.*

SSGN. U.S. designation for a nuclear-powered cruise missile submarine. See also *Submarine.*

SSN. U.S. designation for a nuclear-powered submarine. See also *Submarine.*

Stand-off (missile and carrier). Any system in which a conveyance of any sort delivers any missile to a designated launch point. The missile then proceeds to the target under its own power, while the transport returns to base.

START. See *Strategic Arms Reduction Talks.*

Stealth bomber. See *Advanced Technology Bomber.*

Strategic. Refers to a nation's overall military, economic, and/or political power and its ability to control the course of political/military events. Also refers to the central nuclear weapon systems of the U.S. and the USSR, i.e., ICBMs, SLBMs, and heavy bombers, which are intended for use primarily on an intercontinental basis. See also *Strategic nuclear weapon systems; Tactical; Theater.*

Strategic Air Command (SAC). U.S. military bureau responsible for control of ICBMs and intercontinental bombers.

Strategic Arms Limitation Talks (SALT). The discussions that began in 1970 between the United States and the USSR on the limitation of strategic armaments, now referred to as START. See also *Strategic Arms Reduction Talks.*

Strategic Arms Reduction Talks (START). A series of negotiations begun during the Reagan administration intended to reduce offensive strategic weapon arsenals. See also *Strategic arms limitation talks.*

Strategic bomber. A multi-engine aircraft with intercontinental range, designed specifically to engage targets whose destruction would reduce an enemy's capacity and/or will to wage war. See also *Medium bomber.*

Strategic forces. See *Strategic nuclear weapon systems.*

Strategic nuclear operations. The use of nuclear weapons against an enemy's homeland so as to reduce the enemy's capacity and/or will to wage war. Also includes actions to defend friendly assets from similar forays by foes.

Strategic nuclear parity. See *Essential equivalence.*

Strategic nuclear weapon systems. Offensive nuclear weapon systems designed to be employed against enemy targets for the purpose of effecting the destruction of the enemy's political/economic/military capacity, and defensive nuclear weapon systems designed to counteract those systems.

Strategic stability. A state of equilibrium that encourages prudence by opponents facing the possibility of general war. Tendencies toward an arms race are restrained, since maneuvering for marginal advantage is seen as meaningless.

Strike aircraft. Tactical aircraft used primarily for interdiction and close air support missions.

Strip alert. See *Ground alert.*

Submarine (SS, SSB, SSBN, SSG, SSGN, SSN). A warship designed for operations under the surface of the seas. The standard U.S. naval designation for a diesel-powered submarine (or "submergible ship") is "SS." Nuclear-powered submarines are identified by the designation "N"; those armed with cruise missiles by the letter "G"; and those armed with ballistic missiles by the letter "B." See also *Delta submarine; Polaris submarine; Poseidon submarine; Trident submarine; Typhoon submarine.*

Submarine-launched ballistic missile (SLBM). Any ballistic missile transported by and launched from a submarine. May be short-, medium-, intermediate-, or long-range. See also *Ballistic missile.*

Submarine-launched cruise missile (SLCM). Any airbreathing missile transported by and launched from a submarine. May be short-, medium-, intermediate-, or long-range. See also *Cruise missile.*

Suppliers' club. A name used to refer to those countries that have the ability to make nuclear reactors and other essential equipment, and that have banded together to discuss policies for the sale of nuclear plants to other countries.

Surface-to-air missiles (SAM). A missile fired from the earth's surface against aerial targets.

Surgical strike. U.S. term used to indicate a selective attack with nuclear weapons in contrast to all-out first strike or retaliatory second strike. The desirability of being able to carry out a surgical strike is being used to justify the development and procurement of nuclear weapons with counterforce capabilities.

Survivability. See *Prelaunch survivability; Postlaunch survivability.*

System. See *Nuclear delivery system.*

TAC. See *Tactical Air Command.*

Tactical. Generally, relating to battlefield operations. See also *Battlefield nuclear weapons; Strategic; Theater.*

Tactical Air Command (TAC). U.S. military unit responsible for nonstrategic air operations both in North America and overseas.

Tactical forces. See *General-purpose forces.*

Tactical nuclear delivery vehicle. Nuclear weapon system designed to be employed against enemy targets in a limited conflict. Usually refers to vehicles of shorter range than those necessary for the conduct of strategic and theater operations.

Tactical nuclear weapons. See *Battlefield nuclear weapons.*

Targeting doctrine. Principle governing the selection of targets to be attacked in the event of war, the allocation of weapons to those targets, and the order in which they will or can be attacked.

Terminal guidance. In-flight corrections to the trajectory of a ballistic or cruise missile during its final approach to the target for the purpose of improving accuracy. See also *Mid-course correction.*

Terrain contour matching. A system that correlates contour-map data with terrain being overflown by ballistic or cruise missiles. The results provide position fixes at intervals. These can be used to correct inertial guidance errors and thereby improve accuracy. See also *Mid-course correction.*

Theater. A geographically limited (regional) area of military conflict. See also *Strategic; Tactical; Theater nuclear forces.*

Theater nuclear forces (TNF). All nuclear forces not considered strategic. See also *Alliance and regionally oriented (related) systems.*

Thermonuclear weapon. Nuclear weapon (also referred to as the hydrogen bomb) in which the main part of the explosive energy released results from thermonuclear fusion reactions. The high temperatures required for such reactions are obtained with a fission explosion.

Throw-weight. Ballistic missile throw-weight is the useful weight placed on a trajectory towards the target by the boost stages of the missile. For the purposes of SALT II, throw-weight is defined as the sum of the weight of (a) the RV or RVs; (b) any PBV or similar device for releasing or targeting one or more RVs; and (c) any antiballistic missile penetration aids, including their release devices.

Time-sensitive/time-urgent target. Any target that can move to avoid being struck. Includes weapons that can be launched or redeployed before hostile aircraft or missiles arrive.

TNF. See *Theater nuclear forces.*

Triad. Refers to the basic structure of the U.S. strategic deterrent force, composed of land-based ICBMs, sea-based SLBMs and SLCMs, and manned bombers armed with bombs, SRAMs, and ALCMs.

Trident submarine. The latest U.S. ballistic missile submarine. The Trident is armed with 24 Trident C-4 MIRVed SLBMs. This missile will be replaced by the MIRVed Trident D-5 SLBM in the 1980s, a measure that will provide the U.S. SSBN fleet with counterforce capabilities equivalent to those possessed by U.S. land-based ICBMs.

Typhoon submarine. U.S. designation for the latest Soviet SSBN. The Typhoon carries 20–24 MIRVed SLBMs capable of striking intercontinental targets from waters adjacent to the USSR.

Unacceptable damage. Degree of destruction anticipated from an enemy retaliatory strike sufficient to deter a nuclear power from launching a first strike.

Verification. Inspection and/or surveillance measures to determine compliance with arms-control agreements. See also *Arms control; Arms limitation.*

Vertical proliferation. The development and enlargement of a state's nuclear capacity in terms of further refinement, accumulation, and deployment of nuclear weapons.

War-fighting. Combat actions, as opposed to deterrence (which theoretically is designed to prevent rather than prosecute wars). See also *Counterforce strategy.*

Warhead. That part of a missile, projectile, torpedo, rocket, or other munition that contains either the nuclear or thermonuclear system, the high-explosive system, the chemical or biological agents, or the inert materials intended to inflict damage.

Weapons-grade materials. Radioactive materials suitable for the construction of a nuclear weapon.

Weapon system. See *Nuclear delivery system.*

Worst case. In estimates of future enemy military capabilities, the most extreme situation imaginable.

Yield. The energy released in an explosion. The energy released in the detonation of a nuclear weapon is generally measured in terms of the kilotons or megatons of TNT required to produce the same energy release (1 kiloton = 1,000 tons of TNT; 1 megaton = 1 million tons of TNT).

Appendix B:
Important Nuclear
Weapon Systems

APPENDIX B: IMPORTANT NUCLEAR WEAPON SYSTEMS

NATION	SYSTEM	DATE DEPLOYED	NUMBER DEPLOYED	WEAPONS LOAD; CEP	RANGE (km)	TOTAL WARHEADS
Intercontinental Ballistic Missiles (ICBMs)						
U.S.	Titan II	1962	52[a]	1 x 9 Mt; CEP 1.3km	11,500	52
	Minuteman II	1966	450[b]	1 x 1-2 Mt; CEP 0.4km	9,000	450
	Minuteman III/Mk-12	1970	250	3 x 170 kt MIRV; CEP 0.3km	9,000	750
	Minuteman III/Mk-12A	1979	300	3 x 350 kt MIRV; CEP 0.3km	9,000	900
	Peacekeeper-MX (forthcoming)	1986(?)	100(?)	10 x 335-500 kt MIRV; CEP 0.1km	11,000	1,000
USSR[c]	SS-11	1966	} 580	1 x 1 Mt, CEP 1.0-1.8km; or 3 x 500 kt MRV, CEP 1.0-1.8km	10,500	n.a.[d]
	SS-11 (Model 3)	1973				
	SS-13	1969	60	1 x 1 Mt; CEP 1.3km	8,000	60
	SS-17 (Model 1)	1977	130	4 x 200-750 kt MIRV; CEP 0.4km	10,000	520
	SS-17 (Model 2)	1977	20	1 x 3 Mt; CEP 0.3-0.6km	10,000	20
	SS-18 (Models 1 & 3)	1975/76	} 308	1 x 25-50 Mt; CEP 1km	12,000	n.a.
	SS-18 (Model 2)	1977		8 x 1-2 Mt MIRV; CEP 0.2km	12,000	n.a.
	SS-18 (Model 4)	1979		10 x 1-2 Mt MIRV; CEP 0.2km	12,000	n.a.

Country	System	Year	Number deployed	Warhead	Range (km)	Warheads
	SS-19 (Model 1)	1976	300 }	6 x 200 kt-1 Mt; CEP 0.3-0.45km	9,600	n.a.
	SS-19 (Model 2)	1976		1 x 10-25 Mt; CEP 0.4km	10,000	n.a.
China	CSS-3	1976	2 - 4	1 x 10-25 Mt; CEP n.a.	7,000	2 - 4

Submarine-launched Ballistic Missiles (SLBMs)

Country	System	Year	Number deployed	Warhead	Range (km)	Warheads
U.S.	Poseidon C-3	1970	304	10 x 40 kt MIRV; CEP 0.5km	4,600	3,040
	Trident C-4	1979	240	8 x 100 kt MIRV; CEP 0.5km	7,500	1,920
	Trident D-5 (forthcoming)	1990s(?)	240-264	8 x 350 kt MIRV; CEP 0.2km	11,500	1,920-2,112
USSR[e]	SS-N-5	1964	18	1 x 1 Mt; CEP 1.5km	1,200	18
	SS-N-6 (Models 1 & 2)	1968	n.a.	1 x 1 Mt; CEP 1-2.5km	2,900	n.a.
	SS-N-6 (Model 3)	1973	n.a.	2 x 200 kt MRV; CEP 1-2.5km	2,900	n.a.
	SS-N-8	1973	346	1 x 1 Mt; CEP 1-1.5km	7,900	346
	SS-NX-17	1979	12	1 x 1 Mt; CEP 0.8km	n.a.	12
	SS-N-18	1978	144	3 x 200 kt MIRV; CEP 0.5-1km	7,500	432
	SS-NX-20	1981	20-24	7-12 x 200 kt MIRV; CEP n.a.	7,500	140-288
France	MSBS M-20	1977	80	1 x 1 Mt; CEP n.a.	3,000	80
	MSBS M-4 (forthcoming)	1985(?)	16(?)	6-7 x 150 kt MRV; CEP n.a.	4,000	96-112

APPENDIX B (cont.)

NATION	SYSTEM	DATE DEPLOYED	NUMBER DEPLOYED	WEAPONS LOAD; CEP	RANGE (km)	TOTAL WARHEADS
Britain	Polaris A-3	1967	64	3 x 200 kt MRV; CEP n.a.	4,600	192
Long-Range Sea-launched Cruise Missiles (SLCMs)						
U.S.	BGM-109 Tomahawk (forthcoming)	1980s	1,720	1 x 200 kt; CEP 0.1km	2,500	1,720
USSR	SS-N-3 Shaddock	1962	100	1-? kt; CEP n.a.	700	100
Long Range Strategic Bombers						
U.S.	B-52 C/D/E/F	1956	83	27 tons of bombs	18,500	
	B-52 G/H	1959	265	34 tons of bombs, SRAMs, and Hound Dog ALCMs	20,000	3,100 bombs, SRAMs, and Hound Dog ALCMs
	FB-111A	1970	65	17 tons of bombs and SRAMs	n.a.	
	B-1B (forthcoming)	1989(?)	100(?)	30(?) Tomahawk ALCMs	n.a.	n.a.
USSR	M-4 Bison	1955	45	9 tons of bombs and ALCMs	10,000	n.a.
	Tu-95 Bear	1956	100	18 tons of bombs and ALCMs	12,500	n.a.
Air-launched Strategic Weapons						
U.S.	Bombs	early 1950s	n.a.	200 kt-1 Mt; CEP 0.1km	n.a.	n.a.

	System	Year		Payload		
	Hound Dog ALCM	1961	400	1 x ? kt; CEP n.a.	1,000	400
	Tomahawk ALCM (forthcoming)	1980s	3,300	1 x 200 kt; CEP 0.1km	2,500	3,300
	SRAM	1972	1,020	1 x 170 kt; CEP n.a.	150	1,020
USSR	Bombs	1950s	n.a.	Mt range; CEP 0.1km	n.a.	n.a.
	AS-3 Kangaroo ALCM	1961	n.a.	1 x ? Mt; CEP n.a.	650	n.a.
	AS-4 Kitchen ALCM	1962	800	1 x ? Mt; CEP n.a.	700	800
	AS-5 Kingfish ALCM	1977	n.a.	1 x ? kt; CEP n.a.	n.a.	n.a.
Ballistic Missile Defenses (BMDs)						
USSR	ABM-1 Galosh	1967	64	1 x 2-3 Mt; CEP n.a.	300	64
Medium Range Bombers						
U.S.	FB-111 E/F	1970	300 (165 in Europe)	17 tons of bombs and SRAMs	6,000	n.a.
USSR	Tu-16 Badger	1955	600-700	9 tons of bombs and ALCMs	4,800	n.a.
	Tu-22 Blinder	1961	}	10 tons of bombs and ALCMs	2,250	n.a.
	Tu-22M Backfire	1974	150	9 tons of bombs and ALCMs	3,400	n.a.
Britain	Vulcan B2	1960	40	10 tons of bombs	3,500	n.a.

APPENDIX B (cont.)

NATION	SYSTEM	DATE DEPLOYED	NUMBER DEPLOYED	WEAPONS LOAD; CEP	RANGE (km)	TOTAL WARHEADS
China	Tu-16	n.a.	less than 300	n.a.	n.a.	n.a.
	Tu-4	n.a.		n.a.	n.a.	n.a.
France	Mirage IV-A	1964	35	n.a.	1,600	n.a.

Long Range Theatre Missiles

NATION	SYSTEM	DATE DEPLOYED	NUMBER DEPLOYED	WEAPONS LOAD; CEP	RANGE (km)	TOTAL WARHEADS
U.S.	Pershing II (forthcoming)	1983(?)	108(?)	1 x ? kt; CEP 0.04km	1,800	108[f]
	Tomahawk GLCM	1983(?)	464(?)	1 x ? kt; CEP 0.05km	2,500	464(?)
USSR	SS-4	1959	340	1 x 1 Mt; CEP 2.4km	1,800	340
	SS-5	1961	40	1 x 1 Mt; CEP 1.2km	3,500	40
	SS-20	1977	324	3 x 200 kt MIRV; CEP 0.3km	5,000	972[g]
China	CSS-2	n.a.	50-70	n.a.	2,600	n.a.
	CSS-1	n.a.	40-50	n.a.	1,000	n.a.
France	SSBS S-3	1980	18	1 x 1 Mt; CEP n.a.	3,000	18

Strike Aircraft

NATION	SYSTEM	DATE DEPLOYED	NUMBER DEPLOYED	WEAPONS LOAD; CEP	RANGE (km)	TOTAL WARHEADS
U.S.	F-4	1962	1,400 (250 in Europe)	n.a.	1,100	n.a.

A-6E	1963	150	n.a.	n.a.	n.a.
A-7E	1966	720 (360 active, 48 in Europe)	n.a.	n.a.	n.a.
F-16	1979	380	n.a.	n.a.	n.a.
USSR Su-17	1970	850	n.a.	n.a.	n.a.
Su-24	1974	600	n.a.		n.a.
MiG 23/27	1971	2,000	n.a.	n.a.	n.a.

Short Range Theatre Missiles

U.S. Lance	1972	900 (36 in Europe)	1 x 1-100 kt; ERW capable; CEP n.a.	1,900	900[h]
Pershing 1A	1962	108	1 x 60-400 kt; CEP n.a.	700	108
USSR FROG-series	1965	680 (est.)	1 x 15 kt; CEP n.a.	30-70km	680 (est.)
SS-1c Scud B	1965	620	1 x ? kt; CEP n.a.	300	
SS-12 Scaleboard	1969		1 x 1 Mt; CEP n.a.	800	620
SS-22	1979	100-120	1 x 1 Mt; CEP n.a.	900	100-120
France Pluton	1974	32	1 x 15-25 kt; CEP n.a.	120	32

Artillery

U.S. M-110 203mm howitzer	1962	1,000 (est.)	1 x 1-2 kt; CEP n.a.	15-30km	n.a.
M-109 155mm howitzer	1964	1,000 (est.)	1 x 1-2 kt; CEP n.a.	15-30km	n.a.

APPENDIX B (cont.)

NATION	SYSTEM	DATE DEPLOYED	NUMBER DEPLOYED	WEAPONS LOAD;CEP	RANGE (km)	TOTAL WARHEADS
USSR	M-55 203mm gun	1950s	n.a.	1 x 15 kt; CEP n.a.	15-45km	n.a.

Sources: Information on U.S. nuclear forces is compiled from the following materials: Center for Defense Information, "U.S.-Soviet Military Facts," Defense Monitor, Vol. 11, No. 6 (1982); Cordesman, Anthony H., Deterrence in the 1980s: Part I--American Strategic Forces and Extended Deterrence (London: International Institute for Strategic Studies, 1982), Adelphi Paper No. 175; Forsberg, Randall, "A Bilateral Nuclear Weapon Freeze," Scientific American, Vol. 247, No. 5 (November 1982), pp. 52-61; Freeman, Harold, This Is the Way the World Will End, This Is the Way You Will End, Unless . . . (Edmonton, Canada: Hurtig Publishers, 1983); Ground Zero, Nuclear War: What's in It for You? (New York: Pocket Books, 1982); Lodal, Jan, "U.S. Strategic Nuclear Forces," in America's Security in the 1980s: Part I (London: International Institute for Strategic Studies, 1982), Adelphi Paper No. 173; Millar, Thomas, The East-West Strategic Balance (London: George Allen & Unwin, 1981); North Atlantic Assembly's Special Committee on Nuclear Weapons in Europe, Second Interim Report on Nuclear Weapons in Europe, Report to the Committee on Foreign Relations, United States Senate (Washington, DC: Government Printing Office, 1983); North Atlantic Treaty Organization, NATO and Warsaw Pact Force Comparisons (Brussels: NATO, 1982); Stockholm International Peace Research Institute (SIPRI), The Arms Race and Arms Control (London: Taylor & Francis, 1982); Tsipis, Kosta, and John David Isaacs, "Instruments of War," in The Final Epidemic: Physicians and Scientists on Nuclear War, edited by Ruth Adams and Susan Cullen (Chicago: University of Chicago Press, 1981); United Nations, General and Complete Disarmament--Comprehensive Study on Nuclear Weapons: Report of the Secretary-General, 35 UN, GAOR Annex [Provisional Agenda Item 48(b)], UN Doc. A/35/392 (1980); and U.S. Department of Defense, Report of Secretary of Defense Caspar W. Weinberger to the Congress on the FY 1984 Budget, FY 1985 Authorization Request and FY 1984-88 Defense Programs (Washington, DC: Government Printing Office, 1983).

In addition, the sources of information on U.S. nuclear forces also contain data pertaining to the Soviet nuclear arsenal: International Institute for Strategic Studies (IISS); Strategic Balance Survey 1971-1982 (Colchester, UK: Spottiswoode & Ballantyne, 1982; Kaplan, Fred M., Dubious Specter--A Skeptical Look at the Soviet Nuclear Threat (Washington, DC: Institute for Policy Studies, 1980); McCauseland, Jeff, "The SS-20: Military and Political Threat?" Fletcher Forum, Vol. 6, No. 1 (Winter 1982), pp. 1-32; Menaul, Stewart, Russian Military Power (New York: Bonanza Books, 1982); and U.S. Department of Defense, Soviet Military Power (Washington, DC: Government Printing Office, 1981).

NOTES

a. All Titan II missiles are expected to be deactivated by the end of 1986.

b. Fifty single-warhead Minuteman IIs are scheduled for conversion to three-warhead MIRVed Minuteman IIIs.

c. The number of total warheads associated with single- and multiple-RV versions of the SS-11, SS-18, and SS-19 are subject to substantial variation in the public literature. The total number of Soviet ICBM warheads generally is placed at 5,100, which means that more than 75% of these weapons are deployed in their multiple-RV versions.

d. The abbreviation "n.a." means "not readily available."

e. The total number of SS-N-6s is 274. Publicly available information does not break the number down into separate counts of single- and multiple-RV versions.

f. The Pershing II launch vehicle has a rapid reload/refire capability that enables it to store a second missile on board. Thus, it is likely that the number of Pershing IIs finally deployed will total 216.

g. The SS-20, like the Pershing II, is a rapid reload/refire system, which means that the total number of SS-20 missiles may actually add up to 1,944.

h. The number of Lance warheads in active inventory may be twice the number cited, as the United States Government is stockpiling enhanced radiation warheads compatible with this missile.

General Bibliography

Alford, Jonathan. *The Impact of New Military Technology.* International Institute for Strategic Studies (IISS), Adelphi Hampshire, UK: Gower, Allanheld, and Osmun, 1981.

Allan, Pierre. *Crisis Bargaining and the Arms Race.* Cambridge, MA: Ballinger Publishing Co., 1983.

Aron, Raymond, *Peace and War.* New York: Praeger Publishers, 1967.

Barnet, Richard J., and Richard A. Falk, eds. *Security in Disarmament.* Princeton, NJ: Princeton University Press, 1965.

Beer, Francis A. *Peace Against War: The Ecology of International Violence.* San Francisco: W. H. Freeman and Co., 1981.

Beitz, Charles B., and Theodore Herman, eds. *Peace and War.* San Francisco: W. H Freeman and Co., 1973.

Boulding, Kenneth. *Stable Peace.* Austin, TX: University of Texas Press, 1978.

Brodie, Bernard. *Strategy in the Missile Age.* Princeton, NJ: Princeton University Press, 1959.

Brown, Harrison. *The Human Future Revisited: The World Predicament and Possible Solutions.* New York: W. W. Norton, 1978.

Burns, Richard Dean. *Arms Control and Disarmament: A Bibliography.* Santa Barbara, CA: ABC-Clio Publishers, 1977.

Burrows, Bernard, and Geoffrey Edwards. *The Defense of Western Europe.* Woburn, MA: Butterworth Publishers, 1982.

Cochran, Thomas R., William M. Arkin, and Milton M. Hoenig, eds. *Nuclear Weapons Databook.* Cambridge, MA: Ballinger Publishing Co., 1983.

Cordesman, Anthony H. "American Strategic Forces and Extended Deterrence." In *Deterrence in the 1980s, Part I.* UK: Carlton Berry Co., 1982. (IISS, Adelphi Paper No. 175.)

"Disarmament and Human Survival." *Gandhi Marg*, Vol. 4, Nos. 2–3 (May–June 1982).

Eide, Asbjorn, and Marek Thee, eds. *Problems of Contemporary Militarism.* London: Croom Helm, 1980.

Epstein, William, and Bernard T. Feld, eds. *New Directions in Disarmament.* New York: Praeger Publishers, 1981.

Falk, Richard A., and Samuel S. Kim, eds. *The War System: An Interdisciplinary Approach.* Boulder, CO: Westview Press, 1980.

Falk, Richard A., and Saul H. Mendlovitz, eds. *The Strategy of World Order: Disarmament and Economic Development.* New York: World Law Fund, 1966.

Farrar, L. L., ed. *War: A Historical, Political and Social Study.* London: Oxford University Press, 1978.

Galtung, Johan. *Essays in Peace Research. I: Peace Research, Education, Action; II: Peace, War and Defence.* Copenhagen: Christian Ejlers, 1975/1976.

Geyer, Alan. *The Idea of Disarmament: Rethinking the Unthinkable.* Elgin, IL: Brethren Press, 1982.

Giagolev, I. *Why We Need Disarmament.* Moscow: Novosti Press, 1973.

Gompert, David C., Michael Mandelbaum, Richard L. Garwin, and John H. Barton. *Nuclear Weapons and World Politics: Alternatives for the Future.* New York: McGraw-Hill, 1977.

Graubard, Stephen R., ed. "Arms, Defense Policy, and Arms Control." *Daedalus,* Vol. 104, No. 3 (Summer 1975).

Hanreider, Wolfram F. *Arms and Control and Security: Current Issues.* Boulder, CO: Westview Press, 1979.

Harvard Nuclear Study Group. *Living with Nuclear Weapons.* New York, Toronto, London, and Sydney: Bantam Books, 1983.

Hilgartner, Stephen, Richard C. Bell, and Rory O'Connor. *Nukespeak: The Selling of Nuclear Technology in America.* New York: Penguin Books, 1983.

Hoffman, Stanley. *Primacy or World Order: American Foreign Policy Since the Cold War.* New York: McGraw-Hill, 1978.

International Institute for Strategic Studies. *Strategic Balance Survey 1981–82.* Colchester, UK: Spottiswoode Ballantyne, 1982.

Johansen, Robert C. *The National Interest and the Human Interest: An Analysis of United States Foreign Policy.* Princeton, NJ: Princeton University Press, 1980.

Kaldor, Mary, and Asbjorn Eide. *The World Military Order.* New York: Praeger Publishers, 1979.

Kennedy, Robert, and John M. Weinstein. *The Defense of the West: Strategic and European Security Issues Reappraised.* Boulder, CO: Westview Press, 1983.

Kissinger, Henry A. *Nuclear Weapons and Foreign Policy.* New York: Doubleday Books, 1958.

Lens, Sidney. *Day Before Doomsday: An Anatomy of the Nuclear Arms Race.* Boston: Beacon Press, 1978.

Laszlo, Ervin, and Donald Keys, eds. *Disarmament: The Human Factor.* New York: Pergamon Press, 1981.

Lodal, Jan. "U.S. Strategic Nuclear Forces." In *America's Security in the 1980s, Part I.* (IISS, Adelphi Paper No. 173.) Cambridge, UK: Heffers Printers, 1982.

Mandelbaum, Michael. *The Nuclear Revolution: International Politics Before and After Hiroshima.* Cambridge and New York: Cambridge University Press, 1981.

McVitty, Marion H. *Preface to Disarmament: An Appraisal of Recent Proposals.* Washington, DC: Public Affairs Press, 1970.

Millar, Thomas B. *The East-West Strategic Balance.* London: George Allen and Unwin, 1981.

Pauling, Linus. *No More War.* New York: Dodd, Mead, 1975.

Quester, George. *Nuclear Diplomacy: The First Twenty-five Years.* New York: Dunellen, 1973.

Russett, Bruce. *The Prisoners of Insecurity: Nuclear Deterrance, the Arms Race, and Arms Control.* San Francisco: W. H. Freeman and Co., 1983.

Schell, Jonathan. *The Fate of the Earth.* New York: Alfred A. Knopf, 1982.

Sharp, Jane. *Opportunities for Disarmament.* New York: Carnegie Endowment for International Peace, 1978.

Sims, N. A. *Approaches to Disarmament.* London: Quaker Peace and Service, 1979.

Singer, J. David, ed. *The Correlates of War.* 2 vols. New York: Free Press, 1979/1980.

Stockholm International Peace Research Institute. *Tactical Nuclear Weapons: European Perspectives.* London: Taylor & Francis, 1978.

————. *The Arms Race and Arms Control.* London: Taylor & Francis, 1982.

————. *World Armaments and Disarmaments: Yearbook 1983.* London: Taylor & Francis, 1983.

Thee, Marek. *Armaments, Arms Control and Disarmament.* Paris: UNESCO Press, 1981.

Thompson, E. P., and Dan Smith, eds. *Protest and Survive.* New York and London: Monthly Review Press, 1981.

United Nations Educational, Scientific and Cultural Organization. *Obstacles to Disarmament and Ways of Overcoming Them.* New York: United Nations Publications, 1981.

United States Arms Control and Disarmament Agency. *Arms Control and Disarmament Agreements.* Washington, DC: United States Arms Control and Disarmament Agency, 1982.

Woito, Robert S., ed. *To End War.* New York: Pilgrim Press, 1982.

York, Herbert, ed. *Arms Control: Readings from* Scientific American. San Francisco: W. H. Freeman and Co., 1973.

About the Authors

Chadwick F. Alger is Mershon Professor of Political Science and Public Policy and Director of the Transnational Intellectual Cooperation Program at Ohio State University. He is a member of the Board of Editors of *Peace and Change: A Journal of Peace Research* and a former president of the International Studies Association.

The *Alternative Defence Commission* was established in October 1980 and sponsored by the Lansbury House Trust Fund in conjunction with the School of Peace Studies at Bradford University. It was chaired by Frank Blackaby, Director of the Stockholm International Peace Research Institute. Other members of the Alternative Defence Commission included: Viv Bingham, April Carter, Malcolm Dando, Tony Dumper, Mary Kaldor, Isobel Lindsay, Terry Moran, James O'Connell, Michael Randle, Joseph Rotblat, Elizabeth Sigmund, Dan Smith, Walter Stein, Dafydd Elis Thomas, and Ron Todd.

Georgi A. Arbatov is Director of the Institute of U.S. and Canadian Studies of the Soviet Academy of Sciences. He also is a member of the Central Committee of the Communist Party of the Soviet Union.

Richard J. Barnet is a Senior Fellow at the Institute for Policy Studies in Washington, D.C. Among his recent works is *Real Security: Restoring American Power in a Dangerous Decade* (Simon & Schuster, 1981).

Louis René Beres is Professor of Political Science at Purdue University and author of *Terrorism and Global Security: The Nuclear Threat* (Westview Press, 1979); *Apocalypse: Nuclear Catastrophe in World Politics* (University of Chicago Press, 1980); and *Mimicking Sisyphus: America's Countervailing Nuclear Strategy* (Lexington Books, 1983).

Harvey Brooks is Benjamin Pierce Professor of Technology and Public Policy at Harvard and author of *Science, Technology, and International Relations* (MIT Center for International Studies, 1978).

Silviu Brucan is Professor of Political Science at the University of Bucharest in Rumania. Among his numerous writings is *The Dialectic of World Politics* (Free Press, 1978).

Hedley Bull is Professor of International Relations at Balliol College, Oxford University. Among his more recent books is *The Anarchical Society, A Study in World Politics* (Columbia University Press, 1977).

McGeorge Bundy was Special Assistant to the President for National Security Affairs from 1961 to 1966 and President of the Ford Foundation from 1966 to mid-1979. He currently is Professor of History at New York University.

Walter C. Clemens, Jr., is Professor of Political Science at Boston University and author of *The Superpowers and Arms Control: From Cold War to Interdependence* (Lexington Books, 1973) and *The U.S.S.R. and Global Interdependence* (American Enterprise Institute for Public Policy Research, 1978).

Jonathan Dean is Resident Associate of the Carnegie Endowment for International Peace and was U.S. Ambassador to the Mutual and Balanced Force Reduction Talks from 1978 to 1981.

Robert H. Donaldson is Provost, Dean of the Faculties, and Professor of Political Science at Herbert H. Lehman College, City University of New York. Among his most recent books is *The Soviet Union in the Third World* (Westview Press, 1981).

Lloyd (Jeff) Dumas is Professor of Political Economy at the University of Texas at Dallas and currently is a member of the Nuclear Weapons Control Steering Committee of the American Association for the Advancement of Science. Among his major works are *The Conservation Response: Strategies for the Design and Operation of Energy-Using Systems* (Lexington Books, 1976) and *The Other Half: An Inquiry Into the Causes of Persistent Inflation, Unemployment, and General Economic Decay* (forthcoming).

Richard A. Falk is Albert G. Milbank Professor of International Law and Practice at Princeton University and a Senior Fellow of the World Policy Institute in New York City. Among many scholarly achievements, he is the author of *A Study of Future Worlds* (Free Press, 1975), coeditor (with Burns H. Weston and Anthony A. D'Amato) of *International Law and World Order: A Problem-Oriented Course-book* (West Publishing Co., 1980), and coeditor of *Toward a Just World Order* (Westview Press, 1982).

Dietrich Fischer is Assistant Professor of Economics at New York University and author of *Major Global Trends and Causal Interactions Among Them* (United Nations Publications, 1982).

Roger Fisher is Samuel Williston Professor of Law at the Harvard Law School and Director of the Harvard Negotiation Project. He is the author of *Improving Compliance with International Law* (University Press of Virginia, 1981).

Randall Forsberg, a former staff member of the Stockholm International Peace Research Institute, is the founder and now Director of the Institute for Defense and Disarmament Studies in Brookline, Massachusetts. She also is credited with having initiated the nuclear freeze movement in the United States.

Jerome D. Frank is Professor Emeritus of Psychiatry at the John Hopkins University School of Medicine, a member of the Board of the Directors of SANE, and a member of the National Advisory Board of the Physicians for Social Responsibility.

Harold Freeman is Professor Emeritus at the Massachusetts Institute of Technology and a former consultant to the U.S. Secretary of Defense.

Noel Gayler is a U.S. Navy Admiral (ret.) who served as Commander-in-Chief Pacific Command and as U.S. military advisor to the Southeast Asia Treaty Organization (SEATO), the ANZUS Pact Command, and the U.S.-Japanese Security Consultative Committee.

Ralph M. Goldman is Professor of Political Science at San Francisco State University. He is the author of, among other books, *Contemporary Perspectives on Politics* (Transaction Books, 1976).

The *Group of Experts on a Comprehensive Study on Nuclear Weapons* was chaired by Anders I. Thunborg (Sweden), and in addition included the following governmental officials: F.K.A. Albtey (Ghana), Fathih K. Bouayad-Agha (Algeria), Milutin Civic (Yugoslavia), Francisco Correa-Villalobos (Mexico), Ryukichi Imai (Japan), Albert Legault (Canada), Jamsheed K. A. Marker (Pakistan), Jose Maria Otegui (Argentina), Alan Oxley (Australia), Gheorge Tinca (Rumania), and M. A. Vellsdi (India).

The *Independent Commission on Disarmament and Security Issues* was chaired by Olof Palme (Sweden), and in addition included Georgi Arbatov (USSR), Egon Bahr (Federal Republic of Germany), Gro Harlem Brundtland (Norway), Jozef Cyrankiewicz (Poland), Jean-Marie Daillet (France), Robert A. D. Ford (Canada), Alfonso Garcia-Robles (Mexico), Haruki Mori (Japan), C. B. Muthamma (India), Olusegun Obasanjo (Nigeria), David Owen (United Kingdom), Shridath Ramphal (Guyana), Salim Salim (Tanzania), Soedjatmoko (Indonesia), Joop den Uyl (Netherlands), and Cyrus Vance (U.S.).

Robert C. Johansen is a Senior Fellow of the World Policy Institute in New York City and Director of the Institute's Grenville Clark Project on Disarmament, Security, and Abolition of the War System. He also is the author of *The National Interest and the Human Interest: An Analysis of United States Foreign Policy* (Princeton University Press, 1980).

Mary Kaldor is a Research Fellow at the Science Policy Research Unit, University of Sussex, and author of *The Disintegrating West* (Penguin Books, 1978) and *The Baroque Arsenal* (Hill and Wang, 1982).

Fred M. Kaplan is the author of *The Wizards of Armageddon* (Simon and Schuster, 1983). He also reports regularly on defense policy for the *Boston Globe* and writes for other publications.

George F. Kennan is Professor Emeritus at the Institute for Advanced Study, Princeton University. He served as Minister-Counselor in Moscow in 1944, returned as U.S. Ambassador to the Soviet Union in 1952, and served again as U.S. Ambassador to Yugoslavia from 1961 to 1963. He also is the author of numerous books, including *Soviet-American Relations, 1917–20* (Pantheon Books, 1931), *The Nuclear Delusion: Soviet-American Relations in the Atomic Age* (Pantheon Books, 1982), and *Memoirs* (Pantheon Books, 1983).

Rajni Kothari is Professor of Political Science at the University of Delhi and was founder and Director of the Centre for the Study of Developing Societies (1964–76). Among his major works is *Footsteps Into the Future* (Free Press, 1974).

Allan Krass is Professor of Physics and Science Policy at Hampshire College and author of *Uranium Enrichment and Nuclear Weapon Proliferation* (International Publication Service, 1983).

Louis Kriesberg is Professor of Sociology at Syracuse University, Series Editor of *Research in Social Movements, Conflicts and Change* (JAI Press, Greenwich, CT), and a member of the editorial boards of the

Journal of Political and Military Sociology and *Peace and Change: A Journal of Peace Research.*

The *Lawyers Committee on Nuclear Policy* is an organization of lawyers, legal scholars, and law students dedicated to the prevention of nuclear war and the abolition of nuclear weapons. The Committee is based in New York City.

Robert Jay Lifton is Professor of Psychiatry at the Yale University School of Medicine. Among his many writings is *Home From the War—Vietnam Veterans: Neither Victims Nor Executioners* (Simon & Schuster, 1973).

Robin Luckham is a Fellow of the Institute of Development Studies at the University of Sussex, and author of *Politicians and Soldiers in Ghana, 1966–1972* (Cass, 1975) and *Imperialism* (Institute of Development Studies, 1977).

Robert S. McNamara was Secretary of Defense from 1961 to 1968 and President of the World Bank from 1968 to mid-1981.

The *National Conference of Catholic Bishops* was advised by its Ad Hoc Committee on War and Peace, chaired by Cardinal Joseph Bernardin. Others on the Ad Hoc Committee included Bishop George Fulcher, Auxiliary Bishop Thomas Gumbleton, Auxiliary Bishop John O'Conner, and Bishop Daniel Reilly.

Charles E. Osgood is Professor of Communications and Psychology at the University of Illinois, and Director of the Center for Advanced Studies at the University of Illinois. Among his major works is *An Alternative to War or Surrender* (University of Illinois Press, 1962).

William C. Potter is Associate Director of the Center for International and Strategic Affairs, University of California, Los Angeles. He is coauthor of *SALT and Beyond: A Handbook on Strategic Weapons and Means of Control* (1977), editor of *Verification and SALT: The Challenge of Soviet Strategic Deception* (1980), and co-editor of *Soviet Decisionmaking for National Security* (1983).

Bruce Russett is Professor of Political Science at Yale University and Editor of the *Journal of Conflict Resolution.* Among his many books are *Power and Community in World Politics* (W. H. Freeman and Co., 1974) and *World Politics: The Menu for Choice* (W. H. Freeman and Co., 1974).

Jonathan Schell is staff writer for *New Yorker* and the author of *Time of Illusion* (Knopf, 1975).

Gerard Smith was Chief of the U.S. Delegation to the Strategic Arms Limitations Talks (SALT) from 1969 to 1972, and is author of *Doubletalk: The Story of SALT I* (Doubleday, 1980).